T0181693

Lecture Notes in Computer Science   12123

Founding Editors

Gerhard Goos
  Karlsruhe Institute of Technology, Karlsruhe, Germany
Juris Hartmanis
  Cornell University, Ithaca, NY, USA

Editorial Board Members

Elisa Bertino
  Purdue University, West Lafayette, IN, USA
Wen Gao
  Peking University, Beijing, China
Bernhard Steffen ⓘ
  TU Dortmund University, Dortmund, Germany
Gerhard Woeginger ⓘ
  RWTH Aachen, Aachen, Germany
Moti Yung
  Columbia University, New York, NY, USA

More information about this series at http://www.springer.com/series/7409

Andreas Harth · Sabrina Kirrane ·
Axel-Cyrille Ngonga Ngomo ·
Heiko Paulheim · Anisa Rula ·
Anna Lisa Gentile · Peter Haase ·
Michael Cochez (Eds.)

The Semantic Web

17th International Conference, ESWC 2020
Heraklion, Crete, Greece, May 31–June 4, 2020
Proceedings

 Springer

Editors
Andreas Harth (iD)
University of Erlangen-Nuremberg
Nuremberg, Germany

Axel-Cyrille Ngonga Ngomo (iD)
University of Paderborn
Paderborn, Germany

Anisa Rula (iD)
University of Milano-Bicocca
Milan, Italy

Peter Haase (iD)
metaphacts GmbH
Walldorf, Germany

Sabrina Kirrane (iD)
Vienna University of Economics
and Business
Vienna, Austria

Heiko Paulheim (iD)
University of Mannheim
Mannheim, Germany

Anna Lisa Gentile (iD)
IBM Research - Almaden
San Jose, CA, USA

Michael Cochez (iD)
Vrije Universiteit Amsterdam
Amsterdam, The Netherlands

ISSN 0302-9743 ISSN 1611-3349 (electronic)
Lecture Notes in Computer Science
ISBN 978-3-030-49460-5 ISBN 978-3-030-49461-2 (eBook)
https://doi.org/10.1007/978-3-030-49461-2

LNCS Sublibrary: SL3 – Information Systems and Applications, incl. Internet/Web, and HCI

© Springer Nature Switzerland AG 2020
The chapter "Piveau: A Large-Scale Open Data Management Platform Based on Semantic Web Technologies" is licensed under the terms of the Creative Commons Attribution 4.0 International License (http://creativecommons.org/licenses/by/4.0/). For further details see license information in the chapter.
This work is subject to copyright. All rights are reserved by the Publisher, whether the whole or part of the material is concerned, specifically the rights of translation, reprinting, reuse of illustrations, recitation, broadcasting, reproduction on microfilms or in any other physical way, and transmission or information storage and retrieval, electronic adaptation, computer software, or by similar or dissimilar methodology now known or hereafter developed.
The use of general descriptive names, registered names, trademarks, service marks, etc. in this publication does not imply, even in the absence of a specific statement, that such names are exempt from the relevant protective laws and regulations and therefore free for general use.
The publisher, the authors and the editors are safe to assume that the advice and information in this book are believed to be true and accurate at the date of publication. Neither the publisher nor the authors or the editors give a warranty, expressed or implied, with respect to the material contained herein or for any errors or omissions that may have been made. The publisher remains neutral with regard to jurisdictional claims in published maps and institutional affiliations.

This Springer imprint is published by the registered company Springer Nature Switzerland AG
The registered company address is: Gewerbestrasse 11, 6330 Cham, Switzerland

Preface

This volume contains the main proceedings of the 17th edition of the Extended Semantic Web Conference (ESWC 2020). ESWC is a major venue for presenting and discussing the latest scientific results and technology innovations related to the Semantic Web, Linked Data, and Knowledge Graphs. For almost two decades, researchers, industry specialists, and practitioners from all over the world have come together at ESWC in order to exchange ideas and to shape the future of the Semantic Web community.

ESWC has always been a place for experimenting with innovative practices that deliver added value to the community and beyond. The willingness and ability to experiment with innovative practices was certainly a requirement of ESWC 2020, which took place online. This year's conference was supported by live streaming technology as well as video conferencing systems, online forums, and text chat systems. Without the internet and the web, such remote participation would not have been possible.

The main scientific program of ESWC 2020 consisted of three tracks: the research track, the resource track, and the in-use track. These tracks showcase research and development activities, services and applications, and innovative research outcomes making their way into industry. The research track caters for both long standing and emerging research topics in the form of the following subtracks (i) Ontologies and Reasoning; (ii) Natural Language Processing and Information Retrieval; (iii) Semantic Data Management and Data Infrastructures; (iv) Social and Human Aspects of the Semantic Web; (v) Machine Learning; (vi) Distribution and Decentralization; (vii) Science of Science; (viii) Security, Privacy, Licensing, and Trust; (ix) Knowledge Graphs; and (x) Integration, Services, and APIs. All tracks follow the Open and Transparent Review Policy established by the conference in 2018, however this year both authors and reviewers were afforded more flexibility. Authors could choose to opt in or opt out of being known by the reviewers (i.e., submissions could be anonymous) while reviewers could choose to opt in or opt out of being known by the authors (i.e., reviews could be anonymous).

The main scientific program of ESWC 2020 contained 39 papers: 26 papers in the research track, 8 papers in the resources track, and 5 papers in the in-use track. The papers were selected out of 166 paper submissions, with a total acceptance rate of 23.5% (22% for the research track, 26% for the resources track, and 28% for the in-use track). The main program also includes three invited keynotes from world-renowned researchers and practitioners.

The conference also provided several other opportunities for participation. A poster and demo track, an industry track, a PhD symposium, and several workshops and tutorials catered for work in progress and practical results. These associated events complemented the main program by providing for a discussion-oriented open, diverse, and stimulating environment. Proceedings from these satellite events are available in a separate volume.

The general chair and program chairs would like to thank all those who were involved in making the ESWC 2020 a big success. First of all, our thanks go to the 24 research, resources, and in-use track co-chairs, and over 250 reviewers for the main tracks, for ensuring a rigorous review process that led to an excellent scientific program.

The general chair thanks the program chairs, who did an outstanding job in managing and overseeing a thorough review process. STI International lent a steady hand in strategic matters. However, ESWC 2020 would not have happened without the support and dedication of each and every member of the Organizing Committee (OC). There were always friendly faces showing up in our regular video conferences, and although the OC was focused on its organizational duties, we managed to have a little bit of fun along the way.

We finally thank our sponsors for their support of the 2020 edition of ESWC.

April 2020

Andreas Harth
Sabrina Kirrane
Axel-Cyrille Ngonga Ngomo
Heiko Paulheim
Anisa Rula
Anna Lisa Gentile
Peter Haase
Michael Cochez

Organization

General Chair

Andreas Harth — Friedrich-Alexander University, Erlangen-Nuremberg, Fraunhofer IIS-SCS, Germany

Research Track Program Chairs

Sabrina Kirrane — Vienna University of Economics and Business, Austria
Axel Ngonga — Paderborn University, Germany

Resource Track Program Chairs

Heiko Paulheim — University of Mannheim, Germany
Anisa Rula — University of Milano-Bicocca, Italy

In-Use Track Program Chairs

Anna Lisa Gentile — IBM, USA
Peter Haase — Metaphacts GmbH, Germany

Industry Track Program Chairs

Javier D. Fernández — F. Hoffmann-La Roche AG, Switzerland
Josiane Xavier Parreira — Siemens AG, Austria

Poster and Demo Chairs

Valentina Presutti — University of Bologna, Italy
Raphaël Troncy — Institut Eurécom, France

PhD Symposium Chairs

Maribel Acosta — Karlsruhe Institute of Technology, Germany
Axel Polleres — Vienna University of Economics and Business, Austria

Workshops and Tutorials Chairs

Olaf Hartig — Linköping University, Sweden
Katja Hose — Aalborg University, Denmark

Sponsoring Chair

Victor Charpenay   Friedrich-Alexander University Erlangen-Nuremberg, Germany

Project Networking Chair

Basil Ell   Bielefeld University, Germany

Publicity and Web Presence Chairs

Uldis Bojārs   University of Latvia, National Library of Latvia, Latvia
Valentina Ivanova   RISE Research Institutes of Sweden, Sweden

Semantic Technologies Coordinator

Ruben Taelman   Ghent University, Belgium

Proceedings Chair

Michael Cochez   Vrije Universiteit Amsterdam, The Netherlands

Subtrack Chairs

Social and Human

Amrapali Zaveri   Maastricht University, The Netherlands
Laura Koesten   University of Southampton, UK

Security, Privacy, Licensing and Trust

Víctor Rodríguez Doncel   Universidad Politécnica de Madrid, Spain
Serena Villata   Université Côte d'Azur, CNRS, Inria, I3S, France

Semantic Data Management and Data Infrastructures

Maria Esther Vidal   Leibniz Information Centre For Science and Technology University Library, Germany, and Universidad Simon Bolivar, Venezuela
Philippe Cudre-Mauroux   University of Fribourg, Switzerland

Resources Track

Anisa Rula   University of Milano-Bicocca, Italy
Heiko Paulheim   University of Mannheim, Germany

Science of Science

Paul Groth   University of Amsterdam, The Netherlands
Francesco Osborne   The Open University, UK

Ontologies and Reasoning

Stefan Schlobach   Vrije Universiteit Amsterdam, The Netherlands
Jeff Pan   University of Aberdeen, UK

Natural Language Processing and Information Retrieval

Marieke van Erp   KNAW Humanities Cluster, The Netherlands
Paul Buitelaar   NUI Galway, Ireland

Machine Learning

Mayank Kejriwal   University of Southern California, USA
Stefan Dietze   GESIS, Heinrich-Heine-University Düsseldorf,
                                    Germany

Knowledge Graphs

Antoine Zimmerman   École des Mines de Saint-Étienne, France
Stefan Decker   RWTH Aachen University, Fraunhofer FIT, Germany

Integration, Services and APIs

Maria Maleshkova   University of Bonn, Germany
Ernesto Jimenez Ruiz   City, University of London, UK

In-Use Track

Anna Lisa Gentile   IBM, USA
Peter Haase   Metaphacts GmbH, Germany

Distribution and Decentralization

Ruben Verborgh   Ghent University, Belgium, and Massachusetts Institute
                                    of Technology, USA
Muhammad Saleem   AKSW, Leipzig University, Germany

Program Committee

Ibrahim Abdelaziz   IBM, USA
Alfie Abdul-Rahman   King's College London, UK
Maribel Acosta   Karlsruhe Institute of Technology, Germany
Alessandro Adamou   The Open University, UK
Nitish Aggarwal   Roku Inc., USA
Mehwish Alam   FIZ Karlsruhe, KIT Karlsruhe, Germany
Panos Alexopoulos   Textkernel B.V., The Netherlands

Marjan Alirezaie	Orebro University, Sweden
Natanael Arndt	AKSW, Leipzig University, Germany
Maurizio Atzori	University of Cagliari, Italy
Sören Auer	TIB, University of Hannover, Germany
Nathalie Aussenac-Gilles	IRIT, CNRS, Université de Toulouse, France
Sebastian Bader	Fraunhofer IAIS, Germany
Payam Barnaghi	University of Surrey, UK
Valerio Basile	University of Turin, Italy
Rafael Berlanga	Universitat Jaume I, Spain
Leopoldo Bertossi	Adolfo Ibáñez University, Chile
Christian Bizer	University of Mannheim, Germany
Carlos Bobed	everis, NTT Data, University of Zaragoza, Spain
Fernando Bobillo	University of Zaragoza, Spain
Katarina Boland	GESIS, Germany
Piero Bonatti	University of Naples Federico II, Italy
Georgeta Bordea	Université de Bordeaux, France
Adrian M. P. Brasoveanu	MODUL Technology GmbH, Austria
Carlos Buil Aranda	Universidad Técnica Federico Santa María, Chile
Gregoire Burel	The Open University, UK
Davide Buscaldi	LIPN, Université Sorbonne Paris Nord, France
Anila Sahar Butt	CSIRO, Australia
Elena Cabrio	Université Côte d'Azur, CNRS, Inria, I3S, France
Jean-Paul Calbimonte	HES-SO, Switzerland
Irene Celino	Cefriel, Italy
Thierry Charnois	LIPN, CNRS, University of Paris 13, France
Huiyuan Chen	Case Western Reserve University, USA
Gong Cheng	Nanjing University, China
Michael Cochez	Vrije Universiteit Amsterdam, The Netherlands
Simona Colucci	Politecnico di Bari, Italy
Olivier Corby	Inria, France
Oscar Corcho	Universidad Politécnica de Madrid, Spain
Francesco Corcoglioniti	Free University of Bozen-Bolzano, Italy
Luca Costabello	Accenture Labs, Ireland
Olivier Curé	Université Paris-Est LIGM, France
Hanna Ćwiek-Kupczyńska	IPG PAS, Poland
Claudia d'Amato	University of Bari, Italy
Enrico Daga	The Open University, UK
Victor de Boer	Vrije Universiteit Amsterdam, The Netherlands
Daniele Dell'Aglio	University of Zurich, Switzerland
Gianluca Demartini	The University of Queensland, Australia
Angelo Di Iorio	University of Bologna, Italy
Dennis Diefenbach	University of Lyon, France
Dimitar Dimitrov	GESIS, Germany
Anastasia Dimou	Ghent University, Belgium
Ying Ding	The University of Texas at Austin, USA
Milan Dojchinovski	CTU in Prague, Czech Republic

Mauro Dragoni	FBK-irst, Italy
Aaron Eberhart	Kansas State University, USA
Kemele M. Endris	L3S Research Center, Germany
Vadim Ermolayev	Zaporizhzhia National University, Ukraine
Pavlos Fafalios	ICS-FORTH, Greece
Stefano Faralli	Sapienza University of Rome, Italy
Alessandro Faraotti	IBM, Italy
Daniel Faria	INESC-ID, Universidade de Lisboa, Portugal
Catherine Faron Zucker	Université Nice Sophia Antipolis, France
Nicolas Rodolfo Fauceglia	IBM, USA
Anna Fensel	STI Innsbruck, University of Innsbruck, Austria
Mariano Fernández López	Universidad San Pablo CEU, Spain
Jesualdo Tomás Fernández-Breis	Universidad de Murcia, Spain
Sebastien Ferre	Université Rennes, CNRS, IRISA, France
Besnik Fetahu	L3S Research Center, Germany
Agata Filipowska	Poznan University of Economics, Business, Poland
Valeria Fionda	University of Calabria, Italy
George H. L. Fletcher	Eindhoven University of Technology, The Netherlands
Adam Funk	Sheffield University, UK
Ujwal Gadiraju	Delft University of Technology, The Netherlands
Balaji Ganesan	IBM, India
Daniel Garijo	Information Sciences Institute, Spain
Cristina Gena	University of Turin, Italy
Jose Manuel Gomez-Perez	ExpertSystem, Spain
Rafael S. Gonçalves	Stanford University, USA
Simon Gottschalk	L3S Research Center, Germany
Alasdair Gray	Heriot-Watt University, UK
Dagmar Gromann	University of Vienna, Austria
Christophe Guéret	Accenture Labs, Ireland
Armin Haller	The Australian National University, Australia
Harry Halpin	Inria, France
Ramisa Hamed	Trinity College Dublin, Ireland
Karl Hammar	Jönköping AI Lab, Jönköping University, Sweden
Olaf Hartig	Linköping University, Sweden
Oktie Hassanzadeh	IBM, USA
Nicolas Heist	University of Mannheim, Germany
Nathalie Hernandez	IRIT, France
Sven Hertling	University of Mannheim, Germany
Yusniel Hidalgo Delgado	Universidad de las Ciencias Informáticas, Cuba
Aidan Hogan	DCC, Universidad de Chile, Chile
Geert-Jan Houben	Delft University of Technology, The Netherlands
Dag Hovland	University of Oslo, Norway
Eero Hyvönen	Aalto University, Finland
Yazmin A. Ibanez-Garcia	Cardiff University, UK
Luis Ibanez-Gonzalez	University of Southampton, UK

Ryutaro Ichise	National Institute of Informatics, Japan
Filip Ilievski	University of Southern California, USA
Oana Inel	Delft University of Technology, The Netherlands
Antoine Isaac	Europeana, VU Amsterdam, The Netherlands
Hajira Jabeen	University of Bonn, Germany
Krzysztof Janowicz	University of California, Santa Barbara, USA
Clement Jonquet	University of Montpellier, LIRMM, France
Tobias Käfer	Karlsruhe Institute of Technology, Germany
Maulik R. Kamdar	Elsevier Health, USA
Tomi Kauppinen	Aalto University School of Science, Finland
Takahiro Kawamura	NARO, Japan
Mayank Kejriwal	University of Southern California, USA
Shinsaku Kiyomoto	KDDI Research Inc., Japan
Kjetil Kjernsmo	Inrupt Inc., Norway
Matthias Klusch	DFKI, Germany
Haridimos Kondylakis	ICS-FORTH, Greece
Stasinos Konstantopoulos	NCSR Demokritos, Greece
Roman Kontchakov	Birkbeck, University of London, UK
Manolis Koubarakis	National and Kapodistrian University of Athens, Greece
Maria Koutraki	L3S Research Center, Germany
Ralf Krestel	HPI, University of Potsdam, Germany
Adila A. Krisnadhi	Universitas Indonesia, Indonesia
Christoph Lange	Fraunhofer FIT, RWTH Aachen, Germany
Maxime Lefrançois	Ecole des Mines de Saint-Etienne, France
Maurizio Lenzerini	Sapienza University of Rome, Italy
Yuan-Fang Li	Monash University, Australia
Vanessa Lopez	IBM, Ireland
Gengchen Mai	University of California, Santa Barbara, USA
Maria Maleshkova	University of Bonn, Germany
Ioana Manolescu	Inria, Institut Polytechnique de Paris, France
Claudia Marinica	ETIS, UMR8051, CY University, ENSEA, CNRS, France
Miguel A. Martinez-Prieto	University of Valladolid, Spain
Rory Mc Grath	Accenture AI, Ireland
Nicholas McCarthy	Accenture, Ireland
Fiona McNeill	Heriot-Watt University, UK
Gabriela Montoya	Aalborg University, Denmark
Jose Mora	Universidad Politécnica de Madrid, Spain
Diego Moussallem	Paderborn University, Germany
Raghava Mutharaju	IIIT-Delhi, India
Sebastian Neumaier	WU Vienna, Austria
Vinh Nguyen	National Library of Medicine, NIH, USA
Andriy Nikolov	AstraZeneca, UK
Inah Omoronyia	University of Glasgow, UK
Sergio Oramas	Pandora, Spain

Francesco Osborne   The Open University, UK
Ana Ozaki   Free University of Bozen-Bolzano, Italy
Özgür Lütfü Özcep   University of Lübeck, Germany
Matteo Palmonari   University of Milano-Bicocca, Italy
Harshvardhan J. Pandit   ADAPT Centre, Trinity College Dublin, Ireland
Tassilo Pellegrini   St. Pölten University of Applied Sciences, Austria
Nathalie Pernelle   LRI, Université Paris SUD, France
Catia Pesquita   LASIGE, F. Ciências, Universidade de Lisboa,
                               Portugal
Guangyuan Piao   Nokia Bell Labs, Ireland
Francesco Piccialli   University of Naples Federico II, Italy
Emmanuel Pietriga   Inria, France
Lydia Pintscher   Wikimedia Deutschland, Germany
Giuseppe Pirró   Sapienza University of Rome, Italy
Dimitris Plexousakis   ICS-FORTH, Greece
María Poveda-Villalón   Universidad Politécnica de Madrid, Spain
Freddy Priyatna   Universidad Politécnica de Madrid, Spain
Cédric Pruski   LIST, Luxembourg
Joe Raad   Vrije Universiteit Amsterdam, The Netherlands
Dnyanesh Rajpathak   General Motors, USA
Simon Razniewski   Max Planck Institute for Informatics, Europe
Blake Regalia   University of California, Santa Barbara, USA
Georg Rehm   DFKI GmbH, Germany
Achim Rettinger   Trier University, Germany
Juan L. Reutter   Pontificia Universidad Católica, Chile
Mariano Rico   Universidad Politécnica de Madrid, Spain
Petar Ristoski   IBM, USA
Giuseppe Rizzo   LINKS Foundation, Italy
Mariano Rodríguez Muro   Google, USA
Maria Del Mar   Universidad de Malaga, Spain
   Roldan-Garcia
Francesco Ronzano   Universitat Pompeu Fabra, Spain
Catherine Roussey   Inrae Clermont-Ferrand Center, France
Ana Roxin   University of Burgundy, UMR 6306, CNRS, France
Marta Sabou   Vienna University of Technology, Austria
Sherif Sakr   University of New South Wales, Australia
Angelo Antonio Salatino   The Open University, UK
Muhammad Saleem   AKSW, Leipzig University, Germany
Felix Sasaki   Cornelsen Verlag GmbH, TH Brandenburg, Germany
Kai-Uwe Sattler   TU Ilmenau, Germany
Marco Luca Sbodio   IBM, Ireland
Johann Schaible   GESIS, Germany
Konstantin Schekotihin   Alpen-Adria Universität Klagenfurt, Austria
Gezim Sejdiu   University of Bonn, Germany
Barış Sertkaya   Frankfurt University of Applied Sciences, Germany
Saeedeh Shekarpour   University of Dayton, USA

Gerardo Simari	Universidad Nacional del Sur, CONICET, Argentina
Elena Simperl	King's College London, UK
Hala Skaf-Molli	University of Nantes, LS2N, France
Dezhao Song	Thomson Reuters, USA
Adrián Soto	Pontificia Universidad Católica de Chile, Chile
Dayana Spagnuelo	Vrije Universiteit Amsterdam, The Netherlands
Blerina Spahiu	Università degli Studi di Milano Bicocca, Italy
Marc Spaniol	Université de Caen Normandie, France
Kavitha Srinivas	IBM, USA
Steffen Staab	IPVS, University of Stuttgart, Germany, and WAIS, University of Southampton, UK
Nadine Steinmetz	TU Ilmenau, Germany
Armando Stellato	Tor Vergata University of Rome, Italy
Markus Stocker	Technische Informationsbibliothek (TIB), Germany
Audun Stolpe	FFI, Norway
Heiner Stuckenschmidt	University of Mannheim, Germany
York Sure-Vetter	Nationale Forschungsdateninfrastruktur (NFDI), Germany
Pedro Szekely	University of Southern California, USA
Kerry Taylor	The Australian National University, Australia
Kia Teymourian	Boston University, USA
Andreas Thalhammer	F. Hoffmann-La Roche AG, Switzerland
Veronika Thost	MIT, IBM, USA
Ilaria Tiddi	Vrije Universiteit Amsterdam, The Netherlands
Konstantin Todorov	University of Montpellier, LIRMM, France
Riccardo Tommasini	University of Tartu, Estonia
Sebastian Tramp	eccenca GmbH, Germany
Raphaël Troncy	Institut Eurécom, France
Umair Ulhassan	National University of Ireland Galway, Ireland
Jacopo Urbani	Vrije Universiteit Amsterdam, The Netherlands
Ricardo Usbeck	Paderborn University, Germany
Sahar Vahdati	University of Oxford, UK
Frank Van Harmelen	Vrije Universiteit Amsterdam, The Netherlands
Serena Villata	CNRS, I3S, Université Sophia-Antipolis, France
Domagoj Vrgoc	Pontificia Universidad Católica de Chile, Chile
Kewen Wang	Griffith University, Australia
Rigo Wenning	W3C, France
Cord Wiljes	Bielefeld University, Germany
Gregory Todd Williams	J. Paul Getty Trust, USA
Josiane Xavier Parreira	Siemens AG, Austria
Guohui Xiao	Free University of Bozen-Bolzano, Italy
Fouad Zablith	American University of Beirut, Lebanon
Ondřej Zamazal	University of Economic in Prague, Cech Republic
Ziqi Zhang	Sheffield University, UK
Rui Zhu	University of California, Santa Barbara, USA
Arkaitz Zubiaga	Queen Mary University of London, UK

Subreviewers

Note: some reviewers acted both as a normal reviewer in the PC and as a subreviewer.
Their names are not repeated here.

Ahmed Awad	University of Tartu, Estonia
Mahdi Bennara	École des Mines de Saint-Étienne, France
Russa Biswas	FIZ Karlsruhe, KIT Karlsruhe, Germany
Christoph Braun	Karlsruhe Institute of Technology, Germany
Pieter Colpaert	Ghent University, Belgium
Daniel Daza	Vrije Universiteit Amsterdam, The Netherlands
Helena Deus	Elsevier Inc., USA
Nils Feldhus	DFKI, Germany
Javier D. Fernández	F. Hoffmann-La Roche AG, Switzerland
Richard Figura	University of Duisburg-Essen, Germany
Erwin Filtz	WU Vienna, Austria
Pouya Ghiasnezhad Omran	The Australian National University, Australia
Jonas Halvorsen	FFI, Norway
Bjorn Jervell Hansen	FFI, Norway
Fabian Hoppe	FIZ Karlsruhe, KIT Karlsruhe, Germany
Yasar Khan	INSIGHT Centre for Data Analytics, NUIG, Ireland
Lefteris Koumakis	ICS-FORTH, Greece
Anelia Kurteva	STI Innsbruck, University of Innsbruck, Austria
Elaheh Maleki	EMSE, France
Qaiser Mehmood	INSIGHT Centre for Data Analytics, NUIG, Ireland
Malte Ostendorff	DFKI, Germany
Petros Papadopoulos	Glasgow Caledonian University, UK
Romana Pernischová	University of Zurich, Switzerland
Cosimo Damiano Persia	Free University of Bozen-Bolzano, Italy
Thiviyan Thanapalasingam	University of Amsterdam, The Netherlands
Tabea Tietz	FIZ Karlsruhe, KIT Karlsruhe, Germany
Bo Yan	LinkedIn, USA

Contents

Ontologies and Reasoning

Natural Language Processing and Information Retrieval

Semantic Data Management and Data Infrastructures

Social and Human Aspects of the Semantic Web

Machine Learning

Distribution and Decentralization

Science of Science

Security, Privacy, Licensing and Trust

Knowledge Graphs

Integration, Services and APIs

Resources

In-Use

Ontologies and Reasoning

Handling Impossible Derivations During Stream Reasoning

Hamid R. Bazoobandi, Henri Bal, Frank van Harmelen, and Jacopo Urbani$^{(\boxtimes)}$

Vrije Universiteit Amsterdam, Amsterdam, The Netherlands
h.bazoubandi@vu.nl, {bal,frankh,jacopo}@cs.vu.nl

Abstract. With the rapid expansion of the Web and the advent of the Internet of Things, there is a growing need to design tools for intelligent analytics and decision making on streams of data. Logic-based frameworks like LARS allow the execution of complex reasoning on such streams, but it is paramount that the computation is completed in a timely manner before the stream expires. To reduce the runtime, we can extend the validity of inferred conclusions to the future to avoid repeated derivations, but this is not enough to avoid all sources of redundant computation. To further alleviate this problem, this paper introduces a new technique that infers the impossibility of certain derivations in the future and blocks the reasoner from performing computation that is doomed to fail anyway. An experimental analysis on microbenchmarks shows that our technique leads to a significant reduction of the reasoning runtime.

1 Introduction

In highly dynamic environments like the Web or the Internet of Things, there are many use cases that require an efficient processing of large streams of data to provide complex data analytics or intelligent decision making. For instance, the content of the stream can be used to make predictions about future behaviors (e.g., financial market movement), or to build an accurate representation of the current environment (e.g., crowd control).

In some cases, a semantic-oriented approach is needed to process the stream. An example is given by autonomous driving, which is currently one of the most prominent frontiers of AI. As it was recently shown by Suchan et al. [31], there are situations that cannot (yet) be handled by deep-learning-based computer vision techniques, and this can lead to safety concerns. The *occlusion scenario* is an example of such a situation. This scenario occurs when another vehicle, which is clearly visible in close proximity, suddenly disappears and reappears shortly after (e.g., due to the steering of a third vehicle). When this event occurs, a system that relies only on the input provided by computer vision might erroneously conclude that the vehicle is no longer in close proximity, and consequently act on this false premise. Humans, in contrast, (usually) apply some logic-based reasoning and conclude that the vehicle is still nearby although it is hidden.

Suchan et al. mention this scenario to motivate the need for semantics and logic-based reasoning of temporal data. Currently, one of the most prominent

© Springer Nature Switzerland AG 2020
A. Harth et al. (Eds.): ESWC 2020, LNCS 12123, pp. 3–19, 2020.
https://doi.org/10.1007/978-3-030-49461-2_1

frameworks for this type of processing is LARS [5]. LARS is ideal for use cases like the aforementioned one. First, its semantics is grounded on Answer Set Programming (ASP); thus it provides an AI that is explainable by design, which means that it can be used also by non experts or audited by regulators. Second, LARS offers a variety of operators that are specifically designed for modeling streams to allow the execution of complex reasoning without making it harder than it is in ASP. For instance, LARS offers window operators that allow the restriction of the analysis to the last data in the stream, or other operators like @ which specifies when a derived conclusion will be valid.

Since often the data in the stream expires after a short amount of time, it is paramount that reasoning is performed in a timely manner. Recently, several works have used LARS to implement stream reasoning that reconciles the expressivity of LARS with high performance. One of such reasoner is *Ticker* [6], while a more recent distributed implementation is presented in [14]. Another of such reasoners is *Laser*, which we presented in a previous paper [4]. Laser distinguishes itself from the previous two by focusing on a smaller and more tractable fragment of LARS called *Plain LARS*. Another distinctive feature is that Laser introduces a new technique that annotates the formulae with two timestamps, called *consideration* and *horizon* times, to extend the validity of the formulae in the future to avoid that they are re-derived at each time point. This technique is particularly effective when the body of the rules contains the LARS operators ◇ (validity at *some* time point) or @ (validity at *one specific* time point), and it can lead to significantly faster runtimes. However, this technique does not work with the operator □ (validity at *all* time points) because the semantics of this operator is such that the validity cannot be guaranteed in the future.

In this paper, we present a new technique to further limit the number of redundant derivations. Our technique targets formulae for which the consideration and horizon timestamps are not effective (i.e., the rules that use the □ operator). The main idea is to identify the cases when it will be impossible to produce some derivations in the future and to use this knowledge to disable rules that won't be able to produce any new conclusion. For example, consider the LARS rule $\boxplus^3 \Box p(a) \rightarrow q(a)$. This rule specifies that if the fact $p(a)$ appears in the stream in last three time points, then we can infer $q(a)$. In this case, if the stream does not contain $p(a)$ at the current time point, then we can conclude that for the next three time points the rule will never be able to infer $q(a)$, thus making it an "impossible derivation". Since we know that it is impossible that $q(a)$ will be derived, we can disable the rule and simplify reasoning. Moreover, if other rules use $q(a)$ in their body, then they can also be disabled, with a further improvement of the performance.

We have implemented our technique in a new reasoner called *Laser2*, which is a completely rewritten Plain LARS reasoner in Golang. Our experiments show that our technique returns significant improvements in terms of runtime. The code of Laser2 and other evaluation data can be found at at https://bitbucket.org/hrbazoo/laser.

2 Background

We start our discussion with some background notions on logic programming and LARS [5]. Let $\mathcal{C}, \mathcal{V}, \mathcal{P}$ be disjoint sets of *constants*, *variables*, and *predicates*. A predicate p can be either *extensional* or *intensional* and it is associated to a fixed arity $\mathsf{ar}(p) \geq 0$. A *term* is either a constant or variable. An *atom* is an expression of the form $p(\mathbf{t})$ where p is a predicate, $\mathbf{t} = t_1, \ldots, t_n$ is a list of terms and $n = \mathsf{ar}(p)$. A *ground* expression is an expression without any variable. A *fact* is a ground atom.

Let $\mathcal{A}$ be the set of all facts we can construct from $\mathcal{P}$ and $\mathcal{C}$ and let $\mathcal{A}^{\mathcal{E}} \subseteq \mathcal{A}$ be the subset of facts with extensional predicates. A *timeline* $\mathbf{T}$ is a closed non-empty interval in the set of natural numbers $\mathbb{N}$. We refer to each member in a timeline as a *time point*. Abusing notation, we write $t \in \mathbf{T}$ to indicate a generic time point in $\mathbf{T}$. We are now ready to define the notion of *stream*.

Definition 1. *A stream $S = (\mathbf{T}, v)$ is a pair of a timeline and evaluation function $v : \mathbb{N} \mapsto 2^{\mathcal{A}}$, which maps integers to set of atoms in $\mathcal{A}$ with the constraint that $v(t) \mapsto \emptyset$ for each $t \notin \mathbf{T}$.*

Intuitively, v is used to map time points to sets of facts. We say that S is a *data stream* if v maps only to atoms in $\mathcal{A}^{\mathcal{E}}$. Also, a stream is *ground* if v maps only to facts. Finally, we say that $S' = (\mathbf{T}, v')$ is a *substream* of $S = (\mathbf{T}, v)$, denoted as $S' \subseteq S$, if $v'(t) \subseteq v(t)$ for each time point in $\mathbf{T}$. A *window function* w is a computable function which receives in input a stream S and a time point t and returns in output a stream $S' \subseteq S$. LARS proposes several window functions: a *time-based* window function w_n returns a substream that filters out all the atoms that are not in t or in the previous $n-1$ time points; a *tuple-based* window function returns a substream with the last n facts, etc. In this paper, we consider only time-based windows functions, and leave an extension of our technique to other types of window functions as future work.

In this paper, we focus on a fragment of LARS called *Plain LARS* [4]. Plain LARS restricts some features of LARS in order to enable a fast computation. In Plain LARS, an *extended atom* α is a formula that complies with the grammar

$$\alpha ::= a \mid @_t a \mid \boxplus^n @_t a \mid \boxplus^n \Diamond a \mid \boxplus^n \Box a$$

where $t \in \mathbb{N}$, a is an atom, $@$ is an operator that specifies that a holds at t, $\boxplus^n$ is used to restrict the stream using the time-based window w_n, $\Diamond$ states that a should hold at least in one time point, while $\Box$ states that a should hold at every time point. A (ground) *rule* is an expression of the form:

$$B_1 \wedge \ldots \wedge B_m \to H \tag{1}$$

where $B_1, \ldots, B_m$ are (ground) extended atoms, and H is a (ground) extended atom that is either an atom or of the form $@_t a$. A (ground) *program* is a finite set of (ground) rules. Let r be a rule as shown in (1). Throughout, we use the shortcut $\mathsf{B}(r)$ (body) to refer to the left-side of the rule and $\mathsf{H}(r)$ (head) for the right-side.

We first define the semantics for ground programs. Let $M = \langle S, w_n, \mathcal{B} \rangle$ be a structure where $S = (\mathbf{T}, v)$ is a ground stream of facts in $\mathcal{A}$, w_n is the time-based window function, $\mathcal{B} \subseteq \mathcal{A}$ is a set of facts called *background knowledge*. Then, M *entails* α at time point t, denoted as $M, t \Vdash \alpha$, as follows:

if	$\alpha = a$	then	$M, t \Vdash \alpha$	iff	$a \in v(t)$ or $a \in \mathcal{B}$,
if	$\alpha = \Diamond a$	then	$M, t \Vdash \alpha$	iff	$M, t' \Vdash a$ for some $t' \in \mathbf{T}$,
if	$\alpha = \Box a$	then	$M, t \Vdash \alpha$	iff	$M, t' \Vdash a$ for all $t' \in \mathbf{T}$,
if	$\alpha = @_{t'} a$	then	$M, t \Vdash \alpha$	iff	$M, t' \Vdash a$ and $t' \in \mathbf{T}$,
if	$\alpha = \boxplus^n \beta$	then	$M, t \Vdash \alpha$	iff	$M', t \Vdash \beta$ where $M' = \langle w_n(S, t), w_n, \mathcal{B} \rangle$,
if	$\alpha = \wedge_{i=1}^{m} B_i$	then	$M, t \Vdash \alpha$	iff	$M, t \Vdash B_i$ for all $1 \leq i \leq m$,
if	$\alpha = B \to H$	then	$M, t \Vdash \alpha$	iff	$M, t \not\Vdash B \vee M, t \Vdash H$.

Given a data stream $D = (\mathbf{T}, v_D)$, we say that M is a *model* of P (for D) at time point t, denoted as $M, t \models P$, if $M, t \Vdash r$ for every $r \in P$ and M and S coincides with D on $\mathcal{A}^{\mathcal{E}}$, i.e., $S \supseteq D$ and every fact with extensional predicate in S at time point x is also in D at x. If no other model $M' = \langle S', w_n, \mathcal{B} \rangle \neq M$ exists such that $S' = (\mathbf{T}, v')$ and $v'(t) \subseteq v(t)$ for any $t \in \mathbf{T}$, then M is *minimal*.

The semantics of a non ground program P (i.e., a program where some rules contain variables) equals to the semantics of the ground program that is obtained by grounding all rules in P with all possible substitutions in $\mathcal{C}$. For instance, if $\mathcal{C} = \{c_1, c_2\}$ and $P = \{p(X) \to q(X)\}$ where X is a variable, then $M, t \models t$ iff $M, t \models P'$ where $P' = \{p(c_1) \to q(c_1), p(c_2) \to q(c_2)\}$. Given an input data stream and a program, our goal is to compute *answer streams* and return the derivations to the user.

Definition 2. *Stream S is an* answer stream *of program P for data stream D at time point t if $M = \langle S, w_n, \mathcal{B} \rangle$ is a minimal model of the reduct $P^{M,t} = \{r \in P \mid M, t \models \mathrm{B}(r)\}$.*

We have now all the elements to define the output of our computation.

Definition 3. *Let $S = (\mathbf{T}, v)$ be the answer stream of program P (for D) at time point t. Then, the* output *is the set $v(t) \backslash \mathcal{A}^{\mathcal{E}}$, that is, the set of all the atoms with intensional predicates that can be inferred by P at t.*

3   Intuition

The example below illustrates the computation performed during LARS reasoning and is useful to provide an intuitive description of our technique.

Example 1. Let $\mathcal{P} = \{highTemp, warning, error, shutdown\}$ be a set of predicates where only $highTemp$ is extensional and $\mathcal{C} = \{b_1, b_2\}$. We consider an input stream $D = (\mathbf{T}, v)$ which is defined with the timeline $\mathbf{T} = \langle 1, \ldots, 15 \rangle$ and

$$v = \{2 \mapsto \{highTemp(b_1), highTemp(b_2)\}, 3 \mapsto \{highTemp(b_2)\}\},$$

that is, a high temperature is observed only at time points 2 and 3 (all other time points are mapped to the empty set).

Moreover, let us consider a ground program P with the rules

$$\boxplus^{10}\Diamond highTemp(b_1) \rightarrow warning(b_1) \qquad (r_1)$$

$$\boxplus^{3}\Box highTemp(b_2) \rightarrow error(b_2) \qquad (r_2)$$

$$error(b_2) \rightarrow shutdown(b_2) \qquad (r_3)$$

Given this input, an answer stream of P for D at time point 2 is the stream $S_2 = (\mathbf{T}, v')$ where

$$v' = \{2 \mapsto \{highTemp(b_1), highTemp(b_2), warning(b_1)\}, 3 \mapsto \{highTemp(b_2)\}\}$$

while $S_3 = (\mathbf{T}, v'')$ where

$$v'' = \{2 \mapsto \{highTemp(b_1), highTemp(b_2)\}, 3 \mapsto \{highTemp(b_2), warning(b_1)\}\}$$

is an answer stream at time point 3. In this case, the output will be the set $\{warning(b_1)\}$ both at time point 2 and 3.

Since the output of a LARS program is defined with respect to a single time point, the framework does not put any restriction on the order in which the time points should be considered. In Example 1, for instance, a user could decide to compute first the output at time point 3 and then at time point 2. In practice, however, streams are typically evaluated time point after time point.

This evaluation criterion can be exploited to avoid triggering redundant derivations. In Example 1, a naïve application of rule r_1 will derive $warning(b_1)$ twice; both at time point 2 and 3. However, the second derivation can be avoided since we know that $warning(b_1)$ will hold at least until time point 12 because r_1 fires if $highTemp(b_1)$ appears at least once in the last 10 time points.

In [4], it has been shown how we can exploit this observation by annotating the formulae with two timestamps: a *consideration* and a *horizon* time. The consideration time identifies the first time point where the formula holds, while the horizon time identifies the last time point where the formula is guaranteed to hold. For instance, at time point 2 the formula $\boxplus^{10}\Diamond highTemp(b_1)$ is annotated with a consideration time equals to 2 (i.e., the first time point where this formula is inferred). Instead, the horizon time equals to 12 since we know that the body of the rule will hold until 12. The annotated formula with these timestamps is denoted as $\boxplus^{10}\Diamond highTemp(b_1)_{[2,12]}$. From these annotations, it also follows that the fact $warning(b_1)$ can be annotated as $warning(b_1)_{[2,12]}$. Since these two formulae will hold in the future, they are kept in the working memory until the current time point is greater than the horizon time. When this occurs, they expire and can be removed.

When we execute a rule, we can use the annotations to perform a check that is similar to the one of Semi Naïve Evaluation (SNE) [1] – a well-known Datalog technique to reduce the number of duplicate derivations. The idea behind SNE is to block the firing of the rule if no atom that instantiates the body was derived in the previous step. In our setting, we can apply a similar principle and enforce that at least one formula used in the body has a consideration time equal to the current time point. In our example, this constraint will block the application of r_1 at time point 3 because $\boxplus^{10}\Diamond highTemp(b_1)_{[2,12]}$ has already been considered.

While the consideration and horizon timestamps are useful to reduce the runtime [4], their introduced benefit cannot be extended to formulae that use the operator $\Box$. In fact, a formula like $\Box a$ holds only if a holds at *every* time point. Because of this constraint, we are unable to guarantee that it will hold in the future, hence we cannot extend the horizon time.

The technique presented in this paper aims precisely at overcoming this limitation. The main idea is the following: Although we cannot guarantee that a formula with $\Box$ will hold in the future, sometimes we can guarantee that the formula will *not* hold. Let us consider again Example 1. At time point 1, the absence of facts with the predicate $highTemp$ in the data stream tells us that rule r_2 will never fire for at least the following three time points. Consequently, also r_3 will never fire and therefore can be safely ignored until time point 4. By doing so, our technique complements the usage of consideration and horizon times by covering the formulae where these two time stamps are not beneficial.

4   Formal Description

Algorithm 1 describes the reasoning procedure with our technique enabled to compute the output of a Plain LARS program. Function **reason** receives in input a data stream $D = (\mathbf{T}, v_D)$, background knowledge $\mathcal{B}$ and a program P and returns the *output on* $\mathbf{T}$, i.e., a data structure (*Out* in Algorithm 1) that contains the output at each time point in $\mathbf{T}$ (*Out*[t_1] contains the output at time point t_1, *Out*[t_2] contains the output at time point t_2, etc.). The presented algorithm assumes that the user is interested in computing the output at each time point. If this is not the case, then the algorithm can be easily adapted.

The computation of **reason** can be divided into four parts:

- *Init* (lines 1–7): In this phase the algorithm initializes various data structures;
- *EnableRules* (lines 9–11): Rules that were previously disabled are re-enabled;
- *Reasoning* (lines 12–14): Computes the derivations at a given time point;
- *DisableRules* (lines 15–23): Rules that won't fire in the future are disabled.

Init. The procedure uses four global variables. P_A contains the active rules, i.e., that are considered during reasoning while P_I contains the disabled rules. Initially, P_A equals to P while P_I is empty (line 7). R is a multimap used to collect the rules that can be invalidated for some time points in the future. We use R to retrieve these rules after we observe that there are no facts derived in the current time point. These rules have a formula of the form $\boxplus^x \Box p(\mathbf{t})$ in their body. Let r be such a rule. In this case, R maps p to one tuple of the form $\langle r, x \rangle$ which indicates that r can be disabled for x time points (line 5). The variable S refers to another multimap that point to the rules that derive formulae with a given predicate. We use S to decide whether the exclusion of a rule can trigger the exclusion of other ones.

Algorithm 1: reason($D, \mathcal{B}, P$)

Input	: data stream $D = (\mathbf{T}, v_D)$, background data $\mathcal{B}$, program P
Output	: Output on $\mathbf{T}$
Global vars	: P_A, P_I, R, S

1   $R := \emptyset$ $S := \emptyset$
2   **foreach** $r \in P$
3   Let q be the predicate used in $\mathsf{H}(r)$
4     $S[q] := S[q] \cup \{r\}$
5   **foreach** $\alpha \in \mathsf{B}(r)$ *such that* $\alpha := \boxplus^x \Box p(\mathbf{t})$ **do** $R[p] := R[p] \cup \langle r, x \rangle$
6   Let $\mathbf{T}$ be of the form $\langle t_1, \ldots, t_n \rangle$
7   $P_A := P$ $P_I := \emptyset$ $t_i := t_1$
8   **while** $t_i \leq t_n$ **do**
9   **foreach** $\langle r, t \rangle \in P_I$ *and* $t = t_i$
10       $P_A := P_A \cup \{r\}$
11       $P_I := P_I \setminus \{\langle r, t \rangle\}$
12     $Out[t_i] := \emptyset$
13   Compute answer stream $S = (\mathbf{T}, v)$ of P_A for D at t_i
14     $Out[t_i] := v(t_i) \setminus v_D(t_i)$
15   **foreach** $p \in \mathcal{P}$ *that does not appear in* $v(t_i)$
16   **foreach** $\langle r, t \rangle \in R[p]$ *such that* $r \in P_A$
17         $P_A := P_A \setminus \{r\}$
18   **if** $\langle r, y \rangle \in P_I$
19           $P_I := P_I \setminus \{\langle r, y \rangle\}$
20           $l := \max(t_i + t, y)$
21   **else** $l := t_i + t$
22         $P_I := P_I \cup \{\langle r, l \rangle\}$
23   disable(r, l, t_i)
24     $t_i := t_i + 1$
25 **end**
26 **return** Out

EnableRules. The procedure considers each time point in a sequence (line 8). Before reasoning starts, it checks whether some rules that were previously disabled can be included again. To this end, the procedure considers all rules in P_I which have expired, re-add them to P_A, and remove them from P_I (lines 10–11).

Reasoning. Reasoning is computed in lines 12–14. First, it initializes the data structure Out. Then, it computes the answer stream according to Definition 2 and the corresponding output as specified in Definition 3. Note that these are computed using only the rules in P_A. Our method is agnostic to the procedure that is used to compute the derivations. In our implementation, we rely on the reasoning procedure specified in [4], that is the one that uses consideration and horizon timestamps, but one could in principle use any other routine, as long as it computes a valid answer stream.

DisableRules. After the answer stream is computed, we check whether some rules can be disabled. First, we identify all the predicates which do not appear in

---

Algorithm 2: disable(r_d, l, t_i)

    Input   : r_d is the rule that was deactivated, l the length of the
                            deactivation, t_i is the current time point
    Output   : Modified P_A and P_I

27   Let q be the predicate used in $\mathsf{H}(r_d)$
28   **if** $|S[q]| = 1$
29   **foreach** $r \in P_A$
30          $rm :=$ **false** $g := l$
31   **foreach** $\alpha \in \mathsf{B}(r)$
32   **if** $\alpha = q(\mathbf{t})$ $rm :=$ **true**
33   **if** $\alpha = \boxplus^n \Box q(\mathbf{t})$
34                  $g := \mathsf{max}(l, t_i + n)$
35                  $rm :=$ **true**
36   **if** $rm =$ **true**
37              $P_A := P_A \setminus \{r\}$
38              $P_I := P_I \cup \{\langle r, g \rangle\}$
39   disable(r, g, t_i)

---

the output at the current time point (line 15). If there is a body atom with the operator $\Box$ in a rule in P_A (line 16), then we remove the rule from P_A (line 17) and add it to P_I (line 22). When we add r to P_I, we also specify the number of time points for which the rule should remain disabled. This number corresponds to the size of the window. If the rule is already disabled (this can occur if r has multiple body atoms with $\Box$), then we use the maximum time point (line 20).

If a rule is disabled, then other rules can be disabled as well. To this purpose, we invoke the function disable, reported in Algorithm 2. The function receives in input the rule that was just removed, i.e., r_d, the time point until r_d will be disabled, and the current time point. First, we consider further rules only if r_d is the only rule that derives facts with the predicate in the head (q, see line 28). If this occurs, then some rules that use q in the body won't be able to fire as well. These are the rules where q appears either as body atom or used with the $\Box$ operator (with other operators, the rule can still fire). We identify such rules in the loop in lines 31–35 with the flag rm. If the flag is enabled, then the rule is disabled until the time point g (lines 36–39). Note that if the body atom is used inside a window, then g is updated considering the maximum time point as expiration time point (line 34). After this, the procedure is invoked recursively (termination is ensured because in the worst case all rules in P_A are removed and then the recursive call will not occur).

Example 2. Let us consider the input in Example 1. At time point 1, the stream is empty. Thus, $Out[1]$ will be equal to $v_D(1)$. Therefore, predicate $highTemp$ will be considered in the loop in line 16. The tuple $\langle r_2, 3 \rangle$ is selected and r_2 is disabled by removing it from P_A (line 17) and adding the tuple $\langle r_2, 4 \rangle$ to P_I (line 22). Then, function disable is invoked. The if condition in line 28 succeeds and the for loop selects rule r_3 to be deactivated. Therefore, in line 37 rule r_3 is also removed and the tuple $\langle r_3, 4 \rangle$ is added to P_I. After reasoning at time points 2 and 3, rules r_2 and r_3 will be re-activated at time point 4 by adding them back to P_A (line 10) and removing them from P_I (line 11). In fact, it is only at this time point that these two rules can fire and produce some derivations.

The application of our method to Example 1 as shown before illustrates the benefit of our technique: The facts that some atoms were missing in one time point resulted in disabling two rules and for two time points reasoning was performed considering only r_1, and this can result in a better runtime.

5   Evaluation

We implemented a new reasoner in Golang which includes the optimization introduced in Laser and the technique proposed in this paper. The re-implementation was necessary since the pre-existing implementation of Laser was too prototypical to be extended. Throughout, we refer to the old Laser as "Laser1" and to the new implementation as "Laser2".

Below, we report the results of a number of experiments that we executed to illustrate the benefit introduced by our technique. The experiments can be grouped into four classes:

- *Ours vs. Laser1*: We compare the runtime vs. our old implementation;
- *Runtime single rule (best case)*: We study the runtime in the best case;
- *Runtime single rule (worst case)*: We study the runtime in the worst case;
- *Runtime multiple rules*: We observe the runtime with multiple rules.

Inputs. Although several benchmarks for stream processing exist (e.g., SRBench [38]) we are not aware of any that supports the operators in LARS and that can be used to stress the techniques introduced in this paper. In order to have full control on the experimental setting and to accurately measure the effects with the various configurations, we created, in a similar fashion as done in [4], a number of microbenchmarks that are specifically designed to evaluate our technique.

Evaluation Setup. We ran all the experiments on an iMac equipped with 8-core Intel(R) 2.60 GHz CPU and 8 GB of memory. We used Golang 1.13 to compile and run our system and Pypy 7.2.0 to run Laser1. To minimize the footprint of external effects (e.g., memory garbage collection, etc.) in our results, we run each experiment ten times over 300 time points and report the average result.

Ours vs. Laser1. Before we evaluate our proposal, we report some experiments where we compare the performance of Laser1 and Laser2 (the latter is executed without our proposed optimization). The motivation for doing so is to show that our new implementation is more performant than the old one, and this justifies its usage in the following experiments when we evaluate our technique.

In this set of experiments, we created a number of programs P_n where $n \in \{10, 50, 100\}$ which contain a single rule of the form $\boxplus^n \Diamond p(X, Y) \rightarrow q(X, Y)$.

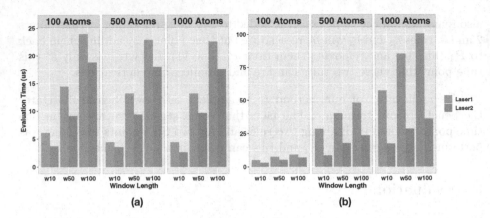

Fig. 1. Runtime of Laser1 and Laser2. In (a), w_n refers to P_n. In (b), w_n refers to P'_n.

Similarly, we have also created other programs P'_n with the rule $\boxplus^n \Box p(X, Y) \rightarrow q(X, Y)$. Intuitively, $P_{10,50,100}$ test the performance of the reasoner with a rule that uses the $\Diamond$ operator while $P'_{10,50,100}$ does the same but with the $\Box$ operator.

In each experiment, we instruct the data generator to create, at each time point, the set of facts $\bigcup_{i:=1}^{m} \{p(a_i, a_i)\}$ where $m \in \{100, 500, 1000\}$. In this way, we can stress the system both varying the window size and the number of facts in input. The average reasoning runtime for processing one input fact with $P_{10,50,100}$ is reported in Fig. 1a while the one with $P'_{10,50,100}$ is reported in Fig. 1b.

From the figures, we can see that in both cases Laser2 outperforms Laser1. In addition, we can make some interesting observations about the operators $\Diamond$ and $\Box$. In Fig. 1a, we can see that if the number of input atoms increases and the window size remains constant, then the average runtime remains relatively constant or even decreases. This behavior is due to the usage of the horizon time introduced in [4] which extends the validity of a formula for as many time points as the window size. Moreover, reasoning at each time point has a fixed cost that is amortized over the input facts. If there are more input facts, this cost becomes less prominent. This explains the slight decrease in the runtime when the input size increases.

The results in Fig. 1b show a different behaviour. In this case, the validity of the body of the rule cannot be extended to the future. Consequently, the runtime increases both when the window size increases (since the reasoner has to check that the facts hold at more time points) and when the size of the stream increases. This shows that the evaluation of $\Box$ can be much more challenging than $\Diamond$. The increase of the runtime is observed with both implementations although with Laser2 it is less pronounced. The reason behind this difference is purely technical and due to the fact that the new implementation does not have the overhead introduced by the interpretation layer of Python.

Runtime Single Rule (Best Case). We now compare the runtime on a simple benchmark with and without activating our technique. We consider a series of

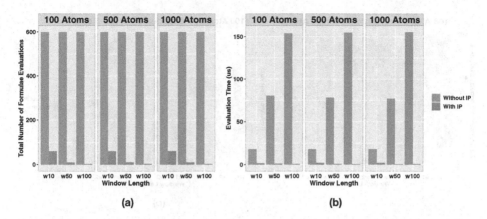

Fig. 2. Total number of evaluated formulae (a) and average runtime per input fact (b) in a best-case scenario.

programs which contain a single rule of the form $\boxplus^n \Diamond p(X,Y), \boxplus^n \Box q(X,Y) \rightarrow m(X,Y)$ where $n \in \{10, 50, 100\}$. We apply the programs on different streams. At time point i, the various streams contain the facts $\bigcup_{i:=1}^m \{p(a_i, a_i)\}$ if i mod $n = 0$ or $\bigcup_{i:=1}^m \{p(a_i, a_i), q(a_i, a_i)\}$ otherwise, where $m \in \{100, 500, 1000\}$. In essence, the idea is to use a stream where every n time points there are no q−facts so that $\boxplus^n \Box q(X,Y)$ does not hold and consequently the rule is disabled. This scenario represents the best case for our method because without it the reasoner would need to evaluate the rule at each time point.

Figures 2a and 2b report the total number of formulae evaluations and the average runtime per input fact with different window and stream sizes. The results marked with "With IP" ("Without IP") use (don't use) our technique. The results show that with our approach the reasoner evaluates many fewer formulae (because the rule is disabled most of the time). Note that when our technique is enabled the number of evaluated formulae is non-zero. The reason is that every n time points the counter for disabling the rule expires and the rule is re-added to the set of active rules. This event occurs less frequently if the window size is larger. This explains why the number of evaluated formulae decreases in Fig. 2a.

As a consequence that some rules are disabled, the runtime decreases to the point it is barely visible in Fig. 2b. It is worth to point out that in Fig. 2b the runtime with our technique is almost constant while, without our technique, it increases with the window size (this behavior was observed also in Fig. 1b). This comparison illustrates the effectiveness of our approach in disabling rules.

Runtime Single Rule (Worst Case). In the previous set of experiments, we evaluated our technique in a best-case scenario. We now present some experiments in a worst-case scenario. To simulate this case, we consider programs with the rule $\boxplus^{10} \Diamond p(X,Y), \boxplus^n \Box q(X,Y) \rightarrow m(X,Y)$ where n (i.e., the window size) is very small. In particular, we considered $n \in \{1, 2, 3\}$. If $n = 1$ and the rule is

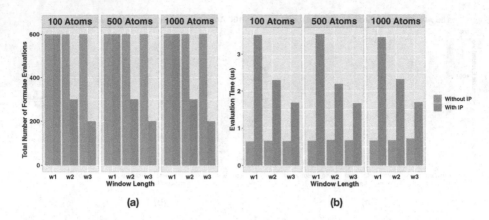

Fig. 3. Total number of evaluated formulae (a) and average runtime per input fact (b) in a worst-case scenario.

disabled, then our approach immediately re-adds it in the next iteration since its invalidity has expired. For this reason, we can use this type of program to measure the overhead of our approach with an input where it is not effective. As input streams, we consider those that add the facts $\bigcup_{i:=1}^{m}\{p(a_i, a_i)\}$ at each time point where $m \in \{100, 500, 1000\}$. Note that since no fact with predicate q appears in the stream, the rule will always try to disable it (unless it was already previously disabled) but in the next 1, 2, or 3 time points the rule will be re-activated.

Figures 3a and 3b report, similarly as before, the number of formulae evaluations and the runtime per input fact. From these results, we observe that when the window size is one (which is the worst scenario), the number of evaluations is the same as when our technique is disabled. However, the overhead incurred by our approach significantly increases the runtime. If the window size increases, then the performance improves because the overhead is less prominent.

Note that there is a simple optimization to overcome the problem observed in this experiment: When we populate R in line 5 of Algorithm 1, we can consider only the formulae where the window size is sufficiently large (e.g., $x > 10$). In this way, we can restrict the application only to the cases whether the saving introduced by our technique outweighs the overhead.

Runtime Multiple Rules. We have shown that sometimes disabling a rule can have a cascading effect that leads to the disabling of more rules. To test the performance in this scenario, we consider a series of programs of the form

$$\boxplus^n \Diamond p(X, Y) \wedge \boxplus^n \Box q(X, Y) \rightarrow h_1(X, Y) \qquad (r_1)$$
$$h_1(X, Y) \rightarrow h_2(X, Y) \qquad (r_2)$$
$$\dots \qquad (r_{3\dots w-1})$$
$$h_{w-1}(X, Y) \rightarrow h_w(X, Y) \qquad (r_w)$$

where $n \in \{10, 50, 100\}$ and $w \in \{10, 20\}$. As input, we use a fixed stream which contains the facts $\bigcup_{i:=1}^{300}\{p(a_i, a_i)\}$ at each time point.

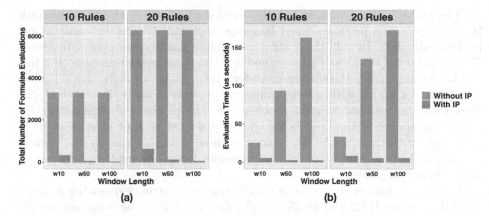

Fig. 4. Total number of evaluated formulae (a) and average runtime per input fact (b) with multiple rules.

Figures 4a and 4b report the total number of formulae evaluations and the average runtime per input fact respectively. We observe a similar trend as in the previous cases: Without our technique, at each time point the reasoner evaluates many more formulae and the runtime is significantly higher. With our technique, the average runtime drops and remains reasonably constant with different window sizes and number of rules (the slight increase is due to the overhead incurred by larger programs). The saving can be very high: In the best case (with $n = 100$ and $w = 20$), the runtime is 31 times faster. Although these numbers are obtained with artificially created datasets, they nevertheless indicate the effectiveness of our proposal in speeding up stream reasoning.

6 Related Work and Conclusion

Related Work. The problem of stream reasoning in the context of the Semantic Web was first introduced by Della Valle et al. in [11,12]. Since then, numerous works have been focused on different aspects of this problem and yearly workshops[1] have further fostered the creation of an active research community.

The surveys at [13,21] provide a first overview of the various techniques. A few influential works have tackled this problem by extending SPARQL with stream operators [2,3,7–9]. Additionally, other stream reasoners either propose a custom processing model [20] or rely on (probabilistic) ASP [15,25,38] or on combinations of the two [22]. Finally, some works focus on improving the scalability [16,26,27] by distributing the computation on multiple machines or with incremental techniques [19]. Since these works support different semantics, it is challenging to compare them. Indeed, providing a fair and comprehensive comparison of the various proposal remains an open problem, despite notable efforts in this direction [30,33,34].

---

[1] The last one was in Apr.'19: https://sr2019.on.liu.se/.

The problem of stream reasoning has been studied also by the AI community. In [18], Koopmann proposes a new language to provide OBQA on temporal and probabilistic data. In [32], the authors investigate stream reasoning with Metric Temporal Logic (MTL) and later extend it with approximate reasoning [10]. In a similar setting, in [36], the authors consider stream reasoning in datalogMTL – an extension of Datalog with metric temporal operators. Finally, Ronca et al. [29] introduced the window validity problem, i.e., the problem of determining the minimum number of time points for which data must be kept in main memory to comply with the window sizes. None of these works address the problem of exploiting the impossibility of future derivations for improving the performance, as we do in this paper.

Finally, a research area that is closely related to stream reasoning is incremental reasoning [17,23,24,28,35,37]. The major difference between incremental reasoning and stream reasoning is that the latter is characterized by the usage of windows functions to focus on the most recent data. Moreover, in a typical stream reasoning scenario data expires after a relatively short amount of time.

Conclusion. In this paper, we tackled the problem of providing efficient stream-based reasoning with (plain) LARS programs. In our previous work [4] we proposed a technique to reduce the number of redundant derivations by extending the time validity of formulae which will *hold* in the future. Here, we presented a technique to extend the time validity of formulae which will *not hold*. This is meant to target formulae where the previous technique is not effective.

Future work can be done in multiple directions. First, it is interesting to study whether more advanced techniques can determine a longer time validity (or invalidity) for formulae which are beyond plain LARS (e.g., nested windows). Moreover, a dynamic strategy can be designed to detect whether for some formulae a naïve recomputation is faster. Such a strategy could be used to mitigate the performance decrease observed in the worst-case scenario. Finally, our technique is triggered when no atoms with a certain predicate appear in the stream. It is possible that a more fine-grained technique, which considers facts rather than predicates, leads to improvements in more cases, but it is not trivial to implement it without introducing significant overhead.

Our experimental evaluation on artificially created microbenchmarks shows that the performance gain is significant. This makes our proposal a valuable addition to the portfolio of techniques for computing logic-based stream reasoning efficiently and at scale.

References

1. Abiteboul, S., Hull, R., Vianu, V.: Foundations of Databases, vol. 8. Addison-Wesley Reading, Boston (1995)
2. Anicic, D., Fodor, P., Rudolph, S., Stojanovic, N.: EP-SPARQL: a unified language for event processing and stream reasoning. In: Proceedings of WWW, pp. 635–644 (2011)

3. Barbieri, D.F., Braga, D., Ceri, S., Valle, E.D., Grossniklaus, M.: C-SPARQL: a continuous query language for RDF data streams. Int. J. Seman. Comput. **4**(1), 3–25 (2010)
4. Bazoobandi, H.R., Beck, H., Urbani, J.: Expressive stream reasoning with laser. In: d'Amato, C., et al. (eds.) ISWC 2017. LNCS, vol. 10587, pp. 87–103. Springer, Cham (2017). https://doi.org/10.1007/978-3-319-68288-4_6
5. Beck, H., Dao-Tran, M., Eiter, T.: Lars: a logic-based framework for analytic reasoning over streams. Artif. Intell. **261**, 16–70 (2018)
6. Beck, H., Eiter, T., Folie, C.: Ticker: a system for incremental ASP-based stream reasoning. Theory and Practice of Logic Programming **17**(5–6), 744–763 (2017)
7. Bolles, A., Grawunder, M., Jacobi, J.: Streaming SPARQL - extending SPARQL to process data streams. In: Bechhofer, S., Hauswirth, M., Hoffmann, J., Koubarakis, M. (eds.) ESWC 2008. LNCS, vol. 5021, pp. 448–462. Springer, Heidelberg (2008). https://doi.org/10.1007/978-3-540-68234-9_34
8. Bonte, P., Tommasini, R., De Turck, F., Ongenae, F., Valle, E.D.: C-Sprite: efficient hierarchical reasoning for rapid RDF stream processing. In: Proceedings of DEBS, pp. 103–114 (2019)
9. Calbimonte, J.-P., Corcho, O., Gray, A.J.G.: Enabling ontology-based access to streaming data sources. In: Patel-Schneider, P.F., et al. (eds.) ISWC 2010. LNCS, vol. 6496, pp. 96–111. Springer, Heidelberg (2010). https://doi.org/10.1007/978-3-642-17746-0_7
10. de Leng, D., Heintz, F.: Approximate stream reasoning with metric temporal logic under uncertainty. In: Proceedings of AAAI, pp. 2760–2767 (2019)
11. Della Valle, E., Ceri, S., Barbieri, D.F., Braga, D., Campi, A.: A first step towards stream reasoning. In: Domingue, J., Fensel, D., Traverso, P. (eds.) FIS 2008. LNCS, vol. 5468, pp. 72–81. Springer, Heidelberg (2009). https://doi.org/10.1007/978-3-642-00985-3_6
12. Valle, E.D., Ceri, S., Van Harmelen, F., Fensel, D.: It's a streaming world! reasoning upon rapidly changing information. IEEE Intell. Syst. **24**(6), 83–89 (2009)
13. Dell'Aglio, D., Della Valle, E., van Harmelen, F., Bernstein, A.: Stream reasoning: a survey and outlook. Data Sci. **1**(1–2), 59–83 (2017)
14. Eiter, T., Ogris, P., Schekotihin, K.: A distributed approach to LARS stream reasoning (System paper). Theor. Pract. Logic Program. **19**(5–6), 974–989 (2019)
15. Gebser, M., Grote, T., Kaminski, R., Obermeier, P., Sabuncu, O., Schaub, T.: Answer set programming for stream reasoning. CoRR, abs/1301.1392 (2013)
16. Hoeksema, J., Kotoulas, S.: High-performance distributed stream reasoning using S4. In: Ordring Workshop at ISWC (2011)
17. Hu, P., Motik, B., Horrocks, I.: Optimised maintenance of datalog materialisations. In: Proceedings of AAAI, pp. 1871–1879 (2018)
18. Koopmann, P.: Ontology-based query answering for probabilistic temporal data. In: Proceedings of AAAI, pp. 2903–2910 (2019)
19. Le-Phuoc, D.: Operator-aware approach for boosting performance in RDF stream processing. J. Web Semant. **42**, 38–54 (2017)
20. Le-Phuoc, D., Dao-Tran, M., Xavier Parreira, J., Hauswirth, M.: A native and adaptive approach for unified processing of linked streams and linked data. In: Aroyo, L., et al. (eds.) ISWC 2011. LNCS, vol. 7031, pp. 370–adaptive approach for unified388. Springer, Heidelberg (2011). https://doi.org/10.1007/978-3-642-25073-6_24
21. Margara, A., Urbani, J., Van Harmelen, F., Bal, H.: Streaming the web: reasoning over dynamic data. J. Web Semant. **25**, 24–44 (2014)

22. Mileo, A., Abdelrahman, A., Policarpio, S., Hauswirth, M.: StreamRule: a non-monotonic stream reasoning system for the semantic web. In: Faber, W., Lembo, D. (eds.) RR 2013. LNCS, vol. 7994, pp. 247–252. Springer, Heidelberg (2013). https://doi.org/10.1007/978-3-642-39666-3_23

23. Motik, B., Nenov, Y., Piro, R., Horrocks, I.: Incremental update of datalog materialisation: the backward/forward algorithm. In: Proceedings of AAAI, pp. 1560–1568 (2015)

24. Motik, B., Nenov, Y., Piro, R., Horrocks, I.: Maintenance of datalog materialisations revisited. Artif. Intell. **269**, 76–136 (2019)

25. Nickles, M., Mileo, A.: Web stream reasoning using probabilistic answer set programming. In: Kontchakov, R., Mugnier, M.-L. (eds.) RR 2014. LNCS, vol. 8741, pp. 197–205. Springer, Cham (2014). https://doi.org/10.1007/978-3-319-11113-1_16

26. Pham, T.-L., Ali, M.I., Mileo, A.: Enhancing the scalability of expressive stream reasoning via input-driven parallelization. Semant. Web **10**(3), 457–474 (2019)

27. Ren, X., Curé, O., et al.: Strider R: massive and distributed RDF graph stream reasoning. In: Proceedings of International Conference on Big Data, pp. 3358–3367 (2017)

28. Ren, Y., Pan, J.Z.: Optimising ontology stream reasoning with truth maintenance system. In: Proceedings of CIKM, pp. 831–836 (2011)

29. Ronca, A., Kaminski, M., Grau, B.C., Horrocks, I.: The window validity problem in rule-based stream reasoning. In: Proceedings of KR, pp. 571–580 (2018)

30. Scharrenbach, T., Urbani, J., Margara, A., Della Valle, E., Bernstein, A.: Seven commandments for benchmarking semantic flow processing systems. In: Cimiano, P., Corcho, O., Presutti, V., Hollink, L., Rudolph, S. (eds.) ESWC 2013. LNCS, vol. 7882, pp. 305–319. Springer, Heidelberg (2013). https://doi.org/10.1007/978-3-642-38288-8_21

31. Suchan, J., et al.: Out of sight but not out of mind: an answer set programming based online abduction framework for visual sensemaking in autonomous driving. In: Proceedings of IJCAI, pp. 1879–1885 (2019)

32. Tiger, M., Heintz, F.: Stream reasoning using temporal logic and predictive probabilistic state models. In: 23rd International Symposium on Temporal Representation and Reasoning, pp. 196–205 (2016)

33. Tommasini, R., Della Valle, E., Balduini, M., Dell'Aglio, D.: Heaven: a framework for systematic comparative research approach for RSP engines. In: Sack, H., Blomqvist, E., d'Aquin, M., Ghidini, C., Ponzetto, S.P., Lange, C. (eds.) ESWC 2016. LNCS, vol. 9678, pp. 250–265. Springer, Cham (2016). https://doi.org/10.1007/978-3-319-34129-3_16

34. Tommasini, R., Della Valle, E., Mauri, A., Brambilla, M.: RSPLab: RDF stream processing benchmarking made easy. In: d'Amato, C., et al. (eds.) ISWC 2017. LNCS, vol. 10588, pp. 202–209. Springer, Cham (2017). https://doi.org/10.1007/978-3-319-68204-4_21

35. Urbani, J., Margara, A., Jacobs, C., van Harmelen, F., Bal, H.: DynamiTE: parallel materialization of dynamic RDF data. In: Alani, H., et al. (eds.) ISWC 2013. LNCS, vol. 8218, pp. 657–672. Springer, Heidelberg (2013). https://doi.org/10.1007/978-3-642-41335-3_41

36. Walega, P.A., Kaminski, M., Grau, B.C.: Reasoning over streaming data in metric temporal datalog. In: Proceedings of AAAI, pp. 3092–3099 (2019)

37. Wang, Y., Luo, J.: An incremental reasoning algorithm for large scale knowledge graph. In: Liu, W., Giunchiglia, F., Yang, B. (eds.) KSEM 2018. LNCS (LNAI), vol. 11061, pp. 503–513. Springer, Cham (2018). https://doi.org/10.1007/978-3-319-99365-2_45

38. Zhang, Y., Duc, P.M., Corcho, O., Calbimonte, J.-P.: SRBench: a streaming RDF/SPARQL benchmark. In: Cudré-Mauroux, P., et al. (eds.) ISWC 2012. LNCS, vol. 7649, pp. 641–657. Springer, Heidelberg (2012). https://doi.org/10.1007/978-3-642-35176-1_40

Modular Graphical Ontology Engineering Evaluated

Cogan Shimizu[1]($\boxtimes$)(iD), Karl Hammar[2](iD), and Pascal Hitzler[1](iD)

[1] Data Semantics Lab, Kansas State University, Manhattan, USA
{coganmshimizu,phitzler}@ksu.edu
[2] Jönköping AI Lab, Jönköping University, Jönköping, Sweden
karl.hammar@ju.se

Abstract. Ontology engineering is traditionally a complex and time-consuming process, requiring an intimate knowledge of description logic and predicting non-local effects of different ontological commitments. Pattern-based modular ontology engineering, coupled with a graphical modeling paradigm, can help make ontology engineering accessible to modellers with limited ontology expertise. We have developed CoMo-dIDE, the Comprehensive Modular Ontology IDE, to develop and explore such a modeling approach. In this paper we present an evaluation of the CoModIDE tool, with a set of 21 subjects carrying out some typical modeling tasks. Our findings indicate that using CoModIDE improves task completion rate and reduces task completion time, compared to using standard Protégé. Further, our subjects report higher System Usability Scale (SUS) evaluation scores for CoModIDE, than for Protégé. The subjects also report certain room for improvements in the CoModIDE tool – notably, these comments all concern comparatively shallow UI bugs or issues, rather than limitations inherent in the proposed modeling method itself. We deduce that our modeling approach is viable, and propose some consequences for ontology engineering tool development.

1 Introduction

Building a knowledge graph, as with any complex system, is an expensive endeavor, requiring extensive time and expertise. For many, the magnitude of resources required for building and maintaining a knowledge graph is untenable. Yet, knowledge graphs are still poised to be a significant disruptor in both the private and public sectors [17]. As such, lowering the barriers of entry is very important. More specifically, it will be necessary to increase the approachability of knowledge graph development best practices, thus reducing the need for dedicated expertise. Of course, we do not mean imply that *no* expertise is desirable, simply that a dedicated knowledge engineer may be out of reach for small firms or research groups. For this paper, we focus on the best practices according to the eXtreme design (XD) [4] and modular ontology modeling (MOM) [12] paradigms. To this point, we are interested in how tooling infrastructure can improve approachability. In the context of our chosen paradigms and focus on

© Springer Nature Switzerland AG 2020
A. Harth et al. (Eds.): ESWC 2020, LNCS 12123, pp. 20–35, 2020.
https://doi.org/10.1007/978-3-030-49461-2_2

tooling infrastructure, approachability may be proxied by *the amount of effort to produce correct and reasonable output*, where effort is a function of tool-user experience (UX) and time taken. Furthermore, by using tooling infrastructure to encapsulate best practices, it improves the maintainability and evolvability accordingly.

In particular, this paper investigates the use of a graphical modeling tool that encapsulates the pattern-driven philosophies of XD and MOM. To do so, we have developed CoModIDE (the *Comprehensive Modular Ontology IDE* – pronounced "commodity"), a plugin for the popular ontology editing platform, Protégé [16]. In order to show that CoModIDE improves approachability of knowledge graph development, we have formulated for the following hypotheses.

H1. When using CoModIDE, a user takes less time to produce correct and reasonable output, than when using Protege.
H2. A user will find CoModIDE to have a higher SUS score than when using Protege alone.

The remainder of this paper is organized as follows. Section 2 presents CoModIDE. Section 3 discusses related work on graphical modeling and ontology design pattern use and development. We present our experimental design in Sect. 4, our results in Sect. 5, and a discussion of those results and their implications in Sect. 6. Finally, Sect. 7 concludes the paper, and suggests possibilities for future research.

2   CoModIDE: A Comprehensive Modular Ontology IDE

2.1   Motivator: A Graphical and Modular Ontology Design Process

CoModIDE is intended to simplify ontology engineering for users who are not ontology experts. Our experience indicates that such non-experts rarely need or want to make use of the full set of language constructs that OWL 2 provides; instead, they typically, at least at the outset, want to model rather simple semantics. Such users (and, indeed also more advanced users) often prefer to do initial modeling in pair or group settings, and to do it graphically – whether that be on whiteboards, in vector drawing software, or even on paper. This further limits the modeling constructs to those that can be expressed somewhat intuitively using graphical notations (such that all involved participants, regardless of their ontology engineering skill level, can understand and contribute).

This initial design process typically iterates rapidly and fluidly, with the modeling task being broken down into individual problems of manageable complexity[1]; candidate solutions to these problem pieces being drawn up, analysed and discussed; a suitable solution selected and documented; and the next step

---

[1] We find that the size of such partial solutions typically fit on a medium-sized whiteboard; but whether this is a naturally manageable size for humans to operate with, or whether it is the result of constraints of or conditioning to the available tooling, i.e., the size of the whiteboards often mounted in conference rooms, we cannot say.

of the problem then tackled. Many times, the formalization of the developed solution into an OWL ontology is carried out after-the-fact, by a designated ontologist with extensive knowledge of both the language and applicable tooling. However, this comes at a cost, both in terms of hours expended, and in terms of the risk of incorrect interpretations of the previously drawn graphical representations (the OWL standard does not define a graphical notation syntax, so such representations are sometimes ambiguous).

The design process discussed above mirrors the principles of *eXtreme Design* (XD) [4]: working in pairs, breaking apart the modeling task into discrete problems, and iterating and refactoring as needed. XD also emphasizes the use of *Ontology Design Patterns* (ODPs) as solutions to frequently recurring modeling problems. Combining ODP usage with the graphical modeling process discussed above (specifically with the need to in an agile manner refactor and modify partial solutions) requires that the partial solutions (or *modules*) derived from ODPs are annotated, such that they can at a later time be isolated for study, modified, or replaced.

In summary it would be useful for our target user group if there were tooling available that supported 1) intuitive and agile graphical modeling, directly outputting OWL ontologies (avoiding the need for the aforementioned postprocessing), and 2) reuse of ODPs to create and maintain ODP-based modules. Hence, CoModIDE.

2.2   Design and Features

The design criteria for CoModIDE, derived from the requirements discussed above, are as follows:

- CoModIDE should support visual-first ontology engineering, based on a graph representation of classes, properties, and datatypes. This graphical rendering of an ontology built using CoModIDE should be consistent across restarts, machines, and operating system or Protégé versions.
- CoModIDE should support the type of OWL 2 constructs that can be easily and intuitively understood when rendered as a schema diagram. To model more advanced constructs (unions and intersections in property domains or ranges, the property subsumption hierarchy, property chains, etc), the user can drop back into the standard Protégé tabs.
- CoModIDE should embed an ODP repository. Each included ODP should be free-standing and completely documented. There should be no external dependency on anything outside of the user's machine[2]. If the user wishes, they should be able to load a separately downloaded ODP repository, to replace or complement the built-in one.

---

[2] Our experience indicates that while our target users are generally enthusiastic about the idea of reusing design patterns, they are quickly turned off of the idea when they are faced with patterns that lack documentation or that exhibit link rot.

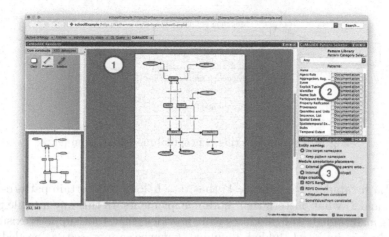

Fig. 1. CoModIDE User Interface featuring 1) the schema editor, 2) the pattern library, and 3) the configuration view.

– CoModIDE should support simple composition of ODPs; patterns should snap together like Lego blocks, ideally with potential connection points between the patterns lighting up while dragging compatible patterns. The resulting ontology modules should maintain their coherence and be treated like modules in a consistent manner across restarts, machines, etc. A pattern or ontology interface concept will need be developed to support this.

CoModIDE is developed as a plugin to the versatile and well-established Protégé ontology engineering environment. The plugin provides three Protégé views, and a tab that hosts these views (see Fig. 1). The *schema editor* view provides an a graphical overview of an ontology's structure, including the classes in the ontology, their subclass relations, and the object and datatype properties in the ontology that relate these classes to one another and to datatypes. All of these entities can be manipulated graphically through dragging and dropping. The *pattern library* view provides a set of built-in ontology design patterns, sourced from various projects and from the ODP community wiki[3]. A user can drag and drop design patterns from the pattern library onto the canvas to instantiate those patterns as modules in their ontology. The *configuration* view lets the user configure the behavior of the other CoModIDE views and their components. For a detailed description, we refer the reader to the video walkthrough on the CoModIDE webpage[4]. We also invite the reader to download and install CoModIDE themselves, from that same site.

When a pattern is dragged onto the canvas, the constructs in that pattern are copied into the ontology (optionally having their IRIs updated to correspond with the target ontology namespace), but they are also annotated using

---

[3] http://ontologydesignpatterns.org/.
[4] https://comodide.com.

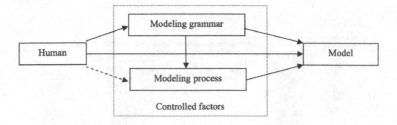

Fig. 2. Factors affecting conceptual modeling, from [9].

the OPLa vocabulary, to indicate 1) that they belong to a certain pattern-based module, and 2) what pattern that module implements. In this way module provenance is maintained, and modules can, provided that tool support exists (see Sect. 7) be manipulated (folded, unfolded, removed, annotated) as needed.

3 Related Work

Graphical Conceptual Modeling [9] proposes three factors (see Fig. 2) that influence the construction of a conceptual model, such as an ontology; namely, the *person* doing the modeling (both their experience and know-how, and their interpretation of the world, of the modeling task, and of model quality in general), the *modeling grammar* (primarily its expressive power/completeness and its clarity), and the *modeling process* (including both initial conceptualisation and subsequent formal model-making). Crucially, only the latter two factors can feasibly be controlled in academic studies. The related work discussed below tends to focus on one or the other of these factors, i.e., studying the characteristics of a modeling language *or* a modeling process. Our work on CoMo-dIDE straddles this divide: employing graphical modeling techniques reduces the grammar available from standard OWL to those fragments of OWL that can be represented intuitively in graphical format; employing design patterns affects the modeling process.

Graphical modeling approaches to conceptual modeling have been extensively explored and evaluated in fields such as database modeling, software engineering, business process modeling, etc. Studying model grammar, [22] compares EER notation with an early UML-like notation from a comprehensibility point-of-view. This work observes that restrictions are easier to understand in a notation where they are displayed coupled to the types they apply to, rather than the relations they range over. [7] proposes a quality model for EER diagrams that can also extend to UML. Some of the quality criteria in this model, that are relevant in graphical modeling of OWL ontologies, include *minimality* (i.e., avoiding duplication of elements), *expressiveness* (i.e., displaying all of the required elements), and simplicity (displaying no more than the required elements).

[1] study the usability of UML, and report that users perceive UML class diagrams (closest in intended use to ontology visualizations) to be less easy-to-use

than other types of UML diagrams; in particular, relationship multiplicities (i.e., cardinalities) are considered frustrating by several of their subjects. UML displays such multiplicities by numeric notation on the end of connecting lines between classes. [13] analyses UML and argues that while it is a useful tool in a design phase, it is overly complex and as a consequence, suffers from redundancies, overlaps, and breaks in uniformity. [13] also cautions against using difficult-to-read and -interpret adornments on graphical models, as UML allows.

Various approaches have been developed for presenting ontologies visually and enabling their development through a graphical modeling interface, the most prominent of which is probably *VOWL*, the *Visual Notation for OWL Ontologies* [15], and its implementation viewer/editor WebVOWL [14,23]. VOWL employs a force-directed graph layout (reducing the number of crossing lines, increasing legibility) and explicitly focuses on usability for users less familiar with ontologies. As a consequence of this, VOWL renders certain structures in a way that, while not formally consistent with the underlying semantics, supports comprehensibility; for instance, datatype nodes and owl:Thing nodes are duplicated across the canvas, so that the model does not implode into a tight cluster around such often used nodes. It has been evaluated over several user studies with users ranging from laymen to more experienced ontologists, with results indicating good comprehensibility. CoModIDE has taken influence from VOWL, e.g., in how we render datatype nodes. However, in a collaborative editing environment in which the graphical layout of nodes and edges needs to remain consistent for all users, and relatively stable over time, we find the force-directed graph structure (which changes continuously as entities are added/removed) to be unsuitable.

For such collaborative modeling use cases, the commercial offering *Grafo*[5] offers a very attractive feature set, combining the usability of a VOWL-like notation with stable positioning, and collaborative editing features. Crucially, however, Grafo does not support pattern-based modular modeling, and as a web-hosted service, does not allow for customizations or plugins that would support such a modeling paradigm.

CoModIDE is partially based on the Protégé plugin *OWLAx*, as presented in [19]. This plugin supports one-way translation from graphical schema diagrams drawn by the user, into OWL ontology classes and properties; however, it does not render such constructs back into a graphical form. There is thus no way of continually maintaining and developing an ontology using only OWLAx. There is also no support for design pattern reuse in this tool.

Ontology Design Patterns. Ontology Design Patterns (ODPs) were introduced by Gangemi [8] and Blomqvist and Sandkuhl [2] in 2005, as a means of simplifying ontology development. ODPs are intended to guide non-expert users, by packaging best practices into reusable blocks of functionality, to be adapted and specialised by those users in individual ontology development projects. Presutti et al. [18] defines a typology of ODPs, including patterns for reasoning, naming, transformation, etc. The eXtreme Design methodology [4] describes how

---

[5] https://gra.fo.

ontology engineering projects can be broken down into discrete sub-tasks, to be solved by using ODPs. Prior studies indicate that the use of ODPs can lower the number of modeling errors and inconsistencies in ontologies, and that they are by the users perceived as useful and helpful [3,5].

Applying the XD method and ODPs requires the availability of both high-quality ODPs, and of tools and infrastructure that support ODP use. Recent work in this area, by the authors and others, includes *XDP*, a fork of the WebProtégé ontology editor [10]; the *OPLa* annotations vocabulary that models how ontology concepts can be grouped into modules, and the provenance of and interrelations between such modules, including to ODPs [11]; and the MODL library, a curated and specially documented collection of high-quality patterns for use in many domains [21]. CoModIDE draws influence from all of these works, and includes the MODL library as its default pattern library, using an OPLa-based representation of those patterns.

4   Research Method

Our experiment is comprised of four steps: a survey to collect subject background data (familiarity with ontology languages and tools), two modeling tasks, and a follow-up survey to collect information on the usability of both Protégé and CoModIDE. The tasks were designed to emulate a common ontology engineering process, where a conceptual design is developed and agreed upon by whiteboard prototyping, and a developer is then assigned to formalizing the resulting white-board schema diagram into an OWL ontology.

During each of the modeling tasks, participants are asked to generate a *reasonable* and *correct* OWL file for the provided schema diagram. In order to prevent a learning effect, the two tasks utilize two different schema diagrams. To prevent bias arising from differences in task complexity, counterbalancing was employed (such that half the users performed the first task with standard Protégé and the second task with CoModIDE, and half did the opposite). The correctness of the developed OWL files, and the time taken to complete each tasks, were recorded (the latter was however, for practical reasons, limited to 20 min per task).

The following sections provide a brief overview of each the steps. The source material for the entire experiment is available online[6].

Introductory Tutorial. As previously mentioned, our intent is to improve the approachability of ontology modeling by making it more accessible to those without expertise in knowledge engineering. As such, when recruiting our participants for this evaluation, we did not place any requirements on ontology modeling familiarity. However, to establish a shared baseline knowledge of foundational modeling concepts (such as one would assume participants would have in the situation we try to emulate, see above), we provided a 10 min tutorial

---

[6] http://urn.kb.se/resolve?urn=urn:nbn:se:hj:diva-47887.

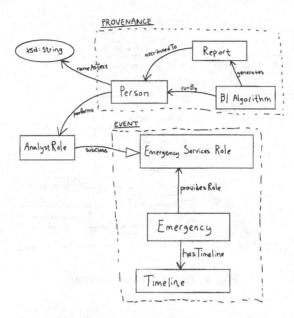

Fig. 3. Task A schema diagram

on ontologies, classes, properties, domains, and ranges. The slides used for this tutorial may be found online with the rest of the experiment's source materials.

a priori **Survey.** The purpose of the *a priori* survey was to collect information relating to the participants base level familiarity with topics related to knowledge modeling, to be used as control variables in later analysis. We used a 5-point Likert scale for rating the accuracy of the following statements.

CV1. I have done ontology modeling before.
CV2. I am familiar with Ontology Design Patterns.
CV3. I am familiar with Manchester Syntax.
CV4. I am familiar with Description Logics.
CV5. I am familiar with Protégé.

Finally, we asked the participants to describe their relationship to the test leader, (e.g. student, colleague, same research lab, not familiar).

Modeling Task A. In Task A, participants were to develop an ontology to model how an analyst might generate reports about an ongoing emergency. The scenario identified two design patterns to use:

- **Provenance**: to track who made a report and how;
- **Event**: to capture the notion of an emergency.

Figure 3 shows how these patterns are instantiated and connected together. Overall the schema diagram contains seven concepts, one datatype, one subclass relation, one data property, and six object properties.

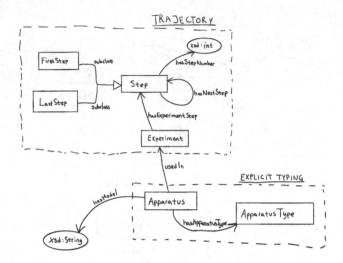

Fig. 4. Task B schema diagram

Modeling Task B. In Task B, participants were to develop an ontology to capture the steps of an experiment. The scenario identified two design patterns to use:

- **Trajectory**: to track the order of the steps;
- **Explicit Typing**: to easily model different types of apparatus.

Figure 4 shows how these patterns are instantiated and connected together. Overall, the schema diagram contains six concepts, two datatypes, two subclass relations, two data properties, and four object properties (one of which is a self-loop).

a posteriori **Survey,** The *a posteriori* survey included the SUS evaluations for both Protégé and CoModIDE. The SUS is a very common "quick and dirty," yet reliable tool for measuring the usability of a system. It consists of ten questions, the answers to which are used to compute a total usability score of 0–100. Additional information on the SUS and its included questions can be found online.[7]

Additionally, we inquire about CoModIDE-specific features. These statements are also rated using a Likert scale. However, we do not use this data in our evaluation, except to inform our future work, as described in Sect. 7. Finally, we requested any free-text comments on CoModIDE's features.

5   Results

5.1   Participant Pool Composition

Of the 21 subjects, 12 reported some degree of familiarity with the authors, while 9 reported no such connection. In terms of self-reported ontology engineering familiarity, the responses are as detailed in Table 1. It should be observed that responses vary widely, with a relative standard deviation (σ/mean) of 43–67%.

---

[7] https://www.usability.gov/how-to-and-tools/methods/system-usability-scale.html.

Table 1. Mean, standard deviation, relative standard deviation, and median responses to *a priori* statements

	mean	σ	relative σ	median
CV1: I have done ontology modeling before	3.05	1.75	57%	3
CV2: I am familiar with Ontology Design Patterns	3.05	1.32	43%	3
CV3: I am familiar with Manchester Syntax	2.33	1.56	67%	1
CV4: I am familiar with Description Logics	2.81	1.33	47%	3
CV5: I am familiar with Protégé	2.95	1.63	55%	3

5.2   Metric Evaluation

We define our two metrics as follows:

- **Time Taken:** number of minutes, rounded to the nearest whole minute and capped at 20 min due to practical limitations, taken to complete a task;
- **Correctness** is a discrete measure that corresponds to the structural accuracy of the output. That is, 2 points were awarded to those structurally accurate OWL files, when accounting for URIs; 1 point for a borderline case (e.g one or two incorrect linkages, or missing a domain statement but including the range); and 0 points for any other output.

For these metrics, we generate simple statistics that describe the data, per modeling task. Tables 2a and 2b show the mean, standard deviation, and median for the Time Taken and Correctness of Output, respectively.

In addition, we examine the impact of our control variables (CV). This analysis is important, as it provides context for representation or bias in our data set. These are reported in Table 2c. CV1-CV5 correspond exactly to those questions asked during the *a priori* Survey, as described in Sect. 4. For each CV, we calculated the bivariate correlation between the sample data and the self-reported data in the survey. We believe that this is a reasonable measure of impact on effect, as our limited sample size is not amenable to partitioning. That is, the partitions (as based on responses in the *a priori* survey) could have been tested pair-wise for statistical significance. Unfortunately, the partitions would have been too small to conduct proper statistical testing. However, we do caution that correlation effects are strongly impacted by sample size.

We analyze the SUS scores in the same manner. Table 4 presents the mean, standard deviation, and median of the data set. The maximum score while using the scale is a 100. Table 2d presents our observed correlations with our control variables.

Finally, we compare the each metric for one tool against the other. That is, we want to know if our results are statistically significant—that as the statistics suggest in Table 2, CoModIDE does indeed perform better for both metrics and the SUS evaluation. To do so, we calculate the probability p that the samples from each dataset come from different underlying distributions. A common tool, and the tool we employ here, is the Paired (two-tailed) T-Test—noting that it

Table 2. Summary of statistics comparing Protege and CoModIDE.

	mean	σ	median
Protégé	17.44	3.67	20.0
CoModIDE	13.94	4.22	13.5

(a) Mean, standard deviation, and median *time taken* to complete each modeling task.

	mean	σ	median
Protégé	0.50	0.71	0.0
CoModIDE	1.33	0.77	1.5

(b) Mean, standard deviation, and median *correctness of output* for each modeling task.

	CV1	CV2	CV3	CV4	CV5
TT (P)	-0.61	-0.18	-0.38	-0.58	-0.62
Cor. (P)	0.50	0.20	0.35	0.51	0.35
TT (C)	0.02	-0.34	-0.28	-0.06	0.01
Cor. (C)	-0.30	0.00	-0.12	-0.33	-0.30

(c) Correlations control variables (CV) on the Time Taken (TT) and Correctness of Output (Cor.) for both tools Protégé (P) and CoModIDE (C).

	CV1	CV2	CV3	CV4	CV5
SUS (P)	0.70	0.52	0.64	0.73	0.64
SUS (C)	-0.34	-0.05	-0.08	-0.29	-0.39

(d) Correlations with control variables (CV) on the SUS scores for both tools Protégé (P) and CoModIDE (C).

is reasonable to assume that the underlying data are normally distributed, as well as powerful tool for analyzing datasets of limited size. The threshold for indicating confidence that the difference is significant is generally taken to be $p < 0.05$. Table 3 summarizes these results.

5.3   Free-Text Responses

18 of the 21 subjects opted to leave free-text comments. We applied fragment-based qualitative coding and analysis on these comments. I.e., we split the comments apart per the line breaks entered by the subjects, we read through the fragments and generated a simple category scheme, and we then re-read the

Table 3. Significance of results.

Time taken	Correctness	SUS evaluation
$p \approx 0.025 < 0.05$	$p \approx 0.009 < 0.01$	$p \approx 0.0003 < 0.001$

Table 4. Mean, standard deviation, and median SUS score for each tool. The maximum score is 100.

	mean	σ	median
Protégé	36.67	22.11	35.00
CoModIDE	73.33	16.80	76.25

fragments and applied these categories to the fragments (allowing at most one category per fragment) [6,20]. The subjects left between 1–6 fragments each for a total of 49 fragments for analysis, of which 37 were coded, as detailed in Table 5.

Of the 18 participants who left comments, 3 left comments containing no codable fragments; these either commented upon the subjects own performance in the experiment, which is covered in the aforementioned completion metrics, or were simple statements of fact (e.g., *"In order to connect two classes I drew a connecting line"*).

6   Discussion

Participant Pool Composition. The data indicates no correlation (bivariate correlation $< \pm 0.1$) between the subjects' reported author familiarity, and their reported SUS scores, such as would have been the case if the subjects who knew the authors were biased. The high relative standard deviation for a priori knowledge level responses indicates that our subjects are rather diverse in their skill levels – i.e., they do not consist exclusively of the limited-experience class of users that we hope CoModIDE will ultimately support. As discussed below, this variation is in fact fortunate as it allows us to compare the performance of more or less experienced users.

Metric Evaluation. Before we can determine if our results confirm H1 and H2 (replicated in Fig. 5 from Sect. 1), we must first examine the correlations between our results and the control variables gathered in the *a priori* survey.

Table 5. Free text comment fragments per category

Code	Fragment #
Graph layout	4
Dragging & dropping	6
Feature requests	5
Bugs	8
Modeling problems	5
Value/preference statements	9

H1. When using CoModIDE, a user takes less time to produce correct and reasonable output, than when using Protege.

H2. A user will find CoModIDE to have a higher SUS score than when using Protege alone.

Fig. 5. Our examined hypotheses, restated from Sect. 1.

In this context, we find it reasonable to use these thresholds for a correlation $|r|$: 0–0.19 very weak, 0.20–0.39 weak, 0.40–0.59 moderate, 0.60–0.79 strong, 0.80–1.00 very strong.

As shown in Table 2c, the metric *time taken* when using Protégé is negatively correlated with each CV. The *correctness* metric is positively correlated with each CV. This is unsurprising and reasonable; it indicates that familiarity with the ontology modeling, related concepts, and Protégé improves (shortens) time taken to complete a modeling task and improves the correctness of the output. However, for the metrics pertaining to CoModIDE, there are only very weak and three weak correlations with the CVs. We may construe this to mean that performance when using CoModIDE, with respect to our metrics, is largely agnostic to our control variables.

To confirm H1, we look at the metrics separately. *Time taken* is reported better for CoModIDE in both mean and median. When comparing the underlying data, we achieve $p \approx 0.025 < 0.05$. Next, in comparing the *correctness* metric from Table 2b, CoModIDE again outperforms Protégé in both mean and median. When comparing the underlying data, we achieve a statistical significance of $p \approx 0.009 < 0.01$. With these together, we reject the null hypothesis and confirm H1.

This is particularly interesting; given the above analysis of CV correlations where we see no (or very weak) correlations between prior ontology modeling familiarity and CoModIDE modeling results, and the confirmation of H1, that CoModIDE users perform better than Protégé users, we have a strong indicator that we have in fact achieved increased approachability.

When comparing the SUS score evaluations, we see that the usability of Protégé is strongly influenced by familiarity with ontology modeling and familiarity with Protégé itself. The magnitude of the correlation suggests that newcomers to Protege do not find it very usable. CoModIDE, on the other hand is weakly, negatively correlated along the CV. This suggests that switching to a graphical modeling paradigm may take some adjusting.

However, we still see that the SUS scores for CoModIDE have a greater mean, tighter σ, and greater median, achieving a very strong statistical significance $p \approx 0.0003 < 0.001$. Thus, we may reject the null hypothesis and confirm H2.

As such, by confirming H1 and H2, we may say that CoModIDE, via graphical ontology modeling, does indeed improve the approachability of knowledge graph development, especially for those not familiar with ontology modeling— with respect to our participant pool. However, we suspect that our results are generalizable, due to the strength of the statistical significance (Table 3) and participant pool composition (Sect. 5.1).

Free-Text Responses. The fragments summarized in Table 5 paints a quite coherent picture of the subjects' perceived advantages and shortcomings of CoModIDE, as follows:

- *Graph layout:* The layout of the included MODL patterns, when dropped on the canvas, is too cramped and several classes or properties overlap, which reduces tooling usability.
- *Dragging and dropping:* Dragging classes was hit-and-miss; this often caused users to create new properties between classes, not move them.
- *Feature requests:* Pressing the "enter" key should accept and close the entity renaming window. Zooming is requested, and an auto-layout button.
- *Bugs:* Entity renaming is buggy when entities with similar names exist.
- *Modeling problems:* Self-links/loops cannot easily be modeled.
- *Value/preference statements:* Users really appreciate the graphical modeling paradigm offered, e.g., *"Mich easier to use the GUI to develop ontologies"*, *"Moreover, I find this system to be way more intuitive than Protégé"*, *"comodide was intuitive to learn and use, despite never working with it before."*

We note that the there is a near-unanimous consensus among the subjects that graphical modeling is intuitive and helpful. When users are critical of the CoModIDE software, these criticisms are typically aimed at specific and quite shallow bugs or UI features that are lacking. The only consistent criticism of the modeling method itself relates to the difficulty in constructing self-links (i.e., properties that have the same class as domain and range).

7   Conclusion

To conclude, we have shown how the CoModIDE tool allows ontology engineers, irrespective of previous knowledge level, to develop ontologies more correctly and more quickly, than by using standard Protégé; that CoModIDE has a higher usability (SUS score) than standard Protégé; and that the CoModIDE issues that concern users primarily derive from shallow bugs as opposed to methodological or modeling issues. Taken together, this implies that the modular graphical ontology engineering paradigm is a viable way to improving the approachability of ontology engineering.

Future Work. CoModIDE is under active development and is not yet feature-complete. Specifically, during the spring of 2020 we will implement the following features:

- Wrapping instantiated modules (e.g., in dashed-line boxes) to indicate cohesion and to allow module folding/unfolding.
- An interface feature, allowing design patterns to express how they can be connected to one another; and adding support for this to the canvas, lighting up potential connection points as the user drags a pattern.
- Support for custom pattern libraries; and vocabulary specifications indicating hos pattern libraries should be annotated to be useful with CoModIDE.

In developing CoModIDE we have come across several trade-offs between usability and expressiveness, as discussed in Sect. 2. We intend to follow these threads, using CoModIDE as test bed, to study more precisely how the need for graphical representability affects the use of modeling constructs and/or ontology engineering methods. For instance, we initially assumed that a graphical modeling paradigm would help users verify the correctness of their designs; but the answers to our *a posteriori* survey questions on this matter proved inconclusive.

Acknowledgement. Cogan Shimizu and Pascal Hitzler acknowledge partial support from the following financial assistance award 70NANB19H094 from U.S. Department of Commerce, National Institute of Standards and Technology and partial support from the National Science Foundation under Grant No. 1936677.

References

1. Agarwal, R., Sinha, A.P.: Object-oriented modeling with uml: a study of developers' perceptions. Commun. ACM **46**(9), 248–256 (2003)
2. Blomqvist, E., Sandkuhl, K.: Patterns in ontology engineering: classification of ontology patterns. In: Proceedings of the 7th International Conference on Enterprise Information Systems, pp. 413–416 (2005)
3. Blomqvist, E., Gangemi, A., Presutti, V.: Experiments on pattern-based ontology design. In: Gil, Y., Noy, N. (eds.) K-CAP 2009: Proceedings of the Fifth International Conference on Knowledge Capture, pp. 41–48. ACM (2009)
4. Blomqvist, E., Hammar, K., Presutti, V.: Engineering ontologies with patterns - the eXtreme design methodology. In: Hitzler, P., Gangemi, A., Janowicz, K., Krisnadhi, A., Presutti, V. (eds.) Ontology Engineering with Ontology Design Patterns: Foundations and Applications, Studies on the Semantic Web, chap. 2, vol. 25, pp. 23–50. IOS Press (2016)
5. Blomqvist, E., Presutti, V., Daga, E., Gangemi, A.: Experimenting with eXtreme design. In: Cimiano, P., Pinto, H.S. (eds.) EKAW 2010. LNCS (LNAI), vol. 6317, pp. 120–134. Springer, Heidelberg (2010). https://doi.org/10.1007/978-3-642-16438-5_9
6. Burnard, P.: A method of analysing interview transcripts in qualitative research. Nurse Educ. Today **11**(6), 461–466 (1991)
7. Cherfi, S.S.-S., Akoka, J., Comyn-Wattiau, I.: Conceptual modeling quality - from EER to UML schemas evaluation. In: Spaccapietra, S., March, S.T., Kambayashi, Y. (eds.) ER 2002. LNCS, vol. 2503, pp. 414–428. Springer, Heidelberg (2002). https://doi.org/10.1007/3-540-45816-6_38
8. Gangemi, A.: Ontology design patterns for semantic web content. In: Gil, Y., Motta, E., Benjamins, V.R., Musen, M.A. (eds.) ISWC 2005. LNCS, vol. 3729, pp. 262–276. Springer, Heidelberg (2005). https://doi.org/10.1007/11574620_21
9. Hadar, I., Soffer, P.: Variations in conceptual modeling: classification and ontological analysis. J. Assoc. Inf. Syst. **7**(8), 20 (2006)
10. Hammar, K.: Ontology design patterns in WebProtégé. In: Proceedings of the ISWC 2015 Posters & Demonstrations Track co-located with the 14th International Semantic Web Conference (ISWC-2015), Betlehem, USA, 11 October 2015 (2015). No. 1486 in CEUR-WS

11. Hitzler, P., Gangemi, A., Janowicz, K., Krisnadhi, A.A., Presutti, V.: Towards a simple but useful ontology design pattern representation language. In: Blomqvist, E., Corcho, Ó., Horridge, M., Carral, D., Hoekstra, R. (eds.) Proceedings of the 8th Workshop on Ontology Design and Patterns (WOP 2017) Co-located with the 16th International Semantic Web Conference (ISWC 2017), Vienna, Austria, 21 October 2017 (2017). No. 2043 in CEUR Workshop Proceedings
12. Hitzler, P., Krisnadhi, A.: A tutorial on modular ontology modeling with ontology design patterns: the cooking recipes ontology. CoRR abs/1808.08433 (2018), http://arxiv.org/abs/1808.08433
13. Krogstie, J.: Evaluating UML using a generic quality framework. In: UML and the Unified Process, pp. 1–22. IGI Global (2003)
14. Lohmann, S., Link, V., Marbach, E., Negru, S.: WebVOWL: web-based visualization of ontologies. In: Lambrix, P., et al. (eds.) EKAW 2014. LNCS (LNAI), vol. 8982, pp. 154–158. Springer, Cham (2015). https://doi.org/10.1007/978-3-319-17966-7_21
15. Lohmann, S., Negru, S., Haag, F., Ertl, T.: Visualizing ontologies with vowl. Semant. Web 7(4), 399–419 (2016)
16. Musen, M.A.: The Protégé project: a look back and a look forward. AI Matters 1(4), 4–12 (2015)
17. Noy, N.F., Gao, Y., Jain, A., Narayanan, A., Patterson, A., Taylor, J.: Industry-scale knowledge graphs: lessons and challenges. Commun. ACM 62(8), 36–43 (2019). https://doi.org/10.1145/3331166
18. Presutti, V., et al.: D2.5.1: a library of ontology design patterns: reusable solutions for collaborative design of networked ontologies. Technical report, NeOn Project (2007)
19. Sarker, M.K., Krisnadhi, A.A., Hitzler, P.: OWLAx: A protégé plugin to support ontology axiomatization through diagramming. In: Kawamura, T., Paulheim, H. (eds.) Proceedings of the ISWC 2016 Posters & Demonstrations Track co-located with 15th International Semantic Web Conference (ISWC 2016), Kobe, Japan, 19 October 2016. CEUR Workshop Proceedings, vol. 1690 (2016)
20. Seaman, C.B.: Qualitative methods. In: Shull, F., Singer, J., Sjøberg, D.I.K. (eds.) Guide to Advanced Empirical Software Engineering, pp. 35–62. Springer, London (2008). https://doi.org/10.1007/978-1-84800-044-5_2
21. Shimizu, C., Hirt, Q., Hitzler, P.: MODL: a modular ontology design library. In: Proceedings of the 10th Workshop on Ontology Design and Patterns (WOP 2019) co-located with 18th International Semantic Web Conference (ISWC 2019). CEUR Workshop Proceedings, vol. 2459, pp. 47–58 (2019)
22. Shoval, P., Frumermann, I.: Oo and eer conceptual schemas: a comparison of user comprehension. J. Database Manag. (JDM) 5(4), 28–38 (1994)
23. Wiens, V., Lohmann, S., Auer, S.: WebVOWL editor: device-independent visual ontology modeling. In: Proceedings of the ISWC 2018 Posters & Demonstrations, Industry and Blue Sky Ideas Tracks. CEUR Workshop Proceedings, vol. 2180 (2018)

Fast and Exact Rule Mining with AMIE 3

Jonathan Lajus[1(✉)], Luis Galárraga[2], and Fabian Suchanek[1]

[1] Télécom Paris, Institut Polytechnique de Paris, Palaiseau, France
jonathan.lajus@telecom-paris.fr
[2] INRIA Rennes, Rennes, France

Abstract. Given a knowledge base (KB), rule mining finds rules such as "If two people are married, then they live (most likely) in the same place". Due to the exponential search space, rule mining approaches still have difficulties to scale to today's large KBs. In this paper, we present AMIE 3, a system that employs a number of sophisticated pruning strategies and optimizations. This allows the system to mine rules on large KBs in a matter of minutes. Most importantly, we do not have to resort to approximations or sampling, but are able to compute the exact confidence and support of each rule. Our experiments on DBpedia, YAGO, and Wikidata show that AMIE 3 beats the state of the art by a factor of more than 15 in terms of runtime.

1 Introduction

Recent years have seen the rise of large knowledge bases (KBs) such as Wikidata, YAGO, DBpedia, and many others. These are large collections of knowledge about the real world in the form of entities (such as organizations, movies, people, and locations) and relations between them (such as *wasBornIn*, *actesIn*, etc.). Today's KBs contain millions of entities and facts about them. They find applications in Web search, text analysis, and chat bots.

Rule mining is the task of automatically finding logical rules in a given KB. For example, a rule mining approach can find that "If X and Y are married, and X lives in Z, then Y also lives in Z". Such rules usually come with confidence scores that express to what degree a rule holds. The rules can serve several purposes: First, they serve to complete the KB. If we do not know the place of residence of a person, we can propose that the person lives where their spouse lives. Second, they can serve to debug the KB. If the spouse of someone lives in a different city, then this can indicate a problem. Finally, rules are useful in downstream applications such as fact prediction [5,12,14,18], data and ontology alignment [7,10], fact checking [2], and error detection [1].

The difficulty in finding such rules lies in the exponential size of the search space: every relation can potentially be combined with every other relation in a rule. This is why early approaches (such as AMIE [8]) were unable to run on large KBs such as Wikidata in less than a day. Since then, several approaches have resorted to sampling or approximate confidence calculations [4,9,15,19]. The more the approach samples, the faster it becomes, but the less accurate

© Springer Nature Switzerland AG 2020
A. Harth et al. (Eds.): ESWC 2020, LNCS 12123, pp. 36–52, 2020.
https://doi.org/10.1007/978-3-030-49461-2_3

the results will be. Another common technique [13,15,16,19] (from standard inductive logic programming) is to mine not all rules, but only enough rules to cover the positive examples. This, likewise, speeds up the computation, but does not mine all rules that hold in the KB.

In this paper, we present AMIE 3, a successor of AMIE [8] and AMIE+ [9]. Our system employs a number of sophisticated strategies to speed up rule mining: pruning strategies, parallelization, and a lazy computation of confidence scores. This allows our system to scale effortlessly to large KBs. At the same time, the system still computes the exact confidence and support values for each rule, without resorting to approximations. Furthermore, unlike her predecessor [9] and other systems, AMIE 3 exhaustively computes all rules that hold in the KB for a given confidence and support threshold.

Our experiments show that AMIE 3 beats the state of the art by a factor of 15 in terms of runtime. We believe that the techniques that we have discovered can be of use for other systems as well—no matter whether they compute the exhaustive set of rules or not.

2   Related Work

First Generation Rule Mining. Inductive Logic Programming (ILP) is the task of learning rules from positive and negative examples. The first of these systems [11,13,16] appeared before the rise of large KBs. Hence, they are generally unsuitable for today's KBs for two reasons: (i) they were not designed to scale to millions of facts, and (ii) they do not account for the Open World Assumption (OWA) made by current KBs. For example, FOIL [16] (as well as its optimized successor [19]) cannot be applied directly to KBs because it assumes the user can provide explicit counter-examples for the rules. Alas, KBs do not store negative statements. In contrast, WARMR [11] generates negative evidence by assuming the KB is complete, i.e., by making a closed world assumption (CWA), whereas [13] uses a positives-only learning function that generates negative evidence from random facts (a similar, but more systematic mechanism is proposed in [15]). It was shown [8] that these strategies work less well on KBs than the partial completeness assumption (PCA), which was explicitly designed for KBs.

Second Generation Rule Mining. AMIE (and its successor AMIE+) [8,9] was the first approach to explicitly target large KBs. While AMIE+ is at least 3 orders of magnitude faster than the first-generation systems, it can still take hours, even days, to find rules in very large KBs such as Wikidata. On these grounds, more recent approaches [3,4,15] have proposed new strategies (parallelism, approximations, etc.) to speed up rule mining on the largest KBs. The Ontological Pathfinding method (OP) [3,4] resorts to a highly concurrent architecture based on Spark[1] to calculate the support and the confidence of a set of candidate rules. The candidates are computed by enumerating all conjunctions of atoms that are allowed by the schema. Like AMIE, OP calculates

---

[1] https://spark.apache.org.

the exact scores of the rules and supports both the CWA and the PCA for the generation of counter-evidence. At the same time, the system supports only path rules of up to 3 atoms. Other types of rules require the user to implement a new mining procedure. We will see in our experiments that AMIE 3 is both more general and faster than OP.

RudiK [15] is a recent rule mining method that applies the PCA to generate explicit counter-examples that are semantically related. For example, when generating counter-facts for the relation *hasChild* and a given person x, RudiK will sample among the non-children of x who are children of someone else ($x' \neq x$). Rudik's strategy is to find all rules that are necessary to predict the positive examples, based on a greedy heuristic that at each step adds the most promising rule (in terms of coverage of the examples) to the output set. Thus, differently from exhaustive rule mining approaches [3,8,9,11], Rudik aims to find rules that make good predictions, not all rules above a given confidence threshold. This non-exhaustivity endows RudiK with comparable performance to AMIE+ and OP. Nevertheless, we show that AMIE 3 outperforms RudiK in terms of runtime while still being exhaustive.

3 Preliminaries

Knowledge Bases. We assume a set $\mathcal{I}$ of entities (such as *Paris*), a set $\mathcal{P}$ of binary relations (such as *locatedIn*), and a set $\mathcal{L}$ of literal values (strings or numbers)[2]. We model a knowledge base (KB) $\mathcal{K}$ as a set of assertions $r(s, o)$, also called *facts*, with a subject $s \in \mathcal{I}$, a relation $r \in \mathcal{P}$ and an object $o \in \mathcal{I} \cup \mathcal{L}$. An example of a fact is *locatedIn(Paris, France)*. Whenever $\mathcal{K}$ is clear from the context, we write $r(s, o)$ to mean $r(s, o) \in \mathcal{K}$.

Relations and Functions. The *inverse* of a relation r, denoted r^-, is the relation consisting of all the facts of the form $r^-(o, s)$ such that $r(s, o) \in \mathcal{K}$. A relation r is a *function* in $\mathcal{K}$, if r has at most one object for each subject. Some relations (e.g., *isCitizenOf*) are *quasi-functions*, i.e. they rarely associate multiple objects to a given subject. Hence, the notion of functions has been generalized to the *functionality score* [17] of a relation r:

$$fun(r) = \frac{|\{s : \exists o : r(s, o) \in \mathcal{K}\}|}{|\{(s, o) : r(s, o) \in \mathcal{K}\}|} \qquad (1)$$

The functionality score is always between 0 and 1 (incl.). It is exactly 1 for strict functions such as *hasBirthPlace*, it is close to 1 for quasi-functions, and it is smaller for relations that have many objects (such as *actedInMovie*).

Atoms and Rules. An *atom* is an expression of the form $r(X, Y)$, where r is a relation and X, Y are either constants or variables. From now on, we denote variables by lowercase letters, whereas constants (entities) are always capitalized. An atom is *instantiated* if at least one of its arguments is a constant, as in

---

[2] In line with the other works [4,8,9,15], we do not consider blank nodes.

livesIn(x, Berlin). If both arguments are constants, the atom is *grounded* and it is tantamount to a fact. We define the operator $var(A)$ so that it returns the set of variables of an atom A. A (conjunctive) *query* is a conjunction of atoms: $B_1 \wedge ... \wedge B_n$. A *substitution* σ is a partial mapping from variables to constants. Substitutions can be straightforwardly extended to atoms and conjunctions. A *result* of a query $B_1 \wedge ... \wedge B_n$ on a KB $\mathcal{K}$ is a substitution σ that (i) maps all variables and (ii) that entails $\sigma(B_i) \in \mathcal{K} \; \forall i \in \{1, ..., n\}$.

A (Horn) *rule* is a formula of the form $\boldsymbol{B} \Rightarrow H$, where the $\boldsymbol{B}$ is a query of *body atoms* $B_1, ..., B_n$, and H is the *head atom*. Two atoms A, A' are *connected* if $var(A) \cap var(A') \neq \emptyset$, i.e., they have common variables. It is common [4,8,9,15] to impose that all atoms in a rule are transitively connected and that rules are closed. A rule is *closed* if all variables appear in at least two atoms. A closed rule is always *safe*, i.e. all head variables appear also in at least one body atom.

Predictions. Given a rule $R = B_1 \wedge ... \wedge B_n \Rightarrow H$ and a substitution σ, we call $\sigma(R)$ an *instantiation* of R. If $\sigma(B_i) \in \mathcal{K} \; \forall i \in \{1, ..., n\}$, we call $\sigma(H)$ a *prediction* of R from $\mathcal{K}$, and we write $\mathcal{K} \wedge R \models \sigma(H)$. If $\sigma(H) \in \mathcal{K}$, we call $\sigma(H)$ a *true prediction*.

A *false prediction* of a rule is a prediction of a counter-example of the rule. There are different approaches to define these counter-examples: Under the *Closed World Assumption* (CWA), any assertion that is not in the KB is considered a counter-example. However, KBs are usually incomplete, and thus the CWA penalizes rules that predict new facts. Under the *Open World Assumption* (OWA), facts that are not in the KB are not necessarily wrong, and hence there are no counter-examples. This entails that a rule mining algorithm will report arbitrary rules as long as these rules make enough true predictions (such as "All people play the violin"). Therefore, AMIE [8] has proposed the *Partial Completeness Assumption* (PCA): If we have $r(s, o)$ in the KB $\mathcal{K}$, and if $fun(r) \geq fun(r^-)$, then we assume that all $r(s, o') \notin \mathcal{K}$ do not hold in the real world. If $fun(r) < fun(r^-)$, then the PCA says that all $r(s', o) \notin \mathcal{K}$ do not hold in the real world. These assertions can thus serve as counter-examples. There are a number of other approaches to generate counter-examples in the literature [18].

Support and Confidence. The *support* of a rule R in a KB $\mathcal{K}$ is the number of true predictions p (of the form $r(X, Y)$) that the rule makes in the KB:

$$support(R) = |\{p : (\mathcal{K} \wedge R \models p) \wedge p \in \mathcal{K}\}| \qquad (2)$$

The *head-coverage* is the proportional variant of the support: It is the ratio of instantiations of the head atom that are predicted by the rule:

$$hc(\boldsymbol{B} \Rightarrow r(x, y)) = \frac{support(\boldsymbol{B} \Rightarrow r(x, y))}{|\{(x, y) : r(x, y) \in \mathcal{K}\}|}$$

The *confidence* of a rule R in a KB $\mathcal{K}$ is the proportion of true predictions out of the true predictions and false predictions:

$$confidence(R) = \frac{support(R)}{support(R) + |\{p : (\mathcal{K} \wedge R \models p) \wedge p \in cex(R)\}|} \qquad (3)$$

Here, $cex(R)$ denotes the set of counter-examples of R. If the counter-examples are chosen by the PCA, we refer to the confidence as the *PCA confidence* and denote it by *pca-conf* (analogously for the CWA).

In general, the support of the rule quantifies its relevance, whereas the confidence quantifies its accuracy. *Rule mining* is the task of finding all rules in a KB that fulfill certain confidence and support thresholds. It is a relaxation of inductive logic programming (ILP), in the sense that it finds also rules that predict some limited number of counter-examples (see [18] for a discussion).

4   AMIE 3

In this section, we first recap the original AMIE algorithm [8] (Sect. 4.1). Then we present a series of optimizations that give rise to AMIE 3 (Sect. 4.2). Finally, we show different quality metrics that AMIE 3 can compute (Sect. 4.3).

4.1   The AMIE Approach

The AMIE algorithm [8,9] is a method to mine closed Horn rules on large KBs. AMIE (Algorithm 1) takes as input a knowledge base $\mathcal{K}$, and thresholds l for the maximal number of atoms per rule, $minHC$ for the minimum head coverage, and $minC$ for the minimum PCA confidence. AMIE uses a classical breadth-first search: Line 1 initializes a queue with all possible rules of size 1, i.e., rules with an empty body. The search strategy then dequeues a rule R at a time and adds it to the output list (Line 6) if it meets certain criteria (Line 5), namely, (i) the rule is closed, (ii) its PCA confidence is higher than $minC$, and (iii) its PCA confidence is higher than the confidence of all previously mined rules with the same head atom as R and a subset of its body atoms. If the rule R has less than l atoms and its confidence can still be improved (Line 7), AMIE refines it. The refinement operator *refine* (Line 8) derives new rules from R by considering all possible atoms that can be added to the body of the rule, and creating one new rule for each of them.

AMIE iterates over all the non-duplicate refinements of rule R and adds those with enough head coverage (Lines 10–11). The routine finishes when the queue runs out of rules. The AMIE algorithm has been implemented in Java with multi-threading. By default, AMIE sets $minHC = 0.01$, $minC = 0.1$, and $l = 3$. AMIE+ [9] optimized this algorithm by a number of pruning strategies, but did not change the main procedure.

4.2   AMIE 3

We now present the optimizations of Algorithm 1 that constitute AMIE 3, the successor of AMIE+.

Algorithm 1: AMIE

Input: a KB: $\mathcal{K}$, maximum rule length: l, head coverage threshold: $minHC$,
      confidence threshold: $minC$
Output: set of Horn rules: *rules*

1   $q = [\top \Rightarrow r_1(x,y), \top \Rightarrow r_2(x,y) \ldots \top \Rightarrow r_m(x,y)]$
2   $rules = \langle \rangle$
3   **while** $|q| > 0$ **do**
4       $R = q.dequeue()$
5   **if** $closed(R) \wedge pca\text{-}conf(R) \geq minC \wedge betterThanParents(R, rules)$ **then**
6         $rules.add(r)$
7   **if** $length(R) < l \wedge pca\text{-}conf(R_c) < 1.0$ **then**
8   **for** *each rule* $R_c \in refine(R)$ **do**
9   **if** $hc(R_c) \geq minHC \wedge R_c \notin q$ **then**
10             $q.enqueue(r_c)$

11 **return** *rules*

Existential Variable Detection. In order to decide whether to output a rule, AMIE has to compute its confidence (Lines 5 and 7 of Algorithm 1), i.e., it has to evaluate Eq. 3. If the PCA confidence is used, this equation becomes:

$$pca\text{-}conf(\boldsymbol{B} \Rightarrow r(x,y)) = \frac{support(\boldsymbol{B} \Rightarrow r(x,y))}{|\{(x,y) : \exists y' : \boldsymbol{B} \wedge r(x,y')\}|}. \tag{4}$$

This is for the case where $fun(r) \geq fun(r^-)$. If $fun(r) < fun(r^-)$, the denominator becomes $|\{(x,y) : \exists x' : \boldsymbol{B} \wedge r(x',y)\}|$. To evaluate this denominator, AMIE first finds every possible value of x. This is the purpose of Algorithm 2: We find the most restrictive atom in the query, i.e., the atom A^* with the relation with the least number of facts. If x appears in this atom, we select the possible instantiation of x in the atom for which the rest of the query is satisfiable (Lines 3 and 4). Otherwise, we recursively find the values of x for each instantiation of this most restrictive atom and add them to the result set $\mathcal{X}$. Once AMIE has found the set of possible values for x with Algorithm 2, it determines, for each value of x, the possible values of y—again by Algorithm 2. This is necessary because we cannot keep in memory all values of y encountered when we computed the values of x, because this would lead to a quadratic memory consumption.

This method can be improved as follows: Assume that our rule is simply $r_1(x,z) \wedge r_2(z,y) \Rightarrow r_h(x,y)$. Then AMIE will compute the number of distinct pairs (x,y) for the following query (the denominator of Eq. 4):

$$r_1(x,z) \wedge r_2(z,y) \wedge r_h(x,y')$$

AMIE will use Algorithm 2 to select the possible values of x. Assume that the most restrictive atom is $r_2(z,y)$. Then AMIE will use all possible instantiations $\sigma : \{z \leftarrow Z, y \leftarrow Y\}$ of this atom, and find the possible values of x for the following query (Lines 5 and 6 of Algorithm 2):

$$r_1(x, Z) \wedge r_2(Z, Y) \wedge r_h(x, y') \tag{5}$$

However, we do not have to try out all possible values of y, because for a fixed instantiation $z \leftarrow Z$ all assignments $y \leftarrow Y$ lead to the same value for x. Rather, y can be treated as an existential variable: once there is a single Y with $r_2(Z, Y)$, we do not need to try out the others. Thus, we can improve Algorithm 2 as follows: If a variable y of $A^* = r(x, y)$ does not appear elsewhere in q, then Line 5 iterates only over the possible values of x in A^*.

Algorithm 2: DistinctValues

Input: variable x, query $q = A_1 \wedge ... \wedge A_n$, KB $\mathcal{K}$,
Output: set of values $\mathcal{X}$
1 $\mathcal{X} := \emptyset$
2 $A^* := argmin_A(|\{(x, y) : A = r(x, y), A \in q\}|)$
3 **if** x *appears in* A^* **then**
4 $\quad$ **return** $\{x : x \in \sigma(A^*) \wedge \sigma(q \setminus A^*) \text{ is satisfiable}\}$
5 **for** *each* $\sigma : \sigma(A^*) \in \mathcal{K}$ **do**
6 $\quad$ $\mathcal{X} := \mathcal{X} \cup DistinctValues(x, \sigma(q \setminus A^*), \mathcal{K})$
7 **return** $\mathcal{X}$

Lazy Evaluation. The calculation of the denominator of Eq. 4 can be computationally expensive, most notably for "bad" rules such as:

$$R : directed(x, z) \wedge hasActor(z, y) \Rightarrow marriedTo(x, y). \tag{6}$$

In such cases, AMIE spends a lot of time computing the exact confidence, only to find that the rule will be pruned away by the confidence threshold. This can be improved as follows: Instead of computing first the set of values for x, and then for each value of x the possible values of y, we compute for each value of x directly the possible values of y—and only then consider the next value of x. Following the principle "If you know something is bad, do not spend time to figure out how bad exactly it is", we stop this computation as soon as the set size reaches the value $support(R) \times minC^{-1}$. If this occurs, we know that $pca\text{-}conf(R) < minC$, and hence the rule will be pruned in Line 5 of Algorithm 1.

Variable Order. To compute the PCA confidence (Eq. 4), we have to count the instantiations of pairs of variables x, y. AMIE counts these asymmetrically: It finds the values of x and then, for each value of x, the values of y. We could as well choose to start with y instead. The number of pairs is the same, but we found that the choice impacts the runtime: Once one variable is fixed, the computation of the other variable happens on a rule that has fewer degrees of freedom than the original rule, i.e., it has fewer instantiations. Thus, one has an interest in fixing first the variable that appears in as many selective atoms as possible. Alas, it is very intricate to determine which variable restricts more efficiently the set of instantiations, because the variables appear in several atoms, and each instantiation of the first variable may entail a different number of instantiations of the second variable. Therefore, estimating the exact complexity is unpractical.

We use the following heuristic: Between x and y, we choose to start with the variable that appears in the head atom of the rule in the denominator of Eq. 4. The reason is that this variable appears in at least two atoms already, whereas the other variable appears only in at least one atom. We show in our experiments that this method improves the runtime by several orders of magnitude for some rules.

Parallel Computation for Overlap Tables. AMIE implements an approximation of Eq. 4. This approximation misses only a small percentage of rules (maximally 5% according to [9]), but speeds up the calculation drastically. In AMIE 3, this feature can be switched off (to have exact results) or on (to have faster results). Here, we show how to further speed up this heuristic. The method finds an efficient approximation of the denominator of Eq. 4 for a rule R. This approximation uses the join structure of the query in combination with the functionality scores and the overlaps of the different relations to estimate the total number of examples (both positive and negative) of a rule. The exact formula and the rationale behind it can be found in [9]. The functionality, domain and overlaps with other relations are pre-computed for all relations. This pre-calculation can be significant for large KBs with many predicates. In our experiments with DBpedia, e.g., precomputing all overlaps takes twice as much time as the mining. In AMIE 3, we exploit the fact that this task is easy parallelizable, and start as many threads as possible in parallel, each treating one pair of relations. This reduces the precomputation time linearly with the number of threads (by a factor of 40 in our experiments).

Integer-Based In-Memory Database. AMIE uses an in-memory database to store the entire KB. Each fact is indexed by subject, by object, by relation, and by pairs of relation/subject and relation/object. In order to be able to load also large KBs into memory, AMIE compresses strings into custom-made *ByteStrings*, where each character takes only 8 bits. AMIE makes sure that ByteString variables holding equivalent ByteStrings point to the same physical object (i.e., the ByteString exists only once). This not just saves space, but also makes hashing and equality tests trivial. Still, we incur high costs of managing these objects and the indexes: ByteStrings have to be first created, and then checked for duplicity; unused ByteStrings have to be garbage-collected; equality checks still require casting checks; and HashMaps create a large memory overhead. Built-in strings suffer from the same problems. Therefore, we migrated the in-memory database to an integer-based system, where entities and relations are mapped to an integer space and represented by the primitive datatype *int*. This is in compliance with most RDF engines and popular serialization formats such as [6]. We use the fastutil library[3] to store the indexes. This avoids the overhead of standard HashMaps. It also reduces the number of objects that the garbage collector has to treat, leading to a significant speedup.

---

[3] http://fastutil.di.unimi.it/.

4.3 Quality Metrics

AMIE is a generic exhaustive rule miner, and thus its output consists of *rules*. These rules can serve as input to other applications, for example, to approaches that predict *facts* [5,15]. Such downstream applications may require different quality metrics. These can be implemented on top of AMIE, as shown here:

Support and head coverage. Support is a standard quality metric that indicates the significance of a rule. Due to the anti-monotonicity property, most approaches use support to prune the search space of rules. AMIE [8,9] uses by default the head coverage (the relative variant of support) for pruning.

PCA Confidence. By default, AMIE uses the PCA confidence to assess the quality of a rule, because it has been shown to rank rules closer to the quality of their predictions than classical metrics such as the CWA confidence [8].

CWA confidence. This confidence is used in OP [3,4]. Many link prediction methods are evaluated under the closed world assumption as well [18].

GPRO confidence. The work of [5] noted that the PCA confidence can underestimate the likelihood of a prediction in the presence of non-injective mappings. Therefore, the authors propose a refinement of the PCA confidence, the GPRO confidence, which excludes instances coming from non-injective mappings in the confidence computation. To judge the quality of a predicted fact, the approach needs the GPRO confidence both on the first and second variable of the head atom. AMIE is not designed to judge the quality of a predicted fact, but can compute the GPRO confidence on both variables.

GRANK confidence. This refinement of the GPRO metric is proposed by [5] in order to take into account the number of instances of the variables of the rule that are not in the head atom.

These metrics are implemented in AMIE 3 and can be enabled by command line switches.

5 Experiments

We conducted two series of experiments to evaluate AMIE 3: In the first series we study the impact of our optimizations on the system's runtime. In the second series, we compare AMIE 3 with two scalable state-of-the-art approaches, namely RudiK [15] and Ontological Pathfinding (OP) [3,4] (also known as ScaleKB) on 6 different datasets.

5.1 Experimental Setup

Data. We evaluated AMIE 3 and its competitors on YAGO (2 and 2s), DBpedia (2.0 and 3.8) and a dump of Wikipedia from December 2014. These datasets were used in evaluations of AMIE+ [9], OP [3] and Rudik [15]. In addition, we used

Table 1. Experimental datasets

Dataset	Facts	Relations	Entities
Yago2	948 358	36	834 750
Yago2s	4 484 914	37	2 137 469
DBpedia 2.0	6 601 014	1 595	2 275 327
DBpedia 3.8	11 024 066	650	3 102 999
Wikidata 12-2014	8 397 936	430	3 085 248
Wikidata 07-2019	386 156 557	1 188	57 963 264

Table 2. Old ByteString database vs. the new integer-based database.

Dataset	Loading time	Wall time		Memory used	
		Integer	ByteString	Integer	ByteString
Yago2	7 s	26.40 s	29.69 s	6Go	9Go
Yago2s	45 s	1 min 55 s	4 min 10 s	16Go	19Go
DBpedia 2.0	55 s	7 min 32 s	34 min 06 s	29Go	32Go
DBpedia 3.8	1 min 20 s	7 min 49 s	52 min 10 s	40Go	42Go
Wikidata 2014	59 s	5 min 44 s	6 min 01 s	27Go	54Go

a recent dump of Wikidata from July 1st, 2019[4]. Table 1 shows the numbers of facts, relations, and entities of our experimental datasets.

Configurations. All experiments were run on a Ubuntu 18.04.3 LTS with 40 processing cores (Intel Xeon CPU E5-2660 v3 at 2.60 GHz) and 500Go of RAM. AMIE 3 and RudiK are implemented in Java 1.8. AMIE 3 uses its own in-memory database to store the KB, whereas RudiK relies on Virtuoso Open Source 06.01.3127, accessed via a local endpoint. OP was implemented in Scala 2.11.12 and Spark 2.3.4.

Unless otherwise noted, the experiments were run using the default settings of AMIE: We used the PCA confidence, computed lazily with a threshold of 0.1, with all the lossless optimizations (no approximations). The threshold on the head coverage is 0.01 and the maximal rule length is 3 [8].

5.2   Effect of Our Optimizations

In-Memory Database. Table 2 shows the performance with the new integer-based in-memory database and the old ByteString database. The change reduces the memory footprint by around 3 GB in most cases, and by 50% in Wikidata. Moreover, the new database is consistently faster, up to 8-fold for the larger KBs such as DBpedia 3.8.

---

[4] Selecting only facts between two Wikidata entities, and excluding literals.

Table 3. Impact of laziness and of switching on the confidence approximation. *Ov. tables* is the time needed to compute the overlap tables.

Dataset	Conf. Approx. off		Confidence approximation on		
	Non-lazy	Lazy	Non-lazy	Lazy	Ov. tables
Yago2	24.12 s	26.40 s	24.39 s	21.41 s	0.2 s
Yago2s	4 min 28 s	1 min 55 s	1 min 42 s	2 min 03 s	2.4 s
DBpedia 2.0	10 min 14 s	7 min 32 s	7 min 42 s	8 min 13 s	23.5 s
DBpedia 3.8	14 min 50 s	7 min 49 s	11 min 07 s	10 min 18 s	15.2 s
Wikidata 2014	19 min 27 s	5 min 44 s	5 min 45 s	4 min 36 s	12 s
Wikidata 2019	>48 h	16h 43 min	17h 06 min	16h 31 min	41.4 s

Laziness. As explained in Sect. 4.2, AMIE can invest a lot of time in calculating the PCA confidence of low-confident rules. The lazy evaluation targets exactly this problem. Table 3 shows that this strategy can reduce the runtime by a factor of 4. We also show the impact of laziness when the PCA confidence approximation is switched on. We observe that the parallel calculation of the overlap tables reduces drastically the contribution of this phase to the total runtime when compared to AMIE+—where it could take longer than the mining itself. We also note that the residual impact of the confidence approximation is small, so that this feature is now dispensable: We can mine rules exhaustively.

Count Variable Order. To measure the impact of the count variable order, we ran AMIE 3 (with the lazy evaluation activated) on Yago2s and looked at the runtimes when counting with the variable that appears in the head atom versus the runtime when counting with the other variable. For every rule with three atoms and a support superior to 100, we timed the computation of the PCA confidence denominator (Eq. 4) in each case. The y-axis of Fig. 1 shows the runtime when we first instantiate the variable that occurs in the head atom, whereas the x-axis shows the runtime when using the other variable.

We see that every query can be run in under 10 s and that most of the queries would run equally fast independently of the order of the variables. However, for some rules, instantiating first the variable that does not appear in the head atom can be worse than the contrary by several orders of magnitude. Some queries would take hours (days in one case) to compute, even with lazy evaluation. In Yago2s, these rules happen to be pruned away by the AMIE+ confidence upper bound (a lossless optimization), but this may not be the case for all KBs. The problematic rules all have bodies of the following shape:

$$\begin{cases} hasGender(x, g) \wedge hasGender(y, g) \\ isLocatedIn(x, l) \wedge isLocatedIn(y, l) \end{cases}$$

Both *hasGender* and *isLocatedIn* are very large relations as they apply to any person and location, respectively. While early pruning of those "hard rules" is the purpose of the confidence approximations and upper bounds of AMIE+, these strategies may fail in a few cases, leading to the execution of expensive

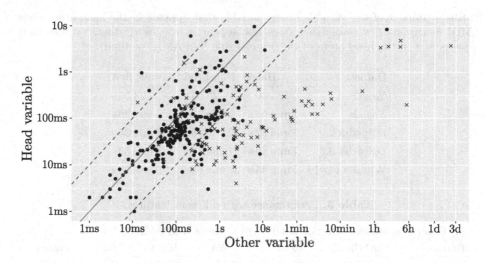

Fig. 1. Impact of the variable order on Yago2s. Each point is a rule. Cross points: pruned by the confidence approximation. Red line: same performance. Dashed lines: relative speedup of 10×.

queries. Finally, we show the overall impact of the count variable order heuristic in Table 4. The results suggest that our heuristic generally yields lower runtimes.

Impact of Existential Variable Detection. Last but not least, the on-the-fly detection of existential variables reduces the number of recursive calls made to Algorithm 2. Table 5a shows the performances of AMIE 3 with and without this optimization. This optimization is critical for AMIE 3 on most datasets. This is less important for DBpedia 2.0 as it contains mostly small relations.

Metrics. Table 5b shows the impact of different quality metrics on the runtime, with iPCA being the PCA with injective mappings. The metrics run slower than the PCA confidence, because we cannot use the PCA upper bound optimization. The GRank metric, in particular, is very sensitive to the number of facts per relation, which explains its performance on Yago2s and DBpedia 3.8. For all other metrics, however, the numbers are very reasonable.

5.3   Comparative Experiments

In this section, we compare the performance of AMIE 3 with two main state-of-the-art algorithms for rule mining in large KBs, RuDiK and OP.

AMIE 3. We ran AMIE 3 in its default settings. In order to compare the improvements to previous benchmarks of AMIE, we had AMIE compute the standard CWA confidence for each rule, in addition to the PCA confidence (except for Wikidata 2019, where no such previous benchmark exists).

Table 4. Impact of the variable order: variable that appears in the head atom (new AMIE 3 heuristic); variable that does not appear in the head atom; variable that appears first in the head atom of the original rule (old AMIE method).

Dataset	Head	Non-head	Always first
Yago2	26.40 s	25.64 s	23.59 s
Yago2s	1 min 55 s	4 min 32 s	4 min 30 s
DBpedia 2.0	7 min 32 s	12 min 46 s	6 min 36 s
DBpedia 3.8	7 min 49 s	21 min 12 s	8 min 53 s
Wikidata 2014	5 min 44 s	36 min 09 s	9 min 50 s

Table 5. Performance with different features.

(a) Existential variable detection (ED)

Dataset	AMIE 3	No ED
Yago2	26.40 s	24.84 s
Yago2s	1 min 55 s	>2 h
DBpedia 2.0	7 min 32 s	9 min 10 s
DBpedia 3.8	7 min 49 s	>2 h
Wikidata 2014	5 min 44 s	>2 h

(b) Different metrics (Sect. 4.3)

CWA	iPCA	GPro	GRank
22.54 s	38.42 s	37.47 s	33.36 s
1 min 56 s	3 min 30 s	2 min 45 s	>2 h
7 min 26 s	12 min 31 s	11 min 53 s	1 h 16 min
6 min 49 s	15 min 22 s	23 min 31 s	>2 h
5 min 48 s	7 min 04 s	11 min 50 s	>2 h

RuDiK. We set the number of positive and negative examples to 500, as advised on the project's github page[5]. We tried to run the system in parallel for different head relations. However, the graph generation phase of the algorithm already runs in parallel and executes a lot of very selective SPARQL queries in parallel. Hence, the additional parallelization flooded the SPARQL endpoint, which rejected any new connection at some point. For this reason, we mined the rules for every possible relation sequentially, using only the original parallelization mechanism. RuDiK also benefits from information on the taxonomic types of the variables. While the built-in method to detect the types of the relations works out-of-the-box for DBpedia (which has a flat taxonomy), it overgeneralizes on the other datasets, inverting the expected benefits. Therefore, we ran RuDiK without the type information on the other datasets.

Ontological Pathfinding. This system first builds a list of candidate rules (Part 5.1 of [4]). Unfortunately, the implementation of this phase of the algorithm is not publicly available. Hence, we had to generate candidate rules ourselves. The goal is to create all rules that are "reasonable", i.e., to avoid rules with empty joins such as $birthPlace(x, y) \land hasCapital(x, z)$. The original algorithm discards all rules where the domain and range of joining relations do not match. However, it does not take into account the fact that an entity can be an instance of multiple classes. Thus, if the domain of $actedIn$ is $Actor$, and the domain of $directed$ is $Director$, the original algorithm would discard any rule that contains

---
[5] https://github.com/stefano-ortona/rudik.

actedIn(*x*, *y*) ∧ *directed*(*x*, *z*)—even though it may have a non-empty support. Hence, we generated all candidate rules where the join between two connected atoms is not empty in the KB. This produces more candidate rules than the original algorithm (around 10 times more for Yago2s, i.e., 29762), but in return OP can potentially mine all rules that the other systems mine.

Table 6. Performances and output of Ontological Pathfinding (OP), RuDiK and AMIE 3. *: rules with support ≥ 100 and CWA confidence ≥ 0.1.

Dataset	System	Rules	Runtime
Yago2s	OP (their candidates)	429 (52*)	18 min 50 s
	OP (our candidates)	1 348 (96*)	3 h 20 min
	RuDiK	17	37 min 30 s
	AMIE 3	97	**1 min 50 s**
	AMIE 3 (support=1)	1 596	7 min 6 s
DBpedia 3.8	OP (our candidates)	7 714 (220*)	>45 h
	RuDiK	650	12 h 10 min
	RuDiK + types	650	11 h 52 min
	AMIE 3	5 084	**7 min 52 s**
	AMIE 3 (support=1)	132 958	32 min 57 s
Wikidata 2019	OP (our candidates)	15 999 (326*)	>48 h
	RuDiK	1 145	23 h
	AMIE 3	8 662	**16 h 43 min**

Results
It is not easy to compare the performance of OP, AMIE 3, and Rudik, because the systems serve different purposes, have different prerequisites, and mine different rules. Therefore, we ran all systems in their default configurations, and discuss the results (Table 6) qualitatively in detail.

Ontological Pathfinding. We ran OP both with a domain-based candidate generation (which finds fewer rules) and with our candidate generation. In general, OP has the longest running times, but the largest number of rules. This is inherent to the approach: OP will prune candidate rules using a heuristic [3] that is similar to the confidence approximation of AMIE+. After this step, it will compute the support and the exact CWA confidence of any remaining candidate. However, it offers no way of pruning rules upfront by support and confidence. This has two effects: First, the vast majority (>90%) of rules found by OP have very low confidence (<10%) or very low support (<100). Second, most of the time will be spent computing the confidence of these low-confidence rules, because the exact confidence is harder to compute for a rule with low confidence.

To reproduce the result of OP with AMIE, we ran AMIE 3 with a support threshold of 100 and a CWA confidence threshold of 10%. This reproduces the rules of OP (and 8 more because AMIE does not use the OP functionality heuristics) in less than two minutes. If we set our support threshold to 1, and our minimal CWA confidence to 10^{-5}, then we mine more rules than OP on Yago2s (as shown in Table 6) in less time (factor 25×). If we mine rules with AMIE's default parameters, we mine rules in less than two minutes (factor 90×).

The large search space is even more critical for OP on DBpedia 3.8 and Wikidata 2019, as the number of candidate rules grows cubically with the number of relations. We generated around 9 million candidate rules for DBpedia and around 114 million candidates for Wikidata. In both cases, OP mined all rules of size 2 in 1 h 20 min ($\approx 21k$ candidates) and 14 h ($\approx 100k$ candidates) respectively. However, it failed to mine any rule of size 3 in the remaining time. If we set the minimal support again to 1 and the CWA confidence threshold to 10^{-5}, AMIE can mine twice as many rules as OP on DBpedia 3.8 in 33 min.

RuDiK. For RuDiK, we found that the original parallelization mechanism does not scale well to 40 cores. The load average of our system, Virtuoso included, never exceeded 5 cores used. This explains the similar results between our benchmark and RuDiK's original experiments on Yago2s with fewer cores. On DBpedia, we could run the system also with type information—although this did not impact the runtime significantly. The loss of performance during the execution of the SPARQL queries is more noticeable due to the multitude of small relations in DBpedia compared to Yago. In comparison, AMIE was more than 20× faster on both datasets. This means that, even if RuDiK were to make full use of the 40 cores, and speed up 4-fold, it would still be 5 times slower. AMIE also found more rules than RuDiK. Among these are all rules that RuDiK found, except two (which were clearly wrong rules; one had a confidence of 0.001).

In our experiment, RuDiK mined rules in Wikidata in 23 h. However, RuDiK was not able to mine rules for 22 of the relations as Virtuoso was not able to compute any of the positive or the negative examples RuDiK requires to operate. This is because RuDiK would timeout any SPARQL query after 20 s of execution[6]. Virtuoso failed to compute the examples during this time frame on the 22 relations, which are the largest ones in our Wikidata dataset: They cover 84% of the facts. Interestingly, RuDiK did also not find rules that contain these relations in the body (except one, which covered 0.5% of the KB).

In comparison, AMIE mined 1703 rules with at least one of these relations, computing the support, confidence and PCA confidence exactly on these huge relations—in less time. For example, it found the rule $inRegion(x, y) \wedge inCountry(y, z) \Rightarrow inCountry(x, z)$, which is not considered by RuDiK, but has a support of over 7 million and a PCA confidence of over 99%.

AMIE 3 outperformed both OP and RuDiK in terms of runtime and the number of rules. Moreover, it has the advantage of being exact and complete. Then again,

---

[6] Increasing the timeout parameter is not necessarily a good solution for two reasons: First, we cannot predict the optimal value so that all queries finish. Second, it would increase the runtime of queries succeeding with partial results thanks to Virtuoso's Anytime Query capability. This would largely increase RuDiK's runtime with no guarantee to solve the issue.

the comparisons have to be seen in context: RuDiK, e.g., is designed to run on a small machine. For this, it uses a disk-based database and sampling. AMIE, in contrast, loads all data into memory, and thus has a large memory footprint (the 500 GB were nearly used up for the Wikidata experiment). In return, it computes all rules exactly and is fast.

6 Conclusion

We have presented AMIE 3, the newest version of the rule mining system AMIE (available at https://github.com/lajus/amie/). The new system uses a range of optimization and pruning strategies, which allow scaling to large KBs that were previously beyond reach. In particular, AMIE 3 can exhaustively mine all rules above given thresholds on support and confidence, without resorting to sampling or approximations. We hope that the optimizations and subtleties exposed in this paper can carry over to other types of databases, and potentially other systems.

Acknowledgements. Partially supported by the grant ANR-16-CE23-0007-01.

References

1. Ahmadi, N., Huynh, V.P., Meduri, V., Ortona, S., Papotti, P.: Mining expressive rules in knowledge graphs. JDIQ **12**(2), 1–27 (2019)
2. Ahmadi, N., Lee, J., Papotti, P., Saeed, M.: Explainable fact checking with probabilistic answer set programming. In: Conference for Truth and Trust online (2019)
3. Chen, Y., Goldberg, S., Wang, D.Z., Johri, S.S.: Ontological pathfinding. In: SIGMOD (2016)
4. Chen, Y., Wang, D.Z., Goldberg, S.: ScaLeKB: scalable learning and inference over large knowledge bases. VLDB J. **25**(6), 893–918 (2016). https://doi.org/10.1007/s00778-016-0444-3
5. Ebisu, T., Ichise, R.: Graph Pattern Entity Ranking Model for Knowledge Graph Completion. In: NAACL-HLT (2019)
6. Fernández, J.D., Martínez-Prieto, M.A., Gutiérrez, C., Polleres, A., Arias, M.: Binary RDF Representation (HDT). Web Semant. **19**, 22–41 (2013)
7. Galárraga, L., Heitz, G., Murphy, K., Suchanek, F.: Canonicalizing open knowledge bases. In: CIKM (2014)
8. Galárraga, L., Teflioudi, C., Hose, K., Suchanek, F.: AMIE: association rule mining under incomplete evidence in ontological knowledge bases. In: WWW (2013)
9. Galárraga, L., Teflioudi, C., Hose, K., Suchanek, F.M.: Fast rule mining in ontological knowledge bases with AMIE+. VLDB J. **24**(6), 707–730 (2015). https://doi.org/10.1007/s00778-015-0394-1
10. Galárraga, L.A., Preda, N., Suchanek, F.M.: Mining rules to align knowledge bases. In: AKBC (2013)
11. Hand, D.J., Adams, N.M., Bolton, R.J. (eds.): Pattern Detection and Discovery. LNCS (LNAI), vol. 2447. Springer, Heidelberg (2002). https://doi.org/10.1007/3-540-45728-3
12. Meng, C., Cheng, R., Maniu, S., Senellart, P., Zhang, W.: Discovering meta-paths in large heterogeneous information networks. In: WWW (2015)

13. Muggleton, S.: Learning from positive data. In: ILP (1997)
14. Niu, F., Ré, C., Doan, A., Shavlik, J.: Tuffy: Scaling up statistical inference in Markov logic networks using an RDBMS. arXiv:1104.3216 (2011)
15. Ortona, S., Meduri, V.V., Papotti, P.: Robust discovery of positive and negative rules in knowledge bases. In: ICDE (2018)
16. Quinlan, J.R.: Learning logical definitions from relations. Machine Learning 5(3), 239–266 (1990). https://doi.org/10.1007/BF00117105
17. Suchanek, F.M., Abiteboul, S., Senellart, P.: PARIS: probabilistic alignment of relations, instances, and schema. In: PVLDB, vol. 5, no. 3 (2011)
18. Suchanek, F.M., Lajus, J., Boschin, A., Weikum, G.: Knowledge representation and rule mining in entity-centric KBs. In: Reasoning Web Summer School (2019)
19. Zeng, Q., Patel, J.M., Page, D.: QuickFOIL: scalable inductive logic programming. In: VLDB, vol. 8, no.3, November 2014

A Simple Method for Inducing Class Taxonomies in Knowledge Graphs

Marcin Pietrasik[1]([✉])[iD] and Marek Reformat[1,2][iD]

[1] University of Alberta, 116 St & 85 Ave, Edmonton, Canada
{pietrasi,reformat}@ualberta.ca
[2] University of Social Sciences, 90-113 Łódź, Poland

Abstract. The rise of knowledge graphs as a medium for storing and organizing large amounts of data has spurred research interest in automated methods for reasoning with and extracting information from this representation of data. One area which seems to receive less attention is that of inducing a class taxonomy from such graphs. Ontologies, which provide the axiomatic foundation on which knowledge graphs are built, are often governed by a set of class subsumption axioms. These class subsumptions form a class taxonomy which hierarchically organizes the type classes present in the knowledge graph. Manually creating and curating these class taxonomies oftentimes requires expert knowledge and is time costly, especially in large-scale knowledge graphs. Thus, methods capable of inducing the class taxonomy from the knowledge graph data automatically are an appealing solution to the problem. In this paper, we propose a simple method for inducing class taxonomies from knowledge graphs that is scalable to large datasets. Our method borrows ideas from tag hierarchy induction methods, relying on class frequencies and co-occurrences, such that it requires no information outside the knowledge graph's triple representation. We demonstrate the use of our method on three real-world datasets and compare our results with existing tag hierarchy induction methods. We show that our proposed method outperforms existing tag hierarchy induction methods, although both perform well when applied to knowledge graphs.

Keywords: Knowledge graphs · Taxonomy induction · Ontologies

1 Introduction

Knowledge graphs are data storage structures that rely on principles from graph theory to represent information. Specifically, facts are stored as triples which bring together two entities through a relation. In a graphical context, these entities are analogous to nodes, and the relations between them are analogous to

© Springer Nature Switzerland AG 2020
A. Harth et al. (Eds.): ESWC 2020, LNCS 12123, pp. 53–68, 2020.
https://doi.org/10.1007/978-3-030-49461-2_4

edges. In recent years, knowledge graphs have garnered widespread attention as a medium for storing data on the web. Public knowledge bases such as DBpedia [13], YAGO [12], and WikiData [28] are all underpinned by large-scale knowledge graphs containing upwards of one billion triples each. These knowledge bases find uses in personal, academic, and commercial domains and are ubiquitous in the research fields of the Semantic Web, artificial intelligence, and computer science broadly. Furthermore, private companies are known to use proprietary knowledge graphs as a component of their data stores. Google, for instance, uses a knowledge graph derived from Freebase [6] to enhance their search engine results by providing infoboxes which summarize facts about a user's query [24].

Ontologies are often used in conjunction with knowledge graphs to provide an axiomatic foundation on which knowledge graphs are built. In this view, an ontology may be seen as a rule book that provides semantics to a knowledge graph and governs how the information contained within it can be reasoned with. One of the core components of an ontology is the class taxonomy: a set of subsumption axioms between the type classes that may exists in the knowledge graph. When put together, the subsumption axioms form a hierarchy of classes where general concepts appear at the top and their subconcepts appear as their descendants.

One of the challenges that arise when working with large knowledge graphs is that of class taxonomy construction. Manual construction is time consuming and requires curators knowledgeable in the area. DBpedia, for instance, relies on its community to curate its class taxonomy. Similarly, YAGO relies on a combination of information from Wikipedia[1] and WordNet[2], both of which are manually curated. On the other hand, automated methods are not able to induce class taxonomies of the quality necessary to reliably apply to complex knowledge bases. Furthermore, they oftentimes rely on external information which may itself be manually curated or may only be applicable to knowledge bases in a particular domain. With this in mind, the impetus for automatically inducing class taxonomies of high quality from large-scale knowledge graphs becomes apparent.

In this paper, we propose a scalable method for inducing class taxonomies from knowledge graphs without relying on information external to the knowledge graph's triples. Our approach applies methods used to solve the problem of tag hierarchy induction, which involves inducing a hierarchy of tags from a collection of documents and the tags that annotate them. Although extensively studied in the field of natural language processing, these methods have yet to be applied to knowledge graphs to the best of our knowledge. In order to use these methods, we reshape the knowledge graph's triple structure to a tuple structure, exploiting the graph's single dimensionality in assigning entities to type classes. Furthermore, we propose a novel approach to inducing class taxonomies which outperforms existing tag hierarchy induction methods both in terms scalability and quality of induced taxonomies.

---

[1] https://www.wikipedia.org/.
[2] https://wordnet.princeton.edu/.

The remainder of this paper proceeds with Sect. 2 which provides an overview of the existing work done on inducing class taxonomies and tag hierarchies. We formalize the problem and introduce notation in Sect. 3. Our proposed method is described in Sect. 4 and evaluated in Sect. 5. Section 6 concludes the paper.

2 Related Work

We divide our discussion of related work into two subsections: class taxonomy induction methods and tag hierarchy induction methods. Both of these methods are used to construct a hierarchy of concepts, however they differ in the type of data they are applied to. Class taxonomy induction methods are used on knowledge graphs and thus operate on data represented as triples. Tag hierarchy induction methods operate on documents and the tags that annotate them. In practice, these documents are often blog posts, images, and videos annotated by users on social networking websites. We can view our proposed method as a combination of the aforementioned categories as it takes the input structure of documents and tags but is applied to knowledge graphs to induce a class taxonomy.

2.1 Methods for Class Taxonomy Induction

Völker and Niepert [27] introduce *Statistical Schema Induction* which uses association rule mining on a knowledge graph's transaction table to generate ontology axioms. Each row in the transaction table corresponds to a subject in the graph along with the classes it belongs to. Implication patterns which are consistent with the table are mined from this table to create candidate ontology axioms. The candidate axioms are then sorted in terms of descending certainty values and added greedily to the ontology only if they are logically coherent with axioms added before them. Nickel et al. [18] propose a method using hierarchical clustering on a decomposed representation of the knowledge graph. Specifically, they extend *RESCAL* [17], a method for factorizing a three-way tensor, to better handle sparse large-scale data and apply *OPTICS* [3], a density based hierarchical clustering algorithm. Ristoski et al. [20] rely on entity and text embeddings in their proposed method, *TIEmb*. The intuition behind this approach is that entities of a subclass will be embedded within their parent class's embeddings. Thus if you calculate the centroid for each class's embeddings, you can infer its subclasses as those whose centroid falls within a certain radius. For instance, the class centroids of `Mammals` and `Reptiles` will fall inside the radius of `Animals` although the converse is not true since `Mammals` and `Reptiles` are more specific classes and are expected to have a smaller radius.

2.2 Methods for Tag Hierarchy Induction

Heymann and Garcia-Molina [11] propose a frequency-based approach using cosine similarity to calculate tag generality. In their approach, tags are assigned vectors based on the amount of times they annotate each document. The pair-wise cosine similarity between tag vectors is used to build a tag similarity graph. The closeness centrality of tags in this graph is used as the generality of tags. To build the hierarchy, tags are greedily added – in order of descending generality – as children to the tag in the hierarchy that has the highest degree of similarity. This approach was extended by Benz et al. [4] to better handle synonyms and homonyms in the dataset. Schmitz [23] proposed a method extending on the work done by Sanderson and Croft [22] which uses subsumption rules to identify the relations between parents and children in the hierarchy. The subsumption rules are calculated by tag co-occurrence and filtered to control for "idiosyncratic vocabulary". These rules form a directed graph which is then pruned to create a tree. Solskinnsbakk and Gulla [25] use the Aprioir algorithm [1] to mine a set of association rules from the tags. Each of these rules has the relationship of premise and consequence which the authors treat as that of class and subclass. This is used to construct a tree which is then verified based on the semantics of each tag. Tang et al. [26] use *Latent Dirichlet Allocation* (LDA) [5] to generate topics comprised of tags. Generality can then be calculated following the reasoning that tags with high frequencies across many topics are more general than ones that have a high frequencies in a single topic. Relations between tags are induced based on four divergence measures calculated on the LDA results. *Agglomerative Hierarchical Clustering for Taxonomy Construction* [14] avoids explicitly computing tag generality by employing agglomerative clustering and selecting cluster medoids to be promoted upwards in the hierarchy. Cluster medoids are chosen based on a similarity metric calculated as the divergence between a tag's topic distributions as learned by LDA. Wang et al. [29] propose a taxonomy generation method based on repeated application of k-medoids clustering. As the distance metric necessary for k-medoids clustering, they propose a similarity score based on the weighted sum of document and textual similarities. Levels in the hierarchy are created by repeated application of k-medoids clustering such that for each cluster, the cluster medoid becomes the parent of all other tags in the cluster. Dong et al. [8] propose a supervised learning approach wherein binary classifiers are trained to predict a "broader-narrower" relation between tags. LDA is used to generate topic distributions for tags which act as a basis for three sets of features used to train the classifier. This approach does not guarantee that the relations between tags will form a rooted tree.

3 Problem Description

A knowledge graph, $\mathcal{K}$, is repository of information structured as a collection of triples where each triple relates the subject, s, to the object, o, through a relation, r. More formally, $\mathcal{K} = \{\langle s, r, o \rangle \in \mathcal{E} \times \mathcal{R} \times \mathcal{E}\}$ where $\langle s, r, o \rangle$ is a triple, $\mathcal{E}$ is the set of entities in $\mathcal{K}$, and $\mathcal{R}$ is the set of relations in $\mathcal{K}$. $\mathcal{K}$ can therefore be viewed as a directed graph with nodes representing entities and edges representing relations.

We can think of relation-object pairs, $\langle r, o \rangle$, as tags that describe the subject. In this view, each entity that takes on the role of subject, s_i, is annotated by tags,

$t_j \in \mathcal{A}_i$, where $\mathcal{A}_i$ is the set of tags that annotate s_i. We call these entities documents, $d_i \in \mathcal{D}$, such that the set of all documents is a subset of all entities, $\mathcal{D} \subseteq \mathcal{E}$. Tags are defined as relation-objects pairs, $t := \langle r, o \rangle$, and belong to the set of all tags, the vocabulary, denoted as $\mathcal{V}$, such that $t_j \in \mathcal{V}$. For a concrete example of this notation consider DBpedia, wherein the entity dbr:Canada is annotated by the tags $\langle$dbo:capital,dbr:Ottawa$\rangle$, $\langle$dbo:currency,dbr:Canadian_dollar$\rangle$, $\langle$rdf:type,dbo:Location$\rangle$, and $\langle$rdf:type,dbo:Country$\rangle$ amongst others. In this view, the knowledge base $\mathcal{K}$ may be represented as the set of document-tag tuples $\mathcal{K} = \{\langle d, t \rangle \in \mathcal{D} \times \mathcal{V}\}$, where $\langle d, t \rangle$ is the tuple that relates document d with tag t. We refer to this notation as the tuple structure for the remainder of the paper.

Information in knowledge graphs is often structured using an ontology, which provides semantics to the knowledge graph's triples through an axiomatic foundation which defines how entities and relations associate with one another. A key component of most ontologies is the class taxonomy which organizes classes through a set of class subsumption axioms. These subsumption axioms may be thought of as is-a relations between classes. For instance, in the DBpedia class hierarchy, the subsumption axioms {dbo:Person → dbo:Artist} and {dbo:Artist → dbo:Painter} imply that dbo:Painter is a dbo:Artist and that dbo:Artist is a dbo:Person. Furthermore, since class subsumption axioms are transitive, dbo:Painter is a dbo:Person. This taxonomy oftentimes takes the form of a rooted tree with a root class of which all other classes are considered logical descendants of.

The problem of class taxonomy induction from knowledge graphs involves generating subsumption axioms from triples to build the class taxonomy. We notice that in most knowledge graphs, subjects are related to their class type by one relation. This has the effect of reducing the knowledge graph's class identifying triples to a single dimension. The property can be exploited in the tuple structure, since all class identifying relations are the same, they can be ignored without loss of information. For instance, in DBpedia the relation which relates subjects to their class is rdf:type. Thus, when compiling a dataset of class identifying tuples, we can treat the tags $\langle$rdf:type,dbo:Country$\rangle$ and dbo:Country as equivalent. Therefore, the tuple $\langle$dbr:Canada, dbo:Country$\rangle$ preserves all information required to induce a class taxonomy. This can be exploited by tag hierarchy induction methods which take documents and their tags as input.

4   Approach

Our proposed method uses class frequencies and co-occurrences to calculate similarity between tags. This approach, inspired by the method proposed by Schmitz, relies on the intuition that subclasses will co-occur in documents with their superclasses more often than with classes they are not logical descendants of. Unlike Schmitz's method which uses this assumption to generate candidate subsumption axioms, our method uses similarity to choose a parent tag which already exists in the taxonomy. In this step, which draws inspiration from Heymann and Garcia-Molina, tags are greedily added to the taxonomy in order of descending generality. Thus, subsumption axioms induced by our method have to abide by the following rules: (1) the parent tag has a higher generality than the child tag; (2) the parent tag is the tag with the highest similarity to the child tag from the tags that exist in the taxonomy when the child tag is being added.

As previously mentioned, our approach leverages the tuple structure of a knowledge graph to induce a class taxonomy in the form of a rooted tree. As such, the first step is data preprocessing wherein all of a knowledge graph's class identifying triples are converted to tuple structure.

4.1 Class Taxonomy Induction Procedure

Before describing the taxonomy induction procedure for our method, we define measures which are calculated on the knowledge graph as required input for our algorithm.

- The number of documents annotated by tag t_a is denoted as D_{t_a}.
- The number of documents annotated by both tags t_a and t_b is denoted as D_{t_a,t_b}. We note that this measure is symmetrical, i.e. $D_{t_a,t_b} = D_{t_b,t_a}$.
- The generality of tag t_a, denoted as G_{t_a}, measures how general the concept described by the tag is and how high it belongs in the taxonomy. The generality is defined as:

$$G_{t_a} = \sum_{t_b \in \mathcal{V}_{-t_a}} \frac{D_{t_a,t_b}}{D_{t_b}} \tag{1}$$

Where $\mathcal{V}_{-t_a}$ is the set of all tags excluding tag t_a.

Having calculated the aforementioned measures, we proceed by sorting tags in the order of descending generality and store them as $\mathcal{V}_{sorted}$. The first element of this list, $\mathcal{V}_{sorted}[0]$, is semantically the most general of all tags and becomes the root tag of the taxonomy. The taxonomy, $\mathcal{T}$, is represented as a set of subsumption axioms between parent and child tags. Formally, each subsumption between parent tag, t_{parent}, and child tag, t_{child}, is represented by $\{t_{parent} \rightarrow t_{child}\}$ such that $\{t_{parent} \rightarrow t_{child}\} \in \mathcal{T}$. The taxonomy is therefore initialized with the root tag as $\mathcal{T} = \{\{\emptyset \rightarrow \mathcal{V}_{sorted}[0]\}\}$ where $\emptyset$ represents a null value, i.e. no parent.

Following initialization, the remaining tags are added to the taxonomy in terms of descending generality by calculating the similarity between the tag being added, t_b, and all the tags already in the taxonomy, $\mathcal{T}*$. The tag $t_a \in \mathcal{T}*$ that has the highest similarity with tag t_b becomes the parent of t_b and $\{t_a \rightarrow t_b\}$ is added to $\mathcal{T}$. The similarity between tags t_a and t_b, denoted as $S_{t_a \rightarrow t_b}$, measures the degree to which tag t_b is the direct descendant of tag t_a. It is calculated as the degree to which tag t_b is compatible with tag t_a and all the ancestors of t_a:

$$S_{t_a \rightarrow t_b} = \sum_{t_c \in \mathcal{P}_{t_a}} \alpha^{l_a - l_c} \frac{D_{t_b,t_c}}{D_{t_b}} \tag{2}$$

Where $\mathcal{P}_{t_a}$ is the path in the taxonomy from the root tag $\mathcal{V}_{sorted}[0]$ to tag t_a. l_a and l_c denote the levels in the hierarchy of tags t_a and t_c, respectively. The levels are counted from the root tag starting at zero. Thus, the level of $\mathcal{V}_{sorted}[0]$, denoted as $l_{\mathcal{V}_{sorted}[0]}$, is equal to zero, the levels of its children are equal to one, and so on. The decay factor, α, is a hyperparameter that controls the effect ancestors of tag t_a have on its similarity when calculating $S_{t_a \to t_b}$. By setting the value of α such that $0 < \alpha < 1$, we ensure that the effect is lower the more distant an ancestor tag is. The cases were $\alpha = 0$ and $\alpha = 1$ correspond to ancestors having no effect and equal effect on the similarity, respectively. We explore the effect various α values have on the induced class taxonomy in the following section. The full details of our method's procedure are outlined in Algorithm 1.

Algorithm 1. Procedure for Class Taxonomy Induction

Input: Knowledge graph in tuple structure, $\mathcal{K}$; Document counts annotated by tag, D; Generality of tags, G; Decay factor, α
Output: Induced class taxonomy, $\mathcal{T}$
 1: Sort tags in order of descending generality, $\mathcal{V}_{sorted}$
 2: Initialize taxonomy with root tag equal to the tag with highest generality, $\mathcal{T} = \{\{\emptyset \to \mathcal{V}_{sorted}[0]\}\}$
 3: Initialize the set of tags that have already been added to the taxonomy, $\mathcal{T}* = \{\mathcal{V}_{sorted}[0]\}$
 4: **for** b = 1, 2, ..., $|\mathcal{V}_{sorted}|$ **do**
 5:     $maxSimTag = \mathcal{V}_{sorted}[0]$
 6:     $maxSimValue = 0$
 7:     **for** $t_a \in \mathcal{T}*$ **do**
 8:         Calculate $S_{t_a \to t_b}$ using Equation 2
 9:         **if** $S_{t_a \to t_b} > maxSimValue$ **then**
10:             $maxSimTag = t_a$
11:             $maxSimValue = S_{t_a \to t_b}$
12:         **end if**
13:     **end for**
14:     $\mathcal{T} = \{maxSimTag \to t_b\} \cup \mathcal{T}$
15:     $\mathcal{T}* = t_b \cup \mathcal{T}*$
16: **end for**

---

5   Evaluation

Evaluation of class taxonomy induction methods is difficult as there may be several equally valid taxonomies for a dataset. Previous works such as Gu et al. [10] and Wang et al. (2009) [30] have opted for human evaluation, wherein domain experts assess the correctness of relations between classes. Wang et al. (2012) [29] used domain experts to rank entire paths on a three point scale. Others, such as Liu et al. [15] and Almoqhim et al. [2], compare class relations against a gold standard taxonomy. In this approach, a confusion matrix between class subsumption axioms is calculated between the induced and gold standard taxonomies. When a gold standard taxonomy can be established, it is the preferred evaluation method as it provides an objective measurement; as such, it is the one we use in our work. We use the confusion matrix to derive the harmonic mean between precision and recall, the F_1 score [7], as our evaluation metric:

$$precision = \frac{TP}{TP + FP} \tag{3}$$

$$recall = \frac{TP}{TP + FN} \tag{4}$$

$$F_1 = 2 * \frac{precision * recall}{precision + recall} \tag{5}$$

where TP, FP, and FN are the number of true positives, false positives, and false negatives, respectively.

For the remainder of this section, we first evaluate the effect of our method's hyperparameter, α, on each of the three datasets and provide suggestions for selecting the α value when applying our method to other datasets. This is followed by a comparing our method to the aforementioned Heymann and Garcia-Molina method, Schmitz method, as well as results from the literature. We also provide visualizations of excerpts from the class taxonomies induced by our method on the Life and DBpedia datasets. Finally, our method's computational complexity and the effect of dataset size on induced taxonomies are evaluated. The method was implemented using Python and has been made public alongside our datasets for reproducibility on Github[3].

5.1   Datasets

We evaluate the method on three real-world datasets generated from public online knowledge bases: Life, DBpedia, and WordNet. All three datasets as well as their respective gold standard class taxonomies were generated during the month of November 2019.

The Life Dataset was generated by querying the Catalogue of Life: 2019 Annual Checklist (CoL) [21], an online database that indexes living organisms by their taxonomic classification. One hundred thousand living organisms were randomly selected from the GBIF Type Specimen Names [9], an online checklist of 1,226,904 organisms, and queried on CoL at each of their taxonomic ranks to generate the document-tag tuples. The resulting dataset takes the form such that each organism is a document and its membership at each taxonomic rank is a tag related by is-a. For instance, the document Canis_latrans (coyote) will have the tags ⟨is-a, Mammalia⟩ and ⟨is-a, Canidae⟩. Furthermore, to anchor the class taxonomy to a root tag, we added the tag ⟨is-a, LivingOrganism⟩ to every document. We note that even though the number of taxonomic ranks is fixed, most organisms in the database are not defined on all of them. As such,

---

[3] https://github.com/mpietrasik/smict.

the number of tags per document varies from two to ten. In total, there are 100,000 documents and 37,368 unique tags. Since the dataset itself is classified in the correct taxonomic order, the Life gold standard taxonomy could simply be obtained by querying for subsumption axioms from the dataset.

The DBpedia Dataset was generated by randomly querying for 50,000 unique subjects in DBpedia for which there exists a triple where the subject is related to a DBpedia class object (an object having the prefix `dbo:`) via the relation `rdf:type`. These 50,000 subjects become the documents in the tuple structure. Following this step, all the triples for each document having the tag form $\langle$`rdf:type, dbo:*`$\rangle$ were queried to make the document-tag tuples. (`dbo:*` represents any object with the prefix `dbo`.) In total, 205,793 triples were used to create the dataset with 418 unique tags. The DBpedia gold standard taxonomy was generated from the DBpedia ontology class mappings which can be found on the DBpedia website[4]. At the time of querying, the ontology had 765 classes, 418 of which were present in the dataset. This difference made it necessary to include only those subsumption axioms for which parent and child tags exist in the dataset when computing the confusion matrix. This is similar to the dataset generated in Ristoski et al. where the number of classes present in their dataset was 415.

The WordNet Dataset was generated by querying DBpedia for subjects of types that exist in WordNet [16], an English language lexical database. Fifty thousand subjects having a WordNet class object related by `rdf:type` were queried. In DBpedia, WordNet class objects use the `yago:` prefix, giving the tag format $\langle$`rdf:type, yago:*`$\rangle$. This process yielded a dataset comprised of 50,000 documents and 1752 unique tags generated from 392,846 triples. To generate the WordNet gold standard taxonomy, DBpedia was queried to learn the relations between WordNet classes through the `rdfs:subClassOf` relation. In this process, `yago:PhysicalEntity100001930` is set as the root class and the taxonomy is built by recursively querying for subclasses using `rdfs:subClassOf` as the relation. This process builds a taxonomy of 30722 tags. To fit the 1752 tags present in the dataset, it was necessary to collapse the gold standard taxonomy. This was done by removing tags in the gold standard taxonomy that are missing in the dataset and adopting orphaned tags with the nearest ancestor existing in the dataset.

5.2 Hyperparameter Sensitivity

We evaluate our method's sensitivity to the decay factor, α, by performing a hyperparameter sweep on each of the three datasets. In this process, our method is applied five times on each dataset for α values starting at $\alpha = 0$ and increasing by increments of 0.05 up until $\alpha = 1$. This process is analogous to increasing

---

[4] http://mappings.dbpedia.org/server/ontology/classes/.

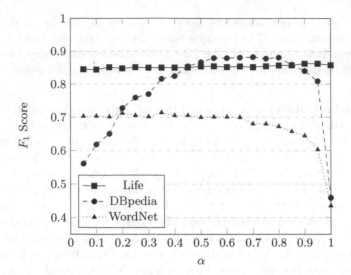

Fig. 1. Comparison of mean test F_1 Scores at varying α values on the Life, DBpedia, and WordNet datasets.

the relative importance of ancestor tags when calculating tag similarity. Furthermore, since similarity is calculated as a summation, increasing α will favour tags lower in the taxonomy. The F_1 scores are calculated and their means at each α value are displayed graphically in Fig. 1. For clarity, we omit graphing the mean F_1 scores at $\alpha = 0$ as the values are disproportionately low for all three datasets ($F_1 < 0.1$). This is because when $\alpha = 0$, the similarity gets reduced to $S_{t_a \to t_b} = D_{t_a,t_b}/D_{t_b}$ which has the effect of inducing shallow taxonomies with most tags as children of the root tag.

Upon cursory inspection of the F_1 scores, we notice that there is no clear behaviour that α exhibits which is constant across datasets. This is also apparent when comparing the optimal α values: 0.95, 0.70, and 0.35 for Life, DBpedia, and WordNet datasets, respectively. Furthermore, we notice that as α increases, the trend follows three different patterns: stable, generally increasing, and generally decreasing. A possible reason for the relative stability of α on the Life dataset is its consistency. Due to the strict requirements for source datasets to be included in CoL, all entries are well scrutinised. As such, tags will always appear with their ancestors in the same documents. For example, all 893 instances of the tag Mammalia co-occur with the tag's ancestors Animalia, Chordata, and LivingOrganism. In this scenario, there is less information to be gained by incorporating information from higher up in the taxonomy. On the other hand, the DBpedia dataset shows improvement with increasing α values until a peak is reached and F_1 declines. The increase in induced taxonomy quality with increasing α values in consistent with the assumption that taking into account a potential parent's path is advantageous when selecting a parent. The decline in F_1 after $\alpha = 0.8$ can be explained by distant ancestor tags having too strong an influence in assigning parent tags to children. One possible explanation for better F_1 scores of lower α values on WordNet is our method's overall lower F_1 scores on this dataset. Errors in the induced taxonomy propagate downwards and their effect increases with the value of α. Thus, in a taxonomy with many errors, it is advantageous to place a relatively higher value on the similarity between the direct parent tag and its child, as is done with lower α values.

In general, it is difficult to predict the optimal α value a priori, however there are a few rules of thumb to guide this process when applying our method. When there is no prior information about a nature of the dataset or its expected class taxonomy, we suggest using α values around 0.5 as these values perform well (although not optimally) in our experiments. Datasets which are complex, or have low co-occurence rates between ancestor and descendent tags will favour lower α values as these ensure errors will propagate less through the taxonomy. On the other hand, well structured datasets will be less affected by varying α values.

5.3   Results

In our experiments, we applied our proposed method to each of the aforementioned datasets at the α values determined optimal in the previous subsection. Each dataset was applied five times to account for the stochasticity in sorting tags of equal generality. The results of our method as well as those of the comparison methods are summarized in Table 1. We implemented Heymann and Garcia-Molina, and Schmitz methods to the best of our understanding and performed hyperparameter exploration for their respective hyperparameters on each dataset. After obtaining the optimal hyperparameters, we ran the methods five times on each dataset and collected the results. We note that Heymann and Garcia-Molina was not able to terminate sufficiently fast enough for us to obtain results on the Life dataset. In the table we also included the results reported in previous work applied on the DBpedia dataset. Although the DBpedia dataset was derived similarly to our own, conclusions in comparing this method to our proposed method should be drawn cautiously. We indicate these entries in the table with a footnote.

In general, our method outperforms the other two tag hierarchy induction methods as shown by the mean F_1 scores. We notice similarly high precision and recall values which suggests that it's both capable of inducing subsumption axioms (recall) while ensuring these axioms are correct (precision). Furthermore, closer inspection of the results reveals that many of the errors can be categorized by two types, which we illustrate by using results from the DBpedia dataset. In the first, the order between parent and child tags are reversed as in the induced {dbo:Guitarist → dbo:Instrumentalist} when the correct order is {dbo:Instrumentalist → dbo:Guitarist}. In the second, a tag is misplaced as the child of its sibling, for instance, the gold standard classification of educational institutions is {{dbo:EducationalInstitution → dbo:University}, {dbo:EducationalInstitution → dbo:College}} while our induced taxonomy gives the following: $\{\{$dbo:EducationalInstitution $\rightarrow$ dbo:University$\}, \{$dbo:University $\rightarrow$ dbo:College$\}\}$. Finally, our induced taxonomy includes subsumption axioms which are considered incorrect as per the gold standard but may not be to a human evaluator. An example of this is that our method induced the subsumption axiom $\{$dbo:SportFacility $\rightarrow$ dbo:Stadium$\}$ while the gold standard considers $\{$dbo:Venue $\rightarrow$ dbo:Stadium$\}$ to be the correct parent for dbo:Stadium. We provide an excerpt of our induced class taxonomies on the Life and DBpedia datasets in Fig. 2.

Table 1. Method results (mean $\pm$ standard deviation) on the Life, DBpedia, and WordNet datasets.

Method	Life			DBpedia			WordNet		
	Precision	Recall	F_1	Precision	Recall	F_1	Precision	Recall	F_1
Heymann and	–	–	–	.7944	.8021	.7982	.6027	.5814	.5918
Garcia-Molina	–	–	–	±.0148	±.0150	±.0149	±.0116	±.0112	±.0114
Schmitz	.8936	.7966	.8423	.8063	.7962	.8013	.8140	.7756	.7943
	±0	±0	±0	±0	±0	±0	±0	±0	±0
Paulheim and	–	–	–	.1040	.2190	.1410	–	–	–
Fümkranz[a] [19,20]	–	–	–	–	–	–	–	–	–
Ristoski	–	–	–	.5940	.4650	.5210	–	–	–
et al. [20] [a]	–	–	–	–	–	–	–	–	–
Völker and	–	–	–	.9920	.9970	.9950	–	–	–
Niepert [27] [a]	–	–	–	–	–	–	–	–	–
Our method	.8740	.8513	.8625	.8781	.8867	.8824	.7275	.7018	.7144
	±.0041	±.0040	±.0040	±.0051	±.0052	±.0052	±.0070	±.0068	±.0069

[a] The result for this method was obtained from the literature.

5.4 Computational Complexity Evaluation

One of the most salient issues that arises when applying class taxonomy induction methods to real-world knowledge graphs is that of scalability. As mentioned previously, DBpedia, Yago, and WikiData have upwards of one billion triples each, thus for a method to operate on these datasets, it has to be computationally efficient. It is important to note, however, that in inducing a class taxonomy, it is not necessary to use all the triples available in the knowledge graph but rather to only use as many as is required to achieve an acceptable result. We discuss this idea in the following subsection.

The most computationally taxing procedure in our method is that of calculating the number of documents annotated by two tags, D_{t_a,t_b}, which has a worst case time complexity of $\mathcal{O}(|\mathcal{D}||\mathcal{V}|^2)$, where $|\mathcal{D}|$ and $|\mathcal{V}|$ are the number of documents and tags, respectively. It is important to note, however, that the worst case only occurs when all documents are annotated by all tags. In this scenario, every subject in a knowledge graph is of every class type in the ontology. The average computation complexity of our algorithm is $\mathcal{O}(|\mathcal{D}||\overline{|\mathcal{A}|}^2)$ where $|\mathcal{A}|$ is the average number of tags that annotate a document. In our experiments our method was faster to terminate than both the Heymann and Garcia-Molina and Schmitz methods on all three datasets.

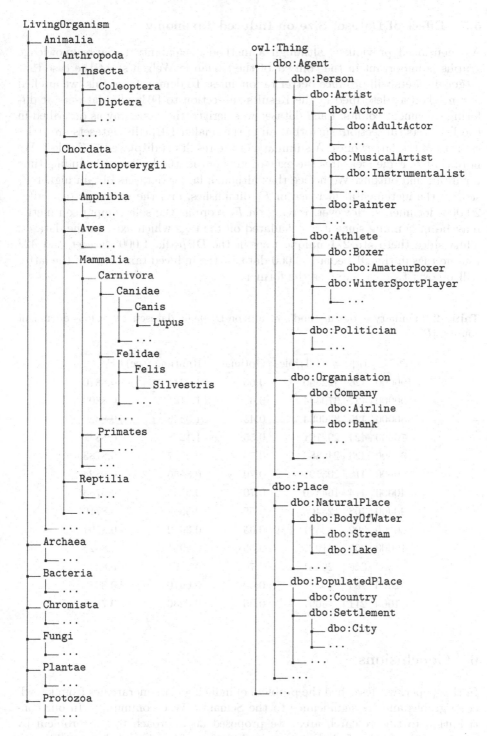

Fig. 2. Excerpts of the induced class taxonomies for the Life (left) and DBpedia (right) datasets. Ellipses denote addition child classes omitted for brevity.

5.5   Effect of Dataset Size on Induced Taxonomy

As mentioned previously, although a method's scalability to large knowledge graphs is important in the context of the Semantic Web, it's not the case that larger datasets will produce better taxonomies. To demonstrate this, we applied our method as described in the Results subsection to DBpedia datasets at differing document counts. Each dataset was derived the same way as described in the Datasets subsection, such that all of the smaller DBpedia datasets are strict subsets of the larger ones. A summary of the results is displayed in Table 2. We note that runtime measures the execution of our method without including time for input and output. We notice that although larger datasets obtain higher F_1 scores, the incremental increase in F_1 diminishes, and the scores plateau after 20,000 documents. However, relying on F_1 score as the sole comparison metric may be misguiding since it is calculated on the tags which exist in the dataset. Thus since there are 211 unique tags in the DBpedia 1,000 dataset and 428 unique tags in the DBpedia 100,000 dataset, the induced taxonomy of the latter will be over twice as large as the former.

Table 2. Summary of our method's results on DBpedia datasets at various document counts, $|\mathcal{D}|$.

$|\mathcal{D}|$	$|\mathcal{V}|$	# of Triples	Optimal α	Runtime (sec)	F_1
100000	428	422860	0.65	1.6311	0.8810
90000	427	379444	0.65	1.5131	0.8808
80000	425	336084	0.45	1.3340	0.8826
70000	424	292791	0.55	1.1248	0.8847
60000	423	249383	0.70	0.9767	0.8783
50000	418	205793	0.70	0.8556	0.8824
40000	414	164470	0.70	0.6545	0.8783
30000	408	123408	0.55	0.5564	0.8716
20000	392	82381	0.65	0.3652	0.8791
10000	365	41081	0.65	0.2001	0.8425
5000	326	20481	0.70	0.1161	0.8354
2500	284	10330	0.60	0.0670	0.8372
1000	211	4097	0.35	0.0280	0.7632

6   Conclusions

In this paper, we described the problem of inducing class hierarchies from knowledge graphs and its significance to the Semantic Web community. In our contribution to this research area, we proposed an approach to the problem by marrying the fields of class taxonomy induction from knowledge graphs with tag hierarchy induction from documents and tags. To this end, we reshaped the knowledge graph to a tuple structure and applied two existing tag hierarchy induction methods to show the viability of such an approach. Furthermore, we proposed a novel method for inducing class taxonomies that relies solely on class frequencies and co-occurrences and can thus be applied on knowledge graphs irrespective of their content. We showed our method's ability to induce class hierarchies by applying it on three real-world datasets and evaluating it against their respective gold standard taxonomies. Results demonstrate that our method induces better taxonomies than other tag hierarchy induction methods and can be reliably applied to large-scale knowledge graphs.

References

1. Agrawal, R., Srikant, R.: Fast algorithms for mining association rules. In: Proceedings 20th International Conference Very Large Data Bases, VLDB. vol. 1215, pp. 487–499 (1994)
2. Almoqhim, F., Millard, D.E., Shadbolt, N.: Improving on popularity as a proxy for generality when building tag hierarchies from folksonomies. In: Aiello, L.M., McFarland, D. (eds.) SocInfo 2014. LNCS, vol. 8851, pp. 95–111. Springer, Cham (2014). https://doi.org/10.1007/978-3-319-13734-6_7
3. Ankerst, M., Breunig, M.M., Kriegel, H.P., Sander, J.: Optics: ordering points to identify the clustering structure. ACM Sigmod record **28**, 49–60 (1999)
4. Benz, D., Hotho, A., Stützer, S., Stumme, G.: Semantics made by you and me: Self-emerging ontologies can capture the diversity of shared knowledge (2010)
5. Blei, D.M., Ng, A.Y., Jordan, M.I.: Latent dirichlet allocation. J. Mach. Learn. Res. **3**(Jan), 993–1022 (2003)
6. Bollacker, K., Evans, C., Paritosh, P., Sturge, T., Taylor, J.: Freebase: a collaboratively created graph database for structuring human knowledge. In: Proceedings of the 2008 ACM SIGMOD International Conference on Management of data, pp. 1247–1250. ACM (2008)
7. Chinchor, N.: Muc-4 evaluation metrics. In: Proceedings of the 4th Conference on Message Understanding, pp. 22–29. Association for Computational Linguistics (1992)
8. Dong, H., Wang, W., Coenen, F.: Rules for inducing hierarchies from social tagging data. In: Chowdhury, G., McLeod, J., Gillet, V., Willett, P. (eds.) iConference 2018. LNCS, vol. 10766, pp. 345–355. Springer, Cham (2018). https://doi.org/10.1007/978-3-319-78105-1_38
9. Döring, M.: Gbif type specimen names (2017). https://doi.org/10.15468/sl9pyf
10. Gu, C., Yin, G., Wang, T., Yang, C., Wang, H.: A supervised approach for tag hierarchy construction in open source communities. In: Proceedings of the 7th Asia-Pacific Symposium on Internetware, pp. 148–152. ACM (2015)
11. Heymann, P., Garcia-Molina, H.: Collaborative creation of communal hierarchical taxonomies in social tagging systems. Technical report (2006)
12. Hoffart, J., Suchanek, F.M., Berberich, K., Weikum, G.: Yago2: a spatially and temporally enhanced knowledge base from wikipedia. Artif. Intell. **194**, 28–61 (2013)
13. Lehmann, J., et al.: Dbpedia-a large-scale, multilingual knowledge base extracted from wikipedia. Semant. Web **6**(2), 167–195 (2015)

14. Li, X., et al.: Inducing taxonomy from tags: an agglomerative hierarchical clustering framework. In: Zhou, S., Zhang, S., Karypis, G. (eds.) ADMA 2012. LNCS (LNAI), vol. 7713, pp. 64–77. Springer, Heidelberg (2012). https://doi.org/10.1007/978-3-642-35527-1_6

15. Liu, K., Fang, B., Zhang, W.: Ontology emergence from folksonomies. In: Proceedings of the 19th ACM International Conference on Information and Knowledge Management, pp. 1109–1118. ACM (2010)

16. Miller, G.A.: Wordnet: a lexical database for english. Commun. ACM **38**(11), 39–41 (1995)

17. Nickel, M., Tresp, V., Kriegel, H.P.: A three-way model for collective learning on multi-relational data (2011)

18. Nickel, M., Tresp, V., Kriegel, H.P.: Factorizing yago: scalable machine learning for linked data. In: Proceedings of the 21st international conference on World Wide Web. pp. 271–280. ACM (2012)

19. Paulheim, H., Fümkranz, J.: Unsupervised generation of data mining features from linked open data. In: Proceedings of the 2nd International Conference on Web Intelligence, Mining and Semantics, p. 31. ACM (2012)

20. Ristoski, P., Faralli, S., Ponzetto, S.P., Paulheim, H.: Large-scale taxonomy induction using entity and word embeddings. In: Proceedings of the International Conference on Web Intelligence, pp. 81–87. ACM (2017)

21. Roskov Y., et al.: Species 2000 & itis catalogue of life, 2019 annual checklist (2019)

22. Sanderson, M., Croft, B.: Deriving concept hierarchies from text. In: Proceedings of the 22nd Annual International ACM SIGIR Conference on Research and Development in Information Retrieval, pp. 206–213. ACM (1999)

23. Schmitz, P.: Inducing ontology from flickr tags. In: Collaborative Web Tagging Workshop at WWW2006, Edinburgh, Scotland, vol. 50, p. 39 (2006)

24. Singhal, A.: Introducing the knowledge graph: things, not strings (2012). https://www.blog.google/products/search/introducing-knowledge-graph-things-not/

25. Solskinnsbakk, G., Gulla, J.A.: A hybrid approach to constructing tag hierarchies. In: Meersman, R., Dillon, T., Herrero, P. (eds.) OTM 2010. LNCS, vol. 6427, pp. 975–982. Springer, Heidelberg (2010). https://doi.org/10.1007/978-3-642-16949-6_22

26. Tang, J., Leung, H.f., Luo, Q., Chen, D., Gong, J.: Towards ontology learning from folksonomies. In: Twenty-First International Joint Conference on Artificial Intelligence (2009)

27. Völker, J., Niepert, M.: Statistical schema induction. In: Antoniou, G., et al. (eds.) ESWC 2011. LNCS, vol. 6643, pp. 124–138. Springer, Heidelberg (2011). https://doi.org/10.1007/978-3-642-21034-1_9

28. Vrandečić, D., Krötzsch, M.: Wikidata: a free collaborative knowledge base (2014)

29. Wang, S., Lo, D., Jiang, L.: Inferring semantically related software terms and their taxonomy by leveraging collaborative tagging. In: 2012 28th IEEE International Conference on Software Maintenance (ICSM), pp. 604–607. IEEE (2012)

30. Wang, W., Barnaghi, P.M., Bargiela, A.: Probabilistic topic models for learning terminological ontologies. IEEE Trans. Knowl. Data Eng. **22**(7), 1028–1040 (2009)

Hybrid Reasoning Over Large Knowledge Bases Using On-The-Fly Knowledge Extraction

Giorgos Stoilos⓪, Damir Juric, Szymon Wartak, Claudia Schulz⁽⊠⁾⓪,
and Mohammad Khodadadi

Babylon Health, London, SW3 3DD, UK
{giorgos.stoilos,damir.juric,szymon.wartak,claudia.schulz,
mohammad.khodadadi}@babylonhealth.com

Abstract. The success of logic-based methods for comparing entities heavily depends on the axioms that have been described for them in the Knowledge Base (KB). Due to the incompleteness of even large and well engineered KBs, such methods suffer from low recall when applied in real-world use cases. To address this, we designed a reasoning framework that combines logic-based subsumption with statistical methods for on-the-fly knowledge extraction. Statistical methods extract additional (missing) axioms for the compared entities with the goal of tackling the incompleteness of KBs and thus improving recall. Although this can be beneficial, it can also introduce noise (false positives or false negatives). Hence, our framework uses heuristics to assess whether knowledge extraction is likely to be advantageous and only activates the statistical components if this is the case. We instantiate our framework by combining lightweight logic-based reasoning implemented on top of existing triple-stores with an axiom extraction method that is based on the labels of concepts. Our work was motivated by industrial use cases over which we evaluate our instantiated framework, showing that it outperforms approaches that are only based on textual information. Besides the best combination of precision and recall, our implementation is also scalable and is currently used in an industrial production environment.

Keywords: Large medical ontologies · Axiom extraction from text · Hybrid reasoning

1 Introduction

Large Knowledge Bases (KBs) have started to play a key role in applications like dialogue systems [29], healthcare [4], and recommendation systems [20]. KBs describe the entities of the domain at hand and their relationships. This enables semantic interpretation of information expressed in terms of knowledge from a

---

G. Stoilos—Since submission Giorgos Stoilos is a member of Huawei Technologies, R&D, UK.

ⓒ Springer Nature Switzerland AG 2020
A. Harth et al. (Eds.): ESWC 2020, LNCS 12123, pp. 69–85, 2020.
https://doi.org/10.1007/978-3-030-49461-2_5

KB, and thus allows the exchange of information between different systems or components expressing information using a shared KB.

To capture real-world meaning, systems may not only use atomic concepts from the KB but also combine concepts to express more complex entities of the domain. For example, in a biomedical application using SNOMED CT to represent medical data, a user profile may contain the concept $C_1 :=$ RecentInjury $\sqcap$ $\exists$findingSite.Head, capturing the condition "recent injury in the head" associated with the patient. Yet, in a symptom-checking service the same condition may be represented as $C_2 :=$ HeadInjury $\sqcap$ $\exists$occurred.Recent. To enable proper information exchange between these services, *subsumption reasoning* over the stored knowledge is crucial to correctly match equivalent information expressed in different ways, i.e. to prove that $\mathcal{K} \models C_1 \sqsubseteq C_2$ and $\mathcal{K} \models C_2 \sqsubseteq C_1$ for a KB $\mathcal{K}$.

In theory, ontology reasoners like ELK [15] can be used for this kind of subsumption checking, however, in practice this is problematic for at least two reasons. First, even large and well-engineered KBs suffer from *incompleteness* [10,21], leading to very low recall of equivalent and subsumed concepts. Indeed, for the above example and for $\mathcal{K}$ the SNOMED CT, we have $\mathcal{K} \not\models C_1 \sqsubseteq C_2$ and $\mathcal{K} \not\models C_2 \sqsubseteq C_1$ since $\mathcal{K}$ is missing an axiom of the form $ax :=$ RecentInjury $\equiv$ Injury $\sqcap$ $\exists$occurred.Recent. SNOMED CT contains many such ill-defined concepts [21] like SevereDepression, which is not defined in terms of concepts Severe and Depression, or CardiacMuscleThickness, not defined in terms of CardiacMuscle and Thick. The same can be observed for other KBs like DBpedia [1], where the category ItalianRenaissancePainters is not connected to concepts Painter or ItalianRenaissance. Second, such reasoners are not designed for reasoning over very large industrial KBs, like DBpedia and Freebase, which are usually stored in triple-stores or graph databases.

To address the above issues, we designed a *hybrid reasoning framework* for subsumption checking that couples logic-based reasoning with on-the-fly knowledge extraction. Knowledge extraction is used to enrich the concepts being compared with intended but missing axioms and hence increase recall of subsumption checking. Since knowledge extraction can produce false positives, i.e. lead to subsumptions that are not intended, the framework incorporates heuristics to decide when to apply knowledge extraction.

We give a concrete instantiation of our framework, where the knowledge extraction component is realised using Natural Language Processing techniques that construct (complex) concepts from the *labels* of the compared concepts. For instance, in our running example, the label of concept RecentInjury in SNOMED CT is "Recent Injury". From that, our knowledge extraction component constructs the more detailed concept Injury $\sqcap$ $\exists$occurred.Recent, thus recovering the missing axiom ax and eventually enabling to prove the subsumption since $\mathcal{K} \cup \{ax\} \models C_1 \sqsubseteq C_2$. Furthermore, to allow reasoning over large industrial KBs we realise logic-based reasoning via a lightweight approximate reasoner implemented on top of existing triple-stores. Finally, we present concrete instantiations of the heuristics controlling the knowledge extraction component.

Importantly, our knowledge extraction method not only forms a crucial part of the hybrid reasoning framework, but it can also be applied as a stand-alone method for constructing complex concepts from short phrases and can thus be useful, e.g., for keyword-based and entity-centric query answering on top of KBs [13,14,23]. This furthermore enables us to apply our hybrid reasoner to textual inputs (short phrases), which can be transformed into concepts using the stand-alone knowledge extraction component, followed by the normal application of our hybrid reasoner.

Our work was motivated by several industrial use cases in Babylon Health[1], a digital health care provider offering services such as AI-based symptom-checking and triaging. Data in all services are encoded using (complex) concepts built from a large medical KB that is stored in a triple-store. It is desirable that different services exchange and compare concepts for the purposes of interoperability, ensuring the delivery of intelligent services to end-users. For example, if new evidence for a "head injury" is encoded in the user profile in the form of concept C_1, other services like triaging or symptom-checking need to be able to interpret C_1 and compare it to concepts used by these services, e.g. C_2, to provide advice to the patient on how to proceed. We tested our implementation in two use cases within this industrial healthcare setting. Our results show the advantage of our knowledge extraction method used internally in our hybrid subsumption checking reasoner compared to pure logic-based reasoning, as well as the high quality of concepts constructed by the extraction method. Furthermore, results reveal that our hybrid reasoner provides the best combination of precision and recall compared to approaches that are purely statistical or purely rule-based.

2   Preliminaries

The concept extraction method we design will construct concepts expressed in the Description Logic (DL) $\mathcal{EL}$ [2], that is, concepts that are defined by the grammar $C := \top \mid A \mid C_1 \sqcap C_2 \mid \exists R.C$ where A is an *atomic concept* and R is an *atomic property*. In addition to the standard DL notation, we assume that every atomic concept A (resp. property R) has an associated label denoted by $\mathscr{L}(A)$ (resp. $\mathscr{L}(R)$). $\mathcal{EL}$-concepts can also be written as $\sqcap_i A_i \sqcap \sqcap_j \exists R_j.C_j$ where each A_i is an atomic concept or $\top$ and each C_j is again an $\mathcal{EL}$-concept. We also consider concepts like $\exists R.B$ to be of the form $\top \sqcap \exists R.B$.

$\mathcal{EL}$ is expressive enough to capture many medical KBs like SNOMED CT. In fact, as noted in [8], the SNOMED CT KB is *primitive*, that is, it can be rewritten as a set of subsumption axioms of the form $A \sqsubseteq D$ where A is atomic. This is because full definitions of the form $A \equiv D$ are acyclic and therefore can be recursively unfolded into axioms of the form $B \sqsubseteq \exists R.A$ to obtain $B \sqsubseteq \exists R.D$ and then discard $A \equiv D$.

The reasoning problem investigated in our work is *subsumption checking* between two concepts C and D of the above form with respect to a KB $\mathcal{K}$—that

---

[1] https://www.babylonhealth.com/.

is, whether $\mathcal{K} \models C \sqsubseteq D$. However, acknowledging the fact that KBs are incomplete [10,21] the problem we study is whether a set of "missing" axioms $\mathcal{K}'$ can be extracted such that $\mathcal{K} \cup \mathcal{K}' \models C \sqsubseteq D$. In order not to modify the KB during subsumption checking, the axioms in $\mathcal{K}'$ can be immediately unfolded into C and D, obtaining new concepts C' and D'. We thus reformulate the original axiom addition problem as a concept rewriting problem and check if $\mathcal{K} \models C' \sqsubseteq D'$.

3   A Framework for Hybrid Reasoning

In theory, given two concepts standard reasoning techniques can be used to compare them w.r.t. subsumption. However, the success of this task heavily depends on the knowledge described in the KB for every concept and, as already pointed out in the literature [21], a lot of relevant knowledge is usually missing.

Example 1. Consider the SNOMED CT KB $\mathcal{K}$ and the phrase "recent head injury", which different services may represent in the following different ways:
$C_1 :=$ RecentInjury $\sqcap$ $\exists$findingSite.Head
$C_2 :=$ Injury $\sqcap$ $\exists$findingSite.Head $\sqcap$ $\exists$occurred.Recently
It can be verified using any DL reasoner that $\mathcal{K} \not\models C_1 \sqsubseteq C_2$ and $\mathcal{K} \not\models C_2 \sqsubseteq C_1$ since $\mathcal{K}$ is missing an axiom of the form RecentInjury $\equiv$ Injury $\sqcap$ $\exists$occurred.Recently.

The above example highlights the need for a method that tries to construct such missing but intended axioms for any two concepts to enable higher recall of traditional subsumption checking algorithms. Looking again at the example, we note that the missing knowledge is in fact encoded in the *label* of the concept RecentInjury, which is "recent injury". More precisely, using this label, our goal is to construct an axiom $ax :=$ RecentInjury $\equiv$ Injury $\sqcap$ $\exists$occurred.Recently and then directly unfold it into C_1 for subsumption checking, yielding $C_1' :=$ Injury $\sqcap$ $\exists$occurred.Recently $\sqcap$ $\exists$findingSite.Head. We would then have $\mathcal{K} \models C_1' \sqsubseteq C_2$ and $\mathcal{K} \models C_2 \sqsubseteq C_1'$, implying the equivalence of C_1 and C_2 (given the missing axiom).
    Although axiom extraction and concept unfolding can improve recall of subsumption checking, they may also introduce false positives (i.e. subsumption of concepts that should be unrelated) or even false negatives (i.e. failure of proving subsumption for concepts that are subsumed without unfolding).

Example 2. Assume that for the concepts in Example 1, we also use the label of concept Injury to unfold C_2, which is "Traumatic AND/OR non-traumatic injury". A concept extraction method is likely to construct an axiom $ax' :=$ Injury $\equiv$ Injury $\sqcap$ $\exists$assocWith. Traumatic $\sqcap$ $\exists$assocWith.NonTraumatic from this. Then, for C_2' the unfolding of ax' in C_2, we will have $\mathcal{K} \not\models C_1' \sqsubseteq C_2'$.

Based on the above, we designed a *hybrid reasoning framework*, given in Algorithm 1, which combines logic-based subsumption checking with on-the-fly statistical knowledge extraction. Given a candidate subsumption $C \sqsubseteq D$, the algorithm first attempts to use standard logic-based reasoning (line 1) to prove

---

Algorithm 1. isSubsumed$_{\mathcal{K}}(C, D)$

Input: Concepts of the form $C := \bigsqcap_i A_i \sqcap \bigsqcap_j \exists R_j.E_j$ and $D := \bigsqcap_k B_k \sqcap \bigsqcap_l \exists S_l.F_l$

1: **if** $\mathcal{K} \models C \sqsubseteq D$ **then return true**
2: **if** $\mathrm{sim}(C, D) < \sigma_1$ **then return false**
3: $C_{ext} := C$
4: **if** $|\mathrm{diff}(C, D)| > \sigma_2$ **then**
5:     $C_{ext} := \bigsqcap_i \mathrm{constructConcepts}(A_i, \mathcal{K}) \sqcap \bigsqcap_j \exists R_j.E_j$
6:     **if** $\mathcal{K} \models C_{ext} \sqsubseteq D$ **then return true**
7: **end if**
8: $D_{ext} := \bigsqcap_k \mathrm{constructConcepts}(B_k, \mathcal{K}) \sqcap \bigsqcap_l \exists S_l.F_l$
9: **if** $\mathcal{K} \models C_{ext} \sqsubseteq D_{ext}$ **then return true**
10: **return false**

---

subsumption over a KB $\mathcal{K}$. If subsumption cannot be proven, the knowledge extraction method may be activated, subject to some applicability conditions. The *first condition* (sim) assesses if the similarity of the compared concepts C and D is sufficiently high (line 2). Intuitively, the higher the similarity, the more likely it is for the axiom extraction step to lead to true positive results.

If the first condition is satisfied, the question is which of the two concepts should be extended with additional knowledge. Due to the monotonicity of the OWL semantics, adding axioms for C would be valuable since failure to prove subsumption implies that D likely has "more constraints" (conjuncts) than C. These additional axioms could then make up for the missing constraints. The *second applicability condition* (diff) thus checks whether D has more constraints than C. If so, the knowledge extraction component is activated to unfold C with an axiom obtained by processing its main atomic concepts (line 5). If the unfolded C is still not subsumed by D, D is also unfolded (line 8).

There are various things to note about our hybrid reasoning framework. First, extraction is only applied on the main atomic concepts (i.e. the A_i and B_k) as these represent the gist of a complex concept. Applying knowledge extraction on more parts of a complex concept would induce further fuzziness, thus increasing the probability for false positives and false negatives. For the same reason, our hybrid reasoner applies knowledge extraction *on-the-fly* instead of extracting all possible axioms from concept labels before reasoning, which would lead to the unrestricted usage of extracted axioms. For small KBs, extracting axioms upfront could allow manual validation, thus providing an advantage over on-the-fly extraction. However for large-scale industrial KBs as investigated here, this is infeasible since there is no way to reliably validate thousands of axioms. Thus, on-the-fly extraction is more beneficial for such KBs.

The exact implementation used for logic-based subsumption checking and knowledge extraction is up to the user and depends on the application at hand. In the following sections, we present concrete instantiations of all parts, targeted at knowledge extraction from *concept labels* and reasoning over *triple-stores*.

4   Extracting Concepts from Text

Our concept extraction method (i.e., the implementation of constructConcepts in Algorithm 1) will be based on the *labels* of concepts. Labels have been used in the past for tasks like ontology enrichment [9,21] as they constitute a good source of additional knowledge that is usually in abundance in ontologies.

The problem of constructing concepts from their labels can be broken down into two parts, as further detailed in the following sections: 1) parsing the label to correctly identify its parts, and 2) linking each part to atomic concepts in the KB and selecting appropriate KB properties to piece them together.

4.1   Parsing the Phrase Structure

Concept labels usually follow a specific pattern, that is, they contain a *central entity*, frequently narrowed down by *modifiers*. For example, in the SNOMED CT concept label "pain in left leg" the central entity is "pain", which is further detailed by "leg", which in turn is narrowed down via modifier "left". Examples of concept labels in other KBs are "Italian Renaissance painters" or "Thriller Movie". Such phrases may include linguistic constructs like prepositions, e.g., "Pain **in** Leg" versus "Leg Pain", and can in some rare cases contain verbs, e.g., "central sleep apnea **caused by** high altitude". Finally, KBs seldom contain concepts representing conjunctions or disjunctions of atomic entities, hence their labels rarely include coordinating conjunctions like "pain in arm **and** chest" and never contain non-$\mathcal{EL}$ constructors like "at least" and "for all".

The above observations motivate the use of dependency parsing [16], which precisely attempts to capture the main word in a phrase (called *root*) and then recursively append the rest of the modifiers to it. At an abstract level, the *dependency tree* of a phrase txt can be characterised as a tree where each node nd is labelled with a corresponding word from txt, denoted $nd.\ell$, and each edge $\langle nd_1, nd_2 \rangle$ is labelled with a *dependency relation* $\langle nd_1, nd_2 \rangle.\ell$ that denotes the linguistic relation between the nodes $nd_1.\ell$ and $nd_2.\ell$.

Figure 1a depicts the dependency tree of the phrase "recent pain caused by injury" obtained using ClearNLP [6]. Since a dependency parser constructs a

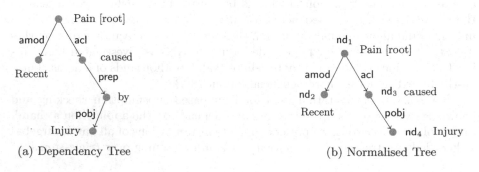

(a) Dependency Tree   (b) Normalised Tree

Fig. 1. Dependency and normalised trees of "recent pain caused by injury".

node for every word in the phrase, compound concepts like "heart attack" are split into separate nodes. However, grouping them is beneficial for better interpreting meaning [27]. Moreover, since prepositions do not carry concept meaning, we prune prepositions and other functional words. In summary, the dependency tree is post-processed as follows:

($\Diamond$) All paths $\langle nd_1, nd_2 \rangle, ..., \langle nd_{n-1}, nd_n \rangle$ with $n \geq 2$ such that each edge is labelled with dependency relation compound are collapsed to one node nd_1 with new label $nd_1.\ell \oplus$ "" $\oplus ... \oplus$ "" $\oplus nd_n.\ell$ where $\oplus$ denotes string concatenation.
($\sharp$) All paths $\langle nd_1, nd_2 \rangle, ..., \langle nd_{n-1}, nd_n \rangle$ with $n \geq 2$ such that each edge is labelled with either prep or case are collapsed to one node nd_1.

Due to ($\sharp$) the dependency tree in Fig. 1a is reduced to the tree in Fig. 1b. This post-processing can be easily realised using a tree traversal algorithm.

4.2 Building Concepts

After parsing the phrase to identify the important parts, atomic concepts from the KB need to be linked to the tree nodes, a problem referred to as entity linking [12]. Furthermore, a KB property between them needs to be established in order to construct a (complex) concept.

Many approaches have been proposed for entity linking, most of them involving supervised machine learning methods [24]. We use a simple, yet effective and scalable, information retrieval approach, which does not require a large training dataset. More precisely, given the label $nd.\ell$ of a node in the tree, *ElasticSearch* is used to search the KB for the concept or property with the most similar label, denoted by $linkC(\ell)$ and $linkR(\ell)$, respectively. If no matching concept can be found, $linkC(\ell) = \bot$, and if no matching property can be found, $linkR(\ell) = assocWith$, using the most common and versatile property.

A concept corresponding to a normalised dependency tree is defined recursively as given in Definition 1. We distinguish two strategies for obtaining a property between two concepts. If the tree contains three adjacent nodes nd_i, nd_j, and nd_k such that nd_j is a verb, $linkR$ links the verb to a property in the KB to connect the concepts represented by nodes nd_i and nd_k; otherwise, a property is "mined" using two adjacent nodes representing concepts.

Definition 1. *For a node nd_i in some dependency tree, the concept corresponding to nd_i is $\bot$ if $linkC(nd_i.\ell) = \bot$, otherwise it is recursively defined as follows:*

$$linkC(nd_i.\ell) = \bigsqcap_{\langle nd_i, nd_j \rangle.\ell=acl, \langle nd_j, nd_k \rangle} \exists linkR(nd_j.\ell).C_k \sqcap \qquad (1)$$
$$\bigsqcap_{\langle nd_i, nd_j \rangle.\ell \neq acl} \exists mine(nd_i.\ell, nd_j.\ell).C_j$$

where C_k and C_j are the concepts corresponding to the sub-trees rooted at nodes nd_k and nd_j, respectively.

Function mine is based on domain and range restrictions of properties. Consider for example nodes nd_1 and nd_2 in Fig. 1b and assume that they have been linked to concepts Pain and Recent from SNOMED CT, respectively. Pain is a sub-concept of ClinicalFinding and Recent is a sub-concept of TemporalConcept. According to the SNOMED CT documentation, property temporalContext has these two concepts as a domain and range, respectively, so we can create concept Pain ⊓ ∃temporalContext.Recent. If no property can be mined this way, mine returns assocWith. Modern KBs often come with such domain and range restrictions (e.g., DBpedia contains almost 2,000). If no such axioms exist then properties between concepts can be mined using, e.g., statistical approaches [19].

Our implementation of constructConcepts returns the concept corresponding to the root of the dependency tree and traverses it using a depth-first algorithm. Applied on the dependency tree of Fig. 1b, exploiting the domain and range restrictions in SNOMED CT and the existence of the verb in the tree, our method constructs concept Pain ⊓ ∃temporalContext.Recent ⊓ ∃causedBy.Injury.

If a dependency tree contains coordinating conjunctions, we split the dependency tree into multiple trees [31], construct a concept for each according to Definition 1 and connect them with conjunction to form an overall concept.

Even though the above method was initially developed as part of our hybrid reasoning framework (i.e. method constructConcepts in Algorithm 1), it can be used as a stand-alone approach for concept extraction from any phrase that follows a structure similar to concept labels. It can thus enable the usage of our hybrid reasoner with *textual input queries* to verify if these queries express the same information: first concepts are constructed from the queries using the stand-alone knowledge extraction component and subsequently the hybrid reasoner is applied as usual. This pipeline approach is further discussed in Sect. 6. In the rest of this paper, we refer to our concept extraction method as *concept builder*.

5 Practical Hybrid Reasoning over Large KBs

Our hybrid reasoning approach presented in Sect. 3 uses logic-based reasoning to check subsumption between two given concepts (lines 1, 6, and 9 in Algorithm 1), which is implemented in SPARQL.

Unfortunately, the concepts we are dealing with may involve a number of conjuncts, existential quantifiers, or even be nested, while SPARQL cannot check subsumption recursively. To address these issues, we use a form of structural subsumption [3], which reduces subsumption checking to subsumption between the atomic elements of a (potentially complex) concept.

Definition 2. *Let* $C := \bigsqcap_i A_i \sqcap \bigsqcap_{j=1}^m \exists R_j.E_j$ *and* $D := \bigsqcap_k B_k \sqcap \bigsqcap_{l=1}^n \exists S_l.F_l$ *be two concepts and let* $\mathcal{K}$ *be a KB. We say that* C *is* structurally subsumed *by* D, *denoted by* $C \sqsubseteq_s D$, *if and only if the following hold:*

1. *For every* B_k *some* A_i *exists such that* $\mathcal{K} \models A_i \sqsubseteq B_k$.
2. *for every* $l \in [1, n]$ *either of the following holds:*
   (a) *there exists* $j \in [1, m]$ *s.t.* $\mathcal{K} \models R_j \sqsubseteq S_l$ *and* $\mathcal{K} \models E_j \sqsubseteq_s F_l$
   (b) *some* $A_i \sqsubseteq \exists T.G \in \mathcal{K}$ *exists s.t.* $\mathcal{K} \models T \sqsubseteq S_l$ *and* $\mathcal{K} \models G \sqsubseteq_s F_l$.

If some conjunct $\exists S_l.F_l$ of D does not subsume any conjunct in C, condition 2b performs an *expansion* on one of the main concepts A_i of C, using the KB to check if A_i is subsumed by some other concept that is subsumed by $\exists S_l.F_l$. Definition 2 can be easily implemented as SPARQL queries over triple-stores.

Example 3. Consider a KB $\mathcal{K}$ containing the following axioms:
FootPain $\sqsubseteq$ $\exists$findingSite.Foot,   FootPain $\sqsubseteq$ Pain, Foot $\sqsubseteq$ Limb
Let C_1 = FootPain and C_2 = Pain $\sqcap$ $\exists$findingSite.Limb and assume we want to check whether $\mathcal{K} \models C_1 \sqsubseteq C_2$, which is indeed the case. According to Definition 2, C_1 is structurally subsumed by C_2 since $\mathcal{K} \models$ FootPain $\sqsubseteq$ Pain and FootPain $\sqsubseteq$ $\exists$findingSite.Foot $\in \mathcal{K}$ such that $\mathcal{K} \models$ Foot $\sqsubseteq_s$ Limb (condition 2b of Definition 2).

As discussed in Sect. 3, concept extraction and unfolding should only be applied in our hybrid reasoning framework if we have reason to believe that it will be helpful for proving a correct subsumption. Since our concept extraction method uses labels of concepts, we also base the instantiation of the applicability condition sim on the *label* similarity of the compared concepts C and D.

Definition 3. *Let concepts C and D of the same form as in Definition 2 be the input of Algorithm 1. Let* str-sim *be some string similarity algorithm and let $\oplus$ denote string concatenation. We instantiate* $\text{sim}(C, D)$ *in line 2 of Algorithm 1 as* str-sim$(\oplus_i \mathscr{L}(A_i) \oplus \oplus_{j=1}^{m} \mathscr{L}(E_j), \oplus_k \mathscr{L}(B_k) \oplus \oplus_{l=1}^{n} \mathscr{L}(F_l))$.

For example, for concepts C = FootPain and D_1 = Pain $\sqcap$ $\exists$findingSite.Head, the similarity score is expected to be lower compared to the one for C and D_2 = Pain $\sqcap$ findingSite.Foot. Using an appropriate threshold σ_1, we can avoid applying concept builder on C when we compare it to D_1 but do apply it when we compare it to D_2, so as to extract conjunct $\exists$findingSite.Foot from label "Foot Pain" of C, which appears in D_2 and thus lets us prove subsumption. We apply Levenshtein distance for str-sim and find that setting σ_2 to half of the shorter string's length works well.

For the instantiation of the second applicability condition diff, we check whether the reason that subsumption failed was that some conjuncts in D do not subsume any conjuncts in C.

Definition 4. *Let C, D be concepts of the same form as in Definition 2 and let $\mathcal{K}$ be a KB. Function* diff(C, D) *returns all $\exists S_l.F_l$ in D such that both of the following hold:*

1. $\forall j \in [1, m]$ either $\mathcal{K} \not\models R_j \sqsubseteq S_l$ or $\mathcal{K} \not\models E_j \sqsubseteq_s F_l$, and
2. no $A_i \sqsubseteq \exists T.G \in \mathcal{K}$ exists such that $\mathcal{K} \models T \sqsubseteq S_l$ and $\mathcal{K} \models G \sqsubseteq_s F_l$

If the set returned has more than σ_2 elements (for our purpose $\sigma_2 = 0$ works well), then Algorithm 1 will try to extract conjuncts from C that are subsumed by those in D using concept builder in line 5. An empty set expresses that the reason for non-subsumption of C and D is that A is not subsumed by B, in which case B rather than A should be unfolded to be able to prove that A is a more specific concept than B.

Table 1. Examples of concepts constructed by concept builder for SNOMED labels

Partially correct concept	
Blood in Urine	Blood ⊓ ∃assocWith.Urine
	Blood ⊓ ∃findingSite.Urine (doctor concept)
Wrong concept	
Prune belly syndrome	Prune ⊓ ∃assocWith.Syndrome ⊓ ∃findingSite.Belly
	PruneBellySyndrome (doctor concept)

Example 4. Consider Example 1, where
$C_1 :=$ RecentInjury ⊓ ∃findingSite.Head
$C_2 :=$ Injury ⊓ ∃findingSite.Head ⊓ ∃occurred.Recently
Then, $\text{diff}_{\mathcal{K}}(C_1, C_2) = \{∃\text{occurred.Recently}\}$, which does not subsume any conjunct of similar form in C_1 and there is no such conjunct in the KB for RecentInjury either. Hence, Algorithm 1 will extract a concept from the label of C_1 as desired (if $\sigma_2 = 0$).

In contrast, $\text{diff}_{\mathcal{K}}(C_2, C_1)$ returns $\emptyset$ since the only conjunct of C_1 also exists in C_2 (∃findingSite.Head). Thus, when calling isSubsumed$_{\mathcal{K}}(C_2, C_1)$ the algorithm will skip the block in lines 4–7 and will only apply concept builder on C_1.

6   Evaluation

Our work was motivated by the need to compare medical knowledge encoded in different services in Babylon Health, such as an AI-based symptom-checking chatbot, triaging, drug prescriptions, and telemedicine. Medical information in all services is encoded using (complex) concepts built from a *large medical KB* [4], curated from sources like SNOMED CT and NCI and stored in GraphDB [26].

Even though the same KB is used, different services (and even humans) may encode the same information in different ways. For example, concepts representing symptoms in the triaging system were manually created by doctors, encoding *"swelling of ear"* as an atomic KB concept SwollenEar. However, during a patient interaction with the chatbot the same phrase may be automatically encoded as Swelling ⊓ ∃findingSite.Ear. To allow interoperability of services, a system able to identify these two concepts as being equivalent needs to be in place. We deploy our hybrid reasoner for this task.

In the following, we evaluate the performance of our hybrid reasoner on two different use cases that require subsumption reasoning. First, however, we evaluate the performance of concept builder in isolation, as it is an integral part of our hybrid reasoner and can be used as a stand-alone concept extraction tool.

6.1   Performance of Concept Builder

We randomly sampled 200 SNOMED CT concept labels containing at least two words and applied concept builder to extract (complex) concepts linked to

Table 2. Number of equivalences and subsumptions proven by hybrid reasoner between complex/atomic doctors' concepts and supposedly equivalent concept builder concepts.

Type of reasoning	Complex					Atomic				
	equiv	subs	none	error	timeout	equiv	subs	none	error	timeout
Logic	0	0	0	0	0	169	8	55	0	0
+ expansion	29	0	0	1	0	68	0	0	0	17
+ builder	36	4	0	0	0	411	68	67	2	2
+ expansion/builder	24	4	100	5	0	83	17	0	0	6
Total	89	8	100	6	0	731	93	122	2	25

the KB. Three doctors then evaluated the quality of concepts constructed by concept builder by classifying each as *correct*, *partially correct*, or *wrong*. Rare disagreements between doctors' judgements were resolved by discussions.

For 19 labels, concept builder failed to extract a concept from the SNOMED label as it was unable to link some of the words in the label to KB concepts. For the remaining 181 SNOMED labels concept builder exhibits good performance, with 60% of extracted concepts evaluated as correct by doctors, 29% as partially correct, and only 11% as wrong. As illustrated in Table 1, the most common reasons for concepts being wrong or only partially correct are an incorrect choice of property (first example in the table) and insufficient tree pruning, resulting in too many atomic concepts in the constructed concept (second example in the table). Overall, we consider the performance of our concept builder sufficiently good to be applied as the knowledge extraction component in our hybrid reasoner and as a stand-alone tool for constructing concepts from short phrases.

6.2 Use Case 1: Constructing the Symptom-Checking Network

The first dataset to evaluate our hybrid reasoner is based on a symptom-checking engine, consisting of a network of 1176 nodes representing symptoms, diseases, and risk factors interconnected with probabilities. A group of doctors created this network manually by associating each medical entity node they wanted the network to contain with an atomic or complex concept based on the KB. For example, the doctors created a node for "Aching Epigastric Pain" and associated it with the concept EpigastricPain ⊓ ∃hasSensation.AchingSensation. Besides the concept, the group of doctors also stored the name of the medical entity they represented.

To test how well our hybrid reasoner can identify equivalent concepts, we apply our concept builder on the name associated with each node to automatically obtain a second concept representation D using the KB. Since D is based on the same entity name as concept C constructed by doctors, C and D should be equivalent. We use the hybrid reasoner to check this, i.e. if $C \sqsubseteq D$ and $D \sqsubseteq C$, giving an insight into how well the hybrid reasoner can identify equivalences.

Table 3. Examples and reasons why our hybrid reasoner could not prove equivalence between two concepts (top concept – concept builder; bottom concept – doctor).

Semantic equivalence	
Poor hygiene	Hygiene ⊓ ∃associatedWith.Poor
	NeglectOfPersonalHygiene
Highly complex concept	
Analgesia overuse	Headache ⊓ ∃hasDef.Analgesia⊓
headache	∃assocWith.RepetitiveStrainInjury
	AnalgesicOveruseHeadache

Our results are summarised in Table 2, distinguishing between atomic and complex concepts created by doctors. The columns "equiv" and "subs" denote cases where both or only one of the above subsumption calls to the reasoner succeeded. Column "none" counts concepts for which our hybrid reasoner could not prove subsumption, "error" denotes cases in which concept builder failed to construct a concept for the given phrase, and "timeout" cases in which the reasoner exceeded the time-out limit of five seconds. Rows distinguish the type of reasoning performed by the reasoner while trying to prove the two subsumption directions, in particular, simple *logic*-based reasoning, i.e. no expansion and no concept extraction (line 1 in Algorithm 1 without using 2b in Definition 2), logic-based reasoning with concept *expansion* (line 1 in Algorithm 1 using 2b in Definition 2), and logic-based reasoning (and concept expansion) with the application of concept *builder* on KB labels (Algorithm 1 past line 1). The last row, *expansion/builder*, denotes cases where one subsumption direction required expansion (without concept builder) and the other direction also required the usage of concept builder.

Table 2 shows that our hybrid reasoner exhibits good performance: in 70% of the cases it can prove the equivalence of concepts and in another 9% it can prove that one is subsumed by the other. Concept expansion has a significant impact in increasing the inference power of determining subsumption. Furthermore, applying concept builder for on-the-fly knowledge extraction from concept labels leads to another huge improvement. Note that for complex concepts, pure logic-based reasoning is unable to prove any equivalences, illustrating the usefulness of our hybrid reasoner.

Further analysis revealed that logic-based reasoning is only able to prove equivalence if the two given concepts C and D are in fact the same atomic concept A, i.e. $C = A$ and $D = A$. In contrast, in all cases in which our hybrid reasoner applied knowledge extraction and expansion to prove equivalence, at least one of the given concepts was a complex concept, making the reasoning much more challenging. Note that for any complex concept by a doctor, concept builder constructed a different complex concept, making subsumption checking extremely difficult. Despite this complexity, our hybrid reasoner is able to prove equivalence in half of these highly challenging cases.

The main reasons why our reasoner failed to prove subsumption between concepts was that the two concepts were semantically equivalent but expressed using completely different concepts and that one concept was way more complex than the other, as illustrated in Table 3. Overall, this use case shows the advantage of our hybrid subsumption reasoning method, which applies knowledge extraction to tackle the inherent incompleteness in KBs, as compared to pure logic-based reasoning.

6.3 Use Case 2: Understanding User Queries for Symptom-Checking

The symptom-checking engine from the first use case is accessed by end-users through a chatbot. Given a user query such as "My stomach hurts", the correct node from the network needs to be activated to initiate symptom-checking.

Before the development of our hybrid reasoner, two different methods were tested to map user queries to nodes in the network. First, the *GATE* text annotation system [7], which applies string matching and hand-crafted rules, was used to identify names of symptom nodes in a query. Second, the Google universal *sentence embedder* [5] (based on Transformer) was used to embed both the user query and all symptom nodes in the network and then the node with the closest vector compared to the query vector (using cosine similarity) was chosen.

Our hybrid reasoner can be used to map queries to nodes as follows: first, concept builder extracts a concept C from user text, then the hybrid reasoner finds a "closest" matching symptom by checking which node in the network is associated with a concept D that subsumes C, i.e. for which D it holds that $C \sqsubseteq D$. We refer to this pipeline as ConBReas(Concept Builder–Reasoner).

To systematically compare the performance of the three methods, doctors created a dataset of 1878 mock user queries[2] and matched each with a node from the network. For example, doctors matched the query "*I can't focus*" to the node associated with concept PoorConcentration. In addition to comparing the performance of GATE and the embedder to ConBReas, we also experiment with using the embedder as a fallback in GATE and ConBReas, that is, if either of these approaches fails to return a node from the network then the embedder is used; we call these settings GATE$_{emb}$ and ConBReas$_{emb}$, respectively.

Table 4. Performance of different methods on our query–symptom dataset.

	GATE	GATE$_{emb}$	emb	ConBReas	ConBReas$_{emb}$
Precision	1.00	0.86	0.72	0.96	0.84
Recall	0.53	0.74	0.72	0.79	0.88

---

[2] For privacy reasons we do not use real user queries.

Table 5. Examples of false positives (FP) and false negatives (FN) of ConBReas.

User query	ConBReas	Correct symptom	Type
I don't sleep well	SleepingWell	RestlessSleep	FP
I'm hungry all the time	Always ⊓ ∃assocWith.Hungry	IncreasedAppetite	FP
I can't speak properly	—	DifficultySpeaking	FN
I'm getting skinnier	—	WeightLoss	FN

Performance results of the different methods are given in Table 4. As expected, GATE offers the lowest recall but highest precision, since it performs an almost exact lexical match between the words in a query and the possible symptom labels. The combination of GATE with an embedder increases its recall, but decreases precision. The embedder provides better recall but the precision is too low for a medical application. ConBReas outperforms the embedder in terms of both precision and recall. Compared to GATE, ConBReas' precision is only slightly lower, while its recall is much higher. ConBReas$_{emb}$ obtains the best trade-off between precision and recall among all methods, and is thus used in production to link user queries to the symptom checking engine.

For future improvement, we performed an error analysis and found that most of ConBReas' mistakes are due to concept construction from the user query, and in particular the entity linking step if sophisticated common-sense reasoning is needed to link the correct concept. Table 5 gives some examples of false positives (wrong concept constructed) and false negatives (no concept constructed).

7   Related Work and Conclusions

To the best of our knowledge, our hybrid reasoning framework is the first approach applying statistical methods as part of logic-based subsumption checking. Conversely, Movshovitz-Attias et al. [18] train a subsumption classifier and include logic-based features using a KB, in particular the overlap of concepts' properties in Biperpedia. Like us they exploit dependency trees, used in terms of a feature expressing whether any paths in the dependency trees of the two concepts match. In contrast to our hybrid reasoner, the results of their classifier are not easily explainable and the classifier needs sufficient training data, whereas our reasoner can be applied without training and can be easily interpreted.

The problem of learning DL axioms from unstructured text has received considerable attention [8,11,22,28]. The structure of text targeted by these works is substantially different to the one usually found in concept labels. These works deal with verb phrases which often have some definitory character, e.g. from text *"Enzymes are proteins that catalyse chemical reactions"* an axiom of the form Enzyme ⊑ Protein ⊓ ∃catalyse.ChemicalReaction can be extracted. In contrast, concept labels – as used by us – are usually short phrases without verbs, so properties between entities need to be inferred as they cannot be extracted from the text. The work by Romacker [25] is close to ours as they also use dependency parsing and then map the dependency tree to DL concepts. However, again full sentences are targeted using a form of reification. For our running example (Fig. 1a) their approach would create Provoking⊓provokingAgent.Injury⊓ ∃provokingPatient.Pain, whereas ours produces simpler and more concise concepts enabling easier subsumption checking.

Concept labels have been previously proven useful for extracting additional information from KBs [9,21]. Fernandez-Breis et al. [9] use manually created patterns to "decompose" concept labels, whereas Pacheco et al. [21] use all sub-words in a concept label and do not consider any dependency relations between them. Our approach is less rigid as it construct concepts dynamically based on the structure of the dependency tree.

The structure of concept labels found in KBs resembles keyword-based and entity-oriented natural language queries [13,17,23]. Compared to Pound et al. [23] we can extract arbitrary (even nested) existentially quantified concepts and do not require training of application-specific template classifiers. Furthermore, we do not require that relations between concepts are expressed by words in the query [13]. Similar to us, Lei et al. [17] derive KB properties to connect concepts from words in the query or, if not present, from the KB structure. However, they construct a tree from the query which needs to be a sub-tree of the KB, whereas our complex concepts are not tied to the KB structure in this way. Xu et al. [30] use dependency trees for relation extraction, however they require task-specific training data, whereas we apply pre-trained dependency parsers.

The comparison with related work highlights the novelty of our hybrid reasoning framework in integrating knowledge extraction from concept labels using NLP methods into logic-based subsumption checking. We have provided an instantiation of our hybrid reasoning framework paying extra care on design choices in order to provide a highly efficient system that can operate in a production environment. Our evaluation on two industrial use cases showed that our approach provides the best combination of precision and recall compared to purely statistical or purely rule-based approaches and our reasoner is thus currently employed in an industrial production environment.

Although our use case and implementation regards the medical domain, all methods are domain independent and can be adapted easily to new domains. For example, concept builder can be used on phrases like "Italian Painters" over DBpedia to construct concept Painter ⊓ ∃birthPlace.Italy or on "Thriller Movies" over the Movie KB[3] to construct concept Movie ⊓ ∃belongsToGenre.Thriller. Future work will target better compounding methods in concept builder to avoid the construction of over-complicated concepts as well as the integration of common-sense reasoning methods to infer equivalence in difficult cases.

---

[3] http://www.movieontology.org/.

References

1. Auer, S., Bizer, C., Kobilarov, G., Lehmann, J., Cyganiak, R., Ives, Z.: DBpedia: a nucleus for a web of open data. In: Aberer, K., et al. (eds.) ASWC/ISWC 2007. LNCS, vol. 4825, pp. 722–735. Springer, Heidelberg (2007). https://doi.org/10.1007/978-3-540-76298-0_52
2. Baader, F., Brandt, S., Lutz, C.: Pushing the EL envelope. In: IJCAI, pp. 364–369 (2005)
3. Baader, F., Calvanese, D., McGuinness, D.L., Nardi, D., Patel-Schneider, P.F. (eds.): The Description Logic Handbook: Theory, Implementation, and Applications. Cambridge University Press, Cambridge (2003)
4. Barisevičius, G., et al.: Supporting digital healthcare services using semantic web technologies. In: Vrandečić, D., et al. (eds.) ISWC 2018. LNCS, vol. 11137, pp. 291–306. Springer, Cham (2018). https://doi.org/10.1007/978-3-030-00668-6_18
5. Cer, D., et al.: Universal sentence encoder. CoRR abs/1803.11175 (2018)
6. Choi, J.D., McCallum, A.: Transition-based dependency parsing with selectional branching. In: ACL, pp. 1052–1062 (2013)
7. Cunningham, H., Tablan, V., Roberts, A., Bontcheva, K.: Getting more out of biomedical documents with gate's full lifecycle open source text analytics. PLoS Comput. Biol. **9**(2), e1002854 (2013)
8. Distel, F., Ma, Y.: A hybrid approach for learning SNOMED CT definitions from text. In: DL, pp. 156–167 (2013)
9. Fernandez-Breis, J.T., Iannone, L., Palmisano, I., Rector, A.L., Stevens, R.: Enriching the gene ontology via the dissection of labels using the ontology pre-processor language. In: Cimiano, P., Pinto, H.S. (eds.) EKAW 2010. LNCS (LNAI), vol. 6317, pp. 59–73. Springer, Heidelberg (2010). https://doi.org/10.1007/978-3-642-16438-5_5
10. Galárraga, L., Razniewski, S., Amarilli, A., Suchanek, F.M.: Predicting completeness in knowledge bases. In: WSDM, pp. 375–383 (2017)
11. Gyawali, B., Shimorina, A., Gardent, C., Cruz-Lara, S., Mahfoudh, M.: Mapping natural language to description logic. In: Blomqvist, E., Maynard, D., Gangemi, A., Hoekstra, R., Hitzler, P., Hartig, O. (eds.) ESWC 2017. LNCS, vol. 10249, pp. 273–288. Springer, Cham (2017). https://doi.org/10.1007/978-3-319-58068-5_17
12. Hachey, B., Radford, W., Nothman, J., Honnibal, M., Curran, J.R.: Evaluating entity linking with wikipedia. Artif. Intell. **194**, 130–150 (2013)
13. Han, S., Zou, L., Yu, J.X., Zhao, D.: Keyword search on RDF graphs - a query graph assembly approach. In: CIKM, pp. 227–236 (2017)
14. Hou, J., Nayak, R.: A concept-based retrieval method for entity-oriented search. In: AusDM, pp. 99–105 (2013)
15. Kazakov, Y., Krötzsch, M., Simancik, F.: The incredible ELK - from polynomial procedures to efficient reasoning with $\mathcal{EL}$ ontologies. J. Autom. Reason. **53**(1), 1–61 (2014)
16. Kübler, S., McDonald, R.T., Nivre, J.: Dependency Parsing. Synthesis Lectures on Human Language Technologies. Morgan & Claypool Publishers, San Francisco (2009)
17. Lei, C., et al.: Ontology-based natural language query interfaces for data exploration. IEEE Data Eng. Bull. **41**(3), 52–63 (2018)
18. Movshovitz-Attias, D., Whang, S.E., Noy, N.F., Halevy, A.Y.: Discovering subsumption relationships for web-based ontologies. In: WebDB, pp. 62–69 (2015)

19. Nickel, M., Murphy, K., Tresp, V., Gabrilovich, E.: A review of relational machine learning for knowledge graphs. Proc. IEEE **104**(1), 11–33 (2016)
20. Oramas, S., Ostuni, V.C., Noia, T.D., Serra, X., Sciascio, E.D.: Sound and music recommendation with knowledge graphs. ACM TIST **8**(2), 21:1–21:21 (2016)
21. Pacheco, E.J., Stenzhorn, H., Nohama, P., Paetzold, J., Schulz, S.: Detecting under specification in SNOMED CT concept definitions through natural language processing. In: AMIA (2009)
22. Petrova, A., et al.: Formalizing biomedical concepts from textual definitions. J. Biomed. Semant. **6**(1), 22 (2015). https://doi.org/10.1186/s13326-015-0015-3
23. Pound, J., Hudek, A.K., Ilyas, I.F., Weddell, G.: Interpreting keyword queries over web knowledge bases. In: CIKM, pp. 305–314 (2012)
24. Raiman, J., Raiman, O.: DeepType: multilingual entity linking by neural type system evolution. In: AAAI, pp. 5406–5413 (2018)
25. Romacker, M., Markert, K., Hahn, U.: Lean semantic interpretation. In: IJCAI, pp. 868–875 (1999)
26. Stoilos, G., Geleta, D., Shamdasani, J., Khodadadi, M.: A novel approach and practical algorithms for ontology integration. In: ISWC (2018)
27. Stuckenschmidt, H., Ponzetto, S.P., Meilicke, C.: Detecting meaningful compounds in complex class labels. In: Blomqvist, E., Ciancarini, P., Poggi, F., Vitali, F. (eds.) EKAW 2016. LNCS (LNAI), vol. 10024, pp. 621–635. Springer, Cham (2016). https://doi.org/10.1007/978-3-319-49004-5_40
28. Völker, J., Hitzler, P., Cimiano, P.: Acquisition of OWL DL axioms from lexical resources. In: Franconi, E., Kifer, M., May, W. (eds.) ESWC 2007. LNCS, vol. 4519, pp. 670–685. Springer, Heidelberg (2007). https://doi.org/10.1007/978-3-540-72667-8_47
29. Wessel, M., Acharya, G., Carpenter, J., Yin, M.: OntoVPA—an ontology-based dialogue management system for virtual personal assistants. In: Eskenazi, M., Devillers, L., Mariani, J. (eds.) Advanced Social Interaction with Agents. LNEE, vol. 510, pp. 219–233. Springer, Cham (2019). https://doi.org/10.1007/978-3-319-92108-2_23
30. Xu, H., Hu, C., Shen, G.: Discovery of dependency tree patterns for relation extraction. In: PACLIC, pp. 851–858 (2009)
31. Zhang, W., Liu, S., Yu, C., Sun, C., Liu, F., Meng, W.: Recognition and classification of noun phrases in queries for effective retrieval. In: CIKM, pp. 711–720 (2007)

Natural Language Processing and Information Retrieval

Partial Domain Adaptation for Relation Extraction Based on Adversarial Learning

Xiaofei Cao(iD), Juan Yang(✉)(iD), and Xiangbin Meng(iD)

Beijing Key Lab of Intelligent Telecommunication Software and Multimedia,
Beijing University of Posts and Telecommunications, Beijing, China
{caoxf,yangjuan,mengxb}@bupt.edu.cn

Abstract. Relation extraction methods based on domain adaptation
have begun to be extensively applied in specific domains to alleviate the
pressure of insufficient annotated corpus, which enables learning by utilizing the training data set of a related domain. However, the negative
transfer may occur during the adaptive process due to differences in data
distribution between domains. Besides, it is difficult to achieve a fine-
grained alignment of relation category without fully mining the multi-
mode data structure. Furthermore, as a common application scenario,
partial domain adaptation (PDA) refers to domain adaptive behavior
when the relation class set of a specific domain is a subset of the related
domain. In this case, some outliers belonging to the related domain will
reduce the performance of the model. To solve these problems, a novel
model based on a multi-adversarial module for partial domain adaptation (MAPDA) is proposed in this study. We design a weight mechanism to mitigate the impact of noise samples and outlier categories, and
embed several adversarial networks to realize various category alignments
between domains. Experimental results demonstrate that our proposed
model significantly improves the state-of-the-art performance of relation
extraction implemented in domain adaptation.

Keywords: Relation extraction · Domain adaptation · Adversarial
learning

1 Introduction

Relation extraction (RE) plays a pivotal role in addressing the issue of information extraction, which aims to detect the semantic relationship between real-
world entities. For instance, the task of RE can be described as discovering the
"cause-effect (e1, e2)" relation between a pair of entities $<microphone, signal>$
in the sentence: the microphone converts sound into an electrical signal. RE
has been widely utilized in various fields of natural language processing (NLP),
such as automatic question and answering system [1] and knowledge graphs
(KG) [2,3]. The semantic web is a general framework proposed to make the data
on the network machine-readable [4], and which utilizes the resource description

© Springer Nature Switzerland AG 2020
A. Harth et al. (Eds.): ESWC 2020, LNCS 12123, pp. 89–104, 2020.
https://doi.org/10.1007/978-3-030-49461-2_6

framework (RDF) to describe network resources. The edge element of RDF represents the relation between entities or the relationship between the entity and its attributes. Therefore, RE indirectly provides data support for the construction of the semantic network.

Extensive research has demonstrated that RE models based on deep learning indicate outstanding performance with a large quantity of corpus. Zeng et al. [5] applied the convolution neural network (CNN) to automatically gain lexical and sentence features. Socher et al. [6] proposed using the recurrent neural network (RNN) to explore the combinatorial vector representation of phrases and sentences of any syntactic type and length. These models based on deep learning can automatically learn the implicit and complex feature expression of text. Therefore, they are considered to be better than those based on traditional machine learning algorithms such as SVM [7] and MaxEnt [8]. However, in some domains, the lack of sufficient annotation data set for model training can lead to poor performance. In order to relieve the pressure of labeled data sparsity, Mintz et al. [9] presented distant supervision (DS). DS takes the triple <e1, r, e2> in the existing knowledge base as the seed. It then matches the text containing e1 and e2 heuristically, and the resulting sentences are used as the annotation data of the r relationship. However, this method will generate much noise. For example, triple <Donald Trump, born in, New York>, may be aligned to "Donald Trump was born in New York", or may be aligned to "Donald Trump worked in New York". The first one is the annotation data that we want to generate, while the second one is the noise data. How to remove the noise data is an important research topic, which to date has had limited exploration. To complicate things further, the precondition of DS is dependent up the existence and quality of the knowledge base.

Pan et al. [10] found that domain adaptation (DA) can assist a target domain training model by using annotation data of the source domain. It has been widely used in computer vision, NLP, and other related fields. For example, predicting the emotion of data generated from the fast-food comment is done by utilizing movie comment data using existing emotional markers [11], or classified picture data on the e-commerce website is used to classify photos taken by mobile phones [12]. By eliminating the limitation that training data and test data must be independent and equally distributed, DA provides an effective way for RE to be applied in a data-sparse domain. Plank et al. [13] combined term generalization approaches and structured kernels to improve the performance of a relation extractor on new domains. Nguyen et al. [14] evaluated embedding words and clustering on adapting feature-based relation extraction systems. All of these research studies were done to find a way to effectively improve the model accuracy on new domains through DA. However, we discover additional problems in DA that required further resolutions.

– **Model collapse.** Model collapse refers to when most DA models focus on reducing the feature-level domain shift, even in the same feature space, category mismatch problem may exist and result in poor migration to the new dataset [15]. For example, some entity pairs are assigned the wrong relation

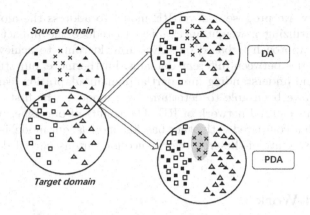

Fig. 1. DA represents the general domain adaptation. PDA is a generalized domain adaptive setting where the classification space of the target domain is a subset of the source domain category space. The red mark x in the figure represents the outlier class. It only appears in the source domain data, which may lead to a negative transfer.

types, which demonstrates that the model lacks robustness. Consequently, a more fine-grained class alignment solution needs to be developed.

- **Outlier classes.** Current DA models are generally based on the assumption that the source domain and target domain share the same category space. However, the PDA usually exists where the class set of target domain is a subset of the source domain. For example, a general domain such as Wikipedia partially adapts to a vertical domain (such as news domain or financial domain) with smaller label space. In this case, outlier classes that only belong to the source domain may lead to the reduction of the classification effect of the source supervised model [16].
- **Negative migration samples.** Because the source and target domain differ at the feature level, there may be some non-migratable samples. If such samples of the source domain are fitted to align with the samples of the target domain, it can negatively affect model performance. It is therefore considered important to determine how to reduce the impact of these samples on the network during migration. This is one of the key issues that need to be resolved to improve the accuracy of the model.

To address the above problems, we work on ways to alleviate negative transfer via the PDA solution with a weight selection mechanism. This approach is expected to reduce negative migration and improve the generalization abilities of the model. As shown in Fig. 1, the ellipse consisting of crosses in the middle of the circle has been separated to limit the migration of the outliers. We subsequently strive to align the labels of source and target domains by embedding multiple adversarial neural networks, aiming to eliminate the hidden dangers of category mismatches.

In summary, we propose a novel RE model to address the aforementioned problems by utilizing a weight mechanism to reduce the impact of negative transfer. This approach is based on adversarial learning to achieve the alignment of categories between different domains. Furthermore, our study provides new insights and understanding into partial domain adaptation learning of RE. As far as we have been able to determine, our model is the first one to apply a multi-layer adversarial network of RE. The results of our experimental study demonstrate that compared with other baseline models, our model is able to consistently achieve state-of-the-art performance for various partial domain adaptation tasks.

2   Related Work

2.1   Relation Extraction

In recent years, the area of DS has received significant research attention. This research was presented to combine the advantages of bootstrapping [17] and supervised learning, to alleviate the pressure of missing training data sets. Subsequent DS research focused on two key aspects. Many classic models have enhanced the robustness of the RE model by reducing the training weight of the noisy sample. In order to solve the problem of error tagging in DS, Zeng et al. [18] proposed a multi-instance learning method to extract a high confidence training corpus for a RE model. Liu et al. [19] introduced a sentence level attention mechanism into multiple-instance learning, which has effectively reduced the weight of noise instances. However, multi-instance learning is based on the assumption that there is at least one correct labeled data in each package. Luo et al. [20] suggested using a noise matrix to fit with the distribution of noise, so as to achieve the purpose of fitting it with the real distribution. Several other models tried to improve the accuracy of the RE model by taking full advantage of the syntactic information. Zhang et al. [21] supported the notion that encoding the main words on the dependency path of sentences by a network block GRU could capture more important information in sentences. Liu et al. [22] applied bidirectional gated recurrent unit to extract sentence feature vectors from each word, and an attention mechanism to give greater weight to keywords.

However, all of these models required sufficient labeling data or prior knowledge to build fake samples, which ignored relevant information in other related domains. Our model focuses on the adaptive learning of RE, which removes restrictions of prior knowledge, to transfer the knowledge acquired by the supervised model of a general domain to a special field.

2.2   Adversarial Domain Adaptation

The research study [25] first proposed the idea of adversarial domain adaptation to embed domain adaption into the process of learning representation, so that the decision making about final classifications thoroughly integrated the characteristics of differences and variances to the domain change. In this way, the

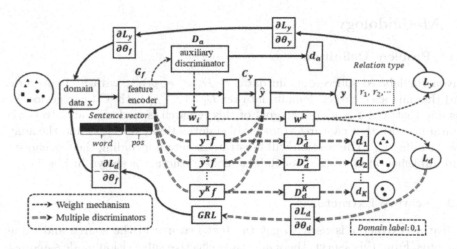

Fig. 2. The architecture of our method. The G_f denotes the feature extractor CNN to capture the text information, and the C_y represents the relation classifier. The auxiliary discriminator D_a is the core structure of the weight mechanism, which is introduced to obtain the sample weight w_i and iteratively updates category weight w^k that is attached to the loss function of the discriminator and the classifier. Besides, K discriminators are applied to capture a multi-mode data structure [23]. For example, the k-th discriminator is denoted as D_d^k. A gradient reversal layer (GRL) [24] is used to illustrate the opposite value of the gradient and achieve the effect of confrontation.

feedforward network could be applied to a new domain without being affected by the displacement influences between the two domains. Subsequently, research studies on adversarial domain adaptation have emerged. Among them, a few papers have drawn attention to the negative effects of transfer [26] and the risk of model collapse [27,28]. One of these papers [23] presented a structure of multiple discriminators to explore the multi-mode structure, while it ignored PDA. Cao et al. [16] weighted the data of the anomaly source class to train the source classifier and to promote positive delivery by matching the feature distribution in the shared label space. Cao et al. [29] found a suitable solution by decreasing the weight of the noise sample or outlier to update network parameters.

However, the research and application direction of DA methods based on adversarial network have mainly focused on the image domain to conduct the image classification [30,31]. There has been a lack of systematic discussion and research work in the field of relation extraction. Plank and Moschitti [13] found that a proper combination of grammar and lexical generalization was useful for DA. Zhang et al. [32] proposed a novel model of relation-gated adversarial learning for relation extraction to extend the adversarial based DA methods. However, this approach may cause problems in that even if the network training converged and the discriminator was completely confused, it would be impossible to tell which domain the sample came from. There was no guarantee that the shared feature distribution of data could be captured.

3 Methodology

3.1 Problem Definition

Given the labeled source domain data set $D_s = (x_i, y_i)_{i=1}^{n_s}$ with $|C_s|$ categories and the unlabeled target domain data set $D_t = (x_i)_{i=1}^{n_t}$ with $|C_t|$ categories. We assume that $|C_s| >> |C_t|$. The goal of this research is to design an adversarial neural network that captures transferable information $f = G_f(x)$ and the adaptive classifier C_y. This section will illustrate in detail, including the mechanisms and implementation of the model. The model structure is shown in Fig. 2.

3.2 Feature Extractor

A feature extractor is used to get the text features in the source and target domains. From this aspect, there are many effective supervision models and network structures, such as CNN [5], Bi-LSTM [33], and PCNN [18]. This paper adopts a CNN structure, which extracts features by concatenating lexical features and sentence features. For input text sample x_i, its semantic features are expressed as $f = G_f(x_i)$. G_f is the symbolic representation of CNN. By giving the characteristics of source domain samples to the C_y classifier, the probability of each relational class and the prediction label can be obtained. The following loss function is established to update the parameters of the classifier and the encoder.

$$(\hat{\theta}_f, \hat{\theta}_y) = \underset{\theta_f, \theta_y}{argmin} \frac{1}{n_s} \sum_{x_i \in D_s} L_y(C_y(G_f(x_i)), y_i) \tag{1}$$

In the above formula, θ_f is the parameter of CNN, θ_y is the parameter of the classifier, and y_i is the true label of sample x_i. L_y adopts a cross-entropy loss function.

3.3 Multi-adversarial Neural Network

The core idea of the adversarial domain adaptation is inspired by generative adversarial networks [34], which consists of a generator and a discriminator. The generator randomly takes samples from the source domain as input, and its output results should imitate the real samples in the target domain. The discriminator takes the real sample of the target domain or the output of the generator as the input. It is designed to focus on distinguishing the output of the generator from the actual sample to the greatest extent, while the generator should cheat the discriminator as far as possible. The two networks constitute an adversarial neural network, confronting each other and continuously adjusting the parameters. The ultimate goal of the adversarial neural network is to make the discriminator unable to judge whether the output of the generator is the target domain sample. This approach can maintain the feature invariance between the source domain and reduce the discrepancy of data distribution.

In this study, the feature extractor acts as a generator, and we use the symbol G_d to represent the discriminator. The symbol L_d denotes the optimizer goal of the adversarial neural network, which can be expressed as follows.

$$\min_{\theta_f} \max_{\theta_d} L_d(\theta_d, \theta_f) = \int_{x_s} p(x_s) logG_d(x_s)dx_s + \int_{x_t} p(x_t) logG_d(G_f(x_t))dx_t \quad (2)$$

The $p(x_s)$ denotes data distribution in the source domain and the $p(x_t)$ represents data distribution in the target domain, noting that $p(x_s) \neq p(x_t)$. The objective of the above optimization function is to align two distributions, $p(x_s)$ and $p(x_t)$.

However, these strategies are far from enough to improve the performance of the RE model in the target domain. From an existing defect, a single domain discriminator does not take advantage of the complex multi-mode structure. Consequently, in this paper, a multi-adversarial domain adaptive (MADA) module [23] is applied to capture the multi-mode structure to ensure the fine-grained alignment of different data distributions.

Assuming that there are K classes in the source domain, the model uses K discriminators, with each discriminator focusing on aligning a certain cross-class in the source domain and the target domain. The optimized objective function of the discriminator is as follows:

$$L_d = \frac{1}{n_s + n_t} \sum_{k=1}^{K} \sum_{x_i \in D} L_d^k(D_d^k(\hat{y}_i^k G_f(x_i)), d_i)) \quad (3)$$

The overall objective function can be expressed as the following formula:

$$L(\theta_f, \theta_y, \theta_d|_{k=1}^{K}) = \frac{1}{n_s} \sum_{x_i \in D_s} L_y(C_y(G_f(x_i)), y_i) \quad (4)$$

$$- \frac{\lambda}{n_s + n_t} \sum_{k=1}^{K} \sum_{x_i \in D} L_d^k(D_d^k(\hat{y}_i^k G_f(x_i)), d_i)$$

Where θ_d^k is the parameter of D_d^k, L_d^k denotes the loss function of the k-th discriminator, and $\hat{y}_i^k$ represents the probability that the sample x_i belongs to class k. In addition, $D = D_s \cup D_t$. The first part of the formula represents the loss function of the relation classifier, while the second part represents the loss function of the K discriminators.

3.4 Adaptive Transfer Weight Selection Mechanism

DA is not expected to the situation of $c \in C_s$ and $c \notin C_t$. The previous network structures saw, the samples of each category in the source domain fitted with target domain data without differences, which was not conducive to the model performance of the target domain. In this paper, the weight mechanism is utilized to control the loss function to mitigate the migration of the negative samples and enhance the adaptability of the positive samples.

Instance Weight Calculating. The sample migration ability can be reflected in the discriminator's prediction of the probability that the sample originated from the source domain. The higher the predicted confidence, the more likely the sample can be distinguished from the target domain sample [26]. On the contrary, if the sample has low predicted confidence, this can suggest that the source domain sample and the target domain sample have a higher similarity. At this stage, the source domain sample has more migration performance, which means that the model needs to increase to fit with the sample. The migration weight therefore can be set by the output of the discriminator so that by using the source domain sample as the input of the classification model, the migration weight can be set according to the migration performance.

In this paper, we are able to improve the influence of the sample with low prediction confidence on neural network parameters. Specifically, an auxiliary discriminator D_a is introduced into the model, and the sample weight is constructed by predicting the result of the auxiliary discriminator. The higher the confidence, the greater the weight. Otherwise, the weight will be smaller. The prediction confidence of the sample is denoted as $D_a(f)$ and its weight w_i can be calculated by using the following formula:

$$w_i = \frac{1}{1 + \frac{D_a(G_f(x_s))}{D_a(G_f(x_t))}} = 1 - D_a(f) \tag{5}$$

Class Weight Updating. In order to resolve the central problem of negative transfer caused by outlier categories, the uncertainty of sample migration is used to calculate the category weight. Obviously, all of the samples in an outlier class should not have the nature of migration, so the mobility of the samples can measure the mobility of the category of relation to a certain extent. If all samples in a relation class have low mobility, the class mobility should also be relatively low. Therefore, the migration weight of the class can be calculated by samples weights, so as to reduce the migration weight of the outlier categories.

The larger the w^k is, the closer the class is to the target domain category. Otherwise, there is a greater probability of it being considered an outlier. The effect of category weight on the model is reflected in the following aspects: it strengthens the influence of the category weight on the relation classifier; or, the influences of the samples in the source domain on the discriminator and feature extractor parameters are enhanced. The formula for calculating the category weight is expressed as $\frac{1}{n_{sk}} \sum_{i=1}^{n_{sk}} w_i$. According to the weights of classes, the influence of outliers on parameter updating is effectively limited. The w^K is initialized to $w^K = [1, 1, \cdots, 1]$. Obviously, for outliers, the migration of the interference samples is finite.

Table 1. ACE05 entity types and relation types.

Entity types	Relation types
FAC (Facility)	ART (artifact)
GPE (Geo-Political Entity)	GEN-AFF (Gen-affiliation)
LOC (Location)	ORG-AFF (Org-affiliation)
ORG (Organization)	PART-WHOLE (part-whole)
PER (Person)	PER_SOC (person-social)
VEH (Vehicle)	PHYS (physical)
WEA (Weapon)	——

3.5 Loss Function

The following formula represents the total loss function of our model. The w_i^k represents the migration weight of the category to which the sample x_i belongs. The first part is the loss of a training relation classifier with the source domain data. It emphasizes the use of samples from high mobility categories to update the classification model parameters, which can enhance the generalization performance of the supervised model in the target domain. The second part is the discriminator loss function of K discriminators. On the one hand, w_i^k avoids assigning each sample point to only one discriminator. On the other hand, each sample point is only aligned with the most relevant class, and the uncorrelated class is filtered out by probability. It is not included in the corresponding domain discriminator, thus avoiding the wrong alignment of the discrimination structure in different distributions. With the updating of the class weight, the probability of outliers will gradually converge. In addition, the impact on parameter updating of the discriminators and feature extractor will reduce.

$$L(\theta_f, \theta_y, \theta_d^k|_{k=1}^K) = \frac{1}{n_s} \sum_{k=1}^K \sum_{x_i \in D_s} w_i^k L_y(C_y(G_f(x_i)), y_i) \tag{6}$$

$$-\lambda \sum_{k=1}^K (\sum_{x_i \in D_t} L_d^k(D_d^k(\hat{y}_i^k G_f(x_i)), d_i) + \sum_{x_i \in D_s} w_i^k L_d^k(D_d^k(\hat{y}_i^k G_f(x_i)), d_i))$$

The optimal parameters of the model are expressed as follows.

$$(\hat{\theta}_f, \hat{\theta}_y) = \underset{\theta_f, \theta_y}{argmin}\, L(\theta_f, \theta_y, \theta_d^k|_{k=1}^K),$$

$$(\hat{\theta}_d^1, \cdots, \hat{\theta}_d^K) = \underset{\theta_d^1, \cdots, \theta_d^k}{argmax}\, L(\theta_f, \theta_y, \theta_d^k|_{k=1}^K) \tag{7}$$

4   Experiments

4.1   Dataset

ACE05 Dataset. ACE05 corpus is a type of data that is released by linguistic data consortium. It consists of entities, relations, and event annotations. It aims at developing automatic content extraction technology, and it supports automatic processing of human language in the form of text. This data set includes seven types of entities and six types of relations (see Table 1). In this study, we used the ACE05 dataset to evaluate our proposed model by dividing its texts from its six genres into domains: broadcast conversation (bc), broadcast news (bn), telephone conversation (cts), newswire (nw), usenet (un) and weblogs (wl). To get an understanding of how these domains differ, Fig. 3 depicts the distribution of relations in each domain.

NYT-10 Dataset. NYT-10 dataset has been extensively used in DS research, which was originally developed by Riedel et al. [35], and it was generated by aligning Freebase relations with the New York Times (NYT) corpus. Entity mentions are determined using the Stanford named entity tagger [36], and they are further matched to the names of Freebase entities. This corpus includes 52 relations and a special relation NA which means that there is no relation between the entity pair in this instance. NYT-10 corpus is composed of training data and testing data, where data from 2005–2006 are used as the training set, and data from 2007 is used for testing. Training data includes 522,611 sentences, 281,270 entity pairs, and 18,252 relational facts. Testing data includes 172,448 sentences, 96,678 entity pairs and 1,950 relational facts. We evaluate the performance of our model under an setting using this dataset.

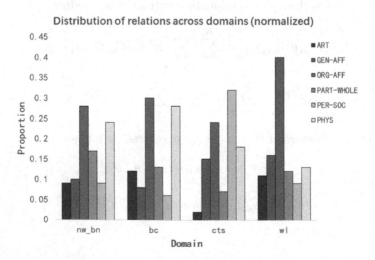

Fig. 3. Distributions of relations in ACE05.

4.2   Hyperparameters Settings

In order to fairly compare the results of our models with those baselines, we follow most of the experimental parameters in existing research [37], which proposed an unsupervised domain adaptation model consisting of a CNN-based relation classifier and a domain-adversarial classifier. We use word embedding that is pre-trained on newswire with 300 dimensions from word2vec [38] as the input of the CNN model. We also choose a cross-validation approach to tune our model and conduct a grid search to determine model parameters.

Table 2. Partition of ACE05 data set and overview of corpus.

Split	Corpus	Documents	Sentences	ASL	Relations
Source domain	nw & bn	298	5029	18.8	3562
Target domain	bc	52	2267	16.3	1297
	wl	114	1697	22.6	677
	cts	34	2696	15.3	603

4.3   Evaluation Results

Results on ACE05. In terms of data set division, previous works [32,37] used newswire (bn & nw) as the source data. The other half of bc, cts, and wl were the target training data, and the other half of bc, cts, and wl as the target test data. We use the same data split process (see Table 2). Our model require unlabeled target domain instances. To meet this requirement and avoid the train-on-test, for all of the three test domains, we separate 20% of the data from the training set as a validation set, in order to adjust the hyperparameters in the model. In terms of experimental settings, several experiments are set up to compare our proposed model with existing models. We choose to design two directions for our comparison. On the one hand, we set a conventional domain adaptation, which extracts some of the relational categories from C_s to make $C_s = C_t$. Reference experiments are as follows: Hybrid [39] combined the traditional feature-based methods, CNN and RNN, and the FCM was used for compositional embedding. CNN+DANN [37] contained a CNN-based relational classifier and a domain-adversarial classifier. CNN+MADA has been modified on the basis of the prototype, replacing the original feature extraction model with a CNN structure. Other parts of the model have not been altered. MADA-weight was designed on the basis of CNN+MADA. The weight mechanism was only valid for the loss function of the classifier and does not affect the loss function of the discriminator.

On the other hand, we promote the adaptive comparison of partial domains. The relational category sets of the three target domains have the following associations, which is to guarantee that $C_t \neq C_s$ and $C_t \in C_s$. CNN + DANN is used as the baseline model to compare with our final MAPDA model.

The experimental results are shown in the following table. The bold word in the table represents that the F1 score of the model has improved compared

Table 3. Comparisons with classical models on F1-score in two aspects: formal domain adaptation and partial domain adaptation. Bold font represents the corresponding model effect, which has demonstrated distinct improvements.

Normal DA	bc	wc	cts	Avg
FCM	61.90	N/A	N/A	N/A
Hybrid	63.26	N/A	N/A	N/A
CNN+DANN	65.16	55.55	57.19	59.30
CNN+MADA	64.23	54.36	55.28	57.96
MADA-weight	**65.86**	**56.10**	56.33	**59.43**
Partial DA	bc	wl	cts	Avg
CNN+DANN	63.17	53.55	53.32	56.68
MAPDA	**65.71**	**56.01**	**55.12**	**59.03**

Table 4. Comparisons of different methods under domain adaptive and non domain adaptive settings.

No DA	Top 100	Top 200	Top 300	Avg
CNN	0.62	0.60	0.60	0.61
PCNN	0.66	0.63	0.62	0.64
DA	Top 100	Top 200	Top 300	Avg
CNN	0.85	0.80	0.76	0.80
PCNN	0.87	0.84	0.82	0.84
CNN+DANN	0.80	0.75	0.71	0.75
MADA-weight	**0.87**	**0.86**	**0.83**	**0.85**

with other models. From the evaluation results that are shown in Table 3, the following points can be observed and summarized. Firstly, in the case of normal DA, the performance of applying MADA directly to relation extraction need to be improved. Our model MADA-weight achieves a performance comparable to that of CNN+DANN, which is a recognized state-of-the-art model. The model demonstrates that it is an effective option to apply sample weight and category weight to the loss function of a classification supervision model, and alleviate the migration of negative samples. Secondly, in the case of partial DA, our model significantly outperforms the plain adversarial DA model. These positive results demonstrate the validity of our weight mechanism and the multi-adversarial adaptive layer.

Results on NYT-10. In our experiment, we take samples of prediction probability Top N (N is 100, 200, 300 respectively), and ignore NA class. We then use the prediction results of this part of the data to evaluate the model performance. The results of the evaluation on NYT-10 can be seen in Table 4. We set up two comparative experiments. One is an experiment without domain adaptive method (No DA), including CNN and PCNN models. In this setting, after training with source domain data, the model is directly applied to the samples in the target domain for prediction. The other experiment use the adaptive domain method (DA), including CNN, PCNN, CNN + DANN, and our model MADA-weight. The models use the source domain data for training, and we then apply the labeled data of the target domain for either fine-tuning or by applying the adaptive domain method for transfer learning.

From the results of the experiment, we can see that the accuracy of the CNN and PCNN models without DA is stable between 0.6 and 0.7. The highest accuracy is 0.66, while CNN and PCNN with DA are found to be 0.8 and above. These results demonstrate that DA is effective in an unsupervised environment and has a positive role in improving the accuracy of the RE model.

Furthermore, in the setting of the top 100, our model MADA with a weight mechanism (MADA-weight) gains 0.87 and exceeds other models by an average of 0.85. It achieved an optimal effect compared with other DA methods in the DA column, which further demonstrates that our weight mechanism is effective.

5   Conclusion

In this study, we propose a novel model based on adversarial learning to extract relation, which successfully obtains an improvement on all three test domains of ACE05 in partial domain adaptation. In addition, the results are able to demonstrate the practicability of the weight mechanism on the NYT-10 dataset. We use multiple adversarial neural networks to learn cross-domain features and align data distribution of the source domain and target domain. It will be a useful instrument for RE to relieve the pressure of data sparsity. Future studies will focus on the scenario where the set of relational categories for the source and target domains only partially overlap. We believe that this research will have a considerable impact on the outcomes, reflects an extensive application value, and generate new research studies in this field.

References

1. Cabrio, E., Cojan, J., Aprosio, A.P., Magnini, B., Lavelli, A., Gandon, F.: QAKIS: an open domain QA system based on relational patterns. In: Proceedings of the 2012 International Conference on Posters and Demonstrations Track-Volume 914 (2012)
2. Lin, Y., Liu, Z., Sun, M., Liu, Y., Zhu, X.: Learning entity and relation embeddings for knowledge graph completion. In: Twenty-Ninth AAAI Conference on Artificial Intelligence (2015)
3. Schlichtkrull, M., Kipf, T.N., Bloem, P., van den Berg, R., Titov, I., Welling, M.: Modeling relational data with graph convolutional networks. In: Gangemi, A., et al. (eds.) ESWC 2018. LNCS, vol. 10843, pp. 593–607. Springer, Cham (2018). https://doi.org/10.1007/978-3-319-93417-4_38

4. Gutierrez, C., Hurtado, C.A., Mendelzon, A.O., Pérez, J.: Foundations of semantic web databases. J. Comput. Syst. Sci. **77**(3), 520–541 (2011)
5. Zeng, D., Liu, K., Lai, S., Zhou, G., Zhao, J., et al.: Relation classification via convolutional deep neural network. In: Proceedings of the 25th International Conference on Computational Linguistics (2014)
6. Socher, R., Huval, B., Manning, C.D., Ng, A.Y.: Semantic compositionality through recursive matrix-vector spaces. In: Proceedings of the 2012 Joint Conference on Empirical Methods in Natural Language Processing and Computational Natural Language Learning, pp. 1201–1211. Association for Computational Linguistics (2012)
7. GuoDong, Z., Jian, S., Jie, Z., Min, Z.: Exploring various knowledge in relation extraction. In: Proceedings of the 43rd Annual Meeting on Association for Computational Linguistics, pp. 427–434. Association for Computational Linguistics (2005)
8. Kambhatla, N.: Combining lexical, syntactic, and semantic features with maximum entropy models for extracting relations. In: Proceedings of the ACL 2004 on Interactive Poster and Demonstration Sessions, p. 22-es (2004)
9. Mintz, M., Bills, S., Snow, R., Jurafsky, D.: Distant supervision for relation extraction without labeled data. In: Proceedings of the Joint Conference of the 47th Annual Meeting of the ACL and the 4th International Joint Conference on Natural Language Processing of the AFNLP: Volume 2, vol. 2, pp. 1003–1011. Association for Computational Linguistics (2009)
10. Pan, S.J., Yang, Q.: A survey on transfer learning. IEEE Trans. Knowl. Data Eng. **22**(10), 1345–1359 (2009)
11. Glorot, X., Bordes, A., Bengio, Y.: Domain adaptation for large-scale sentiment classification: a deep learning approach. In: ICML (2011)
12. Gebru, T., Hoffman, J., Fei-Fei, L.: Fine-grained recognition in the wild: a multitask domain adaptation approach. In: Proceedings of the IEEE International Conference on Computer Vision, pp. 1349–1358 (2017)
13. Plank, B., Moschitti, A.: Embedding semantic similarity in tree kernels for domain adaptation of relation extraction. In: Proceedings of the 51st Annual Meeting of the Association for Computational Linguistics (Volume 1: Long Papers), pp. 1498–1507 (2013)
14. Nguyen, T.H., Grishman, R.: Employing word representations and regularization for domain adaptation of relation extraction. In: Proceedings of the 52nd Annual Meeting of the Association for Computational Linguistics (Volume 2: Short Papers), pp. 68–74 (2014)
15. Long, M., Cao, Z., Wang, J., Jordan, M.I.: Conditional adversarial domain adaptation. In: Advances in Neural Information Processing Systems, pp. 1640–1650 (2018)
16. Cao, Z., Ma, L., Long, M., Wang, J.: Partial adversarial domain adaptation. In: Ferrari, V., Hebert, M., Sminchisescu, C., Weiss, Y. (eds.) ECCV 2018. LNCS, vol. 11212, pp. 139–155. Springer, Cham (2018). https://doi.org/10.1007/978-3-030-01237-3_9
17. Brin, S.: Extracting patterns and relations from the world wide web. In: Atzeni, P., Mendelzon, A., Mecca, G. (eds.) WebDB 1998. LNCS, vol. 1590, pp. 172–183. Springer, Heidelberg (1999). https://doi.org/10.1007/10704656_11
18. Zeng, D., Liu, K., Chen, Y., Zhao, J.: Distant supervision for relation extraction via piecewise convolutional neural networks. In: Proceedings of the 2015 Conference on Empirical Methods in Natural Language Processing, pp. 1753–1762 (2015)

19. Lin, Y., Shen, S., Liu, Z., Luan, H., Sun, M.: Neural relation extraction with selective attention over instances. In: Proceedings of the 54th Annual Meeting of the Association for Computational Linguistics (Volume 1: Long Papers), pp. 2124–2133 (2016)
20. Luo, B., et al.: Learning with noise: enhance distantly supervised relation extraction with dynamic transition matrix. arXiv preprint arXiv:1705.03995 (2017)
21. Zhang, Y., Qi, P., Manning, C.D.: Graph convolution over pruned dependency trees improves relation extraction. arXiv preprint arXiv:1809.10185 (2018)
22. Liu, T., Zhang, X., Zhou, W., Jia, W.: Neural relation extraction via inner-sentence noise reduction and transfer learning. arXiv preprint arXiv:1808.06738 (2018)
23. Pei, Z., Cao, Z., Long, M., Wang, J.: Multi-adversarial domain adaptation. In: Thirty-Second AAAI Conference on Artificial Intelligence (2018)
24. Ganin, Y., et al.: Domain-adversarial training of neural networks. J. Mach. Learn. Res. **17**(1), 2030–2096 (2016)
25. Ganin, Y., Lempitsky, V.: Unsupervised domain adaptation by backpropagation. arXiv preprint arXiv:1409.7495 (2014)
26. Zhang, J., Ding, Z., Li, W., Ogunbona, P.: Importance weighted adversarial nets for partial domain adaptation. In: Proceedings of the IEEE Conference on Computer Vision and Pattern Recognition, pp. 8156–8164 (2018)
27. Luo, Y., Zheng, L., Guan, T., Yu, J., Yang, Y.: Taking a closer look at domain shift: category-level adversaries for semantics consistent domain adaptation. In: Proceedings of the IEEE Conference on Computer Vision and Pattern Recognition, pp. 2507–2516 (2019)
28. Zhang, Y., Tang, H., Jia, K., Tan, M.: Domain-symmetric networks for adversarial domain adaptation. In: Proceedings of the IEEE Conference on Computer Vision and Pattern Recognition, pp. 5031–5040 (2019)
29. Cao, Z., You, K., Long, M., Wang, J., Yang, Q.: Learning to transfer examples for partial domain adaptation. In: Proceedings of the IEEE Conference on Computer Vision and Pattern Recognition, pp. 2985–2994 (2019)
30. Xie, S., Zheng, Z., Chen, L., Chen, C.: Learning semantic representations for unsupervised domain adaptation. In: International Conference on Machine Learning, pp. 5423–5432 (2018)
31. Pan, Y., Yao, T., Li, Y., Wang, Y., Ngo, C.W., Mei, T.: Transferrable prototypical networks for unsupervised domain adaptation. In: Proceedings of the IEEE Conference on Computer Vision and Pattern Recognition, pp. 2239–2247 (2019)
32. Zhang, N., Deng, S., Sun, Z., Chen, J., Zhang, W., Chen, H.: Transfer learning for relation extraction via relation-gated adversarial learning. arXiv preprint arXiv:1908.08507 (2019)
33. Miwa, M., Bansal, M.: End-to-end relation extraction using LSTMs on sequences and tree structures. arXiv preprint arXiv:1601.00770 (2016)
34. Goodfellow, I., et al.: Generative adversarial nets. In: Advances in Neural Information Processing Systems, pp. 2672–2680 (2014)
35. Riedel, S., Yao, L., McCallum, A.: Modeling relations and their mentions without labeled text. In: Balcázar, J.L., Bonchi, F., Gionis, A., Sebag, M. (eds.) ECML PKDD 2010. LNCS (LNAI), vol. 6323, pp. 148–163. Springer, Heidelberg (2010). https://doi.org/10.1007/978-3-642-15939-8_10
36. Finkel, J.R., Grenager, T., Manning, C.: Incorporating non-local information into information extraction systems by Gibbs sampling. In: Proceedings of the 43rd Annual Meeting on Association for Computational Linguistics, pp. 363–370. Association for Computational Linguistics (2005)

37. Fu, L., Nguyen, T.H., Min, B., Grishman, R.: Domain adaptation for relation extraction with domain adversarial neural network. In: Proceedings of the Eighth International Joint Conference on Natural Language Processing (Volume 2: Short Papers), pp. 425–429 (2017)
38. Mikolov, T., Chen, K., Corrado, G., Dean, J.: Efficient estimation of word representations in vector space. arXiv preprint arXiv:1301.3781 (2013)
39. Nguyen, T.H., Grishman, R.: Combining neural networks and log-linear models to improve relation extraction. arXiv preprint arXiv:1511.05926 (2015)

SASOBUS: Semi-automatic Sentiment Domain Ontology Building Using Synsets

Ewelina Dera, Flavius Frasincar(✉) [ID], Kim Schouten, and Lisa Zhuang

Erasmus University Rotterdam,
P.O. Box 1738, 3000 DR Rotterdam, The Netherlands
ewelina.dera@live.com, {frasincar,schouten}@ese.eur.nl,
lisa.zhuang@hotmail.com

Abstract. In this paper, a semi-automatic approach for building a sentiment domain ontology is proposed. Differently than other methods, this research makes use of synsets in term extraction, concept formation, and concept subsumption. Using several state-of-the-art hybrid aspect-based sentiment analysis methods like Ont + CABASC and Ont + LCR-Rot-hop on a standard dataset, the accuracies obtained using the semi-automatically built ontology as compared to the manually built one, are slightly lower (from approximately 87% to 84%). However, the user time needed for building the ontology is reduced by more than half (from 7 h to 3 h), thus showing the usefulness of this work. This is particularly useful for domains for which sentiment ontologies are not yet available.

Keywords: Semi-automatic ontology building · Sentiment domain ontology · Aspect-based sentiment analysis

1 Introduction

With the growth of review data on the Web, as well as its importance, it is no wonder that 80% of consumers read online reviews and 75% of those people consider these reviews important [9]. Currently, the amount of online reviews, as well as other Web-based content, is tremendous. It is nearly impossible for a human to go through even a fraction of those reviews. As a result, it is not surprising that there was and still is, an increased interest in extracting, filtering and summarizing all the available reviews. Consequently, sentiment analysis and the more specific, aspect-based sentiment analysis (ABSA) [22] are very crucial and relevant tasks in the current business world.

This paper focuses on ABSA. ABSA is especially useful since in comparison with sentiment analysis, it gives more in-depth sentiment breakdown. There are many different approaches to conduct ABSA. However, there are two main types of methods, namely, knowledge representation (KR)-based and machine learning (ML)-based. Despite different advantages and disadvantages of those two methods, they both have a relatively good performance [22]. Nevertheless, a hybrid approach, combing ML with KR, was recently found to have an even

© Springer Nature Switzerland AG 2020
A. Harth et al. (Eds.): ESWC 2020, LNCS 12123, pp. 105–120, 2020.
https://doi.org/10.1007/978-3-030-49461-2_7

better performance than the two methods on their own [23]. Therefore, it is not surprising that many researchers tried combining these methods.

The authors of [25] proposed a hybrid model with better performance than other state-of-the-art approaches, including [17,23]. Therefore, [25] will be used as a base for this paper. The aim of this research is to further improve the performance of the methods proposed in [25] by enhancing the employed domain ontology. A new semi-automatic domain ontology is built based on synsets. Employing synsets instead of words should enable a fair and reliable comparison of words, while simultaneously capturing their meaning. Moreover, what is particularly worth emphasizing is the fact that as semi-automatic ontologies save considerable amounts of time, they are already considered to be successful if they have a similar performance to the manual ontologies. This is particularly true for new domains for which sentiment ontologies have not been yet devised.

There are many papers concerned with semi-automatic ontology building, e.g., [8,11,14]. However, these ontologies are neither sentiment ontologies nor are they built specifically for the task of ABSA. Furthermore, the majority of ontologies does not utilise synsets in any of the ontology building steps.

This paper follows with a review of the relevant literature in Sect. 2. Then, in Sect. 3 the used data is briefly explained. Afterwards, in Sect. 4 the used methodology is described. Then, the paper follows with Sect. 5 where the obtained results are presented. This paper concludes with Sect. 6 giving conclusions and suggestions for future work.

2   Related Work

As mentioned in [2], the KR-based techniques for ABSA have a rather good performance if a few major difficulties are overcome. The performance of a KR mainly depends on the quality of the used resource. For it to be extensive, it would need to be built automatically. However, for it to also be precise, it would need to be created manually, thus taking significant amounts of time. Hence, semi-automatic ontologies seem to be the best solution, where automatically extracted information is curated by users. Moreover, ML approaches, such as SVMs or neural networks, have a relatively good performance on their own. Unfortunately, they also need a lot of training data in order to learn properly [2]. That is why hybrid approaches are a good option for ABSA or other text classification tasks [22]. Hybrid approaches combine KR with ML, thus also exploiting the strengths of each of these two methods.

Seeing the potential of ontology as a base model, the authors of [25] decided to implement hybrid approaches. The authors used the same data and the same domain sentiment ontology as in [23]. However, for the ML part they decided to replace the SVM from [23] with neural networks. First, they combined the ontology with the Content Attention Based Aspect-based Sentiment Classification (CABASC) model [13]. By using a context attention mechanism, the model is able to take into consideration correlations between words and, at the same time, also the words' order. Furthermore, the authors also combined the sentiment domain ontology with a Left-Center-Right (LCR) separated neural network

[27]. They used three different variants of the LCR model, namely, LCR-Rot, LCR-Rot-inv and LCR-Rot-hop. The first approach has a rotatory attention mechanism, which first finds the most indicative words from the left and right context. These are, in turn, used to find the most indicative words in the target phrase (for the considered aspect). The second model, LCR-Rot-inv, is very similar - the only difference is that it inverses the order of the rotatory attention mechanism. Finally, the third model just repeats the rotatory attention mechanism of LCR-Rot multiple times. With the above described approaches, the authors obtained an even better performance than [23], with Ont + LCR-Rot-hop having the highest (out-of-sample) accuracy equal to 88% for the 2016 dataset [25]. Furthermore, while not directly compared, based on the reported performance results, [25] also has better results than [17] on the very same dataset.

Based on [25] it can be seen that a sentiment domain ontology is a very useful tool for ABSA. The neural back-up models in the mentioned paper have a high performance and improving them would be a tedious and strenuous task that might give an improvement at the level of a fraction of a percent. Therefore, it is decided that the best way to further enhance the performance of hybrid models for ABSA, is to concentrate on the ontology. Any further improvements to the KR would only make it more reliable and thus, decrease the number of cases when the back-up model has to be used.

Regarding previous efforts in extracting information in relation to aspects and their associated sentiments from text we would like to mention the following works. First, there are works that exploit dependency relations and a sentiment lexicon for finding aspects and their associated sentiment in text [7,21]. Second, there are advanced solutions that make use of an argumentation framework [6] or the rhetorical structure of text [10] in conjunction with a sentiment lexicon for determining aspects and/or the sentiment associated to these. Nevertheless, these works adopt a linguistic approach and not a KR one as considered here.

3   Data

For the purpose of this paper, different datasets are used. The Yelp dataset is used as a domain corpus for building the ontology. It comes from the Yelp Dataset Challenge 2017[1] and it contains 5,001 restaurant-related reviews and 47,734 sentences in total. Except the text representing the opinion of the reviewer, each review also contains a star rating. This rating is represented by an integer value between zero and five.

In addition, some contrastive corpora are also used for ontology learning, namely, six popular and freely available English books obtained from Project Gutenberg[2] as text files. These books are first pre-processed. Each book goes through the NLP pipeline from Stanford CoreNLP 3.8.0[3] toolkit. The following

---

[1] https://www.yelp.nl/dataset/challenge.
[2] http://www.gutenberg.org/wiki/Main_Page.
[3] https://stanfordnlp.github.io/CoreNLP/.

steps are performed: sentence splitting, tokenization, lemmatization and part-of-speech (POS) tagging.

Our proposed approach builds in a semi-automatic manner a sentiment domain ontology that is tested using the methods from [25]. While [25] used two datasets, i.e., SemEval-2015 and SemEval-2016, we only evaluate the afore-mentioned methods with the SemEval-2016 dataset. There is no need for the SemEval-2015 data as it is contained in the SemEval-2016 dataset. In 2016 Task 5[4] of SemEval was performed on ABSA. The used dataset contains reviews regarding different domains. However, as [25] used only the restaurant domain, to enable a reliable comparison, we also only focus on the restaurant domain. The SemEval-2016 data is already split into training and test datasets. The former contains 350 reviews and the latter only 90 reviews. Each review consists of sentences. In total, there are 2,676 sentences (2000 in the training dataset and 676 in the test dataset) and each one of them holds one or more opinions. Each one of the 3,365 opinions has a target word, aspect, and sentiment polarity. The aspect name consists of an entity and an attribute separated by a hash symbol. Furthermore, in Fig. 1 an example sentence in XML format is given. Here, a target word is 'atmosphere' (spans from the '12'th character to the '22'nd character in the text), the aspect category is 'AMBIENCE#GENERAL', and the sentiment polarity is 'positive'. There might be cases where, e.g., word 'meat' implies a food aspect; this is an explicit aspect because it has a clear target word. Nevertheless, there are also situations, when there is no target word. For instance, the sentence 'everything was cooked well' also implies a food aspect but there is no clear target word. In order to stay consistent with [25], all opinions with implicit aspects are removed. Consequently, there are 2,529 opinions remaining (1,870 in the training dataset and 650 in the test dataset). Moreover, all the words are tokenized and lemmatized using the NLTK platform [1] and WordNet.

```
<Sentence id="en_BlueRibbonSushi_478218900:2">
    <Text>I liked the atmosphere very much but the food was not worth the price.</Text>
    <Opinions>
        <Opinion to="22" from="12" polarity="positive" category="AMBIENCE#GENERAL"
        target="atmosphere"/>
        <Opinion to="45" from="41" polarity="negative" category="FOOD#QUALITY" target="food"/>
        <Opinion to="45" from="41" polarity="negative" category="FOOD#PRICES" target="food"/>
    </Opinions>
</Sentence>
```

Fig. 1. An example sentence from the SemEval-2016 dataset.

Moreover, it can be seen from Fig. 2a that for both train and test data, the positive sentiment is most frequently expressed. It accounts for 65–70% of the cases. Negative sentiment is found considerably less (with frequency of 25–30%).

---

[4] Data and tools for SemEval-2016 Task 5 can be found here:
http://alt.qcri.org/semeval2016/task5/index.php?id=data-and-tools.

Furthermore, when it comes to the number of opinions expressed per sentence, it can be seen in Fig. 2b that almost all of the respondents have between 0–3 opinions in a sentence.

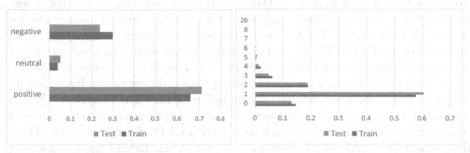

(a) Frequency of different sentiments   (b) Number of opinions per sentences

Fig. 2. Descriptive statistics for the SemEval-2016 dataset.

4   Methodology

All the text pre-processing and ontology learning is performed in the Semi-automatic Sentiment Domain Ontology Building Using Synsets (SASOBUS)[5] framework in Java. Furthermore, the HAABSA[6] framework in Python is used to evaluate the created ontology. Moreover, the Java API for WordNet Searching (JAWS)[7] library is used for obtaining synsets from WordNet.

In order to identify a sense of each word for both, the domain corpus and the contrastive corpora for ontology learning, the Simplified Lesk algorithm [12] is used. The reason behind such choice is that out of all the variants of the Lesk algorithm, this one has the best trade-off between accuracy and speed [5,12,24]. Besides, despite its simplicity it is hard to beat by other more advanced algorithms. The general idea behind the algorithm is that the ambiguous word and its context words are compared based on their glosses. The sense (or synset) having the highest overlap is returned by the algorithm.

4.1   Semi-automatic Ontology Learning

The approach chosen for the ontology building process is based on methods using ordinary words. However, these methods are modified in such a way that words are replaced with their corresponding synsets. Such an approach enables not only the comparison of the manually built ontology from [25] with the semi-automatically built ontology in this paper, but it also facilitates a comparison of two semi-automatically built ontologies: one with ordinary words and one

---

[5] https://github.com/EJDera/SASOBUS.

[6] https://github.com/ofwallaart/HAABSA.

[7] https://github.com/jaytaylor/jaws.

with synsets. Using synsets enables capturing the meaning of words better, thus enabling a more reliable comparison of words.

To the extent of authors' knowledge there is no research so far on ontology learning with synsets as terms. The term extraction method that is used has a score based on domain pertinence (DP) and domain consensus (DC) [16]. There are also other methods for term suggestion, such as, e.g., Term Frequency Inverse Document Frequency (TF-IDF) method based on frequency count [19]. In [3] the authors used TF-IDF and replaced terms by synsets, thus creating Synset Frequency Inverse Document Frequency (SF-IDF) method. The authors obtained better results with terms being synsets rather than ordinary words. Even though, [3] used SF-IDF for news item recommendation rather than for ABSA, there is still reason to believe that synsets as terms have a large potential, for instance, in other term extraction methods such as the DP and DC-based approach. These above mentioned reasons complement the motivation behind using synsets as terms not only for term extraction but also for the whole ontology building process.

Ontology Structure. The built ontology will have the same structure as in [23]. What is important to know is the fact that there are different types of sentiments. Type-1 sentiments are the words that have only one polarity, i.e., positive or negative, irrespective of the context and aspect. Type-2 sentiments are aspect-specific. These are words such as 'delicious' that can only relate to one aspect, i.e., sustenance in this case. When it comes to Type-3 sentiments, these words can have different polarity depending on the mentioned aspect. For instance, 'cold' combined with 'beer' has a positive sentiment, while 'cold' and 'soup' has a negative meaning.

Skeletal Ontology. The skeletal ontology contains two main classes, namely *Mention* and *Sentiment*. The first class encloses all the classes and concepts that represent the reviewed aspect, while the second one encompasses all concepts that relate to the sentiment polarity. The *Mention* class incorporates three subclasses: *ActionMention*, *EntityMention* and *PropertyMention*, which consist only of verbs, nouns and adjectives, respectively. The *Sentiment* class also has three subclasses: *Positive*, *Neutral* and *Negative*, which refer to the corresponding sentiment word. Each of the *Mention* classes has two subclasses called *GenericPositive<Type>* and *GenericNegative<Type>*. Type denotes one of the three types of mention classes, i.e., *Action*, *Entity* and *Property*. Those *Generic<Positive/Negative><Type>* classes are also subclasses of the corresponding *<Positive/Negative>* class.

The first performed step in ontology building is adding some general synsets representing words such as 'hate', 'love', 'good', 'bad', 'disappointment' and 'satisfaction' for each of the *GenericPositive<Type>* and *GenericNegative<Type>* classes. For each of those classes two general properties are added. Each word/synonym in a given synset is added to the concept as a *lex* property. Moreover, the synset ID is added as a *synset* property. However, to make the name of the concept more human-readable and -understandable, the synset ID is not used as the name. Instead the first word contained in the associated synset denotes the name of the given concept. For instance, the synset 'verb@1778057' is added as a (subclass) concept to *GenericNegativeAction*. All the synonyms in this synset, i.e., 'hate' and 'detest' are added as a *lex* property, the ID is added as a *synset* property and the name of this concept is the first synonym of this synset, namely *Hate*. The synset ID has a format of POS@ID, where POS stands for the part-of-speech tag and ID denotes the unique synset ID number from WordNet. What is important to note is that '@' is replaced by '#' because '@' has its own meaning in the RDFS language used for ontology building. An example concept and its properties can be seen in Fig. 3.

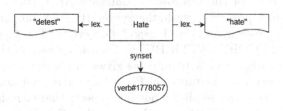

Fig. 3. An example concept from the ontology.

Furthermore, as it was already mentioned in Sect. 3, each aspect has the format of ENTITY#ATTRIBUTE. In this context 'entity' just represents a certain category for a particular aspect. Moreover, as it was also already mentioned *ActionMention*, *EntityMention* and *PropertyMention* classes can only consist of (concepts with) verbs, nouns and adjectives, respectively. Consequently, 'entity' in *EntityMention* means noun. In order not to confuse those two meanings of 'entity', i.e., category or noun, from now on, an aspect has the format of CAT-EGORY#ATTRIBUTE and it consists of a category and attribute. In other words, word 'entity' is replaced with 'category' for this particular context.

The next step in the ontology building process is adding all the classes representing different aspects to the ontology. Just as in [23], for each *<Type>Mention* class, a set of subclasses is added, namely, all the possible *<Category><Type>-Mention* and *<Attribute><Type>Mention* classes are added. For *Attribute* there are only three possible choices, i.e., prices, quality and style&options. General and miscellaneous attributes are skipped as, e.g., *MiscellaneousEntityMention* would be a too generic class. However, what is worth noting is the fact that *Food<Type>Mention* and *Drinks<Type>Mention* classes are not added directly as children of the respective *<Type>Mention* class. Just as in [23], these classes have a parent called *Sustenance<Type>Mention*, which in turn has *<Type>Mention* as a parent.

In the next step, for each $<Category/Attribute><Type>Mention$ class, two new subclasses are created, namely $<Category/Attribute>Positive<Type>$ and $<Category/Attribute>Negative<Type>$ class. These classes also have the respective *Positive* or *Negative* classes as parents. An example with just a few possible classes can be seen in Fig. 4. It can be seen there that, e.g., *PropertyMention* has two subclasses, namely *ServicePropertyMention* (which represents one of the $<Category>PropertyMention$ classes) and *PricesPropertyMention* (which represents one of the $<Attribute>PropertyMention$ classes). Furthermore, *ServicePropertyMention* has two children: *ServicePositiveProperty* and *ServiceNegativeProperty*. These classes also have another parent: *Positive* and *Negative*, respectively. The situation is the same for all the remaining categories, attributes and types.

Furthermore, each of the discussed $<Category/Attribute><Type>Mention$ classes has a *synset* property (with the synset ID), *lex* properties (with the synonyms from a given synset) and *aspect* properties. The last property has the format of CATEGORY#ATTRIBUTE. For each class, all the aspects that contain a certain category or attribute (as given in the class name) are added as the *aspect* property. For instance, in Fig. 5 there is a *LocationEntityMention* class. *Location* is a category so all the possible aspects that contain this category are added as an *aspect* property. Furthermore, location has a meaning of 'a determination of the place where something is'[8] so the corresponding synset 'noun@27167' is added as a *synset* property. All of the synonyms in this synset, i.e., 'location', 'localization' and 'localisation' are added as lexicalisations with the *lex* property.

Additionally, what is also important to know is the fact that there is a *disjointWith* relation between all the $<Category/Attribute>Positive<Type>$ and all the $<Category/Attribute>Negative<Type>$ classes.

Term Selection. To extract useful terms, the relevance score from [16] is used. The first step of this method is related to finding terms that are relevant only for a particular domain but not for another (irrelevant) domain. The DP score is calculated the following way:

$$DP_D(t) = \frac{freq(t/D)}{max_i(freq(t/C_i))},\tag{1}$$

where $freq(t/D)$ denotes the frequency of term t in the domain corpus D and $freq(t/C_i)$ denotes the frequency of the same term t in the contrastive corpus C_i. Index i stands for a particular contrastive corpus [16].

Furthermore, another measure that forms the relevance score is DC, which is defined as the consensus of a term across the domain corpus. The DC score is calculated as follows [16]:

$$DC_D(t) = -\sum_{d\in D} n\_freq(t,d) \times log(n\_freq(t,d)),\tag{2}$$

---

[8] https://wordnet.princeton.edu/.

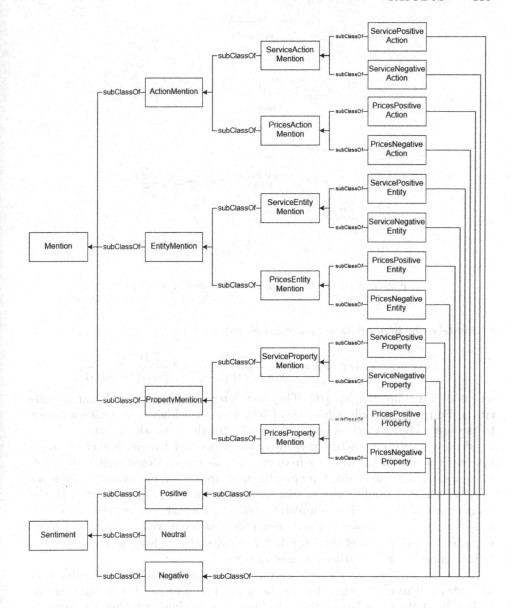

Fig. 4. An excerpt from the ontology with a few example classes.

where $n\_freq(t, d)$, the normalized frequency of term t in document d is defined as follows:

$$n\_freq(t,d) = \frac{freq(t,d)}{max_{d \in D}(freq(t,d))}. \tag{3}$$

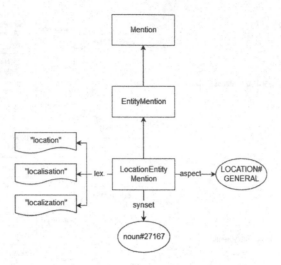

Fig. 5. A simplified example class from the ontology.

Ultimately, the final relevance score is defined as:

$$relevance\_score(t, D) = \alpha \frac{DP_D(t)}{max_t(DP_D(t))} + \beta \frac{DC_D(t)}{max_t(DC_D(t))}, \qquad (4)$$

where α and β are weights [16]. They are determined with a grid search algorithm. Furthermore, only a fraction of terms with the highest score is suggested to the user. These fractions are determined with the same algorithm.

However, terms are substituted by either synsets or lemma. If there exists a synset for a particular word, its frequency is calculated. Consequently, this frequency score is more reliable than just the word frequency. For instance, the noun 'service' has 15 possible senses in WordNet. With ordinary words as terms all the occurrences of this word in completely different contexts are counted together. With synset terms, however, these occurrences are context-dependent. Furthermore, if there is no synset for a word, it is replaced by its lemma. Consequently, in this paper a term is either a synset or a word.

Once all the frequencies and relevance scores are calculated, the (fraction of) extracted terms is suggested to the user. The user can reject the term or accept it. If it is the latter, then the user has to chose whether the term is an aspect concept or sentiment concept. The former just encompasses all the words/synsets relating to a certain aspect but with no polarity in their meaning. The latter are also aspect-related but they have a sentiment as well. For instance, 'sushi' is an aspect concept because it is related to an aspect, specifically to the food category. Also, 'yummy' is aspect-related; however, this word also carries a positive sentiment in its meaning. Therefore, it is a sentiment concept (related to the food aspect).

Hierarchical Relations. Hierarchical methods are derived with the subsumption method [20]. This method is based on co-occurrence and determines potential parents (subsumers) with the following formula:

$$P(x|y) \geq c, P(y|x) < c, \tag{5}$$

where c is a co-occurrence threshold, x is the potential parent and y the potential child [16,20]. In other words, the parent appears in more than a fraction of c documents, where the child also occurs, and the child occurs in less than a fraction of c documents, where the parent also occurs. Just as it was suggested in [20], c is replaced with a value of 1 in the second inequality, and set empirically to 0.2 in the first inequality.

Furthermore, multiple parents can be found by Eq. 5 so only one is chosen based on a parent score defined as:

$$parent\_score(x, y) = P(x|y). \tag{6}$$

All the potential parents are ranked by the score (from highest to lowest). The potential parents for verbs, nouns and adjectives that are aspect concepts are the respective *<Category/Attribute><Type>Mention* classes. However, the potential parent classes for terms that are sentiment concepts are the corresponding *<Category/Attribute><Polarity><Type>* classes. The *Polarity* here denotes the positive or negative sentiment of a concept.

Furthermore, an additional step to calculate the sentiment score of a given concept is added. We adapt the score from [4] as:

$$sentiment\_score(y) = \frac{\sum\limits_{d \in D} \left(rating(d) \times \frac{n(y,d)}{\sum\limits_{sent \in sentiments(D)} n(sent,d)} \right)}{\sum\limits_{d \in D} \frac{n(y,d)}{\sum\limits_{sent \in sentiments(D)} n(sent,d)}}, \tag{7}$$

where $rating(d)$ is a (Min-Max) normalized score of the Yelp star rating of a review d, $n(y,d)$ stands for the number of times concept y is used in review d and $sent$ is a sentiment concept in $sentiments(D)$, the sentiment concepts in D. The polarity is negative if the score is smaller than 0.5, otherwise it is positive.

Consequently, as possible parent classes for aspect concepts are suggested based only on score from Eq. 6, there are two scores that are taken into account when suggesting possible parents for sentiment concepts. The score from Eq. 6 suggests a possible *<Category/Attribute><Polarity>Type*, while the score from Eq. 7 suggests a certain polarity value first. For instance, if Eq. 6 calculates the highest score for *FoodMention* class, Eq. 7 suggests a positive sentiment and the word form is verb then, *FoodPositiveAction* is suggested first, followed by *FoodNegativeAction*.

Additional Steps. What is worth being explicitly mentioned are the Type-3 sentiments. The proposed methods allow the user to accept multiple parents for a concept. Consequently, for instance, concept *Cheap* can have parents *PricesPositiveProperty* and *AmbienceNegativeProperty*.

4.2   Evaluation

In order to evaluate the quality of the created ontology, the same methods as used in [25] are utilised. The hybrid approach Ont + LCR-Rot-hop is performed with the manual ontology and the semi-automatic ontology for the SemEval-2016 dataset. This approach was chosen as it was found to have the best performance by the authors of [25]. Furthermore, similarly to [25] the Ont + CABASC approach is used as a baseline.

5   Results

This section provides all the results related to the ontology building process. First, the parameter optimisation results are described in Sect. 5.1. Then, the effectiveness of the semi-automatically built ontology is evaluated in Sect. 5.2 with three methods: Ont, Ont + LCR-Rot-hop and Ont + CABASC. Furthermore, each of these methods is evaluated with an in-sample, out-of-sample and average (based on 10-fold cross-validations) in-sample accuracy.

5.1   Parameter Optimisation

As it was already mentioned, the parameters α, β and the fraction of suggested verbs, nouns and adjectives were optimised. Let us call these ratios f_v, f_n and f_a, respectively. What is especially worth mentioning, is the fact that in Eq. 4 only the relative ratio between α and β is crucial. Consequently, the restriction of $\alpha + \beta = 1$ is imposed. Furthermore, an important goal of the ontology building process is to extract and suggest terms that the user accepts. Consequently, the grid search has the objective of maximising the term acceptance ratio. However, the user also does not want to go through all the possible terms. Therefore, to keep the number of suggested terms at a reasonable amount and to maximise the amount of accepted terms, the grid search for f_v, f_n, f_a and the respective values of α and β, maximises the harmonic mean between acceptance ratio and the amount of accepted terms. This mean is defined as:

$$objective_{pos} = \frac{2}{\frac{1}{acceptance\_ratio_{pos}} + \frac{1}{accepted\_terms_{pos}}}, \tag{8}$$

where *pos* stands for verbs, nouns and adjectives. The step size for the values of α and β is equal to 0.1 on a range from 0 to 1 and the step size for f_v, f_n and f_a is 0.01 on a range from 0.1 to 0.2 (due to the large number of terms). The resulting parameters can be seen in Table 1.

5.2   Ontology Building Evaluation

The number of added properties and classes in the built ontology can be seen in the left part of Table 2. Based on those numbers it can be observed that the ontology based on synsets as terms (sOnt) has more lexicalisations and classes.

Table 1. Table with the best performing parameters.

	α	β	f
Verbs (v)	1.0	0.0	0.10
Nouns (n)	0.5	0.5	0.11
Adjectives (a)	0.1	0.9	0.14

Furthermore, there are more *synset* properties than concepts, which means that there are some concepts that have more than one meaning. For instance, concept *Atmosphere* has two *synset* properties (and consequently, two meanings), namely, 'a particular environment or surrounding influence' and 'a distinctive but intangible quality surrounding a person or thing'. Moreover, sOnt does not have considerably more concepts than mOnt, however, the number of lexicalisations is significantly higher. While each concept in mOnt, on average, has one *lex* property, in sOnt there are, on average, three *lex* properties.

As can be seen in the right part of Table 2, the total time taken to create sOnt is higher than for mOnt. When it comes to the system time this is due to WSD. However, when it comes to the user time, it is lower by more than half when comparing sOnt to mOnt. In general, the system time cannot be reduced. However, when comparing the user time, it can be seen that sOnt takes considerably less time, while having substantially more concepts and lexicalisations.

Table 2. Table comparing some general statistics between different ontologies.

	lex property	*aspect* property	*synset* property	Classes	Concepts	System time	User time	Total time
sOnt	1324	45	483	558	456	5 h	3 h	8 h
mOnt	374	16	–	365	328	–	7 h	7 h

sOnt denotes the semi-automatic ontology based on synsets that was built using the methods from this paper and mOnt stands for the manual ontology from [23]. Furthermore, word 'classes' denotes here all the ontology classes, while 'concepts' stands for the classes containing the accepted terms.

The upper part of Table 3 shows the KR-based method's results. Unfortunately, sOnt has lower, both in-sample and out-of-sample accuracy than mOnt. However, this difference is rather small (only around 2%). Moreover, another semi-automatic ontology with words as terms (wOnt) has a slightly lower both in-sample and out-of-sample accuracy than sOnt. Therefore, the performance of sOnt is slightly worse than mOnt but it is simultaneously considerably better than a similar semi-automatic ontology but built on words rather than synsets.

Furthermore, it can also be seen in Table 3 that each hybrid method with sOnt has also around 2% lower performance. In addition, for both ontologies the benchmark approach (based on CABASC) has the worst performance when it comes to hybrid methods. The Ont + LCR-Rot-hop approach is significantly better than the benchmark, thus confirming the findings of [25].

Moreover, what is also interesting to see is that the benchmark approach, as well as the KR one has higher out-of-sample than in-sample accuracy for both types of ontology. However, the LCR-Rot method has the accuracy values the other way around. In other words, the KR and the benchmark approach tend to underfit the data, while the LCR-Rot method rather leans towards overfitting.

Table 3. Table comparing the performance of different methods based on SemEval-2016 dataset with in-sample, out-of-sample and 10-fold cross-validation accuracy.

	Out-of-sample	In-sample	Cross-validation	
	Accuracy	Accuracy	Accuracy	St. dev.
mOnt	78.31%	75.31%	75.31%	0.0144
wOnt	72.80%	70.80%	70.90%	0.0504
sOnt	76.46%	73.92%	73.87%	0.0141
mOnt + CABASC	85.11%	82.73%	80.79%	0.0226
mOnt + LCR-Rot-hop	86.80%	88.21%	82.88%	0.0224
sOnt + CABASC	83.16%	79.53%	72.04%	0.1047
sOnt + LCR-Rot-hop	84.49%	86.07%	79.73%	0.0348

wOnt stands for a similar semi-automatic ontology built with the same methods as sOnt but with words (instead of synsets) as terms.

Each of the components used in the implementation is subject to errors due to various reasons. First, the proposed method depends on the domain corpus (as well as the contrastive corpora) for building the sentiment domain ontology (that affects both coverage and precision). Second, the method is sensitive to the errors made by the used NLP components. Given that we mainly use the Stanford CoreNLP 3.8.0 toolkit, which reports very good performance in the considered tasks [15], we expect the number of errors to be limited. The component that gives the largest number of errors is the word sense disambiguation implementation based on the Simplified Lesk algorithm, which obtained an accuracy of 67.2% on the SemCor 3.0 dataset [18] (word sense disambiguation is considered a hard task in natural language processing). Fortunately, some of the errors made by the implementation components can be corrected by the user as we chose for a semi-automatic approach instead of a fully automatic one.

6   Conclusion

This paper's aim was to propose a semi-automatic approach for ontology construction in ABSA. The main focus was on exploiting synsets for term extraction, concept formation and concept subsumption during the ontology learning process. A new semi-automatic ontology was built with synsets as terms. Its accuracy was slightly lower (about 2%) than the accuracy of the manual ontology but the user time is significantly lower (about halved). This result is particularly useful for new domains for which a sentiment ontology has not been devised yet. It can be concluded that the created ontology is successful. It can also be stated that employing synsets in the term extraction, concept formation and taxonomy building steps of the ontology learning process results in better performance than just employing words. As future work it is planned to apply the proposed approach to other domains than restaurants, e.g., laptops. Also, it is desired to experiment with alternative methods to build the concept hierarchy, for instance like the one proposed in [26].

References

1. Bird, S., Klein, E., Loper, E.: Natural Language Processing with Python, Analyzing Text with the Natural Language Toolkit. O'Reilly Media, Inc., Sebastopol (2009)
2. Cambria, E.: Affective computing and sentiment analysis. IEEE Intell. Syst. **31**(2), 102–107 (2016)
3. Capelle, M., Frasincar, F., Moerland, M., Hogenboom, F.: Semantics-based news recommendation. In: 2nd International Conference on Web Intelligence, Mining and Semantics (WIMS 2012), p. 27. ACM (2012)
4. Cesarano, C., Dorr, B., Picariello, A., Reforgiato, D., Sagoff, A., Subrahmanian, V.: OASYS: an opinion analysis system. In: AAAI Spring Symposium on Computational Approaches to Analyzing Weblogs (CAAW 2006), pp. 21–26. AAAI Press (2006)
5. Craggs, D.J.: An analysis and comparison of predominant word sense disambiguation algorithms. Edith Cowan University (2011)
6. Dragoni, M., da Costa Pereira, C., Tettamanzi, A.G.B., Villata, S.: Combining argumentation and aspect-based opinion mining: the SMACk system. AI Commun. **31**(1), 75–95 (2018)
7. Federici, M., Dragoni, M.: A knowledge-based approach for aspect-based opinion mining. In: Sack, H., Dietze, S., Tordai, A., Lange, C. (eds.) SemWebEval 2016. CCIS, vol. 641, pp. 141–152. Springer, Cham (2016). https://doi.org/10.1007/978-3-319-46565-4_11
8. Fortuna, B., Mladenič, D., Grobelnik, M.: Semi-automatic construction of topic ontologies. In: Ackermann, M., et al. (eds.) EWMF/KDO 2005. LNCS (LNAI), vol. 4289, pp. 121–131. Springer, Heidelberg (2006). https://doi.org/10.1007/11908678_8
9. Gretzel, U., Yoo, K.H.: Use and impact of online travel reviews. In: O'Connor, P., Hopken, W., Gretzel, U. (eds.) Information and Communication Technologies in Tourism 2008. Springer, Vienna (2008). https://doi.org/10.1007/978-3-211-77280-5_4
10. Hoogervorst, R., et al.: Aspect-based sentiment analysis on the web using rhetorical structure theory. In: Bozzon, A., Cudre-Maroux, P., Pautasso, C. (eds.) ICWE 2016. LNCS, vol. 9671, pp. 317–334. Springer, Cham (2016). https://doi.org/10.1007/978-3-319-38791-8_18
11. Kietz, J.U., Maedche, A., Volz, R.: A method for semi-automatic ontology acquisition from a corporate intranet. In: 12th International Conference on Knowledge Engineering and Knowledge Management (EKAW 2000) (2000)
12. Kilgarriff, A., Rosenzweig, J.: English senseval: report and results. In: 2nd International Conference on Language Resources and Evaluation (LREC 2000). ELRA (2000)
13. Liu, Q., Zhang, H., Zeng, Y., Huang, Z., Wu, Z.: Content attention model for aspect based sentiment analysis. In: 27th International World Wide Web Conference (WWW 2018), pp. 1023–1032. ACM (2018)

14. Maedche, A., Staab, S.: Semi-automatic engineering of ontologies from text. In: 12th International Conference on Software Engineering and Knowledge Engineering (SEKE 2000), pp. 231–239 (2000)

15. Manning, C.D.: Part-of-speech tagging from 97% to 100%: is it time for some linguistics? In: Gelbukh, A.F. (ed.) CICLing 2011. LNCS, vol. 6608, pp. 171–189. Springer, Heidelberg (2011). https://doi.org/10.1007/978-3-642-19400-9_14

16. Meijer, K., Frasincar, F., Hogenboom, F.: A semantic approach for extracting domain taxonomies from text. Decis. Support Syst. **62**, 78–93 (2014)

17. Meskele, D., Frasincar, F.: ALDONA: A hybrid solution for sentence-level aspect-based sentiment analysis using a lexicalised domain ontology and a neural attention model. In: 34th Symposium on Applied Computing (SAC 2019), pp. 2489–2496. ACM (2019)

18. Mihalcea, R.: SemCor 3.0 (2019). https://web.eecs.umich.edu/~mihalcea/downloads.html#semcor

19. Ramos, J., et al.: Using TF-IDF to determine word relevance in document queries. In: 1st instructional Conference on Machine Learning (iCML 2003), vol. 242, pp. 133–142 (2003)

20. Sanderson, M., Croft, W.B.: Deriving concept hierarchies from text. In: 22nd Annual International ACM SIGIR Conference on Research and Development in Information Retrieval (SIGIR 1999), pp. 206–213. ACM (1999)

21. Schouten, K., Frasincar, F.: The benefit of concept-based features for sentiment analysis. In: Gandon, F., Cabrio, E., Stankovic, M., Zimmermann, A. (eds.) SemWebEval 2015. CCIS, vol. 548, pp. 223–233. Springer, Cham (2015). https://doi.org/10.1007/978-3-319-25518-7_19

22. Schouten, K., Frasincar, F.: Survey on aspect-level sentiment analysis. IEEE Trans. Knowl. Data Eng. **28**(3), 813–830 (2016)

23. Schouten, K., Frasincar, F.: Ontology-driven sentiment analysis of product and service aspects. In: Gangemi, A., et al. (eds.) ESWC 2018. LNCS, vol. 10843, pp. 608–623. Springer, Cham (2018). https://doi.org/10.1007/978-3-319-93417-4_39

24. Vasilescu, F., Langlais, P., Lapalme, G.: Evaluating variants of the lesk approach for disambiguating words. In: 4th International Conference on Language Resources and Evaluation (LREC 2004). ELRA (2004)

25. Wallaart, O., Frasincar, F.: A hybrid approach for aspect-based sentiment analysis using a lexicalized domain ontology and attentional neural models. In: Hitzler, P., et al. (eds.) ESWC 2019. LNCS, vol. 11503, pp. 363–378. Springer, Cham (2019). https://doi.org/10.1007/978-3-030-21348-0_24

26. Zafar, B., Cochez, M., Qamar, U.: Using distributional semantics for automatic taxonomy induction. In: 14th International Conference on Frontiers of Information Technology (FIT 2016), pp. 348–353. IEEE (2016)

27. Zheng, S., Xia, R.: Left-center-right separated neural network for aspect-based sentiment analysis with rotatory attention. arXiv preprint arXiv:1802.00892 (2018)

Keyword Search over RDF Using Document-Centric Information Retrieval Systems

Giorgos Kadilierakis[1,2], Pavlos Fafalios[1(✉)] (iD), Panagiotis Papadakos[1,2] (iD), and Yannis Tzitzikas[1,2] (iD)

[1] Information Systems Laboratory, FORTH-ICS, Heraklion, Greece
kadilier@csd.uoc.gr, {fafalios,papadako,tzitzik}@ics.forth.gr
[2] Computer Science Department, University of Crete, Heraklion, Greece

Abstract. For ordinary users, the task of accessing knowledge graphs through structured query languages like SPARQL is rather demanding. As a result, various approaches exploit the simpler and widely used keyword-based search paradigm, either by translating keyword queries to structured queries, or by adopting classical information retrieval (IR) techniques. In this paper, we study and adapt `Elasticsearch`, an out-of-the-box document-centric IR system, for supporting keyword search over RDF datasets. Contrary to other works that mainly retrieve entities, we opt for retrieving triples, due to their expressiveness and informativeness. We specify the set of functional requirements and study the emerging questions related to the selection and weighting of the triple data to index, and the structuring and ranking of the retrieved results. Finally, we perform an extensive evaluation of the different factors that affect the IR performance for four different query types. The reported results are promising and offer useful insights on how different `Elasticsearch` configurations affect the retrieval effectiveness and efficiency.

1 Introduction

The Web of Data currently contains thousands of RDF datasets available online that includes cross-domain KBs like DBpedia and Wikidata, domain specific repositories like DrugBank and MarineTLO, as well as Markup data through schema.org (see [17] for a recent survey). These datasets are queried through structured query languages (SPARQL), however this is quite complex for ordinary users. Ordinary users are acquainted with keyword search due to the widely used web search engines. Faceted search system is another popular paradigm for interactive query formulation, however even such systems (see [24] for a survey) need a keyword search engine as an entry point to the information space. We conclude that an effective method for keyword search over RDF is indispensable.

© Springer Nature Switzerland AG 2020
A. Harth et al. (Eds.): ESWC 2020, LNCS 12123, pp. 121–137, 2020.
https://doi.org/10.1007/978-3-030-49461-2_8

At the same time we observe a widespread use of out-of-the-box IR systems, like `Elasticsearch`, in different contexts. To this end in this paper we investigate how such existing document-centric Information Retrieval Systems (IRSs), can be used for enabling keyword search over arbitrary RDF datasets, and how they perform compared to dedicated keyword search systems for RDF. Towards this aim, we study the following relevant questions: (a) how to index an RDF dataset, (b) what data we should rank and how, and (c) how the search results should be presented. In this work, we study and propose various methods for tackling the above questions over the popular IR system `Elasticsearch`, and report extensive evaluation results in terms of their effectiveness and efficiency.

The source code of our implementation is available on GitHub as an indexing service[1] and a search API[2]. We also provide a demo named `Elas4RDF`[3] on top of these services over the DBpedia dataset, where the services are configured based on the most effective options reported in this work.

The rest of the paper is organized as follows: Sect. 2 describes the related background, requirements and challenges, Sect. 3 discusses the related work, and Sect. 4 details our adaptation of `Elasticsearch` for RDF. Finally, Sect. 5 discusses the evaluation results, while Sect. 6 concludes the paper and identifies issues for further research.

2   Problem Statement and Requirements

Section 2.1 describes the background and the main objective, Sect. 2.2 discusses the requirements, and Sect. 2.3 identifies the rising questions and challenges.

2.1   Background and Objective

We first define the notions of *RDF triple* and *RDF dataset*. Consider an infinite set of URI references $\mathcal{U}$, an infinite set of blank nodes $\mathcal{B}$ (anonymous resources), and an infinite set of literals $\mathcal{L}$. A *triple* $\langle s, p, o \rangle \in (\mathcal{U} \cup \mathcal{B}) \times \mathcal{U} \times (\mathcal{U} \cup \mathcal{L} \cup \mathcal{B})$ is called an RDF triple, where s is the subject, p the predicate, and o the object of the triple. An RDF dataset (or RDF graph) is a finite set of RDF triples. These triples usually describe information for a set of entities E (subject or object URIs), like persons, locations, etc. Figure 1 depicts an example of a small RDF graph describing three albums of *The Beatles* band. It contains 16 triples, involving 4 entity URIs (black nodes), 2 class URIs (white nodes), and 8 literals (gray nodes). Among the 8 literals, 7 are strings (free text) and 1 is a number.

Our objective is to allow a user submit a free-text query q and get back the most relevant data, for a given set of RDF triples T.

---

[1] https://github.com/SemanticAccessAndRetrieval/Elas4RDF-index.
[2] https://github.com/SemanticAccessAndRetrieval/Elas4RDF-search.
[3] https://demos.isl.ics.forth.gr/elas4rdf.

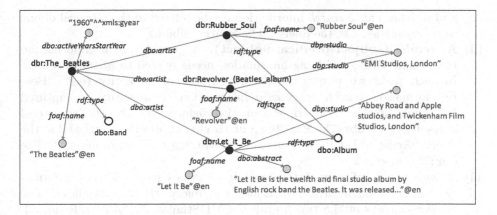

Fig. 1. An example of a small RDF graph.

2.2 Requirements

We consider the following three *functional requirements*:

- *Unrestricted RDF datasets.* A valid RDF dataset contains any set of valid RDF triples. We do not presuppose knowledge of the ontology/schema for describing the underlying data. Thus, triples describing the data schema may not exist. In addition, the dataset might not contain human-friendly URIs.
- *Unrestricted keyword-based/free-text queries.* The only input is a free-text query describing any type of information need (e.g., retrieving an entity, attributes of an entity, etc.). We do not consider query operators like AND/OR, wildcards, the ability to search in specific indexed fields, phrasal queries, or any other input specified at query-time.
- *Exploitation of an existing IR system.* We do not aim at building a new IR system. Instead we want to use an existing widely-used system, exploit its functionalities, and tune it for retrieving RDF data. Whenever possible, we should use its default settings. Any configuration should be made only if this is required by the nature of the RDF data, but without considering any information about the topic or domain of the indexed dataset.

2.3 Challenges

We can identify four basic challenges of keyword search over RDF data:

Challenge 1: Deciding on the Retrieval Unit. Contrary to the classic IR task where the *retrieval unit* is an unstructured or semi-structured textual document, an RDF dataset contains highly-structured data in the form of RDF triples, where each triple consists of three elements: *subject, predicate* and *object*. There are three main options to consider regarding the *retrieval unit*:

(i) **An *entity* corresponding to a single URI.** An RDF dataset usually describes information for a set of resources (e.g., persons or locations). Such a resource can be found either in the subject and/or the object of the triple, and satisfies *entity search* information needs, related to the retrieval of one or more entities, like the query "The Beatles albums".

(ii) **A *triple* (subject-predicate-object).** It provides more information than single URIs, satisfying information needs related to *attribute search*. In such tasks we want to find an attribute of an entity (e.g., "Beatles formation year"), or general information of an entity as captured by string literals. The triple can also help verify the correctness of a result, e.g., (dbr:The_Beatles, dbo:artist, dbr:Let_It_be) for the query "Artist of Let It Be", instead of returning the URI of an entity like dbr:The_Beatles.

(iii) **A *subgraph* (of size *l* triples).** It describes more complex information than a single triple. Consider the query "Beatles studios". The answer consists of the two literals ("EMI Studios...", "Abbey Road..."), connected to the Beatles' albums *Revolver* and *Rubber Soul* through the property dbp:studio, which in turn are connected to *The Beatles* entity through the property dbo:artist. Thus, a correct candidate answer consists of a path or *subgraph* of two triples: <dbr:The_Beatles, dbo:artist, dbr:Rubber_Soul> and <dbr:Rubber_Soul, dbp:studio, "EMI Studios, London">.

Challenge 2: Selecting the Data to Index. An RDF dataset contains elements of different types: i) resource identifiers (URIs/URLs), ii) string literals, iii) numerical and boolean literals, iv) date literals, and v) unnamed elements (blank nodes) that are used for connecting other elements. Types ii–iv are all literals, so there is no need for any special preprocessing, while blank nodes (type v) can be ignored. With respect to type i, the last part of a URI usually reveals the name of the corresponding entity or resource, and is rather useful after some pre-processing (e.g., replacing underscores with space). The domain of the URI usually reveals the knowledge base it belongs to, e.g., DBpedia, and its middle part can reveal the type of the resource (e.g., class, property, etc.), which can be useful for more experienced users. If the retrieval unit is an *entity*, one can index (parts of) its URI as well as all its outgoing properties that provide characteristics and more information about the entity. If the retrieval unit is a *triple*, one can just index all of its parts (subject, predicate, object), or choose to index additional data about the subject and object of the triple, e.g., literal properties like the rdfs:label. Finally, if we consider a *subgraph* as the retrieval unit, then the data to index depends on whether the subgraph has a constant size, independently of the query, or its size is selected dynamically. For the former, one storage-inefficient option is to index all possible subgraphs of size *l*. Thus, a more flexible approach is to index single triples and select the *l* triples that form a subgraph during the retrieval process.

Challenge 3: Weighting the Indexed Fields. Deciding on the importance of each indexed field may be another thing to consider. By assigning weights, important fields can affect more the final ranking. For example, we may assign higher weights to URI's containing certain properties (e.g., label, comment, etc.), or to literals over URIs. By allowing the adjustment of weights of the various fields at query time, we can fine-tune the IRS's query evaluator module at run-time, offering better results for easily identifiable query types (e.g., Q&A queries).

Challenge 4: Structuring the Results. The final challenge is to decide on how to structure and show the results page. One option is to follow a classical IR approach and show a top-K ranked list of individual results (i.e., entities, triples or subgraphs), and its metadata (e.g., relevance score) through a faceted search UI. Another option is to show a top-K graph which depicts how the individual results (entities, triples, or subgraphs), are connected to each other.

We study all these challenges as parameters of `Elasticsearch` (see Sect. 4).

3 Related Work

Keyword search over RDF data can be supported either by translating keyword queries to structured (SPARQL) queries (like in [8,15,22,23]), or by building or adapting a dedicated IRS using classical IR methods for indexing and retrieval.

Since our work falls under the second direction, below we report related works and showcase the difference of our approach. Such systems construct the required indexing structures either from scratch or by employing existing IR engines (e.g., Lucene and Solr), and adapt the notion of a virtual document for the structured RDF data. Usually, they rank the results (entities or subgraphs) according to commonly used IR ranking functions. One of the first such systems was Falcon [2], where each document corresponds to the textual description of the maximum subset of connected RDF triples, while the ranking of the documents is done by mapping keyword terms to documents through cosine similarity and the popularity of each document. In the entity search track of SemSearch10 workshop[4], a number of related systems were presented and evaluated [4,5,16]. Most of those systems are based on variations of the TD-IDF weighting adapted for RDF data, and return a ranked list of entities (i.e., URIs). An approach that uses inverted lists over terms that appear as predicates or objects of triples is described in [3], where the keyword query is translated to a logical expression that returns the ids of the matching entities. Another direction in the bibliography is to return ranked subgraphs instead of relevant entity URIs. For example, in [18] documents represent a literal or a resource, and external knowledge is used to explore relations between the keywords and the dataset components, while the returned subgraphs are ranked using a TF-based function. In [7] the returned subgraphs are computed using statistical language models based on the likelihood estimation of generating the query from each subgraph.

In current state-of-the-art approaches though, RDF data are ranked based on extensions of the BM25 model. For example, BM25F [1,19], takes into account the various fields of a virtual document and computes the normalized term-frequency using the field's length instead of the document's. Further, the recent work described in [6] introduces the TSA + VDP keyword search system, where

---

[4] http://km.aifb.kit.edu/ws/semsearch10/.

initially, the system builds offline an index of documents over a set of subgraphs via a breadth-first search method, while at query-time, it returns a ranked list of these documents based on a BM25 model.

Regarding the retrieval unit, we have seen that most works return either URIs or subgraphs. However, the concept of triple ranking has also emerged in works that do not directly target the task of keyword search over RDF data. For example, the TripleRank algorithm presented in [9] ranks authorities in the Semantic Web, in the same manner as PageRank for the WWW. In [20], the authors propose a learning to rank framework with relation-independent features that aims at developing ranking models that measure triple significance. For a given relation type as input (e.g., *profession*) the computed score of each triple measures how well the triple captures the relevance of the statement that it expresses, compared to other triples from the same relation.

With respect to works that make use of Elasticsearch, LOTUS [11,12] is a text-based entry point to the Linked Data cloud. It makes use of Elasticsearch for supporting keyword search, offering various approaches for matching and ranking the relevant information. Its focus is on scalability and does not study how the different matching and ranking methods affect the retrieval performance. Elasticsearch has been also used for indexing and querying Linked Bibliographic Data in JSON-LD format [14], while the *ElasticSearch RDF River Plugin*[5] uses it as a way to index URIs from various endpoints and enrich the indexed documents with RDF data.[6]

Positioning. In our work, we make use of Elasticsearch for supporting schema-agnostic keyword search over a set of RDF triples, in order to return a ranked list of triples. We also provide ways of constructing a ranked list of entities over this list of triples. Complementary to the approach followed by LOTUS [11,12], which focuses on the scalability and efficiency of query evaluation using Elasticsearch, we study in detail how the various configuration options affect the retrieval accuracy. We aim at gaining a better understanding on how Elasticsearch performs over RDF, so that anyone can use it out-of-the-box over any RDF dataset. Our experimental evaluation (Sect. 5) showed that, a proper (schema-agnostic) configuration in Elasticsearch provides a retrieval accuracy similar to that of dataset-specific approaches built from scratch for the task per se. To our knowledge, our work is the first that studies how the different indexing and retrieval options in Elasticsearch affect the retrieval accuracy.

4   Adapting a Document-Centric IRS for RDF

Here, we describe the selected IRS (Sect. 4.1) and provide an overview of our approach (Sect. 4.2). Then, we detail the various options we experimented with, regarding indexing (Sect. 4.3), retrieval (Sect. 4.4) and ranking (Sect. 4.5).

---

[5] https://github.com/eea/eea.elasticsearch.river.rdf#main-features.
[6] https://www.opensemanticsearch.org/connector/rdf.

4.1   Considered IRS: Elasticsearch

Elasticsearch is a highly-scalable, open-source, full text search engine that allows to store and search big volumes of data. It is based on Apache Lucene and offers a distributed architecture of inverted indexes.

Basic Concepts. All data in Elasticsearch are stored in *indices* containing different types of *documents* (units of search and index) that Elasticsearch can store, update and search. Each document is a JSON object stored with a unique ID that contains a set of *fields*. Each field is a key-value pair of various datatypes (e.g., strings, JSON objects, etc.), organized by a *mapping* type for each index. In our work, we create different mappings depending on the approach we follow. For each field, we need to specify a *type* (e.g., *text*) and an *analyzer*, and also define the used *tokenizer*, *stemmer* and *stopword-list*. Each *index* can be split into multiple *shards*, and each shard can be replicated using *replicas*. A *node* contains multiple shards/replicas and if the number of nodes is greater than one, Elasticsearch balances the load equally. Finally, a single *cluster* may contain one or more nodes that run in parallel and serve multiple requests.

Query Domain Specific Language (DSL). Elasticsearch has a powerful Query DSL which supports advanced search features on top of Lucene's query syntax. There are two main types of query clauses: (a) *filter-context* which answers whether a query matches a document (exact-match), and (b) *query-context* which answers how well does a document matches a query using a relevance score (best-match). Since we are interested in free-text search that provides a ranked-list of results, we will solely be using *query-context* clauses. Queries can be further categorised in *match queries* and *multi-match queries*. A *match query* is executed over a single field, while a *multi-match query* allows searching upon multiple fields. Depending on the way it is executed internally, a *multi-match query* is categorized in: (i) *best-fields*, (ii) *most-fields* and (iii) *cross-fields*. Types *(i)* and *(ii)* follow a field-centric approach, evaluating all query keywords on each field before combining scores from each field. Type (i) assigns as document score the score of the best-matched field, while for type (ii), the final score is the average score of all field scores. Field-centric approaches appear to be problematic in cases where the query terms are scattered across multiple fields (e.g., across the triple's subject, predicate and object). A term-centric approach addresses this issue by searching a query term-by-term on each field. This is implemented in type (iii) where *cross-fields* searches each term across fields, favoring queries whose answer is scattered across multiple fields.

4.2   Overview of the Approach

In this section we describe how we cope with the challenges discussed in Sect. 2.3, and provide an overview of our approach and implementation.

With respect to Challenge 1 (*deciding on the retrieval unit*), we opt for high flexibility and thus consider *triple* as the retrieval unit. A triple is more informative than an entity, provides a means to verify the correctness of a piece of information, since it is closer to Q&A, and offers flexibility on how to structure and present the final results (Challenge 4). For example, one can use various aggregation methods over a ranked list of retrieved triples, for providing a ranked list of entities for entity search or showing graphs of connected entities. Moreover in *RDF*, a triple can be viewed as the simplest representation of a fact. This property is one of the major reasons we chose *triple* as our *virtual document*.

Regarding Challenge 2 (*selecting the data to index*), we experiment and evaluate different approaches on what data to consider for each virtual document. Our *baseline* approach, considers only data from the triple itself (i.e., text extracted from the subject, object and predicate). This simple approach, may appear problematic in a dataset where URI's are IDs, and thus not descriptive of the underlying resource. As a result, we also extend the *baseline* approach to exploit information in the neighborhood of the triple's elements. For example, we consider important outgoing properties such as *rdfs:label* and *rdfs:comment*, and evaluate how various extensions affect the results quality and the index size.

With respect to Challenge 3 (*weighting the indexed fields*), we do not apply any predefined weights in the indexed fields, but instead, adjust the weights of the various fields at query time. In this way, the IRS's query module evaluator can be fine-tuned at run-time for specific query types (e.g., Q&A queries).

Finally, for Challenge 4 *(results structuring)*, we opt for a ranked-list of results since this is the way that traditionally IRS present the results to the user. On top of the ranked-list of triples, we propose a method for mapping the retrieved triples into a ranked list of entities, based on the appearance of URIs either in the subject or the object. Then, the entities are ranked based on a weighted gain factor of the ranking order of the triples in which they appear, similar to the discounted cumulative gain used in the nDCG metric [13]. The evaluation of different visualization methods (e.g., list of resources, top-K graphs, etc.) and the corresponding user experience go beyond the scope of this paper.

Below, we provide details of the different approaches we experimented with for indexing, retrieval and ranking of RDF triples in `Elasticsearch`.

4.3   Indexing

We try variations of two different indexing approaches, the *baseline index* that considers only the triple itself, and the *extended index* that extends the *baseline index* with additional descriptive information about the triple components.

Baseline Index. This index uses only information that exists in the triple's three components (subject, predicate, object). In case the value of one of the components is a URI, the URI is tokenized into keywords, based on a special tokenizer that extracts the last part of the URI (i.e., the text after the last '/' or '#') that usually describes the underlying resource, and its namespace parts.

Extended Index. The *extended index*, includes additional information when one of the triple components is a resource (URI). This is particularly useful when the last part of the URIs are not descriptive of the corresponding resources, and thus not useful for querying. We experiment with three different variations that include the value(s) of: i) the `rdfs:label` property, that usually contains the name of the corresponding resource, ii) the `rdfs:comment` property, which is very descriptive of the underlying resource, and provides much more information than the `rdfs:label`, and iii) all the outgoing properties of the resource. The first two approaches are useful when we are aware of the schema(s) used to describe the data. The latter one, includes all the information that describes the resource. However it can highly increase the size of the index and introduce noise.

4.4 Retrieval

We experimented with various *query types*, *weighting methods* and *similarity models* offered by `Elasticsearch`.

Query Types. Since our indexes contain different sets of fields, we can use multiple types of `Elasticsearch` queries. We study the following two approaches: (i) *single-field*: a single field is created containing the index data, e.g., a super-field containing all keywords describing the subject, the predicate and the object, and (ii) *multi-field*: multiple fields are created, each one containing a specific piece of information, e.g., one field for the subject keywords, one for the predicate keywords and one for the object keywords.

Weighting. Another factor for improving relevance at query retrieval time is applying weights on the various fields. Boosting fields only makes sense upon *multi-field* queries, for specifying the importance of a field over another. For example, we may define that the field containing the object keywords is twice more important than the fields containing the subject and predicate keywords. We experimented with different weighting approaches, by weighting more either: i) only the subject keywords; ii) only the object keywords; iii) both the subject and the object keywords.

Similarity Models (and Parameterization). A similarity model defines how matching documents are scored. In `Elasticsearch` the default model is Okapi BM25, which is a TF/IDF based similarity measure. BM25 has an upper limit in boosting terms with a high TF, meaning that it follows a nonlinear term frequency saturation. Parameter *k1* can control how quickly this saturation will happen based on the TF value. The default value is *1.2* and higher values result in slower saturation. In our case, since the text in our fields is generally short, *k1* will probably perform better towards lower values. The other tuning option of BM25 is the field-length normalization, that can be controlled with parameter *b* which has a default value of *0.75*. Shorter fields gain more weight than longer fields by increasing *b*, and this can be used to boost a short descriptive resource over a long literal inside an object field.

Another available similarity module in `Elasticsearch` is *DFR*, a probabilistic model that measures the divergence from randomness. Parameters include a basic randomness model definition, using inverse term frequency, and a two-level normalization. Language models supported by `Elasticsearch` include the *LM-Dirichlet* similarity, a bayesian smoothing that accepts the μ parameter, and the *LM-Jelinek Mercer* similarity, which can be parameterized with λ. We experimented with all the above-mentioned similarity models.

4.5 Grouping and Final Ranking

At this point we have performed a keyword query and have retrieved a ranked list of triples (1st-level results). Now, we need to decide on how we will present the results to the user. One approach is to group the retrieved triples based on entities (i.e. subject and object URIs), and return a ranked list of entities (2nd-level results) to the user, where each entity is associated with a ranked list of triples. Such an approach offers flexibility on how to display the results to the user, and allows to evaluate the different configurations we experimented with using as ground truth existing datasets for entity search [10] (more below).

For ranking the derived entities, we exploit the ranking order of the triples based on a weighted factor. Thereby, the gain that each entity accumulates works in a logarithmic reduction manner, as in the widely used Discounted Cumulative Gain (DCG) metric [13]. Specifically, each entity collects the discounted gain of each triple based on the ranking position that it appeared on the *1st-level results* ranking. The final score of an entity e for a keyword-query q is given by the formula:

$$score(e, q) = \sum_{t_i}^{t_n} \frac{2^{(n\_score_i)} - 1}{\log_2(i + 1)} \tag{1}$$

where t is the ranked list of triples that the entity e appears in, and n_score_i is the normalized score of triple i in that list for the query q. Since `Elasticsearch` deliberately scores documents with any number > 0, we use *minmax* normalization for the results in list t.

Table 1. Query categories in the 'DBpedia Entity' test collection for entity search.

Category	Description	Example	# queries
SemSearch_ES	Named entity queries	"brooklyn bridge"	113
INEX-LD	IR-style keyword queries	"electronic music genres"	99
QALD2	Natural language questions	"Who is the mayor of Berlin?"	115
ListSearch	Entity-list queries	"Professional sports teams in New York"	140

5 Evaluation

In Sect. 5.1 we describe the setup and the dataset of the evaluation, while Sect. 5.2 and Sect. 5.3 report retrieval effectiveness, and space and time efficiency, respectively. Finally, Sect. 5.4 summarizes the key findings.

5.1   Test Collection and Setup

For our experiments we used the DBpedia-Entity test collection for entity search [10], which is based on a DBpedia dump of 2015–10. The collection contains a set of heterogeneous keyword queries along with relevance judgments obtained using crowdsourcing. There are four categories of queries: i) named-entity queries, ii) IR-style keyword queries, iii) natural language questions, and iv) entity-list queries. Table 1 provides an example and the total number of queries for each query category. In total, over 49K query-entity pairs are labeled using a three-point scale (0: irrelevant, 1: relevant, and 2: highly relevant).

After following the instructions in [10] for building the RDF dataset and removing duplicates, we end up with a collection of approximately 400M triples. In addition to this *full-collection*, we also generated a subset of 15 million triples that forms our *mini-collection* by extracting all judged entity-based triples ($\approx$6M) and randomly adding an extra of 9M unjudged triples. The mini-collection allows us to run a large number of experiments and study how the different factors discussed in the previous section affect the quality of the retrieved results.

We deployed `Elasticsearch` 6.4 as a single node with max heap size set at 32 GB and 6 physical cores running on Debian 9.6. Using Python's multiprocessing pool we initiate 12 indexing instances with a bulk-size of 3,500 documents each. These numbers were assigned empirically based on the collection and our hardware. The number of shards is also assigned empirically and it alters between the *baseline* and the *extended* index. For the *baseline* we select 2 shards while depending on the *extended* approach we alter between 3 and 4 shards.

5.2   Quality of Retrieval

Our objective is to measure how the following parameters affect the quality of search results: i) the various decisions regarding the indexed triple data, ii) the used `Elasticsearch` query type, iii) the weighting of the fields, iv) the additional indexed data for each triple, and iv) the available similarity models in `Elasticsearch`. We first study the effect of all these parameters using the *mini-collection* and then evaluate the best performing methods on the *full-collection*. For measuring the quality, we make use of the evaluation metric nDCG in positions 100 and 10, as in [10].

Examining Field Separation and Query Type (Baseline-Index). We start by examining how each part of the triple (subject, predicate, object) and the different query types (single field, multi-field) affect the quality of the retrieved results using the baseline index, i.e., without considering additional information about the triple subject, predicate or object. Specifically, we examine the following cases: i) *baseline (s)*: only the keywords of the subject are indexed, ii) *baseline (p)*: only the keywords of the predicate are indexed, iii) *baseline (o)*: only the keywords of the object are indexed, iv) *baseline (spo)*: the keywords of all triple's elements are indexed as a single field, v) *baseline (s)(p)(o)*: the keywords of all triple's elements are indexed as different fields. Single-field queries are executed using the *match query* retrieval method while multi-fields using *multi-match query* and *cross-fields*.

Table 2 shows the results. As expected, better results are obtained when all triple elements are indexed. The use of a super-field (spo) seems to perform slightly better in average than using distinct fields, mostly for the query types of SemSearch & INEX-LD. However, the ListSearch type has the best performance when using only the object field, while the Q&A type when the three fields are distinguished. Recall that, as described in Sect. 4.1, the cross-fields query evaluation type of Elasticsearch favors queries whose answer is scattered across multiple fields. This means that in the Q&A query type, the best results come from more than one fields. With respect to the distinct triple elements, we see that considering only the object provides the best results, outperforming the case where we consider only the subject, by more than 14%. This means that the answer usually exists in the object part of the triple. It is interesting also that considering only the object provides better results than considering all the triple elements for the ListSearch queries. Finally, considering only the predicate provides a very poor performance, being relevant mostly to the Q&A and ListSearch query types.

Examining Field Weighting (Baseline-Index). Multiple-field queries allow specifying custom weights, enabling us to boost the importance of specific fields. We examine the following cases: i) *baseline* $(s)^2(p)(o)$: doubling the weight of subject, ii) *baseline* $(s)(p)(o)^2$: doubling the weight of object, and iii) *baseline* $(s)^2(p)(o)^2$: doubling the weight of both subject and object. Table 3 shows the results. We see that doubling the weight of the object keywords provides the best results on average, slightly outperforming both *baseline (spo)* and *baseline* $(s)(p)(o)$ @100 (cf. Table 2). On the contrary, we notice that doubling the importance of the subject keywords drops the performance by around 10%. Thus, we can conclude that, for this collection, object keywords are more useful for keyword searching than subject keywords.

Table 2. nDCG@100 (@10) for different field separation and query type approaches.

Method	SemSearch_ES	INEX-LD	QALD2	ListSearch	AVG
Baseline (s)	0.48 (0.46)	0.28 (0.26)	0.30 (0.20)	0.30 (**0.30**)	0.340 (0.270)
Baseline (p)	0.02 (0.00)	0.04 (0.01)	0.06 (0.03)	0.07 (0.03)	0.04 (0.01)
Baseline (o)	0.63 (0.50)	0.43 (0.30)	0.42 (0.26)	**0.47** (0.26)	0.485 (0.330)
Baseline (spo)	**0.70 (0.61)**	**0.45 (0.33)**	0.43 (0.30)	0.44 (0.26)	**0.505 (0.372)**
Baseline (s)(p)(o)	0.65 (0.55)	0.44 (0.32)	**0.45 (0.31)**	0.46 (0.28)	0.500 (0.358)

Extending the Index. We now study the case where we extend the index with additional information about the triple's elements. We consider the best performing weighting method, i.e. $(s)(p)(o)^2$, and examine the cases described in Sect. 4.3: i) *extended-label*, that includes the rdfs:label property value of the subject and object URIs as two different fields, ii) *extended-comment*, that includes the rdfs:comment property value of the subject and object URIs as two different fields, and iii) *extended-outgoing*, that includes the values of all the

Table 3. nDCG@100 (@10) for different *field weighting* approaches.

Method	SemSearch_ES	INEX-LD	QALD2	ListSearch	AVG
Baseline $(s)^2$ (p)(o)	0.54 (0.50)	0.36 (0.31)	0.36 (0.28)	0.36 (0.23)	0.405 (0.330)
Baseline $(s)(p)(o)^2$	**0.67 (0.55)**	**0.45 (0.31)**	**0.44 (0.28)**	**0.48 (0.28)**	**0.509 (0.355)**
Baseline $(s)^2(p)(o)^2$	0.64 (0.54)	0.44 **(0.32)**	**0.44** (0.29)	0.46 (0.26)	0.495 **(0.355)**

Table 4. nDCG@100 (@10) for different approaches to *extend* the index.

Method	SemSearch_ES	INEX-LD	QALD2	ListSearch	AVG
Extended-label $(s)(p)(o)^2$	0.67 **(0.56)**	0.45 (0.31)	0.44 (0.28)	0.48 (0.28)	0.510 (0.358)
Extended-comment $(s)(p)(o)^2$	**0.68 (0.56)**	**0.53 (0.37)**	**0.50 (0.34)**	**0.54 (0.34)**	**0.562 (0.403)**
Extended-outgoing $(s)(p)(o)^2$	0.61 (0.52)	0.45 (0.34)	0.43 (0.32)	0.49 (0.33)	0.495 (0.378)

Table 5. nDCG@100 (@10) for different similarity models.

Module	SemSearch_ES	INEX-LD	QALD2	ListSearch	AVG
BM25	0.68 (0.56)	0.53 (0.37)	**0.50 (0.34)**	0.54 (0.34)	0.562 (0.403)
DFR	**0.72 (0.61)**	**0.55 (0.38)**	**0.50** (0.33)	0.53 (0.33)	0.575 (0.412)
LM Dirichlet	0.42 (0.38)	0.31 (0.26)	0.29 (0.23)	0.31 (0.23)	0.333 (0.275)
LM Jelinek-Mercer	0.71 (0.59)	**0.55 (0.39)**	**0.50 (0.34)**	**0.55 (0.35)**	**0.578 (0.417)**

outgoing properties of the subject and object URIs as two different fields. The object is enriched only if it is a URI. We do not enrich the predicate because the used collection does not include triples that describe the property URIs.

Table 4 shows the results. We see that including the comment property improves performance by more than 5%. On the contrary, including all outgoing properties drops the performance from 0.510 to 0.495, which means that this extension method introduces noise. With respect to the label property, we see that performance is almost the same. This is an expected result given that, in the DBpedia collection, for the majority of resources the last part of the URI is similar to the value of the rdfs:label property.

Examining Different Similarity Models. We now study the effect of the different similarity models offered by Elasticsearch (on their default setting), as described in Sect. 4.4: BM25 ($k1 = 1.2$, $b = 0.75$), DFR (basic model: g, after effect: l, normalization: z), LM Dirichlet ($\mu = 2,000$), and LM Jelinek-Mercer ($\lambda = 0.1$). Since the performance of a similarity model is highly affected by the indexed data, we consider the best performing *extended* method of our previous experiments, i.e., *extended-comment $(s)(p)(o)^2$*.

Table 5 shows the results. We notice that three of the models (BM25, DFR, and LM Jelinek-Mercer) have a very similar performance, with LM Jelinek-Mercer outperforming the other two in all query categories apart from Sem-Search_ES, the simplest category, for which DFR provides the best results.

Comparative Results on the Full Collection. We now examine the performance of our approach on the full collection and compare it to a set of other available approaches in the bibliography that focus on entity search in DBpedia.

Specifically, we consider the best performing methods for baseline and extended approaches: *baseline (s)(p)(o)^2* and *extended-comment (s)(p)(o)^2* respectively, with both BM25 and LM Jelinek-Mercer similarity models.

Since the proposed methods do not require training, we compare them with the *unsupervised* methods of [10] (BM25, PRMS, MLM-all, LM, SDM). Note also that all the methods in [10] have been particularly designed for *entity search in DBpedia* and, as described in the dataset's github repository[7], a set of more than 25 DBpedia-specific properties was collected for representing an entity and creating the index. On the contrary, we provide general methods that consider an existing IRS (using triple as the retrieval unit), that do not require special dataset-specific information for building the indexes, apart from the use of a very common property, like `rdfs:comment`.

Table 6. nDCG@100 (nDCG@10) results on full collection.

Method	SemSearch_ES	INEX-LD	QALD2	ListSearch	AVG
Elas4RDF$_{BL}$ BM25	0.67 (0.57)	0.45 (0.34)	0.32 (0.23)	0.37 (0.27)	0.455 (0.352)
Elas4RDF$_{EXT}$ BM25	**0.68** (**0.59**)	**0.48** (**0.38**)	**0.41** (**0.29**)	**0.43** (**0.30**)	**0.500** (**0.390**)
Elas4RDF$_{BL}$ LM Jelinek-Mercer	0.67 (0.56)	0.44 (0.32)	0.37 (0.25)	0.37 (0.25)	0.463 (0.345)
Elas4RDF$_{EXT}$ LM Jelinek-Mercer	**0.68** (**0.59**)	0.46 (0.36)	**0.41** (**0.29**)	0.41 (0.29)	0.490 (0.382)
DBpedia-Entity-v2 BM25	0.41 (0.24)	0.36 (0.27)	0.33 (0.27)	0.33 (0.21)	0.358 (0.255)
DBpedia-Entity-v2 PRMS	0.61 (0.53)	0.43 (0.36)	0.40 (0.32)	0.44 (0.37)	0.469 (0.391)
DBpedia-Entity-v2 MLM-all	0.62 (0.55)	0.45 (0.38)	0.42 (0.32)	0.46 (0.37)	0.485 (0.402)
DBpedia-Entity-v2 LM	0.65 (**0.56**)	0.47 (**0.40**)	**0.43** (**0.34**)	0.47 (0.39)	0.504 (0.418)
DBpedia-Entity-v2 SDM	**0.67** (0.55)	**0.49** (**0.40**)	**0.43** (**0.34**)	**0.49** (**0.40**)	**0.514** (**0.419**)

Table 6 shows the results. We see that, on average, `Elas4RDF` achieves the highest performance when using the extended index and BM25. Compared to the DBpedia-Entity-v2 methods, we notice that the performance of our approach is very close to the top-performing SDM method (the difference is 0.014 for nDCG@100 and 0.029 for nDCG@10). SDM performs better on average mainly because of its high performance on the ListSearch query type. This is a rather promising result, given that the DBpedia-Entity-v2 methods are tailored to the DBpedia dataset and the task per se (entity search).

---

[7] https://iai-group.github.io/DBpedia-Entity/index_details.html.

5.3   Space and Efficiency

We report the space requirements and the average query execution time of our best models for *baseline* and *extended* indexes considering the full DBpedia collection (57 GB uncompressed). The number of virtual documents in both cases is 395,569,688. The size of the baseline index is around 72 GB and that of the extended (with `rdfs:comment`) around 160 GB. We see that, as expected, the extended index requires more than 2 times the size of the baseline index. The average query execution time is around 0.7 s for the baseline method and 1.6 s for the extended and depends on the query type. We see that extending the index improves performance, however it affects the space requirements.

5.4   Executive Summary

The key findings of the aforementioned experiments are: i) all triple components contribute on achieving the highest performance; ii) object keywords seem to be more important than subject keywords, thus giving higher weight to the object fields can improve performance; iii) extending the index with additional (descriptive) information about the triple URIs improves performance; however, including all available information about the URIs (all outgoing properties) can introduce noise and drop performance; iv) the default similarity model of `Elasticsearch` (BM25) achieves a satisfactory performance; v) a proper configuration of `Elasticsearch` can provide a performance very close to that of task- and dataset-specific systems built from scratch.

6   Conclusion

The objective of this work was to investigate the use of a classic document-centric IR system, for enabling keyword search over arbitrary RDF datasets. For this study, we decided to use one of the most widely used IR systems, namely `Elasticsearch`. To this end, we specified the requirements and identified the main rising questions and issues, related to the selection of the retrieval unit and the data to index. We selected triple as our retrieval unit due to its expressiveness and informativeness, and developed a mapping of a ranked list of triples to a ranked list of entities. Then we experimented with a large number of implementation approaches, including different indexing structures, query types, field-weighting methods and similarity models offered by `Elasticsearch`. We evaluated the performance of the approaches against the *DBpedia-Entity v2* test collection. The results show that `Elasticsearch` can effectively support keyword search over RDF data if configured properly. The most effective configuration, that weights higher the object part of the triple, performs similarly to systems specifically built for retrieving entities over the DBpedia dataset. This approach is demonstrated in the publicly available `Elas4RDF` demo[8].

---

[8] https://demos.isl.ics.forth.gr/elas4rdf/.

One direction that is worth investigating, is the provision of good answers for *entity-relation* queries, i.e., queries that involve entities that are not directly connected in the indexed RDF graph but they are connected through one or more long paths of triples. In that case, different sets of unconnected triples might be retrieved, each one corresponding to an entity appearing in the query. Thus, in future we plan to study how our approach can be extended for providing answers to such type of queries. Another interesting direction for future work is the automatic detection of the query category and the application of different configuration parameters for each case. Finally, we plan to apply and evaluate our approach in domain-specific RDF datasets, e.g., ClaimsKG [21].

References

1. Blanco, R., Mika, P., Vigna, S.: Effective and efficient entity search in RDF data. In: Aroyo, L., et al. (eds.) ISWC 2011. LNCS, vol. 7031, pp. 83–97. Springer, Heidelberg (2011). https://doi.org/10.1007/978-3-642-25073-6_6
2. Cheng, G., Qu, Y.: Searching linked objects with Falcons: approach, implementation and evaluation. Int. J. Semant. Web Inf. Syst. (IJSWIS) **5**(3), 49–70 (2009)
3. Delbru, R., Campinas, S., Tummarello, G.: Searching web data: an entity retrieval and high-performance indexing model. J. Web Semant. **10**, 33–58 (2012)
4. Delbru, R., Rakhmawati, N.A., Tummarello, G.: Sindice at SemSearch 2010. In: WWW. Citeseer (2010)
5. Demartini, G., Kärger, P., Papadakis, G., Fankhauser, P.: L3S research center at the SemSearch 2010 evaluation for entity search track. In: Proceedings of the 3rd International Semantic Search Workshop (2010)
6. Dosso, D., Silvello, G.: A scalable virtual document-based keyword search system for RDF datasets. In: Proceedings of the 42nd International ACM SIGIR Conference on Research and Development in Information Retrieval, pp. 965–968 (2019)
7. Elbassuoni, S., Blanco, R.: Keyword search over RDF graphs. In: International Conference on Information and knowledge management, pp. 237–242. ACM (2011)
8. Elbassuoni, S., Ramanath, M., Schenkel, R., Weikum, G.: Searching RDF graphs with SPARQL and keywords. IEEE Data Eng. Bull. **33**(1), 16–24 (2010)
9. Franz, T., Schultz, A., Sizov, S., Staab, S.: TripleRank: ranking semantic web data by tensor decomposition. In: Bernstein, A., et al. (eds.) ISWC 2009. LNCS, vol. 5823, pp. 213–228. Springer, Heidelberg (2009). https://doi.org/10.1007/978-3-642-04930-9_14
10. Hasibi, F., et al.: DBpedia-Entity V2: a test collection for entity search. In: SIGIR, pp. 1265–1268. ACM (2017)
11. Ilievski, F., Beek, W., van Erp, M., Rietveld, L., Schlobach, S.: LOTUS: adaptive text search for big linked data. In: Sack, H., Blomqvist, E., d'Aquin, M., Ghidini, C., Ponzetto, S.P., Lange, C. (eds.) ESWC 2016. LNCS, vol. 9678, pp. 470–485. Springer, Cham (2016). https://doi.org/10.1007/978-3-319-34129-3_29
12. Ilievski, F., Beek, W., Van Erp, M., Rietveld, L., Schlobach, S.: LOTUS: linked open text unleashed. In: COLD (2015)
13. Järvelin, K., Kekäläinen, J.: Cumulated gain-based evaluation of IR techniques. ACM Trans. Inf. Syst. (TOIS) **20**(4), 422–446 (2002)
14. Johnson, T.: Indexing linked bibliographic data with JSON-LD, BibJSON and elasticsearch. Code4lib J. **19**, 1–11 (2013)

15. Lin, X., Zhang, F., Wang, D.: RDF keyword search using multiple indexes. Filomat **32**(5), 1861–1873 (2018). https://doi.org/10.2298/FIL1805861L
16. Liu, X., Fang, H.: A study of entity search in semantic search workshop. In: Proceedings of the 3rd International Semantic Search Workshop (2010)
17. Mountantonakis, M., Tzitzikas, Y.: Large-scale semantic integration of linked data: a survey. ACM Comput. Surv. (CSUR) **52**(5), 103 (2019)
18. Ouksili, H., Kedad, Z., Lopes, S., Nugier, S.: Using patterns for keyword search in RDF graphs. In: EDBT/ICDT Workshops (2017)
19. Pérez-Agüera, J.R., Arroyo, J., Greenberg, J., Iglesias, J.P., Fresno, V.: Using BM25F for semantic search. In: Proceedings of the 3rd International Semantic Search Workshop, p. 2. ACM (2010)
20. Shahshahani, M.S., Hasibi, F., Zamani, H., Shakery, A.: Towards a unified supervised approach for ranking triples of type-like relations. In: Pasi, G., Piwowarski, B., Azzopardi, L., Hanbury, A. (eds.) ECIR 2018. LNCS, vol. 10772, pp. 707–714. Springer, Cham (2018). https://doi.org/10.1007/978-3-319-76941-7_66
21. Tchechmedjiev, A., et al.: ClaimsKG: a knowledge graph of fact-checked claims. In: Ghidini, C., et al. (eds.) ISWC 2019. LNCS, vol. 11779, pp. 309–324. Springer, Cham (2019). https://doi.org/10.1007/978-3-030-30796-7_20
22. Tran, T., Cimiano, P., Rudolph, S., Studer, R.: Ontology-based interpretation of keywords for semantic search. In: Aberer, K., et al. (eds.) ASWC/ISWC 2007. LNCS, vol. 4825, pp. 523–536. Springer, Heidelberg (2007). https://doi.org/10.1007/978-3-540-76298-0_38
23. Tran, T., Wang, H., Rudolph, S., Cimiano, P.: Top-k exploration of query candidates for efficient keyword search on graph-shaped (RDF) data. In: 2009 IEEE International Conference on Data Engineering, ICDE 2009, pp. 405–416. IEEE (2009)
24. Tzitzikas, Y., Manolis, N., Papadakos, P.: Faceted exploration of RDF/S datasets: a survey. J. Intell. Inf. Syst. **48**(2), 329–364 (2016). https://doi.org/10.1007/s10844-016-0413-8

Entity Linking and Lexico-Semantic Patterns for Ontology Learning

Lama Saeeda[✉], Michal Med, Martin Ledvinka, Miroslav Blaško, and Petr Křemen

Department of Computer Science and Faculty of Electrical Engineering, Czech Technical University in Prague , Prague, Czech Republic
{lama.saeeda,michal.med,martin.ledvinka,blaskmir,petr.kremen}@fel.cvut.cz

Abstract. Ontology learning from a text written in natural language is a well-studied domain. However, the applicability of techniques for ontology learning from natural language texts is strongly dependent on the characteristics of the text corpus and the language used. In this paper, we present our work so far in entity linking and enhancing the ontology with extracted relations between concepts. We discuss the benefits of adequately designed lexico-semantic patterns in ontology learning. We propose a preliminary set of lexico-semantic patterns designed for the Czech language to learn new relations between concepts in the related domain ontology in a semi-supervised approach. We utilize data from the urban planning and development domain to evaluate the introduced technique. As a partial prototypical implementation of the stack, we present Annotace, a text annotation service that provides links between the ontology model and the textual documents in Czech.

Keywords: Entity linking · Ontology learning · Lexico-semantic patterns

1 Introduction

Ontology is an essential component for building and understanding the context of any domain of interest. For example, in urban planning and development, the master plan is a legal tool for global planning that aims to support the urban character of the various localities. It addresses the future of the city, including the development of infrastructure and areas for new constructions. Different regulations can apply to different parts of the plan, for example, building regulations. Also, it involves many actors in building and developing the plan, including urban planning experts, inhabitants, experts from the legal and regulation department, and even politicians. Communication between all these parties is not an easy process and involves a broad range of ambiguous technical terms and jargon. For this reason, it is crucial to normalize an efficient way of communication through an urban planning ontology that allows a common understanding of the technical terms that might cause confusion among all participants.

© Springer Nature Switzerland AG 2020
A. Harth et al. (Eds.): ESWC 2020, LNCS 12123, pp. 138–153, 2020.
https://doi.org/10.1007/978-3-030-49461-2_9

However, using such ontology depends directly on the availability of this ontology in the target domain. Building the ontology manually is tremendously exhaustive in terms of time and effort spent by human experts. Usually, domain experts, besides knowledge engineers, spend a lot of time revising textual resources and documents in order to build a background knowledge that supports the studied domain. This process can be enhanced by utilizing natural language processing side by side with information extraction techniques to help developing the ontology. Ontology learning from a textual corpus is the set of methods and techniques used for building an ontology from scratch, enriching, or adapting an existing ontology in a semi-automatic fashion using several knowledge and information sources [16]. These techniques are divided into two main types, linguistic and statistical approaches. In this paper, we investigate methods that support building the domain ontology based on a seed ontology and a set of domain-related documents in two main tasks:

- Document processing and entity linking task: this step enhances the documents with syntactic and semantic information. It provides links between the textual documents and the concepts that are defined in the seed ontology to add a semantic context to the processed documents. To perform this task, we introduce **Annotace**, a text annotation service that is further discussed in Sect. 4.
- Learning ontological relations task: in this step, a set of rule-based lexico-semantic patterns is used to enhance the process of learning new relations between concepts in a semi-supervised approach.

To further illustrate our approach, consider the following example taken from an urban planning document in Czech.

Cs: "Správní území Prahy členěno na lokality"
En: "Administrative territory of Prague divided into localities"

At first, the entity linking engine enhances the text with semantic information by providing links to the terms in the ontology.

Cs: "**Správní území Prahy** členěno na **lokality**" Where:
Správní území Prahy is linked to mpp[1]:správní-území-prahy and
lokality is linked to mpp:lokalita

Using this information with the following pattern written in HIEL language [14] to extract a part-whole relation from Czech text,

($subject, hasPart, $object) : −$subject : Concept COMP RB? IN? $object : Concept

reveals the relation between concepts,

mpp:správní-území-prahy *hasPart* **mpp:lokalita**

---

[1] mpp: http://onto.fel.cvut.cz/ontologies/slovnik/datovy-mpp-3.5-np/pojem/.

where "COMP", "RB?", and "IN?" are specific variables used in the pattern's context. This revealed relation then can be suggested to the user to be added to the ontology.

The rest of the paper is organized as follows. In Sect. 2, we present related works in the domain of entity linking and relation extraction methods. Section 3 explains in detail our approach. Sections 4 and 5 provide an overview of the experiments carried in this research work and the evaluation of the proposed approach, respectively. Finally, we conclude by summarizing the contributions and presenting perspectives in Sect. 6.

2   Related Work

As discussed in [24], in order to discover new relationships between entities mentioned in the text, the extracted relation requires the process of mapping entities associated with the relation to the knowledge base before it could be populated into the knowledge base. The entity linking task is highly data-dependent, and it is unlikely for a technique to dominate all others across all data sets [24]. The system requirements and the characteristics of the data sets affect the design of the entity linking system.

Any entity linking system is usually based on two steps: 1) candidate entity selection in a knowledge base that may refer to a given entity mention in the text; 2) similarity score definition for each selected candidate entity. Approaches to candidate entity generation are mainly based on string comparison between the textual representation of the entity mention in the text and the textual representation of the entity in the knowledge base. A wide variety of techniques makes use of redirect pages, disambiguation links and hyperlinks in the text to build a "Name Dictionary" that contains information about the named entities and provides a good base for linkage possibilities, as in [9,11,23]. Surface form expansion helps to find other variants for the surface form of the entity mention, for example, abbreviations that are extracted from the context of the processed document as in [10,15,17,28]. Although some candidate generation and ranking features demonstrate robust and high performance on some data sets, they could perform poorly on others. Hence, when designing features for entity linking systems, the decision needs to be made regarding many aspects, such as the trade-off between accuracy and efficiency, and the characteristics of the applied data set [24]. Using Name Dictionary Based Techniques is not usable in our case since the terms in the domain-specific ontology are similar and some of them share common words, for instance,"lokalita" (en. "locality"), "zastavitelná lokalita" (en. "buildable site"), and "zastavitelná stavební lokalita" (en. "buildable construction site"). Hence, using features like entity pages, redirect pages, hyperlinks, and disambiguation pages as in [9,11,23], bag of words [27] and entity popularity [22], are not useful in our case. Even statistical methods give poor results due to the small corpus and lack of training data. Authors in [16] created a Czech corpus for a simplified entity linking task that focuses on extracting instances of class "Person". Building such a corpus is a costly task considering the different types of domain-specific entities that exist in our data.

The next task is to calculate a proper score for each candidate entity. In [3,21], researchers used a binary classifier to tackle the problem of candidate entity ranking. This method needs many labeled pairs to learn the classifier, and it is not a final-decision method since the final result-set can contain more than one positive class for an entity mention. While researches in [20,26] treated the entity ranking problem as an information retrieval task, probabilistic models are also used to link entity mentions in web free text with a knowledge base. The work in [13] proposed a generative probabilistic model that incorporates popularity, name, and context knowledge into the ranking model. Our method is based mainly on three aspects, the string similarity measures of the tokens and the candidate entity name, the number of matched tokens, and the order of these tokens as they appear in the text.

Ontology learning and population methods can be divided into clustering-based approaches that make use of widely known clustering and statistical methods, and pattern-based approaches that mainly employ linguistic patterns. However, the former approaches require large corpora to work well.

Two types of patterns can be applied to natural language corpora. Lexico-syntactic patterns that use lexical representations and syntactical information, and lexico-semantic patterns that combine lexical representations with syntactic and semantic information in the extraction process. Text2Onto [4] combines machine learning approaches with basic linguistic processing to perform relation extraction from text. FRED [8] is a tool for automatically producing RDF/OWL ontologies and linked data from natural language sentences. Both tools do not provide a direct support for documents in Czech language. Java Annotation Patterns Engine (JAPE) [6] is a language to express patterns within the open-source platform General Architecture for Text Engineering (GATE) [5]. Researchers intensively define the patterns using JAPE rules, taking advantages of the linguistic preprocessing components provided by GATE framework as in [19]. However, it is not possible to use these GATE components with our data since GATE does not have models to support resources in the Czech language. Much cleaner rules with considerably less effort and time to create can be written using Hermes Information Extraction Language (HIEL) [14].

In [19], researchers defined a set of lexico-syntactic patterns corresponding to ontology design patterns (ODPs), namely subClassOf, equivalence, and property rules. Lexico-semantic patterns were defined focusing on domain-specific event relation extraction from financial events in [2], and in [12] to spot customer intentions in micro-blogging. To the best of our knowledge, no work has been done on the topic of lexico-semantic patterns for Slavic languages. In this work, we attempt to define a preliminary set of these patterns corresponding to subClassOf, equivalence, part-whole, and property relations.

3   Proposed Approach

Our approach focuses on the Czech language with prospective usage for a bigger class of languages, for example, Slavic ones. The proposed approach is illustrated in Fig. 1. Following, the main components of the system are discussed in details.

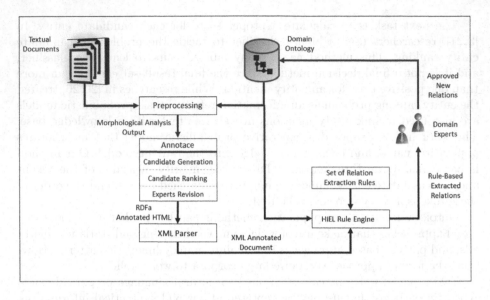

Fig. 1. Entity linking and relation extraction proposed pipeline

3.1   Entity Linking

Preprocessing. Any task that deals with textual documents needs to perform a natural language processing step to enhance the parts of the text with further syntactic pragmatic, morphological, and semantic information. Some of the performed steps include tokenization, sentence splitting, and part-of-speech tagging which are dealt with by a morphological analyzer tool called MorphoDiTa, Morphological Dictionary and Tagger [25]. MorphoDiTa[2] uses trained language models for both Czech and English languages.

For the entity linking task, morphological analysis is important because Czech, like many other Slavic languages, is a highly inflective language. Meaning that a word can have different suffixes to determine a linguistic case so that tokens can have many forms belonging to the same lemma and referring to the same semantic entity. For example, "*Metropolitní plán*" (Metropolitan plan in Czech) can appear in several forms like "*Metropolitním plánem*", "*Metropolitního plánu*" and so on. We perform the same processing on the labels of entities in the ontology for the same reason.

After stop-words removal, it is necessary to match all the remaining tokens since, in the text, most of the tokens might refer to a semantic entity in the ontology. Using regular named entity recognition (NER) tools would not be enough to recognize all the potential mentions. That is because the ontological classes are diverse and not necessarily limited to the standard named entity classes such as geographical location, person, or organization.

---

[2] http://ufal.mff.cuni.cz/morphodita accessed: 2020-05-05.

Candidate Entity Set Generation and Scoring. At this point, we have the clean document enriched with lemmas that should be linked to corresponding semantic classes. First, we find candidate entities in the ontology that may refer to tokens in the text. We apply the famous Jaccard similarity coefficient algorithm on the lemmatized tokens taking into consideration the lexical matching. i.e., the string comparison between the surface form of the entity mention and the name of the entity existing in the knowledge base.

As mentioned earlier, our method is based mainly on three aspects, the string similarity measures of the tokens and the candidate entity name, the number of matched tokens, and the order of these tokens as they appear in the text to ensures a final-decision result.

Given a vocabulary V having a set of entities E, and a processed document D composed of a set of potential entity mentions M_d, we need to find for each entity mention $m \in M_d$ (in our case a sequence of tokens) a mapping to its corresponding entity $e \in E$. In many cases, it can happen that the mapping is not injective since there are more candidate entities in the vocabulary to be linked to a specific mention. Thus, it is needed to rank the entities in the candidate set to choose the most relevant entity and associate it with the sequence of tokens that is considered to be an entity mention of the semantic entity.

For every single token (one word), the annotation service retrieves all possible entities that the surface form of this token might refer to and creates a set of candidate entities for this token E_t. We refer to these annotations as *Words*. A *Word* contains information like the single token's surface form that we are matching the entities against, the lemma, how vital this token is (whether it is extracted as a statistical keyword by Keyword Extractor Tool KER [18]), and a list of Phrases. A *Phrase* contains information like the label and the URI of the retrieved entity in the ontology and whether it is a full match to the token or not.

Even if a phrase indicates a full-match to the token, it does not mean that this token will be annotated with this phrase. The annotation service takes into consideration the neighbors of this token while deciding for the annotation. That means that it looks around the token and it gives a higher score to the phrase if the label of the entity has common sub-strings with the tokens around. In other words, if in the text M_d occurs the sequence $t_1t_2t_3$, t_1 matches the label of the entity e_i in the ontology, but the sequence of tokens, t_1t_2 matches another entity e_j in the ontology, then the service will give a higher score to annotate the multi-word mention t_1t_2 with the entity e_j. In case there is an entity e_k in the ontology with label matching the third token as well, the sequence $t_1t_2t_3$ will be annotated with the entity e_k. For example, let us assume the document contains the sequence of tokens **"součást otevřené krajiny"** (en. "part of an open landscape"), and in the vocabulary there is e_1 : <mpp:otevřená -krajina>, e_2 : <mpp:krajina>, the mention **"otevřené krajiny"** will be annotated with the entity e_1. The current state of the tool does not support overlapping annotations but it is considered in a newer version.

3.2   Lexico-Semantic Ontology Design Patterns

Even though the domain ontology is rich, it is still far from complete. Updating the ontology manually is an exhaustive process, for that, it is crucial to support the process of developing the ontology with automatic suggestions to the user. Statistical information extraction does not provide satisfactory results when running on a small domain-specific corpus. We define a set of rule-based extraction patterns to help the user in building the ontology. Most of the research on lexico-semantic patterns (LSPs) is done for the English language. Only some attempts have been done on other languages like French and German. To the best of our knowledge, no such work exists on Slavic languages as for Czech. In our case, we define a set of lexico-semantic patterns for Czech language focusing on common ontology relations.

For patterns definition, we use the Hermes Information Extraction Language (HIEL) that enables selecting concepts from the knowledge base and incorporate them into the lexical patterns. HIEL patterns are an ordered collection of tokens that are divided by spaces. They are described by two parts, a left-hand side (LHS) that define the relation to be extracted, and a right-hand side (RHS) that describes the pattern that should be extracted from the text. Once the RHS has been matched in the text to be processed, it is annotated as described by the LHS of the pattern. Usually, the syntax of the pattern is denoted as follows:

$$LHS :- RHS$$

The language supports lexical features like a limited list of part-of-speech tags, concepts and relations, literals, logical operators (and, or, not), repetition operators (*, +, ?), and wildcards (%, _). We extended the lexico-syntactic pattern restricted symbols and abbreviations used in [7]. The list of the abbreviations and common lexical categories used to formalize our patterns can be found in Table 1.

In our experiments and by the help of domain experts, we performed linguistic analysis and manually defined a preliminary set of lexico-semantic patterns corresponding to ontology design patterns (ODPs) that captures basic ontology relations, such as *subClassOf*, *equivalence*, *part-whole*, and *hasProperty* relations.

In the following patterns, the LHS for the rules is represented as:

$$LHS = (\$subject, relationOfInterest, \$object)$$

In Tables 2, 3, 4, and 5, we present only the right-hand side part of the rules due to space presentation limit. We also provide examples extracted from our data.

Table 1. LSPs symbols and lexical categories

Symbols & Abbreviations	Description & Examples
CATV	Phrases of classification. For example, rozlišuje (distinguishes), člení se (is divided into), etc.
COMP	Phrases of composition. For example, zahrnuje (includes), tvořený (formed), skládající se (consisting of),členěno na (divided into)
COMPR	Phrases of reverse composition. For example, vyskytující se v (appearing in), tvoří (creates), je součástí (is part[of])
CN	Phrases of generic class names. For example, základní typy (base types of)
SYN	Phrases of synonyms. For example, ekvivalent (equivalent)
PROP	Phrases of properties. For example, je přiřazen (is attached)
BE, CD, DT	Verb to be, Cardinal number, Determiner, respectively
NN, JJ, RB, IN	Noun, Adjective, Adverb, Preposition, respectively

Table 2. LSPs corresponding to subClassOf rules

P_{id}	RHS
P_{11}	*CATV CD CN* $object : Concept$ *DT*? $subject : Concept$ *CATV CD CN* $object : Concept$ *DT*? $Concept$ $('a'|',')$ $subject : Concept$
	example: Metropolitní plán rozlišuje dva základní typy **krajin městskou a otevřenou**
	meaning: Metropolitan plan distinguishes two base types of landscape: municipal landscape and open landscape
P_{12}	$object : Concept$ *IN*? *CATV IN*? $subject : Concept$ $object : Concept$ *IN*? *CATV IN*? $Concept$ $('a'|',')$ $subject : Concept$
	example: **Parkem** [se rozumí] vymezená část území s rozlišením na **městský park** a **krajinný park**.
	meaning: Park [is understood as] delimited part of area, further distinguished into municipal park and landscape park
P_{13}	$subject : Concept$ *BE* $object : Concept$
	example: **Metropolitní plán** je především **plánem** struktury území
	meaning: The metropolitan plan is primarily a plan of the area structure

Table 3. LSPs corresponding to part-whole rules

P_{id}	RHS
P_{21}	$\$subject : Concept\ COMP\ RB?\ IN?\ \$object : Concept$
	example: **Správní území Prahy** členčno na **lokality**
	meaning: Administrative territory of Prague is divided into localities
P_{22}	$\$subject : Concept\ COMP\ RIN?\ \$object : Concept$
	example: **Veřejná prostranství** tvoří **ulice**
	meaning: Public areas are created by streets

Table 4. LSPs corresponding to equivalence rules

P_{id}	RHS
P_{31}	$\$subject : Concept\ BE?\ SYN\ NN?\$object : Concept$
	$\$subject : Concept\ BE?\ SYN\ NN?\ Concept\ ('a'\ \vert\ ',')\ \$object : Concept$
	example: **Metropolitní** je ekvivalentem pojmů **celoměstský** a **nadmístní**
	meaning: Metropolitan is equivalent of terms citywide and supralocal
P_{32}	$\$subject : Concept\ DT?\ SYN\ DT?\ \$object : Concept$
	example: **Krajinou za městem**, syn. **krajinným zázemím města**
	meaning: Landscape outside the city, synonym. city landscape background

4   Implementation of Annotace - Text Annotation Service

As a part of the processing stack, **Annotace**[3], a text annotation service, was
implemented and used in the context of TermIt[4], a terminology management
tool based on Semantic Web technologies developed at Czech Technical University
in Prague. TermIt allows managing vocabularies and documents that use
terms from the vocabularies. The documents can be imported into TermIt document
manager and associated with vocabulary. The vocabulary can be empty
or already augmented with some classes and instances. TermIt allows users to
create and manage vocabularies based on related resources, and the annotation
service helps to automate this process in two scenarios:

– In the first scenario, a new document is uploaded into the TermIt document
manager, and a newly created vocabulary is associated with it. The vocabulary
is empty at this point. The task is to help the user to start building the
vocabulary based on the text present in the document. Annotace starts analyzing
the text based on KER[5] to extract the most significant mentions from
the text as a candidate classes in the vocabulary. This step does not involve

---

[3] Source code is available at https://github.com/kbss-cvut/annotace accessed: 2020-05-05.

[4] https://github.com/kbss-cvut/termit accessed: 2020-05-05.

[5] https://github.com/ufal/ker accessed: 2020-05-05.

Table 5. LSPs corresponding to hasProperty rules

P_{id}	RHS
P_{41}	$\$subject : (Concept|(JJ?NN?))BEPROP\$object : (Concept|(JJNN)|NN)$
	example: **Každé lokalitě** je přiřazen **typ struktury**
	meaning: Every locality has assigned type of structure
P_{42}	$CD\ CN\ Concept\ IN?\ \$subject : Concept\ DT?\ CD?\ \$object : Concept$
	$CD\ CN\ Concept\ IN?\ \$subject : Concept\ DT?\ CD?\ Concept\ ('a'\ |\ ',')$
	$CD?\ \$object : Concept$
	example: Deset typů struktur pro zastavitelné stavební lokality: (01) rostlá struktura, (02) bloková struktura,...
	meaning: Ten types of structures for buildable localitiesa are (01) growing structure, (02) block structure,...

any semantic technology since there is no semantic information present in the knowledge base yet. The extracted information from the text is then presented to the user as a highlighted text with actions. These actions allow the user to create a new term in the vocabulary. The user can reject the suggested term if it is irrelevant to the associated vocabulary.

- The second scenario has a lot in common with the previous one, but it suggests that the vocabulary has already seed classes and instances. Besides the steps introduced in the first scenario, Annotace starts analyzing the document using the classes in the associated vocabulary to find mentions in the text that refer to specific entities in the vocabulary and provides links between them. These mentions are also presented as highlighted text in the document but differ from the extracted terms in the statistical step by providing a link to the associated term directly. Similar to create and reject actions, the user is allowed to approve the suggested association or change the association to a different term in the vocabulary.

Both scenarios suggest human interaction with the system to approve or reject the output of Annotace. The semi-automatic approach is paramount to keep the high precision of building the ontology and save the user time and efforts needed to be spent with the manual process. Annotace handles data in HTML format and the annotations are created using RDFa [1]. RDFa is an extension to HTML5 that allows to inject linked data annotations in the structure of the HTML document. Whenever a token is recognized as an entity mention for an entity in the vocabulary, a new annotation is injected around this token with properties about this annotation like a unique ID, the resource attribute referring to the URI of the entity in the vocabulary, the type of the annotation in the ontology model, and the accuracy of the prediction represented in the score attribute as depicted in Listing 1.

The implementation of the patterns is not part of the stack for the current state of the tool. The patterns are tested separately within Hermes system to evaluate their efficiency. After annotating the document by Annotace with the corresponding ontological classes, Annotace augment the output with their proper tags presented in Table 1 and parse the resulted document to XML-based format that serves as an input for the patterns' implementation tool. We consider integrating the patterns in the pipeline of Annotace as part of the ongoing work.

```
<html prefix="ddo:http://onto.fel.cvut.cz/ontologies/application
  ↪ /termit/pojem/">
          <p> Metropolitní plán vymezuje ve <span about="_:4"
            ↪ property="ddo:je-výskytem-termu" resource="
            ↪ http://onto.fel.cvut.cz/ontologies/slovnik/
            ↪ datovy-mpp-3.5-np/pojem/správní-území-prahy"
            ↪ typeof="ddo:výskyt-termu" score="1.0">správním
            ↪  území Prahy</span> hranici zastavěného území
            ↪ ... </p>
```

Listing 1. Annotated HTML with RDFa (output sample)

5 Evaluation

5.1 Description of the Evaluation Corpus

To perform the evaluation, we used a set of documents and vocabularies related to these documents in the urban planning and development field. The documents are on different levels of details regulating spatial and urban planning in Prague. All documents are in Czech. The main document in this set is the *Metropolitan Plan of Prague (MPP)*[6] which is a spatial plan for the Czech capital. It consists of 168 articles divided into ten parts. The current version of MPP vocabulary corresponding to this document contains 59 terms. Other documents including but not limited to the document of the *Law 2006/183 Col., Building Law*[7], the law of urban planning and building regulations in the Czech Republic and the *Prague Building Regulations*[8] in a version from 2016 *(PSP 2016)*. The *Building Law* has 179 paragraphs divided into seven parts, and its corresponding vocabulary has 15 terms currently. On the other hand, *PSP 2016* that regulates the construction of buildings and urban planning in the Czech capital, is conceptualized as a book with 202 pages, describing 87 paragraphs, and the PSP2016 vocabulary consists of 102 terms.

---

[6] https://plan.iprpraha.cz/uploads/assets/prohlizeni/zavazna-cast/textova-cast/ TZ_00_Textova_cast_Metropolitniho_planu.pdf accessed: 2020-05-05.

[7] https://www.zakonyprolidi.cz/cs/2006-183 accessed 2020-05-05.

[8] Not available online.

5.2   Evaluation of Annotace

To evaluate the entity linking system, we used the set of documents and vocabularies described in Sect. 5.1. The textual files are loaded into TermIt and automatically annotated using the vocabulary related to the respective documents. The annotations are then revised by a human expert and evaluated based on precision, recall, and F1 measures. The scores are calculated as follows, the True Positives (TP), the number of correct links suggested by Annotace, the False Positives (FP), where the links are suggested by Annotace but they are false, and the False Negatives (FN), the number of mentions in the text that are not suggested by Annotace as a term occurrence but the term is present in the vocabulary. These statistics are then used to calculate the well-known precision, recall, and F1 measures.

Annotace achieved average precision, recall, and F1 measures of 83%, 79%, and 80.9% respectively. It is noticeable that the false negatives occur more often than false positives. There are only a few distinct false positives. In most of the cases, terms are defined in the vocabulary and used in different meaning in the context of the document. As illustrated in Fig. 2, in the vocabulary, it happens that the term **"Lokalita"** (en. "Locality") has intrinsic trope **"Cílový charakter lokality"** (en. "Target character of locality") which in turn, is composed of other intrinsic tropes like **"Struktura"** (en. "Structure"), **"Stabilita"** (en. "Stability"), and **"Využití"** (en. "Usage") and in most of the false positive cases, the word "Struktura" is used in a different context. For example, in the following sentence, *"Metropolitní plán je především plánem struktury území"* (en. "The metropolitan plan is primarily a plan of the area structure"), the word "Struktura" is recognized as the term **"Struktura"** in the vocabulary even though, in this sentence, it means the structure of the area (in Czech, "Území") and is not meant to describe the structure of the locality. The link, in this case, should not be suggested, and hence, it is considered as a false positive. To solve this problem, the specialization classes of the class **"Lokalita"** should be considered in the disambiguation process which we will consider in future work.

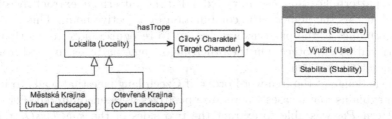

Fig. 2. Example of involving the hierarchy of the ontology in the disambiguation task

On the other hand, false negatives occurred while evaluating the MPP document when some frequently used terms come from other vocabularies and are not present in the vocabulary of MPP and hence, Annotace is not able to retrieve those terms correctly without involving other vocabularies in the process. However, most of the false negative cases happened due to lemma mismatching between the surface form and the term in the ontology, when the morphological tagger erroneously returns different lemmas for the same string.

5.3 Evaluation of Lexico-Semantic Patterns

We evaluated the patterns defined in Sect. 3.2 on the same textual documents that are annotated and parsed by Annotace. Domain experts provided their approval or rejection of the new relations extracted from the annotated documents after applying the patterns. The patterns achieved 65% of precision, 57% of recall, and an average F1 score of 61%. Table 6 allows a closer insight of precision and recall achieved by each pattern.

Table 6. Lexico-semantic patterns evaluation in terms of precision and recall

	Precision	Recall
P11	76%	40%
P12	51%	54%
P13	63%	60%
P21	74%	70%
P22	69%	53%
P31	78%	81%
P32	83%	75%
P41	85%	87%
P42	80%	56%

The false negative cases mostly occurred when the phrase was not recognized in the text as a term occurrence, and hence, the sentence did not match the specified pattern. For this reason, we extended the patterns to extract the subject or the object as the noun or the combination of adjective-noun. This improved the performance of the patterns and helped to recognize more terms that were not retrieved by Annotace. On the other hand, some patterns suffered from the over-generating problem.

The challenge of the free-word order of Czech language that leads to inverse relation explains many cases where false positives were encountered. For example, pattern P_{12} was able to extract the two sides of the *subClassOf* relation correctly but wrongly reversed the assignment of the super-class and the subclass in some cases. A possible solution is to consider the case of the words besides their position. Unfortunately, we could not investigate further because the Hermes language allows only the usage of specific tags. However, the free-word order problem of the Czech language is a challenge even after considering syntactic information. The problem is that, for example, the nominative case is similar to the accusative case when the noun is plural in some situations. This would make it hard even for an expert to get the relation correctly based on the ambiguous syntactic information only. Consider the sentence, "*Zastavitelné území tvoří plochy zastavitelné*" (en. "Buildable area creates buildable surfaces") which represents exactly this case where the verb "tvoří" can be used in both directions, and "zastavitelné území", and "plochy zastavitelné" will have the same form in the nominative and accusative linguistic cases.

The type of the recognized relation is another open issue. Pattern P_{21} wrongly retrieved concepts that had a *hyponym-hypernym* relation as a *part-whole* relation. This happens when a word that, according to our experts, intuitively refers to a *part-whole* relation but is used in the text carelessly. Another common issue we found in the data is that the text does not always provide complete information to be extracted. For example, for the sentence "*Metropolitní plán rozlišuje stanici metra, vestibul stanice metra a depo metra.*" (meaning Metropolitan plan distinguishes subway station, subway station lobby and subway depot), pattern P_{12} extracted **"Stanice metra"**, **"Vestibul stanice metra"** and **"Depo metra"** to be sub-classes of **"Metropolitní plán"**. However, this is not the case since **"Metropolitní plán"** is the term used to represent the document itself and hence, the extracted terms are sub-classes of a super-class that is not mentioned in the text.

Patterns P_3 and P_4 achieved reasonably high scores. However, there are only a few instances found in the corpus. A larger corpus is necessary to perform a more comprehensive evaluation.

6   Conclusion and Future Work

In this paper, we described a rule-based relation extraction approach to support the process of semi-automatic ontology building, based on a domain-specific seed vocabulary and textual documents. We defined a preliminary set of lexico-semantic rules corresponding to common ontological relations to help to extract relations between concepts based on the analysis of annotated documents written in Czech. As a part of the pipeline, we introduced Annotace, an entity linking system for the Czech language that enhances textual documents with conceptual context and supports creating the extraction patterns.

We intend to expand the patterns to cover more common relations. As a larger corpus would give a better overview of the proposed pipeline, we will consider evaluating the system on bigger data and a different domain, namely the aviation domain. In the ongoing work, we consider investigating the available rule-based languages and tools that are more flexible, taking into consideration the availability to plug the Czech language models, which is another problem we faced. We plan to configure the preprocessing component in the pipeline to support language models for other Slavic languages that are similar in nature to the Czech language.

Acknowledgments. This work was supported by grant No. CK01000204 Improving effectiveness of aircraft maintenance planning and execution of Technology Agency of the Czech Republic and grant No. SGS19/110/OHK3/2T/13 Efficient Vocabularies Management Using Ontologies of the Czech Technical University in Prague.

References

1. Adida, B., Birbeck, M., McCarron, S., Herman, I.: RDFA core 1.1. W3C technical reports (2010)
2. Borsje, J., Hogenboom, F., Frasincar, F.: Semi-automatic financial events discovery based on lexico-semantic patterns. Int. J. Web Eng. Technol. **6**(2), 115 (2010)
3. Chen, Z., Ji, H.: Collaborative ranking: a case study on entity linking. In: Proceedings of the 2011 Conference on Empirical Methods in NLP (2011)
4. Cimiano, P., Völker, J.: Text2Onto: a framework for ontology learning and data-driven change discovery. In: Montoyo, A., Muñoz, R., Métais, E. (eds.) NLDB 2005. LNCS, vol. 3513, pp. 227–238. Springer, Heidelberg (2005). https://doi.org/10.1007/11428817_21
5. Cunningham, H.: GATE, a general architecture for text engineering. Comput. Humanit. **36**(2), 223–254 (2002). https://doi.org/10.1023/A:1014348124664
6. Cunningham, H., Maynard, D., Tablan, V.: JAPE: a Java annotation patterns engine (1999)
7. Aguado de Cea, G., Gómez-Pérez, A., Montiel-Ponsoda, E., Suárez-Figueroa, M.C.: Natural language-based approach for helping in the reuse of ontology design patterns. In: Gangemi, A., Euzenat, J. (eds.) EKAW 2008. LNCS (LNAI), vol. 5268, pp. 32–47. Springer, Heidelberg (2008). https://doi.org/10.1007/978-3-540-87696-0_6
8. Gangemi, A., Presutti, V., Recupero, D.R., Nuzzolese, A.G., Draicchio, F., Mongiovi, M.: Semantic web machine reading with FRED. Semant. Web **8**(6), 873–893 (2017)
9. Gattani, A., et al.: Entity extraction, linking, classification, and tagging for social media: a Wikipedia-based approach. In: Proceedings of the VLDB Endowment (2013)
10. Gottipati, S., Jiang, J.: Linking entities to a knowledge base with query expansion. In: Proceedings of the Conference on Empirical Methods in NLP (2011)
11. Guo, S., et al.: To link or not to link? A study on end-to-end tweet entity linking. In: Proceedings of the 2013 Conference of the North American Chapter of the Association for Computational Linguistics (2013)
12. Hamroun, M., et al.: Lexico semantic patterns for customer intentions analysis of microblogging. In: 2015 11th International Conference on Semantics, Knowledge and Grids (SKG) (2015)
13. Han, X., Sun, L.: A generative entity-mention model for linking entities with knowledge base. In: Proceedings of the 49th Annual Meeting of the Association for Computational Linguistics: Human Language Technologies (2011)
14. Ijntema, W., Sangers, J., Hogenboom, F., Frasincar, F.: A lexico-semantic pattern language for learning ontology instances from text. Web Semant. **15**, 37–50 (2012). https://doi.org/10.1016/j.websem.2012.01.002
15. Jain, A., Cucerzan, S., Azzam, S.: Acronym-expansion recognition and ranking on the web. In: 2007 IEEE International Conference on Information Reuse and Integration (2007)
16. Konkol, M.: First steps in Czech entity linking. In: Král, P., Matoušek, V. (eds.) TSD 2015. LNCS (LNAI), vol. 9302, pp. 489–496. Springer, Cham (2015). https://doi.org/10.1007/978-3-319-24033-6_55

17. Lehmann, J., et al.: LCC approaches to knowledge base population at TAC 2010. In: TAC (2010)
18. Libovický, J.: KER - keyword extractor: LINDAT/CLARIN digital library at the Institute of Formal and Applied Linguistics (ÚFAL). Charles University, Faculty of Mathematics and Physics (2016)
19. Maynard, D., Funk, A., Peters, W.: Using lexico-syntactic ontology design patterns for ontology creation and population. In: Proceedings of the 2009 International Conference on Ontology Patterns, vol. 516, pp. 39–52. CEUR-WS. org (2009)
20. Nemeskey, D.M., Recski, G., Zséder, A., Kornai, A.: Budapestacad at TAC 2010. In: TAC (2010)
21. Pilz, A., Paaß, G.: From names to entities using thematic context distance. In: Proceedings of the 20th ACM International Conference on Information and Knowledge Management (2011)
22. Ratinov, L., Roth, D., Downey, D., Anderson, M.: Local and global algorithms for disambiguation to Wikipedia. In: Proceedings of the 49th Annual Meeting of the Association for Computational Linguistics: Human Language Technologies-Volume 1. Association for Computational Linguistics (2011)
23. Shen, W., et al.: Linking named entities in tweets with knowledge base via user interest modeling. In: Proceedings of the 19th ACM SIGKDD (2013)
24. Shen, W., Wang, J., Han, J.: Entity linking with a knowledge base: Issues, techniques, and solutions. IEEE Trans. Knowl. Data Eng. $27(2)$, 443–460 (2015)
25. Straková, J., Straka, M., Hajič, J.: Open-source tools for morphology, lemmatization, POS tagging and named entity recognition. In: Proceedings of 52nd Annual Meeting of the Association for Computational Linguistics: System Demonstrations (2014)
26. Varma, V., et al.: IIIT Hyderabad in guided summarization and knowledge base population (2019)
27. Zhang, W., et al.: NUS-I2R: Learning a combined system for entity linking. In: TAC (2010)
28. Zhang, W., et al.: Entity linking with effective acronym expansion, instance selection and topic modeling. In: 22 International Joint Conference on AI (2011)

Semantic Data Management and Data Infrastructures

Estimating Characteristic Sets for RDF Dataset Profiles Based on Sampling

Lars Heling[(✉)] and Maribel Acosta

Institute AIFB, Karlsruhe Institute of Technology (KIT), Karlsruhe, Germany
{heling,acosta}@kit.edu

Abstract. RDF dataset profiles provide a formal representation of a dataset's characteristics (features). These profiles may cover various aspects of the data represented in the dataset as well as statistical descriptors of the data distribution. In this work, we focus on the characteristic sets profile feature summarizing the characteristic sets contained in an RDF graph. As this type of feature provides detailed information on both the structure and semantics of RDF graphs, they can be very beneficial in query optimization. However, in decentralized query processing, computing them is challenging as it is difficult and/or costly to access and process all datasets. To overcome this shortcoming, we propose the concept of a profile feature estimation. We present sampling methods and projection functions to generate estimations which aim to be as similar as possible to the original characteristic sets profile feature. In our evaluation, we investigate the feasibility of the proposed methods on four RDF graphs. Our results show that samples containing 0.5% of the entities in the graph allow for good estimations and may be used by downstream tasks such as query plan optimization in decentralized querying.

1 Introduction

The characteristics of an RDF dataset can be formally represented as a set of features that compose a dataset profile. They support various applications such as entity linking, entity retrieval, distributed search and federated queries [5]. The features in a dataset profile can range from information on licensing, provenance to statistical characteristics of the dataset. Depending on the granularity of the statistics in a profile feature, the computation can be costly and require access to the entire dataset. For instance, characteristic sets are fine-grained statistic that is difficult to compute as it represents the set of predicates associated with each entity in a graph. Yet, several centralized and decentralized query engines rely on fine-grained dataset profiles for finding efficient query plans [7,11,13]. For example, Odyssey [13] leverages statistics on the characteristic sets of the datasets in the federation to estimate intermediate results when optimizing query plans.

In this work, we focus on the *Characteristic Sets Profile Feature* (CSPF), a statistical feature of RDF graphs that include the characteristic sets, their counts and the multiplicity of their predicates. There are three major reasons why we focus on the CSPF as a representative statistical characterization of RDF graphs. First, it implicitly captures structural features of the underlying graph, such as

© Springer Nature Switzerland AG 2020
A. Harth et al. (Eds.): ESWC 2020, LNCS 12123, pp. 157–175, 2020.
https://doi.org/10.1007/978-3-030-49461-2_10

the average out-degree, distinct number of subjects, and the set of predicates and their counts. Second, the characteristic sets contain semantic information on the entities represented in the graph and, thus, also implicitly reflect its schema. Lastly, the CSPF provides detailed insights into the predicate co-occurrences and, hence, it is well suited to be used by (decentralized) query engines for cardinality estimations and other downstream tasks. While the CSPFs are very beneficial for applications, their computation can be a challenging task. First, obtaining the entire dataset to compute this feature can be too difficult or costly. For example, in federated querying, data dumps are not always available and datasets can only be partially accessed via SPARQL endpoint or Triple Pattern Fragment servers. Second, the complexity of computing the characteristic sets for n triples is in $\mathcal{O}(n \cdot log(n) + n)$ [11]. This may be an additional restriction for very large and constantly evolving datasets.

To overcome these limitations, we propose an approach that estimates accurate statistical profile features based on characteristic sets and that relies only on a sample of the original dataset. Given an RDF graph, we sample entities and compute their characteristic sets to build the CSPF of the sample. Then, we apply a projection function to extrapolate the feature observed in the sample to estimate the original graph's CSPF. It is important to consider that the estimations for the CSPF are very sensitive to the structure of the graph and the sample. Assume, for example, the following characteristic sets S_1, S_2 and S_3 from YAGO and the number of associated subjects (*count*):

$$S_1 = \{\texttt{rdfs:label}, \texttt{skos:prefLabel}\}, count(S_1) = 783, 686,$$
$$S_2 = \{\texttt{rdfs:label}, \texttt{skos:prefLabel}, \texttt{yago:isCitizenOf}\}, count(S_2) = 7, 823,$$
$$S_3 = \{\texttt{rdfs:label}, \texttt{skos:prefLabel}, \texttt{yago:isLocatedIn}\}, count(S_3) = 188, 529.$$

Even though S_1 differs only by a single predicate from S_2 and S_3, S_1 occurs over 100 times more often than S_2, but only about 4 times more often than S_3. Hence, the main objective of our approach is avoiding misestimations when minor differences in characteristic sets lead to major changes in their *count* values. In summary, our contributions are

- a definition of statistical profile feature estimation and the associated problem,
- a formalization of Characteristic Sets Profile Feature (CSPF),
- an approach for generating profile feature estimations for CSPF, and
- an extensive experimental study examining the effectiveness of our approach on four well-known RDF datasets.

The remainder of this work is organized as follows. We present related work in Sect. 2 and introduce preliminaries in Sect. 3. We provide a formal problem definition in Sect. 4 and present our approach in Sect. 5. We evaluate our approach and discuss the results in Sect. 6. In Sect. 7, we draw our conclusions and point to future work.

2   Related Work

RDF Dataset Profiling. Capturing the characteristics of RDF datasets in *dataset profiles* has been studied in previous works. Ellefi et al. [5] present a taxonomy for dataset features represented in such profiles, which includes the categories general, qualitative, provenance, links, licensing, statistical, and dynamics. Regarding statistical features, different approaches have been proposed. Fernández et al. [6] aim to enable efficient RDF data structures, indexes, and compression techniques. To this end, the authors propose various metrics to characterize RDF datasets incorporating the particularities of RDF graphs. LODStats [3] is statement-stream-based approach that comprises 32 schema-level statistical criteria ranging from out-degree to the number of used classes. The ProLOD++ tool [1] supports profiling, mining and cleansing functionalities for RDF datasets. It enables a browser-based visualizations of domain level, schema level, and data level characteristics. ExpLOD [8] is a tool for generating summaries of RDF datasets combining textual labels and bisimulation contractions. These summaries include statistical information such as the class, predicate, and interlinking usage.

In addition to the existing statistical dataset profile feature covered in the literature, we propose and formalize a novel feature based on characteristic sets capturing both structural and semantic properties of the graph.

RDF Graph Sampling. The concept of sampling data from RDF graphs has been proposed for and applied to different problems. Debattista et al. [4] propose approximating specific quality metrics for large, evolving datasets based on samples. They argue that the exact computation of some quality metrics is too time-consuming and expensive and that an approximation of the quality is usually sufficient. They apply reservoir sampling and use the sampled triples to estimate the dereferenceability of URIs and links to external data providers. Rietveld et al. [16] aim to obtain samples that entail as many of the original answers to typical SPARQL queries. They rewrite the RDF graph to compute the network metrics PageRank, in-degree, and out-degree for the nodes. Based on the metrics, the *top-k* percent of all triples are selected as the sample of the graph. Soulet et al. [17] focus on analytical queries, which are typically too expensive to be executed directly over SPARQL endpoints. They propose separating the computation of such queries by executing them over random samples of the datasets. Due to the properties of the queries, the aggregation values converge with an increasing number of samples.

While in the first work sampling is applied to reduce the computational effort for quality metrics, they do not require the sampling method to capture the semantics of the dataset. The second approach aims to obtain a *relevant* sample which allows answering common queries and not a *representative* sample. Furthermore, the first two approaches require local access to the entire dataset for generating the sample. However, our work, similar to Soulet et al., is motivated by the restrictions that occur especially in decentralized scenarios with large, evolving datasets where it is not feasible to have local access to every dataset.

Different to the work by Soulet et al., we aim to sample the data in such a fashion that a single sample can be used to estimate the statistical profile feature and do not rely on the convergence properties induced by repeated sampling.

Network Sampling. Approaches for sampling large non-RDF graphs have also been proposed. Leskovec et al. [9] provide an overview of methods suitable for obtaining representative samples from large networks, considering three major categories for sampling: by selecting random nodes, by selecting random edges or by exploration. To assess the representativeness of the samples, static graph patterns are used, i.e., the distribution of structural network properties. The agreement for the graph pattern between the original graph and the samples is measured by the Kolmogorov-Smirnov D-statistic. No single best method emerges from their experimental study, but their performance depends on the specific application. Ribeiro et al. [15] focus on directed graphs and propose a directed unbiased random walk (DURW) algorithm. They model directed graphs as undirected graphs such that edges can also be traversed backwards when performing random walks. They incorporate random jumps to nodes with a probability that depends on the out-degree of the node as well as the weights of the edges. Ahmed et al. [2] identify two relevant models of computation when sampling from large networks. The *static model* randomly accesses any location in the graph. The *streaming model* merely allows for accessing edges in a sequential stream of edges. For the two models of computation, they propose methods based on the concept of graph induction and show that they preserve key network statistics of the graph, while achieving low space complexity and linear runtime complexity with respect to the edges in the sample.

In contrast to these methods, our approach aims to generate representative samples that allow for estimating statistic profile features of RDF datasets and therefore, the sampling methods need to be tailored to this task and the particularities of RDF graphs.

3   Preliminaries

The Resource Description Framework (RDF) defines a graph-based data model, where statements are represented as tuples (s, p, o) such that a subject s and an object o are connected nodes via a directed labeled edge by predicate p. The terms of the tuples can be Internationalized Resource Identifiers (IRIs), blank nodes, or literals. Assume the pairwise disjoint sets of IRIs I, blank nodes B, and literals L. A tuple $(s, p, o) \in (I \cup B) \times I \times (I \cup B \cup L)$ is an RDF triple. A set of RDF triples is denominated an RDF graph. The set of subjects in an RDF graph is often referred to as its *entities*.

The characteristics of RDF graphs can be summarized in statistic profiles. In traditional database theory, a statistic profile is a "complex object composed of quantitative descriptors" [10]. The quantitative descriptors cover different data characteristics: (i) central tendency (ii) dispersion, (iii) size, and (iv) frequency distribution. Such statistic profiles are used by query optimizers to devise an efficient query plan. Similarly, in RDF, statistic profiles are also commonly used by centralized triple stores and federated query engines for query optimization [7,11,13]. Typically, the query optimizer uses the statistic profiles to estimate the join cardinalities of subqueries. In the following, we consider statistical profile features and follow the terminology by Ellefi et al. [5], denoting an RDF dataset profile as a formal representation of a set of dataset profile features.

Definition 1 (Profile Feature). *Given a RDF graph G, a profile feature $F(G)$ is defined as a characteristic describing a statistical feature F of the graph G.*

An example statistical profile feature of an RDF graph could be derived from its characteristic sets. The concept of characteristic sets for RDF graphs was presented by Neumann et al. [14] and captures the correlations between join predicates in an RDF graph. The idea of characteristic sets is describing semantically similar entities by grouping them according to the set of predicates the entities share. As a result, such a profile feature incorporates both statistical information on the data distribution as well as semantic information of the entities contained within an RDF graph.

Definition 2 (Characteristic Sets [14]). *The characteristic set of an entity s in an RDF graph G is given by: $S_C(s) := \{p \mid \exists o : (s,p,o) \in G\}$. Furthermore, for a given RDF graph G, the set of characteristic sets is given by $\mathcal{S}_C(G) := \{S_C(s) \mid \exists p, o : (s,p,o) \in G\}$.*

To obtain a statistical profile, the counts for the characteristic sets are computed as well as the multiplicities of the predicates within each characteristic set. These additional statistics is required by centralized triple stores as well as federated query engines to determine exact cardinality estimations for distinct queries as well as computing cardinality estimations for non-distinct queries [7,11,13,14]. Similar to Neumann et al. [14], we define the count of a characteristic set $S = \{p_1, p_2, \ldots\}$ in an RDF graph G as

$$count(S) := |\{s \mid \exists p, o : (s,p,o) \in G \wedge S_C(s) = S\}|. \tag{1}$$

In addition, in this work, we focus on the occurrences of predicates in characteristic sets by considering their mean multiplicity. The mean multiplicity is given by

$$multiplicity(p_i, S) := \frac{|\{(s,p_i,o) \mid (s,p_i,o) \in G \wedge S_C(s) = S\}|}{count(S)}. \tag{2}$$

In other words, for a given characteristic set, the multiplicity specifies how often each predicate occurs on average. For example, consider the characteristic set $S_1 = \{\texttt{rdf:type}, \texttt{rdfs:label}\}$ with $count(S_1) = 10$, $multiplicity(\texttt{rdfs:label}, S_1) = 1$ $multiplicity(\texttt{rdf:type}, S_1) = 2$. This indicates that 10 entities belong to S_1 and each of those entities has *exactly* one $\texttt{rdfs:label}$ and *on average* two $\texttt{rdf:type}$ predicates.

4   Problem Definition

As outlined in the introduction, it might be too difficult and/or costly to access an entire dataset for computing its profile features. For example, this might be the case for decentralized querying when the datasets may only be partially accessed via SPARQL endpoints or Triple Pattern Fragment servers. To address this problem, we propose the concept of *Profile Feature Estimation* which aims to estimate the original profile feature using limited data of the original dataset. The goal is generating a profile feature estimation which is as similar as possible to the original profile feature while requiring partial data only. More precisely, in this work, we focus on approaches that rely on a sample from the original RDF graph and employ a projection function to estimate the true profile feature. Hence, we define a profile feature estimation as follows.

Definition 3 (Profile Feature Estimation). *Given an RDF graph G, a projection function ϕ, a subgraph $H \subset G$, and the profile feature $F(\cdot)$, a profile feature estimation $\hat{F}(\cdot)$ for G is defined as*

$$\hat{F}(G) := \phi(F(H))$$

Ideally, a profile feature estimation is identical to the true profile feature. However, the similarity of such estimations to the original feature is influenced by the type of feature to be estimated, the subgraph H and the projection function ϕ. For example, given just a small subgraph, the estimation might be less accurate than for a larger subgraph, as it may cover more characteristics of the original graph. Therefore, the problem is finding an estimation based on a subgraph H and a projection function ϕ for the profile feature which maximizes the similarity to the profile feature of the original RDF graph.

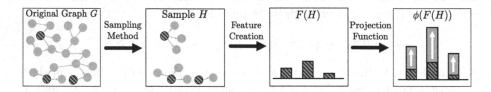

Fig. 1. Overview of the approach to estimate characteristic sets profile features.

Definition 4 (Profile Feature Estimation Problem). *Given an RDF graph G and a profile feature $F(\cdot)$, the problem of profile feature estimation is defined as follows. Determine a profile feature estimation $\hat{F}(\cdot)$, such that $\hat{F}(G) = \phi(F(H))$ and*

$$\max \delta(F(G), \hat{F}(G))$$

with $|H| \ll |G|$ and δ a function assessing the similarity of two statistic profile features.

The method for determining this similarity needs to be defined according to the profile feature. Consider for example a profile feature $F(G)$ counting the literals in a dataset and $\hat{F}(G)$ estimating this value based on a sample. Then the similarity between them may be calculated as the absolute difference between the true count and the estimated value. In network theory, the similarity of a sample is commonly assessed by how well it captures the structural properties of the original graph [2,9,15]. However, since the labels of the edges and nodes in an RDF graph hold semantic information on the entities and concepts described in the graph, merely considering structural features may not be sufficient to assess how representative a sample of an RDF graph is. Hence, we propose a more comprehensive profile feature based on the characteristic sets capturing structural and semantic features of the graph's entities, which we present in the following.

5   Characteristic Sets Profile Feature Estimation

In this work, we present a comprehensive profile feature based on characteristic sets that captures both structural and semantic aspects of RDF graphs. This Characteristic sets profile feature (CSPF) can formally be defined as the following.

Definition 5 (Characteristic Sets Profile Feature (CSPF)). *Given a RDF graph G, the characteristic sets profile feature $F(G)$ is a 3-tuple $(\mathcal{S}, c, m)$ with:*

- *$\mathcal{S} = \mathcal{S}_C(G)$, the set of characteristic sets in G,*
- *$c : \mathcal{S} \rightarrow \mathbb{N}$ a function for count as defined in Eq. 1, and*
- *$m : I \times \mathcal{S} \rightarrow \mathbb{R}^+$ a function for multiplicity as defined in Eq. 2.*

Our approach addressing the profile feature estimation problem for CSPFs is shown in Fig. 1. Given a graph G, we create a sample $H \subset G$ using one of the RDF graph sampling methods presented in Sect. 5.1. Then, we build the CSPF $F(H)$ for the sample H. Finally, we apply one of the projection functions presented in Sect. 5.2, to extrapolate the feature observed in H to estimate those of the original graph as $\phi(F(H))$. We apply a set of similarity measures for characteristic sets defined in Sect. 5.3 to determine the similarity between the original CSPF $F(G)$ and its estimation $\hat{F}(G)$.

5.1   RDF Graph Sampling

The first component of our approach is the sampling method. When designing sampling methods, it is crucial to determine the kind of characteristic that should be captured before the collection of data. In this work, we collect samples to estimate the characteristic sets profile feature. Since each entity is associated with one characteristic set, we define the population as the set of entities in the graph: $E := \{s \mid (s,p,o) \in G\}$. Each observation in the sample corresponds to one entity. The input of a sampling method is an RDF graph G and a sample size n'. The output of the sampling method is a subgraph H induced by n' entities of G. Let E' be the set of sampled entities with $|E'| = n'$, then $H := \{(s,p,o) \mid (s,p,o) \in G \wedge s \in E'\}$. We present three sampling methods differing in the probabilities of an entity being sampled. Thus, they allow for exploring different parts of the search space of possible characteristic sets during sampling.

Unweighted Sampling. It selects n' entities with equal probability from the population E. Thus, the probability $Pr(e)$ of $e \in E$ being a part of the sample is $Pr(e) = 1/|E|$.

Weighted Sampling. We present a biased sampling method which considers the out-degree of each entity e given by $d(e) := |\{(e,p,o) \mid (e,p,o) \in G\}|$. The weighted sampling method selects n' subjects where the probability of a subject to be chosen is proportional to its out-degree. In this way, entities that appear as subjects of many triples in the graph have a higher probability of being selected. Formally, the probability $Pr(e)$ of $e \in E$ being a part of the sample is given by $Pr(e) = d(e)/|G|$.

Hybrid Sampling. This sampling method combines the previous approaches where $\beta \cdot n'$ entities are selected using the unweighted method and $(1 - \beta) \cdot n'$ entities using the weighted method. Accordingly, the probability $Pr(e)$ of entity e being selected is

$$Pr(e) = \beta \cdot \frac{1}{|E|} + (1 - \beta) \cdot \frac{d(e)}{|G|}, \ \beta \in [0,1].$$

The β parameter allows for favoring either the weighted or the unweighted method.

5.2   Profile Feature Projection Functions

Next, the characteristic sets in the sample H are computed to create the corresponding CSPF $F(H)$. This can be done by first sorting the triples in H by subjects and then iterating all subjects determining the characteristic set for each subject. Given a profile feature $F(H) = (\mathcal{S}, c, m)$, the goal of a projection function is to extrapolate the statistical properties observed in sample H to the entire population as $\hat{F}(G) = \phi(F(H))$. In the following, we propose two classes of projection functions for the count values of the characteristic sets in the sample. The multiplicity statistic is not affected by the projection functions as it is a relative measure (the average occurrence of a predicate in a characteristic set) that does not require to be extrapolated. The first class, which we denote *basic projection functions*, only rely on information contained within the sample. The second class of projection functions rely on the information contained in the sample as well as additional high-level information on the dataset. We denote the latter class of functions as *statistics-enhanced projection functions*.

Basic Projection Function. This function simply extrapolates the count values for the given characteristic sets profile feature $F(H)$ based on the relative size of the sample. We define the function ϕ_1 which uses the ratio $r_t := \frac{|G|}{|H|}$ of triples in the sample with respect to the triples in the graph:

$$\phi_1(F(H)) := (\mathcal{S}, r_t \cdot c, m)$$

The assumption of this projection function is that the characteristic sets observed in the sample occur proportionally more often in the original graph. However, it neglects the fact that some characteristics sets might not have been sampled and is affected by potentially skewed distributions of the counts as exemplified in the introduction.

Statistics-Enhanced Projection Functions. The second class of projection functions incorporates additional high-level information about the original graph. In this work, we consider the number of triples per predicate in the original graph as a high-level statistic. The number of triples for predicate p' is given by $t(p') := |\{(s, p', o) \mid (s, p', o) \in G\}|$. We propose the ϕ_2 projection function that applies a true upper bound for the counts:

$$\phi_2(F(H)) := (\mathcal{S}, \dot{c}, m), \text{ with } \dot{c}(S_C) := \min(r_t \cdot c(S_C), \min_{p' \in S_C} t(p'))$$

The idea is that knowing how often a predicate occurs in the original graph allows for limiting the estimated counts for characteristic sets containing that predicate. This reduces the likelihood of overestimating counts without increasing the likelihood of underestimating them. Due to the fact that predicates, especially common ones such as rdf:type, may be used in several characteristic sets of the same graph, the aforementioned upper bound may be limited in its effectiveness. This is because it does not consider the number of characteristic sets a given predicate is part of. Therefore, we propose a third projection function ϕ_3 which "distributes" the upper bound for a predicate p' by considering the sum of counts of the characteristic sets, the predicates occurs in:

$$\phi_3(F(H)) := (\mathcal{S}, \ddot{c}, m), \text{ with } \ddot{c}(S_C) := \min \left(r_t \cdot c(S_C), \min_{p' \in S_C} \left(\frac{t(p') \cdot c(S_C)}{\sum\limits_{S'_C \in \mathcal{S} \wedge p' \in S'_C} c(S'_C)} \right) \right)$$

The projection function ϕ_3 is adjusted by multiplying $t(p')$ with the ratio of the count $c(S_C)$ of S_C and the sum of counts for all characteristic sets p' occurs in. In contrast to ϕ_2, this approach increases the likelihood of underestimating the count of characteristic sets. However, at the same time, it applies a more realistic upper bound by considering all characteristic sets a predicate occurs in and adjusting the upper bound accordingly. Note that further projection functions may be applied. For instance, the size of the characteristic sets or additional statistics about the predicates in the sample could be considered. However, we chose not to include them since they are likely produce projections that are tailored to specific graphs and cannot be generalized to other datasets.

5.3   Similarity Measures for Characteristic Sets

Finally, we define metrics that quantify the similarity between the estimated values and the real values to measure the quality of the profile estimations. Following the profile feature estimation problem defined in Definition 4, the goal is to identify an estimator $\hat{F}(G) = \phi(F(H))$ for the characteristic F that combines a sample H and projection function ϕ which maximizes the similarity δ between the estimated and the original profile feature. The similarity depends on the profile feature and we propose measures tailored to the characteristic sets profile feature (CSPF). Due to the diverse nature of the CSPF, there are multiple criteria to be considered when it comes to defining the similarity $\delta(F(G), \hat{F}(G))$ between the original CSPF $F(G) = (\mathcal{S}, c, m)$ and an estimated CSPF $\hat{F}(G) = (\hat{\mathcal{S}}, \hat{c}, \hat{m})$. In the following, we present a selection of similarity measures which consider both structural as well as statistical aspects captured by the CSPF. These measures take values in $[0, 1]$ and their interpretation is 'higher is better'.

Structural Similarity Measures. Considering the structural properties, the mean out-degree and the predicate coverage can be considered to assess the similarity between the estimation and the original feature. We compute the *out-degree* similarity as

$$\delta^{od}(F(G), \hat{F}(G)) := 1 - \frac{|d_{mean}(F(G)) - d_{mean}(\hat{F}(G))|}{\max(d_{mean}(\hat{F}(G)), d_{mean}(F(G)))}, \text{ with} \quad (3)$$

$$d_{mean}(F(G)) := \frac{|G|}{\sum_{S_C \in \mathcal{S}} c(S_C)}$$

Note that $d_{mean}(\hat{F}(G))$ is computed analogously using H, $\hat{\mathcal{S}}$, and $\hat{c}$ instead. Next, we can assess the *predicate coverage* similarity by computing the ratio of the number predicates covered in the estimation w.r.t. the number of predicates in the original profile feature as

$$\delta^{pc}(F(G), \hat{F}(G)) := \frac{|\{p \mid p \in S_C \wedge S_C \in \hat{\mathcal{S}}\}|}{|\{p \mid p \in S_C \wedge S_C \in \mathcal{S}\}|}. \quad (4)$$

The quality of the characteristic sets that are covered in the sample can be assessed by the following measures. First, the *absolute set coverage* similarity can be computed as the ratio of characteristic sets in the estimation to those in the original statistic profile:

$$\delta^{ac}(F(G), \hat{F}(G)) := |\hat{\mathcal{S}}|/|\mathcal{S}| \quad (5)$$

This measure, however, does not consider the amount of triples that haven been actually covered by the characteristic sets. The *relative set coverage* similarity of a characteristic set S_C of an RDF graph G reflects the relative amount of triples that S_C induces in G. The relative set coverage similarity δ^{rc} of an estimation is calculated as the number of triples induced by all characteristic sets in the estimation on the original graph G:

$$\delta^{rc}(F(G), \hat{F}(G)) := \frac{\sum_{S_C \in \hat{S}} \sum_{p \in S_C} m(p, S_C) \cdot c(S_C)}{|G|}. \tag{6}$$

Note that the characteristic sets in the estimation $\hat{S}$ are considered while the number of triples they cover, i.e. $\sum_{p \in S_C} m(p, S_C) \cdot c(S_C)$, is w.r.t. the original graph. In this way, δ^{rc} reflects the relevance of the characteristic sets captured in the sample. For example, consider an RDF graph G with two characteristic sets S_1 and S_2, where S_1 covers 90% and S_2 10% of all triples in G. Now, given an estimation with $\hat{S} = \{S_1\}$, even though the estimation only capture 50% of the characteristic sets, the importance of S_1 is very high, as it covers 90% of the triples in the original graph.

Table 1. Overview of the similarity measures.

Structural similarity measures				Statistical similarity measures	
Out-degree	Predicate coverage	Absolute set coverage	Relative set coverage	Count similarity	Multiplicity similarity
δ^{od} (3)	δ^{pc} (4)	δ^{ac} (5)	δ^{rc} (6)	$\delta^{count}_{S_C}$ (7)	$\delta^{multiplicity}_{S_C}$ (8)

Statistical Similarity Measures. Next, we focus on similarity measures which consider the *counts* and the *multiplicity* of predicates in the feature estimation. The degree to which counts and the multiplicities can be estimated accurately depends on the characteristic set. There might be characteristic sets for which these estimations may be very accurate, while for others this might not be the case. Hence, to avoid aggregating the similarity values for all characteristic sets to a single value, we define the similarity on the level of characteristic sets. Based on these values, an aggregation, such as mean or the median, may be used to obtain a single similarity value for all sets. For the similarity with respect to the count estimations, we adopt the q-error [12] by computing the maximum of the ratios between true and estimated count. Larger values for the q-error indicate a higher discrepancy between the true value and the estimation, and q-error of 1 indicates that the estimation is correct. Therefore, we use the inverse of the q-error to assess similarity

$$\delta^{count}_{S_C}(F(G), \hat{F}(G)) := \left(\max\left(\frac{c(S_C)}{\hat{c}(S_C)}, \frac{\hat{c}(S_C)}{c(S_C)} \right) \right)^{-1}, \forall S_C \in \hat{S} \tag{7}$$

Note that the q-error measures the magnitude of the estimation error but does not reveal whether values are over- or underestimated. This property avoids that overestimated values cancel underestimated values out when the similarity values for all characteristic sets in the sample are aggregated. Analogously, we compute the similarity of the multiplicities based on the q-error. We aggregate the values for all predicates in the characteristic sets using the mean to obtain a single value, as follows

$$\delta_{S_C}^{multiplicity}(F(G), \hat{F}(G)) := \left(\frac{1}{|S_C|} \sum_{p \in S_C} \max \left(\frac{\hat{m}(p, S_C)}{m(p, S_C)}, \frac{m(p, S_C)}{\hat{m}(p, S_C)} \right) \right)^{-1}, \forall S_C \in \hat{S}$$

(8)

Summarizing, a CSPF implicitly and explicitly captures various characteristics of RDF graphs. The quality of estimating such a feature may not be assessed by a single similarity value but requires considering various metrics which are summarized in Table 1.

6   Experimental Evaluation

In this section, we empirically analyze the different components of our proposed approach. The goal of the evaluation is to investigate the following core questions:

Q1 How do different sampling sizes influence the similarity measures?
Q2 What is the impact of different sampling methods on the similarity measures?
Q3 What are the effects of leveraging additional statistics in the projection functions?
Q4 How do different characteristics of the RDF graph influence the estimation?

Next, we present the setup of our experiments and present and analyze the results of our experiments. Based on our findings, we answer the addressed questions in the conclusions (cf. Sect. 7). The source code and the sample results are available online.[1]

Table 2. Characterization of the four RDF graphs studied in the experiments.

RDF graph	# Triples	# Subj.	# Pred.	# Obj.	d_{mean}	d_{std}	$|S|$	$\frac{|S|}{\text{# Subjects}}$	$\frac{|S^1|}{|S|}$	AUC
DBLP	88,150,324	5,125,936	27	36,413,780	17.2	9.38	270	0.005%	15%	99.13%
LinkedMDB	5,444,664	688,187	220	1,930,703	7.91	5.9	8516	1.24%	62%	97.40%
Wordnet	5,558,748	647,215	64	2,483,030	8.58	10.26	777	0.12%	37%	98.22%
YAGO	82,233,128	6,429,347	79	50,670,009	12.79	15.82	29309	0.46%	49%	98.76%

Datasets. We selected four well-known RDF graphs from different domains: publications (DBLP), movies (LinkedMDB), linguistics (Wordnet), and cross-domain (YAGO). An overview of their characteristics is shown in Table 2. The graphs differ with respect to their size (number of triples), the number of distinct subjects, predicates, and objects as well as the number of characteristic

---

[1] https://github.com/Lars-H/hdt_sampler, https://doi.org/10.5445/IR/1000117614.

sets $|S|$. As the number of potential characteristic sets not only depends on the distinct predicates, but it is bound by the number of distinct subjects in the graph, we also provide the ratio $|S|/\#$ Subjects in percent as a measure of the characteristic sets' diversity. Furthermore, we consider *exclusive* characteristic sets defined as $S^1 := \{S_C \mid count(S_C) = 1 \land S_C \in S\}$ and provide the ratio of exclusive characteristic sets to all characteristic sets. An exclusive characteristic set only occurs once in the entire graph and as a result, introduces two major difficulties when sampling and projecting the characteristic sets: (i) it is unlikely to sample them as they occur only once, and (ii) when projecting them, it is likely to overestimate their counts. However, because the coverage of exclusive characteristic sets is low, it is potentially less important to correctly project them, as they might be less relevant as other characteristic sets.

For each RDF graph, we indicate the area under the curve (AUC) below the relative cumulative coverage curve (cf. Fig. 2). For the relative cumulative coverage curve, the characteristic sets are ranked and sorted in decreasing order according to the number of triples they cover on the x-axis (cf. Sect. 5.3) and on the y-axis, the cumulative sum of the relative number of triples they cover is indicated. For instance, the curve for DBLP shows that the characteristic set with the highest coverage (i.e., the start of the curve on the left), covers almost 40% of all triples and 20% of the characteristic sets cover almost all triples in the graph (relative cumulative coverage ≈ 0.99). As a result, the shape of the curve indicates how evenly the coverage is distributed across the characteristic sets. A diagonal line indicates all characteristic sets covering the same number of triples. The stronger the curve is dented towards the upper left corner the more unevenly is the coverage of the characteristic sets distributed. This indicates that a few sets cover many triples in the graph. Consequently, a large AUC indicates unevenly distributed coverage.

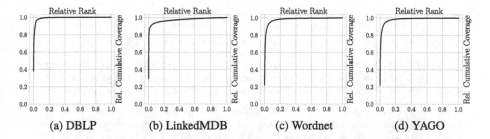

| (a) DBLP | (b) LinkedMDB | (c) Wordnet | (d) YAGO |

Fig. 2. The cumulative relative coverage curve shows the ratio of triples covered with respect to the characteristic sets ordered by decreasing relative coverage.

Sampling Methods. We study the presented unweighted, weighted and hybrid sampling methods. For the hybrid sampling method we chose $\beta = 0.5$. We study four different sample sizes defined relative to the number of entities $|E|$ with

$n' = \{0.1‰ \cdot |E|, 0.5‰ \cdot |E|, 1‰ \cdot |E|, 5‰ \cdot |E|\}$ (Note: 10 ‰ = 1%). We generate 30 samples per dataset, sampling method, and sample size resulting in a total of $30 \cdot 4 \cdot 3 \cdot 4 = 1,440$ samples.

6.1 Results: Structural Similarity Measures

Table 3 presents the results for the measures out-degree δ^{od}, predicate coverage δ^{pc}, and absolute set coverage δ^{ac}, and relative set coverage δ^{rc} for the different sampling methods. Included are also the ratios of triples sampled $|H|/|G|$ in permille (‰).

Considering sample size (Q1), the results show an improvement on the similarity measures as the sample size increases, with a few exceptions for δ^{od}. In particular, in Wordnet and YAGO, the best similarity values δ^{od} are achieved for the highest relative sample size (5.0‰), while for DBLP and LinkedMDB the best performance is achieved with a sample size of 1.0‰. The predicate coverage similarity δ^{pc} also improves with increasing sample sizes. For instance, from 220 predicates in LinkedMDB the sampling methods obtain ≈66 predicates with the smallest sample size and ≈154 with the largest. For all the studied graphs, a similar relation between the absolute (δ^{ac}) and relative set coverage (δ^{rc}) is observed. Even if only a few characteristic sets are sampled (low δ^{ac}), the number of triples in the original graph covered by those sets is very high (high δ^{rc}). For example, in Wordnet, the unweighted sampling (5.0 ‰) obtains 12% ($\delta^{ac} = 0.12$) of all characteristics sets which cover 95% ($\delta^{rc} = 0.95$) of all triples in the graph.

Table 3. Mean similarity values δ^{od}, δ^{pc}, δ^{ac}, δ^{rc} and mean sampled triples ratio $|H|/|G|$ in permille (‰) by sample size and sampling method (h = hybrid, u = unweighted, w = weighted). Best values per RDF graph and similarity measure are indicate in **bold**.

		DBLP					LinkedMDB					Wordnet					YAGO				
		$\frac{|H|}{|G|}$	δ^{od}	δ^{pc}	δ^{ac}	δ^{rc}	$\frac{|H|}{|G|}$	δ^{od}	δ^{pc}	δ^{ac}	δ^{rc}	$\frac{|H|}{|G|}$	δ^{od}	δ^{pc}	δ^{ac}	δ^{rc}	$\frac{|H|}{|G|}$	δ^{od}	δ^{pc}	δ^{ac}	δ^{rc}
0.1 ‰	h	0.11	0.84	0.94	0.09	0.98	0.13	0.72	0.32	0.00	0.70	0.17	0.57	0.46	0.02	0.77	0.17	0.59	0.67	0.01	0.32
	u	0.10	0.95	0.93	0.08	0.98	0.10	0.90	0.31	0.00	0.69	0.10	0.86	0.42	0.02	0.71	0.10	0.93	0.60	0.01	0.31
	w	0.13	0.75	0.94	0.09	0.98	0.16	0.61	0.34	0.00	0.70	0.23	0.43	0.50	0.03	0.80	0.25	0.40	0.75	0.01	0.32
0.5 ‰	h	0.57	0.85	0.98	0.16	0.99	0.64	0.76	0.48	0.01	0.82	0.86	0.57	0.62	0.06	0.90	0.87	0.57	0.88	0.02	0.37
	u	0.50	0.96	0.98	0.16	0.99	0.50	0.94	0.44	0.01	0.82	0.49	0.92	0.56	0.04	0.87	0.50	0.96	0.72	0.02	0.36
	w	0.65	0.75	0.99	0.16	0.99	0.79	0.62	0.46	0.01	0.83	1.22	0.42	0.66	0.07	0.92	1.25	0.40	0.92	0.02	0.37
1.0 ‰	h	1.15	0.86	**1.00**	0.21	**1.00**	1.28	0.78	0.52	0.01	0.85	1.73	0.59	0.70	0.08	0.93	1.74	0.59	0.93	0.03	0.38
	u	1.00	**0.98**	**1.00**	0.20	**1.00**	1.00	**0.97**	0.51	0.01	0.84	1.01	0.95	0.63	0.06	0.91	1.00	**0.97**	0.79	0.02	0.38
	w	1.30	0.77	**1.00**	0.21	**1.00**	1.57	0.64	0.54	0.02	0.85	2.45	0.42	0.74	0.10	0.94	2.43	0.43	0.95	0.03	0.38
5.0 ‰	h	5.74	0.85	**1.00**	0.31	**1.00**	6.42	0.76	0.72	0.04	0.89	8.48	0.58	0.82	0.17	0.97	8.40	0.59	**0.97**	0.08	**0.40**
	u	5.00	0.97	**1.00**	0.31	**1.00**	5.00	0.96	0.73	0.03	0.88	5.02	**0.96**	0.75	0.12	0.95	4.99	**0.97**	0.88	0.06	**0.40**
	w	6.49	0.75	**1.00**	**0.31**	**1.00**	7.75	0.63	**0.74**	**0.06**	**0.90**	11.9	0.42	**0.84**	**0.21**	**0.98**	11.7	0.43	**0.97**	**0.09**	**0.40**

Regarding the sampling methods (Q2), the unweighted approach performs best for the out-degree similarity δ^{od}. This relates to the fact that the hybrid and weighted sampling methods select high out-degree entities with a higher probability. To illustrate this, consider Fig. 3 that shows the characteristic sets that are constructed with two different sampling methods (in color) in comparison to the characteristic sets from the original graph (in gray). The weighted sampling methods (Fig. 3a) leads to characteristic sets with higher set size (highlighted in the rectangle), while the unweighted sampling (Fig. 3b) captures average-sized characteristic sets. Furthermore, a higher the dispersion of the out-degree distribution (d_{std}/d_{mean}) of the original graph (Q4), leads to a higher similarity for the unweighted sampling method in comparison to the other approaches.

In general, the unweighted sampling method exhibits the lowest predicate coverage similarity (δ^{pc}) in comparison to the other approaches. Combining this observation with Fig. 3, we conclude that the unweighted sampling method fails to obtain those predicates used in characteristic sets with high degrees. The only exception where all methods obtain every predicate is DBLP for sample sizes 1.0‰ and 5.0‰, due a high average out-degree w.r.t. the number of predicates (cf. Table 2) in the original graph.

Considering absolute (δ^{ac}) and relative set coverage (δ^{rc}), the unweighted method performs almost as well in most cases while always sampling the fewest triples ($|H|/|G|$). The relation between absolute and relative set coverage is in accordance with the AUC property of the graphs, i.e., most triples are covered by few characteristic sets only.

6.2   Results: Statistical Similarity Measures

Next, we analyze the estimation results for the counts and multiplicity. Instead of presenting the similarity measures δ^{count} and $\delta^{multiplicity}$, we present the q-error as it is more commonly used in the literature. For each sample, mean and median q-error for count and multiplicity estimations across all characteristic sets $S_C \in \hat{S}$ are computed. Note that mean/median for each sample are computed first to assess the performance on the sample level. We present the average of mean and median q-errors in Table 4 to get an indication of how well the average sample per dataset, size and method performs.

Regarding the graphs (Q4), the best count estimations are observed for DBLP and Wordnet where the best median values are between 1.27 and 1.53 indicating that, for half of the characteristic sets, the counts are misestimated by $\leq$27% and $\leq$53%. The difference in the best mean values for Wordnet (6.09) and DBLP (3.55) reflects that in Wordnet there are higher misestimations on average. For YAGO, the best median q-error is 2.12 for the largest sample size and the unweighted method. The corresponding mean (16.0) is almost 8 times higher than the median indicating a strong positive skew of the q-error distribution. For LinkedMDB the best median result 1.49 is achieved with the smallest sample size, however, it needs to be noted that this smaller sample also covers fewer characteristic sets (cf. δ^{ac} in Table 3). Taking the characteristics of the original graphs into consideration, two observation may explain the differences in q-errors: (i) a

Table 4. Mean and median for q-errors of the count estimations for the projection functions ϕ_1, ϕ_2, and ϕ_3 as well as for the multiplicity estimation. Best values per column are **bold** and values for the best projection function are highlighted in gray .

		DBLP								LinkedMDB							
		ϕ_1		ϕ_2		ϕ_3		multiplicity		ϕ_1		ϕ_2		ϕ_3		multiplicity	
		mean	median	mean	median	mean	median	mean	median	mean	median	mean	median	mean	median	mean	median
0.1 ‰	h	6.31	1.61	5.11	1.57	4.16	1.49	1.04	1.02	547	2.56	222	2.14	117	2.01	1.04	1.01
	u	16.4	1.64	10.4	1.59	9.77	1.51	1.04	1.02	262	**2.22**	117	**1.57**	79.2	**1.49**	1.03	1.0
	w	25.6	1.62	25.1	1.61	18.4	1.48	1.04	1.02	600	5.07	298	3.84	155	3.03	1.05	1.01
0.5 ‰	h	3.9	1.51	3.89	1.49	3.54	1.48	1.04	1.02	207	4.76	173	3.68	87.7	3.07	1.05	1.02
	u	4.47	1.38	4.46	1.36	4.12	1.34	1.04	1.02	130	2.44	108	1.84	74.1	1.78	1.04	1.01
	w	5.36	1.51	5.35	1.5	4.94	1.5	1.06	1.02	217	12.2	185	11.6	76.0	6.9	1.06	1.04
1.0 ‰	h	5.51	1.45	5.51	1.44	5.14	1.43	1.04	1.02	117	6.41	106	6.14	57.1	4.45	1.06	1.04
	u	6.85	1.36	6.85	1.35	6.24	1.32	1.04	1.02	95.5	2.81	87.2	2.35	68.6	2.28	1.05	1.02
	w	5.89	1.43	5.88	1.43	5.33	1.43	1.05	1.02	128	13.6	116	13.2	49.7	7.08	1.07	1.05
5.0 ‰	h	4.06	1.33	4.06	1.33	3.88	1.32	1.04	**1.01**	39.9	8.67	39.0	8.64	21.7	5.38	1.07	1.06
	u	**3.6**	**1.28**	**3.6**	**1.28**	3.53	**1.27**	1.03	**1.01**	**35.2**	4.36	**34.5**	4.09	30.9	3.89	1.06	1.04
	w	3.96	1.36	3.96	1.36	3.77	1.38	1.05	1.02	37.9	10.8	37.1	10.8	**16.8**	5.67	1.07	1.06

		Wordnet								YAGO							
		ϕ_1		ϕ_2		ϕ_3		multiplicity		ϕ_1		ϕ_2		ϕ_3		multiplicity	
		mean	median	mean	median	mean	median	mean	median	mean	median	mean	median	mean	median	mean	median
0.1 ‰	h	43.6	2.31	12.5	2.22	9.04	2.01	1.11	1.11	158	3.07	145	3.04	125	2.91	1.3	1.24
	u	74.6	2.42	11.6	2.11	8.98	1.72	**1.1**	1.08	161	3.05	153	3.03	129	2.77	1.25	1.2
	w	53.8	3.34	23.4	2.81	17.8	2.48	1.12	1.11	150	3.67	137	3.65	125	3.49	1.33	1.27
0.5 ‰	h	28.5	2.28	18.9	2.19	14.4	2.04	1.12	1.11	61.2	2.74	58.3	2.74	54.6	2.68	1.29	1.24
	u	22.6	1.85	15.1	1.75	12.2	1.57	**1.1**	1.08	60.0	2.64	59.1	2.64	55.4	2.51	**1.24**	**1.19**
	w	28.0	2.68	23.5	2.6	18.5	2.37	1.13	1.12	56.3	3.23	52.8	3.22	48.5	3.15	1.32	1.26
1.0 ‰	h	24.4	2.18	18.9	2.17	14.6	2.0	1.12	1.1	38.2	2.51	36.7	2.5	34.6	2.47	1.29	1.24
	u	20.3	1.78	15.2	1.71	12.4	1.59	**1.1**	1.09	41.9	2.45	41.6	2.45	39.3	2.37	**1.24**	1.2
	w	21.2	2.7	17.1	2.68	13.7	2.36	1.13	1.12	37.5	3.12	36.2	3.11	33.1	3.01	1.32	1.27
5.0 ‰	h	10.0	2.14	8.72	2.13	7.26	1.95	1.12	1.1	15.5	2.43	15.5	2.43	14.1	2.39	1.29	1.25
	u	**7.55**	**1.6**	6.8	1.58	6.09	1.53	**1.1**	1.08	16.3	**2.14**	16.3	**2.13**	16.0	**2.12**	**1.24**	1.2
	w	9.75	2.52	8.78	2.51	7.07	2.17	1.12	1.11	**14.7**	3.0	**14.7**	2.99	13.1	2.89	1.32	1.27

higher characteristic set diversity ($|S_C|/\#Subjects$) yields higher q-errors, and (ii) a higher ratio of exclusive characteristic sets yield higher q-errors. Regarding (i): with many possible characteristic sets to be sampled from, it is likely to sample few entities per set. However, sampling several entities per characteristic set allows for better estimating their overall occurrences. Considering (ii): many exclusive characteristic sets increase the likelihood of them being sampled and their counts to be overestimated, as the projection function cannot distinguish them from non-exclusive characteristic sets. Inspecting the projection functions (Q3), the statistic-enhanced functions ϕ_2 and ϕ_3 slightly reduce the mean and median q-errors for the count estimations. In all cases, ϕ_3 yields the best estimations and should be favored over ϕ_2 whenever the additional statistics are

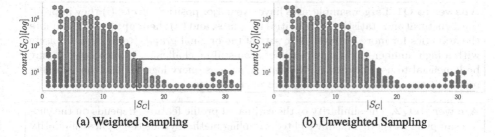

(a) Weighted Sampling   (b) Unweighted Sampling

Fig. 3. Example of the sampled characteristic sets for YAGO with respect to the number of their predicates ($|S_C|$) and their count ($count(S_C)$) on a log-scale. Indicated in gray are all sets of the original dataset and in color those, which are contained in the sample. (Color figure online)

available. Simultaneously, the improvements over the basic projection function ϕ_1 diminish with an increasing sample size indicating that larger samples contain fewer outliers which are corrected by the additional statistics in ϕ_2 and ϕ_3.

For the multiplicity estimations, the mean and median q-errors are below 1.3 in all cases for all graphs. They are less affected by sampling methods and sample sizes reflecting a uniform predicate usage within the characteristic sets with few outliers. Regarding the sample size (Q1), in most cases, a larger sample provides better results for count and multiplicity estimations while at the same time estimating more characteristic sets from the original graph (cf. δ^{ac} in Table 3). As a result, increasing the sampling size not only improves the overall accuracy but also the number of characteristic sets estimated. Similar to previous observations, the unweighted sampling method (Q2) yields the best results in most cases for count and multiplicity estimations.

7   Conclusions and Future Work

We have introduced the problem of RDF dataset profile feature based on characteristic sets and proposed a solution based on sampling. The presented profile feature estimation approach obtains a sample from the original graph, computes the profile feature for the sample, and uses a projection function to estimate the true profile feature. Different applications can benefit from the resulting feature estimations. For instance, query plan optimization in decentralized querying can benefit from the estimations to find efficient query plans, even when the entire dataset may not accessible to compute the complete statistics. We conducted an empirical study to evaluate the similarities between the estimations and the true profile features. We presented and analyzed the results of our study and to conclude our findings, we answer the questions presented in Sect. 6:

Answer to Q1. Larger sample sizes have two major positive effects: (i) they improve the structural and statistical similarities measures, and (ii) they capture and estimate the statistics for more characteristic sets of the original graph. Regardless, datasets with a high number of characteristic sets can still be challenge. In such cases it may be beneficial to use additional information, such as query logs, to lead the sampling method towards the most relevant characteristic sets.

Answer to Q2. The similarity of the estimated profile features depends on the chosen sampling method. The unweighted sampling method yields the highest similarity values in the majority of cases while requiring the fewest triples to be sampled.

Answer to Q3. Projection functions leveraging additional statistics (i.e., overall counts per predicate) achieve better results for projecting the counts of characteristic sets. The improvements over the zero-knowledge projection function diminish with increasing sample size.

Answer to Q4. The structure of the RDF graph affects the similarity values. Especially count values are misestimated for datasets with a large share of exclusive characteristic sets and a larger diversity of characteristic sets. In such scenarios, larger sample sizes can help improving the estimations.

Our future work will focus on investigating the impact of estimated Characteristic Sets Profile Features on the performance of query plan optimizers.

Acknowledgement. This work is funded by the German BMBF in QUOCA, FKZ 01IS17042.

References

1. Abedjan, Z., Grütze, T., Jentzsch, A., Naumann, F.: Profiling and mining RDF data with ProLOD++. In: Proceedings of ICDE (2014)
2. Ahmed, N.K., Neville, J., Kompella, R.R.: Network sampling: from static to streaming graphs. TKDD **8**(2), 7:1–7:56 (2013)
3. Auer, S., Demter, J., Martin, M., Lehmann, J.: LODStats - an extensible framework for high-performance dataset analytics. In: Poceedings of EKAW, pp. 353–362 (2012)
4. Debattista, J., Londoño, S., Lange, C., Auer, S.: Quality Assessment of Linked Datasets Using Probabilistic Approximation. In: Gandon, F., Sabou, M., Sack, H., d'Amato, C., Cudré-Mauroux, P., Zimmermann, A. (eds.) ESWC 2015. LNCS, vol. 9088, pp. 221–236. Springer, Cham (2015). https://doi.org/10.1007/978-3-319-18818-8_14
5. Ellefi, M.B., et al.: RDF dataset profiling - a survey of features, methods, vocabularies and applications. Semant. Web **9**(5), 677–705 (2018)
6. Fernández, J.D., Martínez-Prieto, M.A., de la Fuente Redondo, P., Gutiérrez, C.: Characterising RDF data sets. J. Inf. Sci. **44**(2), 203–229 (2018)
7. Gubichev, A., Neumann, T.: Exploiting the query structure for efficient join ordering in SPARQL queries. In: Proceedings of EDBT (2014)
8. Khatchadourian, S., Consens, M.P.: ExpLOD: summary-based exploration of interlinking and RDF usage in the linked open data cloud. In: Aroyo, L., et al. (eds.) ESWC 2010. LNCS, vol. 6089, pp. 272–287. Springer, Heidelberg (2010). https://doi.org/10.1007/978-3-642-13489-0_19

9. Leskovec, J., Faloutsos, C.: Sampling from large graphs. In: Proceedings of ACM SIGKDD, pp. 631–636 (2006)
10. Mannino, M.V., Chu, P., Sager, T.: Statistical profile estimation in database systems. ACM Comput. Surv. **20**(3), 191–221 (1988)
11. Meimaris, M., Papastefanatos, G., Mamoulis, N., Anagnostopoulos, I.: Extended characteristic sets: graph indexing for SPARQL query optimization. In: Proceedings of ICDE (2017)
12. Moerkotte, G., Neumann, T., Steidl, G.: Preventing bad plans by bounding the impact of cardinality estimation errors. PVLDB **2**(1), 982–993 (2009)
13. Montoya, G., Skaf-Molli, H., Hose, K.: The *Odyssey* approach for optimizing federated SPARQL queries. In: d'Amato, C., et al. (eds.) ISWC 2017. LNCS, vol. 10587, pp. 471–489. Springer, Cham (2017). https://doi.org/10.1007/978-3-319-68288-4_28
14. Neumann, T., Moerkotte, G.: Characteristic sets: accurate cardinality estimation for rdf queries with multiple joins. In: Proceedings of ICDE (2011)
15. Ribeiro, B.F., Wang, P., Murai, F., Towsley, D.: Sampling directed graphs with random walks. In: Proceedings of the IEEE INFOCOM, pp. 1692–1700 (2012)
16. Rietveld, L., Hoekstra, R., Schlobach, S., Guéret, C.: Structural properties as proxy for semantic relevance in RDF graph sampling. In: Mika, P., et al. (eds.) ISWC 2014. LNCS, vol. 8797, pp. 81–96. Springer, Cham (2014). https://doi.org/10.1007/978-3-319-11915-1_6
17. Soulet, A., Suchanek, F.M.: Anytime large-scale analytics of linked open data. In: Ghidini, C., et al. (eds.) ISWC 2019. LNCS, vol. 11778, pp. 576–592. Springer, Cham (2019). https://doi.org/10.1007/978-3-030-30793-6_33

Social and Human Aspects of the Semantic Web

SchemaTree: Maximum-Likelihood Property Recommendation for Wikidata

Lars C. Gleim[1]([⊠]) ⓘ, Rafael Schimassek[1], Dominik Hüser[1], Maximilian Peters[1],
Christoph Krämer[1], Michael Cochez[2,3] ⓘ, and Stefan Decker[1,3] ⓘ

[1] Chair of Information Systems, RWTH Aachen University, Aachen, Germany
{gleim,decker}@dbis.rwth-aachen.de
[2] Department of Computer Science,
Vrije Universiteit Amsterdam, Amsterdam, The Netherlands
m.cochez@vu.nl
[3] Fraunhofer Institute for Applied Information Technology FIT, Sankt Augustin, Germany

Abstract. Wikidata is a free and open knowledge base which can be read and edited by both humans and machines. It acts as a central storage for the structured data of several Wikimedia projects. To improve the process of manually inserting new facts, the Wikidata platform features an association rule-based tool to recommend additional suitable properties. In this work, we introduce a novel approach to provide such recommendations based on frequentist inference. We introduce a trie-based method that can efficiently learn and represent property set probabilities in RDF graphs. We extend the method by adding type information to improve recommendation precision and introduce backoff strategies which further increase the performance of the initial approach for entities with rare property combinations. We investigate how the captured structure can be employed for property recommendation, analogously to the Wikidata Property-Suggester. We evaluate our approach on the full Wikidata dataset and compare its performance to the state-of-the-art Wikidata PropertySuggester, outperforming it in all evaluated metrics. Notably we could reduce the average rank of the first relevant recommendation by 71%.

Keywords: Wikidata · Recommender systems · Statistical property recommendation · Frequent pattern mining · Knowledge graph editing

1 Introduction

Wikidata is a free and open knowledge base which acts as central storage for the structured data of several Wikimedia projects. It can be read and edited by both humans and machines. Related efforts are schema.org [15] and Linked Open Data[1] [7]. Manual editing of knowledge-bases is traditionally an error prone process [23] and requires

---

[1] We provide additional results for the LOD-a-lot dataset [12] together with our implementation in the supplementary material at https://github.com/lgleim/SchemaTreeRecommender.

This work was funded by the Deutsche Forschungsgemeinschaft (DFG, German Research Foundation) under Germany's Excellence Strategy – EXC-2023 Internet of Production – 390621612.

© Springer Nature Switzerland AG 2020
A. Harth et al. (Eds.): ESWC 2020, LNCS 12123, pp. 179–195, 2020.
https://doi.org/10.1007/978-3-030-49461-2_11

intimate knowledge of the underlying information model. Even entities of semantically equal type regularly feature different property sets (also called the attributes or predicates of the entity in the context of RDF [8]), different property orderings, etc. [9].

For Wikidata, much care is taken to create useful properties, which have support from the community[2]. Nevertheless, due to the sheer number of available properties, users often struggle to find relevant and correct properties to add to specific entities of the knowledge base. In order to improve the process of manually incorporating new facts into the knowledge base, the Wikidata platform provides the PropertySuggester tool, which recommends suitable properties for a given subject using an association rule-based approach [25]. Similar recommendation approaches are also employed in more general RDF recommender systems and collaborative information systems [1,2,13,22,26].

The main contribution of this work is the *SchemaTree* in which we make use of frequentist inference to recommend properties; in particular using a compact trie-based representation of property and type co-occurences. We also detail how the approach qualitatively differs from the existing association rule-based approaches, investigate cases in which the baseline SchemaTree does not perform well, and present respective improvement strategies. The results in Sect. 4 show that the recommender performs well on the Wikidata dataset and significantly outperforms the current Wikidata PropertySuggester.

In the following, we first introduce relevant related work in property recommendation systems and frequent pattern learning and discuss potential limitations of these existing systems, before detailing the construction of the SchemaTree and its application to property recommendation. Afterwards, we present an extension of the baseline SchemaTree incorporating type information into the system in Sect. 3 and present back-off strategies to deal with specific cases in Sect. 3 to improve precision and recall further. Subsequently, we evaluate the performance of the proposed approach against a state-of-the-art approach and its applicability to scale to large RDF datasets, before summarizing our results and concluding our work.

2   Related Work

Several data-driven property recommendation systems have been introduced in recent years. In the context of databases and the Web, there are several examples of works which suggest schema elements to designers. As an example, Cafarelle et al. [10] propose the attribute correlation statistics database (AcsDB), which enables property suggestion based on their cooccurences in web tables, assisting database designers with choosing schema elements. Other examples include [5,18].

Also in the context of structured knowledge bases and the Semantic Web, several approaches have been proposed. Many of these are fundamentally based upon the idea of mining association rules [4] from sets of co-occurring properties. Motivated by human abstract association capabilities, association rule-based recommendation hinges on the following underlying rationale: If a number of properties co-occur frequently, the existence of a subset of those properties allows for the induction of the remaining properties with a certain confidence.

---

[2] See for example the discussion at https://www.wikidata.org/wiki/Wikidata:Requests_for_comment/Reforming_the_property_creation_process.

A first example of such work is by Abedjan et al. [1,2], whose RDF enrichment approach employs association rule mining for property suggestion. In their work, recommendations are ranked by the sum of the confidence values of all association rules that respectively entailed them. That work got extended into the Wikidata recommender, which is called *PropertySuggester*[3]. The difference with the basic approach is the introduction of so-called *classifying* properties, which are the properties instanceOf and subclassOf [25]. Subsequently, association rules are not only derived based on the co-occurrence of properties but also on which properties occur on which types of instances, providing additional information for the recommendation computation process.

The Snoopy approach [13,26] is another property recommendation system based on association rules, which distinguishes itself from previous systems by ranking recommendations based on the support – i.e., the number of occurrences of a given rule – across all training data items (in contrast to the sum of confidences used in the previous approaches). Zangerle et al. [25] proposed an extension of the Snoopy approach, inspired by previous work of Sigurbjörnsson et al. [22]. They rank properties by the number of distinct rules that respectively entail them and their total support as a proxy for including contextual information into the ranking process. Zangerle et al. [25] further conducted an empirical evaluation of several state-of-the-art property recommender systems for Wikidata and collaborative knowledge bases and concluded that the Wikidata recommender approach significantly outperforms all evaluated competing systems (including their own). As such, we consider the Wikidata PropertySuggester as state-of-the-art.

Unfortunately, the process of association rule mining can result in misleading rules. Especially due to the spuriousness of the underlying itemset generation, the inability to find negative association rules, and variations in property densities [3]. As such, important information about the context of the mined association rules is lost, leading to deviations between the true conditional probabilities of property occurrence and their association rule approximations. While the previously introduced approaches apply different heuristics in order to rank recommendations based on relevant association rules, they only loosely approximate an ordering based on true likelihoods of the property co-occurrences. In this work, we investigate how a frequentist approximation of this true likelihood can improve recommendations.

Recently, Balaraman et al. [6] developed Recoin, a statistical indicator for relative completeness of individual Wikidata entities. The system can also be repurposed to propose potentially missing properties based on the class information (only). However, this cannot take into account other properties of the entity. It will only suggest properties which a sufficient fraction of other instances of the same class also has. This system has not been shown to outperform the Wikidata PropertySuggester, which includes both class membership and property information.

Dessi and Atzori [11] presented an approach applying supervised, feature-based Machine Learning to Rank algorithms to the task of ranking RDF properties. The approach focuses on flexible personalization of properties' relevance according to user preferences for specific use cases in a supervised training approach. Given this context, a direct comparison between this and the other presented approaches is not feasible.

---

[3] http://gerrit.wikimedia.org/r/admin/projects/mediawiki/extensions/PropertySuggester.

HARE [19] is a generalized approach for ranking triples and entities in RDF graphs, capable of property recommendation, which is based on random walks in a bi-partite graph representation. Its scalability to large datasets has however also not been shown, nor compared to the state-of-the-art.

Razniewski et al. [20] further introduced an approach incorporating human interest-ingness ratings of properties into the property recommendation process, outperforming the state-of-the-art with respect to agreement with human interestingness annotations. The general applicability of the approach is however hindered by the limited availabil-ity of data on human preferences of individual properties and the fact that knowledge graphs are not necessarily created to maximize the interestingness of their contents for humans but often also for algorithmic and specific technical applications.

Next, we introduce our approach for property recommendation in the context of manual knowledge-base statement authoring, based on maximum-likelihood recom-mendation directly employing a frequent pattern tree (FP-tree) for efficient probability computations.

3   SchemaTree: Design and Construction

In this section, we introduce the design and construction of a data structure used for efficient pattern support lookup. A Knowledge Base (KB) generally consists of entities with associated properties and values. An entity can have the same property multiple times and entities in the KB can also have type information[4].

Preliminaries. The task of recommending properties is defined as proposing a relevant property for a given entity, which was previously not attributed to it. In this work, we limit ourselves to proposing properties with respect to their maximum-likelihood as determined from a set of training data. Hence, in the scope of this paper, we define the task of property recommendation as follows:

Definition 1 (Maximum-likelihood Property Recommendation). *Given an entity E with properties $S = \{s_1, \ldots, s_n\} \subseteq \mathcal{A}$ in a Knowledge Graph KG where $\mathcal{A}$ is the set of all properties of all entities, maximum-likelihood property recommendation is the task of finding the property $\hat{a} \in \mathcal{A} \setminus S$ such that*

$$\hat{a} = \operatorname*{argmax}_{a \in (\mathcal{A} \setminus S)} P(a \mid \{s_1, \ldots, s_n\}) = \operatorname*{argmax}_{a \in (\mathcal{A} \setminus S)} \frac{P(\{a, s_1, \ldots, s_n\})}{P(\{s_1, \ldots, s_n\})} \tag{1}$$

where $P(\{t_1, \ldots, t_m\})$ is the probability that a randomly selected entity has at least *the properties $t_1, \ldots, t_m$.*

Intuitively, we need to find the property a which is most often observed together with the properties which the entity already has ($\{s_1, \ldots, s_n\}$). This directly corresponds to a maximum-likelihood estimation over the true probability distribution P of property co-occurrence. To obtain k recommendations, this definition can be extended such that we obtain a list of the k properties which have the highest k maximum-likelihood prob-abilities, as sorted by that probability.

---

[4] These requirements are fulfilled by both Wikidata and RDF graphs in general.

Given a sufficiently large amount of training data, the true joint probabilities can be reasonably well approximated by their relative frequency of occurrence, using a frequentist probability interpretation. We borrow the common approach of grouping RDF triples by subject (i.e. entity in a KB KG) to derive the multiset $\mathfrak{P}$ of all per subject property sets [14,24,25], formally $\mathfrak{P} = \{Q|E \in KG, Q$ is the set of properties of $E\}$. Then, we can determine the absolute frequency (or support count) $\text{supp}(A)$ of a set of properties $A = \{a_1,\ldots,a_{|A|}\} \subseteq \mathcal{A}$ (i.e. a pattern) as the number of subject property sets that include it:

$$\text{supp}(A) = \text{supp}(a_1,\ldots,a_{|A|}) = |\{Q \in \mathfrak{P}|A \subseteq Q\}| \tag{2}$$

Subsequently, we can determine the most likely property recommendation by reformulating Eq. (1) via frequentist inference as:

$$\hat{a} \simeq \underset{a \in (\mathcal{A}\setminus S)}{\operatorname{argmax}} \frac{\text{supp}(a, s_1, \ldots, s_n)}{\text{supp}(s_1, \ldots, s_n)} \tag{3}$$

If we naively computed recommendations according to this definition, it would be impossible to produce these in a timely manner. This is because creating a recommendation will force us to scan trough the complete dataset, which for a realistically sized one like Wikidata will already take prohibitively long. Hence, to make the proposed technique usable, we need efficient lookup of these frequencies. However, given that the number of possible property combinations for n properties is 2^n, it is infeasible to precompute and store them in a simple lookup table. Hence, we introduce a suitable data structure which makes it possible to compute them in a short time in the next subsection.

Construction. To allow for efficient learning, storage, and retrieval of these patterns, we adapt the trie construction idea of the FP-tree, first introduced by Han et al. [17], in order to serve as a highly condensed representation of the property sets. We are not aware of prior work using this approach for frequentist inference. In contrast to common applications in association rule learning, we do not prune the tree based on minimum support but retain the full tree. While various optimized and specialized adaptations of the original FP-tree construction have been proposed in recent years (see, for example, the comparative study in [21]), we build upon the original 2-pass tree construction to enable a more transparent analysis of the tree's properties. Moreover, in order to ensure deterministic construction of the FP-tree, we do adopt the usage of a support descending property ordering together with a lexicographic order as proposed by [16]. As the tree is representing a higher level abstraction of the properties used in the KB, we call this tree the *SchemaTree*. Building the tree is done as follows:

1) For each property $a \in \mathcal{A}$, determine its support $\text{supp}(a)$ in one scan through the data and cache it. Additionally, create an empty lookup index to maintain a list of occurrences of each property within the tree, to later allow for efficient traversal of the tree.
2) Determine a fixed ordering of properties $p_1, \ldots, p_{|\mathcal{A}|}$, first by descending support and second by lexicographical ordering $\text{lex}(p_i)$.

3) Construct the prefix tree from all patterns, respectively sorted according to order-ing $p_1, \ldots, p_{|\mathcal{A}|}$, by inserting the properties into the tree, starting from the root node (representing the empty set, contained in all patterns). Each node in the tree main-tains a counter of its prefix-conditional support (the support for the set of properties between the root and the node in question) and a backlink to its parent. The root node thus counts the total number of patterns inserted. Whenever a new child node is created, it is additionally appended to the list of occurrences of the corresponding property.

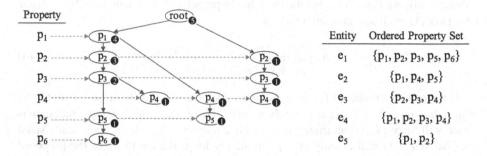

Fig. 1. The SchemaTree derived from the property sets depicted on the right.

Figure 1 illustrates the SchemaTree (left) derived from the example KB of five sub-jects with their respective property sets (right). Patterns are inserted starting from the root node at the top. The blue, solid arrows indicate the pattern tree hierarchy, the green, dashed arrows illustrate the links of the per-property occurrence index, depicted on the left side. The white numbers on black background denote the prefix-conditional support. Once this tree is constructed, it can be used to recommend properties.

Maximum-Likelihood Recommendation. The property recommendations for a given entity with non-empty property set $A \subseteq \mathcal{A}$ can be computed using the following proce-dure:

1) Make a candidate set $C = \mathcal{A} \setminus A$ of support counters for possible property recom-mendations and a support counter for A with respective initial support 0.
2) Sort A using property ordering $p_1, \ldots, p_{|\mathcal{A}|}$ by ascending support to get sorted prop-erties $a_1, \ldots, a_{|A|}$, i.e. where a_1 is the least frequent property.
3) For each occurrence a_1' of a_1 in the SchemaTree (directly retrievable via per-property occurrence index) with associated support s_1':
   a) Check whether the remaining properties in A are contained in the prefix path (i.e. its ancestors).
   b) If yes, increment the support counter of all property candidates contained in the prefix but not already in A by s_1', the support counter of A by s_1' and the support counter of all property candidates that occur as part of the suffix of a_1' (i.e. its children) by their respective occurrence support, as registered in the tree.

4) Sort the candidate set by descending support to receive the ranked list of property recommendations. The respective likelihood approximation of each recommendation can be obtained as its support divided by the support of A.

The reason all candidates occurring in the prefix of a_1' are incremented by s_1' in step 3 (b) and not by their respective individual occurrence support, is that they only occurred s_1'-many times together with the entire pattern A on this branch. Further, note that branches may be discarded early in step 3 (a) based on the known property ordering. More specifically, if the currently inspected prefix node has a lower sort order then the next expected node according to the sorted property set A, the expected property can no longer be encountered and the branch gets ignored immediately. Hereby, the strategy of checking prefix containment, starting with properties of minimal overall support, has a higher selectivity (i.e. specificity or true negative rate) then starting the search from the most likely properties at the root and is thus expected to lead to earlier search terminations.

Suppose we want to make property suggestions for an entity with properties $A = p_2, p_3$, based on p_i as in the SchemaTree depicted in Fig. 1. Ordering reveals p_3 to be the least frequent property. Inspection of the per-property occurrence index of p_3 reveals two occurrences in the tree, p_3^l (left) and p_3^r (right). Since the prefix of p_3^l does contain p_2, the support counters of p_1 (only candidate in the prefix) and A (i.e. the set support counter) are incremented by 2 (the support of p_3^l). The suffixes of p_3^l lead to the respective incrementation of support counters of p_4, p_5 and p_6 by their respective occurrence support of 1. Inspection of the prefix of p_3^r reveals that p_2 is also contained in its prefix, leading us to incremented A by 1 (the support of p_3^r). Since no other candidates are part of the prefix, we can directly continue with the suffix p_4, whose support counter is accordingly incremented by 1. Sorting of the candidate list and division by the support of A results in the final list of recommendations: p_1 and p_4 ($2/3 \simeq 66,67\%$ likelihood each) and p_5 and p_6 ($1/3 \simeq 33,33\%$ likelihood each). Note that we can further deduct that all other properties are unlikely to co-occur with the given set of properties. Depending on the application this knowledge may also have significant value by itself, e.g. in the context of data quality estimation. As such, the approach is also capable of capturing negative relationships, i.e. associations, between properties.

Employing Classifying Properties. The recommendation precision is expected to be limited by a lack of context information when only a small set of existing properties are provided as input to the recommender. This is especially true when these few properties are themselves rather common, since they occur together with a large number of other properties. To improve the recommender's precision in such cases, type information is integrated into the SchemaTree by employing the concept of classifying properties as implemented by the Wikidata PropertySuggester. [25] As such, any value of a classifying property can be considered a *type*. Correspondingly, any value of an instanceOf property (Property:P31) is a type in the sense of the Wikidata data model and can be extracted as such. Equivalently, it is possible to use e.g. the DBpedia type property or RDF type for generic RDF datasets.

To build the SchemaTree, we treat types as additional properties: In the first scan, we count the frequencies of properties as well as types. We create a strict totally ordered set including properties and types – again ordered first by descending support and second by lexicographical order – and redefine the per subject property set as the ordered set of all corresponding properties and types. During the second pass, we insert all subjects' property sets (now including types) into the SchemaTree.

In the recommendation algorithm, we search for paths in the tree that contain both all properties and all types of the provided input set. When the list of recommendations is created, only properties (not types) are considered as possible candidates. Note that this makes it also possible to recommend properties for an entity that only has class information and that this approach could also be used to recommend suitable additional types for a provided input set.

Employing Backoff Strategies. Association rule-based approaches excel at generalizing to property sets not encountered in the training set, due to the typically small size of any given rule's precondition item set. The SchemaTree recommender, however, by default often fails to provide recommendations in this case, since the required lookup of the support of the provided input set and its super-sets will not return any results. To give an example, suppose that we want to compute recommendations for the input set $\{p_1, p_2, p_3, p_4\}$, given the SchemaTree depicted in Fig. 1, then p_4 is the property with the lowest support and therefore the starting point for the recommender. Only the leftmost p_4 node of the SchemaTree meets the condition that properties p_1, p_2, p_3 are on the path from p_4 to the root, so that this is the only node we regard. Unfortunately, there is no other property on that path, neither as predecessor nor successor. Therefore, the recommender does not recommend any new property to the set. Similarly, large input sets generally correlate to fewer corresponding examples in the training set and thus to tendentially less reliable recommendations of the SchemaTree recommender, while association rule-based approaches generally remain unaffected by this issue and rather suffer from the challenge of combining the tendentially many applicable association rules into a comprehensive property ranking.

In order to address these border cases, we designed two **backoff strategies**, which either reduce the set of employed input properties or split it into multiple input sets:

SplitPropertySet. Splits the input property set into two smaller input sets:
1) Sort incoming properties according to the global property support ordering $p_1, \ldots, p_{|\mathcal{A}|}$ of the SchemaTree.
2) Split the ordered property set P into 2 subsets P_1' and P_2' $(P_1' \cup P_2' = P)$.
   We consider two ways to perform splitting of ordered property set P:
   a) *Every Second Item.* The items are split in the sets such that each item in even position in the sorted set P comes in P_1, the others in P_2.
   b) *Two Frequency Ranges.* The first half of sorted set P is put in P_1, the last half in $P2$.
3) Perform recommendation on both subsets in parallel, obtaining two recommendations R_1' and R_2'.
4) Delete those properties from the recommendations which were in the other input property subset resulting in cleaned recommendations R_1 and R_2.
5) Merge recommendation R_1 and R_2 to for the recommendation R, which is finally returned as result of the backoff strategy. This we do, by either taking the *maximum* or the *average* of the two probabilities per individual recommended property.

DeleteLowFrequency. Reduces the size of the input property set by removing a varying number of properties with lowest support and computing recommendations for
multiple such reduced input sets in parallel. In the end, one of these resulting sets of
recommendations is selected. the procedure goes as follows:

1) Sort incoming properties according to the global property support ordering
   $p_1, \ldots, p_{|\mathcal{A}|}$ of the SchemaTree.
2) Create q subsets $P_i, i \in [q]$ by deleting the $d(i)$ least frequent items from the
   original input set P. Here, $d(i)$ determines the number of low frequent properties
   deleted form P in run i, we discuss options below.
3) Run the recommender on the subsets in parallel, obtaining recommendations
   sets R_i.
4) Choose the recommendation R_i with the least number of deleted properties
   which does no longer trigger a backoff condition.
5) Delete any recommendation already contained in the original input set P and
   return the remaining recommendations as the final result. We consider two possible ways to define the number of least frequent properties $d(i)$, which are
   deleted from P in run $i \in [p]$:
   a) *Linear Stepsize* $d_L(i) = i$, i.e. set P_i does not contain the least i properties.
      i.e. with every further parallel execution we remove one more item from the
      property set.
   b) *Proportional Stepsize* $d_P(i) = a * n * \frac{i}{q}, 0 \le a \le 1$. Here, n is the number of
      properties in P, a the largest fraction we want to remove, and q the number
      of runs. So, we remove up to a fraction a of the properties in q equally large
      steps.

The linear approach may result in many parallel executions of the recommender in
cases where multiple properties have to be erased until no backoff condition are triggered anymore. In contrast, the proportional approach covers a wider range of input set
reductions with fewer parallel executions at the cost of a less tight stepsize function,
possibly deleting too many properties to find a condition satisfying recommendation,
negatively impacting the recommender's precision.

We consider two **backoff conditions** to trigger the invocation of a backoff strategy:

a) *TooFewRecommendations.* A minimum threshold T_1 for the number of returned
   properties of the standard recommender.
b) *TooUnlikelyRecommendations.* A minimum threshold T_2 for the average probability
   of the top 10 recommendations returned by the standard recommender.

4   Evaluation

This section describes the conducted evaluation procedures and their respective results
with respect to the performance and quality of the recommender. Furthermore, the effect
of the proposed aggregation strategies and metrics will be demonstrated.

The described approach was implemented[5] using Golang for usage with arbitrary
RDF datasets and evaluations were conducted on a machine with Intel Core i7 8700k

---

[5] https://github.com/lgleim/SchemaTreeRecommender.

processor ($6 \times 3, 7$ GHz, Hyper-threading enabled) and 64 GB of RAM. Note, however, that for the SchemaTree approach much less RAM would have been sufficient since the entire in-memory SchemaTree for the Wikidata dataset uses less then 1.3 GB of RAM. Further, the two-pass creation of the SchemaTree for this dataset takes about 20 min in total, whereas the runtime is largely dominated by disk IO and dataset decompression.

Dataset and Preparation. In order to evaluate the different variants of the Schema-Tree recommender and compare its performance to the state-of-the-art Wikidata PropertySuggester, we employ the full Dumps of Wikidata as of July 29th, 2019[6]. We split the dataset into training set (99.9% = 58810044 of the subjects in the dataset) and test set (0.1% = 58868 of the subjects in the dataset) by splitting off every 1000th subject off into the test- and all others into the training set. The training set is then used to construct the SchemaTree, while the test set is used to measure performance. For technical reasons, the full Wikidata PropertySuggester association rules were generated from the full dataset, theoretically giving that system an unfair performance advantage, due to test data being part of its training process. However, as we will see later, even this additional advantage does not make it outperform the proposed approach. All recommenders are subsequently evaluated using the same test set.

Evaluation Procedure. To evaluate we use the procedure proposed by Zangerle et al. [25]. For each evaluated entity, we gather its full set of properties, order the properties by descending support in the training set, and split it into two subsets: the input set and the left-out set. Then, we call the recommender on the input set and evaluate how well it performs at recommending the very same properties that were initially left out. We start with an input set that contains all properties and repeatedly remove the least frequent non-type property in the input set, adding it to the left-out set. On each step, we run an evaluation with the current pair of input and left-out sets. This process is repeated as long as any non-type properties exist in the input set.

Recommender systems capable of employing type information will receive the entity types as additional context in their input set, while the other systems are evaluated without this additional information. Each evaluation run requires that both the input and left-out sets are non-empty.

The results are grouped by the amount of non-type properties in the input sets and left-out sets. This aggregation will guarantee that each entity will belong to the same group across evaluation runs with all models, whether the model uses the additional type properties or not. Ensuring that entities always belong to the same grouping, irrespective of the recommender system used, eases the direct comparison of the different model performances.

Metrics. In order to evaluate the quality of the computed recommendations we employ the following metrics, which are respectively computed for each group of entities:

---

[6] https://dumps.wikimedia.org/wikidatawiki/entities/20190729/.

- ∅Rank: The average position of the first correct recommendation in the top-most 500 recommendations, respectively incurring 500 if not contained.
- Stddev: The standard deviation of the ranks.
- Prec@L: The average precision considering only the first L recommendations, i.e., the ratio of relevant properties found regarding only the first L recommendations to L, where L equals the number of left-outs in each individual run of the recommender.
- TopX: The percentage of all conducted recommendations, where the first correct result was contained in the top X recommendations, where TopL employs X equal to the number of left-outs L in each individual run of the recommender.
- ∅Latency: The average time until the list of recommendations was received over all recommender calls in milliseconds.
- Recall: The average number of properties that could be found in the recommendations list, divided by the total number of left-out properties.
- Modified F1: The harmonic mean of Prec@L and Recall, with an optimal value of 1 (perfect precision and recall) and worst of 0.

Choosing a Backoff Strategy. The large number of possible configuration options, resulting from the different backoff conditions, strategies and parameters introduced in Sect. 3, motivates a preparatory empirical evaluation of different backoff configurations. The control variables include merger and splitter strategies inside the *SplitPropertySet* backoff strategy (c.f. Sect. 3), as well as several options to choose a stepsize function and the number of parallel executions inside the *DeleteLowFrequency* backoff strategy (c.f. Sect. 3). Additionally, it is necessary to set trigger thresholds for the backoff conditions, which can be combined arbitrarily with any backoff strategy above.

To find a good selection of parameters and a suiting combination of condition and backoff strategy, we perform a grid search in which we evaluate 96 different configurations, using the procedure described in Sect. 4 in conjunction with every 10th subject of the test set described in Sect. 4 and metrics computed over all conducted recommendations. We chose different parameters for each condition and backoff strategy by combining the different backoff strategies (depicted in the upper sub-table of Table 1) with the different combinations of the condition configurations (depicted in the lower sub-table of Table 1). We choose $a = 0.4$ as parameter for the linear *Delete Low Frequency Backoff Strategy*.

Table 1. Tested combinations of workflow configurations.

Backoff strategy	Variable	Configuration variants
Split property set	Splitter	Every second item, two frequency ranges
	Merger	avg, max
Delete low frequency	Stepsize	Linear, proportional
	Parallel runs	$\{1,..,6\}$
Backoff condition	**Variable**	**Configuration variants**
TooFewRecommendations	Threshold	$\{1, 2, 3\}$
TooUnlikelyRecommendations	Threshold	$\{0.033, 0.066, 0.1\}$

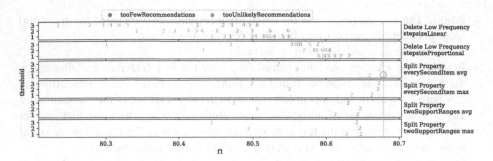

Fig. 2. Comparison of 96 different backoff configurations (c.f. Table 1) w.r.t. their modified F1 score. Higher is better. The six subplots compare the six principal backoff *strategy* configurations outlined in Sect. 3. Sample color indicates the employed backoff *condition* and the position on the respective y-axis the associated backoff *threshold*. *TooUnlikelyRecommondations* thresholds are scaled by factor three for better visual comparability. The number markers indicated the respective number of parallel recommender runs. The best performing strategy is highlighted in red. The F1 score for the system without any backoff startegy is 71.52%.

The evaluation results of all 96 configurations w.r.t. their modified F1 score are illustrated in Fig. 2. First, we observe that any backoff strategy significantly improves the system as without any we obtained an F1 score of 71.52% while all backoff strategies result in more than 80.2%. Comparing the two backoff conditions *TooFewRecommendations* and *TooUnlikelyRecommendations*, the superior performance of the *TooFewRecommendations* strategy is immediately obvious. Comparing the different backoff strategies, we see that the *DeleteLowFrequency* approach with a linear stepsize function performed clearly worst and only reaches comparably better results at the cost of multiple parallel executions. This is likely a direct result of removing an insufficient amount of properties from the initial property set to observe the desired backoff characteristic. In contrast, the *DeleteLowFrequency* strategy with proportional stepsize function achieves much better results, likely because a more optimal, larger amount of properties is left out of the input set compared to the linear stepsize function. In comparison to the *DeleteLowFrequency* approach, the *SplitPropertySet* backoff strategy generally appears to achieve higher recall, which intuitively makes sense, due to the fact that no properties providing context are deleted from the effective input to the recommender system. The respective average merging strategy appears to performs slightly better in most cases then taking the maximum per item probability across the splits.

Concluding, we choose the *SplitPropertySet* backoff approach in conjunction with *everySecondItem* splitter and average merging strategy, triggered by the *TooFewRecommendations* condition with threshold 1, which maximized the modified F1 score over all evaluated strategies.

Evaluation Results. In order to compare the different variants of the SchemaTree recommender with the state-of-the-art Wikidata PropertySuggester (PS) system, we evaluated each system using the procedure described in Sect. 4. We first discuss the overall evaluation results as summarized in Table 2, before examining selected metrics in more detail for different input property set sizes.

All three variants of the SchemaTree recommender (Standard, with type information and with both type information and backoff strategies enabled) clearly outperform the state-of-the-art in terms of ØRank of the first correct recommendation. Additionally the Stddev of that rank is significantly lower, leading to more predictable recommendation results. When comparing only systems with or without usage of type information, the SchemaTree recommender consistently achieves higher Prec@L, F1 and TopX scores, as well as lower average recommendation ØLatency. It thus outperforms the state-of-the-art Wikidata PropertySuggester in every evaluated metric, at the cost of about 1.3 GB of RAM for keeping the SchemaTree data structure in RAM.

With a relative reduction of 71% compared to the PropertySuggester baseline, the average rank of the first correct recommended property for the *Typed & Backoff* approach improves significantly, which directly results in an improved user experience. Note also that the *Typed & Backoff* method leads to relative improvement of 44.83% of the average rank of the first correct property recommendation over the simpler *Typed* approach and a 7.54% relative improvement of correct Top10 results, which in turn means that users will actually see relevant recommendations significantly more often.

Table 2. Benchmark results of the evaluated systems. At the top, we have the PropertySuggester, first without and second with type information for comparison. The three systems at the bottom are the variations of the SchemaTree recommender.

Recommender	ØRank	Stddev	Prec@L	F1	Top1	Top5	Top10	TopL	ØLatency
PS wo/ Types	156.67	179.04	3.31%	6.26%	3.83%	10.15%	12.64%	10.97%	350.58 ms
Wikidata PS	13.05	70.84	64.57%	76.83%	74.34%	90.11%	93.28%	83.65%	29.18 ms
Standard	8.00	40.43	56.48%	71.87%	67.14%	83.38%	89.76%	77.64%	119.66 ms
Typed	6.73	46.25	67.90%	80.49%	78.97%	93.07%	96.02%	87.16%	**25.01 ms**
Typed & Backoff	**3.78**	**24.38**	**68.00%**	**80.76%**	**79.07%**	**93.30%**	**96.32%**	**87.40%**	25.73 ms

To provide a more detailed breakdown of the performance characteristics, we drill down into the results of the metrics Top5, ØRank and modified F1 score and inspect each measure in relation to their respective input set sizes to the recommender systems. Figure 3(a) illustrates the distribution of the respective input set sizes. Note that all following figures depict results for property set sizes of 2 to 55 non-type input parameters. Whereas the lower limit 2 directly results from the requirement to have non-empty input- and left-out sets for the evaluation, the upper limit 55 is selected because of the limited amount of subjects with corresponding larger set size in the test set and the resulting reduced reliability of the evaluation results.

When comparing the Top5 results, depicted in Fig. 3(b), the PropertySuggester without provided type information (*PS wo/ Types*) only achieves a low sub-40% Top5 score throughout the entire test set. In comparison, the *Standard* SchemaTree already results in a significant performance gain, reaching its peak of close to 90% at around 13 input properties, sustaining a score of about 80% as more properties are added to the input set.

The introduction of typing information favours both the PropertySuggester and the SchemaTree, as seen in the results obtained by *Wikidata PS* and *Typed*. As anticipated in Sect. 3, the typing information significantly boosts recommendation performance when only a limited amount of input properties is provided to the recommender. Effectively, the Top5 score of the *Typed* SchemaTree recommender rises by up to more than 75% absolute compared to its untyped *Standard* counterpart. As more and more properties exist on an entity, type information plays a less important role as properties become more specialized and the existing input properties provide more context information. Notably, the SchemaTree (without type information) outperforms the Property-Suggester (with type information) on recalling left-out properties, especially after the 15 properties mark.

While the effect of introducing backoff strategies can be seen in Fig. 3(b) in the general slight performance improvement of the *Typed & Backoff* recommender w.r.t. to the *Typed* SchemaTree, its effect is more obvious when inspecting the ∅Rank of the first correct recommendation in Fig. 3(c). While all characteristics of the different systems described w.r.t. the Top5 score can also be observed for the ∅Rank, it is clearly visible how the introduction of backoff improves the recommendation especially for larger input set sizes. Better recommendations are especially given for entities that are already rather complete. Due to the backoff, properties that co-occur with a subset of the given input can also be recommended, whereas without it only recommends properties that co-occurred with the complete input in the training data. As such, the backoff mechanism clearly fulfills its intended behaviour, as described in Sect. 3. As explained there, the performance degradation of the Wikidata PS likely stems from error accumulation when combining the confidence scores of the potentially many applicable association rules, compared to the frequentist inference approach of the SchemaTree recommender.

Finally, we examine the modified F1 score (Fig. 3(d)) as a measure of the overall quality of the recommendations with varying degrees of left-out properties. Highlighting only the SchemaTree variants, we see a clear confirmation of our previous findings,

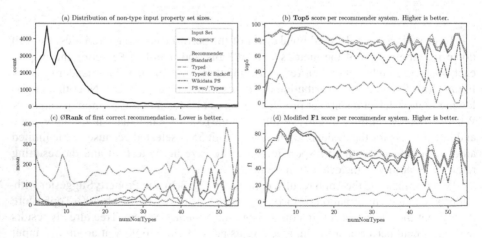

Fig. 3. Detailed results of the recommender system evaluation for different non-type input set sizes.

that type information improves the recommendation quality especially for low numbers of input properties. The incorporation of backoff strategies, on the other hand, only seems to have a slight positive impact with regards to this metric.

Overall, the proposed approach tends to recommend properties that are more contextually relevant (since it can take more context information into account). The Wikidata PropertySuggester, however, can only recommend contextually relevant properties as long as there are meaningful association rules.

5   Conclusion and Future Work

In this work, we introduced a trie-based data structure, capable of efficiently learning and representing property set coocurrence frequencies in RDF graphs. We refer to this data structure as the SchemaTree. We have shown how to use it to efficiently compute the support count of arbitrary property sets in the encoded graph and how it can be employed for maximum-likelihood property recommendation to assist in the manual creation of knowledge graphs, analogously to the Wikidata PropertySuggester. We showed how to improve recall and precision of the recommender system for entities with sparse property sets by incorporating type information from classifying properties into the recommender system. We then presented different novel backoff strategies to improve the capability of the recommender to generalize to unseen property combinations, further improving upon the state-of-the-art, and evaluated the approaches on the Wikidata dataset. We evaluated the performance of different backoff configurations and compared the resulting variations of the SchemaTree property recommender to the state-of-the-art Wikidata PropertySuggester system, demonstrating that our system clearly outperforms the state-of-the-art in all evaluated metrics. Finally, we provided qualitative reasoning as to the limitations of the popular association-rule based recommender systems and how our system overcomes them, as well as advantages and drawbacks of the approach.

One current limitation of this and other existing works is that qualifiers are not taken into account, nor predicted, providing additional directions for further investigations. Further, while we have shown that the presented backoff strategies already significantly improve the performance of the presented recommender, we want to investigate further backoff strategies in future work. Additional theoretical understanding of the current backoff approaches will likely lead to further improvements. To gain this understanding, one would also want to have experimental evidence on how the recommender works for rare properties in heterogeneous graphs.

Further aspects for future work include the inclusion of the values of properties into the property recommendations; one can assume that these also have additional information that can indicate relevance (e.g., typically only people born after 1900 have a personal homepage). Besides, one could also investigate the prediction of values for the properties.

However, due to the combinatorial explosion of options, these are not feasible with the current approach alone (when employing the same approach currently used for classifying properties). For value prediction, if only a small amount of values are possible for a given property, one could attempt to adapt the SchemaTree approach separately for each specific property. For more involved cases, recommending values could be done in a second stage with a different algorithm. Note that value recommendation would also need to work for effectively infinite and/or continuous domains (e.g., floating point numbers), while the current approach only chooses from a finite set of discrete options.

Besides improving the quality of the recommendations themselves, we see also a need fur improving how they are presented to the user. For example, some recommended properties are closely related to each other and presenting them in some sort of clustered or hierarchical form might lead to a better user experience. Further, the conducted evaluation is an attempt to mimic the manual entity authoring process (analogously to evaluations in previous work), we envision a future user study to validate our findings in practice.

References

1. Abedjan, Z., Naumann, F.: Improving RDF data through association rule mining. Datenbank-Spektrum **13**(2), 111–120 (2013). https://doi.org/10.1007/s13222-013-0126-x
2. Abedjan, Z., Naumann, F.: Amending RDF entities with new facts. In: Presutti, V., Blomqvist, E., Troncy, R., Sack, H., Papadakis, I., Tordai, A. (eds.) ESWC 2014. LNCS, vol. 8798, pp. 131–143. Springer, Cham (2014). https://doi.org/10.1007/978-3-319-11955-7_11
3. Aggarwal, C.C., Philip, S.Y.: A new framework for itemset generation. In: Proceedings of the 17th Symposium on Principles of Database Systems, pp. 18–24 (1998)
4. Agrawal, R., Srikant, R., et al.: Fast algorithms for mining association rules. In: Proceedings of the 20th International Conference on Very Large Data Bases, VLDB, vol. 1215, pp. 487–499 (1994)
5. Alonso, O., Kumar, A.: System and method for search and recommendation based on usage mining, US Patent 7,092,936, 15 August 2006
6. Balaraman, V., Razniewski, S., Nutt, W.: Recoin: relative completeness in Wikidata. In: Companion Proceedings of the Web Conference, pp. 1787–1792 (2018)
7. Bauer, F., Kaltenböck, M.: Linked open data: the essentials. In: A Quick Start Guide for Decision Makers, January 2012
8. Berners-Lee, T., Hendler, J., Lassila, O., et al.: The semantic web. Sci. Am. **284**(5), 28–37 (2001)
9. Buneman, P.: Semistructured data. In: Proceedings of the 16th Symposium on Principles of Database Systems, pp. 117–121. ACM (1997)
10. Cafarella, M.J., Halevy, A., Wang, D.Z., Wu, E., Zhang, Y.: WebTables: exploring the power of tables on the web. Proc. VLDB Endowment **1**(1), 538–549 (2008)
11. Dessi, A., Atzori, M.: A machine-learning approach to ranking RDF properties. Future Gener. Comput. Syst. **54**, 366–377 (2016)
12. Fernández, J.D., Beek, W., Martínez-Prieto, M.A., Arias, M.: LOD-a-lot. In: d'Amato, C., et al. (eds.) ISWC 2017. LNCS, vol. 10588, pp. 75–83. Springer, Cham (2017). https://doi.org/10.1007/978-3-319-68204-4_7
13. Gassler, W., Zangerle, E., Specht, G.: Guided curation of semistructured data in collaboratively-built knowledge bases. Future Gener Comput. Syst. **31**, 111–119 (2014)
14. Gleim, L.C., et al.: Schema extraction for privacy preserving processing of sensitive data. In: Joint Proceedings of the MEPDaW, SeWeBMeDA and SWeTI 2018, pp. 36–47. CEUR WS Proceedings, vol. 2112 (2018)
15. Guha, R.V., Brickley, D., Macbeth, S.: Schema.org: evolution of structured data on the web. Commun. ACM **59**(2), 44–51 (2016)

16. Gyorodi, C., Gyorodi, R., Cofeey, T., Holban, S.: Mining association rules using Dynamic FP-trees. In: Proceedings of the Irish Signals and Systems Conference, pp. 76–81 (2003)
17. Han, J., Pei, J., Yin, Y.: Mining frequent patterns without candidate generation. ACM SIG-MOD Rec. **29**, 1–12 (2000)
18. Lee, T., Wang, Z., Wang, H., Hwang, S.W.: Attribute extraction and scoring: a probabilistic approach. In: 29th International Conference on Data Engineering (ICDE), pp. 194–205. IEEE (2013)
19. Ngomo, N., Hoffmann, M., Usbeck, R., Jha, K., et al.: Holistic and scalable ranking of RDF data. In: International Conference on Big Data, pp. 746–755. IEEE (2017)
20. Razniewski, S., Balaraman, V., Nutt, W.: Doctoral advisor or medical condition: towards entity-specific rankings of knowledge base properties. In: Cong, G., Peng, W.-C., Zhang, W.E., Li, C., Sun, A. (eds.) ADMA 2017. LNCS (LNAI), vol. 10604, pp. 526–540. Springer, Cham (2017). https://doi.org/10.1007/978-3-319-69179-4_37
21. Said, A.M., Dominic, P., Abdullah, A.B.: A comparative study of FP-growth variations. Int. J. Comput. Sci. Netw. Secur. **9**(5), 266–272 (2009)
22. Sigurbjörnsson, B., Van Zwol, R.: Flickr tag recommendation based on collective knowledge. In: Proceedings of the 17th International Conference on World Wide Web, pp. 327–336. ACM (2008)
23. Suen, C.Y., Shinghal, R.: Operational Expert System Applications in Canada. Elsevier, Amsterdam (2014)
24. Völker, J., Niepert, M.: Statistical schema induction. In: Antoniou, G., et al. (eds.) ESWC 2011. LNCS, vol. 6643, pp. 124–138. Springer, Heidelberg (2011). https://doi.org/10.1007/978-3-642-21034-1_9
25. Zangerle, E., Gassler, W., Pichl, M., Steinhauser, S., Specht, G.: An empirical evaluation of property recommender systems for Wikidata and collaborative knowledge bases. In: Proceedings of the 12th International Symposium on Open Collaboration, p. 18. ACM (2016)
26. Zangerle, E., Gassler, W., Specht, G.: Recommending structure in collaborative semistructured information systems. In: Proceedings of the 4th Conference on Recommender Systems, pp. 261–264. ACM (2010)

Machine Learning

Hyperbolic Knowledge Graph Embeddings for Knowledge Base Completion

Prodromos Kolyvakis[1]([✉]), Alexandros Kalousis[2], and Dimitris Kiritsis[1]

[1] École Polytechnique Fédérale de Lausanne (EPFL), Lausanne, Switzerland
{prodromos.kolyvakis,dimitris.kiritsis}@epfl.ch
[2] Business Informatics Department, University of Applied Sciences,
Western Switzerland Carouge, HES-SO, Carouge, Switzerland
alexandros.kalousis@hesge.ch

Abstract. Learning embeddings of entities and relations existing in knowledge bases allows the discovery of hidden patterns in them. In this work, we examine the contribution of geometrical space to the task of knowledge base completion. We focus on the family of translational models, whose performance has been lagging. We extend these models to the hyperbolic space so as to better reflect the topological properties of knowledge bases. We investigate the type of regularities that our model, dubbed *HyperKG*, can capture and show that it is a prominent candidate for effectively representing a subset of Datalog rules. We empirically show, using a variety of link prediction datasets, that hyperbolic space allows to narrow down significantly the performance gap between translational and bilinear models and effectively represent certain types of rules.

Keywords: Knowledge graph embeddings · Hyperbolic embeddings · Knowledge base completion

1 Introduction

Learning in the presence of structured information is an important challenge for artificial intelligence [18,31,41]. Knowledge Bases (KBs) such as WordNet [29], Freebase [8], YAGO [47] and DBpedia [27] constitute valuable such resources needed for a plethora of practical applications, including question answering and information extraction. However, despite their formidable number of facts, it is widely accepted that their coverage is still far from being complete [44,58]. This shortcoming has opened the door for a number of studies addressing the problem of automatic knowledge base completion (KBC) or link prediction [34]. The impetus of these studies arises from the hypothesis that statistical regularities lay in KB facts, which when correctly exploited can result in the discovery of missing

Electronic supplementary material The online version of this chapter (https://doi.org/10.1007/978-3-030-49461-2_12) contains supplementary material, which is available to authorized users.

© Springer Nature Switzerland AG 2020
A. Harth et al. (Eds.): ESWC 2020, LNCS 12123, pp. 199–214, 2020.
https://doi.org/10.1007/978-3-030-49461-2_12

true facts [60]. Building on the great generalisation capability of distributed representations, a great line of research [10,35,36,51,62] has focused on learning KB vector space embeddings as a way of predicting the plausibility of a fact.

An intrinsic characteristic of knowledge graphs is that they present power-law (or scale-free) degree distributions as many other networks [15,46]. In an attempt of understanding scale-free networks' properties, various generative models have been proposed such as the models of Barabási and Albert [6] and Van Der Hofstad [53]. Interestingly, Krioukov et al. [25] have shown that scale-free networks naturally emerge in the hyperbolic space. Recently, the hyperbolic geometry was exploited in various works [17,37,38,42] as a means to provide high-quality embeddings for hierarchical structures. Hyperbolic space has the potential to bring significant value in the task of KBC since it offers a natural way to take the KB's topological information into account. Furthermore, many of the relations appearing in KBs lead to hierarchical and hierarchical-like structures [28].

At the same time, the expressiveness of various KB embedding models has been recently examined in terms of their ability to express any ground truth of facts [23,56]. Moreover, Gutiérrez-Basulto and Schockaert [21] have proceeded one step further and investigated the compatibility between ontological axioms and different types of KB embeddings. Specifically, the authors have proved that a certain family of rules, i.e., the quasi-chained rules which form a subset of Datalog rules [1], can be exactly represented by a KB embedding model whose relations are modelled as convex regions; ensuring, thus, logical consistency in the facts induced by this KB embedding model. In the light of this result, it seems important that the appropriateness of a KB embedding model should not only be measured in terms of fully expressiveness but also in terms of the rules that it can model.

In this paper, we explore geometrical spaces having the potential to better represent KBs' topological properties and rules and examine the performance implications on KBC. We focus on the family of translational models [10] that attempt to model the statistical regularities as vector translations between entities' vector representations, and whose performance has been lagging. We extend the translational models by learning embeddings of KB entities and relations in the Poincaré-ball model of hyperbolic geometry. We do so by learning compositional vector representations [30] of the entities appearing in a given fact based on translations. The implausibility of a fact is measured in terms of the hyperbolic distance between the compositional vector representations of its entities and the learned relation vector. We prove that the relation regions captured by our proposed model are convex. Our model becomes, thus, a prominent candidate for representing effectively quasi-chained rules.

Among our contributions is the proposal of a novel KB embedding model as well as a regularisation scheme on the Poincaré-ball model, whose effectiveness we prove empirically. Furthermore, we prove that translational models do not suffer from the restrictions identified by Kazemi and Poole [23] in the case where a fact is considered valid when its implausibility score is below a certain non-zero threshold. We evaluate our approach on various benchmark datasets and our experimental results show that our work makes a big step towards (i) closing the performance gap between translational and bilinear models and (ii) enhancing our understanding of which KBs mostly benefit from exploiting hyperbolic embeddings. Last but not least, our work demonstrates that the choice of geometrical space plays a significant role for KBC and illustrates the importance of taking both the topological and the formal properties of KBs into account. The implementation code and the datasets are publicly available on: https://github.com/prokolyvakis/hyperkg.

2   Related Work

Shallow KB Embedding Models. There has been a great line of research dedicated to the task of learning distributed representations for entities and relations in KBs. To constrain the analysis, we only consider shallow embedding models that do not exploit deep neural networks or incorporate additional external information beyond the KB facts. For an elaborated review of these techniques, please refer to Nickel et al. [34] and Wang et al. [55]. We also exclude from our comparison recent work that explores different types of training regimes such as adversarial training, and/or the inclusion of reciprocal facts [11,23,26,48] to make the analysis less biased to factors that could overshadow the importance of the geometrical space.

In general, the shallow embedding approaches can be divided into two main categories; the translational [10] and the bilinear [36] family of models. In the translational family, the vast majority of models [13,22,57,59] generalise TransE [10], which attempts to model relations as translation operations between the vector representations of the *subject* and *object* entities, as observed in a given fact. In the bilinear family, most of the approaches [35,51,62] generalise RESCAL [36] that proposes to model facts through bilinear operations over entity and relations vector representations. In this paper, we focus on the family of translational models, whose performance has been lagging, and propose extensions in the hyperbolic space which by exploiting the topological and the formal properties of KBs bring significant performance improvements.

Hyperbolic Embeddings. There has been a growing interest in embedding scale-free networks in the hyperbolic space [7,39]. Hyperbolic geometry was also exploited in various works as a way to exploit hierarchical information and learn more efficient representations [17,37,38,42]. However, this line of work has only focused on single-relational networks. Recently and in parallel to our work, two other works have explored hyperbolic embeddings for KBs. Contrary to our work where Möbius or Euclidean addition is used as a translational operation, Suzuki et al. [49] exploit vector fields with an attractive point to generalise translation in Riemannian manifolds. Their approach, although promising, shows a degraded performance on commonly used benchmarks. Similarly to our approach, Balažević et al. [5] extend to the hyperbolic space the family of translational models demonstrating significant performance improvements over state-of-the-art. However, the authors exploit both the hyperbolic as well as the Euclidean space by using the *Möbius Matrix-vector multiplication* and Euclidean scalar biases.[1] Unlike our experimental setup, the authors also include reciprocal facts. Although their approach is beneficial for KBC, it becomes hard to quantify the contributions of hyperbolic space. This is verified by the fact that their Euclidean model analogue performs in line with their "hybrid" hyperbolic-Euclidean model. Finally, neither of these works studies the types of rules that their proposed models can effectively represent.

3   Methods

3.1   Preliminaries

We introduce some definitions and additional notation that we will use throughout the paper. We denote the vector concatenation operation by the symbol $\oplus$ and the inner product by $\langle \cdot, \cdot \rangle$. We define the *rectifier* activation function as: $[\cdot]_+ := \max(\cdot, 0)$.

Quasi-Chained Rules. Let $\mathbf{E}, \mathbf{N}$ and $\mathbf{V}$ be disjoint sets of *entities, (labelled) nulls* and *variables*, respectively.[2] Let $\mathbf{R}$ be the set of relation symbols. A *term* t is an element in $\mathbf{E} \cup \mathbf{N} \cup \mathbf{V}$; an *atom* α is an expression of the form $R(t_1, t_2)$, where R is a *relation* between the terms t_1, t_2. Let $\mathsf{terms}(\alpha) := \{t_1, t_2\}$; $\mathsf{vars}(\alpha) := \mathsf{terms}(\alpha) \cap \mathbf{V}$ and B_n for $n \geq 0$, H_k for $k \geq 1$ be atoms with terms in $\mathbf{E} \cup \mathbf{V}$. Additionally, let $X_j \in \mathbf{V}$ for $j \geq 1$. A *quasi-chained (QC) rule* σ [21] is an expression of the form:

$$B_1 \wedge \ldots \wedge B_n \rightarrow \exists X_1, \ldots, X_j. H_1 \wedge \ldots \wedge H_k, \tag{1}$$

where for all $i : 1 \leq i \leq n$

$$|(\mathsf{vars}(B_1) \cup \ldots \cup \mathsf{vars}(B_{i-1})) \cap \mathsf{vars}(B_i)| \leq 1$$

The QC rules constitute a subset of Datalog rules. A *database* D is a finite set of *facts*, i.e., a set of atoms with terms in $\mathbf{E}$. A *knowledge base (KB)* $\mathcal{K}$ consists of a pair (Σ, D) where Σ is an ontology whose axioms are QC rules and D a database. It should be noted that no constraint is imposed on the number of available axioms in the ontology. The ontology could be minimal in the sense of only defining the relation symbols. However, any type of rule, whether it is the product of the ontological design or results from formalising a statistical regularity, should belong to the family of QC rules. The Gene Ontology [4] constitutes one notable example of an ontology that exhibits QC rules.

Circular Permutation Matrices. An orthogonal matrix is defined as a real square matrix whose columns and rows are orthogonal unit vectors (i.e., orthonormal vectors), i.e.,

$$Q^{\mathrm{T}}Q = QQ^{\mathrm{T}} = I \tag{2}$$

---

[1] The matrix, used in Möbius multiplication, and the biases are defined on Euclidean space and are learned through Euclidean SGD.

[2] Only existential variables can be mapped to labelled nulls.

where I is the identity matrix. Orthogonal matrices preserve the vector inner product and, thus, they also preserve the Euclidean norms. Let $1 \le i < n$, we define the *circular permutation matrix* Π_i to be the orthogonal $n \times n$ matrix that is associated with the following circular permutation of a n-dimensional vector $\boldsymbol{x}$:

$$\begin{pmatrix} x_1 & \cdots & x_{n-i} & x_{n-i+1} & \cdots & x_n \\ x_{i+1} & \cdots & x_n & x_1 & \cdots & x_i \end{pmatrix} \tag{3}$$

where x_i is the ith coordinate of $\boldsymbol{x}$ and i controls the number of $n - i$ successive circular shifts.

Hyperbolic Space. In this work, we exploit the Poincaré-ball model of the hyperbolic geometry. The Poincaré-ball model is the Riemannian manifold $\mathbb{P}^n = (\mathbb{B}^n, d_p)$, where $\mathbb{B}^n = \{\boldsymbol{x} \in \mathbb{R}^n : \|\boldsymbol{x}\| < 1\}$ and d_p is the distance function:

$$d_p(\boldsymbol{u}, \boldsymbol{v}) = \operatorname{acosh}\ (1 + 2\delta(\boldsymbol{u}, \boldsymbol{v})) \tag{4}$$

$$\delta(\boldsymbol{u}, \boldsymbol{v}) = \frac{\|\boldsymbol{u} - \boldsymbol{v}\|^2}{(1 - \|\boldsymbol{u}\|^2)(1 - \|\boldsymbol{v}\|^2)}$$

The Poincaré-ball model presents a group-like structure when it is equipped with the *Möbius addition* [40,52], defined by:

$$\boldsymbol{u} \boxplus \boldsymbol{v} := \frac{(1 + 2\langle \boldsymbol{u}, \boldsymbol{v} \rangle + \|\boldsymbol{v}\|^2)\boldsymbol{u} + (1 - \|\boldsymbol{u}\|^2)\boldsymbol{v}}{1 + 2\langle \boldsymbol{u}, \boldsymbol{v} \rangle + \|\boldsymbol{u}\|^2\|\boldsymbol{v}\|^2} \tag{5}$$

The isometries of $(\mathbb{B}^n, d_p)$ can be expressed as a composition of a left gyrotranslation with an orthogonal transformation restricted to $\mathbb{B}^n$, where the *left gyrotranslation* is defined as $L_u : v \mapsto u \boxplus v$ [2,40]. Therefore, circular permutations constitute zero-left gyrotranslation isometries of the Poincaré-ball model.

3.2   HyperKG

The database of a KB consists of a set of facts in the form of $R(subject, object)$. We will learn hyperbolic embeddings of entities and relations such that valid facts will have a lower implausibility score than the invalid ones. To learn such representations, we extend the work of Bordes et al. [10] by defining a translation-based model in the hyperbolic space; embedding, thus, both entities and relations in the same space.

Let $\boldsymbol{s}, \boldsymbol{r}, \boldsymbol{o} \in \mathbb{B}^n$ be the hyperbolic embeddings of the *subject, relation and object*, respectively, appearing in the $R(subject, object)$ fact. We define a *term embedding* as a function $\xi \colon \mathbb{B}^n \times \mathbb{B}^n \to \mathbb{B}^n$, that creates a composite vector representation for the pair $(subject, object)$. Since our motivation is to generalise the translation models to the hyperbolic space, a natural way to define the term embeddings is by using the Möbius addition. However, we found out empirically that the normal addition in the Euclidean space generalises better than the Möbius addition. We provide a possible explanation for this behaviour in

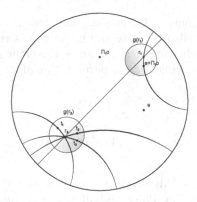

Fig. 1. A visualisation of HyperKG model in the $\mathbb{P}^2$ space. The geodesics of the disk model are circles perpendicular to its boundary. The zero-curvature geodesic passing from the origin corresponds to the line $\epsilon : y - x = 0$ in the Euclidean plane. Reflections over the line ϵ are equivalent to Π_1 permutations in the plane. $s, \Pi_1 o, s + \Pi_1 o$ are the subject vector, the permuted object vector and the composite term vector, respectively. $g(r_1), g(r_2)$ denote the geometric loci of term vectors satisfying relations R_1, R_2, with relation vectors $r1, r2$. t_1, t_2, t_3 are valid term vectors for the relation R_2.

an ablation study presented in the Results & Analysis section. To introduce non-commutativity in the term composition function, we use a circular permutation matrix to project the object embeddings. Non-commutativity is important because it allows to model asymmetric relations with compositional representations [35]. Therefore, we define the term embedding as: $s + \Pi_\beta o$, where β is a hyperparameter controlling the number of successive circular shifts. To enforce the term embeddings to stay in the Poincaré-ball, we constrain all the entity embeddings to have a Euclidean norm less than 0.5. Namely, $\|e\| < 0.5$ and $\|r\| < 1.0$ for all entity and relation vectors, respectively. It should be noted that the entities' norm constraints do not restrict term embeddings to span the Poincaré-ball. We define the implausibility score as the hyperbolic distance between the term and the relation embeddings. Specifically, the implausibility score of a fact is defined as:

$$f_R(s, o) = d_p(s + \Pi_\beta o, r) \tag{6}$$

Figure 1 provides an illustration of the HyperKG model in $\mathbb{P}^2$. We follow previous work [10] to minimise the following hinge loss function:

$$\mathcal{L} = \sum_{\substack{R(s,o) \sim P, \\ R'(s',o') \sim N}} [\gamma + f_R(s, o) - f_{R'}(s', o')]_+ \tag{7}$$

where P is the training set consisting of valid facts, N is a set of corrupted facts. To create the corrupted facts, we experimented with two strategies. We replaced randomly either the subject or the object of a valid fact with a random entity (but not both at the same time). We denote with $\#negs_E$ the number of negative examples. Furthermore, we experimented with replacing randomly the relation while retaining intact the entities of a valid fact. We denote with $\#negs_R$ the number of "relation-corrupted" negative examples. We employ the *"Bernoulli"* sampling method to generate incorrect facts [22,57,60].

As pointed out in different studies [10,12,26], regularisation techniques are really beneficial for the task of KBC. Nonetheless, very few of the classical regu-larisation methods are directly applicable or easily generalisable in the Poincaré-ball model of hyperbolic space. For instance, the ℓ_2 regularisation constraint imposes vectors to stay close to the origin, which can lead to underflows. The same holds for dropout [45], when a rather large dropout rate was used.[3] In our experiments, we noticed a tendency of the word vectors to stay close to the origin. Imposing a constraint to the vectors to stay away from the origin stabilised the training procedure and increased the model's generalisation capa-bility. It should be noted that as the points in the Poincaré-ball approach the ball's boundary their distance $d_p(\boldsymbol{u}, \boldsymbol{v})$ approaches $d_p(\boldsymbol{u}, \boldsymbol{0}) + d_p(\boldsymbol{0}, \boldsymbol{v})$, which is analogous to the fact that in a tree the shortest path between two siblings is the path through their parent [42]. Building on this observation, our regulariser further imposes this "tree-like" property. Additionally, since the volume in hyper-bolic space grows exponentially, our regulariser implicitly penalises crowding. Let $\Theta := \{e_i\}_{i=1}^{|\mathbf{E}|} \bigcup \{r_i\}_{i=1}^{|\mathbf{R}|}$ be the set of all entity and relation vectors, where $|\mathbf{E}|, |\mathbf{R}|$ denote the cardinalities of the sets $\mathbf{E}, \mathbf{R}$, respectively. $\mathcal{R}(\Theta)$ defines our proposed regularisation loss function:

$$\mathcal{R}(\Theta) = \sum_{i=1}^{|\mathbf{E}|+|\mathbf{R}|} (1 - \| \boldsymbol{\theta}_i \|^2) \tag{8}$$

The overall embedding loss is now defined as $\mathcal{L}'(\Theta) = \mathcal{L}(\Theta) + \lambda \mathcal{R}(\Theta)$, where λ is a hyperparameter controlling the regularisation effect. We define $a_i := 0.5$, if θ_i corresponds to an entity vector and $a_i := 1.0$, otherwise. To minimise $\mathcal{L}'(\Theta)$, we solve the following optimisation problem:

$$\Theta' \leftarrow \arg\min_{\Theta} \mathcal{L}'(\Theta) \qquad \text{s.t. } \forall \boldsymbol{\theta}_i \in \Theta : \|\boldsymbol{\theta}_i\| < a_i. \tag{9}$$

To solve Eq. (9), we follow Nickel and Kiela [37] and use Riemannian SGD (RSGD; [9]). In RSGD, the parameter updates are of the form:

$$\theta_{t+1} = \mathfrak{R}_{\theta_t} (-\eta \nabla_R \mathcal{L}'(\theta_t))$$

where $\mathfrak{R}_{\theta_t}$ denotes the retraction onto the open d-dimensional unit ball at θ_t and η denotes the learning rate. The Riemannian gradient of $\mathcal{L}'(\boldsymbol{\theta})$ is denoted by $\nabla_R \in \mathcal{T}_\theta \mathbb{B}$. The Riemannian gradient can be computed as $\nabla_R = \frac{(1-\|\theta_t\|^2)^2}{4} \nabla_E$, where ∇_E denotes the Euclidean gradient of $\mathcal{L}'(\boldsymbol{\theta})$. Similarly to Nickel and Kiela [37], we use the following retraction operation $\mathfrak{R}_\theta(v) = \boldsymbol{\theta} + v$.

---

[3] In our experiments, we noticed that a rather small dropout rate had no effect on the model's generalisation capability.

To constrain the embeddings to remain within the Poincaré ball and respect the additional constraints, we use the following projection:

$$\text{proj}(\boldsymbol{\theta}, a) = \begin{cases} a\boldsymbol{\theta}/(\|\boldsymbol{\theta}\| + \varepsilon) & \text{if } \|\boldsymbol{\theta}\| \geq a \\ \boldsymbol{\theta} & \text{otherwise}, \end{cases} \tag{10}$$

where ε is a small constant to ensure numerical stability. In all experiments we used $\varepsilon = 10^{-5}$. Let a be the constraint imposed on vector $\boldsymbol{\theta}$, the full update for a single embedding is then of the form:

$$\boldsymbol{\theta}_{t+1} \leftarrow \text{proj}\left(\boldsymbol{\theta}_t - \eta \frac{(1 - \|\boldsymbol{\theta}_t\|^2)^2}{4} \nabla_E, a\right). \tag{11}$$

We initialise the embeddings using the Xavier initialization scheme [19], where we use Eq. (10) for projecting the vectors whose norms violate the imposed constraints. Finally, it should be noted that the space complexity of HyperKG is the same as that of TransE and, based on our measurements, the running time of HyperKG is almost double compared to that of TransE [10] and ComplEx [51].

3.3   Convex Relation Spaces

In this section, we investigate the type of rules that HyperKG can model. Recently, Wang et al. [56] proved that the bilinear models are universal, i.e., they can represent every possible fact given that the dimensionality of the vectors is sufficient. The authors have also shown that the TransE model is not universal. In parallel, Kazemi and Poole [23] have shown that the FTransE model [16], which is the most general translational model proposed in the literature, imposes some severe restrictions on the types of relations the translational models can represent. In the core of their proof lies the assumption that the implausibility score defined by the FTransE model approaches zero for all given valid facts. Nonetheless, this condition is less likely to be met from an optimisation perspective [59].

Additionally, Gutiérrez-Basulto and Schockaert [21] studied the types of regularities that KB embedding methods can capture. To allow for a formal characterisation, the authors considered hard thresholds λ_R such that a fact $R(s, o)$ is considered valid iff $s_R(\boldsymbol{s}, \boldsymbol{o}) \leq \lambda_R$, where $s_R(.,.)$ is the implausibility score. It should be highlighted that KB embeddings are often learned based on a maximum-margin loss function, which ideally leads to hard-threshold separation. The vector space representation of a given relation R can then be viewed as a region $n(R)$ in $\mathbb{R}^{2n}$, defined as follows:

$$n(R) = \{\boldsymbol{s} \oplus \boldsymbol{o} \mid s_R(\boldsymbol{s}, \boldsymbol{o}) \leq \lambda_R\} \tag{12}$$

Based on this view of the relation space, the authors prove that although bilinear models are fully expressive, they impose constraints on the type of rules they can learn. Specifically, let $R_1(X, Y) \to S(X, Y)$, $R_2(X, Y) \to S(X, Y)$ be two valid rules. The bilinear models impose either that $R_1(X, Y) \to R_2(X, Y)$ or

$R_2(X, Y) \rightarrow R_1(X, Y)$; introducing, thus, a number of restrictions on the type of subsumption hierarchies they can model. Gutiérrez-Basulto and Schockaert [21], additionally, prove that there exists a KB embedding model with convex relation regions that can correctly represent knowledge bases whose axioms belong to the family of QC rules. Equivalently, any inductive reasoning made by the aforementioned KB embedding model would be logically consistent and deductively closed with respect to the ontological rules. It can be easily verified that the relation regions of TransE [10] are indeed convex. This result is in accordance with the results of Wang et al. [56]; TransE is not fully expressive. However, it could be a prominent candidate for representing QC rules consistently. Nonetheless, this result seems to be in conflict with the results of Kazemi and Poole [23]. Let $s_R^{TE}(s, o)$ be the implausibility score of TransE, we demystify this seeming inconsistency by proving the following lemma:

Lemma 1. *The restrictions proved by Kazemi and Poole [23] do not apply to the TransE model when a fact is considered valid iff $s_R^{TE}(s, o) \leq \lambda_R$ for sufficient $\lambda_R > 0$.*

We prove Lemma 1 in the Supplemental Material, which is also provided in [24], by constructing counterexamples for each one of the restrictions. Since the restrictions can be lifted for the TransE model, we can safely conclude that they are not, in general, valid for all its generalisations. In parallel, we built upon the formal characterisation of relations regions, defined in Eq. (12) and we prove that the relation regions captured by HyperKG are indeed convex. Specifically, we prove:

Proposition 1. *The geometric locus of the term vectors, in the form of $s + \Pi_\beta o$, that satisfy the equation $d_p(s + \Pi_\beta o, r) \leq \lambda_R$ for some $\lambda_R > 0$ corresponds to a d-dimensional closed ball in the Euclidean space. Let $\rho = \frac{\cosh(\lambda_R) - 1}{2}(1 - \|r\|^2)$, the geometric locus can be written as $\|s + \Pi_\beta o - \frac{r}{\rho + 1}\|^2 \leq \frac{\rho}{\rho + 1} + \frac{\|r\|^2}{(\rho + 1)^2} - \frac{\|r\|^2}{\rho + 1}$, where the ball's radius is guaranteed to be strictly greater than zero.*

The proof of Proposition 1 can also be found in the Supplemental Material – also provided in [24]. By exploiting the triangle inequality, we can easily verify that the relation regions captured by HyperKG are indeed convex. Figure 1 provides an illustration of the geometric loci captured by HyperKG in $\mathbb{B}^2$. This result shows that HyperKG constitutes another one prominent embedding model for effectively representing QC rules.

4   Experiments

We evaluate our HyperKG model on the task of KBC using two sets of experiments. We conduct experiments on the WN18RR [12] and FB15k-237 [50] datasets. We also construct two datasets whose statistical regularities can be expressed as QC rules to test our model's performance in their presence. WN18RR and FB15k-237 constitute refined subsets of WN18 and FB15K that

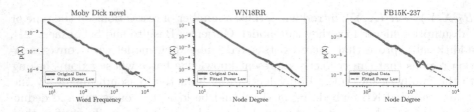

Fig. 2. A visualisation of the probability density functions using a histogram with log-log axes.

were introduced by Bordes et al. [10]. Toutanova and Chen [50] identified that WN18 and FB15K contained a lot of reversible relations, enabling, thus, various KB embedding models to generalise easily. Exploiting this fact, Dettmers et al. [12] obtained state-of-the-art results only by using a simple reversal rule. WN18RR and FB15k-237 were carefully created to alleviate this leakage of information.

To test whether the scale-free distribution provides a reasonable means for modelling topological properties of knowledge graphs, we investigate the degree distributions of WN18RR and FB15k-237. Similarly to Steyvers and Tenenbaum [46], we treat the knowledge graphs as undirected networks. We also compare against the distribution of the frequency of word usage in the English language; a phenomenon that is known to follow a power-law distribution [63]. To do so, we used the frequency of word usage in Herman Melville's novel "Moby Dick" [32]. We followed the procedure described by Alstott et al. [3]. In Fig. 2, we show our analysis where we demonstrate on a histogram with log-log axes the probability density function with regard to the observed property for each dataset, including the fitted power-law distribution. It can be seen that the power-law distribution provides a reasonable means for also describing the degree distribution of KBs; justifying the work of Steyvers and Tenenbaum [46]. The fluctuations in the cases of WN18RR and FB15k-237 could be explained by the fact that the datasets are subsets of more complete KBs; a fact that introduces noise which in turn can explain deviations from the perfection of a theoretical distribution [3].

4.1 Datasets

To test our model's performance on capturing QC rules, we extract from Wikidata [14,54] two subsets of facts that satisfy the following rules:

(a) $is\_a(X, Y) \wedge part\_of(Y, Z) \rightarrow part\_of(X, Z)$
(b) $part\_of(X, Y) \wedge is\_a(Y, Z) \rightarrow part\_of(X, Z)$

The relations is_a, $part\_of$ correspond to the subsumption and the mereology relation, respectively, which are two of the most common relations encountered in KBs [43]. Recent studies have noted that many real world KB relations have very few facts [61], raising the importance of generalising with limited number of facts. To test our model in the presence of sparse long-tail relations, we kept the created datasets sufficiently small. For each type of the aforementioned rules, we extract 200 facts that satisfy them from Wikidata. We construct two datasets that we dub WD and WD$_{++}$. The dataset WD contains only the facts that satisfy rule (a). WD$_{++}$ extends WD by also including the facts satisfying rule (b). The evaluation protocol was the following: For every dataset, we split all the facts randomly in train (80%), validation (10%), and test (10%) set, such that the validation and test sets only contain a subset of the rules' consequents in the form of $part\_of(X, Z)$. Table 1 provides details regarding the respective size of each dataset.

Table 1. Statistics of the experimental datasets.

Dataset	$|E|$	$|R|$	#Train	#Valid	#Test
WN18RR	40,943	11	86,835	3,034	3,134
FB15k-237	14,541	237	272,115	17,535	20,466
WD	418	2	550	25	25
WD$_{++}$	763	2	1,120	40	40

4.2   Evaluation Protocol and Implementation Details

In the KBC task the models are evaluated based on their capability to answer queries such as $R(subject, ?)$ and $R(?, object)$ [10]; predicting, thus, the missing entity. Specifically, all the possible corruptions are obtained by replacing either the *subject* or the *object* and the entities are ranked based on the values of the implausibility score. The models should assign lower implausibility scores to valid facts and higher scores to implausible ones. We use the "**Filtered**" setting protocol [10], i.e., not taking any corrupted facts that exist in KB into account. We employ three common evaluation metrics: mean rank (MR), mean reciprocal rank (MRR), and Hits@10 (i.e., the proportion of the valid/test triples ranking in top 10 predictions). Higher MRR or higher Hits@10 indicate better performance. On the contrary, lower MR indicates better performance.

   The reported results are given for the best set of hyperparameters evaluated on the validation set using grid search. Varying the batch size had no effect on the performance. Therefore, we divided every epoch into 10 mini-batches. The hyperparameter search space was the following: $\#negs_E \in \{1, 2, 3, 4, 5, 8, 10, 12, 15\}$, $\#negs_R \in \{0, 1, 2\}$, $\eta \in \{0.8, 0.5, 0.2, 0.1, 0.05, 0.01, 0.005\}$, $\beta \in \{\lfloor \frac{3n}{4} \rfloor, \lfloor \frac{n}{2} \rfloor, \lfloor \frac{n}{4} \rfloor, 0\}$, $\gamma \in \{7.0, 5.0, 2.0, 1.5, 1.0, 0.8, 0.5, 0.2, 0.1\}$, the embeddings' dimension $n \in \{40, 100, 200\}$, and $\lambda \in \{2.0, 1.5, 1.0, 0.8, 0.6, 0.4, 0.2, 0.1, 0.0\}$. We used early stopping based on the validation's set filtered MRR performance, computed every 50 epochs with a maximum number of 2000 epochs. Due to space limitation, we report the best hyper-parameters in the Supplemental Material provided in [24].

4.3   Results and Analysis

Table 2 compares the experimental results of our HyperKG model with previous published results on WN18RR and FB15k-237 datasets. We have experimentally validated that both datasets present power-law degree distributions. Additionally, WN18RR contains more hierarchical-like relations compared to FB15k-237 [5]. We compare against the shallow KB embedding models DISTMULT [62], ComplEx [51] and TransE [10], which constitute important representatives of bilinear and translational models. We exclude from our comparison recent work that explores different types of training regimes such as adversarial training, the inclusion of reciprocal facts and/or multiple geometrical spaces [5,11,23,26,48] to make the analysis less biased to factors that could overshadow the importance of the embedding space. We give the results of our algorithm under the HyperKG listing. When we compare the performance of HyperKG and TransE on WN18RR, we see that HyperKG achieves almost the double MRR score. This shows that the lower MRR performance on certain datasets is not an intrinsic characteristic of the translational models, but a restriction that can be lifted by the right choice of geometrical space. On the WN18RR dataset, HyperKG exhibits slightly lower Hits@10 performance compared to ComplEx. Moreover, HyperKG achieves a better MR score compared to the bilinear models on WN18RR, but worse compared to TransE. On the FB15k-237 dataset, HyperKG and TransE demonstrate almost the same behaviour outperforming DISTMULT and ComplEx in terms of MRR and Hits@10. Since this performance gap is small, we hypothesise that this is due to a less fine-grained hyperparameter tuning. Interestingly, HyperKG achieves a better MR score compared to TransE on FB15k-237, but, still, worse compared to DISTMULT.

Table 2. Experimental results on WN18RR and FB15k-237 test sets. [⋆]: Results are taken from Nguyen et al. [33].

Method	Type	WN18RR			FB15k-237		
		MR	MRR	Hits@10	MR	MRR	Hits@10
DISTMULT [62] [⋆]	Bilinear	5110	0.43	0.49	254	0.24	0.41
ComplEx [51] [⋆]	Bilinear	5261	0.44	0.51	339	0.24	0.42
TransE [10] [⋆]	Translational	3384	0.22	0.50	347	0.29	0.46
HyperKG (Möbius addition)	Translational	4668	0.30	0.44	822	0.19	0.32
HyperKG (no regularisation)	Translational	5569	0.30	0.46	318	0.25	0.41
HyperKG	Translational	4165	0.41	0.50	272	0.28	0.45

We also report in Table 2 two additional experiments where we explore the performance boost that our regularisation scheme brings as well as the behaviour of HyperKG when the Möbius addition is used instead of the Euclidean one. In the experiment where the Möbius addition was used, we removed the constraint for the entity vectors to have a norm less than 0.5. Although the Möbius addition is non-commutative, we found beneficial to keep the permutation matrix. Nonetheless, we do not use our regularisation scheme. Therefore, the implausibility score is $d_p(s \boxplus \Pi_\beta o, r)$. To investigate the effect of our proposed regularisation scheme, we show results where our regularisation scheme, defined in Eq. 8, is not used, keeping, however, the rest of the architecture the same. Comparing the performance of the HyperKG variation using the Möbius addition against the performance of the HyperKG without regularisation, we can observe that we can achieve better results in terms of MRR and Hits@10 by using the Euclidean addition. This can be explained as follows. Generally, there is no unique and universal geometrical space adequate for every dataset [20]. To recover Euclidean Space from the Poincaré-ball model equipped with the Möbius addition, the ball's radius should grow to infinity [52]. Instead, by using the Euclidean addition and since the hyperbolic metric is locally Euclidean, HyperKG can model facts for which the Euclidean Space is more appropriate by learning to retain small distances. Last but not least, we can observe that our proposed regularisation scheme is beneficial in terms of MR, MRR and Hits@10 on both datasets. Overall, the hyperbolic space appears more beneficial for datasets that contain many hierarchical-like relations such as WN18RR, without a significant performance degradation in the other case.

Table 3 reports the results on the WD and WD$_{++}$ datasets. We compare HyperKG performance against that of TransE and ComplEx. It can be observed that none of the models manages to totally capture the statistical regularities of these datasets. All the models undergo similar Hits@10 performance on both datasets. HyperKG and TransE, that both have convex relation spaces, outperform ComplEx on both datasets in terms of MRR and Hits@10. Furthermore, the translational models show a relatively steady performance compared to ComplEx, whose performance deteriorates in the presence of the two rules appearing in WD$_{++}$. With regard to MR, HyperKG closes the gap between translational and bilinear models on WD and shows the best performance on WD$_{++}$. Our results point to a promising direction for developing less expressive KB embedding models which can, however, better represent certain types of rules.

Table 3. Experimental results on WD and WD$_{++}$ test sets.

Method	WD			WD$_{++}$		
	MR	MRR	Hits@10	MR	MRR	Hits@10
ComplEx	1.22	0.92	0.98	2.42	0.81	0.92
TransE	2.52	0.88	0.96	2.01	0.89	0.98
HyperKG	1.32	0.98	0.98	1.36	0.93	0.98

5   Conclusion and Outlook

In this paper, we examined the importance of the geometrical space for the task of KBC. We showed that the lagging performance of translational models compared to the bilinear ones is not an intrinsic characteristic of them but a restriction that can be lifted in the hyperbolic space. Our results validated that the right choice of geometrical space is a critical decision that impacts the performance of KB embedding models. Our findings also shed light on understanding which KBs mostly benefit from the use of hyperbolic embeddings. Moreover, we demonstrated a new promising direction for developing models that, although not fully expressive, allow to better represent certain families of rules; opening up for more fine-grained reasoning tasks. In the future, we plan to extend our approach to the bilinear family of models.

Acknowledgments. We would like to thank the anonymous reviewers for their insightful comments on the paper.

References

1. Abiteboul, S., Hull, R., Vianu, V.: Foundations of Databases: The Logical Level. Addison-Wesley Longman Publishing Co. Inc., Boston (1995)
2. Ahlfors, L.V.: Invariant operators and integral representations in hyperbolic space. Math. Scand. **36**(1), 27–43 (1975)
3. Alstott, J., Bullmore, E., Plenz, D.: powerlaw: a Python package for analysis of heavy-tailed distributions. PloS One **9**(1), e85777 (2014)
4. Ashburner, M., et al.: Gene ontology: tool for the unification of biology. Nat. Genet. **25**(1), 25 (2000)
5. Balažević, I., Allen, C., Hospedales, T.: Multi-relational Poincaré graph embeddings. In: NeurIPS (2019)
6. Barabási, A.L., Albert, R.: Emergence of scaling in random networks. Science **286**(5439), 509–512 (1999)
7. Boguná, M., Papadopoulos, F., Krioukov, D.: Sustaining the internet with hyperbolic mapping. Nat. Commun. **1**, 62 (2010)
8. Bollacker, K., Evans, C., Paritosh, P., Sturge, T., Taylor, J.: Freebase: a collaboratively created graph database for structuring human knowledge. In: SIGMOD (2008)
9. Bonnabel, S.: Stochastic gradient descent on Riemannian manifolds. IEEE Trans. Automat. Contr. **58**(9), 2217–2229 (2013)
10. Bordes, A., Usunier, N., Garcia-Duran, A., Weston, J., Yakhnenko, O.: Translating embeddings for modeling multi-relational data. In: NeurIPS (2013)
11. Cai, L., Wang, W.Y.: KBGAN: adversarial learning for knowledge graph embeddings. In: NAACL, June 2018. https://www.aclweb.org/anthology/N18-1133
12. Dettmers, T., Minervini, P., Stenetorp, P., Riedel, S.: Convolutional 2D knowledge graph embeddings. In: AAAI (2018)
13. Ebisu, T., Ichise, R.: TorusE: knowledge graph embedding on a lie group. In: AAAI (2018)
14. Erxleben, F., Günther, M., Krötzsch, M., Mendez, J., Vrandečić, D.: Introducing Wikidata to the linked data web. In: Mika, P., et al. (eds.) ISWC 2014. LNCS, vol. 8796, pp. 50–65. Springer, Cham (2014). https://doi.org/10.1007/978-3-319-11964-9_4
15. Faloutsos, M., Faloutsos, P., Faloutsos, C.: On power-law relationships of the internet topology. ACM SIGCOMM Comput. Commun. Rev. **29**, 251–262 (1999). ACM
16. Feng, J., Huang, M., Wang, M., Zhou, M., Hao, Y., Zhu, X.: Knowledge graph embedding by flexible translation. In: KR (2016)
17. Ganea, O., Becigneul, G., Hofmann, T.: Hyperbolic entailment cones for learning hierarchical embeddings. In: ICML, pp. 1646–1655 (2018)

18. Getoor, L., Taskar, B.: Introduction to Statistical Relational Learning, vol. 1. MIT Press, Cambridge (2007)
19. Glorot, X., Bengio, Y.: Understanding the difficulty of training deep feedforward neural networks. In: AISTATS, pp. 249–256 (2010)
20. Gu, A., Sala, F., Gunel, B., Ré, C.: Learning mixed-curvature representations in product spaces. In: ICLR (2018)
21. Gutiérrez-Basulto, V., Schockaert, S.: From knowledge graph embedding to ontology embedding? An analysis of the compatibility between vector space representations and rules. In: KR (2018)
22. Ji, G., He, S., Xu, L., Liu, K., Zhao, J.: Knowledge graph embedding via dynamic mapping matrix. In: ACL-IJCNLP, pp. 687–696 (2015)
23. Kazemi, S.M., Poole, D.: Simple embedding for link prediction in knowledge graphs. In: NeurIPS, pp. 4284–4295 (2018)
24. Kolyvakis, P., Kalousis, A., Kiritsis, D.: HyperKG: hyperbolic knowledge graph embeddings for knowledge base completion. arXiv preprint arXiv:1908.04895 (2019)
25. Krioukov, D., Papadopoulos, F., Kitsak, M., Vahdat, A., Boguñá, M.: Hyperbolic geometry of complex networks. Phys. Rev. E **82**, 036106 (2010)
26. Lacroix, T., Usunier, N., Obozinski, G.: Canonical tensor decomposition for knowledge base completion. In: ICML (2018)
27. Lehmann, J., et al.: DBpedia-a large-scale, multilingual knowledge base extracted from Wikipedia. Semant. Web **6**(2), 167–195 (2015)
28. Li, M., Jia, Y., Wang, Y., Li, J., Cheng, X.: Hierarchy-based link prediction in knowledge graphs. In: WWW (2016). https://doi.org/10.1145/2872518.2889387
29. Miller, G.: WordNet: An Electronic Lexical Database. MIT Press, Cambridge (1998)
30. Mitchell, J., Lapata, M.: Vector-based models of semantic composition. In: Proceedings of ACL-08: HLT (2008). http://aclweb.org/anthology/P08-1028
31. Muggleton, S., De Raedt, L.: Inductive logic programming: theory and methods. J. Log. Program. **19**, 620–670 (1994)
32. Newman, M.E.: Power laws, Pareto distributions and Zipf's law. Contemp. Phys. **46**(5), 323–351 (2005)
33. Nguyen, D.Q., Nguyen, T.D., Nguyen, D.Q., Phung, D.: A novel embedding model for knowledge base completion based on convolutional neural network. In: NAACL (2018). http://aclweb.org/anthology/N18-2053
34. Nickel, M., Murphy, K., Tresp, V., Gabrilovich, E.: A review of relational machine learning for knowledge graphs. Proc. IEEE **104**(1), 11–33 (2016)
35. Nickel, M., Rosasco, L., Poggio, T.: Holographic embeddings of knowledge graphs. In: AAAI (2016). http://dl.acm.org/citation.cfm?id=3016100.3016172
36. Nickel, M., Tresp, V., Kriegel, H.P.: A three-way model for collective learning on multi-relational data. In: ICML (2011)
37. Nickel, M., Kiela, D.: Poincaré embeddings for learning hierarchical representations. In: NeurIPS (2017)
38. Nickel, M., Kiela, D.: Learning continuous hierarchies in the Lorentz model of hyperbolic geometry. In: ICML (2018)
39. Papadopoulos, F., Aldecoa, R., Krioukov, D.: Network geometry inference using common neighbors. Phys. Rev. E **92**(2), 022807 (2015)
40. Rassias, T.M., Suksumran, T.: An inequality related to Möbius transformations. arXiv preprint arXiv:1902.05003 (2019)
41. Richardson, M., Domingos, P.: Markov logic networks. Mach. Learn. **62**(1–2), 107–136 (2006). https://doi.org/10.1007/s10994-006-5833-1
42. Sala, F., De Sa, C., Gu, A., Re, C.: Representation tradeoffs for hyperbolic embeddings. In: ICML (2018). http://proceedings.mlr.press/v80/sala18a.html

43. Schwarz, U., Smith, B.: Ontological relations. Appl. Ontol. Introduction **219**, 234 (2008)
44. Socher, R., Chen, D., Manning, C.D., Ng, A.: Reasoning with neural tensor networks for knowledge base completion. In: NeurIPS, pp. 926–934 (2013)
45. Srivastava, N., Hinton, G., Krizhevsky, A., Sutskever, I., Salakhutdinov, R.: Dropout: a simple way to prevent neural networks from overfitting. J. Mach. Learn. Res. **15**, 1929–1958 (2014)
46. Steyvers, M., Tenenbaum, J.B.: The large-scale structure of semantic networks: statistical analyses and a model of semantic growth. Cogn. Sci. **29**(1), 41–78 (2005)
47. Suchanek, F.M., Kasneci, G., Weikum, G.: Yago: a core of semantic knowledge. In: WWW (2007)
48. Sun, Z., Deng, Z.H., Nie, J.Y., Tang, J.: Rotate: knowledge graph embedding by relational rotation in complex space. In: ICLR (2019)
49. Suzuki, A., Enokida, Y., Yamanishi, K.: Riemannian TransE: multi-relational graph embedding in non-euclidean space (2019). https://openreview.net/forum?id=r1xRW3A9YX
50. Toutanova, K., Chen, D.: Observed versus latent features for knowledge base and text inference. In: Proceedings of the 3rd Workshop on Continuous Vector Space Models and their Compositionality (2015). http://aclweb.org/anthology/W15-4007
51. Trouillon, T., Welbl, J., Riedel, S., Gaussier, É., Bouchard, G.: Complex embeddings for simple link prediction. In: ICML (2016)
52. Ungar, A.A.: Beyond the Einstein Addition Law and its Gyroscopic Thomas Precession: The Theory of Gyrogroups and Gyrovector Spaces. Fundamental Theories of Physics, vol. 117, 1st edn, p. 464. Springer, Netherlands (2012). https://doi.org/10.1007/0-306-47134-5
53. Van Der Hofstad, R.: Random graphs and complex networks, vol. 11 (2009). http://www.win.tue.nl/rhofstad/NotesRGCN.pdf
54. Vrandečić, D., Krötzsch, M.: Wikidata: a free collaborative knowledgebase. Commun. ACM **57**(10), 78–85 (2014). https://doi.org/10.1145/2629489
55. Wang, Q., Mao, Z., Wang, B., Guo, L.: Knowledge graph embedding: a survey of approaches and applications. IEEE Trans. Knowl. Data Eng. **29**(12), 2724–2743 (2017)
56. Wang, Y., Gemulla, R., Li, H.: On multi-relational link prediction with bilinear models. In: AAAI (2018)
57. Wang, Z., Zhang, J., Feng, J., Chen, Z.: Knowledge graph embedding by translating on hyperplanes. In: AAAI (2014)
58. West, R., Gabrilovich, E., Murphy, K., Sun, S., Gupta, R., Lin, D.: Knowledge base completion via search-based question answering. In: WWW (2014)
59. Xiao, H., Huang, M., Zhu, X.: From one point to a manifold: knowledge graph embedding for precise link prediction. In: IJCAI (2016)
60. Xie, Q., Ma, X., Dai, Z., Hovy, E.: An interpretable knowledge transfer model for knowledge base completion. In: ACL (2017)
61. Xiong, W., Yu, M., Chang, S., Guo, X., Wang, W.Y.: One-shot relational learning for knowledge graphs. In: EMNLP, October-November 2018
62. Yang, B., Yih, W.T., He, X., Gao, J., Deng, L.: Embedding entities and relations for learning and inference in knowledge bases. In: ICLR (2015)
63. Zipf, G.K.: Human Behaviour and the Principle of Least Effort. Addison-Wesley, Boston (1949)

Unsupervised Bootstrapping of Active Learning for Entity Resolution

Anna Primpeli[(✉)], Christian Bizer, and Margret Keuper

Data and Web Science Group, University of Mannheim, Mannheim, Germany
{anna,chris}@informatik.uni-mannheim.de, keuper@uni-mannheim.de

Abstract. Entity resolution is one of the central challenges when integrating data from large numbers of data sources. Active learning for entity resolution aims to learn high-quality matching models while minimizing the human labeling effort by selecting only the most informative record pairs for labeling. Most active learning methods proposed so far, start with an empty set of labeled record pairs and iteratively improve the prediction quality of a classification model by asking for new labels. The absence of adequate labeled data in the early active learning iterations leads to unstable models of low quality which is known as the cold start problem. In our work we solve the cold start problem using an unsupervised matching method to bootstrap active learning. We implement a thresholding heuristic that considers pre-calculated similarity scores and assigns matching labels with some degree of noise at no manual labeling cost. The noisy labels are used for initializing the active learning process and throughout the whole active learning cycle for model learning and query selection. We evaluate our pipeline with six datasets from three different entity resolution settings using active learning with a committee-based query strategy and show it successfully deals with the cold start problem. Comparing our method against two active learning baselines without bootstrapping, we show that it can additionally lead to overall improved learned models in terms of F_1 score and stability.

Keywords: Active learning · Unsupervised matching · Entity resolution

1 Introduction

Entity resolution methods often rely on supervised learning for matching entity descriptions from different data sources [3,5]. This means that a specific set of training record pairs is required for each pair of sources to be matched. The required amount of training data thus grows quickly with the number of data sources to be integrated. Labeling large amounts of data is a tedious task. Active learning for entity resolution aims at minimizing the human labeling effort by iteratively selecting only an informative subset of record pairs for labeling. In each active learning iteration, one or more informative record pairs are selected and provided to a human annotator for labeling. One way to measure the degree

© Springer Nature Switzerland AG 2020
A. Harth et al. (Eds.): ESWC 2020, LNCS 12123, pp. 215–231, 2020.
https://doi.org/10.1007/978-3-030-49461-2_13

of informativeness is to calculate the disagreement among the predictions of a classifier ensemble known as the Query-by-Committee strategy [2,19,21]. The most informative record pairs are the ones that cause the highest disagreement among the members of the committee.

A problem which frequently arises in active learning, is the lack of labeled data in the early iterations, known as the cold start problem [9]. In these cases, the model does not have adequate data to learn from and is therefore of low predictive quality. To circumvent the cold start problem, existing active learning methods for entity resolution require the human annotator to label a small set of record pairs. This set is either selected randomly [9,18] or based on the distribution of pre-calculated similarity scores [2,19] before the active learning starts. However, solving the cold start problem by manually annotating a subset of the data is contradicting the main principle of active learning, that of minimizing the human labeling effort.

We propose an alternative method for dealing with the cold start problem. Our method uses unsupervised matching to bootstrap active learning and therefore comes at no additional labeling cost. More concretely, we use datatype specific similarity metrics and assign a similarity score to all record pairs. The similarity score distribution is accounted for setting a suitable threshold value. Considering the threshold boundary, we assign binary labels *match* or *non-match* and confidence weights to the record pairs with some degree of noise. The noisy set of unsupervised weighted labeled record pairs is used to bootstrap active learning. In addition, it is part of the complete active learning cycle as it is used for model training and record pair selection. We show that our thresholding heuristic gives better unsupervised matching results in comparison to commonly used thresholding methods, independently of the underlying similarity distribution. Bootstrapping active learning with unsupervised labeled pairs guarantees high anytime performance and stability. Our experiments show that our proposed method can improve the model quality in terms of absolute F_1 score by 86% in the cold start phase and up to 3% after the cold start phase in comparison to baseline active learning methods that do not use unsupervised bootstrapping. The contributions of our work are summarized as follows:

- We propose a thresholding heuristic that uses a domain independent scoring function and outperforms existing thresholding methods.
- We propose a method for warm-starting active learning that comes at no additional labeling cost and guarantees high anytime performance.
- We perform an extensive evaluation on three types of entity resolution problems: structured, textual, and dirty data.

This paper is organized as follows: Sect. 2 explains our methodology for bootstrapping active learning with unsupervised matching. Section 3 presents the evaluation of our pipeline and comparison to related work and baseline methods. Section 4 discusses the related work in the areas of unsupervised matching and active learning. Section 5 concludes the paper and summarizes our main findings. The code and data used for the evaluation are publicly available[1].

---

[1] https://github.com/aprimpeli/UnsupervisedBootAL.

2 Methodology

This section gives first an overview of our proposed method and then all methodological steps are explained in detail. Our proposed methodology starts with the unsupervised matching of record pairs which includes the feature vector creation, the feature values aggregation to one similarity score per record pair and a thresholding function. We compare the aggregated similarity scores to the threshold value and assign labels and weights to the record pairs. The unsupervised labeled and weighted record pairs are added in the noisy weighted pool and used for training a Random Forest classifier [1]. In every active learning iteration, a committee of models selects the most informative record pair from the noisy pool to be manually labeled which is then removed from the noisy pool and added in the labeled set. The labeled set is used to expand the Random Forest classifier by incrementally training new trees which are added to the existing forest. Figure 1 presents our complete proposed method.

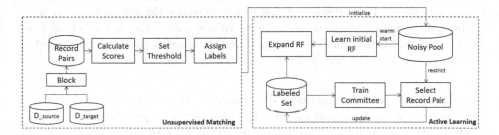

Fig. 1. Unsupervised Bootstrapping for Entity Matching with Active Learning.

2.1 Unsupervised Matching

Feature Vector Creation. We consider the matching problem between two datasets, source and target, with aligned schemata. In order to reduce the number of calculations, we filter out obvious non-matches by blocking using the most identifying domain-specific attribute which we manually define. The blocks are created using Relaxed Jaccard with inner Levenshtein distance and a threshold of 0.2. We create pairwise features from the individual attributes of each record for all remaining record pairs after blocking. Each feature corresponds to a datatype specific similarity score, similarly to the Magellan entity matching system [8]. Feature values of datatype string are compared using the following similarity metrics: Levenshtein, Jaccard, Jaccard with inner Levenshtein, overlap and containment. String attributes with an average length larger than six tokens are considered long strings and the cosine similarity score with tfidf weighting per feature is additionally computed. For numeric attributes the absolute difference is calculated. For date attributes, the day difference, month difference, and year difference are computed. Finally, we calculate the cosine score with tfidf weighting over the concatenated values of all attributes. We rescale all scores to the

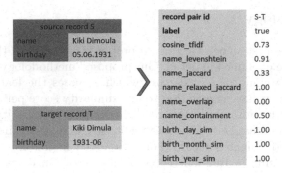

Fig. 2. Feature vector creation example.

range of $[0, 1]$ and convert the difference based features to similarity ones. In the case that the similarity score cannot be computed for an attribute combination because either the source, the target or both values are missing, we assign the out of range score -1. This allows any classifier to consider the relevant record pairs without dropping or replacing the missing values. Figure 2 shows an example of the created feature vector considering a source record S and a target record T describing the same author entity.

Similarity-Score Aggregation. We summarize the feature vector values into one value per record pair and assign this score as its aggregated similarity score. A similarity score close to 1 gives a strong signal that the record pair matches whereas a similarity score close to 0 indicates that it does not match. We calculate the aggregated similarity score per record pair as a weighted linear combination of all its non-missing feature values. The overall cosine similarity receives a weight of 0.5 while all other features share equally a weight of 0.5. We additionally weight every feature value with the overall density of the corresponding feature as dense features tend to be more important than non-dense ones. The aggregated similarity score of a record pair p with n features with density d is calculated using Eq. (1).

$$s_p = 0.5 \times \text{cosine\_tfidf} + 0.5 \times \frac{\sum_{i=1, \text{f}_{ip} \neq -1}^{n} \text{f}_{ip} \times d_i}{|i, \text{f}_{ip} \neq -1|} \qquad (1)$$

Thresholding. After the feature values have been aggregated to one similarity score per record pair, a threshold value t needs to be defined for assigning matching labels. We propose a thresholding method which determines the threshold value t as the *elbow point* (also denoted knee or point of maximum curvature [20]) of the cumulative histogram of the similarity scores of all record pairs after blocking. The elbow value can be approximated as the point with the maximum perpendicular distance to the vector between the first and the last point

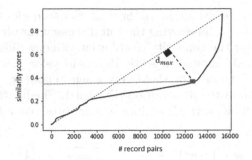

Fig. 3. Elbow point at 0.368 of the cumulative histogram of similarity scores for the dbpedia_dnb record pairs.

of the cumulative histogram. Figure 3 shows the elbow point of the cumulative histogram of similarity scores for author record pairs. From the histogram we can see that 12.8 K pairs in this dataset have a similarity score below the elbow point.

In our experiments, we will compare the elbow method to static thresholding which sets the threshold to the middle value of the similarity score range [7,15] and to Otsu's threshoding method [13]. Otsu's method selects as threshold the value that maximizes the variance between the two classes and therefore expects that the distribution of values is bimodal, i.e. two clear peaks appear in the histograms of similarity scores without any long-tail values.

As an additional thresholding baseline, we consider a variation of Otsu's method, known as the *valley-emphasis* threshold which aims to bypass the bimodality assumption [12]. The valley-emphasis threshold, which has also been used in the area of image segmentation, is calculated using Eq. (2), where p_t is the relative frequency of gray scale t, ω is the probability of each class and μ is the mean gray-level value of each class.

$$t\_valley = ArgMax \left\{ (1 - p_t)\left(\omega_1(t)\mu_1^2(t) + \omega_2(t)\mu_2^2(t)\right) \right\} \tag{2}$$

For the task of image segmentation the relative frequency is calculated as $p_t = n_i/n$, where n_i is the number of occurrences of gray level i and n is the total number of pixels. We adjust the valley-emphasis method to fit the matching task by performing the following two adaptations: (1) We round the similarity scores to the second decimal and calculate n_i as the frequency of the rounded similarity score. In this way we aggregate the occurrences of infrequent values which can allow for reasonable n_i, as the similarity scores can have an arbitrary number of decimal digits. (2) We set n as the number of occurrences of the most frequent similarity score and not to the total number of record pairs which would be the direct equivalent to the number of pixels. The reason for this adaptation is to allow the valley-emphasis method to have an effect over Otsu's method as otherwise the weighting factor $(1 - p_t)$ will always be very close to 1. To the best of our knowledge, we are the first ones to explore and adapt image segmentation thresholding methods to the matching task.

Figure 4 presents the histograms of the similarity scores for three datasets and the threshold boundaries considering the four discussed thresholding methods. It becomes obvious that the similarity distributions among different datasets can vary significantly and therefore a static threshold value cannot fit any distribution. Additionally, Otsu's threshold even when bimodality appears is moved towards the long-tail of the distribution (Fig. 4(a)). Finally, the adjusted valley and the proposed elbow method produce similar threshold values.

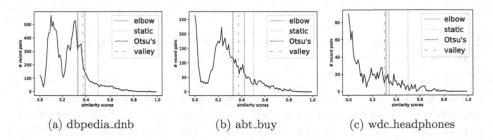

(a) dbpedia_dnb   (b) abt_buy   (c) wdc_headphones

Fig. 4. Histograms of similarity scores and threshold boundaries per method.

Confidence Weights. Apart from their unsupervised matching labels, the record pairs are assigned weights which indicate how confident our unsupervised method is for the predicted label. This is necessary as the record pairs that are expected to be more noisy should affect less the warm start of active learning in comparison to more confident pairs. The confidence weight of a record pair is calculated as the normalized distance of its aggregated similarity score s_p to the threshold value t. Therefore, record pairs close to the decision boundary t will receive a confidence weight close to 0 while record pairs whose similarity scores are the highest or the lowest in the similarity score distribution, will receive a confidence weight close to 1. We use Eq. (3) for calculating the confidence weight c_p of a record pair p given a threshold value t and a similarity score distribution S.

$$
c_p = \begin{cases} \frac{|s_p - t|}{t - \min(S)} & \text{, if } s_p < t \\[2ex] \frac{|s_p - t|}{\max(S) - t} & \text{, if } s_p > t \\[2ex] 0 & \text{, if } s_p = t \end{cases} \tag{3}
$$

2.2 Active Learning

Warm Start. The unsupervised labeled and weighted record pairs are added in the noisy pool. In a typical pool-based active learning setting the pool contains unlabeled data. In our proposed method the noisy pool contains unsupervised labeled data subject to some degree of noise. The existence of labels in the pool allows us to bootstrap the active learning model as well as the committee of models used as part of the query strategy at no manual labeling cost.

Bootstrapping the Active Learning Model. Before starting the active learning process, we use the record pairs of the noisy pool and train a Random Forest classifier with 10 estimators, a minimum split size of 2 while allowing sample replacement and maximum depth. The confidence weights of the record pairs are considered as training weights upon learning. This allows near to zero weighted leaf nodes of the individual trees of the Random Forest classifier to be ignored. In this way, we avoid the over fitting of the initial Random Forest classifier to the most unconfident positive and negative record pairs of the pool.

Bootstrapping the Committee. We bootstrap the models of the committee for our query strategy by adding one most confident positive and one most confident negative pair of the noisy pool to the labeled set. Thus we can ensure that the labeled set is initialized with record pairs of both classes, match and non-match. The initialized labeled set can be used for training the committee models even at the first active learning iteration where no manual labels are provided.

Modified Query-by-Committee Strategy. We use a heterogeneous committee for selecting the most informative record pair for labeling. This has been shown to perform better than committees of the same classification model with different model parameterizations [2]. Our committee comprises out of five linear and non-linear classification models: Logistic Regression, Linear SVM, Decision Tree, XGBoost, and Random Forest. The first four classifiers have been shown to achieve good accuracy with little training data [2]. As we apply a Random Forest classifier for model learning, we add this classifier to the committee. In every query iteration, each classification model in the committee is trained on the current labeled set. Next, it votes its predictions on all record pairs of the noisy pool, i.e. every record pair receives five votes. The record pairs with the maximum disagreement are considered to be the most informative. We measure disagreement using vote entropy. We restrict the number of most informative pairs to the ones whose majority vote disagrees with the unsupervised label of the record pair. From this restricted set, one pair is randomly selected for labeling. In this way we aim to select pairs to query whose unsupervised label might be wrong and can therefore lead to the addition of new information to the Random Forest model learned in the warm start phase.

Model Learning. We propose the incremental training of a classification model per query iteration to allow for a gradual *fading away* effect of the initial model learned in the warm start phase. As this cannot be achieved with the ensemble of committee models designed for the query strategy, we use a Random Forest classifier to which we gradually add more estimators, i.e. trees. Therefore, the model learned in the previous query iterations is not overwritten, a common practice in active learning settings, but expanded. We start our training (active learning iteration 0) with the bootstrapping of the active learning model, as explained previously, by fitting an initial number of trees on the noisy pool of record pairs. Each query iteration adds a small number of new trees to the model of the previous iteration. The added trees are trained on the current labeled set. In the early training iterations, we expect the added estimators to be of low quality and high disagreement on their predictions as they are trained on small amounts of clean data. Therefore, in the early iterations the initial ensemble trained in the warm start phase dominates its predictions over the ones of the added estimators. Once the added estimators become of better quality given the expansion of the labeled set, their prediction agreements will increase, dominate the ones of the initial model and lead to model correction. We set the number of trees learned in the warm start phase to 10 and the increment size of estimators per iteration to 2.

3   Experimental Evaluation

In this section we present the experimental results of our proposed method. First, a detailed description of the datasets used throughout the experimental phase is given. Next, we present and discuss the results of our proposed unsupervised matching method. Finally, the combination of unsupervised matching with active learning is evaluated and compared to two baseline methods.

3.1   Datasets

We use six pairs of datasets for our experimental evaluation from the author and the product domains. The six datasets cover three types of entity resolution problems: structured, textual and dirty, a distinction set by Mudgal et al. [11].

We retrieve two pairs of structured author datasets by exploiting the *owl: sameas* links provided in DBpedia. We use the *owl:sameas* links that link DBpedia author entities to author entities of the DNB[2] (Deutsche Nationalbibliothek) knowledge base and create the *dbpedia_dnb* dataset as well as the VIAF[3] (Virtual International Authority File) knowledge base and create the *dbpedia_viaf* dataset. In total we extract 2887 matching record pairs between DBpedia and DNB and 3353 matching record pairs between DBpedia and VIAF. The DBpedia and DNB datasets have the following attributes in common: *author_name*, *birthdate*, *deathdate*, and *gender*. Between DBpedia and VIAF the attributes *author_name*, *birthdate*, *deathdate*, *gender* and a list of *works* are provided.

---

[2] https://www.dnb.de/wir.
[3] http://viaf.org/.

We use two pairs of benchmark e-commerce datasets that contain textual attributes. The *abt_buy* datasets [10] derive from two online retailers. A ground truth of 1097 positive correspondences between product entities of the two datasets is provided[4]. The common attributes are: *product name, product description* and *product price*. The *product price* attribute has a low density of 18%. The *amazon_google* [10] e-commerce datasets also include product entities described with the following four common attributes: *product name, product description, manufacturer*, and *price*. The provided ground truth contains 1300 positive correspondences between the amazon and the google product entities.

For the dirty active learning setting we use two e-commerce datasets describing *phones* and *headphones* from the Web Data Commons Project[5]. The datasets have many missing attribute values while existing values are neither normalized nor necessarily correct and therefore fall under the dirty entity matching setting. For our experiments, we disregard all attributes that have a density lower than 0.10. After this filtering, the *wdc_phones* dataset has attributes with densities that range between 11% and 93%. The densities of the attributes for the *wdc_headphones* range between 10% and 91%. The gold standard contains 257 matches for phone products and 225 matches for headphone products [17].

The provided ground truth for all pairs of datasets is complete which allows us to easily create non-matching record pairs. We split the ground truth record pairs after blocking into training (80%) and test (20%). We use the training subset for experimenting with our unsupervised and active learning methods while all results are reported using the test set. Table 1 summarizes the profiling information of the datasets we use for experimentation in terms of initial attributes as well as number of matching and non-matching training and test record pairs. We provide all original and transformed datasets, after feature engineering, for public download[6].

Table 1. Datasets profiling information.

	Dataset	# Aligned attributes	Train		Test	
			# pos.	# neg.	# pos.	# neg.
Structured	dbpedia_dnb	4	2,310	11,554	577	2,888
	dbpedia_viaf	5	2,552	12,764	801	4,006
Textual	abt_buy	3	878	4,854	219	1,213
	amazon_google	4	1,041	5,714	259	1,428
Noisy	wdc_phones	18	206	1,556	51	389
	wdc_headphones	14	180	983	45	245

---

[4] https://dbs.uni-leipzig.de/research/projects/object_matching/benchmark_datasets_for_entity_resolution.

[5] http://webdatacommons.org/productcorpus.

[6] https://github.com/aprimpeli/UnsupervisedBootAL/tree/master/datasets.

3.2   Experimental Setup

We run two sets of experiments. First, we evaluate the proposed elbow thresholding method and compare it to the other thresholding methods presented in Sect. 2.1. Next we compare the model performance and stability per active iteration of our proposed bootstrapping method against two baseline methods that do not use unsupervised bootstrapping.

3.3   Thresholding Method Results

We evaluate the elbow point thresholding method proposed for unsupervised matching and compare it to static thresholding, for which the threshold is set to 0.5. Additionally, we perform a comparison to two thresholding methods for binary problems from the field of image segmentation, Otsu's method [13] and the valley-emphasis method [12] after the adjustments explained in Sect. 2.1.

Table 2 presents the results of the four compared thresholding methods in terms of sample correctness (accuracy) and F_1 score. To put the unsupervised matching results into context, we present the difference Δ to the F_1 score achieved in a passive supervised learning scenario, in which all training record pairs are manually labeled and used to train a Random Forest classifier. Additionally, for the four product datasets we compare the results of our passive learning setting to the results reported by state-of-the-art matching systems [11,16]. The reason for this comparison is two-fold: first, to show that our passive learning setting achieves comparable or better results to state-of-the art matchers and second, to indicate that our passive learning baseline sets a competitive upper boundary for comparing our proposed active learning method.

Comparing the results of the four thresholding methods, we can observe that our proposed elbow point method achieves better results in terms of F_1 score for five of the six datasets in comparison to static thresholding, with the exception of wdc_phones where it underperforms by 2%. However, for the rest of the datasets the elbow method significantly dominates static thresholding by an absolute F_1 margin varying from 1% to 20%.

Otsu's thresholding method underperforms the adjusted valley method by a maximum absolute margin of 32%. It is interesting to observe that the valley method achieves very similar results to our proposed elbow method. However, the elbow method significantly outperforms the valley method for the wdc_phones dataset by 8%. Therefore, we consider the elbow method to generalize the best over all other compared thresholding methods despite the underlying similarity score distribution which can greatly vary among the different datasets as shown in Fig. 4. Finally, the elbow thresholding method achieves 11%–32% lower results in terms of F_1 in comparison to the results achieved with full supervision and has an accuracy of 88% or higher. For the rest of the experimental evaluation we consider the elbow thresholding method.

Table 2. Unsupervised matching results. Comparison of thresholding methods and difference to Supervised Learning.

Dataset	Thresholding method	Unsupervised		Supervised F_1	Δ to Supervised F_1
		Accuracy	F_1		
dbpedia_dnb	elbow	0.918	0.722	0.976	**−0.254**
	static	0.894	0.538		−0.438
	Otsu's	0.833	0.602		−0.374
	valley	0.906	0.707		−0.269
dbpedia_viaf	elbow	0.956	0.862	0.983	**−0.121**
	static	0.915	0.663		−0.320
	Otsu's	0.743	0.542		−0.441
	valley	0.958	0.861		−0.122
amazon_google	elbow	0.892	0.588	0.699 (0.693 [11])	−0.111
	static	0.882	0.441		−0.258
	Otsu's	0.825	0.600		−0.099
	valley	0.827	0.602		**−0.097**
abt_buy	elbow	0.896	0.674	0.818 (0.628 [11])	**−0.144**
	static	0.912	0.660		−0.158
	Otsu's	0.794	0.562		−0.256
	valley	0.857	0.630		−0.188
wdc_phones	elbow	0.881	0.523	0.851 (0.849 [16])	−0.328
	static	0.881	0.544		**−0.307**
	Otsu's	0.759	0.438		−0.413
	valley	0.757	0.438		−0.413
wdc_headphones	elbow	0.907	0.734	0.966 (0.940 [16])	−0.232
	static	0.898	0.539		−0.427
	Otsu's	0.877	0.682		−0.284
	valley	0.910	0.738		**−0.228**

3.4   Active Learning Results

We run each active learning experiment 5 times and allow 100 iterations for each run. Each iteration corresponds to exactly one manual annotation. We report the average F_1 scores per iteration and the standard deviation (σ) to account for model stability using a separate test set. We compare our proposed method, which we abbreviate with *boot*, to two baseline methods:

Baseline 1: As the first baseline, abbreviated with *no_boot*, we consider an active learning setting with a pool containing all record pairs without labels or weights and a labeled set which is initially empty. As a query strategy, we apply initially random selection until at least one positive and one negative pair is included in the labeled set. After that, we apply a query-by-committee strategy while considering the same model types and disagreement measure explained in Sect. 2.2. A Random Forest classifier is trained in every iteration with the pairs of the labeled set using 10 estimators.

Baseline 2: The second baseline, abbreviated with *no_boot_warm*, is designed in the same way like the first one apart from the model training step. In this case, we use a warm start setting like in our proposed method with a Random Forest classifier being incrementally expanded. Once the labeled set includes at least one positive and one negative pairs, an initial Random Forest is learned using 10 estimators. Similarly to our *boot* approach, in every iteration two new estimators, i.e. trees, are trained using the labeled set and are added to the initial Random Forest classifier. This baseline guarantees that in every iteration the same number of trees like in the *boot* setting are retrained. In addition, it ensures that the total number of estimators of the Random Forest classifier in every iteration is the same as the one used for our method.

Figures 5, 6, and 7 show the F_1 scores per iteration for the *boot* method in comparison to the two baseline methods and the upper learning bound of passive learning in which all available training data is used. Additionally, we plot the standard deviation σ for every iteration of each active learning setting using the light coloured area around the plotted F1 curves. We observe that for all datasets our method manages to solve the cold start problem while producing stable models at any iteration. In the first active learning iterations (1–40 depending on the dataset) *boot* produces training models of better quality in comparison to the two baselines for all datasets. Considering an active learning setting with a limited budget in terms of manual annotations, our method is preferable as stopping at any iteration produces acceptable results, which is not the case when unsupervised bootstrapping is not applied.

Once the baseline methods go through the cold start phase, their F_1 curves approach the one of the *boot* method and stability increases. In the case of structured datasets, the curves overlap after 30 iterations, signifying that the bootstrapping does not contribute to learning a better model in terms of quality and stability anymore. However, this is not the case for the textual and dirty datasets, for which the *boot* F_1 curve dominates the baseline F_1 curves until the final iteration or until the model converges to the upper learning bound of passive learning, a situation that happens for the wdc_headphones dataset. Therefore, bootstrapping continues to help learning models of better quality even after the cold start phase has passed for the used textual and dirty datasets. A final observation that can be drawn from the three figures, is that the *no_boot_warm* baseline underperforms the *no_boot* baseline in every active learning iteration. This shows that the warm start setting can perform well only when the initially learned model is of an acceptable quality which is guaranteed when it is bootstrapped with unsupervised labeled data but not otherwise.

Table 3 presents the average F_1 scores and standard deviation (σ) for each dataset and method for three snapshots on the 20th, 60th and final iteration. Already in the 20th iteration the *boot* method gives very stable results as the standard deviation ranges from 0.01 to 0.05. At the same iteration point, both baseline methods are significantly more unstable independently from the dataset with the standard deviation ranging from 0.08 to 0.38. This shows that in the cold start phase our proposed *boot* method does not only perform better in terms of F_1 score in comparison to the baseline methods but also produces more stable models. On the 60th iteration all models have recovered from the cold start

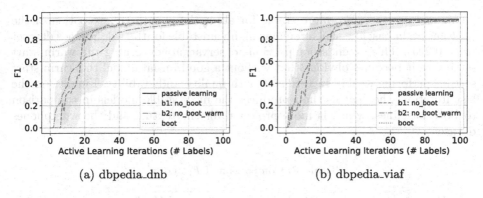

(a) dbpedia_dnb   (b) dbpedia_viaf

Fig. 5. F1 and σ per Active Learning Iteration - Structured datasets.

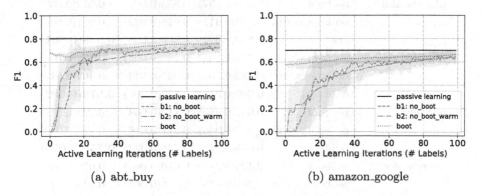

(a) abt_buy   (b) amazon_google

Fig. 6. F1 and σ per Active Learning Iteration - Textual datasets.

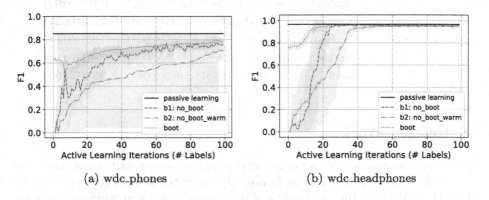

(a) wdc_phones   (b) wdc_headphones

Fig. 7. F1 and σ per Active Learning Iteration - Dirty datasets.

phase and are therefore more stable for all methods with the exception of the *no_boot_warm* baseline which remains highly unstable for the wdc_phones dataset ($\sigma = 0.206$). This extends our previous observation concerning the warm start setting as it becomes obvious that without a good initial model the warm start setting performs weakly in terms of both quality and stability. Finally, on the last iteration, the *boot* method produces the most stable models in comparison to both baselines, which is more profound for the textual and the wdc_phones datasets.

Table 3. Comparison of F_1 and σ.

Dataset	AL method	F1(std)		
		20th iter.	60th iter.	100 iter.
dbpedia_dnb	no_boot	0.756(0.197)	0.953(0.007)	0.952(0.009)
	no_boot_warm	0.628(0.317)	0.916(0.022)	0.961(0.009)
	boot	0.850(0.022)	0.958(0.008)	**0.969(0.001)**
dbpedia_viaf	no_boot	0.725(0.363)	0.967(0.005)	0.972(0.005)
	no_boot_warm	0.782(0.108)	0.937(0.043)	0.964(0.014)
	boot	0.909(0.014)	0.970(0.006)	**0.979(0.002)**
abt_buy	no_boot	0.637(0.080)	0.719(0.034)	0.723(0.031)
	no_boot_warm	0.602(0.086)	0.671(0.046)	0.722(0.039)
	boot	0.685(0.048)	0.738(0.033)	**0.759(0.029)**
amazon_google	no_boot	0.425(0.214)	0.610(0.063)	0.628(0.046)
	no_boot_warm	0.381(0.231)	0.581(0.063)	0.643(0.049)
	boot	0.594(0.055)	0.636(0.041)	**0.663(0.034)**
wdc_phones	no_boot	0.480(0.137)	0.712(0.063)	0.755(0.058)
	no_boot_warm	0.374(0.330)	0.555(0.206)	0.707(0.077)
	boot	0.649(0.050)	0.747(0.053)	**0.783(0.027)**
wdc_headphones	no_boot	0.816(0.242)	0.957(0.008)	0.957(0.008)
	no_boot_warm	0.464(0.386)	0.948(0.006)	0.946(0.004)
	boot	0.945(0.033)	0.955(0.007)	**0.957(0.005)**

4   Related Work

Entity resolution, also referred as record deduplication and entity matching, aims to identify records in one or more datasets that refer to the same real-world entity [3,5]. Depending on the availability of pre-labeled data, matching methods are divided into unsupervised, weakly supervised and supervised methods [3].

Feature Engineering: In order to calculate the similarity between two entities, it is necessary to create features from the combinations of their attributes. Traditionally, features can be created using different similarity functions [3].

The Magellan entity matching system [8] uses data type specific similarity functions per attribute combination. For table row similarity Oulabi et al. [14] suggest the addition of one overall similarity feature using the similarity of the concatenated attribute values. Recent methods propose the use of word embeddings [4] which however lack interpretability and can perform poorly when the attribute values lack semantic meaning, e.g. in the case of person names or birth dates.

Unsupervised Matching: In an unsupervised matching scenario the matching decision for a record pair can be drawn by implementing a set of boolean heuristics [15]. Designing such heuristics requires manual effort. Alternatively, a global threshold can be pre-defined or calculated against which the aggregated pair similarities will be compared [7,15]. We showed that our elbow thresholding method performs consistently better in comparison to these methods.

Active Learning: In the area of supervised matching, many methods have been proposed that aim to reduce the human labeling effort by applying active learning [18,19,21]. Typically, committee-based query strategies are applied for selecting informative pairs for labeling [6,19,21]. Committee members are usually different parametrizations of the same classification model [19,21]. Recent work, has shown that having a committee of different classification models is more efficient [2]. Starting active learning pre-assumes the existence of both matching and non-matching pairs in the labeled set. In existing works, the labeled set is initialized with randomly selected labeled pairs [9,18] or by selecting and labeling record pairs from different areas of the similarity score distribution [2,19]. Both lines of work increase the human labeling effort in contrast to our method which solely relies on unsupervised matching. Additionally, the methods that rely on selecting and labeling pairs from the similarity score distribution need to predefine a number of similarity groups and the number of pairs from each group that needs to be labeled. However, in our experiments we showed that the similarity score distributions of different datasets may significantly vary and therefore the amount of similarity groups would need to be individually defined for each dataset. Additionally, fixing the labeled set size e.g. to ten pairs, before active learning starts is not optimal as different matching settings can behave very differently in terms of convergence which we showed in our experimental evaluation. Our proposed method achieves good performance, even at the very early iterations while we showed that depending on the difficulty of the matching setting ten pairs can even be enough for reaching maximum performance.

5   Conclusion

We presented a method for bootstrapping active learning for entity resolution using unsupervised matching. In the context of unsupervised matching, we assign labels based on thresholding pre-calculated similarity scores. Our proposed thresholding relies on the elbow point of the cumulative histogram of similarity scores. We showed that the elbow thresholding method performs better in comparison to static thresholding and two thresholding methods from the area of image segmentation. Using the unsupervised labeled data to bootstrap active learning and incrementally expanding a Random Forest classifier after every query iteration, leads to the elimination of the cold start problem appearing in active learning settings that do not apply bootstrapping. Our method guarantees high anytime performance as it produces even at early active learning iterations better models in terms of quality and stability, compared to methods that do not apply bootstrapping. On top of the improved high anytime performance, our approach continues showing higher stability and F_1 score after 100 iterations especially for datasets containing many missing values as well as rather textual data.

References

1. Breiman, L.: Random forests. Mach. Learn. **45**(1), 5–32 (2001). https://doi.org/10.1023/A:1010933404324
2. Chen, X., Xu, Y., Broneske, D., Durand, G.C., Zoun, R., Saake, G.: Heterogeneous committee-based active learning for entity resolution (HeALER). In: Welzer, T., Eder, J., Podgorelec, V., Kamišalić Latifić, A. (eds.) ADBIS 2019. LNCS, vol. 11695, pp. 69–85. Springer, Cham (2019). https://doi.org/10.1007/978-3-030-28730-6_5
3. Christophides, V., et al.: End-to-end entity resolution for big data: a survey. arXiv:1905.06397 [cs] (2019)
4. Ebraheem, M., et al.: Distributed representations of tuples for entity resolution. Proc. VLDB **11**, 1454–1467 (2018)
5. Halevy, A., Rajaraman, A., Ordille, J.: Data integration: the teenage years. In: Proceedings of VLDB, pp. 9–16 (2006)
6. Isele, R., Bizer, C.: Learning linkage rules using genetic programming. In: Proceedings of Ontology Matching, pp. 13–24 (2011)
7. Kejriwal, M., Miranker, D.P.: An unsupervised instance matcher for schema-free RDF data. Web Semant **35**(P2), 102–123 (2015)
8. Konda, P., et al.: Magellan: toward building entity matching management systems over data science stacks. PVLDB **13**, 1581–1584 (2016)
9. Konyushkova, K., Sznitman, R., Fua, P.: Learning active learning from data. In: In Proceedings of NIPS, pp. 4225–4235 (2017)
10. Köpcke, H., Rahm, E.: Training selection for tuning entity matching. In: Proceedings of QDB/MUD, pp. 3–12 (2008)
11. Mudgal, S., et al.: Deep learning for entity matching: a design space exploration. In: Proceedings of SIGMOD, pp. 19–34 (2018)
12. Ng, H.F.: Automatic thresholding for defect detection. Pattern Recogn. Lett. **27**(14), 1644–1649 (2006)
13. Otsu, N.: A threshold selection method from gray-level histograms. IEEE Trans. Syst. Man Cybern. **9**(1), 62–66 (1979)
14. Oulabi, Y., Bizer, C.: Extending cross-domain knowledge bases with long tail entities using web table data. In: Proceedings of EDBT, pp. 385–396 (2019)
15. Oulabi, Y., Bizer, C.: Using weak supervision to identify long-tail entities for knowledge base completion. In: Acosta, M., Cudré-Mauroux, P., Maleshkova, M., Pellegrini, T., Sack, H., Sure-Vetter, Y. (eds.) SEMANTiCS 2019. LNCS, vol. 11702, pp. 83–98. Springer, Cham (2019). https://doi.org/10.1007/978-3-030-33220-4_7

16. Petrovski, P., Bizer, C.: Learning expressive linkage rules from sparse data. Semant. Web (Preprint), 1–19 (2019)
17. Petrovski, P., Primpeli, A., Meusel, R., Bizer, C.: The WDC gold standards for product feature extraction and product matching. In: Bridge, D., Stuckenschmidt, H. (eds.) EC-Web 2016. LNBIP, vol. 278, pp. 73–86. Springer, Cham (2017). https://doi.org/10.1007/978-3-319-53676-7_6
18. Qian, K., Popa, L., Sen, P.: Active learning for large-scale entity resolution. In: Proceedings of CIKM, pp. 1379–1388 (2017)
19. Sarawagi, S., Bhamidipaty, A., Kirpal, A., Mouli, C.: ALIAS: an active learning led interactive deduplication system. In: Proceedings of VLDB, pp. 1103–1106 (2002)
20. Satopaa, V., et al.: Finding a "kneedle" in a haystack: detecting knee points in system behavior. In: Proceedings of ICDCS-Workshops, pp. 166–171. IEEE (2011)
21. Tejada, S., Knoblock, C.A., Minton, S.: Learning object identification rules for information integration. Inf. Syst. **26**(8), 607–633 (2001)

Distribution and Decentralization

Processing SPARQL Aggregate Queries
with Web Preemption

Arnaud Grall[1,2], Thomas Minier[1], Hala Skaf-Molli[1(✉)], and Pascal Molli[1]

[1] LS2N – University of Nantes, Nantes, France
{arnaud.grall,thomas.minier,hala.skaf,pascal.molli}@univ-nantes.fr
[2] GFI Informatique - IS/CIE, Nantes, France

Abstract. Executing aggregate queries on the web of data allows to compute useful statistics ranging from the number of properties per class in a dataset to the average life of famous scientists per country. However, processing aggregate queries on public SPARQL endpoints is challenging, mainly due to quotas enforcement that prevents queries to deliver complete results. Existing distributed query engines allow to go beyond quota limitations, but their data transfer and execution times are clearly prohibitive when processing aggregate queries. Following the web preemption model, we define a new preemptable aggregation operator that allows to suspend and resume aggregate queries. Web preemption allows to continue query execution beyond quota limits and server-side aggregation drastically reduces data transfer and execution time of aggregate queries. Experimental results demonstrate that our approach outperforms existing approaches by orders of magnitude in terms of execution time and the amount of transferred data.

1 Introduction

Context and Motivation: Following the Linked Open Data principles (LOD), data providers published billions of RDF triples [4,15]. Executing SPARQL aggregate queries on the web of data allows to compute useful statistics ranging from the number of properties per class in a dataset [8] to the average life of famous scientists per country. However, processing aggregate queries on public SPARQL endpoints is challenging, mainly due to quotas enforcement that prevents queries to deliver complete results as pointed out in [8,17].

Related Works: To overcome quotas limitations, Knowledge Graph providers publish dumps of their data. However, re-ingesting billions of triples on local resources to compute SPARQL aggregate queries is extremely costly and raises issues with freshness. Another approach is to build servers that only process queries that **complete** in a predefined time, *i.e.*, deliver complete results under quotas. Then a smart client interacts with the server to process full SPARQL queries. The Triple Pattern Fragments (TPF) [19] relies on a server that only processes paginated triple pattern queries. The TPF smart client decomposes SPARQL queries into paginated triple pattern subqueries and recombines results

© Springer Nature Switzerland AG 2020
A. Harth et al. (Eds.): ESWC 2020, LNCS 12123, pp. 235–251, 2020.
https://doi.org/10.1007/978-3-030-49461-2_14

to deliver final query answers. However, processing aggregate queries with TPF generates tremendous data transfer and delivers poor performance. Recently, the Web preemption approach [12] relies on a preemptable server that suspends queries after a quantum of time and resumes them later. The server supports joins, projections, unions, and some filters operators. However, aggregations are not supported natively by the preemptable server. Consequently, the server transfers all required mappings to the smart client to finally compute groups and aggregation functions locally. As the size of mappings is much larger than the size of the final results, the processing of aggregate queries is inefficient. This approach allows to avoid quotas, but delivers very poor performance for aggregate queries, and could not be a sustainable alternative.

Approach and Contributions: In this paper, we propose a novel approach for efficient processing of aggregate queries in the context of web preemption. Thanks to the decomposability of aggregate functions, web preemption allows to compute partial aggregates on the server-side while the smart client combines incrementally partial aggregates to compute final results. The contributions of the paper are the following: (i) We introduce the notion of partial aggregations for web preemption. (ii) We extend the SaGe preemptive server and the SaGe smart client [12] with new algorithms for the evaluation of SPARQL aggregations. The new algorithms use partial aggregations and the decomposability property of aggregation functions. (iii) We compare the performance of our approach with existing approaches used for processing aggregate queries. Experimental results demonstrate that the proposed approach outperforms existing approaches used for processing aggregate queries by orders of magnitude in terms of execution time and the amount of transferred data.

This paper is organized as follows. Section 2 reviews related works. Section 3 introduces SPARQL aggregation queries and the web preemption model. Section 4 presents our approach for processing aggregate queries in a preemptive SPARQL server. Section 5 presents experimental results. Finally, conclusions and future work are outlined in Sect. 6.

2   Related Works

SPARQL Endpoints. SPARQL endpoints follow the SPARQL protocol[1], which "describes a means for conveying SPARQL queries and updates to a SPARQL processing service and returning the results via HTTP to the entity that requested them". Without quotas, SPARQL endpoints execute queries using a First-Come First-Served (FCFS) execution policy [7]. Thus, by design, they can suffer from *convoy effect* [5]: one long-running query occupies the server resources and prevents other queries from executing, leading to long waiting time and degraded average completion time for queries.

To prevent the convoy effect and ensure a fair sharing of resources among end-users, most SPARQL endpoints configure quotas on their servers. They mainly

---

[1] https://www.w3.org/TR/2013/REC-sparql11-protocol-20130321/.

restrict the arrival rate per IP address and limit the execution time of queries. Restricting the arrival rate allows end-users to retry later, however, limiting the execution time leads some queries to deliver only partial results. Delivering partial results is a serious limitation for public SPARQL services [2,12,17].

Centralized Query Answering. Big data processing approaches are able to process aggregate queries efficiently on a large volume of data. Data has to be first ingested in a distributed datastore such as HBase [20], then SPARQL queries can be translated to Map/reduce jobs or massively parallelized with parallel scans and joins. Many proposals exist in the semantic web including [3,14]. All these approaches require to download datasets and ingest data on a local cluster to process aggregate queries. Consequently, they require a high-cost infrastructure which can be amortized only if a high number of aggregate queries have to be executed. Our approach processes aggregate queries on available public servers without copying the data and delivers exact answers.

Query Answering by Samples. Approximate query processing is a well-known approach to speedup aggregate query processing [11]. The approach relies on sampling, synopses or sketches techniques to approximate results with bounded errors. The sampling approach proposed in [17] scales with large knowledge graphs, and overcomes quotas but computes approximate query answers. In this paper, we aim to compute the exact results of aggregate queries and not approximate answers.

Distributed Query Processing Approaches. Another well-known approach to overcome quotas is to decompose a query into smaller subqueries that can be evaluated under quotas and recombine their results [2]. Such decomposition requires a *smart client* which allows for performing the decomposition and recombine intermediate results. In that sense, the query processing is *distributed* between a server and smart client that collaborate to process SPARQL queries. However, ensuring that subqueries can be completed under quotas remains hard [2]. Another approach is to build servers with a restricted interface that processes queries that **completes** within bounded times, *i.e.*, quotas. A smart client interacts with such a server to process full SPARQL queries. The Triple Pattern Fragments approach (TPF) [19] decomposes SPARQL queries into a sequence of paginated triple pattern queries. As paginated triple patterns queries can be executed in bounded times, the server does not need quotas. However, as the TPF server only processes triple pattern queries, joins and aggregates are evaluated on the smart client. This requires to transfer all required data from server to client to perform joins, and then to compute aggregate functions locally, which leads to poor query execution performance.

Web preemption [12] is another approach to process SPARQL queries on a public server without quota enforcement. Web preemption allows the web server to suspend a running SPARQL query after a quantum of time and return a link to the smart client. Sending this link back to the web server, allows executing the query for another quantum of time. Compared to First-Come First-Served (FCFS) scheduling policy, web preemption provides a fair allocation of server resources across queries, a better average query completion time per query and a better time for first results. However, if Web preemption allows processing projections and joins on server-side, aggregate operators are still evaluated on a smart client. So, data transfer may be intensive especially for aggregate queries.

In this paper, we extend the web preemption approach to support partial aggregates. Partial aggregates are built during the execution of quanta and sent to the smart client. The smart client recombines partial aggregates to compute the final results.

3   Preliminaries

SPARQL Aggregation Queries: We follow the semantics of aggregation as defined in [10]. We recall briefly definitions related to the proposal of the paper. We follow the notation from [10,13,16] and consider three disjoint sets I (IRIs), L (literals) and B (blank nodes) and denote the set T of RDF terms $I \cup L \cup B$. An RDF triple $(s,p,o) \in (I \cup B) \times I \times T$ connects subject s through predicate p to object o. An RDF graph $\mathcal{G}$ (called also RDF dataset) is a finite set of RDF triples. We assume the existence of an infinite set V of variables, disjoint with previous sets. A mapping μ from V to T is a partial function $\mu : V \to T$, the domain of μ, denoted $dom(\mu)$ is the subset of V where μ is defined. Mappings μ_1 and μ_2 are compatible on the variable $?x$, written $\mu_1(?x) \sim \mu_2(?x)$ if $\mu_1(?x) = \mu_2(?x)$ for all $?x \in dom(\mu_1) \cap dom(\mu_2)$.

A SPARQL graph pattern expression P is defined recursively as follows.

1. A tuple from $(I \cup L \cup V) \times (I \cup V) \times (I \cup L \cup V)$ is a triple pattern.
2. If $P1$ and $P2$ are graph patterns, then expressions (P1 AND P2), (P1 OPT P2), and (P1 UNION P2) are graph patterns (a conjunction graph pattern, an optional graph pattern, and a union graph pattern, respectively).
3. If P is a graph pattern and R is a SPARQL built-in condition, then the expression (P FILTER R) is a graph pattern (a filter graph pattern).

The evaluation of a graph pattern P over an RDF graph $\mathcal{G}$ denoted by $[\![P]\!]_{\mathcal{G}}$ produces a *multisets of solutions mappings* $\Omega = (S_{\Omega}, card_{\Omega})$, where S_{Ω} is the *base set* of mappings and the multiplicity function $card_{\Omega}$ which assigns a cardinality to each element of S_{Ω}. For simplicity, we often write $\mu \in \Omega$ instead of $\mu \in S_{\Omega}$. The SPARQL 1.1 language [18] introduces new features for supporting aggregation queries: i) A collection of *aggregate functions* for computing values, like COUNT, SUM, MIN, MAX and AVG; ii) GROUP BY and HAVING. HAVING restricts the application of aggregate functions to groups of solutions satisfying certain conditions.

Both groups and aggregate deal with lists of expressions $E = [E1, \ldots, En]$, which evaluate to v-lists: lists of values in $T \cup \{error\}$. More precisely, the evaluation of a list of expressions according to a mapping μ is defined as: $[\![E]\!]_{\mu} = [[\![E_1]\!]_{\mu}, \ldots, [\![E_n]\!]_{\mu}]$. Inspired by [10,18], we formalize Group and Aggregate.

:s1 :p1 :o1 .	**SELECT** ?c	**SELECT** ?c
:s1 :a :c2, :c3.	(COUNT(?o) AS ?z)	(COUNT(Distinct (?o)) AS ?z)
:s2 :p1 :o1 .	**WHERE** { ?s :a ?c .	**WHERE** { ?s :a ?c .
:s2 :a :c1, :c3.	?s ?p ?o . ?s :p1 :o1}	?s ?p ?o . ?s :p1 :o1}
	GROUP BY ?c	**GROUP BY** ?c
(a) $\mathcal{G}_1$	(b) SPARQL query Q_1	(c) SPARQL query Q_2

Fig. 1. Aggregate queries $Q1$ and Q_2 on RDF graph $\mathcal{G}_1$

Definition 1 (Group). *A group is a construct $G(E, P)$ with E is a list of expressions[2], P a graph pattern, $\mathcal{G}$ an RDF graph. Let $\Omega = [\![P]\!]_{\mathcal{G}}$, the evaluation of $[\![G(E, P)]\!]_{\mathcal{G}}$ produces a set of partial functions from keys to solution sequences.*

$$[\![G(E, P)]\!]_{\mathcal{G}} = \{[\![E]\!]_{\mu} \mapsto \{\mu' \mid \mu' \in \Omega, [\![E]\!]_{\mu} = [\![E]\!]_{\mu'}\} \mid \mu \in \Omega\}$$

Definition 2 (Aggregate). *An aggregate is a construct $\gamma(E, F, P)$ with E is a list of expressions, F a set of aggregation functions, P a graph pattern, $\mathcal{G}$ an RDF Graph, and $\{k_1 \mapsto \omega_1, \ldots, k_n \mapsto \omega_n\}$ a multiset of partial functions produced by $[\![G(E, P)]\!]_{\mathcal{G}}$. The evaluation of $[\![\gamma(E, F, P)]\!]_{\mathcal{G}}$ produces a single value for each key.*

$$[\![\gamma(E, F, P)]\!]_{\mathcal{G}} = \{(k, F(\Omega)) \mid k \mapsto \Omega \in \{k_1 \mapsto \omega_1, \ldots, k_n \mapsto \omega_n\}\}$$

To illustrate, consider the query Q_1 of Fig. 1b, which returns the total number of objects per class for subjects connected to the object o_1 through the predicate p_1. Here, $P_{Q_1} = \{?s$:a ?c.?s ?p ?o.?s :p1 :o1} denotes the graph pattern of Q_1, and $?c$ is the group key. For simplicity, for each key group, we represent only the value of the variable $?o$, as $?o$ is the only variable used in the COUNT aggregation. $[\![G(?c, P_{Q_1})]\!]_{\mathcal{G}_1} = \{:c3 \mapsto \{:c3, :c1, :c2, :o1, :c3, :o1, \}, :c1 \mapsto \{:o1, :c3, :c1\}, :c2 \mapsto \{:o1, :c3, :c2\}\}$ and the query Q_1 is evaluated as $[\![\gamma(\{?c\}, \{COUNT(?o)\}, P_{Q_1})]\!]_{\mathcal{G}_1} = \{(:c3, 6), (:c1, 3), (:c2, 3)\}$.

Web Preemption and SPARQL Aggregation Queries. *Web preemption* [12] is the capacity of a web server to suspend a running query after a fixed quantum of time and resume the next waiting query. When suspended, partial results and the state of the suspended query S_i are returned to the smart web client[3]. The client can resume query execution by sending S_i back to the web server. Compared to a First-Come First-Served (FCFS) scheduling policy, web preemption provides *a fair allocation of web server resources across queries, a better average query completion time per query and a better time for first results* [1]. To illustrate, consider three SPARQL queries Q_a, Q_b, and Q_c submitted concurrently by three different clients. The execution time of Q_a, Q_b and Q_c are respectively 60 s, 5 s and 5 s. Figure 2a presents a possible execution of these queries with a FCFS policy. In this case, the throughput of FCFS is $\frac{3}{70} = 0.042$ queries per second, the average completion time per query is $\frac{60+65+70}{3} = 65$ s

---

[2] We restrict E to variables, without reducing the expressive power of aggregates [10].
[3] S_i can be returned to the client or saved server-side and returned by reference.

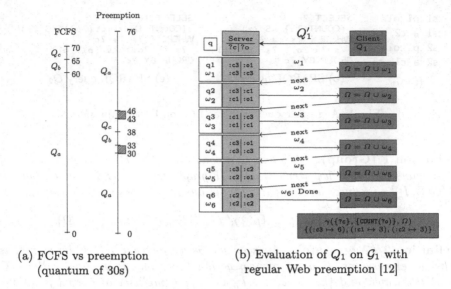

(a) FCFS vs preemption
(quantum of 30s)

(b) Evaluation of Q_1 on $\mathcal{G}_1$ with
regular Web preemption [12]

Fig. 2. Evaluation of SPARQL aggregation queries with web preemption

and the average time for first results is also 65 s. Figure 2a presents the execution of Q_a, Q_b, and Q_c using Web preemption, with a time quantum of 30 s. Web preemption adds an overhead for the web server to suspend the running query and resume the next waiting query, of about in 3 s (10% of the quantum) our example. In this case, the throughput is $\frac{3}{76} = 0.039$ query per second but the average completion time per query is $\frac{76+38+43}{3} = 52.3$ s and the average time for first results is approximately $\frac{30+38+43}{3} = 37$ s. If the quantum is set to 60 s, then Web preemption is equivalent to FCFS. If the quantum is too low, then the throughput and the average completion time are deteriorated due to overhead. Consequently, the challenges with Web preemption are *to bound the preemption overhead in time and space* and *determine the time quantum* to amortize the overhead.

To address these challenges, in [12], the SPARQL operators are divided into two categories: *mapping-at-a-time operators* and *full-mappings operators*. For mapping-at-a-time operators, the overhead in time and space for suspending and resuming a query Q is bounded by $\mathcal{O}(|Q| \times \log(|\mathcal{G}|))$, where $|Q|$ is the number of operators required to evaluate Q. Graph patterns composed of AND, UNION, PROJECTION, and most FILTERS can be implemented using mapping-at-a-time operators. So, this fragment of SPARQL can be efficiently executed by a preemptable Web server. Full-mappings operators, such as OPTIONAL, GROUP BY, Aggregations, ORDER BY, MINUS and EXISTS require full materialization of solution mappings to be executed, so they are executed by Smart clients.

Figure 2b illustrates how web preemption processes the query Q_1 of Fig. 1b over the dataset D_1. The smart client sends the BGP of Q_1 to the server, *i.e.*, the query Q_1': **SELECT** ?c ?o **WHERE** { ?s :a ?c ; ?p ?o ; :p1 :o1}. In this example,

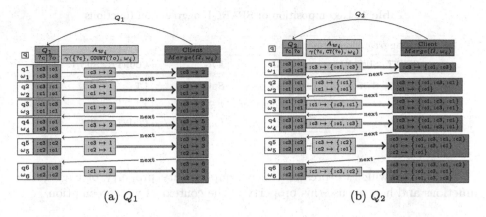

(a) Q_1 (b) Q_2

Fig. 3. Evaluation of Q_1 and Q_2 on $\mathcal{G}_1$ with a partial aggregate P_{Q_1}.

Q'_1 requires six quanta to complete. At the end of each quantum q_i, the client receives mappings ω_i and asks for the next results (*next* link). When all mappings are obtained, the smart client computes $\gamma(\{?c\}, \{\text{COUNT}(?o)\}, \bigcup_i \omega_i)$. Finally, to compute the set of three solutions mappings $\{\{:c3 \mapsto 6\}, \{:c1 \mapsto 3\}, \{:c2 \mapsto 3\}\}$, the server transferred $6 + 3 + 3 = 12$ mappings to the client.

In a more general way, to evaluate $[\![\gamma(E, F, P)]\!]_{\mathcal{G}}$, the smart client first asks a preemptable web server to evaluate $[\![P]\!]_{\mathcal{G}} = \Omega$, the server transfers incrementally Ω, and finally the client evaluates $\gamma(E, F, \Omega)$ locally. The main problem with this evaluation is that the size of Ω, is usually much bigger than the size of $\gamma(E, F, \Omega)$.

Reducing data transfer requires reducing $|[\![P]\!]_{\mathcal{G}}|$ which is impossible without deteriorating answer completeness. Therefore, the only way to reduce data transfer when processing aggregate queries is to process the aggregation on the preemptable server. However, the operator used to evaluate SPARQL aggregation is a full-mapping operator, as it requires to materialize $|[\![P]\!]_{\mathcal{G}}|$, hence *it cannot be suspended and resumed in constant time.*

Problem Statement: Define a preemptable aggregation operator γ such that the complexity in time and space of suspending and resuming γ is bounded in constant time[4].

4   Computing Partial Aggregations with Web Preemption

Our approach for building a preemptable evaluator for SPARQL aggregations relies on two key ideas: (i) First, web preemption naturally creates a partition of mappings over time. Thanks to the decomposability of aggregation functions [21], we compute partial aggregation on the partition of mappings on the server side and recombine partial aggregates on the client side. (ii) Second, to control the size of partial aggregates, we can adjust the size of the quantum for aggregate queries.

---
[4] We only consider aggregate queries with Basic Graph Patterns without OPTIONAL.

Table 1. Decomposition of SPARQL aggregation functions

SPARQL aggregations functions								
	COUNT	SUM	MIN	MAX	AVG	COUNT_D	SUM_D	AVG_D
f_1	COUNT	SUM	MIN	MAX	SaC	CT		
$v \diamond v'$	$v + v'$		$min(v, v')$	$max(v, v')$	$v \oplus v'$	$v \cup v'$		
h	Id				$(x, y) \mapsto x/y$	COUNT	SUM	AVG

In the following, we present the decomposability property of aggregation functions and how we use this property in the context of web preemption.

4.1 Decomposable Aggregation Functions

Traditionally, the *decomposability property* of aggregation functions [21] ensures the correctness of the distributed computation of aggregation functions [9]. We adapt this property for SPARQL aggregate queries in Definition 3.

Definition 3 (Decomposable aggregation function). *An aggregation function f is decomposable if for some grouping expressions E and all non-empty multisets of solution mappings Ω_1 and Ω_2, there exists a (merge) operator $\diamond$, a function h and an aggregation function f_1 such that:*

$$\gamma(E, \{f\}, \Omega_1 \uplus \Omega_2) = \{k \mapsto h(v_1 \diamond v_2) \mid k \mapsto v_1 \in \gamma(E, \{f_1\}, \Omega_1),$$
$$k \mapsto v_2 \in \gamma(E, \{f_1\}, \Omega_2)\}$$

In the above, $\uplus$ denotes the multi-set union as defined in [10], abusing notation using $\Omega_1 \uplus \Omega_2$ instead of P. Table 1 gives the decomposition of all SPARQL aggregations functions, where Id denotes the identity function and $\oplus$ is the *point-wise sum of pairs, i.e.,* $(x_1, y_1) \oplus (x_2, y_2) = (x_1 + x_2, y_1 + y_2)$.

To illustrate, consider the function $f = \text{COUNT}(?c)$ and an aggregation query $\gamma(V, \{f\}, \Omega_1 \uplus \Omega_2)$, such as $\gamma(V, \{f\}, \Omega_1) = \{\{?c \mapsto 2\}\}$ and $\gamma(V, \{f\}, \Omega_2) = \{\{?c \mapsto 5\}\}$. The intermediate aggregation results for the COUNT aggregation can be merged using an arithmetic addition operation, *i.e.*, $\{\{?c \mapsto 2 \diamond 5 = 2+5 = 7\}\}$.

Decomposing SUM, COUNT, MIN and MAX is relatively simple, as we need only to merge partial aggregation results to produce the final query results. However, decomposing AVG and aggregations with the DISTINCT modifier are more complex. We introduce two auxiliary aggregations functions, called SaC (*SUM-and-COUNT*) and CT (*Collect*), respectively. The first one collects information required to compute an average and the second one collects a set of distinct values. They are defined as follows: $\text{SaC}(X) = \langle \text{SUM}(X), \text{COUNT}(X) \rangle$ and $\text{CT}(X)$ is the base set of X as defined in Sect. 3. For instance, the aggregation function of the query $Q = \gamma(V, \text{COUNT}_D(?o), \Omega_1 \uplus \Omega_2)$ is decomposed as $Q' = \text{COUNT}(\gamma(V, \text{CT}(?o), \Omega_1) \cup \gamma(V, \text{CT}(?o), \Omega_2))$.

4.2   Partial Aggregation with Web Preemption

Using a preemptive web server, the evaluation of a graph pattern P over $\mathcal{G}$ naturally creates *a partition of mappings over time* $\omega_1, ..., \omega_n$, where ω_i is produced during the quantum q_i. Intuitively, a *partial aggregations* A_i, formalized in Definition 4, is obtained by applying some aggregation functions on a partition of mappings ω_i.

Definition 4 (Partial aggregation). *Let E be a list of expressions, F a set of aggregation functions, and $\omega_i \subseteq [\![P]\!]_{\mathcal{G}}$ such that $[\![P]\!]_{\mathcal{G}} = \bigcup_{i=1}^{i=n} \omega_i$ where n is the number of quanta required to complete the evaluation of P over $\mathcal{G}$. A partial aggregation A_i is defined as $A_i = \gamma(E, F, \omega_i)$.*

As a partial aggregation operates on ω_i, partial aggregation can be implemented server-side as a *mapping-at-a-time operator*. Suspending the evaluation of aggregate queries using partial aggregates does not require to materialize intermediate results on the server. Finally, to process the SPARQL aggregation query, the smart client computes $[\![\gamma(E, F, P)]\!]_{\mathcal{G}} = h(A_1 \diamond A_2 \diamond \cdots \diamond A_n)$.

Figure 3a illustrates how a smart client computes Q_1 over D_1 using partial aggregates. We suppose that Q_1 is executed over six quanta $q_1, \ldots, q_6$. At each quantum q_i, two new mappings are produced in ω_i and the partial aggregate $A_i = \gamma(\{?c\}, \{COUNT(?o)\}, \omega_i)$ is sent to the client. The client merges all A_i thanks to the $\diamond$ operator and then produces the final results by applying g. Figure 3b describes the execution of Q_2 with partial aggregates under the same conditions. As we can see, the DISTINCT modifier requires to transfer more data, however, a reduction in data transfer is still observable compared with transferring all ω_i for $q_1, q_2, q_3, q_4, q_5, q_6$.

The duration of the quantum seriously impacts query processing using partial aggregations. Suppose in Fig. 3a, instead of six quanta of two mappings, the server requires twelve quanta with one mapping each, therefore, partial aggregates are useless. If the server requires two quanta with six mappings each, then only two partial aggregates $A_1 = \{(:c3, 3), (:c1, 3)\}$ and $A_2 = \{(:c3, 3), (c2, 3)\}$ are sent to the client and data transfer is reduced. If the quantum is infinite, then the whole aggregation is produced on the server-side, the data transfer is optimal. Globally, for an aggregate query, the larger the quantum is, the smaller the data transfer and execution time are.

However, if we consider several aggregates queries running concurrently (as presented in Fig. 2a), the quantum also determines the average completion time per query, the throughput and time for first results. The time for the first result is not significant for aggregate queries. A large quantum reduces overheads and consequently, improves throughput. However, a large quantum degrades the average completion time per query, *i.e.*, the responsiveness of the server as demonstrated in experiments of [12]. Consequently, setting the quantum mainly determines a trade-off between efficiency of the partial aggregates that can be measured in data transfer and the responsiveness of the server that can be measured in average completion time per query. The administrator of a public server is responsible for setting the value of the quantum according to the workload and dataset size.

Algorithm 1: A Server-Side Preemptable SPARQL Aggregation Iterator

Require: I_p: predecessor in the pipeline of iterators, K: grouping variables,
        A: set of aggregations functions.

Data: G: multisets of solutions mappings

```
 1  Function Open():
 2  │  G ← ∅

 3  Function Save():
 4  │  return G

 5  Function GetNext():
 6  │  if I_p.HasNext() then
 7  │  │  μ ← I_p.GetNext()
 8  │  │  non interruptible
 9  │  │  │  Ω ← γ(K, A, {μ})
10  │  │  │  if G = ∅ then
11  │  │  │  │  G ← Ω
12  │  │  │  else
13  │  │  │  │  G ← Merge(K, A, G, Ω)
14  │  return nil

15  Function Merge(K,A,X,Y):
16  │  Z ← ∅
17  │  for μ ∈ X do
18  │  │  if ∃μ' ∈ Y, [[K]]_μ = [[K]]_μ' then
19  │  │  │  for k ↦ v ∈ μ' do
20  │  │  │  │  if type(k, A) ∈ {COUNT, SUM} then
21  │  │  │  │  │  μ[k] ← μ[k] + v
22  │  │  │  │  else if type(k, A) = SaC then
23  │  │  │  │  │  μ[k] ← μ[k] ⊕ v
24  │  │  │  │  else if type(k, A) = MIN then
25  │  │  │  │  │  μ[k] ← min(μ[k], v)
26  │  │  │  │  else if type(k, A) = MAX then
27  │  │  │  │  │  μ[k] ← max(μ[k], v)
28  │  │  │  │  else
29  │  │  │  │  │  μ[k] ← μ[k] ∪ v
30  │  │  else if ∃μ' ∈ Y, μ' ∉ X, K ∈ dom(μ')
          then
31  │  │  │  Z ← Z ∪ {μ'}
32  │  │  Z ← Z ∪ {μ}
33  │  return Z
```

This is not a new constraint imposed by web preemption, DBpedia and Wikidata administrators already set their quotas to 60 s for the same reason. We offer them the opportunity to replace a quota that stops query execution by a quantum that suspends query execution.

4.3   Implementing Decomposable Aggregation Functions

For evaluating SPARQL aggregation queries on the preemptive server SaGe [12], we introduce the *preemptable SPARQL aggregation iterator*. The new iterator incrementally computes partial aggregation during a time quantum and then returns the results to the smart client, as shown in Algorithm 1. It can also be suspended and resumed in *constant time*.

When query processing starts, the server calls the Open() method to initialize a multiset of solution mappings G. At each call to GetNext(), the iterator pulls a set of solutions μ from its predecessor (Line 7). Then, it computes the aggregation functions on μ and merges the intermediate results with the content of G (Lines 8–13), using the $\diamond$ operator. These operations are **non-interruptibles**, because if they were interrupted by preemption, the iterator could end up in a non-consistent state that cannot be saved or resumed. The function *Merge(K, A, X, Y)*

Algorithm 2: Client-side merging of partial aggregates

Require: Q_γ: SPARQL aggregation query, S: url of a SAGE server.

1 **Function** $EvalQuery(Q_\gamma, S)$:
2    $K \leftarrow$ Grouping variables of Q_γ
3    $A \leftarrow$ Aggregation functions of Q_γ
4    $Q'_\gamma \leftarrow DecomposeQuery(Q_\gamma)$
5    $\Omega \leftarrow \emptyset$
6    $\Omega', next \leftarrow$ Evaluate Q'_γ at S
7   **while** $next \neq nil$ **do**
8      $\Omega \leftarrow Merge(K, A, \Omega, \Omega')$
9      $\Omega', next \leftarrow$ Evaluate $next$ at S
10   **return** ProduceResults(Ω, K, A)

11 **Function** $ProduceResults(\Omega, K, A)$:
12    $\Omega_r \leftarrow \emptyset$
13   **for** $\mu \in \Omega$ **do**
14   **for** $k \mapsto v \in \mu, k \notin K$ **do**
15   **if** $type(k, A) = AVG$ **then**
16          $(s, c) \leftarrow v$
17          $\mu[k] = s/c$
18   **else if** $type(k, A) = COUNT_D$ **then**
19          $\mu[k] = |v|$
20   **else if** $type(k, A) = SUM_D$ **then**
21          $\mu[k] = SUM(v)$
22   **else if** $type(k, A) = AVG_D$ **then**
23          $\mu[k] - AVG(v)$
24      $\Omega_r \leftarrow \Omega_r \cup \{\mu\}$
25   **return** Ω_r

(Lines 15–33) merges the content of two solution mappings X, Y. For each $\mu \in X$, it finds a $\mu' \in Y$ that has the same group key as μ (Line 18). If so, the algorithm iterates over all aggregations results in μ (Lines 19–32) to merge them with their equivalent in μ', using the different merge operators shown in Table 1. If the aggregation is a COUNT or SUM (Lines 20–21), then the aggregation results are merged using an addition. If the aggregation is a SaC aggregation (Lines 22–23), then the two results are merged using the *pointwise sum of pairs*, as defined in Sect. 4.2. If it is a MIN (Lines 24–25) or MAX aggregation (Lines 26–27), then the results are merged by keeping the minimum or maximum of the two values, respectively. Finally, in the case of a CT aggregation (Lines 28–29), the two sets of values are merged using *the set union operator*. When preemption occurs, the server waits for its non-interruptible section to complete and then suspends query execution. The section can block the program for at most the computation of γ on a single set of mappings, which can be done in constant time. Then, the iterator calls the Save() method and sends all partial SPARQL aggregation results to the client. When the iterator is resumed, it starts back query processing where it was left, but with an empty set G, *i.e.*, the preemptable SPARQL aggregation iterator is fully stateless and resuming it is done in constant time.

We also extend the SAGE smart web client to support the evaluation of SPARQL aggregation using partial aggregates, as shown in Algorithm 2. To execute a SPARQL aggregation query Q_γ, the client first decomposes Q_γ into Q'_γ to replace the AVG aggregation function and the DISTINCT modifier as described in Sect. 4.2. Then, the client submits Q'_γ to the SAGE server S, and follows the **next** links sent by S to fetch and merge all query results, following the Web preemption model (Lines 6–9). The client transforms the set of partial

Table 2. Statistics of RDF datasets used in the experimental study

RDF dataset	# Triples	# Subjects	# Predicates	# Objects	# Classes
BSBM-10	4 987	614	40	1 920	11
BSBM-100	40 177	4 174	40	11 012	22
BSBM-1k	371 911	36 433	40	86 202	103
DBpedia 3.5.1	153M	6 085 631	35 631	35 201 955	243

SPARQL aggregation results returned by the server to produce the final aggregation results (Lines 11–25): for each set of solutions mappings $\mu \in \Omega$, the client applies the *reducing function* on all aggregation results. For an AVG aggregation, it computes the average value from the two values stored in the pair computed by the SaC aggregation (Lines 15–17). For a $COUNT_D$ (Lines 18–19) aggregation, it counts the size of the set produced by the CT aggregation. For SUM_D (Lines 20–21) and AVG_D (Lines 22–23) aggregations, the client simply applies the SUM and AVG aggregation function, respectively, on the set of values. Finally, for all other aggregations, like SUM or COUNT, the client does not perform any reduction, as the values produced by the merge operator already are final results.

5   Experimental Study

We want to empirically answer the following questions: (i) What is the data transfer reduction obtained with partial aggregations? (ii) What is the speed up obtained with partial aggregations? (iii) What is the impact of time quantum on data transfer and execution time?

We implemented the partial aggregator approach as an extension of the SAGE query engine[5]. The SAGE server has been extended with the new operator described in Algorithm 1. The Java SAGE client is implemented using Apache Jena and has been extended with Algorithm 2. All extensions and experimental results are available at https://github.com/folkvir/sage-sparql-void.

Dataset and Queries: We build a workload (*SP*) of 18 SPARQL aggregation queries extracted from SPORTAL queries [8] (queries without ASK and FILTER). Most of the extracted queries have the DISTINCT modifier. SPORTAL queries are challenging as they aim to build VoID description of RDF datasets[6]. In [8], the authors report that most queries cannot complete over DBpedia due to quota limitations. To study the impact of DISTINCT on performances of aggregate queries processing, we defined a new workload, denoted *SP-ND*, by removing the DISTINCT modifier from the queries of *SP*. We run the *SP* and

---

[5] https://sage.univ-nantes.fr.
[6] https://www.w3.org/TR/void/.

SP-ND workloads on synthetic and real-world datasets: Berlin SPARQL Benchmark (BSBM) with different sizes, and a fragment of DBpedia *v3.5.1*, respectively. The statistics of datasets are detailed in Table 2.

Approaches: We compare the following approaches:

- SAGE: We run the SAGE query engine [12] with a time quantum of 150 ms and a maximum page size of results of 5000 mappings. The data are stored in a PostgreSQL server, with indexes on *(SPO)*, *(POS)* and *(OSP)*.
- SAGE-AGG: is our extension of SAGE with partial aggregations. It runs with the same configuration as the regular SAGE.
- *TPF*: We run the TPF server [19] (with no Web cache) and the Communica client, using the standard page size of 100 triples. Data are stored in HDT format.
- *Virtuoso:* We run the Virtuoso SPARQL endpoint [6] (v7.2.4) **without quotas** in order to deliver complete results and optimal data transfer. We also configured Virtuoso with *a single thread* to fairly compare with other engines.

Servers Configurations: We run experimentations on Google Cloud Platform, on a n1-standard-2: 2 vCPU, 7,5 Go memory with a SSD local disk.

Evaluation Metrics: Presented results correspond to the average obtained of three successive executions of the queries workloads. (i) *Data transfer*: is the number of bytes transferred to the client when evaluating a query. (ii) *Execution time*: is the time between the start of the query and the production of the final results by the client.

Experimental Results

Data Transfer and Execution Time over BSBM. Figure 4 presents data transfer and execution time for BSBM-10, BSBM-100 and BSBM-1k. The plots on the left detail the results for the SP workload and on the right, the results for the SP-ND workload. Virtuoso with no quota is presented as the optimal in terms of data transfer and execution time. As expected, TPF delivers the worst performance because TPF does not support projections and joins on server-side. Consequently, the data transfer is huge even for small datasets. SAGE delivers better performance than TPF mainly because it supports projection and joins on the server side. SAGE-AGG significantly improves data transfer but not execution time. Indeed, partial aggregations allow to reduce data transfer but do not allow to speed up the scanning of data on disk. When comparing the 2 workloads, we can see that processing queries without DISTINCT (on the right) is much more efficient in data transfer than with DISTINCT (on the left). For DISTINCT queries, partial aggregations can only remove duplicates observed during a time quantum only and not those observed during the execution of the query.

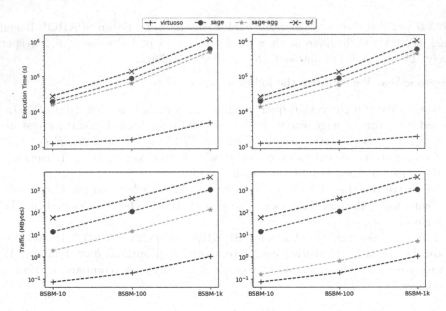

Fig. 4. Data transfer and execution time for BSBM-10, BSBM-100 and BSBM-1k, when running the *SP* (left) and *SP-ND* (right) workloads

Impact of Time Quantum. Figure 5 reports the results of running SAGE, SAGE-AGG and Virtuoso with a quantum of 150 ms, 1,5 s and 15 s on BSBM-1k. The plots on the left detail the results for the SP workload and on the right the SP-ND workload. As we can see, increasing the quantum significantly improves execution times of SAGE-AGG but not of SAGE. Indeed, SAGE transfers the same amount of mappings to the client even with a large quantum. Increasing the quantum reduces data transfer for the SP workload. Indeed, a large quantum allows deduplicating more elements.

Data Transfer and Execution Time over DBPedia. Figure 6 reports the results of running SAGE-AGG with the SP-ND workload on a fragment of DBPedia with a quantum of 30 s compared with Virtuoso. As expected, Virtuoso delivers better performance in data transfer and execution times. Concerning execution time, the difference of performance between Virtuoso and SAGE-AGG is mainly due to the lack of query optimisation in the SAGE-AGG implementation: no projection push-down, no merge-joins. Concerning data transfer, Virtuoso computes full aggregation on the server, while SAGE-AGG performs only partial aggregation. However, Virtuoso cannot ensure termination of queries under quotas. Five queries are interrupted after 60 s. SAGE-AGG replaces a quota that stops query execution by a quantum that suspends query execution. Consequently, SAGE-AGG ensures termination of all queries.

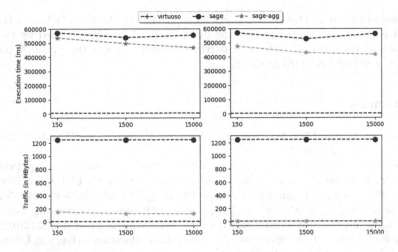

Fig. 5. Time quantum impacts executing *SP* (left) and *SP-ND* (right) over BSBM1k

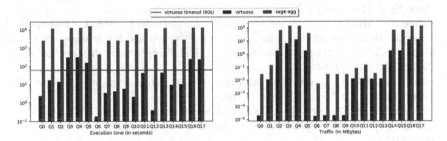

Fig. 6. Execution time and data transferred for *SP-ND* over DBpedia

6   Conclusion and Future Works

In this paper, we demonstrated how the partitioning of mappings produced by
Web preemption can be used to extend a preemptable SPARQL server with
a preemptable aggregation operator. As a large part of aggregations are now
executed on the server-side, it drastically reduces data transfer and improves
execution time of SPARQL aggregation queries compared to SaGe and TPF.
However, in the current implementation, the execution time still exhibits low
performance which limit the application to very large knowledge graphs such as
Wikidata or DBpedia. Fortunately, there are many ways to improve execution
times. First, the current implementation of SaGe has no query optimizer on the
server-side. Just applying state of art optimisation techniques, including filter
and projection push-down, aggregate push down or merge-joins should greatly
improve execution times. Second, web preemption currently does not support
intra-query parallelization techniques. Defining how to suspend and resume parallel scans is clearly in our research agenda.

Acknowledgments. This work is partially supported by the ANR DeKaloG (Decentralized Knowledge Graphs) project, program CE23. A. Grall is funded by the GFI Informatique company. T. Minier is partially funded through the FaBuLA project, part of the AtlanSTIC 2020 program.

References

1. Anderson, T., Dahlin, M.: Operating Systems: Principles and Practice. 2nd edn. Recursive Books (2014)
2. Buil-Aranda, C., Polleres, A., Umbrich, J.: Strategies for executing federated queries in SPARQL1.1. In: Mika, P., et al. (eds.) ISWC 2014. LNCS, vol. 8797, pp. 390–405. Springer, Cham (2014). https://doi.org/10.1007/978-3-319-11915-1_25
3. Auer, S., Demter, J., Martin, M., Lehmann, J.: LODStats - an extensible framework for high-performance dataset analytics. In: EKAW 2012, pp. 353–362 (2012)
4. Bizer, C., Heath, T., Berners-Lee, T.: Linked data - the story so far. Int. J. Semantic Web Inf. Syst. **5**(3), 1–22 (2009)
5. Blasgen, M.W., Gray, J., Mitoma, M.F., Price, T.G.: The convoy phenomenon. Oper. Syst. Rev. **13**(2), 20–25 (1979)
6. Erling, O., Mikhailov, I.: RDF support in the virtuoso DBMS. In: Pellegrini, T., Auer, S., Tochtermann, K., Schaffert, S. (eds.) Networked Knowledge - Networked Media. SCI, vol. 221, pp. 7–24. Springer, Heidelberg (2009). https://doi.org/10.1007/978-3-642-02184-8_2
7. Fife, D.W.: R68-47 computer scheduling methods and their countermeasures. IEEE Trans. Comput. **17**(11), 1098–1099 (1968)
8. Hasnain, A., Mehmood, Q., e Zainab, S.S., Hogan, A.: SPORTAL: profiling the content of public SPARQL endpoints. Int. J. Semantic Web Inf. Syst. **12**(3), 134–163 (2016)
9. Jesus, P., Baquero, C., Almeida, P.S.: A survey of distributed data aggregation algorithms. CoRR abs/1110.0725 (2011). http://arxiv.org/abs/1110.0725
10. Kaminski, M., Kostylev, E.V., Grau, B.C.: Query nesting, assignment, and aggregation in SPARQL 1.1. ACM Trans. Database Syst. **42**(3), 1–46 (2017)
11. Li, K., Li, G.: Approximate query processing: what is new and where to go? Data Sci. Eng. **3**(4), 379–397 (2018)
12. Minier, T., Skaf-Molli, H., Molli, P.: SaGe: web preemption for public SPARQL query services. In: The World Wide Web Conference, WWW 2019, San Francisco, CA, USA, 13–17 May 2019, pp. 1268–1278 (2019)
13. Pérez, J., Arenas, M., Gutiérrez, C.: Semantics and complexity of SPARQL. ACM Trans. Database Syst. **34**(3), 16:1–16:45 (2009)
14. Schätzle, A., Przyjaciel-Zablocki, M., Skilevic, S., Lausen, G.: S2RDF: RDF querying with SPARQL on spark. VLDB Endow. **9**(10), 804–815 (2016)
15. Schmachtenberg, M., Bizer, C., Paulheim, H.: Adoption of the linked data best practices in different topical domains. In: Mika, P., et al. (eds.) ISWC 2014. LNCS, vol. 8796, pp. 245–260. Springer, Cham (2014). https://doi.org/10.1007/978-3-319-11964-9_16
16. Schmidt, M., Meier, M., Lausen, G.: Foundations of SPARQL query optimization. In: Database Theory - ICDT 2010, pp. 4–33 (2010)
17. Soulet, A., Suchanek, F.M.: Anytime large-scale analytics of Linked Open Data. In: Ghidini, C., et al. (eds.) ISWC 2019. LNCS, vol. 11778, pp. 576–592. Springer, Cham (2019). https://doi.org/10.1007/978-3-030-30793-6_33

18. Steve, H., Andy, S.: SPARQL 1.1 query language. In: Recommendation W3C (2013)
19. Verborgh, R., et al.: Triple pattern fragments: a low-cost knowledge graph interface for the web. J. Web Sem. **37–38**, 184–206 (2016)
20. Vora, M.N.: Hadoop-HBase for large-scale data. In: International Conference on Computer Science and Network Technology, vol. 1, pp. 601–605. IEEE (2011)
21. Yan, W.P., Larson, P.A.: Eager aggregation and lazy aggregation. In: 21st International Conference on Very Large Data Bases, VLDB, pp. 345–357 (1995)

Science of Science

Embedding-Based Recommendations on Scholarly Knowledge Graphs

Mojtaba Nayyeri[1]([✉]), Sahar Vahdati[2], Xiaotian Zhou[1],
Hamed Shariat Yazdi[1], and Jens Lehmann[1,3]

[1] University of Bonn, Bonn, Germany
{nayyeri,jens.lehmann}@cs.uni-bonn.de, 6xizhou@uni-bonn.de,
shariatyazdi@gmail.com
[2] University of Oxford, Oxford, UK
sahar.vahdati@cs.ox.ac.uk
[3] Fraunhofer IAIS, Dresden, Germany
jens.lehmann@iais.fraunhofer.de

Abstract. The increasing availability of scholarly metadata in the form of Knowledge Graphs (KG) offers opportunities for studying the structure of scholarly communication and evolution of science. Such KGs build the foundation for knowledge-driven tasks e.g., link discovery, prediction and entity classification which allow to provide recommendation services. Knowledge graph embedding (KGE) models have been investigated for such knowledge-driven tasks in different application domains. One of the applications of KGE models is to provide link predictions, which can also be viewed as a foundation for recommendation service, e.g. high confidence "co-author" links in a scholarly knowledge graph can be seen as suggested collaborations. In this paper, KGEs are reconciled with a specific loss function (Soft Margin) and examined with respect to their performance for co-authorship link prediction task on scholarly KGs. The results show a significant improvement in the accuracy of the experimented KGE models on the considered scholarly KGs using this specific loss. TransE with Soft Margin (TransE-SM) obtains a score of 79.5% Hits@10 for co-authorship link prediction task while the original TransE obtains 77.2%, on the same task. In terms of accuracy and Hits@10, TransE-SM also outperforms other state-of-the-art embedding models such as ComplEx, ConvE and RotatE in this setting. The predicted co-authorship links have been validated by evaluating profile of scholars.

Keywords: Scholarly knowledge graph · Author recommendation · Knowledge graph embedding · Scholarly communication · Science graph · Metaresearch queries · Link prediction · Research of research

1 Introduction

With the rapid growth of digital publishing, researchers are increasingly exposed to an incredible amount of scholarly artifacts and their metadata. The complexity of science in its nature is reflected in such heterogeneously interconnected

© Springer Nature Switzerland AG 2020
A. Harth et al. (Eds.): ESWC 2020, LNCS 12123, pp. 255–270, 2020.
https://doi.org/10.1007/978-3-030-49461-2_15

information. Knowledge Graphs (KGs), viewed as a form of information representation in a semantic graph, have proven to be extremely useful in modeling and representing such complex domains [8]. KG technologies provide the backbone for many AI-driven applications which are employed in a number of use cases, e.g. in the scholarly communication domain. Therefore, to facilitate acquisition, integration and utilization of such metadata, Scholarly Knowledge Graphs (SKGs) have gained attention [3,25] in recent years. Formally, a SKG is a collection of scholarly facts represented in triples including entities and a relation between them, e.g. (Albert Einstein, co-author, Boris Podolsky). Such representation of data has influenced the quality of services which have already been provided across disciplines such as Google Scholar[1], Semantic Scholar [10], OpenAIRE [1], AMiner [17], ResearchGate [26]. The ultimate objective of such attempts ranges from service development to measuring research impact and accelerating science. Recommendation services, e.g. finding potential collaboration partners, relevant venues, relevant papers to read or cite are among the most desirable services in research of research enquiries [9,25]. So far, most of the approaches addressing such services for scholarly domains use semantic similarity and graph clustering techniques [2,6,27].

The heterogeneous nature of such metadata and variety of sources plugging metadata to scholarly KGs [14,18,22] keeps complex metaresearch enquiries (research of research) challenging to analyse. This influences the quality of the services relying only on the explicitly represented information. Link prediction in KGs, i.e. the task of finding (not explicitly represented) connections between entities, draws on the detection of existing patterns in the KG. A wide range of methods has been introduced for link prediction [13]. The most recent successful methods try to capture the semantic and structural properties of a KG by encoding information as multi-dimensional vectors (embeddings). Such methods are known as knowledge graph embedding (KGE) models in the literature [23]. However, despite the importance of link prediction for the scholarly domains, it has rarely been studied with KGEs [12,24] for the scholarly domain.

In a preliminary version of this work [11], we tested a set of embedding models (in their original version) on top of a SKG in order to analyse suitability of KGEs for the use case of scholarly domain. The primary insights derived from results have proved the effectiveness of applying KGE models on scholarly knowledge graphs. However, further exploration of the results proved that the many-to-many characteristic of the focused relation, co-authorship, causes restrictions in negative sampling which is a mandatory step in the learning process of KGE models. Negative sampling is used to balance discrimination from the positive samples in KGs. A negative sample is generated by a replacement of either subject or object with a random entity in the KG e.g., (Albert Einstein, co-author, Trump) is a negative sample for (Albert Einstein, co-author, Boris Podolsky). To illustrate the negative sampling problem, consider the following case: Assuming that $N = 1000$ is the number of all authors in a SKG, the probability of generating false negatives for an author with 100 true or sensible

---

[1] https://scholar.google.de/.

but unknown collaborations becomes $\frac{100}{1000} = 10\%$. This problem is particularly relevant when the in/out-degree of entities in a KG is very high. This is not limited to, but particularly relevant, in scholarly KGs with its network of authors, venues and papers. To tackle this problem, we propose a modified version of the Margin Ranking Loss (MRL) to train the KGE models such as TransE and RotatE. The model is dubbed SM (Soft Margins), which considers margins as soft boundaries in its optimization. Soft margin loss allows false negative samples to move slightly inside the margin, mitigating the adverse effects of false negative samples. Our main contributions are:

- proposing a novel loss function explicitly designed for KGs with many-to-many relations (present in co-authorship relation of scholarly KGs),
- showcasing the effect of the proposed loss function for KGE models,
- providing co-authorship recommendations on scholarly KGs,
- evaluating the effectiveness of the approach and the recommended links on scholarly KGs with favorable results,
- validating the predicted co-authorship links by a profile check of scholars.

The remaining part of this paper proceeds as follows. Section 2 represents details of the scholarly knowledge graph that is created for the purpose of applying link discovery tools. Section 3 provides a summary of preliminaries required about the embedding models and presents some of the focused embedding models of this paper, TransE and RotatE. Moreover, other related works in the domain of knowledge graph embeddings are reviewed in Sect. 3.2. Section 4 contains the given approach and description of the changes to the MRL. An evaluation of the proposed model on the represented scholarly knowledge graph is shown in Sect. 5. In Sect. 6, we lay out the insights and provide a conjunction of this research work.

2   A Scholarly Knowledge Graph

A specific scholarly knowledge graphs has been constructed in order to provide effective recommendations for the selected use case (co-authorship). This knowledge graph is created after a systematic analysis of the scholarly metadata resources on the Web (mostly RDF data). The list of resources includes DBLP[2], Springer Nature SciGraph Explorer[3], Semantic Scholar[4] and the Global Research Identifier Database (GRID)[5] with metadata about institutes. A preliminary version of this KG has been used for experiments of the previous work [11] where suitability of embedding models have been tested of such use cases. Through this research work we will point to this KG as *SKGOLD*. Towards this objective, a domain conceptualization has been done to define the classes and relations of

---

[2] https://dblp2.uni-trier.de/.
[3] https://springernature.com/scigraph.
[4] https://semanticscholar.org.
[5] https://www.grid.ac.

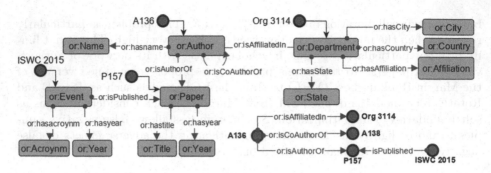

Fig. 1. Ontology of a scholarly knowledge graph for experimenting embedding models in co-authorship link prediction.

focus. Figure 1 shows the ontology that is used for the creation of these knowledge graphs. In order to define the terms, the OpenResearch [20] ontology is reused.

Each instance in the scholarly knowledge graph is equipped with a unique ID to enable the identification and association of the KG elements. The knowledge graphs consist of the following core entities of Papers, Events, Authors, and Departments.

In the creation of the our KG[6] which will be denoted as *SKGNEW* a set of 7 conference series have been selected (namely ISWC, ESWC, AAAI, NeurIPS, CIKM, ACI, KCAP and HCAI have been considered in the initial step of retrieving raw metadata from the source). In addition, the metadata flitted for the temporal interval of 2013–2018. The second version of the same KG has been generated directly from Semantic Scholar.

Table 1. Dataset statistics. The number of triples that are used in different datasets are shown per each entity and relationship.

Dataset	Entities			Relations		
	Author	Publication	Venue	hasAuthor	hasCoauthor	hasVenue
SKGOLD	4,660	2,870	7	9,934	12,921	6,614
SKGNEW	12,472	5,001	42	14,933	21,279	5,001

The datasets, used for model training, which in total comprise 70,682 triples where 29,469 triples are coming from the *SKGOLD* and 41,213 triples are generated in *SKGNEW*. In each set of experiments, both datasets are split into triples

---

[6] The datasets created for SKGs are available here: https://github.com/SmartData Analytics/OpenResearch.

of training/validation/test sets. Table 1 includes the detailed statistics about the datasets only considering three relationships between entities namely hasAuthor (paper - author), hasCoauthor (author - author), hasVenue (author/paper - venue). Due to the low volume of data, isAffiliated (author - organization) relationship is eliminated due in SKGNEW.

3 Preliminaries and Related Work

In this section we focus on providing required preliminaries for this work as well as the related work. The definitions required to understand our approach are:

- **Knowledge Graph.** Let $\mathcal{E}, \mathcal{R}$ be the sets of entities and relations respectively. A Kg is roughly represented as a set $\mathcal{K} = \{(h, r, t)|h, t \in \mathcal{E}, r \in \mathcal{R}\}$ in which h, t, r refer to the subject and object and relation respectively.
- **Embedding Vectors.** The vector representation of symbolic entities and relations in a KG are considered as embeddings. The vectors of a triple h, r, t are depicted as $\mathbf{h, r, t} \in \mathbb{R}^d$, where d refers to the dimension of the embedding space.
- **Score Function.** Each KGE model defines an score function $f_r(h, t)$. The score function gets the embedding vectors of a triple (h, r, t) and returns a value determining if the triple is a fact or not. A lower value for the score function indicates that the triple is more plausible comparing to those triples with higher values.
- **Loss Function.** Each KGE model utilizes a loss function to adjust embedding. In the beginning of the learning process, the model initializes the embedding vectors randomly. Then it updates the vectors by optimizing a loss function $\mathcal{L}$. Since typically many variables should be adjusted in the learning process, Stochastic Gradient Descent (SGD) method is commonly used for the optimization of the loss function.
- **Negative Sampling.** KGs contain only positive samples. Most of KGE models generate artificial negative samples to have a better discrimination from positive ones. Uniform negative sampling ($unif$) is the most widely used negative sampling technique in which a negative sample is generated for a triple (h, r, t) by replacement of either h or t with a random entity (h' or t') existing in $\mathcal{E}$.

3.1 Review of TransE and RotatE Models

The proposed loss is trained on a classical translation-based embedding models named TransE and a model for complex space as RotatE. Therefore, we mainly provide a description of TransE and RotatE and further focus on other state-of-the-art models.

TransE. It is reported that TransE [4], as one of the simplest translation based models, outperformed more complicated KGEs in [11].

The initial idea of TransE model is to enforce embedding of entities and relation in a positive triple (h, r, t) to satisfy the following equality:

$$\mathbf{h} + \mathbf{r} = \mathbf{t} \tag{1}$$

where $\mathbf{h}$, $\mathbf{r}$ and $\mathbf{t}$ are embedding vectors of head, relation and tail respectively. TransE model defines the following scoring function:

$$f_r(h, t) = \|\mathbf{h} + \mathbf{r} - \mathbf{t}\| \tag{2}$$

RotatE. Here, we address RotatE [16] which is a model designed to rotate the head to the tail entity by using relation. This model embeds entities and relations in Complex space. By inclusion of constraints on the norm of entity vectors, the model would be degenerated to TransE. The scoring function of RotatE is

$$f_r(h, t) = \|\mathbf{h} \circ \mathbf{r} - \mathbf{t}\|$$

in which ∘ is the element-wise product.

Loss Function. Margin ranking loss (MRL) is one of the most used loss functions which optimizes the embedding vectors of entities and relations. MRL computes embedding of entities and relations in a way that a positive triple gets lower score value than its corresponding negative triple. The least difference value between the score of positive and negative samples is margin (γ). The MRL is defined as follows:

$$\mathcal{L} = \sum_{(h,r,t) \in S^+} \sum_{(h',r',t') \in S^-} [f_r(h,t) + \gamma - f_r(h',t')]_+ \tag{3}$$

where $[x]_+ = \max(0, x)$ and S^+ and S^- are respectively the set of positive and negative samples.

MRL has two disadvantages: 1) the margin can slide, 2) embeddings are adversely affected by false negative samples. More precisely, the issue of margin sliding is described with an example. Assume that $f_r(h_1, t_1) = 0$ and $f_r(h'_1, t'_1) = \gamma$, or $f_r(h_1, t_1) = \gamma$ and $f_r(h'_1, t'_1) = 2\gamma$ are two possible scores for a triple and its negative sample. Both of these scores get minimum value for the optimization causing the model to become vulnerable to a undesirable solution. To tackle this problem, Limited-based score [28] revises the MRL by adding a term to limit maximum value of positive score:

$$\mathcal{L}_{RS} = \sum\sum [f_r(h,t) + \gamma - f_r(h',t')]_+ + \lambda[f_r(h,t) - \gamma_1]_+ \tag{4}$$

It shows $\mathcal{L}_{RS}$ significantly improves the performance of TransE. Authors in [28] denote TransE which is trained by $\mathcal{L}_{RS}$ as TransE-RS. Regarding the second disadvantage, MRL enforces a hard margin in the side of negative samples. However, using relations with many-to-many characteristic (e.g., co-author), the rate of false negative samples is high. Therefore, using a hard boundary for discrimination adversely affects the performance of a KGE model.

3.2   Review of Other State-of-the-Art Models

With a systematic evaluation (performance under reasonable set up) of suitable embedding models to be considered in our evaluations, we have selected two other models that are described here.

ComplEx. One of the embedding models focusing on semantic matching model is ComplEx [19]. In semantic matching models, the plausibility of facts are measured by matching the similarity of their latent representation, in other words it is assumed that similar entities have common characteristics i.e. are connected through similar relationships [13,23]. In ComplEx the entities are embedded in the complex space. The score function of ComplEx is given as follows:

$$f(h,t) = \Re(\mathbf{h}^T \operatorname{diag}(\mathbf{r})\,\bar{\mathbf{t}})$$

in which $\bar{\mathbf{t}}$ is the conjugate of the vector $\mathbf{t}$.

ConvE. Here we present a multi-layer convolutional network model for link prediction named as ConvE. The score function of the ConvE is defined as below:

$$f(h,t) = g(\operatorname{vec}(g([\bar{\mathbf{h}}, \bar{\mathbf{r}}] * \omega))\,\mathbf{W})\mathbf{t}$$

in which g denotes a non-linear function, $\bar{\mathbf{h}}$ and $\bar{\mathbf{r}}$ are 2D reshape of head and relation vectors respectively, ω is a filter and $\mathbf{W}$ is a linear transformation matrix. The core idea behind the ConvE model is to use 2D convolutions over embeddings to predict links. ConvE consists of a single convolution layer, a projection layer to the embedding dimension as well as an inner product layer.

4   Soft Marginal Loss

This section proposes a new model independent optimization framework for training KGE models. The framework fixes the second problem of MRL and its extension mentioned in the previous section. The optimization utilizes slack variables to mitigate the negative effect of the generated false negative samples.

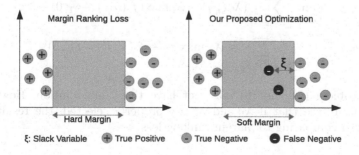

Fig. 2. Optimization of margin ranking loss.

In contrast to margin ranking loss, our optimization uses soft margin. Therefore, uncertain negative samples are allowed to slide inside of margin.

Figure 2 visualizes the separation of positive and negative samples using margin ranking loss and our optimization problem. It shows that the proposed optimization problem allows false negative samples to slide inside the margin by using slack variables (ξ). In contrast, margin ranking loss doesn't allow false negative samples to slide inside of the margin. Therefore, embedding vectors of entities and relations are adversely affected by false negative samples. The mathematical formulation of our optimization problem is as follows:

$$
\begin{cases}
\min_{\xi_{h,t}^r} \sum_{(h,r,t)\in S^+} {\xi_{h,t}^r}^2 \\
\text{s.t.} \\
f_r(h,t) \leq \gamma_1, \ (h,r,t) \in S^+ \\
f_r(h',t') \geq \gamma_2 - \xi_{h,t}^r, \ (h',r,t') \in S^- \\
\xi_{h,t}^r \geq 0
\end{cases}
\tag{5}
$$

where $f_r(h,t)$ is the score function of a KGE model (e.g., TransE or RotatE), S^+, S^- are positive and negative samples sets. $\gamma_1 \geq 0$ is the upper bound of score of positive samples and γ_2 is the lower bound of negative samples. $\gamma_2 - \gamma_1$ is margin ($\gamma_2 \geq \gamma_1$). $\xi_{h,t}^r$ is slack variable for a negative sample that allows it to slide in the margin. $\xi_{h,t}^r$ helps the optimization to better handle uncertainty resulted from negative sampling.

The term ($\sum \xi_{h,t}^r$) represented in the problem 5 is quadratic. Therefore, it is convex which results in a unique and optimal solution. Moreover, all three constraints can be represented as convex sets. The constrained optimization problem (5) is convex. As a conclusion, it has a unique optimal solution. The optimal solution can be obtained by using different standard methods e.g. penalty method [5]. The goal of the problem (5) is to adjust embedding vectors of entities and relations. A lot of variables participate in optimization. In this condition, using batch learning with stochastic gradient descent (SGD) is preferred. In order to use SGD, constrained optimization problem (5) should be converted to unconstrained optimization problem. The following unconstrained optimization problem is proposed instead of (5).

$$
\min_{\xi_{h,t}^r} \sum_{(h,r,t)\in S^+} (\lambda_0 {\xi_{h,t}^r}^2 + \lambda_1 \max(f_r(h,t) - \gamma_1, 0) +
$$
$$
\sum_{(h',r,t')\in S^-_{h,r,t}} \lambda_2 \max(\gamma_2 - f_r(h',t') - \xi_{h,t}^r, 0))
\tag{6}
$$

The problem (5) and (6) may not have the same solution. However, we experimentally see that if λ_1 and λ_2 are properly selected, the results would be improved comparing to margin ranking loss.

5   Evaluation

This section presents the evaluations of TransE-SM and RotatE-SM (TransE and RotatE trained by SM loss), over a scholarly knowledge graph. The evaluations are motivated for a link prediction task in the domain of scholarly communication in order to explore the ability of embedding models in support of metaresearch enquiries. In addition, we provide a comparison of our model with other state-of-the-art embedding models (selected by performance under a reasonable set up) on two standard benchmarks (FreeBase and WordNet). Four different evaluation methods have been performed in order to approve: 1) better *performance* and *effect* of the proposed loss, 2) *quality and soundness* of the results, 3) *validity* of the discovered co-authorship links and 4) *sensitivity* of the proposed model to the selected hyperparameters. More details about each of these analyses are discussed in the remaining part of this section.

5.1   Performance Analysis

The proposed loss is model independent, however, we prove its functionality and effectiveness by applying it on different embedding models. In the first evaluation method, we run experiments and assess *performance* of TransE-SM model as well as RotatE-SM in comparison to the other models and the original loss functions. In order to discuss this evaluation further, let (h, r, t) be a triple fact with an assumption that either head or tail entity is missing (e.g., $(?, r, t)$ or $(h, r, ?)$). The task is to aim at completing either of these triples $(h, r, ?)$ or $(?, r, t)$ by predicting head (h) or tail (t) entity. Mean Rank (MR), Mean Reciprocal Rank (MRR) [23] and Hits@10 have been extensively used as standard metrics for evaluation of KGE models on link prediction.

In computation of Mean Rank, a set of pre-processing steps have been done such as:

- head and tail of each test triple are replaced by all entities in the dataset,
- scores of the generated triples are computed and sorted,
- the average rank of correct test triples is reported as MR.

Let $rank_i$ refers to the rank of the $i-$th triple in the test set obtained by a KGE model. The MRR is obtained as follows:

$$MRR = \sum_i \frac{1}{rank_i}.$$

The computation of Hits@10 is obtained by replacing all entities in the dataset in terms of head and tail of each test triples. The result is a sorted list of triples based on their scores. The average number of triples that are ranked at most 10 is reported as Hits@10 as represented in Table 2.

Table 2. Link prediction results. Results of TransE (reported from [11]), TransRS, and our proposed model (TransE-SM) are obtained. The others are obtained from original code. Dashes: results could not be obtained. The underlined values show the best competitor model and the bold results refer to the cases where our model outperforms other competitors.

	SKGOLD – Filtered			SKGNEW – Filtered		
	FMR	FHits@10	FMRR	FMR	FHits@10	FMRR
TransE [4]	<u>647</u>	50.7	–	1150	<u>77.2</u>	–
ComplEx [19]	–	56.2	0.326	–	73.9	<u>0.499</u>
ConvE [7]	1215	49.3	0.282	1893	71.3	0.442
RotatE [15]	993	<u>60.6</u>	<u>0.346</u>	1780	69.5	0.486
TransE-RS [28]	–	–	–	<u>762</u>	75.8	0.443
TransE-SM (our work)	910	**61.4**	**0.347**	550	**79.5**	0.430
RotatE-SM (our work)	990	60.9	0.347	1713	76.7	**0.522**

Experimental Setup. A Python-based computing package called PyTorch[7] has been used for the implementation of TransE-SM and RotatE-SM[8]. Adagrad was selected as an optimizer. The whole training set is reshuffled in each epoch. Then 100 mini-batches are generated on the reshuffled samples. Batches are taken sequentially and the parameters of the model are optimized on the selected batches in each iteration. The parameters λ_1, λ_2 are set to one for simplicity of our experiments. Sub-optimal embedding dimension (d) is selected among the values in $\{50, 100, 200\}$. Upper bound of positive samples (γ_1) and lower bound of negative samples (γ_2) are selected from the sets $\{0.1, 0.2, ..., 2\}, \{0.2, 0.3, ..., 2.1\}$ respectively. It should be noted that $\gamma_1 \leq \gamma_2$. The regularization term (λ_0) is adjusted among the set $\{0.01, 0.1, 0, 1, 10, 100\}$. For each positive sample in a batch, we generate a set of $\alpha = \{1, 2, ..., 10\}$ negative samples.

Both for TransE-SM and RotatE-SM, the optimal configurations are $\lambda_0 = 10, \gamma_1 = 0.6, \gamma_2 = 0.7, \alpha = 1, d = 100$ for SKGOLD and $\lambda_0 = 10, \gamma_1 = 0.2, \gamma_2 = 0.7, \alpha = 5, d = 200$ for SKGNEW. The results of TransE and TransE-RS are obtained by our implementation. The results corresponding to ConvE, ComplEx are obtained by running their codes.

The results mentioned in the Table 2 validate that TransE-SM and RotatE-SM significantly outperformed other embedding models in all metrics.

In addition, evaluation of the state-of-the-art models have been performed over the two benchmark datasets namely FB15K and WN18. While our focus has been resolving problem of KGEs in presence of many-to-many relationships, the evaluations of the proposed loss function (SM) on other datasets show the effectiveness of SM in addressing other types of relationships.

---

[7] https://pytorch.org/.
[8] The code for Soft margin loss is available here: https://github.com/mojtabanayyeri/Soft-Margin-Loss.

Table 3. Experimental results for FB15K and WN18. Results of TransE-RS and TransE-SM are based on our code. For RotatE we ran the code of authors. Results of other models are taken from the original papers.

	FB15k			WN18		
	FMR	FMRR	FHits@10	FMR	FMRR	FHits@10
TransE [4]	125	–	47.1	251	–	89.2
ComplEx [19]	106	67.5	82.6	543	94.1	94.7
ConvE [7]	51	<u>68.9</u>	85.1	504	94.2	<u>95.5</u>
RotatE [15]	49	68.8	85.9	388	<u>94.6</u>	<u>95.5</u>
TransE-RS [28]	<u>38</u>	57.2	<u>82.8</u>	<u>189</u>	47.9	95.1
TransE-SM	46	64.8	**87.2**	201	47.8	95.2
RotatE-SM	**40**	**70.4**	**87.2**	213	**94.7**	**96.1**

Table 3 shows the results of experiments for TransE, ComplEx, ConvE, RotatE, TransE-RS, TransE-SM and RotatE-SM. The proposed model significantly outperforms the other models with an accuracy of 87.2% on FB15K. The evaluations on WN18 shows that RotatE-SM outperforms other evaluated models. The optimal settings for our proposed model corresponding to this part of the evaluation are $\lambda_0 = 100, \gamma_1 = 0.4, \gamma_2 = 0.5, \alpha = 10, d = 200$ for FB15K and $\lambda_0 = 100, \gamma_1 = 1.0, \gamma_2 = 2.0, \alpha = 10, d = 200$ for WN18.

5.2   Quality and Soundness Analysis

With the second evaluation method, we aim at approving quality and soundness of the results. In order to do so, we additionally investigate the quality of the recommendation of our model. A sample set of 9 researchers associated with the Linked Data and Information Retrieval communities [21] are selected as the foundation for the experiments of the predicted recommendations. Table 4 shows the number of recommendations and their ranks among the top 50 predictions for all of the 9 selected researchers. These top 50 predictions are filtered for a closer look. The results are validated by checking the research profile of the recommended researchers and the track history of co-authorship. In the profile check, we only kept the triples which are indicating:

1. close match in research domain interests of scholars by checking profiles,
2. none-existing scholarly relation (e.g., supervisor, student),
3. none-existing affiliation in the same organization,
4. none-existing co-authorship.

For example, out of all the recommendations that our approach has provided for researcher with id A136, 10 of them have been identified sound and new collaboration target. The rank of each recommended connection is shown in the third column.

Table 4. Co-authorship recommendations. The rank links of discovered potential co-authorship for 9 sample researchers.

Author	#Recom.	Rank of Recom.
A136	10	23, 26, 31, 32, 34, 35, 37, 38, 47, 49
A88	4	2, 19, 30, 50
A816	10	3, 7, 8, 9, 12, 13, 15, 44, 48
A1437	1	21
A138	6	5, 27, 28, 29, 36, 40
A128	1	24
A295	7	1, 11, 14, 18, 22, 39, 41
A940	3	1, 16, 17
A976	8	6, 20, 25, 33, 42, 43, 45, 46

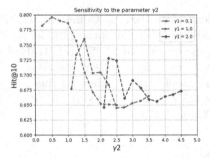 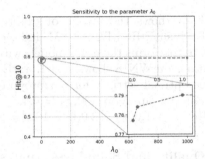

(a) Sensitivity to γ_2 when γ_1 is 0.1, 1.0 and 2.0.

(b) Sensitivity to λ_0 when γ_1 and γ_2 are fixed.

Fig. 3. Sensitivity analysis of TransE-EM to the parameter γ_2 (with fixed values of γ_1) and λ_0.

5.3 Validity Analysis

Furthermore, the discovered links for co-authorship recommendations have been examined with a closer look to the online scientific profile of two top machine learning researchers, *Yoshua Bengio*[9], *A860* and *Yann LeCun*[10], *A2261*. The recommended triples have been created in two patterns of $(A860, r, ?)$ and $(?, r, A860)$ and deduplicated for the same answer. The triples are ranked based on scores obtained from TransE-SM and RotatE-SM. For evaluations, a list of top 50 recommendations has been selected per considered researcher, Bengio and LeCun. In order to validate the profile similarity in research and approval of not existing earlier co-authorship, we analyzed the profile of each recommended author to "Yoshua Bengio" and "Yann LeCun" as well as their own profiles.

---

[9] http://www-labs.iro.umontreal.ca/~bengioy/.
[10] http://yann.lecun.com/.

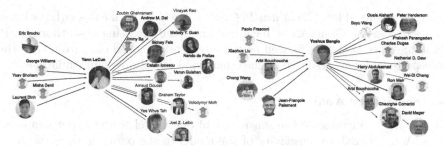

(a) Discovered network of "Yann Le-Cun" among top 50 links without a history of co-authorship in the the time interval of KG.

(b) Discovered network of "Yoshua Bengio" among top 50 links without a history of co-authorship in the time interval of KG.

Fig. 4. Example of co-authorship recommendations.

We analyzed the scientific profiles of the selected researchers provided by the most used scholarly search engine, Google Citation[11]. Due to author name-ambiguity problem, this validation task required human involvement. First, the research areas indicated in the profiles of researchers have been validated to be similar by finding matches. In the next step, some of the highlighted publications with high citations and their recency have been controlled to make sure that the profiles of the selected researchers match in the machine learning community close to the interest of "Yoshua Bengio" – to make sure the researchers can be considered in the same community. As mentioned before, the knowledge graphs that are used for evaluations consist of metadata from 2013 till 2018. In checking the suggested recommendations, a co-authorship relation which has happened before or after this temporal interval is considered valid for the recommendation. Therefore, the other highly ranked links with none-existed co-authorship are counted as valid recommendations for collaboration. Figure 4b shows a visualization of such links found by analyzing top 50 recommendations to and from "Yoshua Bengio" and Fig. 4a shows the same for "Yann LeCun".

Out of the 50 discovered triples for "Yoshua Bengio" being head, 12 of them have been approved to be a valid recommendation (relevant but never happened before) and 8 triples have been showing an already existing co-authorship. Profiles of 5 other researchers have not been made available by Google Citation. Among the triples with "Yoshua Bengio" considered in the tail, 8 of triples have been already discovered by the previous pattern. Profile of 5 researchers were not available and 7 researchers have been in contact and co-authorship with "Yoshua Bengio". Finally, 5 new profiles have been added as recommendations.

Out of 50 triples $(YannLeCun, r, ?)$, 14 recommendations have been discovered as new collaboration cases for "Yann LeCun". In analyzing the triples with a

---

[11] https://scholar.google.com/citations?.

pattern of the fixed tail $(?, r, YannLeCun)$, there have been cases either without profiles on Google Citations or have had an already existing co-authorship. By excluding these examples as well as the already discovered ones from the other triple pattern, 5 new researchers have remained as valid recommendations.

5.4 Sensitivity Analysis

In this part we investigate the sensitivity of our model to the hyperparameters $(\gamma_1, \gamma_2, \lambda_0)$. To analyze sensitivity of the model to the parameters γ_2, we fix γ_1 to 0.1, 1 and 2. Moreover, λ_0 is also fixed to one. Then different values for γ_2 are tested and visualized. Regarding the red dotted line in Fig. 3a, the parameter γ_1 is set to 0.1 and $\lambda_0 = 1$. It is shown that by changing γ_2 from 0.2 to 3, the performance increases to reach the peak and then decreases by around 15%. Therefore, the model is sensitive to γ_2. The significant waving of results can be seen when $\gamma_1 = 1, 2$ as well (see Fig. 3a). Therefore, proper selection of γ_1, γ_2 is important in our model.

We also analyze the sensitivity of the performance of our model on the parameter λ_0. To do so, we take the optimal configuration of our model corresponding to the fixed γ_1, γ_2. Then the performance of our model is investigated in different setting where the $\lambda_0 \in \{0.01, 0.1, 1, 10, 100, 1000\}$. According to Fig. 3b, the model is less sensitive to the parameter λ_0. Therefore, to obtain hyper parameters of the model, it is recommended that first (γ_1, γ_2) are adjusted by validation when λ_0 is fixed to a value (e.g., 1). Then the parameter λ_0 is adjusted while (γ_1, γ_2) are fixed.

6   Conclusion and Future Work

The aim of the present research was to develop a novel loss function for embedding models used on KGs with a lot of many-to-many relationships. Our use case is scholarly knowledge graphs with the objective of providing predicted links as recommendations. We train the proposed loss on embedding model and examine it for graph completion of a real-world knowledge graph in the example of scholarly domain. This study has identified a successful application of a model free loss function namely SM. The results show the robustness of our model using SM loss function to deal with uncertainty in negative samples. This reduces the negative effects of false negative samples on the computation of embeddings. We could show that the performance of the embedding model on the knowledge graph completion task for scholarly domain could be significantly improved when applied on a scholarly knowledge graph. The focus has been to discover (possible but never happened) co-author links between researchers indicating a potential for close scientific collaboration. The identified links have been proposed as collaboration recommendations and validated by looking into the profile of a list of selected researchers from the semantic web and machine learning communities. As future work, we plan to apply the model on a broader scholarly knowledge graph and consider other different types of links for recommendations e.g, recommend events for researchers, recommend publications to be read or cited.

Acknowledgement. This work is supported by the EPSRC grant EP/M025268/1, the WWTF grant VRG18-013, the EC Horizon 2020 grant LAMBDA (GA no. 809965), the CLEOPATRA project (GA no. 812997), and the German national funded BmBF project MLwin.

References

1. Alexiou, G., Vahdati, S., Lange, C., Papastefanatos, G., Lohmann, S.: OpenAIRE LOD services: scholarly communication data as linked data. In: González-Beltrán, A., Osborne, F., Peroni, S. (eds.) SAVE-SD 2016. LNCS, vol. 9792, pp. 45–50. Springer, Cham (2016). https://doi.org/10.1007/978-3-319-53637-8_6
2. Ammar, W., et al.: Construction of the literature graph in semantic scholar. arXiv preprint arXiv:1805.02262 (2018)
3. Auer, S., Kovtun, V., Prinz, M., Kasprzik, A., Stocker, M., Vidal, M.E.: Towards a knowledge graph for science. In: Proceedings of the 8th International Conference on Web Intelligence, Mining and Semantics, p. 1. ACM (2018)
4. Bordes, A., Usunier, N., Garcia-Duran, A., Weston, J., Yakhnenko, O.: Translating embeddings for modeling multi-relational data. In: Advances in NIPS (2013)
5. Boyd, S., Vandenberghe, L.: Convex Optimization. Cambridge University Press, Cambridge (2004)
6. Cai, X., Han, J., Li, W., Zhang, R., Pan, S., Yang, L.: A three-layered mutually reinforced model for personalized citation recommendation. IEEE Trans. Neural Netw. Learn. Syst. **99**, 1–12 (2018)
7. Dettmers, T., Minervini, P., Stenetorp, P., Riedel, S.: Convolutional 2D knowledge graph embeddings. In: AAAI (2018)
8. Färber, M., Ell, B., Menne, C., Rettinger, A.: A comparative survey of DBpedia, Freebase, OpenCyc, Wikidata, and YAGO. Semant. Web J. **1**(1), 1–5 (2015)
9. Fortunato, S., et al.: Science of science. Science **359**(6379), eaao0185 (2018)
10. Fricke, S.: Semantic scholar. J. Med. Libr. Assoc. JMLA **106**(1), 145 (2018)
11. Henk, V., Vahdati, S., Nayyeri, M., Ali, M., Yazdi, H.S., Lehmann, J.: Metaresearch recommendations using knowledge graph embeddings. In: RecNLP Workshop of AAAI Conference (2019)
12. Mai, G., Janowicz, K., Yan, B.: Combining text embedding and knowledge graph embedding techniques for academic search engines. In: Semdeep/NLIWoD@ISWC, pp. 77–88 (2018)
13. Nickel, M., Murphy, K., Tresp, V., Gabrilovich, E.: A review of relational machine learning for knowledge graphs. Proc. IEEE **104**(1), 11–33 (2016)
14. Schirrwagen, J., Manghi, P., Manola, N., Bolikowski, L., Rettberg, N., Schmidt, B.: Data curation in the openaire scholarly communication infrastructure. Inf. Stand. Q. **25**(3), 13–19 (2013)
15. Sun, Z., Deng, Z.H., Nie, J.Y., Tang, J.: Factorizing YAGO: scalable machine learning for linked data. In: ICLR, pp. 271–280 (2019)
16. Sun, Z., Deng, Z.H., Nie, J.Y., Tang, J.: Rotate: knowledge graph embedding by relational rotation in complex space. In: International Conference on Learning Representations (2019). https://openreview.net/forum?id=HkgEQnRqYQ
17. Tang, J., Zhang, J., Yao, L., Li, J., Zhang, L., Su, Z.: ArnetMiner: extraction and mining of academic social networks. In: Proceedings of the 14th ACM SIGKDD International Conference on Knowledge Discovery and Data Mining, pp. 990–998. ACM (2008)

18. Tharani, K.: Linked data in libraries: a case study of harvesting and sharing bibliographic metadata with BIBFRAME. Inf. Technol. Libr. **34**(1), 5–19 (2015)
19. Trouillon, T., Welbl, J., Riedel, S., Gaussier, É., Bouchard, G.: Complex embeddings for simple link prediction. In: International Conference on Machine Learning, pp. 2071–2080 (2016)
20. Vahdati, S., Arndt, N., Auer, S., Lange, C.: OpenResearch: collaborative management of scholarly communication metadata. In: Blomqvist, E., Ciancarini, P., Poggi, F., Vitali, F. (eds.) EKAW 2016. LNCS (LNAI), vol. 10024, pp. 778–793. Springer, Cham (2016). https://doi.org/10.1007/978-3-319-49004-5_50
21. Vahdati, S., Palma, G., Nath, R.J., Lange, C., Auer, S., Vidal, M.-E.: Unveiling scholarly communities over knowledge graphs. In: Méndez, E., Crestani, F., Ribeiro, C., David, G., Lopes, J.C. (eds.) TPDL 2018. LNCS, vol. 11057, pp. 103–115. Springer, Cham (2018). https://doi.org/10.1007/978-3-030-00066-0_9
22. Wan, H., Zhang, Y., Zhang, J., Tang, J.: AMiner: search and mining of academic social networks. Data Intell. **1**(1), 58–76 (2019)
23. Wang, Q., Mao, Z., Wang, B., Guo, L.: Knowledge graph embedding: a survey of approaches and applications. IEEE TKDE **29**(12), 2724–2743 (2017)
24. Wang, R., et al.: AceKG: a large-scale knowledge graph for academic data mining. ACM (2018)
25. Xia, F., Wang, W., Bekele, T.M., Liu, H.: Big scholarly data: a survey. IEEE Trans. Big Data **3**(1), 18–35 (2017)
26. Yu, M.C., Wu, Y.C.J., Alhalabi, W., Kao, H.Y., Wu, W.H.: ResearchGate: an effective altmetric indicator for active researchers? Comput. Hum. Behav. **55**, 1001–1006 (2016)
27. Yu, S., et al.: PAVE: personalized academic venue recommendation exploiting co-publication networks. J. Netw. Comput. Appl. **104**, 38–47 (2018)
28. Zhou, X., Zhu, Q., Liu, P., Guo, L.: Learning knowledge embeddings by combining limit-based scoring loss. In: Proceedings of the 2017 ACM on Conference on Information and Knowledge Management, pp. 1009–1018. ACM (2017)

Investigating Software Usage in the Social Sciences: A Knowledge Graph Approach

David Schindler[1]([⊠])(iD), Benjamin Zapilko[2](iD), and Frank Krüger[1](iD)

[1] Institute of Communications Engineering, University of Rostock, Rostock, Germany
{david.schindler,frank.krueger}@uni-rostock.de
https://www.int.uni-rostock.de/
[2] GESIS - Leibniz Institute for the Social Sciences, Cologne, Germany
Benjamin.Zapilko@gesis.org
https://www.gesis.org/

Abstract. Knowledge about the software used in scientific investigations is necessary for different reasons, including provenance of the results, measuring software impact to attribute developers, and bibliometric software citation analysis in general. Additionally, providing information about whether and how the software and the source code are available allows an assessment about the state and role of open source software in science in general. While such analyses can be done manually, large scale analyses require the application of automated methods of information extraction and linking. In this paper, we present SoftwareKG—a knowledge graph that contains information about software mentions from more than 51,000 scientific articles from the social sciences. A silver standard corpus, created by a distant and weak supervision approach, and a gold standard corpus, created by manual annotation, were used to train an LSTM based neural network to identify software mentions in scientific articles. The model achieves a recognition rate of .82 F-score in exact matches. As a result, we identified more than 133,000 software mentions. For entity disambiguation, we used the public domain knowledge base DBpedia. Furthermore, we linked the entities of the knowledge graph to other knowledge bases such as the Microsoft Academic Knowledge Graph, the Software Ontology, and Wikidata. Finally, we illustrate, how SoftwareKG can be used to assess the role of software in the social sciences.

Keywords: Software in science · Scientific articles · Information extraction · Knowledge graph

1 Introduction

Software is used during the entire research life-cycle and thus has significant influence on the research and its results. Knowledge about the software that was used during a scientific investigation is of interest for various reasons [11],

© Springer Nature Switzerland AG 2020
A. Harth et al. (Eds.): ESWC 2020, LNCS 12123, pp. 271–286, 2020.
https://doi.org/10.1007/978-3-030-49461-2_16

for instance to track the impact of software to attribute its developers, to ana-lyze citation patterns, or to assess provenance information with respect to the research workflow. This is of particular interest, as software might contain issues that can affect the scientific results, as for instance reported by [4,30,31]. More-over, research often relies on closed source software which is often not fully val-idated [25], eventually creating uncertainty about the reliability of the results.

Recently, software citation standards [27] have gained increasing interest in the scientific community but are not consistently used, which hampers the iden-tification of such information on a large scale. Moreover, researchers are surpris-ingly creative when it comes to spelling variations of the actual software name (see Table 6). Named entity recognition (NER) provides a convenient method to identify entities in textual documents and could thus be employed to extract software mentions from scientific articles. The objective is to identify all soft-ware with an assigned name while ignoring unspecific statements such as 'custom script' or 'custom code'. We employed an LSTM based approach to NER, which was trained using transfer learning based on distant and weak supervision and a small corpus of manually annotated articles [26]. The resulting information was then structured, interlinked, and represented in a knowledge graph which enables structured queries about software mentions in and across scientific pub-lications. By exploiting this information as a knowledge graph, we follow W3C recommendations and best practices [7].

In this paper, we present SoftwareKG, a knowledge graph that links 51,165 scientific articles from the social sciences to software that was mentioned within those articles. SoftwareKG is further curated with additional information about the software, such as the availability of the software, its source and links to other public domain knowledge graphs. Using this information and exploiting additional information via links to other knowledge graphs, SoftwareKG provides the means to assess the current state of software usage, free and open source software in particular, in the social sciences. Links to other knowledge bases play an important role since additional information about software and scientific articles can be accessed which is not available directly from the article. All software and data associated with SoftwareKG is publicly available [26].

The remainder of this paper is structured as follows: First we describe how the information from articles was extracted, curated and structured. Afterwards, we provide a brief description of SoftwareKG including entity and relation statistics. We then discuss potential error sources and illustrate how SoftwareKG could be employed for the analysis of software usage in the social sciences. Finally, we discuss related work, summarize, conclude and lay out potential further work.

2   Document Selection and Corpus Generation

2.1   Gold Standard Corpus Generation

The gold standard corpus (GSC) was created by randomly selecting 500 arti-cles from PLoS[1] using the keyword "Social Science". All articles were scanned

---

[1] https://www.plos.org/.

Table 1. Overview of the GSC.

GSC statistics		Most frequent software	
# Sentences	31,915	R	77
# Annotations	1380	SPSS	60
# Distinct	599	SAS	44
Train	847 (+1005)	Stata	41
Devel	276	MATLAB	38
Test	257	Matlab	28

for Methods & Materials (M&M) sections, based on the assumption that those sections contain most of the software usage statements [2]. From the initial set of 500 articles, M&M sections were found in and extracted from 480, which then served as a base for the GSC. The remaining articles did not contain a M&M or similar section and were thus omitted. Ground truth annotation was performed by seven annotators using the BRAT v1.3 [28] web based annotation tool. Annotators were instructed to label all software usage statements, excluding any version or company information (see Example 1). Inter-rater reliability was assessed on 10% of all sentences and showed almost perfect agreement [14] (Cohen's $\kappa = .82$). The GSC was then split into training, development and test sets with relative amounts of 60%, 20%, and 20%, respectively. The training set was extended by 807 sentences with software names to increase the amount of positive samples. The set of positive samples was retrieved by selecting sentences that contain at least one of the 10 most common software names of a previous analysis [2]. An overview of the resulting GSC is provided in Table 1. The GSC is publicly available [26].

2.2 Silver Standard Corpus Generation

Named entity extraction methods, in particular those relying on neural networks, require large amounts of training data to achieve reasonable recognition results. Annotated training data, however, is often unavailable and expensive to produce. The application of silver standard corpora [22] and transfer learning [24] has been shown to increase the recognition rates in such cases [5]. Silver standard corpora (SSCs) are annotated corpora that are not annotated by a manual process but rather provide "suggestive labels" created by employing distant or weak supervision [1]. In this work, we utilize the Snorkel data programming framework [21] which allows the specification of rules and dictionaries to provide such labels. The labeling rules are developed based on open knowledge bases and existing literature and generalize to other scientific domains even so they were optimized towards the social science corpus. Given those rules, Snorkel trains an unsupervised model for annotation by weighted combination of labeling rules by analyzing the correlations between the matches of the different rules. Finally, Snorkel provides scores to rank text candidates that were previously extracted from the text by using n-grams with a maximum length which was set to six

Table 2. Aliases for the software 'Statistical Package for the Social Sciences'.

Wikidata category	Label
label (English)	Statistical Package for the Social Sciences
alias (English)	SPSS
alias (German)	PASW statistics; PASW
alias (French)	SPSS Inc.; PASW

tokens. The maximum length was determined from the GSC. As we optimize the recall, we include all candidates that exceeded the default scoring threshold of .5. In the following, the distant and weak supervision approach is highlighted in more detail.

Distant Supervision. Distant supervision uses external knowledge bases [17] to retrieve information about candidates of interest. As Wikidata[2] is recommended for distant supervision [29], we queried the knowledge graph for software names. To cover spelling variations and aliases for the different software, we considered various subcategories of software and different software types, and included all aliases from Wikidata's "Also known as" attribute in the languages English, German, Spanish and French. The different languages were included because abbreviations may differ based on the authors' language background even if the articles were written in English. We chose these languages as they represent the major languages in Wikipedia. An overview of Wikidata's variations for SPSS is provided in Table 2. Variations are considered as potential candidates if they do not appear in the regular English dictionary. Using the English dictionary for exclusion of potential candidates was successfully used by Duck et al. [2].

Weak Supervision with Context Rules. In addition to the use of external knowledge bases, we implemented labeling functions based on the context of the software usage statements. To this end, we distinguished between general and exact context rules. The first examines the context of a candidate for special words or phrases indicating a software mention based on head word rules [2], while the latter implements the set of rules resulting from training an iterative bootstrapping for software identification [19]. The general rules employ information about the presence of particular tokens in the context of the candidates, such as 'software', 'tool' or 'package' or the presence of version numbers such as 'v0.3', 'version 2' or '2.0.12'. Furthermore, a rule is used that scans for the presence of the developer's name in the context of the candidate. The identification of the potential candidate's context was done after stop word removal. Part of Speech tags were employed for selecting from overlapping n-grams. The exact context rules that determine the context based on a specific pattern are based

---

[2] https://www.wikidata.org/.

on the literature [19]. Examples for the top two rules are: `use <> software` and `perform use <>` where the software position is marked by `<>`. Example 1 illustrates both the positive application of general context rule (dashed line) and the exact context rule (dotted line). The exact context rules are applied on the lemmatized context on the training set as in the original rules. Of the top 10 exact rules, the top 8 were used because the others did not extract any true positives.

Example 1. *We used SPSS software version 23 (SPSS Inc., Chicago, USA) for non-image-based statistical analyses and to compare volumes of subcortical structures.*

SSC Retrieval and Tagging. Snorkel's generative model was used in its default configuration to generate the suggestive annotations and not further fine-tuned. As a final rule the most common false positive n-grams in the training corpus with no true positives were negatively weighted. To assess the quality of the suggestive labels, the Snorkel generative model was applied on both the training and development corpus and evaluated against the gold standard annotated labels with Snorkel's internal evaluation. We trained the Snorkel model on the training set of our corpus and tested if adding further unlabeled data improves the results, since Snorkel is able to learn unsupervised. However, it was observed that the quality did not improve when adding up to five times the size of the original dataset. Overall, the Snorkel model achieved a precision of .33 (.32), a recall of .69 (.64) and an F-score of .45 (.42) on the development (training) set.

The articles for the SSC were obtained by retrieving all articles from PLoS for the keyword "Social Science" on 27th of August 2019. As for the GSC, the M&M sections were extracted and tagged by Snorkel's model, resulting in a corpus of 51,165 labeled documents. In total 282,650 suggestive labels were generated for the entire corpus. Example 2 illustrates a correctly tagged new sample and one partially correct example where a redundant tag was inserted.

Example 2. *All statistical procedures were performed using IBM SPSS Statistics software version 22. Task accuracy and response times were analyzed using the SPSS software package (SPSS v17.0, Chicago, Illinois, USA).*

3 Extraction of Software Mentions

3.1 Model

For the extraction of software from scientific articles we used a bidirectional Long Short Term Memory Network [8] in combination with a Conditional Random Field Classifier [12] (bi-LSTM-CRF) derived from the description by Lample et al. [13]. This model achieves state of the art performance for Named Entity Recognition. We used a feature vector consisting of: 1) pretrained word-embeddings from scientific publications [20], and 2) bi-LSTM based character-embeddings. Word embeddings capture multi-level semantic similarities between

Table 3. Summary of the extraction model hyper-parameter settings.

Hyper-parameter	Setting
Word embedding size	200 (pre-trained, not trainable)
Character embedding size	50 (trainable)
Character LSTM size	25
Main LSTM size	100
Number of labels	3 ('O', 'B-software', 'I-software')

words [16] while character based features allow learning from the orthography of words directly. The input layer is followed by a bidirectional LSTM layer to consider the surrounding context of software mentions, a fully connected layer for classification, and a final CRF layer for the estimation of the most likely tagging sequence [13]. The model's hyper-parameters are summarized in Table 3.

3.2 Training

As discussed above, training of the model was based on two different corpora, an SSC and a GSC. Sequential transfer learning [24] was employed to transfer information learned from the suggestive labels of the SSC to the GSC with the high quality labels to cope with the small amount of training data. For SSC training we selected all positive samples per epoch and used one negative sample per positive sample. We used different negative samples for each epoch until all were seen once. The number of pre-training epochs was optimized by training with up to 25 consecutive epochs on the SSC, after each of which we tested the performance to be expected by applying a standard, optimized re-training routine on the GSC training set. This procedure was selected due to the high computational requirements. For the SSC training, 2 epochs were found to provide the best basis. To optimize the SSC training, different learning and drop-out rates were considered. The best performing model was then selected for further optimization of the GSC training. All optimizations and evaluations were done with *rmsprop* to perform stochastic gradient descent.

During GSC training optimization, the following hyper-parameters were systematically considered: 1) *drop-out rate* in range of .3–.6, 2) *learning rate* in the range of .0001–.003, 3) *learning rate decay*, and 4) *sample weighting* adjusts the loss function label specific in a range of 0–.2 to increase the weight of positive samples. For GSC training we stop the training after 22 epochs. The final hyper-parameters for SSC and GSC training are provided in Table 4.

3.3 Evaluation and Extraction

To determine the expected quality of the final software mention identification, the selected model's performance was evaluated in precision, recall and F-score on both, the development and the test set. We consider both precision and recall

Table 4. Hyper-parameter settings for the training process.

Hyper-parameter	SSC	GSC
Learning rate	.002	.0015
Learning decay	.0001 (linear)	.0007 (exponential)
Dropout rate	.5	.4
Sample weight	.1	.1
Epochs	2	22

Table 5. Overview of the recognition results of the software identification.

Evaluation	Training	Precision		Recall		F-score	
		test	dev	test	dev	test	dev
B-software	SSC	.21	(.21)	.72	(.70)	.32	(.32)
	GSC	.83	(.75)	.74	(.68)	.78	(.71)
	SSC→GSC	**.86**	(.83)	**.85**	(.78)	**.86**	(.80)
I-software	SSC	.36	(.31)	.68	(.35)	.47	(.33)
	GSC	**.86**	(.75)	.66	(.47)	.75	(.58)
	SSC→GSC	.76	(.77)	**.82**	(.61)	**.79**	(.68)
Partial match	SSC	.21	(.22)	.72	(.74)	.32	(.34)
	GSC	.85	(.75)	.76	(.69)	.80	(.72)
	SSC→GSC	**.87**	(.84)	**.85**	(.80)	**.86**	(.82)
Exact match	SSC	.20	(.20)	.68	(.64)	.30	(.30)
	GSC	.80	(.72)	.72	(.66)	.76	(.69)
	SSC→GSC	**.83**	(.81)	**.82**	(.78)	**.82**	(.79)

as highly important for the intended applications of the model. Precision allows, for instance, to give accurate impact measures while a high recall is beneficial for discovering rare, domain specific software. For testing on the development set the final model was trained on the training set alone while for testing on the test set the model was trained on both the training and development sets. This approach enables the estimation of the influence additional training data has. There are four relevant evaluation methods: 1) B-software: a match of the first token in a software name, 2) I-software: a match of all other words in a software name except for the first, 3) partial match: an overlap of the estimated and the true software name, and 4) exact match: the exact identification of the entire software name. To also assess the effect of the manually annotated data and the transfer learning, the following evaluations were performed: 1) SSC: the model resulting from SSC training only, 2) GSC: the model resulting from GSC training only, and 3) SSC→GSC: the final model resulting from transfer learning based on SSC and GSC training. The performance scores are summarized in Table 5.

Table 6. Overview of the most frequent spelling variations for SPSS.

Software mention	Frequency
SPSS	7068
Statistical Package for the Social Sciences	944
IBM SPSS statistics	875
Statistical Package for Social Sciences	784
IBM SPSS	480

For comparison we also tested a CRF based on a set of standard features[3] on the GSC which achieved an F-Score of .41 (.36) with a precision of .30 (.24) and a recall .66 (.70) and on test (devel) set for exact recognition.

As we found an increase in the recognition performance from increasing the amount of training data for all evaluation metrics, the model used for information extraction was trained on the full GSC. It was then applied to all 51,165 M&M section from PLoS to identify software usage statements, resulting in 133,651 software names, 25,900 of which are unique. This seems plausible, as it reflects a similar frequency of mentions per article (2.6) as in the GSC (2.9).

3.4 Entity Disambiguation and Additional Information

Software names in scientific literature contain many variations in spelling and level of detail. This ranges from including the manufacturer's name to using version information and different interpretations of software name abbreviations. Table 6 gives an overview of the most common spelling variations of the statistical software SPSS. In total, 179 different spellings for SPSS were identified, most of which were not in the GSC. This means the model is able to generalize to previously unknown software names.

To disambiguate the different spelling variations, a three part entity linking was employed to reflect software mention specific variations: 1) analysis of simple spelling variations based on mentions, 2) abbreviation based linking, and 3) exploitation of information from the DBpedia knowledge graph. Software mentions were normalized by case folding and removal of special characters such as numbers and Greek letters. Furthermore, syllables such as "pro" were removed from the end of software names and the remaining words were stemmed to match common variations such as 'statistical' and 'statistic'. The result of this step was a transformed version of the software mention. To match the different interpretations of abbreviations, stop-words were removed and abbreviations were created from the first letters of the remaining words. The transformed name and the abbreviations were then used to cluster the first software names in the hierarchical linking pipeline.

For further disambiguation all software from DBpedia including *label, name, wikiPageRedirects* and *wikiPageDisambiguates* was retrieved and used to link the

---

[3] https://sklearn-crfsuite.readthedocs.io.

software names and select unique names as previously suggested [29]. Here, programming languages were included and software of type "video game" excluded. As for the Wikidata query, the languages English, German, French and Spanish were considered. If available the developer of a software was also included. The actual linking was performed as follows:

1) labels from DBpedia were used to further group spelling variations,
2) aliases from all languages were used, and
3) if neither of the previous provided a match, a combination of label and developer was employed.

The representative name used in the final data model was then created from the DBpedia label of the software, if exists, or the most frequent matched name, otherwise. DBpedia entries were retrieved for 66,899 (1160 unique) of the software names. As a result of the entity disambiguation, the set of unique software names was reduced from 25,900 to 20,227.

If available, the following additional information was collected in a manual process for the most frequent software: 1) the corresponding identifier in the Software ontology, Wikidata, and Wikipedia, 2) the URL of the software, 3) the manufacturer of the software, 4) whether the software is freely available, 5) whether the source code of the software is freely available, and 6) the license that was used for the publication of the source code. Additional information was retrieved for 133 software products covering 67,477 software mentions, representing half of all software mentions.

4   SoftwareKG: Data Model and Lifting to RDF

SoftwareKG was generated from the extracted and additionally collected information. In particular, it contains metadata about the publications, the authors and the software used in the publications. The graph contains 3,998,194 triples, 1,013,216 resources which are represented in 5 distinct types and 25 distinct properties. The graph holds 51,165 *Publication* resources, 20,227 *Software* resources, 334,944 *Author* resources, and 473,229 *Organization* resources. In total, the graph contains 133,651 software mentions. The most frequent software mentioned in the papers are *SPSS* (11,145 mentions), *R* (11,102 mentions), and *STATA* (5,783 mentions). Of the included software, 75 software applications are available for free, while 58 are not free. For the remaining software, this information is missing. Similarly, the source code is available of 52 software applications.

The SoftwareKG data model exploits terms from established vocabularies, mostly from schema.org[4]. For designing the data model, established vocabularies have been reused as it is seen as best practice [7]. The model can easily be extended by further properties, e.g. by terms of the CodeMeta Project[5] for describing software metadata. For some very specific properties, we had to define our own properties which are denoted in the model by the namespace skg.

---

[4] https://schema.org/.
[5] https://codemeta.github.io/.

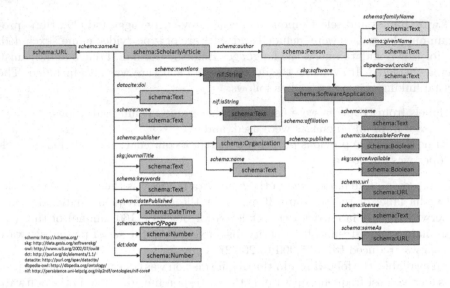

Fig. 1. Illustration of the data model

The core elements of the model are *Software*, *Publication*, *Author*, and *Organization* as shown in Fig. 1. The class *Software* represents a software application. It gathers properties for representing the name of the software application, the publisher, the homepage, the license under which the software has been published, whether it is available for free, and whether the source code is available or not. The property `schema:sameAs` gathers links to Wikipedia, Wikidata, the Software Ontology, and to DBpedia. The class *Publication* represents a scientific article. Here, we use properties to represent title, author(s), DOI, publisher, the publication date, and other metadata. We link to the same publication in the Microsoft Academic Graph by using `schema:sameAs`. The property `schema:mentions` captures the detected software mentions in a publication. Each mention is from the type `nif:String` which connects to the precise string in the paper (`nif:isString`) and to the meant *Software* (`skg:software`). The class *Author* represents each of the authors of a publication with his/her name, affiliation, and Orcid ID. Eventually, to the class *Organization* it is linked to by authors (as their affiliation), publications (as their publisher), and software (also as publisher).

All extracted and linked information is generated in JSON-LD following the data model. SoftwareKG is published under the Creative Commons BY 4.0 license. The KG can be accessed from a Virtuoso triple store with a SPARQL endpoint[6] and is downloadable as a dump [26]. It can also be accessed through its official website[7] which also contains statistics and a set of SPARQL queries.

---

[6] https://data.gesis.org/softwarekg/sparql.
[7] https://data.gesis.org/softwarekg/site/.

5   Use Cases and Exploitation

As initially stated, knowledge about the software employed in scientific investigations is important for several reasons. The previous sections describe how
SoftwareKG, a knowledge graph about software mentions in scientific publication was created. This section illustrates the usage of SoftwareKG and how to
leverage information from other knowledge graphs to perform analyses about
software in science. The queries and the plots illustrating their results can also
be found at the accompanying website.

The frequency of software mentions in scientific articles allow to assess the
impact of individual software to science. Moreover, it allows to attribute the
developers of such software. Figure 2 illustrates the frequencies of the 10 most
common software per year in absolute numbers with respect to our corpus. The
data was obtained by using the query in Listing 1.1. It can be seen that both,
SPSS and R are predominantly used in the social sciences, reflecting their usage
for statistical analyses. In general, statistical analysis software is the most frequently used type of software.

The availability of software used for the original analyses of scientific investigations plays a central role in its reproducibility. Moreover, the usage of open
source software allows researchers to inspect the source code, reducing uncertainty about the reliability of the scientific analyses and the results [25]. Figure 3
illustrates the usage of free and open source software over time.

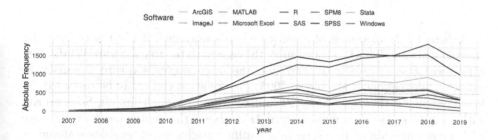

Fig. 2. Absolute amount of the 10 most common software per year.

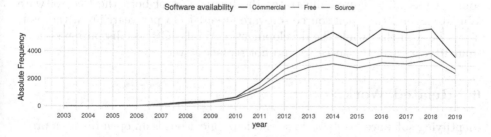

Fig. 3. Absolute frequency of the usages of commercial, free, and open source software.

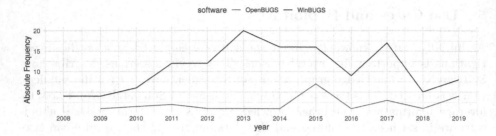

Fig. 4. Absolute frequency of the usages of OpenBUGS and WinBUGS.

```
select ?name ?year (count(?name) as ?count)
 WHERE {
  ?s rdf:type <http://schema.org/SoftwareApplication> .
  ?s <http://schema.org/name> ?name .
  ?m <http://data.gesis.org/softwarekg/software> ?s .
  ?p <http://schema.org/mentions> ?m .
  ?p <http://purl.org/dc/elements/1.1/date> ?year .
 }
 GROUP BY ?name ?year
 HAVING (count(?name) > 1)
 ORDER by DESC(?count)
```

Listing 1.1. SPARQL query to retrieve frequency of software mention per year

When the development of a software is discontinued, it is often replaced by another software. This is, for instance, the case with the free software WinBUGS, with the latest release from 2007 and the open source software OpenBUGS, where the development started in 2005. This relation can easily be retrieved via Wikidata using the *replaced-by*(P1366) relation. Through linking SoftwareKG with WikiData we combined information about the replacement of software with knowledge about its usage in scientific articles which enables statements about when and how such transitions arrive in science. The query linking SoftwareKG and WikiData is available on the SoftwareKG website and with the source code [26]. Figure 4 illustrates the frequencies of both the free software WinBUGS and the open source software OpenBUGS per year. From the plot, it can be seen that while the development of WinBUGS was discontinued more than 10 years ago, the successor did not replace it yet.

6   Related Work

Identifying software mentions in scientific publications is an open research problem and can serve several different purposes: 1) mapping of available software, 2) measuring the impact of software, and 3) analyzing how software is used, shared and cited in science. A more detailed overview of the problem and the reasons can be found in [11]. Besides manual extraction, as for example done by Howison et al. [9] to investigate software citations and their completeness, automated extraction enables the analysis of software usage in a larger context. Greuel and Sperber [6] create a mapping of mathematical software through automated filtering of potential mentions and manual review. Duck et al. [2] use a fully automated, rule-based scoring system configured by hand and based on a dictionary of known software and databases which was later improved by applying machine learning onto the rule set to achieve .67 F-score in the domain of Bioinformatics [3]. Pan et al. [19] use iterative bootstrapping to learn common mentioning patterns and software names starting from an initial set of seed software entities achieving .58 F-score and use the extraction results to provide impact measures. While those investigations all deal with the extraction of software they are not concerned with entity linking and can therefore only argue about distinct software mentions.

Automatically generating knowledge graphs from information about scientific publications allows the analysis of scientific workflows and enable large scale meta-analyses. The Open Academic Graph[8], for instance, captures metadata of scientific publications, while the Scholarlydata project [18] captures linked data about scientific conferences and workshops. Jaradeh et al. [10] create the Open Research Knowledge Graph which captures semantic information from scientific publications. They apply deep learning methods to capture information about process, method, material and data in publications and use DBpedia for entity linking. However, they do not provide a quantitative evaluation of their text mining approach. Recupero et al. [23] employ different existing classifiers to extract knowledge from scientific articles, perform disambiguation between extracted targets and create a knowledge graph based on the gathered information. Luan et al. [15] create a knowledge graph from tasks, methods, metrics, materials, and other entities and their relations from scientific publications.

The work presented here is the first that creates a knowledge graph particularly tailored for analyses of software in science based on recognition performance that outperforms previous approaches and the first to include entity disambiguation for software mentions.

7   Limitations and Potential Sources of Uncertainty

Most of the results presented in this work are based on methods of machine learning and automatic analyses which mainly rely on the quality of the provided labeled corpus. For the entire pipeline we identified several sources of uncertainty, which might accumulate and may result in a bias for further analyses:

- The corpus was retrieved from PLoS by using the keyword "Social Science" potentially resulting in the following two issues: The employed keyword did not only result in articles from the social sciences, but also from the bio medicine and related research domains. On the other hand this aspect facilitates the transfer of the model to the domain of life sciences. Additionally, the

---

[8] https://www.openacademic.ai/oag/.

PLoS corpus itself contains a bias towards the open access general purpose journal, which might not reflect the preferred publication target of researchers from the target domain.

- While the GSC annotation is of high quality in terms of inter-rater reliability the annotation task proved to be a complex task for the annotators, for instance when differentiating between algorithms and software with the same name. The absence of version information makes this decision even harder.
- The SSC is constructed with suggestive labels, with false positives that may be carried over to the final model. Indeed, we found examples, such as *Section* and *ELISA*, which both are software names, but also commonly appear in scientific publications without a connection to the software.
- The employed model achieves a high recognition performance. As suggested by the improvement of the test set evaluation, there is still potential to increase the performance by using a larger GSC.
- Reliably estimating the error of the entity disambiguation is difficult due to the absence of a ground truth. However, the method benefits from just working on extracted names which strongly restricts the chance of errors. We found some cases in which a linking to DBpedia was not possible because of multiple matches with DBpedia entries for which we could not automatically determine which match is the correct one.

In summary, SoftwareKG provides a reasonable quality in terms of knowledge identification, but automatic analyses should carried out carefully.

8   Conclusion and Future Work

In this work we introduce SoftwareKG and a method for creating a large scale knowledge graph capturing information about software usage in the social science. It was generated by employing a bi-LSTM for the automatic identification of software mentions in the plain text of publications. The proposed method achieves a high recognition score of .82 F-score in terms of exact match, which is a strong improvement over the state of the art. By using transfer learning based on data programming with distant and weak supervision rules, the performance could be significantly improved. The proposed approach is the first to integrate entity linking for the disambiguation of software names and the first to construct a knowledge graph to facilitate reasoning by allowing running queries against the constructed graph. Additionally, the available information in our graph was enhanced by manual annotation to support further analyses regarding free and open source software where otherwise no analysis would be possible. To create a large scale basis for reasoning and illustrate how such a basis can be constructed we applied our method to construct a knowledge graph over all articles published by PLoS tagged with "Social Science". Finally, we employed SoftwareKG to illustrate potential analyses about software usage in science.

Future work includes the automatic collection of additional information about the software such as the version or the source code repositories which implies an extension of the data model, e.g. by including properties of CodeMeta.

This enables the identification of the particular implementation by employing software preservation services such as SoftwareHeritage[9].

Acknowledgements. This work was partially carried out at GESIS - Leibniz Institute for the Social Sciences and was financially supported by the GESIS research grant GG-2019-015 and by the Deutsche Forschungsgemeinschaft (DFG, German Research Foundation) - SFB 1270/1 - 299150580.

References

1. Boland, K., Krüger, F.: Distant supervision for silver label generation of software mentions in social scientific publications. In: Proceedings of the BIRNDL 2019, Paris, France, July 2019. http://ceur-ws.org/Vol-2414/paper3.pdf
2. Duck, G., Nenadic, G., Brass, A., Robertson, D.L., Stevens, R.: bioNerDS: exploring bioinformatics' database and software use through literature mining. BMC Bioinformatics **14**(1), 194 (2013)
3. Duck, G., Nenadic, G., Filannino, M., Brass, A., Robertson, D.L., Stevens, R.: A survey of bioinformatics database and software usage through mining the literature. PLoS ONE **11**(6), e0157989 (2016)
4. Eklund, A., Nichols, T.E., Knutsson, H.: Cluster failure: why fMRI inferences for spatial extent have inflated false-positive rates. In: Proceedings of the National Academy of Sciences, p. 201602413 (2016)
5. Giorgi, J.M., Bader, G.D.: Transfer learning for biomedical named entity recognition with neural networks. Bioinformatics **34**(23), 4087–4094 (2018). https://doi.org/10.1093/bioinformatics/bty449
6. Greuel, G.-M., Sperber, W.: swMATH – an information service for mathematical software. In: Hong, H., Yap, C. (eds.) ICMS 2014. LNCS, vol. 8592, pp. 691–701. Springer, Heidelberg (2014). https://doi.org/10.1007/978-3-662-44199-2_103
7. Heath, T., Bizer, C.: Linked data: evolving the web into a global data space. Synth. Lect. Semant. Web Theory Technol. **1**(1), 1–136 (2011)
8. Hochreiter, S., Schmidhuber, J.: Long short-term memory. Neural Comput. **9**(8), 1735–1780 (1997)
9. Howison, J., Bullard, J.: Software in the scientific literature: problems with seeing, finding, and using software mentioned in the biology literature. J. Assoc. Inf. Sci. Technol. **67**(9), 2137–2155 (2016)
10. Jaradeh, M.Y., et al.: Open research knowledge graph: next generation infrastructure for semantic scholarly knowledge. In: Proceedings of the K-Cap, pp. 243–246. ACM (2019)
11. Krüger, F., Schindler, D.: A literature review on methods for the extraction of usage statements of software and data. IEEE Comput. Sci. Eng. (2019). https://doi.org/10.1109/MCSE.2019.2943847
12. Lafferty, J.D., McCallum, A., Pereira, F.C.N.: Conditional random fields: probabilistic models for segmenting and labeling sequence data. In: Proceedings of the Eighteenth International Conference on Machine Learning, ICML 2001, pp. 282–289. Morgan Kaufmann Publishers Inc., San Francisco (2001)
13. Lample, G., Ballesteros, M., Subramanian, S., Kawakami, K., Dyer, C.: Neural architectures for named entity recognition. arXiv preprint arXiv:1603.01360 (2016)
14. Landis, J.R., Koch, G.G.: The measurement of observer agreement for categorical data. Biometrics **33**(1), 159–174 (1977)

---

[9] https://www.softwareheritage.org/.

15. Luan, Y., He, L., Ostendorf, M., Hajishirzi, H.: Multi-task identification of entities, relations, and coreference for scientific knowledge graph construction. In: Proceedings of the EMNLP (2018)

16. Mikolov, T., Sutskever, I., Chen, K., Corrado, G.S., Dean, J.: Distributed representations of words and phrases and their compositionality. In: Advances in Neural Information Processing Systems, pp. 3111–3119 (2013)

17. Mintz, M., Bills, S., Snow, R., Jurafsky, D.: Distant supervision for relation extraction without labeled data. In: Proceedings of the Joint Conference of the 47th Annual Meeting of the ACL and the 4th International Joint Conference on Natural Language Processing of the AFNLP: Volume 2-Volume 2, pp. 1003–1011. Association for Computational Linguistics (2009)

18. Nuzzolese, A.G., Gentile, A.L., Presutti, V., Gangemi, A.: Conference linked data: the scholarlydata project. In: Groth, P., et al. (eds.) ISWC 2016. LNCS, vol. 9982, pp. 150–158. Springer, Cham (2016). https://doi.org/10.1007/978-3-319-46547-0_16

19. Pan, X., Yan, E., Wang, Q., Hua, W.: Assessing the impact of software on science: a bootstrapped learning of software entities in full-text papers. J. Informetr. **9**(4), 860–871 (2015)

20. Pyysalo, S., Ginter, F., Moen, H., Salakoski, T., Ananiadou, S.: Distributional semantics resources for biomedical text processing. In: Proceedings of LBM 2013 (2013)

21. Ratner, A.J., Bach, S.H., Ehrenberg, H.R., Ré, C.: Snorkel: fast training set generation for information extraction. In: Proceedings of the 2017 ACM International Conference on Management of Data, pp. 1683–1686. ACM (2017)

22. Rebholz-Schumann, D., et al.: CALBC silver standard corpus. J. Bioinform. Comput. Biol. **08**(01), 163–179 (2010). https://doi.org/10.1142/s0219720010004562

23. Buscaldi, D., Dessì, D., Motta, E., Osborne, F., Reforgiato Recupero, D.: Mining scholarly publications for scientific knowledge graph construction. In: Hitzler, P., et al. (eds.) ESWC 2019. LNCS, vol. 11762, pp. 8–12. Springer, Cham (2019). https://doi.org/10.1007/978-3-030-32327-1_2

24. Ruder, S.: Neural transfer learning for natural language processing. Ph.D. thesis, National University of Ireland, Galway (2019)

25. Russo, D., Voigt, C.C.: The use of automated identification of bat echolocation calls in acoustic monitoring: a cautionary note for a sound analysis. Ecol. Ind. **66**, 598–602 (2016). https://doi.org/10.1016/j.ecolind.2016.02.036

26. Schindler, D., Zapilko, B., Krüger, F.: SoftwareKG (1.0), March 2020. https://doi.org/10.5281/zenodo.3715147

27. Smith, A.M., Katz, D.S., Niemeyer, K.E.: Software citation principles. PeerJ Comput. Sci. **2**, e86 (2016). https://doi.org/10.7717/peerj-cs.86

28. Stenetorp, P., Pyysalo, S., Topić, G., Ohta, T., Ananiadou, S., Tsujii, J.: BRAT: a web-based tool for NLP-assisted text annotation. In: Proceedings of the Demonstrations at the 13th Conference of the European Chapter of the ACL, pp. 102–107. ACL (2012)

29. Weichselbraun, A., Kuntschik, P., Brasoveanu, A.M.: Name variants for improving entity discovery and linking. In: Proceedings of the LDK 2019. Schloss Dagstuhl-Leibniz-Zentrum fuer Informatik (2019)

30. Zeeberg, B.R., et al.: Mistaken identifiers: gene name errors can be introduced inadvertently when using excel in bioinformatics. BMC Bioinformatics **5**(1), 80 (2004). https://doi.org/10.1186/1471-2105-5-80

31. Ziemann, M., Eren, Y., El-Osta, A.: Gene name errors are widespread in the scientific literature. Genome Biol. **17**(1) (2016). https://doi.org/10.1186/s13059-016-1044-7

Fostering Scientific Meta-analyses with Knowledge Graphs: A Case-Study

Ilaria Tiddi(✉)(iD), Daniel Balliet, and Annette ten Teije

Vrije Universiteit Amsterdam, Amsterdam, The Netherlands
{i.tiddi,d.p.balliet,annette.ten.teije}@vu.nl

Abstract. A meta-analysis is a Science of Science method widely used in the medical and social sciences to review, aggregate and quantitatively synthesise a body of studies that address the same research question. With the volume of research growing exponentially every year, conducting meta-analyses can be costly and inefficient, as a significant amount of time and human efforts needs to be spent in finding studies meeting research criteria, annotating them, and properly performing the statistical analyses to summarise the findings. In this work, we show these issues can be tackled with semantic representations and technologies, using a social science scenario as case-study. We show how the domain-specific content of research outputs can be represented and used to facilitate their search, analysis and synthesis. We present the very first representation of the domain of human cooperation, and the application we built on top of this to help experts in performing meta-analyses semi-automatically. Using few application scenarios, we show how our approach supports the various phases meta-analyses, and more in general contributes towards research replication and automated hypotheses generation.

Keywords: Knowledge graphs · Meta-analysis · Science of Science · e-Science

1 Introduction

Systematic literature reviews and meta-analyses in particular are a scientific method used in a number disciplines ranging from (bio-)medical to social sciences to summarise vast amounts of research outputs on a specific topic [27]. In a nutshell, a meta-analysis exploits statistical models to quantify, aggregate and compare evidence from a set of (dozens, sometimes hundreds) experimental studies addressing the same research question, in order to derive generalisable conclusions [11]. In this way, meta-analyses offer a snapshot of a research topic, supporting research transparency, reproducibility and re-usability – a more and more urgent topic in various research disciplines [19].

© Springer Nature Switzerland AG 2020
A. Harth et al. (Eds.): ESWC 2020, LNCS 12123, pp. 287–303, 2020.
https://doi.org/10.1007/978-3-030-49461-2_17

Performing meta-analyses is a knowledge-intensive process that can take months, sometimes years, due to methodological and technical barriers. And with the volume of research outputs growing exponentially every year, this problem is becoming more and more difficult [3]. A new meta-analysis can require authors to spend a significant amount of time and effort to find studies that meet their criteria, identify the evidence in them, annotate their contents and statistically aggregate their results, before reaching any significant conclusion. Moreover, meta-analyses can be large in scope, and planning for time and human resource allocation can be a hard task. This calls for new methods to help researchers in summarising scientific evidence in a more automated way, and more in general to facilitate publication and sharing of large bodies of scientific findings.

Our motivation stems from the COoperation DAtabank[1] (CODA or Data-Bank henceforth), a large data repository aiming at analysing the entire history of laboratory and field research on human cooperation using social dilemmas. The goal of the DataBank is to encourage and facilitate sharing experiments as well as null findings (that tend to be hardly ever published), and consequently reduce the publication bias that currently affects the area [15]. Over the last 5 years, a small pool of domain experts manually annotated approx. 3,000 studies collecting 60 years of research publications with experimental settings, measured/manipulated variables of observation, and quantitative results, with the goal of establishing an open access database that researchers worldwide could consult to identify studies to include in their systematic literature reviews, as well as to directly conduct their own statistical (meta-)analyses.

In this work, we show how semantic technologies, which provide support for scaling, reuse, and interoperability, can be exploited to tackle the scalability, methodological and technical issues of conducting meta-analyses. Using a social science scenario, we show how the content of research outputs can be represented using semantic descriptions, and how to leverage this structured, domain-specific knowledge to facilitate search, analysis and synthesis of research outputs. Our main contributions are (1) the first structured representation of the field of human cooperation, that researchers from the field can easily reuse and extend; and (2) a Science of Science application to help experts in performing meta-analyses semi-automatically, supporting the correct evaluation and interpretation of research conclusions. We discuss on the multiple benefits of our approach using few use-cases that demonstrate how the various phases of the meta-analytic process can be facilitated and, more in general, how this can significantly contribute to research replication and automated hypotheses generation.

2   Background and Related Work

We introduce here the basic notions of scientific meta-analyses, the best practices and current applications, and overview the semantic approaches supporting scientific research.

---

[1] https://amsterdamcooperationlab.com/databank/.

Principles of Meta-analysis. A meta-analysis is a process used to synthesise knowledge from studies addressing the same research question by using comparable methods. Each study may observe a relation between two (one independent, one dependent) variables, which can be quantified as an effect size. Meta-analytic techniques are then used to estimate an overall effect size average through aggregating the effect sizes observed in single studies [22]. Effect sizes can represent the differences observed between the experimental variations (treatments) of the independent variable and the dependent variable (such as a standardised difference between means d), or could also be the relation between two measured variables (such as a correlation coefficient ρ). In order to derive the overall estimate, a researcher first frames a problem statement, defining the research question, inclusion criteria, independent and dependent variables of observation etc., and then collects relevant studies (both published and non-published material) across scientific sources. Conducting a meta-analysis then consists in: (1) *Coding*, i.e. annotating the studies with the relevant characteristics, including independent and dependent variables and effect sizes; (2) *Analysis*, i.e. estimating the overall effects using fixed and random effects models, determining heterogeneity in the studies, assessing publication bias, conducting moderator analyses through meta regression, performing statistical power analysis; (3) *Interpretation*, i.e. the presentation of the obtained results along with conclusions and graphical support, often including graphs such as forests, funnel, violin/scatter-box plots. These steps make a meta-analysis significantly different from a literature review conducted, for instance, in computer science, as the researcher numerically "pools" results from the studies (i.e. the effects sizes) and arrives at a statistical summary that can be integrated into the narrative of a publication.

Methods and Applications. While meta-analyses are now established in the field, they are still seen as a controversial tool, as even small methodological violations can lead to misleading conclusions [20]. Researchers have argued that significant conclusions can only be derived from meta-analyses with large number of studies, while smaller meta-analyses can only support framing new research hypotheses [14]. In response to this, a number of methodologies across disciplines have been published to assist experts in deriving reliable conclusions, e.g. the Cochrane Handbook by the Campbell organisation [23], the York Centre for Reviews and Dissemination guidelines for health care [29], the Evidence for Policy and Practice Information and Co-ordinating Centre[2]. A considerable amount of statistical expertise is also needed to avoid deriving incorrect conclusions. A number of statistical tools are now available to overcome the technical barriers, resulting in tools and libraries such as RevMan [8], Comprehensive Meta-Analysis [4], Stata, and R packages such as *meta*, *rmeta* and *metafor*. Finally, with the volume of research outputs growing exponentially, identifying relevant studies and annotate the evidence can require significant efforts. As a result, a number of research projects emerged in the latest years with the goal of making

---

[2] https://eppi.ioe.ac.uk/cms/.

large bodies of research findings openly available, offering summaries of scientific evidence and, more in general, automating meta-analyses [1,5].

Supporting Science with Semantic Technologies. Semantic web technologies have been used to provide an interoperable and machine-interpretable infrastructure for scientific enquiry in the context of Semantic e-Science [7].

Ontology engineering techniques have widely been employed to formally organise domain-specific knowledge and provide interactive, semantically-enhanced data querying, exploration, and visualisation in a number of cross-disciplinary settings [12,24,25]. A large number of vocabularies to semantically describe research outputs have been proposed, e.g. document publication [9,16]; provenance, versioning, attribution and credits through research objects[3] or nanopublications [21]; description of research hypotheses [18] and scientific datasets [6]. The benefit of using controlled vocabularies to describe research outputs guarantees them to be findable, exchangeable and interpretable across different applications (interoperability).

Another strand of research has focused on capturing knowledge from scientific processes, in order to support design and management of workflows [26], identify common patterns and motifs in them [13,17], or recommend activities to tackle the cold start problem of experimental design [10]. These works demonstrated that research reproducibility and support to frame research hypotheses can be supported by semantically describing and mining workflow components.

A semantic approach could be used support conducting meta-analyses. Domain vocabularies and descriptions could express the scientific knowledge contained in research outputs to facilitate search, analysis and synthesis. At the same time, replication of published results and support to derive the correct conclusions could be offered by the relying on semantic technologies, that enable scalability, interoperability and reuse. In the following, we show how our hypothesis was tested to support research replication and automated hypotheses generation in a social science scenario.

3   Motivating Scenario and Contribution

The COoperation DAtabank (2015–2020) is a large-scale effort involving a trained team of international researchers working with the goal of representing and publishing an open-access repository of over 60 years of research on human cooperation using social dilemmas. Social dilemmas are social situations that involve a conflict of interests and people must choose between doing what is best for themselves or what is best for the collective, either a dyad or group [30]. In these situations, there is always one choice that results in the best outcome for each individual, regardless of what others choose to do. However, if everyone decides to behave this way, then the entire group receives a worse outcome, relative to when everyone decides to do what is best for the group. Common social

---

[3] http://www.researchobject.org/.

dilemma paradigms used to study cooperation include the prisoner's dilemma, public goods dilemma, and the resource dilemma. Cooperation in these situations is operationalised as deciding to do what it best for the collective.

In the DataBank, around 3,000 studies from the social and behavioural sciences published in English, Chinese, and Japanese were annotated with more than 60 cooperation-related features. These features can be grouped in three categories, i.e. (a) characteristics of the sample participating in the study (e.g. sample size, average age of sample, percentage of males, country of participants), (b) characteristics of the experimental paradigm (structure of the social dilemma, incentives, repeated trial data, etc.), and (c) quantitative results (e.g., mean levels of cooperation, variance in cooperation, and effect sizes with cooperation). In this scenario, the CODA experts are required to annotate and include new data (i.e. findings gathered from researchers worldwide) to the dataset in a continuous way. This can be inconvenient, costly and time-consuming, especially as data are not always directly accessible [2]. In the long-term, we aim at supporting CODA's maintainers in capturing and sharing knowledge more efficiently. Starting with the assumption that scholars that consult the repository online act as domain experts, the solution we target is to crowdsource the meta-analyses that users conduct online to automatically enrich, fix and update the dataset. The procedural nature of the meta-analyses allows in fact to model them as scientific workflows of sequential activities, that we wish to capture and use to update the dataset, in a way that data maintainers do not have to input new data themselves. Besides relieving the workload of the dataset maintainers, collecting workflows could benefit data consumers, as the expertise of previous scholars could support new users when performing their own analyses.

In order to achieve this, our first goal is to make the DataBank available to the field to allow exploring data and conducting meta-analyses with it. Following similar approaches, we use an ontology engineering approach to represent the DataBank as a structured dataset, describing both the bibliographic information and the domain-specific knowledge from the collected studies, and then to build semantically-enhanced application to perform meta-analyses. Our work has two contributions, namely (i) we provide a detailed semantic description of the domain of human cooperation, so far never published in a structured way, that researchers from the field can easily reuse and extend; and (ii) we build a tool to conduct meta-analyses semi-automatically, reducing the time researchers need to test their new hypotheses. More in general, our work shows how semantic technologies can be used to tackle the limitations of meta-analyses at different levels (search, analysis and synthesis), fostering research reproducibility while facilitating the framing and testing of research hypotheses.

4   Performing Meta-analyses over Knowledge Graphs

In order to allow conducting meta-analyses over a knowledge graph, we follow two simple steps: first, we deal with the generation of the DataBank, by describing the research studies and their content and generating a knowledge graph from this; second, we focus on building the application conduct meta-analyses on it. In the following, we will imagine the example of a meta-analysis performed to study the impact (effect) of using communication (independent variable) over cooperation (dependent variable) in a control group.

4.1 DataBank Generation

The first step is gathering the raw data annotated by the CODA team and build a structured knowledge graph from it. The dataset consists a series of CSV tables, roughly divided by topic, where published studies are annotated according to the features described in Sect. 3, including both generic information (study characteristics such as country or year of publication) and specific characteristics (information relevant to cooperation games, e.g. types of priming or incentives given to the study participants). We therefore divide this task in three steps, i.e. establishing a general schema for papers, DOIs, authors, experiments (domain-independent knowledge), providing a more fine-grained model to describe the cooperation situations (domain-specific knowledge), and populating the knowledge graph accordingly.

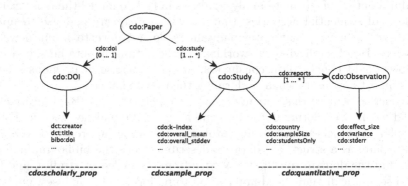

Fig. 1. Domain-independent schema for data annotation.

Modelling Domain-Independent Knowledge. Figure 1 presents the domain-independent schema we used[4], where a publication consists of a `cdo:Paper` that includes an arbitrary set of `cdo:Study`, i.e. experiments performed in different settings and with different goals. In the example of Listing 1.1, for instance, resource `:ENG00073` represents a paper written by H. Varian in 1999 reporting his experimental study `:ENG00073_1` where 48 students from the US played a prisoner's dilemma game. Additional metadata about the paper such as publication date, authors etc. are collected directly by dereferencing the paper's

---

[4] All CODA's namespaces are used here for illustrative purposes. We recommend to follow the links at https://amsterdamcooperationlab.com/databank/ for the most recent versions.

DOIs and by including the collected triples as properties of a `cdo:DOI` class. We then define these properties as `cdo:scholarly_prop`. In our example, the DOI allows to gather the paper's scholar information, such as his author H. Varian and its year of publication (1999).

Each `cdo:Study` has also specific properties, which we divided in `cdo:sample_prop` and `cdo:quantitative_prop` depending if they represent information about the study sample settings or the experimental quantitative/statistical information. For example, `cdo:country`, `cdo:sample_size`, `cdo:country`, `cdo:studentsOnly` and `cdo:game` are subproperties of `cdo:sample_props`, while `cdo:overall_coop` (that measures the overall participants' cooperation rate across different tests in an experiment) is a quantitative property defined as subproperty of `cdo:quant_prop`.

As said, a `cdo:Study` reports one or more tests, modelled as `cdo:Observation`. The significance of the tests is estimated in terms of statistical `cdo:quantitative_prop` of an observation, e.g. effect size values, standard errors, variance, etc. In our example, study `:ENG00073_1` reports one observation called `:ENG00073_1.1.1.2.7`, reporting a measured effect size value of $\sim$0.60 and a standard error of $\sim$0.24.

```
1   @prefix cdo: <http://data.coda.org/coda/vocab/> .
2   @prefix    : <http://data.coda.org/coda/resource/> .
3   @prefix dct: <http://purl.org/dc/terms/>
4
5   :ENG00073 a cdo:Paper ;
6         cdo:includes  :ENG00073_1  ;
7      cdo:doi <http://dx.doi.org/10.1073/pnas.96.19.10933>  .
8    <http://dx.doi.org/10.1073/pnas.96.19.10933> a cdo:DOI ;
9      dct:title "Preplay contracting in the Prisoners' Dilemma";
10     dct:creator [ a foaf:Person;
11              foaf:name "H. Varian" ].
12     dct:date "1999"^^xsd:gYear .
13   :ENG00073_1 a cdo:Study;
14     cdo:country :USA  ;
15     cdo:game :prisoner-s-dilemma  ;
16     cdo:sampleSize "48"^^xsd:integer ;
17     cdo:studentOnly "true"^^xsd:boolean ;
18     cdo:overall_coop "0.413"^^xsd:double ;
19     cdo:reports :ENG00073_1.1.1.2.7 ;
20   :ENG00073_1.1.1.2.7 a cdo:Observation;
21     cdo:effect_size "0.6057"^^xsd:double ;
22     cdo:stder "0.2431"^^xsd:double .
23     cdo:compares (:ENG00073_1.1.1, ENG00073_1.1.2)
24   :ENG00073_1.1.1 a cdo:Treatment.
25     cdo:communicationBaseline "True"^^xsd:boolean .
26   :ENG00073_1.1.2 a cdo:Treatment ;
27     cdo:communicationBaseline "False"^^xsd:boolean .
28     cdo:realCommunication "True"^^xsd:boolean .
29     cdo:communicationContent :promise .
30   :promise a cdo:CommunicationContent .
31   :prisoner-s-dilemma a cdo:Game .
```

Listing 1.1. Example of CODA resources.

Note that the current work only focuses on using a semantic-based approach as a mean to simplify meta-analyses. In other words, vocabulary and data model are not finalised, and while alignments at schema and instance level are already under way, they remain out of this paper's scope.

Modelling Domain-Specific Knowledge. In order to allow experts to understand the factors affecting cooperation, the next step is describe the content of each study in a fine-grained way. We model observations as comparisons of one or two different cdo:Treatment, consisting in the experimental settings that an experimenter modifies with the goal of assessing how and if the cooperation between participants of a game varies significantly. For example, observation :ENG00073_1.1.1.2.7 compares a treatment in which participants were not allowed to communicate (line 24–25) with a second treatment, in which participants were playing with real partners (line 28) and could only exchange promises about future game behaviours (line 29). These experimental settings, modified across different treatments of the same independent variable (IV), are fundamental to perform meta-analyses. An experimenter could be interested in observing the effects of allowing or denying communication within participants of a game, or on the impact of specific characteristics (called moderators) such as age, gender or personality of the participants, type of communication exchanged.

We therefore take all RDF properties whose domain is the class cdo:Treatment, and organise them in a domain-specific taxonomy of information relative to cooperation in social dilemmas. The resulting taxonomy, shown in Fig. 2, was built in a bottom-up fashion, i.e. (i) an initial list of key variables and definitions was drafted by the CODA's team given their extensive expertise in the domain; (ii) the list was used to perform an initial annotation of ∼1k studies across universities, to report potential problems and additions, and (iii) further revised by a scientific advisory board of 12 senior domain experts; (iv) existing papers were revised and new ones were annotated accordingly.

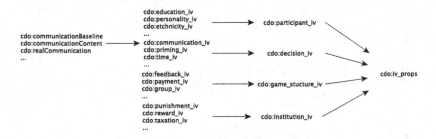

Fig. 2. Property taxonomy for annotation of domain-specific knowledge (simplified).

All properties are by definition subproperties of a generic rdf:Property called cdo:iv_props, and can be either cdo:measured_iv or cdo:manipulated_iv, depending if it consists in a discrete (e.g. type of communication) or continuous (e.g. amount of money incentive) variable. Additionally, up to four categories of properties can describe the cooperative game in a treatment, namely:

- *participant variables* (cdo:participant_iv), i.e. all variables related to the people taking part of a cooperation, including personal background (age, ethnicity, education), stable personality traits (e.g. HEXACO/Social Value Orientation), dynamic psychological states (e.g., emotions, moods);

- *decision variables* (`cdo:decision_iv`), i.e. all variables related to the decisions that people take during the game, e.g. intrapersonal features (priming, time constraints), or interpersonal features (communication, gossip);
- *game structure variables* (`cdo:game_structure_iv`), consisting in all variables related to the structural aspects of the game, e.g. payment of the participants, protocol for forming teams, composition of the team etc;
- *institution variables* (`cdo:institution_iv`), involving the rules and norms for participants, such as punishment, reward or taxation during the game.

Taking back the example of Listing 1.1, `cdo:communicationBaseline`, `cdo:realCommunication`, `cdo:communicationContent` are subproperties of `cdo:communication _iv`, indicating that in his study, the experimenter only manipulated communication as an independent variable. Of course, this is a rather simplified example, and treatments describe on average multiple IVs.

Knowledge Graph Population and Storage. Once defined the two parts of the schema, we create statements with the support of Python's RDFlib library, additionally dividing them across a number of named graphs (i.e. studies, papers, observations, treatments, vocabulary descriptions) for storage and querying convenience. The generated dataset is hosted as a triplyDB instance[5], allowing to easily upload and update datasets and expose them through APIs such as SPARQL, RESTful, and textual search. While the complete dataset is in the process of being iteratively published, its preliminary online version currently includes 330,655 statements, including approx. 1.1k studies and 61 specific independent variables (cfr. Table 1).

Table 1. DataBank status, as of Dec. 2019. Observations are still being computed.

Knowledge	Class	Statements	Annotated resources	Total resources
Domain independent	Papers	6,411	1,454	2,922
	DOIs	22,545	1,276	2,588
	Studies	78,523	2,095	2,102
	Observations	115,881	8,288	n/a
	Treatments	43,844	2,219	11,432
Domain specific	Participant IVs	2,527	23	42
	Decision IVs	799	12	20
	GameStr. IVs	629	9	45
	Institution IVs	4,209	18	31

4.2 Conducting Meta-analyses with the DataBank

In the second phase, we build a web-based interface allowing experts to conduct their meta-analysis over the generated knowledge graph. The application, shown in Fig. 3, is accessible through the main website, and allows to (i) explore the DataBank; (ii) select relevant studies and (iii) performing meta-analyses online.

---

[5] https://triplydb.com/.

Data Exploration. At first, users are presented a global overview of the data. Studies and the effect sizes they report can be explored using a number of criteria, e.g. year of publication, sample size, country of publication (as in Fig. 3). At the bottom, a tabular condensed view of the data is also offered, and users are given the possibility to click on studies, papers and observations to explore their properties in-depth directly from the triplyDB instance. An additional panel at the top offers the possibility of visualising the taxonomy of independent variables described in the previous section.

Search&Selection. The left panel allows users to select the desired studies before starting their statistical computations. The selection can be performed based on independent variables that are manipulated during treatments of a study (cfr. Fig. 2). In the example of Fig. 3, the user selected observations from studies manipulating some `cdo:communication_iv`, and specifically studies manipulating the properties `cdo:realCommunication` and `cdo:communicationContent`, resulting in a selection of 21 observations from 6 different studies.

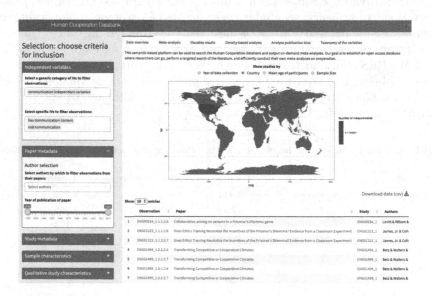

Fig. 3. Main view of the CODA web-app, allowing data visualisation (bottom), search&selection (left), meta-analytic activities (top, and Fig. 4).

Multiple selection is allowed, e.g. one could additionally include `cdo:personality_iv` or `cdo:emotion_iv` variables. Studies can be additionally filtered based on sample and quantitative properties, e.g. one could choose to include in the meta-analysis only observations from studies published between 2000 and 2010, or those with at least 100 participants. In order to foster data sharing and reuse, the portion of desired data can be downloaded in tabular format. In this way, as authors are relieved from the coding step, as the provided data are already annotated, and the model can be extended according to the meta-analysis' purposes.

Meta-analytic Activities. Once selected the desired data, the user can perform his meta-analysis using the tabs in the app. Due to space restrictions, Fig. 4 shows a simplified view of the meta-analytic steps, but the reader is invited to consult the online version to replicate our example. Typical meta-analysis steps include:

1. *Fitting a meta-analytic model* (Fig. 4a). This operation consists in choosing the model type (fixed, random and mixed effects), the method (maximum or restricted likelihood estimators), and the variables (single, or aggregated) to obtain the estimate of the overall population effect size. Models can also be fitted by specific moderators (e.g. mean age of the sample as in Fig. 4b), corresponding to the IVs and study characteristics in the KG schema.
2. *Exploring the heterogeneity of single studies.* Using forest plots (Fig. 4c), a meta-analysts can illustrate the effect sizes of the studies ordered by year of publication, using confidence intervals that reflect the precision with which effects were estimated (the narrower the confidence interval, the greater precision). Effect sizes can also be plotted to check their distribution and density

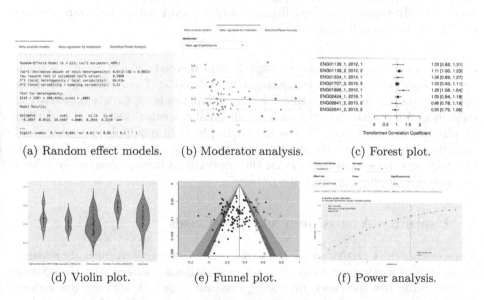

(a) Random effect models.   (b) Moderator analysis.   (c) Forest plot.

(d) Violin plot.   (e) Funnel plot.   (f) Power analysis.

Fig. 4. Example of a meta-analysis: (a) fitted models to estimate the global effect size; (b) linear regression to assess the relation between the moderator and the effect size; (c) forest plot to determine heterogeneity of effect sizes (X-axis) per study (Y-axis); (d) violins to visualise the studies distribution in details; (e) funnels to assess symmetry of the results (X-axis) based on their error degree (Y-axis); (f) power analysis to estimate the required sample size in future experiments.

using violin plots (Fig. 4d), where relevant statistics such as median and its 95% confidence interval, the quartiles and outliers are also shown.

3. *Checking for publication bias.* Using funnel plots (Fig. 4e), the user can plot effects sizes against the sample sizes in a symmetrical inverted funnel centred on the average effect, in a way that asymmetries in the distribution of the data should be revealed. An additional data-augmentation method called "trim&fill" can also be selected in order to estimate the number of studies that are missing from the meta-analysis.

4. *Computing power analysis.* This activity (Fig. 4f) allows to derive the optimal sample size for a desired effect size (either obtained by the fitted model, or specified by the user) with a given power and p-value. Determining the optimal effect size given a desired sample size and p-value is also possible. With this operation, researchers can calculate the required sample size necessary to obtain high statistical power in future studies.

Similarly to the data selection, all meta-analytic results can also be comfortably downloaded through the interface. This is particularly beneficial to less experienced meta-analysts, as they can be relieved from the often tedious and time consuming task of writing efficient code. Additionally, all statistical computations and activities are presented sequentially in order to support methodological design – thoroughly crafted using meta-analytic experts. Finally, by allowing to compute meta-analyses online, published and unpublished meta-analyses can also be easily reproduced, benefitting study reproducibility and transparency for the whole research field.

Implementation. The above web-app is implemented using R Shiny[6], a package for dashboard development straight from R code. The advantage of using Shiny lies mostly in the fact that we can exploit the large variety of statistical techniques (linear/nonlinear modelling, classical statistical tests etc.) and their graphical outputs (funnel, forests and violin plots) to manipulate, interact and visualise data from the DataBank knowledge graph. Data are selected through SPARQL queries stored as APIs on the triplyDB instance, allowing to further decouple the application from the dataset.

5   Usability Assessment via Use-Cases

Since neither the CODA app nor the dataset in its entirety have officially released at the time of writing, we focus here on a qualitative assessment with the domain experts using few use-cases, discussing how our approach support the various phases of the meta-analysis. A usability testing with users is under preparation, and will be held further the official release.

---

[6] https://shiny.rstudio.com/.

Offloading Data Maintainers. Here, we are interested in reducing the workload of the experts in maintaining and updating the dataset. We therefore asked the CODA team to quantify the time it takes the editorial board to include a new study in the dataset. Table 2 shows the main activities they need to perform, i.e. searching studies, skimming publications to assess if they fall under the eligibility criteria, coding studies based on the chosen characteristics, and computing the aggregate effect sizes if a work reports separate splits (e.g. a paper reporting 10 different cooperation rates, because 10 rounds of a game were experimented). We report answers of three experts E_n supervising the DataBank, as well as one annotator A of more limited expertise. These are then compared with the data provided by [28], an established reference that analysed the problem of performing meta-analyses in the medical domain.

Table 2. Time for data maintenance. Aggregation (*) is not always performed. The ranges relate to the difficulty of the studies, which can go from easy studies (small analyses from psychology/economics) to complex meta-analyses that require additional computations.

	Searching (hours)	Skimming (mins/paper)	Coding (mins/paper)	Aggregating* (mins)
E_1	80	5–10	20–90	3
E_2	160–200	3–5	20–90	3
E_3	160–240	5–10	60–120	3
A	–	10–20	45–180+	10
[28]	20–60	60	90–100	640

The table illustrates that data maintainers invest most of their efforts in searching, skimming and annotating papers, reported as the most time-expensive activities needed to be performed. A straightforward conclusion here is that the this workload could be significantly reduced by allowing users consulting the DataBank to upload their studies using the same annotation schema. This would allow maintainers to focus only on the light-weight refinement and validation of the uploaded data. Finally, the disproportion in time between activities in the social science and medical domain suggests that a substantial difference lies in the type of studies that experts need to analyse (e.g. lengths, regression analyses).

Improving Study Exploration. Here, we look at estimating how our approach supports meta-analysts in searching data. We asked the experts to write a set of competency questions, which can indicate how well the knowledge graph support the search phase through requirement fulfilment.

Table 3. Competency questions to assess data exploration.

Competency question	Before	After
1 *Find studies on variable X*	✓	✓
2 *Find studies on N variables*	✗	✓
3 *Find studies with X and Y characteristics, comparing N variables*	✗	✓
4 *Find effects of studies with X or Y characteristics*	✗	✓
5 *Find effects comparing X and Y properties, both of variable Z*	✗	✓
6 *Find negative effects of continuous variables*	✗	✓
7 Number of independent variables	n/a	86

Table 3 shows that a number of requirement, particularly related to the selection of studies with multiple characteristics or using effect sizes, could not be answered with the original the dataset. This means that a user would mostly have to go through the process of extracting and re-coding the studies of interests, before performing a new meta-analysis. Additionally, the DataBank now includes over 86 independent variables (vs. the original dataset with no controlled vocabulary for independent variables), which can be used both for the study selection and the moderator analyses at finer or coarser grain (e.g. users can decide to simply consider all communication variables, or to some specific communication characteristics). This is a great opportunity for the behavioural science community, which can easily investigate different research questions in a more automated and assisted way.

Support in Performing Statistical Analyses. We are interested in understanding if our approach facilitates users performing the statistical computations needed to finalise and publish a meta-analysis. Table 4 provides an estimate of the resources necessary to compute meta-analytic models in a normal setting (i.e. when not supported by the CODA application) based on the answers of two experts that recently run a meta-analysis (ma_1, ma_2), as well as the information provided by [28]. We used lines of code as a measure for data preparation, model fitting and result plotting to show that users might be relieved from writing a significant part of code when using a semantically-enriched system, as opposed to a database of meta-analyses.

Of course, resource allocation is highly dependent on the type meta-analysis performed (i.e. number of studies analysed, complexity of the question framed, number of moderator analyses...), and the same would lie when conducting meta-analyses with the support of our framework. Yet, users would be relieved from the data preparation and programming tasks, offered by the CODA app as interactive activities to be performed in a customised way. To give a baseline over the current application, a simple sequence of model fitting, heterogeneity analysis and moderator analysis takes on average 5 to 10 min.

Table 4. Resource allocation for manually running a meta-analysis.

	Manual resources (#people)	Data prep. (#lines)	Model fitting (#lines)	Plots (#lines)	Tot (h) (time)
ma_1	1 expert 1 assistant	~200	~250	~400	80–100
ma_2	1 expert	~100	~400	~500	160–200
[28]	1 expert 1 statistician	–	–	–	360

Fostering Reproducible Research Through Recommendations. Finally our approach offers quality improvement for the research field in terms of (1) reproducibility, (2) domain description and (3) best practice workflows. First, we offer a dataset of annotated and reproduced experimental studies openly available for consultation and download (both studies and the meta-analyses computed online). Secondly, by relying on a taxonomical representation of the domain, recommendations of variables to explore and analyse can be offered to users as "if you are looking at studies where [$specific\_var_1$] variables were manipulated, you might want to explore other [$parent\_var$] as [$specific\_var$]$_{2, 3}$ ...", where $specific\_var_n$ are siblings of a parent variable (e.g. cdo:communication_iv and cdo:priming_iv are children of cdo:decision_iv). Additionally, by relying on SPARQL queries over the dataset, we can monitor the users' activities, and offer recommendations of new variables to meta-analyse based on popularity (i.e. suggesting the most popular moderators for specific variables) or anti-patterns (i.e. suggesting to choose less popular and unexplored queries for the meta-analysis). Finally, by describing meta-analysis as scientific workflows that manipulate data with specific parameters, we can collect and offer them as recommended practices to users. In this sense, the expertise of previous users could be leveraged to offer inexperienced practitioners a more automated way of performing meta-analyses – tackling to the cold start problem of designing experiments.

6 Conclusions

In this work, we have shown how to use semantic technologies to support researchers in conducting meta-analyses and summarise scientific evidence in a more automated way. Meta-analysis are a Science of Science method for research synthesis, which tend to suffer from scalability, methodological and technical issues also due to the exponentially growing volume of research. Using a social science scenario, we showed how the content of research outputs can be semantically described and used to build an application to help meta-analysts in searching, analysing and synthesising their results in a more automated way. The use-cases we discussed have shown that the approach is beneficial at several levels of the meta-analysis, and has the potential of fostering research replication and facilitating the framing and testing of research hypotheses in the field of behavioural science.

Future work will be focused on: (i) publishing the DataBank following the FAIR principles[7], which will require alignment to existing vocabularies (e.g. Data Cubes) and linking instances to available datasets (e.g. Microsoft Academics); (ii) improving the web application with more advanced analyses, e.g. dynamics of citations, multivariate analyses, integration of cross-societal moderators from the linked open datasets (e.g GDP or GINI indices from Eurostats); (iii) implementing the collection and documentation of meta-analytic workflows using PROV[8]; (iv) evaluation through user-testing, quantifying the time they take to perform a meta-analytic tasks with and without the support of the knowledge-based recommendations, workflows and documentation.

References

1. Bergmann, C., et al.: Promoting replicability in developmental research through meta-analyses: insights from language acquisition research. Child Dev. **89**(6), 1996–2009 (2018)
2. Berman, N.G., Parker, R.A.: Meta-analysis: neither quick nor easy. BMC Med. Res. Methodol. **2**(1), 10 (2002). https://doi.org/10.1186/1471-2288-2-10
3. Borah, R., Brown, A.W., Capers, P.L., Kaiser, K.A.: Analysis of the time and workers needed to conduct systematic reviews of medical interventions using data from the prospero registry. BMJ Open **7**(2), e012545 (2017)
4. Borenstein, M., Hedges, L.V., Higgins, J.P., Rothstein, H.R.: Introduction to Meta-Analysis. Wiley, Hoboken (2011)
5. Bosco, F.A., Uggerslev, K.L., Steel, P.: Metabus as a vehicle for facilitating meta-analysis. Hum. Resour. Manag. Rev. **27**(1), 237–254 (2017)
6. Brickley, D., Burgess, M., Noy, N.: Google dataset search: building a search engine for datasets in an open web ecosystem. In: The World Wide Web Conference, pp. 1365–1375. ACM (2019)
7. Brodaric, B., Gahegan, M.: Ontology use for semantic e-science. Semant. Web **1**(1, 2), 149–153 (2010)
8. Collaboration, C., et al.: Review manager (revman)[computer program] (2014)
9. Belhajjame, K., et al.: Workflow-centric research objects: a first class citizen in the scholarly discourse. In: SePublica@ ESWC, pp. 1–12 (2012)
10. Daga, E., d'Aquin, M., Gangemi, A., Motta, E.: An incremental learning method to support the annotation of workflows with data-to-data relations. In: Blomqvist, E., Ciancarini, P., Poggi, F., Vitali, F. (eds.) EKAW 2016. LNCS (LNAI), vol. 10024, pp. 129–144. Springer, Cham (2016). https://doi.org/10.1007/978-3-319-49004-5_9
11. DerSimonian, R., Laird, N.: Meta-analysis in clinical trials. Control. Clin. Trials **7**(3), 177–188 (1986)
12. Dietze, H., Schroeder, M.: GoWeb: a semantic search engine for the life science web. BMC Bioinformatics **10**(10), S7 (2009)
13. Ferreira, D.R., Alves, S., Thom, L.H.: Ontology-based discovery of workflow activity patterns. In: Daniel, F., Barkaoui, K., Dustdar, S. (eds.) BPM 2011. LNBIP, vol. 100, pp. 314–325. Springer, Heidelberg (2012). https://doi.org/10.1007/978-3-642-28115-0_30

---

[7] https://www.go-fair.org/fair-principles/.

[8] https://www.w3.org/TR/2013/REC-prov-o-20130430/.

14. Flather, M.D., Farkouh, M.E., Pogue, J.M., Yusuf, S.: Strengths and limitations of meta-analysis: larger studies may be more reliable. Control. Clin. Trials **18**(6), 568–579 (1997)
15. Franco, A., Malhotra, N., Simonovits, G.: Publication bias in the social sciences: unlocking the file drawer. Science **345**(6203), 1502–1505 (2014)
16. Gangemi, A., Peroni, S., Shotton, D., Vitali, F.: The publishing workflow ontology (PWO). Semant. Web **8**(5), 703–718 (2017)
17. Garijo, D., Alper, P., Belhajjame, K., Corcho, O., Gil, Y., Goble, C.: Common motifs in scientific workflows: an empirical analysis. Future Gener. Comput. Syst. **36**, 338–351 (2014)
18. Garijo, D., Gil, Y., Ratnakar, V.: The DISK hypothesis ontology: capturing hypothesis evolution for automated discovery. In: K-CAP Workshops, pp. 40–46 (2017)
19. Gonzalez-Beltran, A., et al.: From peer-reviewed to peer-reproduced in scholarly publishing: the complementary roles of data models and workflows in bioinformatics. PLoS ONE **10**(7), e0127612 (2015)
20. Greco, T., Zangrillo, A., Biondi-Zoccai, G., Landoni, G.: Meta-analysis: pitfalls and hints. Heart Lung Vessels **5**(4), 219 (2013)
21. Groth, P., Gibson, A., Velterop, J.: The anatomy of a nanopublication. Inf. Serv. Use **30**(1–2), 51–56 (2010)
22. Gurevitch, J., Koricheva, J., Nakagawa, S., Stewart, G.: Meta-analysis and the science of research synthesis. Nature **555**(7695), 175 (2018)
23. Higgins, J.P.T., Green, S., et al.: Cochrane Handbook for Systematic Reviews of Interventions. Wiley (2019)
24. Hoekstra, R., et al.: The datalegend ecosystem for historical statistics. J. Web Semant. **50**, 49–61 (2018)
25. Hu, W., Qiu, H., Huang, J., Dumontier, M.: Biosearch: a semantic search engine for Bio2RDF. Database **2017** (2017)
26. Khan, F.Z., Soiland-Reyes, S., Sinnott, R.O., Lonie, A., Goble, C., Crusoe, M.R.: Sharing interoperable workflow provenance: a review of best practices and their practical application in CWLProv. GigaScience **8**(11), giz095 (2019)
27. Olkin, I.: Keynote addresses. Meta-analysis: reconciling the results of independent studies. Stat. Med. **14**(5–7), 457–472 (1995)
28. Steinberg, K., et al.: Comparison of effect estimates from a meta-analysis of summary data from published studies and from a meta-analysis using individual patient data for ovarian cancer studies. Am. J. Epidemiol. **145**(10), 917–925 (1997)
29. Tacconelli, E.: Systematic reviews: CRD's guidance for undertaking reviews in health care. Lancet. Infect. Dis. **10**(4), 226 (2010)
30. Van Lange, P.A., Balliet, D.P., Parks, C.D., Van Vugt, M.: Social Dilemmas: Understanding Human Cooperation. Oxford University Press, Oxford (2014)

Security, Privacy, Licensing and Trust

SAShA: Semantic-Aware Shilling Attacks on Recommender Systems Exploiting Knowledge Graphs

Vito Walter Anelli, Yashar Deldjoo, Tommaso Di Noia, Eugenio Di Sciascio, and Felice Antonio Merra[✉]

Politecnico di Bari, Bari, Italy
{vitowalter.anelli,yashar.deldjoo,tommaso.dinoia,
eugenio.disciascio,felice.merra}@poliba.it

Abstract. Recommender systems (RS) play a focal position in modern user-centric online services. Among them, collaborative filtering (CF) approaches have shown leading accuracy performance compared to content-based filtering (CBF) methods. Their success is due to an effective exploitation of similarities/correlations encoded in user interaction patterns, which is computed by considering common items users rated in the past. However, their strength is also their weakness. Indeed, a malicious agent can alter recommendations by adding fake user profiles into the platform thereby altering the actual similarity values in an engineered way.

The spread of well-curated information available in knowledge graphs ($\mathcal{KG}$) has opened the door to several new possibilities in compromising the security of a recommender system. In fact, $\mathcal{KG}$ are a wealthy source of information that can dramatically increase the attacker's (and the defender's) knowledge of the underlying system. In this paper, we introduce *SAShA*, a new attack strategy that leverages semantic features extracted from a knowledge graph in order to strengthen the efficacy of the attack to standard CF models. We performed an extensive experimental evaluation in order to investigate whether *SAShA* is more effective than baseline attacks against CF models by taking into account the impact of various semantic features. Experimental results on two real-world datasets show the usefulness of our strategy in favor of attacker's capacity in attacking CF models.

Keywords: Recommender system · Knowledge graph · Shilling attack

---

Authors are listed in alphabetical order.

© Springer Nature Switzerland AG 2020
A. Harth et al. (Eds.): ESWC 2020, LNCS 12123, pp. 307–323, 2020.
https://doi.org/10.1007/978-3-030-49461-2_18

1 Introduction

Recommender Systems (RS) are nowadays considered as the pivotal technical solution to assist users' decision-making process. They are gaining momentum as the overwhelming volume of products, services, and multimedia contents on the Web has made the users' choices more difficult. Among them, Collaborative filtering (CF) approaches have shown very high performance in real-world applications (e.g., Amazon [26]). Their key insight is that users prefer products experienced by similar users and then, from an algorithmic point of view, they mainly rely on the exploitation of user-user and item-item similarities. Unfortunately, malicious users may alter similarity values. Indeed, these similarities are vulnerable to the insertion of fake profiles. The injection of such manipulated profiles, named shilling attack [20], aims to *push* or *nuke* the probabilities of items to be recommended.

Recently, several works have proposed various types of attacks, classified into two categories [9]: *low-knowledge* and *informed* attack strategies. In the former attacks, the malicious user (or adversary) has poor system-specific knowledge [25,28]. In the latter, the attacker has precise knowledge of the attacked recommendation model and the data distribution [12,25].

Interestingly, the astonishing spread of knowledge graphs ($\mathcal{KG}$) may suggest new knowledge-aware strategies to mine the security of RS. In a Web mainly composed of unstructured information, $\mathcal{KG}$ are the foundation of the Semantic Web. They are becoming increasingly important as they can represent data exploiting a manageable and inter-operable semantic structure. They are the pillars of well-known tools like IBM Watson [7], public decision-making systems [34], and advanced machine learning techniques [2,4,13]. Thanks to the Linked Open Data (LOD) initiative[1], we have witnessed the growth of a broad ecosystem of linked data datasets known as LOD-cloud[2]. These $\mathcal{KG}$ contain detailed information about several domains. In fact, if a malicious user would attack one of these domains, items' semantic descriptions would be priceless.

The main contributions envisioned in the present work is to study the possibility of leveraging semantic-encoded information with the goal to improve the efficacy of an attack in favor/disfavor of (a) given target item(s). Particularly, one of the features distinguishing this work from previous ones is that it exploits publicly available information resources obtained from $\mathcal{KG}$ to generate more influential fake profiles that are able to undermine the performance of CF models. This attack strategy is named semantic-aware shilling attack *SAShA* and extends state-of-the-art shilling attack strategies such as *Random*, *Love-hate*, and *Average* based on the gathered semantic knowledge. It is noteworthy that the extension we propose solely relies on publicly available information and does not provide to the attacker any additional information about the system.

---

[1] https://data.europa.eu/euodp/en/linked-data.
[2] https://lod-cloud.net/.

In this work, we aim at addressing the following research questions:

RQ1 Can public available semantic information be exploited to develop more effective shilling attack strategies against CF models, where the effectiveness is measured in terms of overall prediction shift and overall hit ratio?

RQ2 Can we assess which is the most impactful type of semantic information? Is multiple hops extraction of semantic-features from a knowledge graph more effective than single-hop features?

To this end, we have carried out extensive experiments to evaluate the impact of the proposed *SAShA* against standard CF model using two real-world recommender systems datasets (`LibraryThing` and `Yahoo!Movies`). Experimental results indicate that $\mathcal{KG}$ information is a rich source of knowledge that can in fact worryingly improve the effectiveness of attacks.

The remainder of the paper is organized as follows. In Sect. 2, we analyze the state-of-the-art of CF models as well as shilling attacks. In Sect. 3, we describe the proposed approach (SAShA). Section 4 focuses on experimental validation of the proposed attacks scenarios, where we provide a discussion of the experimental results. Finally, in Sect. 5, we present conclusions and introduce open challenges.

2   Related Work

In this Section, we focus on related literature on recommender systems and state-of-the-art of attacks on collaborative recommender models.

2.1   Recommender Systems (RSs)

Recommendation models can be broadly categorized as content-based filtering (CBF), collaborative filtering (CF) and hybrid. On the one hand, CBF uses items' content attributes (features) together with target user's own interactions in order to create a user profile characterizing the nature of her interest(s). On the other hand, CF models generate recommendation by solely exploiting the similarity between interaction patterns of users. Today, CF models are the mainstream of academic and industrial research due to their state-of-the-art recommendation quality particularly when sufficient amount of interaction data—either explicit (e.g., rating scores) or implicit (previous clicks, check-ins etc.)—are available. Various CF models developed today can be classified into two main groups: memory-based and model-based. While memory-based models make recommendations exclusively based on similarities in user's interactions (user-based CF [23,32]) or items' interactions (item-based CF [23,33]), model-based approaches compute a latent representation of items and users [24], whose linear interaction can explains an observed feedback. Model-based approaches can be implemented by exploiting different machine learning techniques. Among them, matrix factorization (MF) models play a paramount role.

It should be noted, that modern RS nowadays may exploit a variety of side information such as metadata (tags, reviews) [29], social connections [6], image and audio signal features [14] and users-items contextual data [3] to build more in-domain (i.e., domain-dependent) or context-aware recommendations models. $\mathcal{KG}$ are another rich source of information that have gained increased popularity in the community of RS for building knowledge-aware recommender systems (KARS). These models can be classified into: (i) path-based methods [19,37], which use meta-paths to evaluate the user-item similarities and, (ii) $\mathcal{KG}$ embedding-based techniques, that leverages $\mathcal{KG}$ embeddings to semantically regularize items latent representations [16,21,35]. More recently, $\mathcal{KG}$ have also been used to support the reasoning and explainability of recommendations [5,36].

For the simplicity of the presentation, in this work we step our attention aside (shilling attacks against) CF models leveraging these side information for the core task of recommendation, and leave it for an extension in future works. We do however make a fundamental assumption in all considered scenarios that the "attacker can have access to $\mathcal{KG}$, given their free accessibility and use them to shape more in-domain attacks."

2.2   Shilling Attacks on Recommender System

Despite the widespread application of customer-oriented CF models by online services adopted to increase their traffic and promote sales, the reliance of these models on the so-called "word-of-mouth" (i.e., what other people like and dislike), makes them at the same time vulnerable to meticulously crafted profiles that aim to alter distribution of ratings so to misuse this dependency toward a particular (malicious) purpose. The motivation for such shilling attacks can be many unfortunately, including personal gain, market penetration by rival companies [25], malicious reasons and even causing complete mischief on an underlying system [20].

In the literature, one standard way to classify these shilling attacks is based on the *intent* and amount of *knowledge* required to perform attacks. According to the intent, generally attacks are classified as *push attacks* that aim to increase the appeal of some targeted items, and *nuke items*, which conversely aim to lower the popularity of some targeted items. As for the knowledge level, they can be categorized according to *low-knowledge attacks* and *informed attack* strategies. Low-knowledge attacks require little or no knowledge about the rating distribution [25,28], while, informed attacks assume adversaries with knowledge on dataset rating distribution, which use this knowledge to generate effective fake profiles for shilling attacks [25,30].

A large body of research work has been devoted on studying shilling attacks from multiple perspectives: altering the performance of CF models [12,15,25], implementation attack detection policies [8,11,38] and building robust recommendation models against attacks [28,30]. Regardless, a typical characteristic of the previous literature on shilling attack strategies is that they usually target the relations between users, and items, based on similarities scores estimated on their past feedback (e.g., ratings). However, these strategies do not consider the possibility of exploiting publicly available $\mathcal{KG}$ to gain more information on the semantic similarities between the items available in the RS catalogue.

Indeed, considering that product or service providers' catalogues are freely accessible to everyone, this work presents a novel attack strategy that exploits a freely
accessible knowledge graph (DBpedia) to assess if attacks based on semantic similarities between items are more effective than baseline versions that rely only
on rating scores of users.

3   Approach

In this section, we describe the development of a novel method for integrating
information obtained from a knowledge graph into the design of shilling attacks
against targeted items in a CF system. We first introduce the characteristics of
$\mathcal{KG}$ in Sect. 3.1. Afterwards, we present the proposed semantic-aware extensions
to variety of popular shilling attacks namely: *Random*, *Love-Hate*, and *Average*
attacks in Sect. 3.2.

3.1   Knowledge Graph: Identification of Content from $\mathcal{KG}$

A knowledge graph can be seen as a structured repository of knowledge, represented in the form a graph, that can encode different types of information:

- **Factual.** General statements as *Rika Dialina was born in Crete* or *Heraklion
  is the capital of Crete* where we describe an entity by its attributes which are
  in turn connected to other entities (or literal values);
- **Categorical.** These statements bind the entity to a specific category (i.e.,
  the categories associated to an article in Wikipedia pages). Often, categories
  are part of a hierarchy. The hierarchy lets us define entities in a more generic
  or specific way;
- **Ontological.** We can classify entities in a more formal way using a hierarchical structure of classes. In contrast to categories, sub-classes and super-classes
  are connected through IS-A relations.

In a knowledge graph we can represent each entity through the triple structure
$\sigma \xrightarrow{\rho} \omega$, with a *subject* ($\sigma$), a *relation* (*predicate*) ρ and an *object* (ω). Among
the multiple ways to represent features coming from a knowledge graph, we have
chosen to represent each distinct triple as a single feature [5]. Hence, given a set
of items $I = \{i_1, i_2, \ldots, i_N\}$ in a collection and the corresponding triples $\langle i, \rho, \omega \rangle$
in a knowledge graph, we can build the set of 1-hop features as $1\text{-}HOP\text{-}F =
\{\langle \rho, \omega \rangle \mid \langle i, \rho, \omega \rangle \in \mathcal{KG} \text{ with } i \in I\}$.

In an analogous way we can identify 2-hop features. Indeed, we can continue
exploring $\mathcal{KG}$ by retrieving the triples $\omega \xrightarrow{\rho'} \omega'$, where ω is the *object* of a 1-hop
triple and the *subject* of the new triple. Here, the double-hop *relation* (*predicate*)
is denoted by ρ' while the new *object* is referred as (ω'). Hence, we define the
overall feature set as $2\text{-}HOP\text{-}F = \{\langle \rho, \omega, \rho', \omega' \rangle \mid \langle i, \rho, \omega, \rho', \omega' \rangle \in \mathcal{KG} \text{ with } i \in
I\}$. With respect to the previous classification of different types of information
in a knowledge graph, we consider a 2-hop feature as Factual if and only if both
relations (ρ, and ρ') are Factual. The same holds for the other types of encoded
information.

3.2 Strategies for Attacking a Recommender System

A shilling attack against a recommendation model is based on a set of fake profiles meticulously created by the attacker and inserted into the system. The ultimate goal is to alter recommendation in favor of (push scenario) or organist (nuke scenario) a single target item i_t. In this work, we focus on the push attack scenario but everything can be reused also in case of a nuke one. The fake user profile (attack profile) follows the general structure proposed by Bhaumik [8] shown in Fig. 1. It is built up of a rating vector of dimensionality N where N is the entire items in the collection ($N = |I_S| + |I_F| + |I_\emptyset| + |I_T|$). The profile is subdivided into four non-overlapping segments:

I_S			I_F			$I_\emptyset$			I_T
$i_s^{(1)}$	...	$i_s^{(\alpha)}$	$i_f^{(1)}$	...	$i_f^{(\phi)}$	$i_\emptyset^{(1)}$	...	$i_\emptyset^{(\chi)}$	i_t

Fig. 1. General form of a fake user profile

- I_T: This is the *target item* for which a rating score will be predicted by the recommendation model. Often, this rating is assigned to be the maximum or minimum possible score based on the attack goal (push or pull).
- $I_\emptyset$: This is the *unrated item* set, i.e., items that will not contain any ratings in the profile.
- I_F: The *filler item* set. These are items for which rating scores will be assigned specific to each attack strategy.
- I_S: The *selected item* set. These items are selected in the case of *informed attack* strategies, which exploit attacker's knowledge to maximize the attack impact, for instance by selecting items with the higher number of ratings.

The ways I_S and I_F are chosen depend on the attack strategy. The attack size is defined as the number of injected fake user profiles. Hereafter, $\phi = |I_F|$ indicates the filler size, $\alpha = |I_S|$ the selected item set size and $\chi = |I_\emptyset|$ is the size of unrated items. In this paper, we focus our attention on the selection process of I_F since I_S is built by exploiting the attacker's knowledge of the data distribution.

Semantic-Aware Shilling Attack Strategies (SAShA). While previous work on RS has investigated the impact of different standard attack models on CF system, in this work, we propose to strengthen state-of-the-art strategies via the exploitation of semantic similarities between items.

This attack strategy generates fraudulent profiles by exploiting $\mathcal{KG}$ information to fill I_F. The key idea is that we can compute the semantic similarity of the target item i_t with all the items in the catalog using $\mathcal{KG}$-derived features. Then, we use this information to select the filler items of each profile to generate the set I_F.

The insight of our approach is that a similarity value based on semantic features leads to more natural and coherent fake profiles. These profiles are indistinguishable from the real ones, and they effortlessly enter the neighborhood of users and items. In order to compute the semantic similarity between items, in our experimental evaluation, we exploit the widely adopted Cosine Vector Similarity [17].

To test our semantic-aware attacks to recommender systems, we propose three original variants of low-knowledge and informed attack strategies: random attack, love-hate attack, and s average attack.

- *Semantic-aware Random Attack (SAShA-random)* is an extension of Random Attack [25]. The baseline version is a naive attack in which each fake user is composed only of random items ($\alpha = 0, \phi = profile\text{-}size$). The fake ratings are sampled from all items using a uniform distribution. We modify this attack by changing the set to extract the items. In detail, we extract items to fill I_F from a subset of items that are most similar to i_t. We compute the item-item *Cosine Similarity* using the semantic features as introduced in Sect. 3.1. Then, we build a set of most-similar items, considering the first quartile of similarity values. Finally, we extract ϕ items from this set, adopting a uniform distribution.
- *Semantic-aware Love-Hate Attack (SAShA-love-hate)* is a low-knowledge attack that extends the standard Love-Hate attack [28]. This attack randomly extracts filler items I_F from the catalog. All these items are associated with the minimum possible rating value. The Love-Hate attack aims to reduce the average rating of all the platform items but the target item. Indeed, even though the target item is not present in the fake profiles, its relative rank increases. We have re-interpreted the rationale behind the Love-Hate attack by taking into account the semantic description of the target item and its similarity with other items within the catalogue. In this case, we extract items to fill I_F from the 2nd, 3rd, and 4th quartiles. As in the original variant, the rationale is to select the most dissimilar items.
- *Semantic-aware Average Attack (SAShA-average)* is an informed attack that extends the AverageBots attack [28]. The baseline attack takes advantage of the mean and the variance of the ratings. Then, it randomly samples the rating of each filler item from a normal distribution built using the previous mean and variance. Analogously to *SAShA-random*, we extend the baseline by extracting the filler items from the sub-set of most similar items. We use as candidate items the ones in the first quartile regarding their similarity with i_t.

4   Experimental Evaluation

This section is devoted to comparing the proposed approaches against baseline attack strategies. We first introduce the experimental setup, where we present the two well-known datasets for recommendation scenarios. Then, we describe the feature extraction and selection procedure we have adopted to form semantic-aware shilling attacks. Finally, we detail the three canonical CF models we have analyzed. We have carried extensive experiments intented to answer the research questions in Sect. 1. In particular, we aim to assess: (i) whether freely available semantic knowledge can help to generate stronger shilling attacks; (ii) if $\mathcal{KG}$ features types have a different influence on *SAShA* effectiveness; (iii) what is the most robust CF-RS against *SAShA* attacks.

4.1 Experimental Setting

Datasets. In the experiments, we have exploited two well-known datasets with explicit feedbacks to simulate the process of a recommendation engine: Library-Thing [18] and Yahoo!Movies. The first dataset is derived from the social cataloging web application LibraryThing[3] and contains ratings ranging from 1 to 10. To speed up the experiments, we have randomly sampled with a uniform distribution the 25% of the original items in the dataset. Moreover, in order to avoid cold situations (which are usually not of interest in attacks to recommender systems) we removed users with less than five interactions. The second dataset contains movie ratings collected on Yahoo!Movies[4] up to November 2003. It contains ratings ranging from 1 to 5, and mappings to MovieLens and EachMovie datasets. For both datasets, we have used the items-features sets 1-*HOP-F* and 2-*HOP-F* extracted from DBpedia by exploiting mappings which are publicly available at https://github.com/sisinflab/LinkedDatasets. We show datasets statistics in Table 1.

Table 1. Datasets statistics.

Dataset	#Users	#Items	#Ratings	Sparsity	#F-1Hop	#F-2Hops
LibraryThing	4816	2,256	76,421	99.30%	56,019	4,259,728
Yahoo!Movies	4000	2,526	64,079	99.37%	105733	6,697,986

Feature Extraction. We have extracted the semantic information to build *SAShA* exploiting the public available item-entity mapping to DBpedia. We did not consider noisy features containing the following predicates: owl:sameAs, dbo:thumbnail, foaf:depiction, prov:wasDerivedFrom, foaf:isPrimaryTopicOf, as suggested in [5].

Feature Selection. To analyze the impact of different feature types, we have performed experiments considering categorical (CS), ontological (OS) and factual (FS) features. We have chosen to explore those classes of features since they are commonly adopted in the community [5]. For the selection of single-hop (1H) features, the employed policies are:

---

[3] http://www.librarything.com/.
[4] http://research.yahoo.com/Academic_Relations.

- **CS-1H**, we select the features containing the property `dcterms:subject`;
- **OS-1H**, we consider the features including the property `rdf:type`;
- **FS-1H**, we pick all the features but ontological and categorical ones.

For the selection of double-hops (2H) features, the applied policies are:

- **CS-2H**, we select the features with properties equal to either `dcterms:subject` or `skos:broader`;
- **OS-2H**, we consider the features including the properties `rdf:type`, `rdf-schema:subClassOf` or `owl:equivalentClass`;
- **FS-2H**, we pick up the features which are not in the previous two categories.

Noteworthy, we have not put any categorical/ontological features into the noisy list. If some domain-specific categorical/ontological features are not in the respective lists, we have considered them as factual features.

Feature Filtering. Following the aforementioned directions, we have extracted $1H$, and $2H$ features for `LibraryThing`, and `Yahoo!Movies`. Due to the extent of the catalogs, we obtained millions of features. Consequently, we removed irrelevant features following the filtering technique proposed in [18,31]. In detail, we dropped off all the features with more than 99.74% (t) of missing values and more than t of distinct values. In detail, we dropped off all the features with more than 99.74% of missing values and distinct values. The statistics of the resulting datasets is depicted in Table 2.

Table 2. Selected features in the different settings either for single and double hops.

Dataset	CS-1H		OS-1H		FS-1H		CS-2H		OS-2H		FS-2H	
	Tot.	Selected	Tot.	Selected	Tot.	Selected	Tot.	Selected	Tot.	Selected	Tot.	Selected
LibraryThing	3890	458	2090	367	53929	2398	9641	1140	3723	597	4256005	306289
Yahoo!Movies	5555	1125	3036	691	102697	7050	8960	1956	3105	431	6694881	516114

Recommender Models. We have conducted experiments considering all the attacks described in Sect. 3.2 on the following baseline Collaborative Filtering Recommender Systems:

- **User-kNN** [23,32] predicts the score of unknown user-item pairs ($\hat{r}_{ui}$) considering the feedback of the users in the neighborhood. We have tested *SAShA* using the formulation mentioned in [23]. It considers the user and item's ratings biases. Let u be a user inside the set of users U, and i be an item in the set of items I, we estimate the rating given by u to i based on the following Equation:

$$\hat{r}_{ui} = b_{ui} + \frac{\sum_{v \in U_i^k(u)} \delta(u, v) \cdot (r_{vi} - b_{vi})}{\sum_{v \in U_i^k(u)} \delta(u, v)} \tag{1}$$

where δ is the distance metric to measure the similarity between users, $U_i^k(u)$ is the set of k-neighborhood users v of u. We define b_{ui} as $\mu + b_u + b_i$, where μ, b_u, b_i are the overall average rating, the observed bias of user u and item i, respectively. Following directions suggested in [10], we apply as distance metric δ the *Pearson Correlation* and a number of neighbors k equal to 40.

– **Item-kNN** [23,33] estimates the user-item rating score ($\hat{r}_{ui}$) using the recorded feedback given by u to the k-items j in the neighborhood of the item i. Equation 2 defines the rating prediction formula for Item-kNN.

$$\hat{r}_{ui} = b_{ui} + \frac{\sum_{j \in I_u^k(i)} \delta(i,j) \cdot (r_{uj} - b_{uj})}{\sum_{j \in I_u^k(i)} \delta(i,j)} \tag{2}$$

In Eq. 2, the set of k items inside the i neighborhood is denoted as $I_u^k(i)$. The similarity function δ and the number of considered neighbors k are selected as in User-kNN.

– **Matrix Factorization (MF)** [24] is a latent factor model used for items recommendation task that learns user-item preferences, by factorizing the sparse user-item feedback matrix. The learned user and item representation, fitted on previously recorder interactions, are exploited to predict $\hat{r}_{ui}$ as follows:

$$\hat{r}_{ui} = b_{ui} + \mathbf{q}_i^T \mathbf{p}_u \tag{3}$$

In Eq. 3, $\mathbf{q}_i \in \mathbb{R}^f$ and $\mathbf{p}_u \in \mathbb{R}^f$ are the latent vectors for item i and user u learned by the model. We set the number of latent factors f to 100, as suggested in [22].

Evaluation Metrics. We have evaluated our attack strategy by adopting *Overall Prediction Shift*, and *Overall Hit-Ratio@k*. Let I_T be the set of attacked items, and U_T be the set of users that have not rated the items in I_T. We define the *Overall Prediction Shift* (PS) [1] as the average variation of the predicted score for the target item.

$$PS(I_T, U_T) = \frac{\sum_{i \subset I_T, u \subset U_T} (\hat{r}_{ui} - r_{ui})}{|I_T| \times |U_T|} \tag{4}$$

where $\hat{r}_{ui}$ is the predicted rating on item i for user u after the shilling attack, and r_{ui} is the prediction without (before) attack. We define the *Overall Hit-Ratio@k* ($HR@k$) [1] as the average of $hr@k$ for each attacked item. Equation 5 defines $HR@k$ as:

$$HR@k(I_T, U_T) = \frac{\sum_{i \subset I_T} hr@k(i, U_T)}{|I_T|} \tag{5}$$

where $hr@k(i, U_T)$ measures the number of occurrences of the attacked item i in the top-k recommendation lists of the users in $|U_T|$.

Evaluation Protocol. Inspired by the evaluation proposed in [25,27], we have performed a total of 126 experiments. For each dataset, we have generated the recommendations concerning all users using the selected CF models (i.e., User-kNN, Item-kNN and MF). Then, we have added the fake profiles generated according to the baseline attack strategies, and we have re-computed the recommendation lists. We have evaluated the effectiveness of each attack by measuring the above-mentioned metrics on both the initial and the new recommendation lists. After this step, we have performed a series of *SAShA* attacks as described in Sect. 3. In detail, we have considered different feature types (i.e., categorical, ontological and factual) extracted at 1 or 2 hops. Finally, we have evaluated the $HR@k$ and PS for each *SAShA* variant comparing it against baselines. It is worth to note that, in our experiments, each attack is a *push attack*. Indeed, the attacker's purpose is to increase the probability that the target item is recommended. Moreover, by adopting the evaluation protocol proposed in [15,28], we have performed the attacks considering a different amount of added fake user profiles: 1%, 2.5% and 5% of the total number of users. We have tested the attacks considering 50 randomly sampled target items.

4.2   Results and Discussion

The discussion of results is organized accordingly to the research questions stated in Sect. 1. Firstly, we describe the influence of semantic knowledge on attack strategies. Later, we compare the impact of the different types of semantic information.

Analysis of the Effectiveness of Semantic Knowledge on Shilling Attacks. The first Research Question aims to check whether the injection of Linked Open Data as a new source of knowledge can represent a 'weapon' for attackers against CF-RS. Table 3 reports the results of the $HR@10$ for each attack. For both the baseline and semantic-aware variants, we highlight in bold the best results.

Starting from the analysis of the low-informed *random attack*, experiments show that the semantic-aware attacks are remarkably effective. For instance, the semantic-attacks with ontological information at single hop (*SAShA-OS-1H*), outperforms the baselines independently of the attacked model. To support these insights, we can observe the PS resulting from random attacks. Figure 2a shows that any variant of *SAShA* has a higher prediction shift w.r.t. the baseline for Yahoo! Movies. In Fig. 2b, we can notice that the semantic strategy is the most effective one for each model. As an example, the PS of *Rnd-SAShA-OS-1H* increases up to 6.82% over the corresponding baseline in the case of attacks against User-kNN on Yahoo! Movies dataset. The full results are online available[5].

In Table 3, we observe that the injection of semantic information for *love-hate* attack is not particularly effective. This can be due to the specific

---

[5] https://github.com/sisinflab/papers-results/tree/master/sasha-results.

Table 3. Experimental results for *SAShA* at single and double hops.

Metric: HR@10		LibraryThing									YahooMovies								
		User-kNN			Item-kNN			MF			User-kNN			Item-kNN			MF		
		1%	2.5%	5%	1%	2.5%	5%	1%	2.5%	5%	1%	2.5%	5%	1%	2.5%	5%	1%	2.5%	5%
Rnd	baseline	.074	.157	.230	.281	.457	.557	.767	.900	.942	.189	.366	.449	.329	.508	.598	.410	.580	.702
	CS-1H	.068*	.143*	.213*	.271*	.441*	.558	.778*	.898	.940	.202	.372	.455*	.336	.522*	.609*	.430*	.607*	.707
	OS-1H	**.081***	**.170***	**.250***	**.290***	**.467***	**.576***	**.786***	**.902**	**.944**	**.217***	**.394***	**.477***	**.345***	**.535***	**.622***	**.446***	**.635***	**.742***
	FS-1H	.072	.154	.229	.280	.455	.570*	.786*	.901	.942	.213*	.381*	.468*	.338*	.530*	.619*	.442*	.623*	.728*
L-H	baseline	.502	.518	.518	.874	.952	.978	.955	.987	**.995**	.604	.608	.605	.888	.930	**.958**	.956	.967	**.980**
	CS-1H	.502	.518	.518	**.876***	**.953**	**.979**	**.957**	.987	.994	.604	.608	**.605***	**.889**	.932	.957	.956	.967	.979
	OS-1H	.502	.518	.518	.870*	.950*	.974*	.955*	.986	.994	.604	.605	.605	.887	**.933**	.955*	.956	.967	.979
	FS-1H	.502	.518	.518	.874	.951	.977	.955	.987	.993	.604*	.608	.605	.888	**.933**	.956	.956	.967	.979
Avg	baseline	.086	.197	.285	.313	**.508**	.605	.803	.915	.951	.233	**.416**	.494	**.374**	**.574**	**.654**	**.489**	**.685**	**.788**
	CS-1H	.081*	.187*	.269*	.301*	.507	.621*	.814*	.915	.950	.220*	.399*	.479*	.357*	.554*	.639*	.467*	.652*	.744*
	OS-1H	**.093***	**.202**	**.289**	.313	.507	**.610***	**.810***	.911	**.948**	**.237**	.412	.494	.371	.563*	.646*	.475	.656*	.754*
	FS-1H	.084	.190*	.272*	.305*	.504	.614*	.811	.911	.946*	.215*	.397*	.473*	.350*	.547*	.634*	.448*	.627*	.729*
Rnd	baseline	.074	.157	.230	.281	**.457**	.557	.767	.900	.942	.189	.366	.449	.329	.508	.598	.410	.580	.702
	CS-2H	.068*	.143*	.213*	.270*	.441*	.558	**.799***	.897	.940	**.234***	**.410***	**.494***	**.368***	**.564***	**.644***	**.473***	**.667***	**.772***
	OS-2H	**.075**	.157	**.231**	.252	.455	**.567***	.783*	**.901**	.941	.172	.337*	.428*	.304*	.482*	.577*	.399	.560	.652*
	FS-2H	.073	.155	.229	.281	.455	.567*	.787*	**.901**	.942	.208*	.386*	.466*	.341*	.531*	.616*	.440*	.616*	.717*
L-H	baseline	.502	.518	.518	.874	.952	.978	.955	.987	**.995**	.604	.608	.605	.888	.930	**.958**	.956	.967	**.980**
	CS-2H	.502	.518	.518	**.876**	.952	**.979**	**.956**	.987	.993	.604	.608	.605	.887	**.933**	.955*	.956	.967	.979
	OS-2H	.502	.518	.518	.873	.951	.976	**.956**	.986*	.994	.604	.608	.605	.888	**.933**	.957	.956	.967	.979
	FS-2H	.502	.518	.518	.874	.951	.976*	**.956**	.987	.994	.604	.608	.605*	.888	**.934**	.957	.956	.967	.979
Avg	baseline	.086	.197	.285	.313	**.508**	.605	.803	.915	**.951**	.233	.416	**.494**	.374	.574	.654	.489	.685	.788
	CS-2H	.081*	.188*	.269*	.301*	.507	.621*	.815*	.914	.949	.204*	.384*	.466*	.338*	.532*	.621*	.408*	.587*	.688*
	OS-2H	.084*	**.198**	.281	.309	.506	.614*	**.816***	.914	.949	**.249***	**.429***	.493	**.400***	**.593***	**.668***	**.539***	**.720***	**.804***
	FS-2H	.084	.190*	**.273***	.306	.503	.614*	.812*	.913	.948*	.227	.401*	.479*	.364	.557*	.642*	.466*	.646*	.743*

We denote statistically significant results with * *with a p-value less than 0.05 using a paired-t-test statistical significance test.*

attack strategy. A possible interpretation is that, since the rationale is to decrease the overall mean rating of all items but the target one, exploiting similarity does not strengthen the approach.

In the informed attacks (i.e., the *average* attack), results show that semantic integration can be a useful source of knowledge. For instance, *Avg-SAShA-OS-2H* improves performance on Item-kNN by 10.2% compared to the baseline.

It is noteworthy that in the semantic variant of the random attack on the movie domain, *Rnd-SAShA-CS-2H*, reaches performance that is comparable with the baseline *average* attack. This observation shows that even an attacker that is not able to access system knowledge can perform powerful attacks by exploiting public (semantic) available knowledge bases.

Analysis of the Impact of Different Semantic Information Types, and Multi-hops Influence. In the previous analysis, we have focused on the effectiveness of *SAShA* strategy irrespective of different types of semantic properties (Sect. 4.1). Table 3 shows that each attack that exploits ontological information is generally the most effective one if we consider single-hop features.

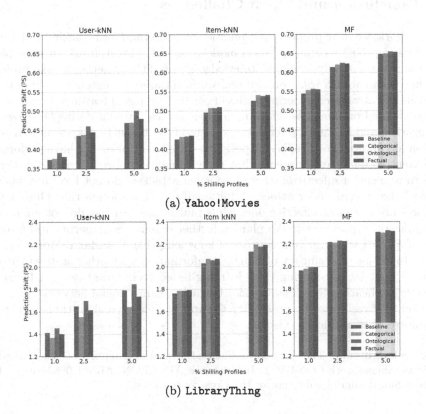

(a) Yahoo!Movies

(b) LibraryThing

Fig. 2. (a) Prediction Shift on Yahoo!Movies for random attacks at single hop. (b) Prediction Shift on LibraryThing for random attacks at single hop.

We motivate this finding with the ontological relation between the fake profiles and the target item. Exploiting ontological relations we can compute similarities without the "noisy" factual features. A possible interpretation is that a strong ontological similarity is manifest for humans, but for an autonomous agent it can be "hidden" by the presence of other features. Moreover, the exploitation of items' categorization is particularly effective to attack CF-RS since CF approaches recommend items based on similarities.

Table 3 shows the results for double-hop features. Also in this case, the previous findings are mostly confirmed but for random attacks on Yahoo!Movies.

Finally, we focus on the differences between the impact of single-hop and double-hops features. Experimental results show that the variants that consider the second hop have not a big influence on the effectiveness of attacks. In some cases, we observe a worsening of performance as in LibraryThing. For instance, the performance of random *SAShA* at double-hops considering ontological features decreases by 13.1% compared to the same configuration at single-hop (when attacking Item-kNN).

5   Conclusion and Open Challenges

In this work, we have proposed a semantic-aware method for attacking collaborative filtering (CF) recommendation models, named *SAShA*, in which we explore the impact of publicly available knowledge graph data to generate fake profiles. We have evaluated *SAShA* on two real-world datasets by extending three baseline Shilling attacks considering different semantic types of features. In detail, we have extended *random*, *love-hate* and *average* attacks by considering Ontological, Categorical and Factual $\mathcal{KG}$ features extracted from DBpedia. Experimental evaluation has shown that *SAShA* outperforms baseline attacks. We have performed an extensive set of experiments that show semantic information is a powerful tool to implement effective attacks also when attackers do not have any knowledge of the system under attack. Additionally, we have found that Ontological features are the most effective one, while multi-hops features do not guarantee a significant improvement. We plan to further extend the experimental evaluation of *SAShA* with different sources of knowledge like Wikidata. Moreover, we intent to explore the efficacy of semantic information with other state-of-the-art attacks (e.g., by considering deep learning-based techniques), with a focus on possible applications of semantic-based attacks against social networks. Finally, we plan to investigate the possibility to support defensive algorithms that take advantage of semantic knowledge.

Acknowledgments. The authors acknowledge partial support of the following projects: Innonetwork CONTACT, Innonetwork APOLLON, ARS01_00821 FLET4.0, Fincons Smart Digital Solutions for the Creative Industry.

References

1. Aggarwal, C.C.: Attack-resistant recommender systems. In: Recommender Systems, pp. 385–410. Springer, Cham (2016). https://doi.org/10.1007/978-3-319-29659-3_12

2. Alam, M., Buscaldi, D., Cochez, M., Osborne, F., Recupero, D.R., Sack, H. (eds.): Proceedings of the Workshop on Deep Learning for Knowledge Graphs (DL4KG2019) Co-located with the 16th Extended Semantic Web Conference 2019 (ESWC 2019). CEUR Workshop Proceedings, Portoroz, Slovenia, 2 June 2019, vol. 2377. CEUR-WS.org (2019)

3. Anelli, V.W., Bellini, V., Di Noia, T., Bruna, W.L., Tomeo, P., Di Sciascio, E.: An analysis on time- and session-aware diversification in recommender systems. In: UMAP, pp. 270–274. ACM (2017)

4. Anelli, V.W., Di Noia, T.: 2nd workshop on knowledge-aware and conversational recommender systems - KaRS. In: CIKM, pp. 3001–3002. ACM (2019)

5. Anelli, V.W., Di Noia, T., Di Sciascio, E., Ragone, A., Trotta, J.: How to make latent factors interpretable by feeding factorization machines with knowledge graphs. In: Ghidini, C., et al. (eds.) ISWC 2019. LNCS, vol. 11778, pp. 38–56. Springer, Cham (2019). https://doi.org/10.1007/978-3-030-30793-6_3

6. Backstrom, L., Leskovec, J.: Supervised random walks: predicting and recommending links in social networks. In: Proceedings of the Forth International Conference on Web Search and Web Data Mining, WSDM 2011, Hong Kong, China, 9–12 February 2011, pp. 635–644 (2011)

7. Bhatia, S., Dwivedi, P., Kaur, A.: That's interesting, tell me more! finding descriptive support passages for knowledge graph relationships. In: Vrandečić, D., et al. (eds.) ISWC 2018, Part I. LNCS, vol. 11136, pp. 250–267. Springer, Cham (2018). https://doi.org/10.1007/978-3-030-00671-6_15

8. Bhaumik, R., Williams, C., Mobasher, B., Burke, R.: Securing collaborative filtering against malicious attacks through anomaly detection. In: Proceedings of the 4th Workshop on Intelligent Techniques for Web Personalization (ITWP 2006), Boston, vol. 6, p. 10 (2006)

9. Burke, R., O'Mahony, M.P., Hurley, N.J.: Robust collaborative recommendation. In: Ricci, F., Rokach, L., Shapira, B. (eds.) Recommender Systems Handbook, pp. 961–995. Springer, Boston (2015). https://doi.org/10.1007/978-1-4899-7637-6_28

10. Candillier, L., Meyer, F., Boullé, M.: Comparing state-of-the-art collaborative filtering systems. In: Perner, P. (ed.) MLDM 2007. LNCS (LNAI), vol. 4571, pp. 548–562. Springer, Heidelberg (2007). https://doi.org/10.1007/978-3-540-73499-4_41

11. Cao, J., Wu, Z., Mao, B., Zhang, Y.: Shilling attack detection utilizing semi-supervised learning method for collaborative recommender system. World Wide Web 16(5), 729–748 (2012). https://doi.org/10.1007/s11280-012-0164-6

12. Chen, K., Chan, P.P.K., Zhang, F., Li, Q.: Shilling attack based on item popularity and rated item correlation against collaborative filtering. Int. J. Mach. Learn. Cybernet. 10(7), 1833–1845 (2018). https://doi.org/10.1007/s13042-018-0861-2

13. Cochez, M., et al. (eds.): Proceedings of the First Workshop on Deep Learning for Knowledge Graphs and Semantic Technologies (DL4KGS) Co-located with the 15th Extended Semantic Web Conerence (ESWC 2018). CEUR Workshop Proceedings, Heraklion, Crete, Greece, 4 June 2018, vol. 2106. CEUR-WS.org (2018)

14. Deldjoo, Y., et al.: Movie genome: alleviating new item cold start in movie recommendation. User Model. User-Adap. Inter. 29(2), 291–343 (2019). https://doi.org/10.1007/s11257-019-09221-y

15. Deldjoo, Y., Di Noia, T., Merra, F.A.: Assessing the impact of a user-item collaborative attack on class of users. In: ImpactRS@RecSys. CEUR Workshop Proceedings, vol. 2462. CEUR-WS.org (2019)

16. Di Noia, T., Magarelli, C., Maurino, A., Palmonari, M., Rula, A.: Using ontology-based data summarization to develop semantics-aware recommender systems. In: Gangemi, A., et al. (eds.) ESWC 2018. LNCS, vol. 10843, pp. 128–144. Springer, Cham (2018). https://doi.org/10.1007/978-3-319-93417-4_9

17. Di Noia, T., Mirizzi, R., Ostuni, V.C., Romito, D., Zanker, M.: Linked open data to support content-based recommender systems. In: Proceedings of the 8th International Conference on Semantic Systems, pp. 1–8. ACM (2012)

18. Di Noia, T., Ostuni, V.C., Tomeo, P., Di Sciascio, E.: SPrank: semantic path-based ranking for top-N recommendations using linked open data. ACM TIST 8(1), 9:1–9:34 (2016)

19. Gao, L., Yang, H., Wu, J., Zhou, C., Lu, W., Hu, Y.: Recommendation with multi-source heterogeneous information. In: IJCAI, pp. 3378–3384. ijcai.org (2018)

20. Gunes, I., Kaleli, C., Bilge, A., Polat, H.: Shilling attacks against recommender systems: a comprehensive survey. Artif. Intell. Rev. 42(4), 767–799 (2012). https://doi.org/10.1007/s10462-012-9364-9

21. Hildebrandt, M., et al.: A recommender system for complex real-world applications with nonlinear dependencies and knowledge graph context. In: Hitzler, P., et al. (eds.) ESWC 2019. LNCS, vol. 11503, pp. 179–193. Springer, Cham (2019). https://doi.org/10.1007/978-3-030-21348-0_12

22. Hug, N.: Surprise, a Python library for recommender systems (2017). http://surpriselib.com

23. Koren, Y.: Factor in the neighbors: scalable and accurate collaborative filtering. TKDD 4(1), 1:1–1:24 (2010)

24. Koren, Y., Bell, R.M., Volinsky, C.: Matrix factorization techniques for recommender systems. IEEE Comput. 42(8), 30–37 (2009)

25. Lam, S.K., Riedl, J.: Shilling recommender systems for fun and profit. In: WWW, pp. 393–402. ACM (2004)

26. Linden, G., Smith, B., York, J.: Amazon.com recommendations: item-to-item collaborative filtering. IEEE Internet Comput. 7(1), 76–80 (2003)

27. Mobasher, B., Burke, R., Bhaumik, R., Williams, C.: Effective attack models for shilling item-based collaborative filtering systems. In: Proceedings of the WebKDD Workshop, pp. 13–23. Citeseer (2005)

28. Mobasher, B., Burke, R.D., Bhaumik, R., Williams, C.: Toward trustworthy recommender systems: an analysis of attack models and algorithm robustness. ACM Trans. Internet Technol. 7(4), 23 (2007)

29. Ning, X., Karypis, G.: Sparse linear methods with side information for top-n recommendations. In: Cunningham, P., Hurley, N.J., Guy, I., Anand, S.S. (eds.) Sixth ACM Conference on Recommender Systems, RecSys 2012, Dublin, Ireland, 9–13 September 2012, pp. 155–162. ACM (2012)

30. O'Mahony, M.P., Hurley, N.J., Kushmerick, N., Silvestre, G.C.M.: Collaborative recommendation: a robustness analysis. ACM Trans. Internet Technol. 4(4), 344–377 (2004)

31. Paulheim, H., Fürnkranz, J.: Unsupervised generation of data mining features from linked open data. In: WIMS, pp. 31:1–31:12. ACM (2012)

32. Resnick, P., Iacovou, N., Suchak, M., Bergstrom, P., Riedl, J.: GroupLens: an open architecture for collaborative filtering of netnews. In: CSCW, pp. 175–186. ACM (1994)

33. Sarwar, B.M., Karypis, G., Konstan, J.A., Riedl, J.: Item-based collaborative filtering recommendation algorithms. In: Shen, V.Y., Saito, N., Lyu, M.R., Zurko, M.E. (eds.) Proceedings of the Tenth International World Wide Web Conference, WWW 10, Hong Kong, China, 1–5 May 2001, pp. 285–295. ACM (2001)
34. Shadbolt, N., et al.: Linked open government data: lessons from data.gov.uk. IEEE Intell. Syst. **27**(3), 16–24 (2012)
35. Wang, H., Zhang, F., Xie, X., Guo, M.: DKN: deep knowledge-aware network for news recommendation. In: WWW, pp. 1835–1844. ACM (2018)
36. Wang, X., Wang, D., Xu, C., He, X., Cao, Y., Chua, T.S.: Explainable reasoning over knowledge graphs for recommendation. In: Proceedings of the AAAI Conference on Artificial Intelligence, vol. 33, pp. 5329–5336 (2019)
37. Yu, X., et al.: Personalized entity recommendation: a heterogeneous information network approach. In: WSDM, pp. 283–292. ACM (2014)
38. Zhou, W., Wen, J., Xiong, Q., Gao, M., Zeng, J.: SVM-TIA a shilling attack detection method based on SVM and target item analysis in recommender systems. Neurocomputing **210**, 197–205 (2016)

Knowledge Graphs

Entity Extraction from Wikipedia List Pages

Nicolas Heist[(✉)] and Heiko Paulheim

Data and Web Science Group, University of Mannheim, Mannheim, Germany
{nico,heiko}@informatik.uni-mannheim.de

Abstract. When it comes to factual knowledge about a wide range of domains, Wikipedia is often the prime source of information on the web. DBpedia and YAGO, as large cross-domain knowledge graphs, encode a subset of that knowledge by creating an entity for each page in Wikipedia, and connecting them through edges. It is well known, however, that Wikipedia-based knowledge graphs are far from complete. Especially, as Wikipedia's policies permit pages about subjects only if they have a certain popularity, such graphs tend to lack information about less well-known entities. Information about these entities is oftentimes available in the encyclopedia, but not represented as an individual page. In this paper, we present a two-phased approach for the extraction of entities from Wikipedia's list pages, which have proven to serve as a valuable source of information. In the first phase, we build a large taxonomy from categories and list pages with DBpedia as a backbone. With distant supervision, we extract training data for the identification of new entities in list pages that we use in the second phase to train a classification model. With this approach we extract over 700k new entities and extend DBpedia with 7.5M new type statements and 3.8M new facts of high precision.

Keywords: Entity extraction · Wikipedia list pages · Distant supervision · DBpedia

1 Introduction

Knowledge graphs like DBpedia [13] and YAGO [14] contain huge amounts of high-quality data on various topical domains. Unfortunately, they are - as their application on real-world tasks show - far from complete: IBM's DeepQA system uses both of them to answer Jeopardy! questions [11]. While the component that uses this structured information gives correct answers 87% of the time (compared to 70% correctness of the complete system), it is only able to provide answers for 2.3% of the questions posed to it. Given that they find in another analysis that around 96% of the answers to a sample of 3,500 Jeopardy! questions can be answered with Wikipedia titles [3], it is safe to say that there is a lot of information in Wikipedia yet to be extracted.

© Springer Nature Switzerland AG 2020
A. Harth et al. (Eds.): ESWC 2020, LNCS 12123, pp. 327–342, 2020.
https://doi.org/10.1007/978-3-030-49461-2_19

List of Japanese speculative fiction writers

From Wikipedia, the free encyclopedia

This is a **list of Japanese speculative fiction writers**. Writers are sorted alphabetically by surname.

A [edit]

- Kimifusa Abe (安部公房, real name of Kōbō Abe)
- Kōbō Abe (安部公房, 1924–1993)
- Hirotaka Adachi (安達寛高, real name of Otsuichi)
- Jirō Akagawa (赤川次郎, b. 1948)
- Mizuhito Akiyama (秋山瑞人, b. 1971)
- Motoko Arai (新井素子, b. 1960)
- Mizuhito Akiyama (秋山瑞人, b. 1971)
- Kunio Aramaki (荒巻邦夫, real name of Yoshio Aramaki)
- Yoshimasa Aramaki (荒巻義雅, real name of Yoshio Aramaki)
- Yoshio Aramaki (荒巻義雄, b. 1933)
- Hiroshi Aramata (荒俣宏, b. 1947)
- Alice Arisugawa or Arisu Arisugawa (有栖川有栖, b. 1959)
- Taku Ashibe (芦辺拓, b. 1958)
- Yukito Ayatsuji (綾辻行人, b. 1960)

B–D [edit]

- Chen Shunchen (陳舜臣, pseudonym of Chin Shunshin)
- Chen Soon Shin (陳舜臣, pseudonym of Chin Shunshin)
- Kimio Chiba (千葉喜美雄, real name of Ryu Mitsuse)
- Chihitsudō (遅筆堂, pseudonym of Hisashi Inoue)
- Chin Shunshin (陳舜臣, 1924–2015)
- Gakuto Coda, Gakuto Kōda (甲田学人, b. 1977)

Fig. 1. Excerpt of the Wikipedia page `List of Japanese speculative fiction writers` displaying the subjects in an **enumeration** layout.

While Wikipedia's infoboxes and categories have been the subject of many information extraction efforts of knowledge graphs already, list pages have - despite their obvious wealth of information - received very little attention. For entities of the page `List of Japanese speculative fiction writers` (shown in Fig. 1), we can derive several bits of information: *(type, Writer)*, *(nationality, Japan)*, and *(genre, Speculative Fiction)*.

In contrast to finding entities of a category, finding such entities among all the entities mentioned in a list page is a non-trivial problem. We will refer to these entities, that are instances of the concept expressed by the list page, as its *subject entities*. Unlike categories, list pages are an informal construct in Wikipedia. Hence, the identification of their subject entities brings up several challenges: While list pages are usually formatted as enumeration or table, they have no convention of how the information in them is structured. For example, subject entities can be listed somewhere in the middle of a table (instead of in the first column) and enumerations can have multiple levels. Furthermore, context information may not be available (it is difficult to find *Japanese speculative fiction writers* in a list if one doesn't know to look for *writers*).

In this paper, we introduce an approach for identifying subject entities in Wikipedia list pages and provide the following contributions in particular:

- An approach for the construction of a combined taxonomy of Wikipedia categories, lists and DBpedia types.

- A distantly supervised machine learning approach for the extraction of subject entities from Wikipedia list pages.
- 700k new entities, 7.5M additional type statements, and 3.8M additional facts for DBpedia that are published as RDF triples and as a standalone knowledge graph called CaLiGraph[1].

The rest of this paper is structured as follows. Section 2 frames the approach described in this paper in related works. Section 3 introduces the idea of entity extraction from list pages, followed by a description of our approach in Sect. 4. In Sect. 5, we discuss results and present an empirical evaluation of our approach. We close with a summary and an outlook on future developments.

2 Related Work

The extraction of knowledge from structured elements in Wikipedia is mostly focused on two fields: Firstly, the field of taxonomy induction, where most of the approaches use the category graph of Wikipedia to derive a taxonomy, and, secondly, the application of information extraction methods to derive facts from various (semi-)structured sources like infoboxes, tables, lists, or abstracts of Wikipedia pages.

The approach of Ponzetto and Navigli [18] was one of the first to derive a large taxonomy from Wikipedia categories by putting their focus on the lexical head of a category. They exploit the fact that almost exclusively categories with plural lexical heads are useful elements of a taxonomy. Hence, they are able to clean the category graph from non-taxonomic categories and relationships. Several other approaches create a combined taxonomy of the category graph and additional resources like WordNet (YAGO [14]) or Wikipedia pages (WiBi [4]).

The distant supervision paradigm [15] is used extensively for information extraction in Wikipedia as it provides an easy way to automatically gather large amounts of training data with a low error rate. Usually, some form of knowledge base is used as background knowledge to generate training data from a target corpus. In the original work, Mintz et al. use Freebase as background knowledge to extract information from Wikipedia. [1] extend this approach by using DBpedia as background knowledge.

Regarding list pages, Paulheim and Ponzetto [17] frame their general potential as a source of knowledge in Wikipedia. They propose to use a combination of statistical and NLP methods to extract knowledge and show that, by applying them to a single list page, they are able to extract a thousand new statements. [12] infer types for entities on list pages and are thus most closely related to our approach. To identify subject entities of the list pages, they rely on information from DBpedia (e.g. how many relations exist between entities on the list page) and are consequently only able to infer new types for existing DBpedia entities. They use a score inspired by TF-IDF to find the type of a list page

---

[1] http://caligraph.org.

and are able to extract 303,934 types from 2,000 list pages with an estimated precision of 86.19%.

Apart from list pages, entity and relation extraction in Wikipedia is applied to structured sources like infoboxes [21], abstracts [8,19], and tables [2,16].

With the exploitation of the structured nature of list pages to extract previously unknown entities as well as factual information about them, we see our approach as a useful addition to the existing literature where the focus is set primarily on enriching the ontology or adding information for existing entities.

3   Categories and List Pages in Wikipedia

The Wikipedia Category Graph (WCG) has been used extensively for taxonomy induction (e.g. in [4,14]) and has proven to yield highly accurate results. The WCG has a subgraph consisting of list categories,[2] which organizes many of the list page articles in Wikipedia. The list page List of Japanese speculative fiction writers (Fig. 1), for example, is a member of the list category Lists of Japanese writers, which in turn has the parent list category Lists of writers by nationality, and so on.

As this subgraph is part of the WCG, we can use the list categories as a natural extension of a taxonomy induced by the WCG (e.g., by linking Lists of Japanese writers to the respective category Japanese writers). This comes with the benefit of including list pages into the taxonomy (i.e., we can infer that List of Japanese speculative fiction writers is a sub-concept of the category Japanese writers). Despite their obvious potential, neither list categories nor list pages have yet explicitly been used for taxonomy induction.

In each list page, some of the links point to entities in the category the list page reflects, others do not. In the list page List of Japanese speculative fiction writers, for example, some links point to pages about such writers (i.e. to its subject entities), while others point to specific works by those writers. To distinguish those two cases, the unifying taxonomy is of immense value. Through the hierarchical relationships between categories and list pages, we can infer that if an entity is mentioned in both a list page *and* a related category, it is very likely a subject entity of the list page. Consequently, if an entity is mentioned in the list page List of Japanese speculative fiction writers and is contained in the category Japanese writers, it is almost certainly a Japanese speculative fiction writer.

In the remainder of this section we provide necessary background information of the resources used in our approach.

The Wikipedia Category Graph. In the version of October 2016[3] the WCG consists of 1,475,015 categories that are arranged in a directed, but not acyclic

---

[2] A list category is a Wikipedia category that starts with the prefix *Lists of*.

[3] We use this version in order to be compatible with the (at the time of conducting the experiments) most recent release of DBpedia: https://wiki.dbpedia.org/develop/datasets.

graph. This graph does not only contain categories used for the categorisation of content pages, but also ones that are used for administrative purposes (e.g., the category Wikipedia articles in need of updating). Similar to [9], we use only transitive subcategories of the category Main topic classifications while also getting rid of categories having one of the following keywords in their name: *wikipedia, lists, template, stub*.

The resulting filtered set of categories $\mathcal{C}^F$ contains 1,091,405 categories that are connected by 2,635,718 subcategory edges. We denote the set of entities in a category c with $\mathcal{E}_c$, the set of all types in DBpedia with $\mathcal{T}$ and the set of types of an entity e with $\mathcal{T}_e$.

The Wikipedia List Graph. The set of list categories $\mathcal{C}^L$ contains 7,297 list categories (e.g., Lists of People), connected by 10,245 subcategory edges (e.g., Lists of Celebrities being a subcategory of Lists of People). The set of list pages $\mathcal{L}$ contains 94,562 list pages. Out of those, 75,690 are contained in at least one category in $\mathcal{C}^F$ (e.g., List of Internet Pioneers is contained in the category History of the Internet), 70,099 are contained in at least one category in $\mathcal{C}^L$ (e.g., List of Internet Pioneers is contained in the category Lists of Computer Scientists), and 90,430 are contained in at least one of the two.[4]

The Anatomy of List Pages. List pages can be categorised into one of three possible layout types [12]: 44,288 pages list entities in a bullet point-like **enumeration**. The list page List of Japanese speculative fiction writers in Fig. 1 lists the subject entities in an enumeration layout. In this case, the subject entities are most often mentioned at the beginning of an enumeration entry. As some exceptions on the page show, however, this is not always the case.

46,160 pages list entities in a **table** layout. An example of this layout is given in Fig. 2, where an excerpt of the page List of Cuban-American writers is shown. The respective subjects of the rows are listed in the first column, but this can also vary between list pages.

The remaining 4,114 pages do not have a consistent layout and are thus categorised as **undefined**[5]. As our approach significantly relies on the structured nature of a list page, we exclude list pages with an undefined layout from our extraction pipeline.

For a list page l, we define the task of identifying its subject entities $\mathcal{E}_l$ among all the mentioned entities $\widehat{\mathcal{E}_l}$ in l as a binary classification problem. A mentioned entity is either classified as being a subject entity of l or not. If not, it is usually mentioned in the context of an entity in $\mathcal{E}_l$ or for organisational purposes (e.g. in a *See also* section). Looking at Figs. 1 and 2, mentioned entities are marked in blue (indicating that they have an own Wikipedia page and are thus contained in DBpedia) and in red (indicating that they do not have a Wikipedia page and

---

[4] Note that $\mathcal{C}^F$ and $\mathcal{C}^L$ are disjoint as we exclude categories with the word *lists* in $\mathcal{C}^F$.

[5] We heuristically label a list page as having one of the three layout types by looking for the most frequent elements: enumeration entries, table rows, or none of them.

List of Cuban-American writers

From Wikipedia, the free encyclopedia
  (Redirected from List of Cuban American writers)

This is a list of the most notable Cuban-American writers.

Name	Year of birth/death	Portrait	Notes
Alex Abella	1950–		Mystery/crime novelist, non-fiction writer, and journalist
Iván Acosta			Playwright; works include *El Super* (movie version 1979) and *Un cubiche en la luna* (1989)[1]
Mercedes de Acosta	1893–1968		
Robert Arellano	1969–		Novelist; works include *Havana Lunar* (2010 Edgar Award finalist) and *Havana Libre* (2017).
Reinaldo Arenas[2]	1943–1990		
René Ariza	1940–1994		
Octavio Armand [es]	1946–		Poet[1]
Joaquín Badajoz	1972–		Poet, author, essayist (North American Academy of the Spanish Language, fellow member)
Jesús J. Barquet[3]			
José Barreiro[4]	1948–		
Ruth Behar[5]	1956–		

Fig. 2. Excerpt of the Wikipedia page `List of Cuban-American writers` displaying the subjects in a **table** layout.

are consequently no entities in DBpedia). Additionally, we could include possible entities that are not tagged as such in Wikipedia (e.g. *Jesús J. Barquet* in the first column of Fig. 2) but we leave this for future work as it introduces additional complexity to the task. Of the three types of possible entities, the latter two are the most interesting as they would add the most amount of information to DBpedia. But it is also beneficial to identify entities that are already contained in DBpedia because we might be able to derive additional information about them through the list page they are mentioned in.

Note that for both layout types, **enumeration** and **table**, we find at most one subject entity per enumeration entry or table row. We inspected a subset of $\mathcal{L}$ and found this pattern to occur in every one of them.

Learning Category Axioms with Cat2Ax. The approach presented in this paper uses axioms over categories to derive a taxonomy from the category graph. Cat2Ax [9] is an approach that derives two kinds of axioms from Wikipedia categories: type axioms (e.g., for the category `Japanese writers` it learns that all entities in this category are of the type *Writer*), and relation axioms (e.g., for the same category it learns that all entities have the relation *(nationality, Japan)*). The authors use statistical and linguistic signals to derive the axioms and report a correctness of 96% for the derived axioms.

4   Distantly Supervised Entity Extraction from List Pages

The processing pipeline for the retrieval of subject entities from list pages in $\mathcal{L}$ is summarized in Fig. 3. The pipeline consists of two main components: In the

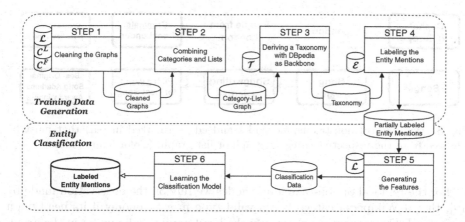

Fig. 3. Overview of the pipeline for the retrieval of subject entities from list pages. Small cylindrical shapes next to a step indicate the use of external data, and large cylindrical shapes contain data that is passed between pipeline steps.

Training Data Generation we create a unified taxonomy of categories, lists, and DBpedia types. With distant supervision we induce positive and negative labels from the taxonomy for a part of the mentioned entities of list pages.

The resulting training data is passed to the **Entity Classification** component. There we enrich it with features extracted from the list pages and learn classification models to finally identify the subject entities.

4.1 Training Data Generation

Step 1: Cleaning the Graphs
The initial category graph ($\mathcal{C}^F$ as nodes, subcategory relations as edges) and the initial list graph ($\mathcal{C}^L$ and $\mathcal{L}$ as nodes, subcategory relations and category membership as edges) both contain nodes and edges that have to be removed in order to convert them into valid taxonomies. Potential problems are shown in an abstract form in Fig. 4 and on an example in Fig. 5. In particular, we have to remove nodes that do not represent proper taxonomic types (e.g. London in Fig. 5).
Additionally, we have to remove

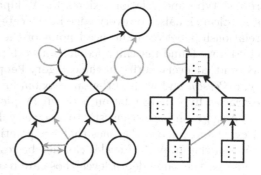

Fig. 4. Possible invalid nodes and edges (marked in red) in the category graph (circles) and list graph (rectangles). (Color figure online)

edges that either do not express a valid subtype relation (e.g. the edge from Songs to Song awards in Fig. 5), or create cycles (e.g. the self-references in Fig. 4).

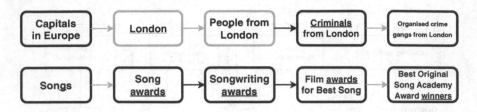

Fig. 5. Examples of non-taxonomic nodes and edges (marked in red) that must be removed from the respective category graph or list graph. (Color figure online)

For the removal of non-taxonomic nodes we rely on the observation made by [18], that a Wikipedia category is a valid type in a taxonomy if its head noun is in plural. Consequently, we identify the head nouns of the nodes in the graph and remove all nodes with singular head nouns.[6]

For the removal of invalid edges we first apply a domain-specific heuristic to get rid of non-taxonomic edges and subsequently apply a graph-based heuristic that removes cycles in the graphs. The domain-specific heuristic is based on [18]: An edge is removed if the head noun of the parent is not a synonym or a hypernym of the child's head noun. In Fig. 5 the head nouns of nodes are underlined; we remove, for example, the edge from Songs to Song awards as the word *songs* is neither a synonym nor a hypernym of *awards*.

We base our decision of synonym and hypernym relationships on a majority vote from three sources: (1) We parse the corpus of Wikipedia for Hearst patterns [6].[7] (2) We extract them from WebIsALOD [10], a large database of hypernyms crawled from the Web. (3) We extract them directly from categories in Wikipedia. To that end, we apply the Cat2Ax approach [9] which computes robust type and relation axioms for Wikipedia categories from linguistic and statistical signals. For every edge in the category graph, we extract a hypernym relationship between the head noun of the parent and the head noun of the child if we found matching axioms for both parent and child. E.g., if we find the axiom that every entity in the category People from London has the DBpedia type *Person* and we find the same axiom for Criminals from London, then we extract a hypernym relation between *People* and *Criminals*.

As a graph-based heuristic to resolve cycles, we detect edges that are part of a cycle and remove the ones that are pointing from a deeper node to a higher node in the graph.[8] If cycles can not be resolved because edges point between nodes on the same depth level, those are removed as well.

Through the cleaning procedure we reduce the size of the category graph from 1,091,405 nodes and 2,635,718 edges to 738,011 nodes and 1,324,894 edges, and we reduce the size of the list graph from 77,396 nodes and 105,761 edges to 77,396 nodes and 95,985 edges.

---

[6] We use spaCy (http://spacy.io) for head noun tagging.

[7] Patterns that indicate a taxonomic relationship between two words like "X is a Y".

[8] We define the depth of a node in the graph as the length of its shortest path to the root node Main topic classifications.

Step 2: Combining Categories and Lists

For a combined taxonomy of categories and lists, we find links between lists and categories based on linguistic similarity and existing connections in Wikipedia. As Fig. 6 shows, we find two types of links: equivalence links and hypernym links. We identify the former by looking for category-list pairs that are either named similar (e.g. `Japanese writers` and `Lists of Japanese writers`) or are synonyms (e.g. `Media in Kuwait` and `Lists of Kuwaiti media`). With this method we find 24,383 links.

We extract a hypernym link (similar to the method that we applied in Step 1) if the head noun of a category is a synonym or hypernym of a list's head noun. However, we limit the candidate links to existing edges in Wikipedia (i.e. the subcategory relation between a list category and a category, or the membership relation between a list page and a category) in order to avoid false positives. With this method we find 19,015 hypernym links. By integrating the extracted links into the

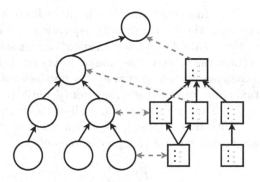

Fig. 6. Possible connections between the category graph and the list graph.

two graphs, we create a category-list graph with 815,543 nodes (738,011 categories, 7,416 list categories, 70,116 list pages) and 1,463,423 edges.

Step 3: Deriving a Taxonomy with DBpedia as Backbone

As a final step, we connect the category-list graph with the DBpedia taxonomy (as depicted in Fig. 7). To achieve that, we again apply the Cat2Ax approach to our current graph to produce type axioms for the graph nodes. E.g., we discover the axiom that every entity in the category `Japanese writers` has the DBpedia type *Writer*, thus we use the type as a parent of `Japanese writers`. Taking the transitivity of the taxonomy into account, we find a DBpedia supertype for 88% of the graph's nodes.

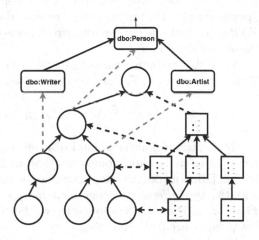

Fig. 7. Extension of the category-list taxonomy with DBpedia as a backbone.

Step 4: Labeling the Entity Mentions

We parse all entity mentions in list pages directly from the Wikitext using the dumps provided by DBpedia and using WikiTextParser[9] as a markup parser.

We compute the training data for mentioned entities $\widehat{\mathcal{E}}_l$ of a list page l directly from the taxonomy. To that end, we define two mapping functions:

$$related : \mathcal{L} \to P(\mathcal{C}^F) \tag{1}$$

$$types : \mathcal{L} \to P(\mathcal{T}) \tag{2}$$

The function $related(l)$ from Definition 1 returns the subset of $\mathcal{C}^F$ that contains the taxonomically equivalent or most closely related categories for l. For example, $related($List of Japanese speculative fiction writers$)$ returns the category Japanese writers and all its transitive subcategories (e.g. Japanese women writers). To find $related(l)$ of a list page l, we traverse the taxonomy upwards starting from l until we find a category c that is contained in $\mathcal{C}^F$. Then we return c and all of its children.

With this mapping, we assign positive labels to entity mentions in l, if they are contained in a category in $related(l)$:

$$\widehat{\mathcal{E}}_l^+ = \left\{ e | e \in \widehat{\mathcal{E}}_l \land \exists c \in related(l) : e \in \mathcal{E}_c \right\} \tag{3}$$

In the case of List of Japanese speculative fiction writers, $\widehat{\mathcal{E}}_l^+$ contains all entities that are mentioned on the list page *and* are members of the category Japanese writers or one of its subcategories.

The function $types(l)$ from Definition 2 returns the subset of the DBpedia types $\mathcal{T}$ that best describes entities in l. For example, $types($List of Japanese speculative fiction writers$)$ returns the DBpedia types *Agent, Person*, and *Writer*. To find $types(l)$, we retrieve all ancestors of l in the taxonomy and return those contained in $\mathcal{T}$.

With this mapping, we assign a negative label to an entity e mentioned in l, if there are types in $\mathcal{T}_e$ that are disjoint with types in $types(l)$:

$$\widehat{\mathcal{E}}_l^- = \left\{ e | e \in \widehat{\mathcal{E}}_l \land \exists t_e \in \mathcal{T}_e, \exists t_l \in types(l) : disjoint(t_e, t_l) \right\} \tag{4}$$

To identify disjointnesses in Eq. 4, we use the disjointness axioms provided by DBpedia as well as additional ones that are computed by the methods described in [20]. DBpedia declares, for example, the types *Person* and *Building* as disjoint, and the type *Person* is contained in $types($List of Japanese speculative fiction writers$)$. Consequently, we label any mentions of buildings in the list page as negative examples.

In addition to the negative entity mentions that we retrieve via Eq. 4, we label entities as negative using the observation we have made in Sect. 3: As soon as we find a positive entity mention in an enumeration entry or table row, we label all the remaining entity mentions in that entry or row as negative.

---

[9] https://github.com/5j9/wikitextparser.

Table 1. Features of the machine learning model grouped by list page type and by feature type. Page features are computed for the complete list page (LP) and do not vary between entity mentions. For page features, we include standard deviations as features in addition to averages.

	Feature type	Features
Shared	Page	# sections
	Positional	Position of section in LP
	Linguistic	Section title, POS/NE tag of entity and its direct context
Enum	Page	# entries, Avg. entry indentation level, Avg. entities/ words/characters per entry, Avg. position of first entity
	Positional	Position of entry in enumeration, Indentation level of entry, # of sub-entries of entry, Position of entity in entry
	Custom	# entities in current entry, # mentions of entity in same/other enumeration of LP
Table	Page	# tables, # rows, # columns, Avg. rows/columns per table, Avg. entities/words/characters per row/column, Avg. first column with entity
	Positional	Position of table in LP, Position of row/column in table, Position of entity in row
	Linguistic	Column header is synonym/hyponym of word in LP title
	Custom	# entities in current row, # mentions of current entity in same/other table of LP

For enumeration list pages, we find a total of 9.6M entity mentions. Of those we label 1.4M as positive and 1.4M as negative. For table list pages, we find a total of 11M entity mentions. Of those we label 850k as positive and 3M as negative.

4.2 Entity Classification

Step 5: Generating the Features

For a single data point (i.e. the mention of an entity in a specific list page), we generate a set of features that is shown in Table 1. Shared features are created for entity mentions of both enumeration and table list pages.

Features of the type *Page* encode characteristics of the list page and are hence similar for all entity mentions of the particular page. Features of the type *Positional, Linguistic, Custom* describe the characteristics of a single entity mention and its immediate context.

Step 6: Learning the Classification Model

To find a suitable classification model, we conduct an initial experiment on six classifiers (shown in Table 2) and compare them with the obvious baseline of always picking the first entity mention in an enumeration entry or table row.

Table 2. Precision (P), Recall (R), and F-measure (F1) in percent for the positive class (i.e. true subject entities in a list page) of various classification models.

Algorithm	Enum			Table		
	P	R	F1	P	R	F1
Baseline (pick first entity)	74	96	84	64	53	58
Naive Bayes	80	90	84	34	**91**	50
Decision Tree	82	78	80	67	66	67
Random Forest	85	**90**	**87**	85	71	**77**
XG-Boost	**90**	83	86	**90**	53	67
Neural Network (MLP)	86	84	85	78	72	75
SVM	86	60	71	73	33	45

We compute the performance using 10-fold cross validation while taking care that all entity mentions of a list page are in the same fold. In each fold, we use 80% of the data for training and 20% for validation. For all the mentioned classifiers, we report their performances after tuning their most important parameters with a coarse-grained grid search.

Table 2 shows that all applied approaches outperform the baseline in terms of precision. The XG-Boost algorithm scores highest in terms of precision while maintaining rather high levels of recall. Since we want to identify entities in list pages with highest possible precision, we use the XG-Boost model. After a fine-grained parameter tuning, we train models with a precision of 91% and 90%, and a recall of 82% and 55% for enumeration and table list pages, respectively.[10] Here, we split the dataset into 60% training, 20% validation, and 20% test data.

5   Results and Discussion

Entities. In total, we extract 1,549,893 subject entities that exist in DBpedia already. On average, an entity is extracted from 1.86 different list pages. Furthermore, we extract 754,115 subject entities that are new to DBpedia (from 1.07 list pages on average). Based on the list pages they have been extracted from, we assign them DBpedia types (i.e., the supertypes of the list page in the derived taxonomy). Figure 8 shows the distribution of new entities over various high-level types.

Entity Types. Overall, we generate 7.5M new type statements for DBpedia: 4.9M for entities in DBpedia (we assign a type to 2M previously untyped entities), and 2.6M for new entities (we find an average of 3.5 types per new entity). This is an increase of 51.15% in DBpedia's total type statements. We especially

---

[10] The models are trained using the scikit-learn library: https://scikit-learn.org/.

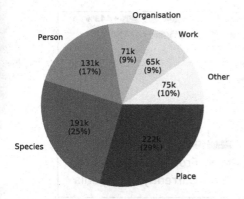

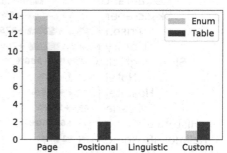

Fig. 8. Distribution of entities that are added to DBpedia based on high-level types.

Fig. 9. The 15 most important features used by XG-Boost grouped by respective feature type.

generate statements for types that are rather specific, i.e., deep in the ontology.[11] Adding all the generated type statements to DBpedia, the average type depth increases from 2.9 to 2.93. For new entities, we have an average type depth of 3.06. Figure 10 shows the increase of type statements for the subtypes of the DBpedia type *Building*. For almost all of them, we increase the amount of type statements by several orders of magnitude.

Entity Facts. Besides type statements, we also infer relational statements using the relation axioms that we generated via Cat2Ax. In total, we generate 3.8M relational statements: 3.3M for existing entities in DBpedia and 0.5M for new entities. For some previously unknown entities we discover quite large amounts of facts. For the moth species *Rioja*[12], for example, we discover the type *Insect* and information about its *class, family, order,* and *phylum*. For *Dan Stulbach*[13] we discover the type *Person* and information about his *birth place, occupation,* and *alma mater*.

Evaluation. We evaluate the correctness of both the constructed taxonomy and the inferred statements.

To validate the taxonomy we conducted an evaluation on the crowd-sourcing platform Amazon MTurk.[14] We randomly sampled 2,000 edges of the taxonomy graph and asked three annotators each whether the edge is taxonomically correct. The edges have been evaluated as correct in 96.25% (±0.86%) of the cases using

---

[11] We define the depth of a type in DBpedia as the length of its shortest path to the root type *owl:Thing*.

[12] http://caligraph.org/resource/Rioja_(moth).

[13] http://caligraph.org/resource/Dan_Stulbach.

[14] https://mturk.com.

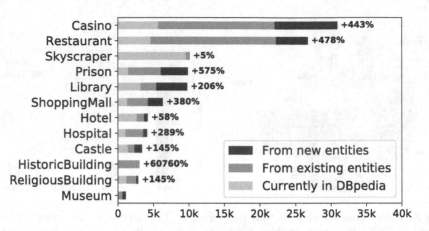

Fig. 10. Comparison of the number of type statements that are currently in DBpedia with additional statements found by our approach for all subtypes of the DBpedia type *Building*.

majority vote (with an inter-annotator agreement of 0.66 according to Fleiss' kappa [5]).

The correctness of the inferred type and relation statements are strongly dependent on the Cat2Ax approach as we use its axioms to generate the statements. The authors of Cat2Ax report a correctness of 96.8% for type axioms and 95.6% for relation axioms. For the resulting type and relation statements (after applying the axioms to the entities of the categories) they report a correctness of 90.8% and 87.2%, respectively. However, the original Cat2Ax approach does not rely on a complete taxonomy of categories but computes axioms for individual categories without considering hierarchical relationships between them. In contrast, we include information about the subcategories of a given category while generating the axioms. An inspection of 1,000 statements[15] by the authors yields a correctness of 99% (±1.2%) for existing and 98% (±1.7%) for new type statements, and 95% (±2.7%) for existing and 97% (±2.1%) for new relation statements.

Classification Models. With values of 91% and 90% the precision of the classification models is significantly lower than the correctness of the extracted type and relation statements. At first glance this is a contradiction because, although the models extract entities and not statements, a statement is obviously incorrect if it has been created for the wrong entity. But we have to consider that the training data, which was used to train and evaluate the models, has been created using distant supervision. Hence, it is likely to contain errors (e.g. due to wrong inheritance relations in the taxonomy). The fact that the final output of the processing pipeline has a higher correctness than the evaluation results of

---

[15] We inspect 250 type and relation statements for both existing and new entities.

the models imply, indicates that the models are in fact able to learn meaningful patterns from the training data.

Figure 9 shows the feature types of the 15 features that have the highest influence on the decision of the final XG-Boost models. Almost all of them are features of the type *Page*, i.e. features that describe the general shape of the list page the entities are extracted from. Features of the other types, that describe the immediate context of an entity, are used only very sparsely. This might be an indicator that, to bridge the gap in recall between the classification models and the baseline, we have to develop models that can make better use of the structure of a list page. Accordingly, we see the biggest potential in an adapted machine learning approach that, instead of classifying every entity mention in isolation, uses a holistic perspective and identifies the set of mentions that fit the list page best, given its structure.

6 Conclusion

In this paper we have presented an approach for the extraction of entities from Wikipedia list pages in order to enrich DBpedia with additional entities, type statements, and facts. We have shown that by creating a combined taxonomy from the WCG, its subgraph formed of lists, and DBpedia, we are able to train highly precise entity extraction models using distant supervision.

To extend our approach, we investigate in two directions. Firstly, we want to further improve the entity extraction by considering entities that are not explicitly tagged as such in list pages. In alignment with that we are developing a method to extract entities of a list page based on a joint likelihood instead of evaluating each entity mention in isolation. To that end we are experimenting with additional features that take the visual layout of a list page and alignment of entities into account.

As soon as we include untagged entities in the extraction, we will have to develop an entity disambiguation mechanism in order to create separate entities for homonyms. For this, we expect the distance between entities in the taxonomy to be a helpful indicator.

Secondly, we investigate an application of our extraction approach to any kind of structured markup in Wikipedia (e.g. enumerations and tables that occur anywhere in Wikipedia), and, ultimately, to markup of arbitrary pages on the web. To achieve that, we want to combine the information about entity alignment on the web page with the available semantic information as outlined in [7].

Code and results of this paper are published on http://caligraph.org.

References

1. Aprosio, A.P., Giuliano, C., Lavelli, A.: Extending the coverage of DBpedia properties using distant supervision over Wikipedia. In: NLP-DBPEDIA@ ISWC (2013)
2. Bhagavatula, C.S., et al.: Methods for exploring and mining tables on Wikipedia. In: ACM SIGKDD Workshop on Interactive Data Exploration and Analytics, pp. 18–26. ACM (2013)

3. Chu-Carroll, J., Fan, J., et al.: Textual resource acquisition and engineering. IBM J. Res. Dev. **56**(3.4), 4:1–4:11 (2012)
4. Flati, T., et al.: Two is bigger (and better) than one: the Wikipedia bitaxonomy project. In: 52nd Annual Meeting of the ACL, vol. 1, pp. 945–955 (2014)
5. Fleiss, J.L.: Measuring nominal scale agreement among many raters. Psychol. Bull. **76**(5), 378 (1971)
6. Hearst, M.A.: Automatic acquisition of hyponyms from large text corpora. In: 14th Conference on Computational Linguistics, vol. 2, pp. 539–545. ACL (1992)
7. Heist, N.: Towards knowledge graph construction from entity co-occurrence. In: Doctoral Consortium at 21st International Conference on Knowledge Engineering and Knowledge Management (2018)
8. Heist, N., Paulheim, H.: Language-agnostic relation extraction from Wikipedia abstracts. In: d'Amato, C., et al. (eds.) ISWC 2017. LNCS, vol. 10587, pp. 383–399. Springer, Cham (2017). https://doi.org/10.1007/978-3-319-68288-4_23
9. Heist, N., Paulheim, H.: Uncovering the semantics of Wikipedia categories. In: Ghidini, C., et al. (eds.) ISWC 2019. LNCS, vol. 11778, pp. 219–236. Springer, Cham (2019). https://doi.org/10.1007/978-3-030-30793-6_13
10. Hertling, S., Paulheim, H.: WebIsALOD: providing hypernymy relations extracted from the web as linked open data. In: d'Amato, C., et al. (eds.) ISWC 2017. LNCS, vol. 10588, pp. 111–119. Springer, Cham (2017). https://doi.org/10.1007/978-3-319-68204-4_11
11. Kalyanpur, A., Boguraev, B.K., et al.: Structured data and inference in DeepQA. IBM J. Res. Dev. **56**(3.4), 10:1–10:14 (2012)
12. Kuhn, P., Mischkewitz, S., Ring, N., Windheuser, F.: Type inference on Wikipedia list pages. Informatik **2016**, 1–11 (2016)
13. Lehmann, J., Isele, R., Jakob, M., et al.: DBpedia-a large-scale, multilingual knowledge base extracted from Wikipedia. Semant. Web **6**(2), 167–195 (2015)
14. Mahdisoltani, F., Biega, J., Suchanek, F.M.: YAGO3: a knowledge base from multilingual Wikipedias. In: CIDR (2013)
15. Mintz, M., et al.: Distant supervision for relation extraction without labeled data. In: Joint Conference of the 47th Annual Meeting of the ACL and the 4th International Joint Conference on NLP of the AFNLP, vol. 2, pp. 1003–1011. ACL (2009)
16. Muñoz, E., Hogan, A., Mileo, A.: Using linked data to mine RDF from Wikipedia's tables. In: 7th ACM International Conference on Web Search and Data Mining, pp. 533–542. ACM (2014)
17. Paulheim, H., Ponzetto, S.P.: Extending DBpedia with Wikipedia list pages. In: NLP-DBPEDIA@ ISWC 13 (2013)
18. Ponzetto, S.P., Navigli, R.: Large-scale taxonomy mapping for restructuring and integrating Wikipedia. In: 21st International Joint Conference on Artificial Intelligence (2009)
19. Schrage, F., Heist, N., Paulheim, H.: Extracting literal assertions for DBpedia from Wikipedia abstracts. In: Acosta, M., Cudré-Mauroux, P., Maleshkova, M., Pellegrini, T., Sack, H., Sure-Vetter, Y. (eds.) SEMANTiCS 2019. LNCS, vol. 11702, pp. 288–294. Springer, Cham (2019). https://doi.org/10.1007/978-3-030-33220-4_21
20. Töpper, G., et al.: DBpedia ontology enrichment for inconsistency detection. In: 8th International Conference on Semantic Systems, pp. 33–40. ACM (2012)
21. Wu, F., Weld, D.S.: Autonomously semantifying Wikipedia. In: 16th ACM Conference on Information and Knowledge Management, pp. 41–50. ACM (2007)

The Knowledge Graph Track at OAEI
Gold Standards, Baselines, and the Golden Hammer Bias

Sven Hertling(✉) and Heiko Paulheim

Data and Web Science Group, University of Mannheim,
B6 26, 68159 Mannheim, Germany
{sven,heiko}@informatik.uni-mannheim.de

Abstract. The Ontology Alignment Evaluation Initiative (OAEI) is an annual evaluation of ontology matching tools. In 2018, we have started the Knowledge Graph track, whose goal is to evaluate the simultaneous matching of entities and schemas of large-scale knowledge graphs. In this paper, we discuss the design of the track and two different strategies of gold standard creation. We analyze results and experiences obtained in first editions of the track, and, by revealing a hidden task, we show that all tools submitted to the track (and probably also other tracks) suffer from a bias which we name the *golden hammer bias*.

Keywords: Ontology matching · Instance matching · Knowledge graph

1 Introduction

The Ontology Alignment Evaluation Initiative (OAEI)[1] was started in 2004 as a forum to collect benchmark datasets for ontology matching tools, and a regular evaluation of those tools [4]. Over the years, new tracks with different foci have been added, e.g., for instance matching in 2009 [7], for multi-lingual ontology matching in 2012 [22], for interactive matching in 2013 [23], and for the discovery of complex alignments in 2018 [28].

The general setup of OAEI tracks is that users can download pairs of input ontologies and have to provide the correspondences (in general: pairs of equivalent classes, properties, and/or instances). Up to 2009, participants in the challenge ran their tools on their own machines and submitted the results, which gave way to over-tuning to specific tasks (i.e., finding optimal parameter sets for individual tasks rather than developing tools that deliver decent results consistently across different tracks).

From 2010 on, the format of OAEI was subsequently changed from the submission of *results* to the submission of *systems*, which where then run centrally by the organizers using the SEALS platform [30]. This also gave way for controlled measurements of computational performance. Since 2012, all tracks of OAEI are

---

[1] http://oaei.ontologymatching.org/.

© Springer Nature Switzerland AG 2020
A. Harth et al. (Eds.): ESWC 2020, LNCS 12123, pp. 343–359, 2020.
https://doi.org/10.1007/978-3-030-49461-2_20

conducted using the SEALS platform, since 2018, the HOBBIT platform is used as second platform next to SEALS [15].

In 2018, we introduced a new track, i.e., the Knowledge Graph track [1]. Since most of the other tracks focused *either* on schema or instance matching, the objective was to evaluate tools that solve both tasks in a real-world setting: as more and more knowledge graphs are developed, the discovery of links both on the instance and schema level becomes a crucial task in combining such knowledge graphs [25].

The rest of this paper is structured as follows. Section 2 describes the track, the datasets used and the two different strategies employed to create the gold standard for the 2018 and 2019 edition of the track. Section 3 discusses the results from the 2019 edition, as well as the observation of the golden hammer bias in an additional evaluation. We close with a summary and an outlook on future work.

2   Data for the Matching Tasks

The data for the knowledge graph matching track is taken from the DBkWik project [8,10]. In that project, we execute the DBpedia Extraction Framework [19] on several different Wikis from *Fandom*[2], which is one of the most popular *Wiki Farms*, comprising more than 385,000 individual Wikis totaling more than 50 million articles. The result is a multitude of disconnected knowledge graphs, i.e., one knowledge graph extracted per Wiki, where each entity is derived from one page in a Wiki. In order to fuse those into one coherent knowledge graphs, we have to identify instance matches (i.e., entities derived from pages about the same real-world entity in different Wikis) as well as schema matches (i.e., classes and properties derived from different constructs in different Wikis).

2.1   Knowledge Graphs

For the 2018 and 2019 edition of the track, we picked groups of Wikis with a high topical overlap (RuneScape, Marvel comics, Star Trek, and Star Wars). Those are depicted in Table 1. The groups cover different topics (movies, games, comics, and books)[3].

Moreover, as a hidden evaluation task for the 2019 edition, we added one more Wiki which has almost *no* topical overlap with the above, but a large likelihood of having many instances with the same name. To that end, we chose the Lyric Wiki, containing around 2M instances (mostly songs, albums, and artists). For example, there are multiple songs named *Star Wars* and *Star Trek*, which, however, should *not* be matched to the movie or series of the same name.

---

[2] http://www.fandom.com/.

[3] More details are available at http://oaei.ontologymatching.org/2019/knowledge graph/index.html.

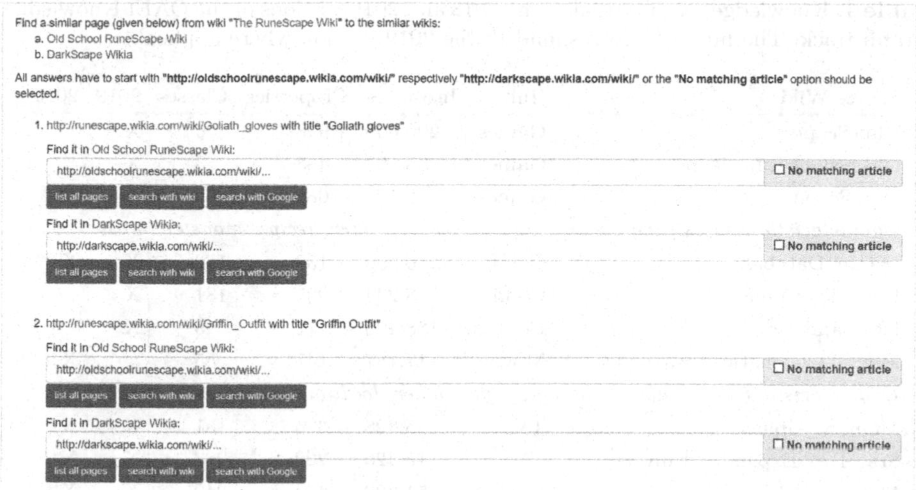

Find a.simliar page (given below) from wiki "The RuneScape Wiki" to the similar wikis:
   a. Old School RuneScape Wiki
   b. DarkScape Wikia

All answers have to start with "**http://oldschoolrunescape.wikia.com/wiki/**" respectively "**http://darkscape.wikia.com/wiki/**" or the "**No matching article**" option should be selected.

   1. http://runescape.wikia.com/wiki/Goliath_gloves with title "Goliath gloves"

      Find it in Old School RuneScape Wiki:

      http://oldschoolrunescape.wikia.com/wiki/...   ☐ No matching article

      list all pages | search with wiki | search with Google

      Find it in DarkScape Wikia:

      http://darkscape.wikia.com/wiki/...   ☐ No matching article

      list all pages | search with wiki | search with Google

   2. http://runescape.wikia.com/wiki/Griffin_Outfit with title "Griffin Outfit"

      Find it in Old School RuneScape Wiki:

      http://oldschoolrunescape.wikia.com/wiki/...   ☐ No matching article

      list all pages | search with wiki | search with Google

      Find it in DarkScape Wikia:

      http://darkscape.wikia.com/wiki/...   ☐ No matching article

      list all pages | search with wiki | search with Google

Fig. 1. Crowd-sourcing interface.

2.2   Gold Standard 2018

For creating the gold standard for evaluation, we took a two-fold approach. The schema level (i.e., classes and properties) are mapped by experts.

For mapping the instance-level, we used a crowd-sourcing approach on Amazon MTurk. As shown in Fig. 1, users were presented a page link to a Wiki page for one Wiki (these pages were randomly sampled), and asked to identify a matching page in two other Wikis. In order to ease the task, they were provided with links to the Wiki's search function and Google site search. Each task was evaluated by five crowdworkers, and we added mappings to our gold standard if the majority agreed on it. Since the task was to match an entity in one source Wiki to two target Wikis, we also add mappings *between* the two target Wikis if the entity is matched to both. This setting was executed for 3 groups of Wikis sharing the same domain and each Wiki of each group was used once as a source. Overall, the inter annotator agreement was 0.87 (according to [18], this is an *almost perfect agreement*).

The result is a partial gold standard for nine pairs of knowledge graphs, as depicted in Table 2. A special characteristic of this gold standard is that non-matching entities are also contained explicitly (i.e., crowdworkers agreed that they could not find a matching page in the other Wiki).

From Table 2, it can be observed that the gold standard contains mostly trivial matches (92.6% of the class matches, 82.4% of the property matches, and 93.6% of the instance matches) which is an exact string match of the label. One possible reason is that crowdworkers were probably not motivated to search for matching pages if they could not find them easily based on matching names, and the provision of search links to ease the task might have increased that bias. Another reason might be the random sampling of source pages. In most cases

Table 1. Knowledge Graphs used in the 2018 and 2019 editions of the OAEI Knowledge Graph track. The numbers correspond to the 2019 version where applicable.

Source Wiki	Hub	Instances	Properties	Classes	2018	2019
RuneScape	Games	200,605	1,998	106	X	
Old School RuneScape	Games	38,563	488	53	X	
DarkScape	Games	19,623	686	65	X	
Characteristic classes: item, bonus, non-player character, recipe, monster, music						
Marvel Database	Comics	210,996	139	186	X	X
Hey Kids Comics	Comics	158,234	1,925	181	X	
DC Database	Comics	128,495	177	5	X	
Marvel Cinematic Universe (mcu)	Movies	17,187	147	55		X
Characteristic classes: actor, character, filmmaker, location, music, episode, event						
Memory Alpha	TV	45,828	325	181	X	X
Star Trek Expanded Universe	TV	13,426	202	283	X	X
Memory Beta	Books	51,323	423	240	X	X
Characteristic classes: actor, individual, character, starship, comic, planet, species						
Star Wars	Movies	145,033	700	269		X
The Old Republic	Games	4,180	368	101		X
Star Wars Galaxies	Games	9,634	148	67		X
Characteristic classes: character, planet, species, battle, weapon, comic book, item						
Lyrics	Music	1,062,920	270	67		X
Characteristic classes: song, album, artist, translation, collaboration						

the page creators give the same name to a well-known concept and only a few pages have different titles. With the given sampling method, the probability to have such pages in the resulting sample is rather low.

During OAEI 2018, five systems were evaluated on the KG track: AML [5], POMap++ [17], Holontology [26], DOME [9], and three variants of LogMap (LogMap, LogMapBio, LogMapLt) [14]. Additionally, we also used a string equivalence baseline. Due to the large number of trivial correspondences, none of the systems was able to beat the simple string equivalence baseline [1].

2.3   Gold Standard 2019

For the 2019 edition of the knowledge graph track, we followed a different approach. While the schema level interlinks were still created by experts, we exploited explicit interlinks between Wikis for the instance level, pages in Wikis with links to a corresponding page in another Wiki. To that end, we selected five pairs of Wikis which have a large number of such interlinks.

Due to the fact that not all inter wiki links on a page link two pages aout the same entity, a few restrictions were made: 1) Only links in sections with

Table 2. Size of the Gold Standard used for OAEI 2018. The numbers in parentheses also count the negative mappings.

	Class		Property		Instance	
	Total	Non-trivial	Total	Non-trivial	Total	Non-trivial
darkscape-oldschoolrunescape	11 (18)	2	14 (20)	1	46 (84)	2
runescape-darkscape	15 (20)	1	10 (20)	0	73 (86)	1
runescape-oldschoolrunescape	13 (17)	1	12 (20)	1	51 (88)	4
heykidscomics-dc	2 (15)	0	10 (20)	2	25 (78)	4
marvel-dc	2 (5)	0	8 (20)	1	7 (72)	2
marvel-heykidscomics	2 (12)	0	10 (20)	2	22 (64)	1
memoryalpha-memorybeta	0 (11)	0	10 (20)	7	19 (68)	0
memoryalpha-stexpanded	0 (3)	0	9 (20)	1	9 (69)	1
memorybeta-stexpanded	0 (14)	0	8 (20)	1	12 (67)	2
Total	54 (115)	4	91 (180)	16	264 (676)	17

a header containing *link* are used e.g. as in "External links"[4], 2) all links are removed where the source page links to *more than one* page in another wiki (ensures the alignments are functional), and 3) multiple links which point to the same concept are also removed (ensures injectivity). The underlying assumption of the latter two steps is that in each wiki (similar to Wikipedia), only one page per entity (e.g., person, song, movie) exists. As a preprocessing step, for each of those links, we executed an HTTP request to resolve potential redirects. Thus we always end up with the same identifier (URL) for one concept. Like the 2018 gold standard, this gold standard is only a *partial gold standard*, but without any explicit negative mappings.

Table 3 shows the resulting gold standard. It can be observed that the fraction of non-trivial matches is considerably larger, especially on the instance level. Moreover, the absolute number of instance matches is also two magnitudes larger than in the 2018 gold standard.

3   Results and Observations

The two gold standards were used in the 2018 and 2019 editions of OAEI for a new knowledge graph track. Different tools were submitted to both editions, which allowed for a variety of insights.

In both years, the evaluation was executed on a virtual machine (VM) with 32 GB of RAM and 16 vCPUs (2.4 GHz), with Debian 9 operating system and Openjdk version 1.8.0_212, using the SEALS client (version 7.0.5). The alignments generated by the participating tools were evaluated based on precision,

---

[4] An example page with such a section is https://memory-alpha.fandom.com/wiki/William_T._Riker.

Table 3. Size of the gold standard used for OAEI 2019

	Class matches		Property matches		Instance matches	
	Total	Non-trivial	Total	Non-trivial	Total	Non-trivial
starwars-swg	5	2	20	0	1,096	528
starwars-swtor	15	3	56	6	1,358	220
mcu-marvel	2	0	11	0	1,654	726
memoryalpha-memorybeta	14	10	53	4	9,296	2,140
memoryalpha-stexpanded	13	6	41	3	1,725	274
Total	49	21	181	13	15,129	3,888

recall, and f-measure for classes, properties, and instances (each in isolation). Moreover, we report the overall precision, recall, and f-measure across all types.

As a baseline, we employed two simple string matching approaches. The source code for these baseline matchers is publicly available.[5]

3.1 Results from OAEI 2018

In 2018, only a simple string equivalence across normalized strings was used, whereas in 2019, we also incorporated similarities of the alternative labels (skos:altLabel) present in the knowledge graphs as a second baseline. These labels were generated by using all titles of redirect pages in the Wikis, and they often contain synonym or shorter versions of the original title. This should in general increase the recall but lower the precision of a matching approach. For example, *Catarina* redirects to *Kathryn Janeway* in the *memoryalpha* Wiki [6], so the baseline would consider all entities with the label *Catarina* as matches for the entity *Kathryn Janeway* derived from that Wiki.

The results for OAEI 2018 are depicted in Table 4. Precision was computed based on the explicit negative mappings present in the 2018 gold standard. Four key observations can be made:

1. Except for LogMap, LogMapLt, and AML, all participating systems could solve all tasks.
2. The runtime varies greatly, ranging from five minutes to almost four hours for solving all nine tasks.
3. Except for DOME, no matcher is capable of matching properties.
4. Overall, the string baseline is hard to beat. Only two matchers (DOME and LogMapBio) outperform the baseline for classes, none for properties and instances.

---

[5] http://oaei.ontologymatching.org/2019/results/knowledgegraph/kgBaseline Matchers.zip.

[6] https://memory-alpha.fandom.com/wiki/Special:WhatLinksHere/Kathryn_Jane way?hidelinks=1\&hidetrans=1.

The first two observations show that in principle, existing ontology matching tools can actually match knowledge graphs, although with different computational behavior.

The third observation is due to a special characteristic of the underlying datasets. While standard ontology matching tools expect OWL Lite or DL ontologies, in which properties are properly typed as `owl:ObjectProperty` and `owl:DatatypeProperty`, the DBkWik knowledge graphs have a very shallow schema which does not make that distinction. Instead, all properties are marked as `rdf:Property`.

The fourth observation may be attributed to the characteristics of the 2018 gold standard: as discussed above, a (probably overestimated) large fraction of matches is trivial, so that trivial matching approaches have an unrealistic advantage in this setup. This observation, together with the desire to have a larger-scale gold standard, lead to the new gold standard used in the 2019 edition.

3.2   Results from OAEI 2019

For the evaluation of the 2019 tracks, we did not have any explicit negative mappings. Hence, we exploited the fact that our partial gold standard contained only 1:1 correspondences, and we further assume that in each knowledge graph, only one representation of each entity exists (typically, a Wiki does not contain two pages about the same real-world entity). This means that if we have a correspondence $<a, b>$ in our gold standard, and a matcher produces a correspondence $<a, b'>$ to a different entity, we count that as a false positive. The count of false negatives is only increased if we have a 1:1 correspondence and it is not found by a matcher. The whole source code for generating the evaluation results is also available.[7]

As a pre-evaluation check, we evaluated all SEALS participants in the OAEI (even those not registered for the track) on a very small matching task.[8] This revealed that not all systems were able to handle the task, and in the end, only the following systems were evaluated: AGM [21], AML [6], DOME [11], FCAMap-KG [3], LogMap [13], LogMapBio, LogMapKG, LogMapLt, POMap++ [16], Wiktionary [24]. Out of those, only LogMapBio, LogMapLt and POMap++ were not registered for this track. Holontology, which participated in 2018, did not submit a system to OAEI 2019.

In comparison to 2018, more matchers participated and returned meaningful correspondences. Moreover, there are systems and system variations which especially focus on the knowledge graph track, e.g., FCAMap-KG and LogMapKG.

Table 5 shows the aggregated results for all systems in 2019, including the number of tasks in which they were able to generate a non-empty alignment (#tasks) and the average number of generated correspondences in those tasks (size). Like in the previous year, three systems (AML, DOME, and LogMapLt)

---

[7] http://oaei.ontologymatching.org/2019/results/knowledgegraph/matching-eval-trackspecific.zip.

[8] http://oaei.ontologymatching.org/2019/results/knowledgegraph/small_test.zip.

Table 4. Knowledge graph track results for 2018, divided into class, property, instance, and overall correspondences. [1]

System	Time	# tasks	Size	Prec.	F-m.	Rec.
Class performance						
AML	24:34:08	5	11.6	0.85 (0.85)	0.64 (0.87)	0.51 (0.88)
POMAP++	0:07:18	9	15.1	0.79	0.74	0.69
Holontology	0:05:18	9	16.8	0.80	0.83	0.87
DOME	3:49:07	9	16.0	0.73	0.73	0.73
LogMap	3:54:43	7	21.7	0.66 (0.66)	0.77 (0.80)	0.91 (1.00)
LogMapBio	0:39:00	9	22.1	0.68	0.81	1.00
LogMapLt	0:08:20	6	22.0	0.61 (0.61)	0.72 (0.76)	0.87 (1.00)
Baseline	0:06:52	9	18.9	0.75	0.79	0.84
Property performance						
AML	24:34:08	5	0.0	0.0	0.0	0.0
POMAP++	0:07:18	9	0.0	0.0	0.0	0.0
Holontology	0:05:18	9	0.0	0.0	0.0	0.0
DOME	3:49:07	9	207.3	0.86	0.84	0.81
LogMap	3:54:43	7	0.0	0.0	0.0	0.0
LogMapBio	0:39:00	9	0.0	0.0	0.0	0.0
LogMapLt	0:08:20	6	0.0	0.0	0.0	0.0
Baseline	0:06:52	9	213.8	0.86	0.84	0.82
Instance performance						
AML	24:34:08	5	82380.9	0.16 (0.16)	0.23 (0.26)	0.38 (0.63)
POMAP++	0:07:18	9	0.0	0.0	0.0	0.0
Holontology	0:05:18	9	0.0	0.0	0.0	0.0
DOME	3:49:07	9	15688.7	0.61	0.61	0.61
LogMap	3:54:43	7	97081.4	0.08 (0.08)	0.14 (0.15)	0.81 (0.93)
LogMapBio	0:39:00	9	0.0	0.0	0.0	0.0
LogMapLt	0:08:20	6	82388.3	0.39 (0.39)	0.52 (0.56)	0.76 (0.96)
Baseline	0:06:52	9	17743.3	0.59	0.69	0.82
Overall performance						
AML	24:34:08	5	102471.1	0.19 (0.19)	0.23 (0.28)	0.31 (0.52)
POMAP++	0:07:18	9	16.9	0.79	0.14	0.08
Holontology	0:05:18	9	18.8	0.80	0.17	0.10
DOME	3:49:07	9	15912.0	0.68	0.68	0.67
LogMap	3:54:43	7	97104.8	0.09 (0.09)	0.16 (0.16)	0.64 (0.74)
LogMapBio	0:39:00	9	24.1	0.68	0.19	0.11
LogMapLt	0:08:20	6	88893.1	0.42 (0.42)	0.49 (0.54)	0.60 (0.77)
Baseline	0:06:52	9	17976.0	0.65	0.73	0.82

Table 5. Knowledge graph track results for 2019, divided into class, property, instance, and overall correspondences. [2]

System	Time	# tasks	Size	Prec.	F-m.	Rec.
Class performance						
AGM	10:47:38	5	14.6	0.23	0.09	0.06
AML	0:45:46	4	27.5	0.78 (0.98)	0.69 (0.86)	0.61 (0.77)
baselineAltLabel	0:11:48	5	16.4	1.0	0.74	0.59
baselineLabel	0:12:30	5	16.4	1.0	0.74	0.59
DOME	1:05:26	4	22.5	0.74 (0.92)	0.62 (0.77)	0.53 (0.66)
FCAMap-KG	1:14:49	5	18.6	1.0	0.82	0.70
LogMap	0:15:43	5	26.0	0.95	0.84	0.76)
LogMapBio	2:31:01	5	26.0	0.95	0.84	0.76)
LogMapKG	2:26:14	5	26.0	0.95	0.84	0.76)
LogMapLt	0:07:28	4	23.0	0.80 (1.0)	0.56 (0.70)	0.43 (0.54)
POMAP++	0:14:39	5	2.0	0.0	0.0	0.0
Wiktionary	0:20:14	5	21.4	1.0	0.8	0.67
Property performance						
AGM	10:47:38	5	49.4	0.66	0.32	0.21
AML	0:45:46	4	58.2	0.72 (0.91)	0.59 (0.73)	0.49 (0.62)
baselineAltLabel	0:11:48	5	47.8	0.99	0.79	0.66
baselineLabel	0:12:30	5	47.8	0.99	0.79	0.66
DOME	1:05:26	4	75.5	0.79 (0.99)	0.77 (0.96)	0.75 (0.93)
FCAMap-KG	1:14:49	5	69.0	1.0	0.98	0.96
LogMap	0:15:43	5	0.0	0.0	0.0	0.0
LogMapBio	2:31:01	5	0.0	0.0	0.0	0.0
LogMapKG	2:26:14	5	0.0	0.0	0.0	0.0
LogMapLt	0:07:28	4	0.0	0.0	0.0	0.0
POMAP++	0:14:39	5	0.0	0.0	0.0	0.0
Wiktionary	0:20:14	5	75.8	0.97	0.98	0.98
Instance performance						
AGM	10:47:38	5	5169.0	0.48	0.25	0.17
AML	0:45:46	4	7529.8	0.72 (0.90)	0.71 (0.88)	0.69 (0.86)
baselineAltLabel	0:11:48	5	4674.2	0.89	0.84	0.80
baselineLabel	0:12:30	5	3641.2	0.95	0.81	0.71
DOME	1:05:26	4	4895.2	0.74 (0.92)	0.70 (0.88)	0.67 (0.84)
FCAMap-KG	1:14:49	5	4530.6	0.90	0.84	0.79
LogMap	0:15:43	5	0.0	0.0	0.0	0.0
LogMapBio	2:31:01	5	0.0	0.0	0.0	0.0
LogMapKG	2:26:14	5	29190.4	0.40	0.54	0.86
LogMapLt	0:07:28	4	6653.8	0.73 (0.91)	0.67 (0.84)	0.62 (0.78)
POMAP++	0:14:39	5	0.0	0.0	0.0	0.0
Wiktionary	0:20:14	5	3483.6	0.91	0.79	0.70

Table 5. (*continued*)

System	Time	# tasks	Size	Prec.	F-m.	Rec.
Overall performance						
AGM	10:47:38	5	5233.2	0.48	0.25	0.17
AML	0:45:46	4	7615.5	0.72 (0.90)	0.70 (0.88)	0.69 (0.86)
baselineAltLabel	0:11:48	5	4739.0	0.89	0.84	0.80
baselineLabel	0:12:30	5	3706.0	0.95	0.81	0.71
DOME	1:05:26	4	4994.8	0.74 (0.92)	0.70 (0.88)	0.67 (0.84)
FCAMap-KG	1:14:49	5	4792.6	0.91	0.85	0.79
LogMap	0:15:43	5	26.0	0.95	0.01	0.0
LogMapBio	2:31:01	5	26.0	0.95	0.01	0.0
LogMapKG	2:26:14	5	29216.4	0.40	0.54	0.84
LogMapLt	0:07:28	4	6676.8	0.73 (0.91)	0.66 (0.83)	0.61 (0.76)
POMAP++	0:14:39	5	19.4	0.0	0.0	0.0
Wiktionary	0:20:14	5	3581.8	0.91	0.8	0.71

were not able to solve all tasks. Again, the runtime differences are drastic, ranging from less than ten minutes to more than ten hours.

In addition to the global average precision, F-measure, and recall results, in which tasks where systems produced empty alignments were counted, we also computed F-measure and recall ignoring empty alignments which are shown in parentheses in the table, where applicable.

Nearly all systems were able to generate class correspondences. In terms of F-Measure, AML is the best one (when considering only completed test cases). Many matchers were also able to beat the baseline. The highest recall is about 0.77 which shows that some class correspondences are not easy to find.

In comparison to the 2018 edition, more matchers are able to produce property correspondences. Only the systems of the LogMap family and POMAP++ do not return any alignments. While Wiktionary and FCAMap-KG achieve an F-Measure of 0.98, other systems need more improvement here because they are not capable of beating the baseline (mostly due to low recall).

With respect to instance correspondences, AML and DOME are the best performing systems, but they outperform the baselines only by a small margin. On average, the systems returned between 3,000 and 8,000 instance alignments. Only LogMapKG returned nearly 30,000 mappings. The latter is interesting because LogMapKG is developed to prefer 1:1 alignments, but deviates here. Thus, we conducted a deeper analysis of the alignment arity. The results are shown in Table 6. To account for matchers which return a mix of 1:n, n:1 or n:m mappings, not only the arity itself is reported, but also the count how often each appear in a mapping. For computing those numbers, the source of each correspondence is analyzed. If it links to only one concept, it counts as 1:1 if no other source is mapped to it, and otherwise as n:1. If the source links

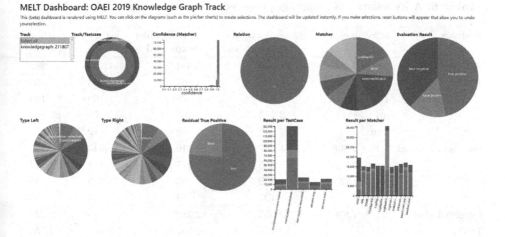

MELT Dashboard: OAEI 2019 Knowledge Graph Track

This (beta) dashboard is rendered using MELT. You can click on the diagrams (such as the pie/bar charts) to create selections. The dashboard will be updated instantly. If you make selections, reset buttons will appear that allow you to undo yourselection.

Fig. 2. Dashboard for analyzing matcher results.

to multiple targets, it counts as 1:n and if one of those targets participate in multiple correspondences, the count for n:m is increased.

A strict 1:1 mapping is only returned by AGM, DOME and POMAP++, and the string matching baseline using only labels. LogMap and LogMapBio return n:1 mappings in two test cases, whereas FCAMap-KG, Wiktionary, as well as the string matching baseline utilizing alternative labels, return a few n:m mappings in all test cases. AML and LogMapLt returned even more of those cases, and LogMapKG has the highest amount of n:m mappings. As discussed above, this is somewhat unexpected because the tool is tailored towards a track focusing only on 1:1 mappings.

For a further detailed analysis of the track results, an online dashboard[9] is implemented. The user interface is shown in Fig. 2. It is mainly intended for matcher developers to analyze their results and improve their systems. The basis is a table of all correspondences together with the evaluation result. The charts at the top allow a filtering of these correspondences by different criteria which can also be combined. The code for generating the dashboard is included in the MELT framework [12] to enable system developers to generate their own analyses.

Some of the key observations of the 2019 edition of the knowledge graph track include:

1. There is no one-size-fits-all solution. Instead, we can observe that different matchers produce the best results for classes, properties, and instances.
2. Scalability is an issue, since not all matchers are capable of solving all tracks, and the runtime varies drastically between the different systems.

---

[9] http://oaei.ontologymatching.org/2019/results/knowledgegraph/ knowledge_graph_dashboard.html.

Table 6. Arity analysis of mappings produced in the knowledge graph track 2019.

Matcher	arity	mcu-marvel	memoryalpha-memorybeta	memoryalpha-stexpanded	starwars-swg	starwars-swtor
AMG	1:1	9,085	11,449	3,684	1,101	847
AML	1:1	–	14,935	3,568	3,323	3,755
	1:n	–	243	78	169	164
	n:1	–	3,424	281	74	103
	n:m	–	240	69	12	24
baselineAltLabel	1:1	2,368	11,497	2,710	1,535	2,469
	1:n	54	855	277	114	131
	n:1	150	1,059	195	59	58
	n:m	2	103	48	4	7
baselineLabel	1:1	1,879	10,552	2,582	1,245	2,272
DOME	1:1	–	12,475	2,727	2,024	2,753
FCAMap-KG	1:1	2,510	12,423	2,985	1,828	2,620
	1:n	28	288	94	240	125
	n:1	138	382	76	47	37
	n:m	6	78	19	25	14
LogMap	1:1	12	32	33	14	29
	n:1	0	8	0	0	2
LogMapBio	1:1	12	32	33	14	29
	n:1	0	8	0	0	2
LogMapKG	1:1	2,919	10,453	2,600	1,663	2,122
	1:n	1,363	4,741	2,857	6,596	7,797
	n:1	3,207	2,963	1,016	410	218
	n:m	33,593	36,382	9,089	6,668	9,425
LogMapLt	1:1	–	12,935	3,349	2,500	3,217
	1:n	–	270	119	205	293
	n:1	–	2,881	36	50	95
	n:m	–	602	73	52	30
POMAP++	1:1	9	20	25	14	29
Wiktionary	1:1	1,757	9,274	1,975	1,494	2,321
	1:n	26	246	110	72	104
	n:1	74	162	58	18	14
	n:m	8	156	24	8	8

3.3   Hidden Task in OAEI 2019 and the Golden Hammer Bias

So far, we have only analyzed settings in which matchers were provided with two knowledge graphs from the same domain. In other words: it is already known that some correspondences are to be found. This is the usual setup in OAEI tracks, where correspondences between the input ontologies are always expected.

Table 7. Test cases with lyric wiki as target. For each matcher and test case 50 correspondences were analyzed.

Matcher	mcu lyrics		memoryalpha lyrics		starwars lyrics	
	matches	precision	matches	precision	matches	precision
AML	2,642	0.12	7,691	0.00	3,417	0.00
baselineAltLabel	588	0.44	1,332	0.02	1,582	0.04
baselineLabel	513	0.54	1,006	0.06	1,141	0.06
FCAMap-KG	755	0.40	2,039	0.14	2,520	0.02
LogMapKG	29,238	0.02	–	–	–	–
LogMapLt	2,407	0.08	7,199	0.00	2,728	0.04
Wiktionary	971	0.12	3,457	0.02	4,026	0.00

In many real world scenarios, we cannot make that assumption. We refer to those scenarios as *open* scenarios, in contrast to *closed domain* scenarios, where the input ontologies share a domain. All OAEI tracks evaluate the latter kind, i.e., using ontologies from the conference or medical domain etc. In contrast, the matching in DBkWik, where thousands of knowledge graphs from different domains are to be integrated, is an open scenario. In such a scenario, where thousands of knowledge graphs co-exist, a random pair of two knowledge graphs may or may not have a certain share of entities in common.

In order to find out whether tools are over-tuned towards closed-domain scenarios, we introduced a *hidden track* to the 2019 edition, i.e., an evaluation which we did not inform the participants about. For this track, we used the single graph within the DBkWik set with the largest number of instances – i.e., the one extracted from *LyricWiki*[10], which has more than 1.7M instances (we took a sample of about one million instances to reduce the runtime of the matchers). Since the main classes are songs, albums, and music artists, we expect a rather low overlap with the other graphs in the KG track, which come from different domains. At the same time, we expect a high overlap of trivial string matches, since there are songs, albums, or artists called *Star Trek*, *Star Wars*, etc., contained in the KG.

All matchers which participated in the knowledge graph track in 2019 were executed on three test cases. Those test cases always have the lyrics Wiki has the target and the following three Wikis as a source: Marvel Cinematic Universe (mcu), Memory Alpha and Star Wars. Since we cannot rule out true positives completely, we evaluated the precision manually by sampling 50 correspondences from the result sets for each matcher and testcase, which totals more than 1k samples (7 matchers × 3 test cases × 50 samples). With this sample size the maximum error is 15% at a 0.95 confidence level. A web front end depicted in Fig. 3 is developed to help the annotators judging if two concepts are the same. It shows two images of the corresponding Wiki page (which are created with

---

[10] https://lyrics.fandom.com/.

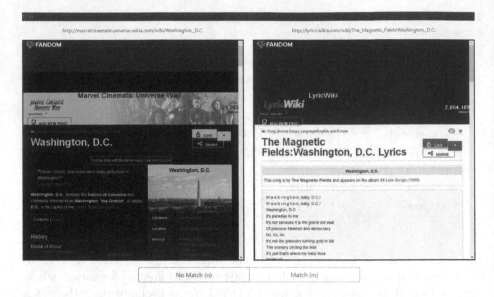

Fig. 3. User interface for judging if two Wiki pages correspond to the same concept.

phantomjs[11]) to provide a constant, browser-independent visualization, and to prevent clicking on links.

Not all matchers are able to execute this hidden task. LogMap, LogMapBio and POMAP++ find only schema mappings and DOME needs more than the provided memory (even when provided with 100 GB of RAM). AGM throws a tool exception, and LogMapKG is only able to finish one test case (in all other cases it runs into a 24 h timeout). These findings, involving a larger knowledge graph (despite smaller than, e.g., DBpedia or Wikidata) illustrate that scalability is still an issue.

The results are shown in Table 7. We can see that all matchers find a considerable amount of instance matches, on average more than one thousand per pair of knowledge graphs. At the same time, the precision is really low. If we contrast those precision figures with the ones in Table 5, we can observe some crucial differences. For all matchers, including the baselines, the precision figures in the latter are significantly higher than those in the hidden track.

This illustrates that all tools make an implicit assumption that some overlap between the ontologies provided exists, and create a certain amount of nonsensical results if that assumption is not met. We can observe this very drastically in the case of matching memoryalpha to lyrics, where the tools match between 2% and 17% of the instances in the smaller Wiki, with most of those matchings being false positives.

We refer to this observation as the *golden hammer bias*: in evaluation setups such as the OAEI (as well as most other evaluations of matching tools), the

---

[11] https://phantomjs.org/.

performance of the matching tools is systematically over-estimated. In contrast, when applying a tool in an open scenario where a positive outcome is not guaranteed a priori, the approaches at hand assume such a positive outcome nevertheless, and, hence, cannot solve the task properly. In particular, this is the case for LogMapKG, which creates a very large number of mappings at a very low precision, at least for the task it is able to solve.

The case of mcu is particularly interesting, since a significant portion of true matches can actually be found here (e.g., songs used in movies). Nevertheless, the precision of all tools is much lower than the precision on tasks in pure closed domain scenarios.

As a conclusion, we can see that existing matching tools cannot be used in open domain scenarios out of the box. Further filtering or a priori class-wise or even knowledge-graph wise blocking would be necessary, although, in the latter case, a significant amount of true positives, like in the case of mcu, would be missed.

4   Conclusion and Outlook

In this paper, we have described the design of knowledge graph track at the OAEI which focuses on the simultaneous matching of instances and schemas. We have introduced the datasets based on the DBkWik knowledge graph extracted from thousands of Wikis, and we have discussed two different strategies for creating the gold standard for instance links – i.e., by crowdsourcing and by utilizing explicit interlinks between Wikis. Moreover, we have introduced a hidden track to inspect the effect of tools expecting a positive outcome of a task, which we named the *golden hammer bias*.

From the results in 2018 and 2019, we can make different observations. First, the task is inherently hard, with most of the tools outperforming a simple string matching baseline only by a small margin. Second, there are strategies for individual subtasks – i.e., matching classes, properties, and instances – which clearly outperform others, including the baseline, but no tool implements a strategy that consistently outperforms the others. Third, many tools have difficulties handling larger-scale input data, i.e., knowledge graphs with millions of instances.

An additional evaluation using a hidden track revealed yet another issue with current knowledge graph matching tools. All of them make the tacit assumptions that the knowledge graphs to be matched have something in common. When confronted with two unrelated knowledge graphs, we have shown that they produce thousands of mostly false matches. We call this effect the *golden hammer bias* – the tools are applied without considering whether they are actually applicable.

Since we observe a growing number of tools that use supervised methods for matching knowledge graphs, we plan to create a sub-track which supports this setting, e.g., by providing separate training, testing, and validation sets.

In sum, those findings show that the task of knowledge graph matching is far from being solved. With our ongoing evaluation efforts – the KG track will be part of OAEI 2020 again – we provide a testbed for new and improved solutions in that field. Moreover, a few approaches for the task of knowledge graph matching have been published in the recent past (e.g., [20,27,29]), which have been evaluated on different datasets (and in closed domain settings only), hence, their results are not directly comparable. By providing a generic benchmark including both open and closed domain settings, we enable a more systematic comparison for such works in the future.

References

1. Algergawy, A., et al.: Results of the ontology alignment evaluation initiative 2018. In: OM@ISWC, vol. 2288, pp. 76–116 (2018)
2. Algergawy, A., et al.: Results of the ontology alignment evaluation initiative 2019. In: OM@ISWC, vol. 2536, pp. 46–85 (2019)
3. Chang, F., Chen, G., Zhang, S.: FCAMap-KG results for OAEI 2019. In: OM@ISWC, vol. 2536, pp. 138–145 (2019)
4. Euzenat, J., Meilicke, C., Stuckenschmidt, H., Shvaiko, P., Trojahn, C.: Ontology alignment evaluation initiative: six years of experience. In: Spaccapietra, S. (ed.) Journal on Data Semantics XV. LNCS, vol. 6720, pp. 158–192. Springer, Heidelberg (2011). https://doi.org/10.1007/978-3-642-22630-4_6
5. Faria, D., Pesquita, C., Santos, E., Palmonari, M., Cruz, I.F., Couto, F.M.: The AgreementMakerLight ontology matching system. In: Meersman, R., et al. (eds.) OTM 2013. LNCS, vol. 8185, pp. 527–541. Springer, Heidelberg (2013). https://doi.org/10.1007/978-3-642-41030-7_38
6. Faria, D., Pesquita, C., Tervo, T., Couto, F.M., Cruz, I.F.: AML and AMLC results for OAEI 2019. In: OM@ISWC, vol. 2536, pp. 101–106 (2019)
7. Ferrara, A., Nikolov, A., Noessner, J., Scharffe, F.: Evaluation of instance matching tools: the experience of OAEI. Web Semant. Sci. Serv. Agents World Wide Web 21, 49–60 (2013)
8. Hertling, S., Paulheim, H.: DBkWik: a consolidated knowledge graph from thousands of wikis. In: 2018 IEEE International Conference on Big Knowledge (ICBK), pp. 17–24. IEEE (2018)
9. Hertling, S., Paulheim, H.: Dome results for OAEI 2018. In: OM@ISWC, vol. 2288, pp. 144–151 (2018)
10. Hertling, S., Paulheim, H.: DBkWik: extracting and integrating knowledge from thousands of Wikis. Knowl. Inf. Syst. 62, 1–22 (2019)
11. Hertling, S., Paulheim, H.: DOME results for OAEI 2019. In: OM@ISWC, vol. 2536, pp. 123–130 (2019)
12. Hertling, S., Portisch, J., Paulheim, H.: Melt-matching evaluation toolkit. In: SEMANTICS (2019)
13. Jiménez-Ruiz, E.: LogMap family participation in the OAEI 2019. In: OM@ISWC, vol. 2536, pp. 160–163 (2019)
14. Jiménez-Ruiz, E., Cuenca Grau, B.: LogMap: logic-based and scalable ontology matching. In: Aroyo, L., et al. (eds.) ISWC 2011. LNCS, vol. 7031, pp. 273–288. Springer, Heidelberg (2011). https://doi.org/10.1007/978-3-642-25073-6_18
15. Jiménez-Ruiz, E., et al.: Introducing the HOBBIT platform into the ontology alignment evaluation campaign. In: Ontology Matching (2018)
16. Laadhar, A., Ghozzi, F., Megdiche, I., Ravat, F., Teste, O., Gargouri, F.: POMap++ results for OAEI 2019: fully automated machine learning approach for ontology matching. In: OM@ISWC, vol. 2536, pp. 169–174 (2019)

17. Laadhar, A., Ghozzi, F., Megdiche Bousarsar, I., Ravat, F., Teste, O., Gargouri, F.: OAEI 2018 results of POMap++. In: OM@ISWC, vol. 2288, pp. 192–196 (2018)
18. Landis, J.R., Koch, G.G.: The measurement of observer agreement for categorical data. Biometrics **33**, 159–174 (1977)
19. Lehmann, J., et al.: DBpedia - a large-scale, multilingual knowledge base extracted from Wikipedia. Semant. Web J. **6**(2), 167–195 (2013)
20. Li, C., Cao, Y., Hou, L., Shi, J., Li, J., Chua, T.S.: Semi-supervised entity alignment via joint knowledge embedding model and cross-graph model. In: Proceedings of the 2019 Conference on Empirical Methods in Natural Language Processing and the 9th International Joint Conference on Natural Language Processing (EMNLP-IJCNLP), pp. 2723–2732 (2019)
21. Lütke, A.: AnyGraphMatcher submission to the OAEI knowledge graph challenge 2019. In: OM@ISWC, vol. 2536, pp. 86–93 (2019)
22. Meilicke, C., et al.: MultiFarm: a benchmark for multilingual ontology matching. Web Semant. Sci. Serv. Agents World Wide Web **15**, 62–68 (2012)
23. Paulheim, H., Hertling, S., Ritze, D.: Towards evaluating interactive ontology matching tools. In: Cimiano, P., Corcho, O., Presutti, V., Hollink, L., Rudolph, S. (eds.) ESWC 2013. LNCS, vol. 7882, pp. 31–45. Springer, Heidelberg (2013). https://doi.org/10.1007/978-3-642-38288-8_3
24. Portisch, J., Hladik, M., Paulheim, H.: Wiktionary matcher. In: OM@ISWC, vol. 2536, pp. 181–188 (2019)
25. Ringler, D., Paulheim, H.: One knowledge graph to rule them all? Analyzing the differences between DBpedia, YAGO, Wikidata & co. In: Kern-Isberner, G., Fürnkranz, J., Thimm, M. (eds.) KI 2017. LNCS (LNAI), vol. 10505, pp. 366–372. Springer, Cham (2017). https://doi.org/10.1007/978-3-319-67190-1_33
26. Roussille, P., Megdiche Bousarsar, I., Teste, O., Trojahn, C.: Holontology: results of the 2018 OAEI evaluation campaign. In: OM@ISWC, vol. 2288, pp. 167–172 (2018)
27. Sun, Z., Hu, W., Zhang, Q., Qu, Y.: Bootstrapping entity alignment with knowledge graph embedding. In: IJCAI, pp. 4396–4402 (2018)
28. Thiéblin, E., Cheatham, M., Trojahn, C., Zamazal, O., Zhou, L.: The first version of the OAEI complex alignment benchmark (2018)
29. Trisedya, B.D., Qi, J., Zhang, R.: Entity alignment between knowledge graphs using attribute embeddings. In: Proceedings of the AAAI Conference on Artificial Intelligence, vol. 33, pp. 297–304 (2019)
30. Wrigley, S.N., García-Castro, R., Nixon, L.: Semantic evaluation at large scale (seals). In: Proceedings of the 21st International Conference on World Wide Web. pp. 299–302. ACM (2012)

Detecting Synonymous Properties
by Shared Data-Driven Definitions

Jan-Christoph Kalo$^{(\boxtimes)}$, Stephan Mennicke, Philipp Ehler, and Wolf-Tilo Balke

Institut für Informationssysteme, Technische Universität Braunschweig,
Mühlenpfordtstraße 23, 38106 Braunschweig, Germany
{kalo,mennicke,balke}@ifis.cs.tu-bs.de, p.ehler@tu-bs.de

Abstract. Knowledge graphs have become an essential source of entity-centric information for modern applications. Today's KGs have reached a size of billions of RDF triples extracted from a variety of sources, including structured sources and text. While this definitely improves completeness, the inherent variety of sources leads to severe heterogeneity, negatively affecting data quality by introducing duplicate information. We present a novel technique for detecting synonymous properties in large knowledge graphs by mining interpretable definitions of properties using association rule mining. Relying on such shared definitions, our technique is able to mine even synonym rules that have only little support in the data. In particular, our extensive experiments on DBpedia and Wikidata show that our rule-based approach can outperform state-of-the-art knowledge graph embedding techniques, while offering good interpretability through shared logical rules.

Keywords: Synonym detection · Association rule mining · Knowledge graphs

1 Introduction

In recent years, knowledge graphs have gained more attention because of the popularity of projects like the Google Knowledge Graph [5], Wikidata [25], DBpedia [2], Freebase [3], and YAGO [22]. The size of these knowledge graphs nowadays comprises hundreds of millions of entities associated by ten thousands of properties, providing a comprehensive knowledge repository for several modern applications, e.g., semantic search, question answering and natural language understanding.

The size of these knowledge graphs has steadily been growing over the last years, due to advances in relation extraction and open information extraction. Often large knowledge graphs are created manually in collaborative knowledge graph projects [25], automatically by extracting information from text or tables [2], by integrating existing knowledge into a single ontology, or by a combination of these three methods. However, integrating knowledge from various

© Springer Nature Switzerland AG 2020
A. Harth et al. (Eds.): ESWC 2020, LNCS 12123, pp. 360–375, 2020.
https://doi.org/10.1007/978-3-030-49461-2_21

sources and by different curators into a single knowledge graph comes with serious heterogeneity issues in practice. Particularly, duplicate concepts, either entities, classes or properties, may cause problems in subsequent querying. As an example, DBpedia contains at least 19 different IRIs for the property `birthplace` ranging from synonymous properties as `placeOfBirth` to French-named properties like `lieuDeNaissance`. Some of them are can be found in thousands of triples, whereas others are very rare, only being used in a couple of triples. But all of them hamper applications working with the data and may lead to incorrect and incomplete query results.

These *synonyms* may either be prevented by controlled vocabularies or strict manual supervision mechanisms as for example seen in Wikidata, or by data cleaning methods that are able to automatically identify synonyms from the data in an efficient way. Previous work has shown that property synonyms can automatically be identified by either frequent item set mining-based techniques [1] or by knowledge graph embedding-based techniques as in one of our previous works [14]. Whereas frequent item set mining lacks in precision, embedding-based techniques usually show a high quality, but are not interpretable. Furthermore, knowledge graph embeddings have been shown to have difficulties in correctly representing closely related properties: most embeddings for example will identify **north** and **south** as synonymous. Also the lack of interpretability is problematic, when the approach is used in a semi-automatic manner to support manual data cleaning.

In this work, we present an interpretable and scalable method for data-driven synonym detection in large-scale knowledge graphs that mines equivalent property definitions using rule mining techniques. We have developed a procedure that mines logical rules in the form of $birthplace(x, y) \Leftrightarrow placeOfBirth(x, y)$ indirectly, such that the rule does not need to be directly supported by triples. That means `birthplace` and `placeOfBirth` do not need to occur for the same entity pairs, but the respective represented concepts need to have a shared definition. Our mining technique is thus able to find synonyms that occur in thousands of triples as well as very rare synonyms with quite high quality. In fact, our synonym detection quality outperforms existing embedding-based techniques, while offering good explainability. For every synonym pair that has been found, our method provides similarities and dissimilarities of the properties in the form of logical rules.

The contributions of this work can be shortly summarized as follows:

- We develop a novel technique for synonym detection based on rule mining, finding and matching property definitions in a data-driven fashion.
- We perform extensive experiments on Wikidata and DBpedia outperforming state-of-the-art techniques for synonym detection, while offering explainable results in the form of shared definitions.
- For reproducibility, we provide all our source code, datasets, and results in a publicly available Github repository[1].

---

[1] https://github.com/JanKalo/RuleAlign.

2 Related Work

Synonym Detection in Knowledge Graphs. So far there is only little research on detecting synonyms in knowledge graphs or RDF data. An early work, on synonymous predicates for query expansion uses frequent item set mining [1]. Given a knowledge graph, for each property, they mine frequent item sets, consisting of object entities. Properties with high overlap with regard to their objects, but low overlap in their subjects are identified as synonym. However, another work has shown that synonyms often cannot be identified by this approach, because they have no overlap in their extension [14].

To tackle this problem, in a previous work, we have proposed a technique based on knowledge graph embeddings [14]. We trained knowledge graph embeddings and compute similarities between properties and use an outlier detection to separate synonyms from only similar properties. This approach is highly dependent on the quality of the embeddings, which varies massively from property to property, from knowledge graph to knowledge graph and from embedding model to embedding model. Furthermore, the results are not interpretable and therefore it is hardly foreseeable for properties, whether synonym detection works well and where it does not. To overcome these drawbacks, we have developed a technique going back to using a symbolic approach based on explicit feature representations in the form of logical rules.

Both approaches, frequent item set mining [1] and knowledge graph embeddings [14] are evaluated and compared to our technique in the experimental section of the paper.

Ontology Matching is about identifying corresponding concepts in two (or more) ontologies or knowledge graphs. Particularly the Ontology Alignment Evaluation Initiative (OAEI) at the Ontology Matching Workshop co-located with the International Semantic Web Conference plays an important role in advancing ontology matching research[2]. Ontology matching systems are primarily concerned with matching corresponding entities and classes from two or more distinct RDF datasets [10,12,13]. Some systems are also capable of matching properties [9,21]. Techniques often heavily rely on string metrics between URLs and labels, but also on structural graph measures.

In contrast to synonym detection, ontology matching systems usually can only align two distinct knowledge graphs and heavily rely on some existing correspondences between these two [21]. Finding duplicate information (e.g. property synonyms) within a single knowledge graph is therefore often not possible. Furthermore, several techniques are relying on manually built ontologies in OWL [12,13]. Heterogeneous real-world knowledge graphs however, often do not provide high quality ontological information.

Open Knowledge Graph Canonicalization. Building knowledge graphs from text is a well researched topic in the natural language processing community. One approach is to rely on open information extraction techniques that extract triples

---

[2] http://om2019.ontologymatching.org/.

directly from text, without sticking to some fixed vocabulary provided by an ontology or knowledge graph [17]. However, this often leads to heterogeneity issues like duplicate entities and paraphrased properties. Cleaning the extracted entity and property mentions from text is known under the term knowledge graph canonicalization [6, 24]. In [6], synonym property mentions from text are identified by equivalence rules among these properties. But in contrast to our approach, their technique only mines rules that are supported by the data. This indeed works well for canonicalization where triple stem directly from text, but not for synonym detection in existing knowledge graphs. Also CESI [24] mines this kind of synonym rules as side information. Their main method however uses knowledge graph embeddings on the textual mentions of properties to canonicalize them. A comparable technique has been explored in our previous work for synonym detection in knowledge graphs and is evaluated in our experimental section [14].

Relational Learning. Representing properties in some feature space is an important topic in the relational learning domain. Relational learning in general is about machine learning from relational data. In context of knowledge graphs, relational learning techniques are usually used for knowledge base completion, i.e. predicting triples from existing knowledge [18].

Recent works in knowledge graph completion rely on so called knowledge graph embeddings [4, 19, 23]. Entities and properties are represented as vectors/matrices satisfying mathematical expressions given by a model. They are usually used to predict new triples. Furthermore, the semantic similarity between properties may be measured by computing similarity metrics between these embeddings. As previously mentioned, these embeddings may be used for synonym detection, but have some problems [14].

Other techniques for knowledge graph completion rely on symbolic representations, usually logical rules or graph features [8, 15]. Here, it has been shown that logical rules, in particular Horn rules, can compete with embedding based techniques for knowledge graph completion. In this work, we analyze whether these logical representations of properties are also well suited for detecting synonyms.

3 Preliminaries

Without limiting the generality of our approach, we assume an arbitrary knowledge graph (KG) to be represented in the Resource Description Framework (RDF) [20]. Thus, a KG consists of a set of facts being subject, predicate, object *triples*: $(s, p, o) \in E \times R \times (E \cup L)$. A subject is an entity or concept from E, a predicate from a universe of properties R and an object is either an entity (i.e., from E) or a literal value from L. Although entities and predicates are technically represented through IRIs, we use suggestive identifiers for the sake of readability.

Our notation of logical rules over KGs stems from Galárraga et al. [8].

An *atom* for the triple (s, p, o) is written as $p(s, o)$. Beyond the RDF format for subject s and object o, rule atoms allow for variables $x, y, z, z_1, z_2, \ldots$ from

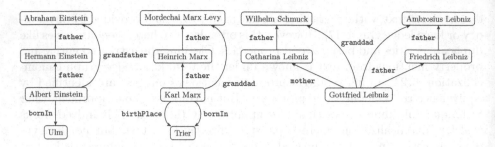

Fig. 1. An example knowledge graph about persons and their ancestors. Nodes are entities and edges are relationships.

a universe of variables V. A rule is a logical implication from a *body* term to a *head* term, where the body is a conjunction of multiple atoms b_i ($i \in \{1, ..., k\}$) while the head is a single atom: $b_1 \land ... \land b_k \Rightarrow r(s, o)$. Throughout this paper, our rules follow strictly this format, i.e., they are *Horn rules*. A rule in which every variable occurs at least twice is a *closed rule*. As an example, consider the following rule:

$$\texttt{father}(x,y) \land \texttt{father}(y,z) \Rightarrow \texttt{granddad}(x,z) \tag{1}$$

The meaning of such a rule w.r.t. a KG is whatever matches the body of the rule (i.e., an assignment of actual KG subjects/objects to the variables) also matches the head. Regarding (1), if y is the *father of* x and z is the *father of* y, then z is the *granddad of* x. We can use this closed rule to predict new facts or to justify existing ones in a KG, like the one depicted in Fig. 1. The KG delivers the facts $\texttt{father}$(Karl M., Heinreich M.) and $\texttt{father}$(Heinrich M., Mordechai M.L.), which implies the fact $\texttt{granddad}$(Karl M., Mordechai M.L.) according to (1). Similarly, we can infer the granddad property between Gottfried Leibniz and Ambrosius Leibniz.

Since rules are usually mined for prediction purposes from an incomplete real-world KG, we need a way to assess their quality. Galárraga et al. use two measures for assessing the quality of a rule $B \Rightarrow r(x, y)$ [8]. First, the *support* of a rule is the absolute number of instances the rule is correct in the KG:

$$supp(B \Rightarrow r(x,y)) = \#(x,y) : \exists z_1, \ldots, z_n : B \land r(x,y), \tag{2}$$

where $z_1, \ldots, z_n$ are the variables occurring in B distinct from x and y. Thus, the support quantifies the number of predictions that are already instances of the KG (*true positives*). For our example rule (1) and KG in Fig. 1, the support is 2 because the rule can only be instantiated by Karl Marx, Gottfried Leibniz and their ancestors. We count $\texttt{granddad}$(Karl M., Mordechai M. L.) and $\texttt{granddad}$(Gottfried L., Ambrosius L.) exactly once. The absolute support value is difficult to interpret if the frequency of a property in the KG and the size of the KG itself is unknown [8]. A support of 1 has a totally different meaning if there are thousands of properties in the KG, as opposed to only a single one in our example.

For $\text{father}(x, y) \wedge \text{father}(y, z) \Rightarrow \text{grandfather}(x, z)$, the support is only 1 but grandfather also only occurs once in the KG.

To become independent of the size of the KG and the frequency of property occurrences, the *head coverage* was introduced as a relative support. It measures the support of a rule relative to the number of occurrences of the respective head relation in the given KG:

$$hc(B \Rightarrow r(x, y)) = \frac{supp(B \Rightarrow r(x, y))}{\#(x', y') : r(x', y')} \tag{3}$$

The head coverage for (1) is thus 0.66 because its support is 2 and the granddad relation occurs three times in Fig. 1.

Since rules are usually mined from the data, we need a second measure assessing the prediction quality of a rule by means of its *standard confidence*:

$$conf(B \Rightarrow r(x, y)) = \frac{supp(B \Rightarrow r(x, y))}{\#(x, y) : \exists z_1, \ldots, z_n : B} \tag{4}$$

The number of true positives relative to the number of all predictions (due to the rule) shows us how many of the predictions are part of the current knowledge graph. Hence, a high confidence entails that the rule is justified by the data in the KG. Regarding (1), the confidence w.r.t. Fig. 1 is 0.66 because the rule's body matches three times while the whole rule comes with a support of 2.

We restrict ourselves to closed Horn rules because this allows the mining process to finish in reasonable time [8].

4 Rule Mining for Synonym Detection

From an RDF point of view, two distinct properties refer to two distinct concepts [20], as described by distinct resources. However, as KGs grow at an enormous pace, extraction and/or human error bring forth properties, such as birthPlace, born, or placeOfBirth, which refer to the same real-world concept. Therefore, we qualify such properties as *synonymous*. Even at this informal stage, *synonymity* is recognized as an equivalence relation. Hence, if two or more properties $r_1, \ldots, r_m \in R$ are synonymous, they can be united to a single URI.

This section is devoted to characterizing synonymous properties in a way that enables us to use existing rule mining techniques, e.g., AMIE+ [7], to identify them as equivalence rules

$$r_1(x, y) \Leftrightarrow r_2(x, y), \tag{5}$$

i.e., r_1 may be replaced by r_2 and vice versa. For properties $r_1, r_2 \in R$, we call (5) a *synonym rule*. An obvious *rule mining*-based solution tries to find two rules $r_1(x, y) \Rightarrow r_2(x, y)$ and $r_2(x, y) \Rightarrow r_1(x, y)$ which culminates to synonymity of r_1 and r_2. Confidence values greater than 0 would require r_1 and r_2 to co-occur for the same subject-object pairs: In Fig. 1, rules $\text{bornIn}(x, y) \Rightarrow \text{birthPlace}(x, y)$ and $\text{birthPlace}(x, y) \Rightarrow \text{bornIn}(x, y)$ may be inferred with confidence values of 0.5 and 1.0. Since both rules have high confidence values, we could take them as being correct and therefore infer the synonym rule `bornIn`(x, y) $\Leftrightarrow$ `birthPlace`(x, y). Mining this kind of synonym rules is the classical approach to detect synonyms using rule mining [6,24].

However, the just stated scenario is quite artificial: In real-world KGs, synonyms often stem from integrated triples from multiple sources, e.g., different extraction tools or persons. Often these triples have totally different domains and share no entities at all. In such cases, rule mining solely relying on the data instances is not very helpful. As another example, we observe that we have no support for the rule `grandfather`(x, y) $\Rightarrow$ `granddad`(x, y) in our example. They simply occur for totally different entities, although a unification of both properties is appropriate.

4.1 Mining Property Definitions

Instead, we try to indirectly mine synonym rules by first mining *property definitions*. Intuitively speaking, a definition is a paraphrase of a property through other properties. Thus, it is an equivalent logical formula to some property. In case of **granddad**, we may find

$$
\begin{aligned}
\texttt{granddad}(x,z) \Leftrightarrow &(\texttt{father}(x,y) \wedge \texttt{father}(y,z)) \vee \\
&(\texttt{mother}(x,y) \wedge \texttt{father}(y,z))
\end{aligned} \tag{6}
$$

an appropriate definition. We identify synonymous properties r_1 and r_2 indirectly by mining their property definitions. More formally, we mine property definitions D such that

$$
r_1(x,y) \Leftrightarrow D \Leftrightarrow r_2(x,y),
$$

which lets us conclude (5) by transitivity of logical equivalence.

Since state-of-the-art rule induction systems usually are only able to mine Horn rules, due to performance reasons, we adapt our notion of property definitions accordingly. Applying a standard rule mining system on the KG from Fig. 1, using the `granddad` relation as a head relation, we mine two rules culminating to the definition given in (6): (a) the paternal granddad

$$
\texttt{father}(x,y) \wedge \texttt{father}(y,z) \Rightarrow \texttt{granddad}(x,z)
$$

but also (b) the maternal granddad

$$
\texttt{mother}(x,y) \wedge \texttt{father}(y,z) \Rightarrow \texttt{granddad}(x,z).
$$

The confidence of (a) is 0.66 and its head coverage is also 0.66. The confidence of rule (b) is 1.0, but the head coverage therefore is only 0.33. Both rules pretty much cover what the `granddad` property expresses. The hypothetical rule

$$
\begin{aligned}
\texttt{granddad}(x,z) \Leftarrow &(\texttt{father}(x,y) \wedge \texttt{father}(y,z)) \vee \\
&(\texttt{mother}(x,y) \wedge \texttt{father}(y,z))
\end{aligned}
$$

has a head coverage of 1.0 and a confidence 0.75. We observe that indeed the disjunction of the rule bodies of the mined Horn rules exceeds the head coverage values of the single rules. The higher the head coverage, the more likely it is to observe the body (or one of the bodies) whenever the head is matched. The extreme case of a head coverage of 1.0 means that whenever the head property is observed, the body can also be matched. In our example, the head coverage is even the sum of the head coverages of both rules because the bodies cover totally different entities. More generally, however, instantiations of different Horn clauses in a definition might overlap, which needs to be considered for head coverage computation by counting distinct instances.

Our example already suggests that the combined rule (6) is valid. This observation can be justified by the rule's head coverage and standard confidence. In general, confidence and head coverage have the rule support in the numerator. While confidence considers the number of matches of the body in the denominator, head coverage uses the size of the head relation. From this, we obtain

$$conf(B \Rightarrow r(x,y)) = hc(B \Leftarrow r(x,y)). \qquad (7)$$

Thus, a rule having a high standard confidence and a high head coverage may imply that rule body and rule head are equivalent.

Driven by the interpretations and observations above, a *property definition* for $r \in R$ is a disjunction of Horn clauses, i.e., $D = b_1 \vee ... \vee b_k$, such that the rule $D \Leftrightarrow r$ holds. In the best case, confidence and head coverage of a definition are as close to 1.0 as possible. Note that a head coverage and confidence of 1.0 is only possible if the property and its definition share all their entities, which is rarely the case in KGs. If directly synonymous properties, sharing several entities, exist in the KG, this yields synonym rules with high confidence and high head coverage, being part of the respective definitions. In most cases, mining Horn rules on real-world KGs yields high confidence but a large number of rules with low head coverage values. Hence, a definition usually consists of a disjunction of hundreds of Horn clauses, covering a very diverse set of entities, and therefore achieving a high overall head coverage for the definition.

4.2   Mining Synonym Rules by Matching Definitions

In heterogeneous and large-scale knowledge graphs, only very few identical definitions can be found: Reconsidering the mined example definition and trying to find properties, such as grandfather, with an equal definition will almost surely fail. The mining process for grandfather returns a single Horn rule:

$$grandfather(x,z) \Leftarrow father(x,y) \wedge father(y,z) \qquad (8)$$

This rule even has a head coverage of 1.0 and a confidence of 0.33. Due to the high head coverage and confidence, it follows that the body is a definition for grandfather (w.r.t. to the KG in Fig. 1). The mined definitions for grandfather and granddad are different but share the clause $father(x, y) \wedge father(y, z)$. This is a typical situation for real-world definitions that have been created in a purely data-driven fashion. To overcome this mismatch of definitions, we relax our indirect mining approach, such that also only partial matches can be used to find synonymous properties. For our example, this would imply that we find the following indirect synonym rule:

$$\text{granddad}(x,z)$$
$$\Leftrightarrow\text{father}(x,y) \wedge \text{father}(y,z) \tag{9}$$
$$\Leftrightarrow\text{grandfather}(x,z)$$

Since this rule leaves out parts of the definition of granddad, we obtain a lower head coverage for this definition, which negatively influences the definition's quality. Since the matched definition only covers a restricted proportion of the entities that are taking part in the granddad relation, also the quality of the synonym rule may be affected negatively. Therefore, in our mining process, we aim at maximizing the overlap of the definitions of two properties, in order to classify them as synonymous. Here, the Jaccard coefficient of the definitions $\frac{D_1 \cap D_2}{D_1 \cup D_2}$ determines the quality of the overlap. Bodies from the definitions are thereby identical if they are structurally identical (isomorphic), respecting the head properties' direction. As a result, we obtain a Jaccard coefficient between 0 and 1 for each property pair which can be interpreted as a confidence for the indirect rule mining. In our granddad and grandfather example above, the Jaccard coefficient is $\frac{1}{2} = 0.5$.

The overall matching process consists of two steps: (1) First of all, we start a rule mining process on a knowledge graph to obtain definitions for all properties. (2) A comparison of all definitions for all property pairs is performed to compute respective Jaccard coefficients. As a result, a ranked list of property pairs with confidence values is returned. If no definition could be mined for some property, all its confidence values are automatically set to 0.0 since no matching definition can be found.

5   Evaluation

In our experiments, we evaluate our rule-based technique against a frequent item set-based technique [1] and our previously published approach based on knowledge graph embeddings [14] on two large real-world knowledge graphs. Our implementation, a description on how to reproduce the experiments and the datasets are all available through our Github repository[3].

For all experiments we employ an existing tool for mining Horn rules: we use AMIE+ [7] with a minimum head coverage of 0.005, a minimum confidence of 0.05 and a minimum initial support to mine closed and connected Horn rules on the datasets. If the rule mining algorithm did not output new rules for more than 10 h, we preliminary stopped the mining process and used the rules mined so far.

Overall, two experiments using 7 baseline approaches are performed: (1) To assess, whether the quality of synonym detection methods is ready for cleaning real-world knowledge graphs, we perform a manual evaluation of the systems

---

[3] https://github.com/JanKalo/RuleAlign.

quality on DBpedia. (2) In the other experiment, we want to analyze the recall and precision of synonym detection techniques on synthetically created synonyms in Wikidata.

Overall, we compare the approaches on two very large real-world datasets Wikidata and DBpedia. Since both datasets have several hundred millions of triples which is unfeasible for training knowledge graph embeddings as well as for mining rules in a feasible time, we stick to the sampled datasets that have been built in [14]. This also allows for a better comparison of our results to previous works. In their work, the authors have presented a sampling technique that keeps triples with every existing property in the respective knowledge graph, while reducing the overall number of triples. Our gold standard datasets containing our manually labeled synonyms for DBpedia and the synthetic synonyms for Wikidata are available online[4].

Frequent Item Set Baseline. The approach presented in [1] uses frequent item set mining to detect synonymously used predicates to perform query expansion. In this work, we used the implementation and results of this baseline from [14]. In that work, we re-implemented the approach using *Range Content Filtering* and *Reversed Correlation Coefficient* as described in the original paper using Python and Spark. The implementation of the approach is also openly available on Github. As an input parameter for frequent item set mining, the approach requires the user to provide a minimum support value. For both experiments, a grid search optimizing for optimal F1-measures was performed.

Knowledge Graph Embedding Baselines. In our previous work [14], it was shown that knowledge graph embeddings may be used to detect synonymous properties, by using outlier detection techniques on the property representation in state-of-the-art embeddings. In the original paper 8 different embedding techniques have been presented using L1 metric as well as cosine similarity. For this work, we only take the top 6 embeddings with the metrics that worked best: TransH [26], TransD [11] ComplEx [23], DistMult [27], ANALOGY [16] and HolE [19]. All these techniques achieve very high quality in the top results, the recall however is problematic in some of the presented experiments. We will further analyze the differences of the fundamentally different approaches embeddings vs. logical rules in various settings here.

5.1   Manual Quality Evaluation in DBpedia

The DBpedia sample comprises 12 million triples with around 15,000 different properties with several natural synonyms, ranging from very rare synonyms only occurring in around 100 triples up to synonyms being part of hundreds of thousands triples. The evaluation on DBpedia is performed manually for the top 500 results of each of the approach classifying pairs of properties in either being

---

[4] https://doi.org/10.6084/m9.figshare.11343785.v1.

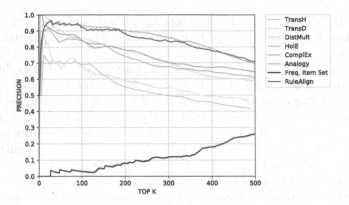

Fig. 2. Experimental results from our approach RuleAlign in red to several baselines on DBpedia manually evaluated with precision at k up to $k = 500$. (Color figure online)

synonyms or not. For the base line approaches, we rely on the datasets classified in [14] extended by a manual classification performed for our newly proposed approach.

In this experiment, we have performed a manual evaluation for the precision@k up to $k = 500$ on a DBpedia sample comparing 8 different approaches. The results are presented as line graphs in Fig. 2.

The frequent item set-based baseline has an increasing precision for higher k values, due to a ranking function that assumes that synonymous properties are not occurring for similar subject entities. This assumption is not true for DBpedia. The precision for this baseline always is below 30% and also does not exceed 30% for k values above 500. The best embedding-based baseline is HolE, having a maximum precision of over 90% in the top 200 results and a precision around 70% at $k = 500$.

Our approach, presented as RuleAlign in red, shows the best results in this experiments together with the embedding model HolE finding at least 352 correct synonyms. Overall, the number should go into the thousands when we extended our manual evaluation. In comparison to a direct rule mining approach for equivalence rules, our indirect approach finds at least 77 correct synonym pairs on our DBpedia dataset which cannot be found by the other approach because they have no support.

But as an additional feature, our approach is able to propose explanations for the synonym predictions in form of property definitions. The top explanations are having a high head coverage, covering lots of entities and have a high confidence. In Table 1, we present some example definitions from DBpedia. Since for many properties around 100 Horn clauses are in the definition, we only present top matched Horn clauses. These explanations are very natural definitions of the respective properties that would also be used in the real-world. Note, that besides these human readable example definitions, many synonym

Table 1. Matched property definitions mined from DBpedia as an explanation for the result.

Property	Definition
grandsire(x, z)	sire(x, y) $\wedge$ sire(y, z)
nationality(x, y)	stateOfOrigin(x, y)
nationality(x, z)	birthPlace(x, y) $\wedge$ country(y, z)
north(x, y)	east(y, z) $\wedge$ northeast(x, z)

pairs are entirely different in their respective URI labels, e.g. "dbp:ff" (father of the father) and "dbp:grandsire" and are therefore very difficult to be identified by humans without our automatic data-driven approach.

A closer look at our predictions reveal some shortcomings of our approach. First of all, our approach is not able to distinguish the gender within some properties. We classify for example father and mother as synonyms, because no rule is able to capture the gender correctly. One reason for that is, that the gender is only mentioned as a literal, which is ignored by the rule mining approach. A second problem are properties that hardly can be distinguished by their data instances, because they are extremely similar. As an example firstDriver and secondDriver representing a person's placement in a race, cannot be distinguished. Furthermore, false-positives in the form of hyponyms as for example genre and musicGenre are returned.

5.2 Precision-Recall Evaluation in Wikidata

The Wikidata sample has more than 11 million triples and more than 1,500 properties. In contrast to DBpedia, it is supposed to be free of synonyms due to intensive manual curation. Therefore, in [14] have introduced synthetic synonyms here by randomly re-naming existing properties. For the triple (Albert E., father, Hermann E.) we instead use (Albert E., father_synonym, Hermann E.). Thus, the properties father and father_synonym can be treated as synonyms, but never co-occur for the same subject-object pair. Overall, 343 synonymous properties have been introduced that need to be identified for the approach. A more detailed description on the creation of the dataset can be found in the original paper.

We again start in having a look at the frequent item set baseline in black. It starts with a very high precision for very low recall values and then drops sharply to under 20%. The maximum precision is at 21% at a recall value of around 35%. Due to the minimum support value that lead to best F1-measure, no higher recall value is achieved here. Embedding-based approaches achieve a very high precision up to a recall of 30%. The best approach is again HolE, starting at 90% precision for a recall of 10% and a precision of 10% for 70% recall. In contrast, our approach (red) is having a perfect precision for recall values up to 30% and still a precision over 90% for a recall of 70%. The recall of our approach sharply drops never achieving 80% recall.

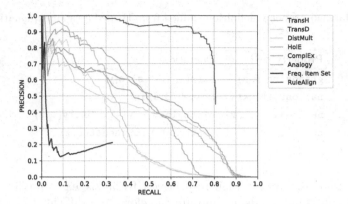

Fig. 3. Experimental results from our approach RuleAlign on Wikidata. We provide a precision-recall analysis for synthetic synonyms.

The second experiment measures precision and recall for 343 synonyms in a Wikidata sample. Our results regarding this experiment are presented as precision-recall curves in Fig. 3. For Wikidata, our approach achieves an extremely high precision, but also has problems in recall due to two reasons: (1) For 32 properties, no rule could be mined due to the minimum head coverage in the rule mining process. (2) The other synonyms could not be found, since none of the mined rules fulfilled our minimum confidence threshold. The few false positives that have been returned by our approach often were hyponyms instead of synonyms.

5.3 Discussion

The rule-based approach matching data-driven property definitions for detecting synonymous properties achieves very high precision. In both datasets, we could observe that a high Jaccard coefficient often implies that the respective property pair is synonymous. In the Wikidata experiment, all pairs with a confidence above 0.9 are synonyms and also in DBpedia a high confidence leads to good results.

However, in DBpedia only very few synonyms with high confidence could be found. For lower Jaccard coefficients, a higher proportion of false positives is returned, because these properties often were in a hyponym relation. These could be solved by an improved matching process that also takes into account the head coverages of the rules when computing the Jaccard coefficient. However, this might further decrease the recall of our approach, which has already been observed as a problem for the Wikidata dataset. The simple Jaccard coefficient as used in this work, achieves very high precision with a reasonable recall.

A low recall could also be prevented by mining rules with lower head coverage, mining more expressive rules or by decreasing the minimum confidence threshold. In turn, this might further decrease the performance of the rule mining tool, resulting in enormous rule sets.

Several false positives that were returned in DBpedia, had a high overlap in their data instances and therefore also very similar definitions. These properties were very similar, but from the labels or IRIs, we observed that they were not synonym. These cases can hardly be identified in a data-driven fashion, because they often need detailed domain knowledge.

6 Conclusion

We have presented a novel approach adapting classical rule mining for knowledge graphs to detect synonymous properties in a data-driven way using property definitions. In two large-scale experiments on two real-world knowledge graphs, we have shown that our approach is able to identify a large proportion of existing synonyms with a precision of over 80% without making any assumptions on the data. In contrast to existing work in this area, our approach is providing human understandable explanations of its decisions in the form of logical Horn clauses, while achieving a higher precision in existing benchmark datasets.

This work shows that symbolic approaches, like rule mining in our case, are capable of competing with latent approaches (i.e., knowledge graph embeddings), when it comes to identifying synonymous properties. In particular with regard to precision and interpretability our rule-based approach is superior over existing systems. However, as shown in our evaluation, our rule-based approach is stretching a purely data-driven approach to its limits. Most false positives that have been produced by our system, cannot be detected purely automatically, because it cannot be observed from the triples nor the property label. Here, it seems promising to have a semi-automatic approach with humans manually checking the matched definitions.

With regard to scalability, however, both paradigms seem to have problems when it comes to real-world knowledge graphs. Knowledge graph embedding training needs powerful GPUs which currently are very restricted with regard to their memory, preventing the training for large datasets. Rule mining, on the other hand, requires the computation of huge joins for a possibly exponential number of rules. These joins sometimes comprise hundred thousands triples which already takes several minutes for a single rule candidate on state-of-the-art hardware, when working with large datasets like Wikidata.

As a future work, we plan to extend the approach to also detect hyponyms between properties and inverse properties. More importantly, we would like to use more expressive rules instead of just closed Horn clauses to improve precision even more. So far, existing rule mining approaches have major performance issues for these kinds of rules on larger datasets.

References

1. Abedjan, Z., Naumann, F.: Synonym analysis for predicate expansion. In: Cimiano, P., Corcho, O., Presutti, V., Hollink, L., Rudolph, S. (eds.) ESWC 2013. LNCS, vol. 7882, pp. 140–154. Springer, Heidelberg (2013). https://doi.org/10.1007/978-3-642-38288-8_10

2. Auer, S., Bizer, C., Kobilarov, G., Lehmann, J., Cyganiak, R., Ives, Z.: DBpedia: a nucleus for a web of open data. In: Aberer, K., et al. (eds.) ASWC/ISWC -2007. LNCS, vol. 4825, pp. 722–735. Springer, Heidelberg (2007). https://doi.org/10.1007/978-3-540-76298-0_52

3. Bollacker, K., Evans, C., Paritosh, P., Sturge, T., Taylor, J.: Freebase: a collaboratively created graph database for structuring human knowledge. In: Proceedings of the 2008 ACM SIGMOD International Conference on Management of Data, SIGMOD 2008, pp. 1247–1250 (2008)

4. Dettmers, T., Minervini, P., Stenetorp, P., Riedel, S.: Convolutional 2D knowledge graph embeddings. In: Thirty-Second AAAI Conference on Artificial Intelligence (2018)

5. Dong, X., et al.: Knowledge vault: a web-scale approach to probabilistic knowledge fusion. In: Proceedings of the 20th International Conference on Knowledge Discovery and Data Mining, SIGKDD 2014, pp. 601–610 (2014)

6. Galárraga, L., Heitz, G., Murphy, K., Suchanek, F.M.: Canonicalizing open knowledge bases. In: Proceedings of the 23rd ACM International Conference on Conference on Information and Knowledge Management, CIKM 2014, pp. 1679–1688 (2014)

7. Galárraga, L., Teflioudi, C., Hose, K., Suchanek, F.M.: Fast rule mining in ontological knowledge bases with AMIE+. VLDB J. 24(6), 707–730 (2015)

8. Galárraga, L.A., Teflioudi, C., Hose, K., Suchanek, F.: AMIE: association rule mining under incomplete evidence in ontological knowledge bases. In: Proceedings of the 22nd International Conference on World Wide Web, WWW 2013, pp. 413–422 (2013)

9. Hertling, S., Paulheim, H.: DOME results for OAEI 2018. In: OM 2018: Proceedings of the 13th International Workshop on Ontology Matching co-located with the 17th International Semantic Web Conference (ISWC 2018), Monterey, CA, USA, 8 October 2018, vol. 2288, pp. 144–151 (2018)

10. Jain, P., Hitzler, P., Sheth, A.P., Verma, K., Yeh, P.Z.: Ontology alignment for linked open data. In: Patel-Schneider, P.F., et al. (eds.) ISWC 2010, Part I. LNCS, vol. 6496, pp. 402–417. Springer, Heidelberg (2010). https://doi.org/10.1007/978-3-642-17746-0_26

11. Ji, G., He, S., Xu, L., Liu, K., Zhao, J.: Knowledge graph embedding via dynamic mapping matrix. In: Proceedings of the 53rd Annual Meeting of the Association for Computational Linguistics and the 7th International Joint Conference on Natural Language Processing, ACL 2015, pp. 687–696 (2015)

12. Jiménez-Ruiz, E., Cuenca Grau, B.: LogMap: logic-based and scalable ontology matching. In: Aroyo, L., et al. (eds.) ISWC 2011. LNCS, vol. 7031, pp. 273–288. Springer, Heidelberg (2011). https://doi.org/10.1007/978-3-642-25073-6_18

13. Juanzi Li, J., Jie Tang, J., Yi Li, Y., Qiong Luo, Q.: RiMOM: a dynamic multistrategy ontology alignment framework. IEEE Trans. Knowl. Data Eng. 21(8), 1218–1232 (2009)

14. Kalo, J.-C., Ehler, P., Balke, W.-T.: Knowledge graph consolidation by unifying synonymous relationships. In: Ghidini, C., et al. (eds.) ISWC 2019. LNCS, vol. 11778, pp. 276–292. Springer, Cham (2019). https://doi.org/10.1007/978-3-030-30793-6_16

15. Lao, N., Mitchell, T., Cohen, W.W.: Random walk inference and learning in a large scale knowledge base. In: Proceedings of the Conference on Empirical Methods in Natural Language Processing, EMNLP 2011, pp. 529–539 (2011)

16. Liu, H., Wu, Y., Yang, Y.: Analogical inference for multi-relational embeddings. In: Proceedings of the 34th International Conference on Machine Learning, ICML 2017, pp. 2168–2178 (2017)
17. Mausam, S.M., Bart, R., Soderland, S., Etzioni, O.: Open language learning for information extraction. In: Proceedings of the 2012 Joint Conference on Empirical Methods in Natural Language Processing and Computational Natural Language Learning, EMNLP-CoNLL 2012, pp. 523–534 (2012)
18. Nickel, M., Murphy, K., Tresp, V., Gabrilovich, E.: A review of relational machine learning for knowledge graphs. Proc. IEEE **104**(1), 11–33 (2016)
19. Nickel, M., Rosasco, L., Poggio, T.: Holographic embeddings of knowledge graphs. In: Proceedings of the 30 AAAI Conference on Artificial Intelligence, AAAI 2016, pp. 1955–1961. AAAI Press (2016)
20. Schreiber, A., Raimond, Y.: RDF 1.1 Primer. W3C Working Group Note, World-Wide Web Consortium (2014). https://www.w3.org/TR/rdf11-primer/
21. Suchanek, F.M., Abiteboul, S., Senellart, P.: PARIS: probabilistic alignment of relations, instances, and schema. Proc. VLDB Endowement **5**(3), 157–168 (2011)
22. Suchanek, F.M., Kasneci, G., Weikum, G.: YAGO: a core of semantic knowledge. In: Proceedings of the 16th International Conference on World Wide Web, WWW 2007, p. 697 (2007)
23. Trouillon, T., Welbl, J., Riedel, S., Gaussier, E., Bouchard, G.: Complex embeddings for simple link prediction. In: Proceedings of the 33rd International Conference on International Conference on Machine Learning - Volume 48, ICML 2016, pp. 2071–2080 (2016)
24. Vashishth, S., Jain, P., Talukdar, P.: CESI: canonicalizing open knowledge bases using embeddings and side information. In: Proceedings of the 2018 World Wide Web Conference, WWW 2018, pp. 1317–1327 (2018). https://doi.org/10.1145/3178876.3186030
25. Vrandečić, D.: Wikidata: a new platform for collaborative data collection. In: Proceedings of the 21st International Conference Companion on World Wide Web, WWW 2012 Companion, p. 1063 (2012)
26. Wang, Z., Zhang, J., Feng, J., Chen, Z.: Knowledge graph embedding by translating on hyperplanes. In: Proceedings of the Twenty-Eighth AAAI Conference on Artificial Intelligence, AAAI 2014, pp. 1112–1119 (2014)
27. Yang, Q., Wooldridge, M.J., Codocedo, V., Napoli, A.: Twenty-Fourth International Joint Conference on Artificial Intelligence, IJCAI 2015, Buenos Aires, Argentina, 25–31 July 2015 (2015)

Entity Summarization with User Feedback

Qingxia Liu[1], Yue Chen[1], Gong Cheng[1(✉)], Evgeny Kharlamov[2,3], Junyou Li[1],
and Yuzhong Qu[1]

[1] National Key Laboratory for Novel Software Technology, Nanjing University,
Nanjing, China
{qxliu2013,mg1933005,141220056}@smail.nju.edu.cn,
{gcheng,yzqu}@nju.edu.cn
[2] Department of Informatics, University of Oslo, Oslo, Norway
evgeny.kharlamov@ifi.uio.no
[3] Bosch Center for Artificial Intelligence, Robert Bosch GmbH, Renningen, Germany
evgeny.kharlamov@de.bosch.com

Abstract. Semantic Web applications have benefited from entity summarization techniques which compute a compact summary for an entity by selecting a set of key triples from underlying data. A wide variety of entity summarizers have been developed. However, the quality of summaries they generate are still not satisfying, and we lack mechanisms for improving computed summaries. To address this challenge, in this paper we present the first study of entity summarization with user feedback. We consider a cooperative environment where a user reads the current entity summary and provides feedback to help an entity summarizer compute an improved summary. Our approach represents this iterative process as a Markov decision process where the entity summarizer is modeled as a reinforcement learning agent. To exploit user feedback, we represent the interdependence of triples in the current summary and the user feedback by a novel deep neural network which is incorporated into the policy of the agent. Our approach outperforms five baseline methods in extensive experiments with both real users and simulated users.

Keywords: Entity summarization · User feedback · Reinforcement learning · Deep neural network

1 Introduction

Entity summarization is the task of computing an optimal compact summary for an entity by selecting a size-constrained subset of triples [13]. It has found application in many domains. For example, in Google's Knowledge Graph, an entity may be described by dozens or hundreds of triples. Showing all of them in an entity card would overload users. Google performs entity summarization by selecting key triples that users are likely to need for that particular entity.

An entity summarizer is a tool that computes entity summaries. A wide variety of entity summarizers have been developed [13]. They generate summaries for general purposes [4,7,21,22] or for specific applications such as Web

© Springer Nature Switzerland AG 2020
A. Harth et al. (Eds.): ESWC 2020, LNCS 12123, pp. 376–392, 2020.
https://doi.org/10.1007/978-3-030-49461-2_22

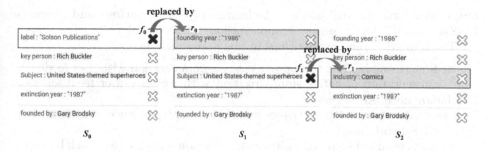

Fig. 1. Two iterations in the cross-replace scenario for entity `Solson Publications`.

browsing [9,23], Web search [10,28], and crowdsourcing [5,6]. However, entity summarization is a difficult task. Recent evaluation results [14] show that summaries generated by existing entity summarizers still differ significantly from ground-truth summaries created by human experts (F1 < 0.6). Moreover, current entity summaries are static. There is a lack of mechanisms for improving an entity summary when its quality could not satisfy users' information needs.

Research Challenges. One promising direction to improve entity summarization is to exploit user feedback. This idea has been practiced in related research such as document summarization [1,27] and document retrieval [15,24]. One can establish a cooperative environment where a user reads the current entity summary and conveniently provides feedback to help an entity summarizer compute an improved summary, which in turn is a motivation for user feedback. To effectively incorporate user feedback into entity summarization, there are two research challenges. First, we need to *represent the cooperative process* using a formal model. Second, to exploit user feedback, we need to *represent the interdependence of the current summary and the user feedback*. This is non-trivial because triples have both textual semantics and structural features.

Contributions. We address these challenges and study entity summarization with user feedback in the following cross-replace scenario, while our approach can be easily extended to support other scenarios. As illustrated in Fig. 1, a user reads a computed summary S_i for entity `Solson Publications` and provides negative feedback by crossing off an irrelevant triple f_i. An entity summarizer analyzes the connection between S_i and f_i, and then replaces f_i with a more relevant triple r_i to form an improved summary S_{i+1}. The process can be repeated. To represent this cooperative process, we model an entity summarizer as a reinforcement learning agent, and model the iterative process as a Markov decision process. Further, we represent the interdependence of triples in the current summary and the user feedback by a novel deep neural network which is incorporated into the policy of the agent. Our approach is referred to as DRESSED, short for **D**eep **R**einforced **E**ntity **S**ummarization with u**S**er f**E**e**D**back. We carry out a user study to demonstrate the effectiveness of DRESSED. We also conduct extensive offline evaluation based on two benchmarks for evaluating entity summarization and a standard framework of simulating user behavior. DRESSED outperforms five baseline methods including entity summarizers and relevance feedback models for document summarization/retrieval.

To summarize, our contributions in this paper include

- the first research effort to improve entity summarization with user feedback,
- a representation of entity summarization with iterative user feedback as a Markov decision process,
- a representation of sets of triples and their interdependence as a novel deep neural network, and
- the first empirical study of entity summarization with user feedback based on both real users and simulated users.

The remainder of the paper is organized as follows. We formulate the problem in Sect. 2, and describe our approach in Sect. 3. Online user study and offline evaluation with simulated users are reported in Sects. 4 and 5, respectively. We discuss related work in Sect. 6 before we conclude in Sect. 7.

2   Problem Statement

In this section we define the terms used in the paper and formulate the problem.

Entity Description. Let I, B, L be the sets of all IRIs, blank nodes, and literals in RDF, respectively. An RDF dataset T is a set of RDF triples:

$$T \subseteq (I \cup B) \times I \times (I \cup B \cup L). \tag{1}$$

For triple $t \in T$, let $\text{subj}(t), \text{pred}(t), \text{obj}(t)$ return the subject, predicate, and object of the triple, respectively. The description of an entity e comprises all the triples in T where e is described as the subject or as the object:

$$\text{Desc}(e) = \{t \in T : \text{subj}(t) = e \text{ or } \text{obj}(t) = e\}. \tag{2}$$

Entity Summarization. Given an integer size constraint k, a summary of entity e is a subset of triples $S \subseteq \text{Desc}(e)$ such that $|S| \le k$. The problem of entity summarization is to generate an optimal summary from the original entity description by selecting an optimal subset of triples. Optimality could depend on the task and/or the context. We follow most existing researches to generate entity summaries for general purposes.

User Feedback. Users and an entity summarizer work in a cooperative environment towards obtaining optimal summaries to best satisfy users' information needs. We consider the following *cross-replace scenario* where a user reads a computed summary and can provide *negative feedback*. Specifically, the summarizer computes and presents a summary S_i for entity e. The user reads S_i and crosses off an irrelevant triple $f_i \in S_i$. Based on this negative feedback, the summarizer selects a new candidate triple $r_i \in (\text{Desc}(e) \setminus S_i)$ to replace f_i and form an improved summary $S_{i+1} = (S_i \setminus \{f_i\}) \cup \{r_i\}$. The process can be repeated until the user provides no further feedback due to satisfaction or loss of patience, or the candidate triples are used up. The problem we study in this paper is how a summarizer *exploits user feedback to identify relevant triples for replacement*.

3   Approach

In the cross-replace scenario, an entity summarizer interacts with a user by iteratively exploiting user feedback to compute improved summaries. We want to optimize the user experience during the entire iterative process. It inspires us to model the summarizer as a reinforcement learning agent. Furthermore, an irrelevant triple crossed off by the user should not be presented again. Therefore, the iterative process has states and hence can be modeled as a Markov decision process (MDP), which we will describe in Sect. 3.1. The core problem for an MDP is to find a policy with which the summarizer can exploit irrelevant triples in user feedback to identify relevant triples for replacement. Representing such triple interdependence in a state is non-trivial, for which we propose a novel deep neural network in Sect. 3.2. We solve the learning problem in a standard way and present implementation details in Sect. 3.3. The proposed approach, referred to as DRESSED, is open source under the Apache License.[1]

3.1   Representation of the Cross-replace Scenario

We firstly review MDP and then we model the cross-replace scenario as an MDP.

MDP. An MDP is represented as a state-action-reward-transition quadruple denoted by $\langle \mathcal{Z}, \mathcal{A}, \rho, \tau \rangle$. An agent interacts with the environment in discrete time steps: $i = 0, 1, \ldots, I$. At time step i, the agent is in state $Z_i \in \mathcal{Z}$, and follows a θ-parameterized policy $\pi_\theta : \mathcal{A} \times \mathcal{Z} \to [0, 1]$ to choose an action $A_i \subset \mathcal{A}$ to take. For action $A \in \mathcal{A}$ and state $Z \in \mathcal{Z}$, the policy $\pi_\theta(A|Z)$ gives the probability of taking action A when the agent is in state Z. At time step $i + 1$, the agent receives a real-valued immediate reward $R_{i+1} \in \mathbb{R}$, and enters state Z_{i+1}. We assume immediate rewards and state transition can be deterministically characterized by functions $\rho : \mathcal{Z} \times \mathcal{A} \to \mathbb{R}$ and $\tau : \mathcal{Z} \times \mathcal{A} \to \mathcal{Z}$, respectively. An iterative process in the cross-replace scenario is represented as a trajectory denoted by ξ:

$$\xi : Z_0, \ A_0, \ R_1 = \rho(Z_0, A_0), \ Z_1 = \tau(Z_0, A_0), \ A_1, \ \ldots, \ R_I, \ Z_I. \tag{3}$$

The main learning problem here is to find a policy π_θ that will maximize the expected discounted sum of the immediate rewards over ξ:

$$J(\boldsymbol{\theta}) = \mathbb{E}_{\xi \sim \pi_\theta}[\sum_{i=1}^{I} \gamma^{i-1} R_i], \tag{4}$$

where $\gamma \in [0, 1]$ is a discount-rate parameter.

MDP-Based Modeling. We model an iterative process in the cross-replace scenario as an MDP. For integer $i \geq 0$, let S_i be the summary computed at time step i, i.e., in the i-th iteration. User feedback is part of the environment. Let f_i be the irrelevant triple crossed off by the user at time step i. Let $F_i = \{f_j : 0 \leq j \leq i - 1\}$ represent all the irrelevant triples crossed off prior to time

---

[1] https://github.com/nju-websoft/DRESSED.

step i. An entity summarizer is an agent. The set of candidate triples for time step i is $C_i = \texttt{Desc}(e) \setminus (F_i \cup S_i)$. An action A_i of the summarizer is to select a replacement triple $r_i \in C_i$ to form an improved summary $S_{i+1} = (S \setminus \{f_i\}) \cup \{r_i\}$. We record S_i, F_i, C_i, and f_i in state Z_i. The full model is defined as follows:

$$
\begin{aligned}
\text{state:} \quad & Z_i = \langle S_i, F_i, C_i, f_i \rangle, \\
\text{action:} \quad & A_i = r_i, \\
\text{policy:} \quad & \pi_\theta(t|Z_i) = \frac{\exp(\texttt{score}(t|Z_i, \boldsymbol{\theta}))}{\sum_{t' \in C_i} \exp(\texttt{score}(t'|Z_i, \boldsymbol{\theta}))}, \\
\text{reward:} \quad & R_{i+1} = \rho(Z_i, A_i) = \frac{\texttt{rel}(r_i)}{\log(i+2)}, \\
\text{transition:} \quad & Z_{i+1} = \tau(Z_i, A_i) = \langle S_{i+1}, F_{i+1}, C_{i+1}, f_{i+1} \rangle, \\
\text{initialization:} \quad & Z_0 = \langle S_0, \emptyset, (\texttt{Desc}(e) \setminus S_0), f_0 \rangle.
\end{aligned}
\tag{5}
$$

The policy π_θ uses a softmax function to map the scores of candidate triples to a probability distribution. Scores are computed by a θ-parameterized deep neural network shown in Fig. 2, which we will describe in Sect. 3.2. In the computation of reward during training, $\texttt{rel}(r_i)$ is the binary relevance label of triple r_i: either $\texttt{rel}(r_i) = 1$ (relevant) or $\texttt{rel}(r_i) = 0$ (irrelevant). We will describe the generation of labeled data in Sect. 3.3.

3.2 Representation of Triple Interdependence

The core of our MDP is the representation of policy. A learned policy informs an entity summarizer of how to exploit irrelevant triples in user feedback to identify relevant triples in candidates for replacement. The decision should be conditioned on the current summary and user feedback as well as the user feedback in history. Therefore, the key to the design of our policy in the following is to properly represent all of these triples and their interdependence in a state.

We design a novel deep neural network in Fig. 2 to represent θ-parameterized policy π_θ. All the parameters in the network are collectively referred to as θ and will be jointly learned. We rewrite the four elements $\langle S_i, F_i, C_i, f_i \rangle$ of a state as three sets of triples which are fed into the network as input:

- $S_i \setminus \{f_i\}$, the set of triples in S_i that will remain in S_{i+1},
- $F_i \cup \{f_i\}$, the set of irrelevant triples crossed off till now, and
- C_i, the set of candidate triples for replacement.

Below we detail the four modules of our policy network in Fig. 2. We describe the encoding of a single triple, the encoding of a set of triples, and the encoding of triple interdependence. Based on the encoded triple interdependence in a state as the context, a candidate triple will be selected for replacement.

Encoding Triples. For each input triple t, we jointly encode its textual semantics and structural features using an embedding layer converting t into a vector representation. Specifically, for each element of t, i.e., the subject, the predicate,

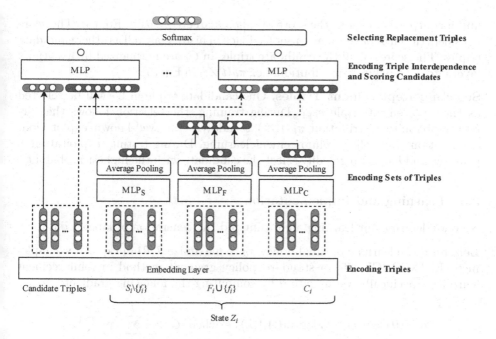

Fig. 2. Policy network.

or the object of t, we obtain its textual form from its `rdfs:label` if it is an IRI or a blank node, or from its lexical form if it is a literal. We average the pre-trained fastText embeddings [3] for all the words in this textual form as a vector representation of the element to encode its textual semantics. Then we concatenate the vector representations of the three elements of t to jointly encode its textual semantics and structural features.

Encoding Sets of Triples. A state Z_i is fed into the network as three sets of triples: $S_i \setminus \{f_i\}$, $F_i \cup \{f_i\}$, and C_i. A representation of a set should be permutation invariant to the order of elements. Networks that are sensitive to the order of elements in the input (e.g., RNN) are not suitable. We use a multilayer perceptron (MLP) with two fully connected hidden layers of size 300 and 150, applying Leaky ReLU activations, to process each triple in a set. Then we perform average pooling over all the triples in the set to generate a vector representation for the set, which satisfies permutation invariance. Separate copies of this network (MLP$_S$, MLP$_F$, MLP$_C$ in Fig. 2) are used to encode the three input sets. Their vector representations are concatenated to represent state Z_i.

Encoding Triple Interdependence and Scoring Candidates. Finally we encode the interdependence of the three sets in Z_i and each candidate triple $t \in C_i$ to score t. We concatenate the vector representation of Z_i with the vector representation of t, and feed the result into an MLP with two fully connected hidden layers of size 64 and 1, applying Leaky ReLU activations. This MLP intercorrelates t and the three sets of triples in Z_i to encode their interdependence, and its output is taken as the score of t, i.e., $\texttt{score}(t|Z_i, \boldsymbol{\theta})$ in Eq. (5). The score considers the current summary, user feedback in history, as well as other candidate triples. The scores of all the candidate triples in C_i are normalized by a softmax layer into a probability distribution, i.e., $\pi_{\boldsymbol{\theta}}(t|Z_i)$ in Eq. (5).

Selecting Replacement Triples. One candidate triple in C_i will be selected as the replacement triple r_{i+1}. During training, the selection follows the current probability distribution $\pi_{\boldsymbol{\theta}}(t|Z_i)$ to address the well-known exploration-exploitation trade-off in reinforcement learning. During testing, exploitation is primary, and hence we greedily select the candidate with the highest probability.

3.3   Learning and Implementation

Now we describe our learning algorithm and the generation of labeled data.

Learning. To learn an optimal policy $\pi_{\boldsymbol{\theta}}$ to maximize $J(\boldsymbol{\theta})$ in Eq. (4), we implement REINFORCE [25], a standard policy gradient method in reinforcement learning. Specifically, we update $\boldsymbol{\theta}$ by computing the following gradient:

$$\nabla_{\boldsymbol{\theta}} J(\boldsymbol{\theta}) = \gamma^i G_i \nabla_{\boldsymbol{\theta}} \log \pi_{\boldsymbol{\theta}}(A_i|Z_i), \quad \text{where } G_i = \sum_{j=i+1}^{I} \gamma^{j-i-1} R_j. \quad (6)$$

Our implementation uses the Adam optimizer based on TensorFlow with learning rate $= 0.01$. In Eq. (6), we set the discount rate $\gamma = 0.6$ to reduce the influence of rewards after 10 iterations below 1% (i.e., $0.6^{10-1} \approx 0.01$) because users may not be patient with many iterations of interaction.

Generating Labeled Data. It is expensive and inflexible to train with real user feedback. We follow a standard synthetic setting in recent information retrieval research [11] to train our model with simulated user behavior. Simulation is based on relevance labels on triples, which can be easily obtained from ground-truth summaries provided by existing benchmarks for evaluating entity summarization such as ESBM [14].

Specifically, for an entity description $\texttt{Desc}(e)$ and a ground-truth summary S_{gt} thereof, a triple $t \in \texttt{Desc}(e)$ is relevant if it appears in S_{gt}, otherwise irrelevant. The $\texttt{rel}$ function in Eq. (5) is defined accordingly:

$$\texttt{rel}(t) = \begin{cases} 1 & \text{if } t \in S_{\text{gt}}, \\ 0 & \text{if } t \notin S_{\text{gt}}. \end{cases} \quad (7)$$

We follow a standard framework of simulating user behavior [11] and we adapt it to the cross-replace scenario over the entity summarization task. For entity e, an initial summary S_0 is generated under size constraint $k = |S_{\text{gt}}|$ using any standard entity summarizer. Then in the i-th iteration of the cross-replace scenario, a simulated user: (a) needs to decide whether to provide any feedback, and if so, (b) needs to select an irrelevant triple f_i from the current summary S_i to cross off. In our implementation we simulate a perfect user [11] who: (a) will stop providing feedback if and only if $S_i = S_{\text{gt}}$, and (b) always provides noise-free feedback, i.e., never mistakenly crosses off triples in $S_i \cap S_{gt}$. We leave experiments with other user models (e.g., with noise) as future work.

When $S_i \neq S_{gt}$, there may be more than one irrelevant triple in S_i. Any of them could be crossed off. To let our simulated user behave consistently, we compute and cross off the triple with the highest degree of irrelevance (doi). We learn the doi of triple t by exploiting all the available ground-truth summaries, denoted by $\mathcal{S}_{GT}$. Existing benchmarks such as ESBM usually provide multiple ground-truth summaries created by different human experts for an entity. A triple that appears in fewer ground-truth summaries is more irrelevant. We implement this idea by feeding the vector representation of t defined in Sect. 3.2 into a two-layer neural network which outputs $\mathtt{doi}(t) \in [0,1]$. We train this network on $\mathcal{S}_{GT}$ to minimize the following logistic loss function:

$$- \sum_{S_{gt} \in \mathcal{S}_{GT}} \sum_{t \in \mathtt{Desc}(e)} (1 - \mathtt{rel}(t)) \log(\mathtt{doi}(t)) + \mathtt{rel}(t) \log(1 - \mathtt{doi}(t)), \quad (8)$$

where S_{gt} is a ground-truth summary for entity e, and $\mathtt{rel}$ is defined by Eq. (7).

4   Experiment 1: Online User Study

In our first experiment, we carry out a preliminary user study with 24 participants. They are graduate students with at least a basic background in RDF and/or knowledge graphs.

4.1   Participating Systems

To the best of our knowledge, DRESSED is the first entity summarizer that can exploit user feedback. We compare it with 2 baselines: a state-of-the-art entity summarizer that cannot exploit user feedback, and a document summarizer that can exploit user feedback and is adapted to perform entity summarization.

FACES-E [8] is a state-of-the-art entity summarizer. We obtain its implementation and configuration from its authors. FACES-E relies on UMBC's Sim-Service which is no longer available. We replace it with a string metric [20]. For entity e, FACES-E generates a ranking of triples in $\mathtt{Desc}(e)$ and chooses k top-ranked triples as a summary. While it cannot exploit user feedback, in each iteration we take the top-ranked candidate triple as the replacement triple.

IPS [27] is a popular document summarizer that exploits user feedback to compute an improved document summary by selecting a new set of sentences. To adapt it to entity summarization, we transform each triple into a sentence by concatenating the textual forms of the three elements of the triple. We constrain the search space of IPS such that a re-computed summary differs from the current summary by exactly one triple. This triple will become the replacement triple. Originally, IPS only supports positive feedback. In our implementation we negate the effect of feedback to fit negative feedback in our scenario.

Training and Tuning. Following Sect. 3.3, we train DRESSED with simulated user behavior over ground-truth summaries from ESBM v1.0.[2] Each ground-truth summary of an entity consists of 5 triples selected by a human expert from

---

[2] https://w3id.org/esbm.

Table 1. Results of online user study (mean ± standard deviation). For each method, significant improvements and losses ($p < 0.01$) over other methods are indicated by ▲ and ▼, respectively. Insignificant differences are indicated by ○.

	I	Q_{stop}	Q_{rplc}
FACES-E	$3.26_{\pm 2.83}$ $^{-▲○}$	$4.25_{\pm 0.85}$ $^{-▲○}$	$3.51_{\pm 1.05}$ $^{-▲▼}$
IPS	$4.18_{\pm 4.99}$ $^{▼-▼}$	$3.95_{\pm 1.05}$ $^{▼-▼}$	$3.09_{\pm 1.22}$ $^{▼-▼}$
DRESSED	$3.05_{\pm 2.70}$ $^{○▲-}$	$4.25_{\pm 0.87}$ $^{○▲-}$	$3.65_{\pm 1.04}$ $^{▲▲-}$

the original entity description. We set epoch = 100 and batchsize = 16. We also use this dataset to tune the two hyperparameters δ and λ of IPS. Their optimal values are found in the range of 0–10 using grid search.

We use CD [26] to generate initial summaries throughout the experiment. However, we could not compare with CD because its output cannot be treated as a ranking of candidate triples like FACES-E.

4.2 Procedure and Metrics

For each participant, we randomly sample 35 entities, including 25 entities from DBpedia version 2015-10 and 10 entities from LinkedMDB. Different entities may be assigned to different participants, and they are disjoint from the entities in ESBM which we use for training and parameter tuning. As a within-subject design, for each entity, the participant starts from the initial summary and separately interacts with each summarizer to help to improve the summary. The three summarizers are provided in random order. The experiment is blind, i.e., the participant does not know the order of systems.

In each iteration, the participant is required to cross off an irrelevant triple and then rate the relevance of the replacement triple. This rating, Q_{rplc}, is in the range of 1–5. Participants are instructed to assess relevance with reference to a satisfying general-purpose summary. When the participant decides to stop providing feedback for this entity, s/he rates the quality of the final summary. This rating, Q_{stop}, is in the range of 1–5. We also record the number of iterations till termination denoted by I.

4.3 Results

Table 1 presents the results of the online user study. We compare DRESSED with the two baselines and we perform two-tailed t-test to analyze whether their differences are statistical significant ($p < 0.01$).

DRESSED is generally the best-performing approach. First, with FACES-E and DRESSED, participants stop quickly ($I < 4$) and obtain reasonably good summaries ($Q_{stop} > 4$). The replacement triples selected by the feedback-aware DRESSED during the iterative process are significantly better than those of the feedback-unaware FACES-E according to the results of Q_{rplc}, demonstrating the usefulness of user feedback and the effectiveness of our approach. Second, compared with DRESSED, participants using IPS perform significantly more iterations but the replacement triples and final summaries they receive are significantly worse. We will justify the performance of these systems in Sect. 5.5.

5 Experiment 2: Offline Evaluation

Compared with evaluation with real user feedback, in recent information retrieval research [11] it has been more common to evaluate with simulated user behavior. By conducting this kind of offline evaluation, it would be more achievable and affordable to evaluate many methods at different time steps in varying conditions and, more importantly, the results would be easily reproducible. Our second experiment follows such a standard synthetic setting [11], which has been adapted to the cross-replace scenario over the entity summarization task in Sect. 3.3.

5.1 Datasets

As described in Sect. 3.3, simulated user behavior is derived from ground-truth summaries. We obtain ground-truth summaries from the two largest available benchmarks for evaluating entity summarization: ESBM[3] and FED.[4]

ESBM v1.0 provides 600 ground-truth summaries for entities in DBpedia version 2015-10, which we refer to as **ESBM-D**. It also provides 240 ground-truth summaries for entities in LinkedMDB, which we refer to as **ESBM-L**. **FED** provides 366 ground-truth summaries for entities in DBpedia version 3.9. In all these datasets, a ground-truth summary of an entity consists of 5 triples selected by a human expert from the original entity description.

For each dataset, we partition ground-truth summaries and the derived user simulation into 5 equal-sized subsets to support 5-fold cross-validation: 60% for training, 20% for validation, and 20% for test.

5.2 Participating Systems

We compare DRESSED with 5 baselines. **FACES-E** [8] and **IPS** [27] have been described in Sect. 4.1. In this experiment we add three relevance feedback models for document retrieval as baselines. For document retrieval, **NRF** [24] is a well-known work that exploits negative relevance feedback, and PDGD [15] represents the state of the art in online learning to rank. Both of them re-rank documents based on user feedback. To adapt them to entity summarization, we transform each triple into a document by concatenating the textual forms of the three elements of the triple. The name of the entity to summarize is treated as a keyword query. After re-ranking, the top-ranked candidate triple is selected as the replacement triple. NRF has three strategies, among which we implement the

---

[3] https://w3id.org/esbm.
[4] http://wiki.knoesis.org/index.php/FACES.

SingleQuery strategy. In fact, the three strategies are essentially equivalent in our scenario where user feedback in each iteration is a single triple. For PDGD, we obtain its implementation and configuration from its authors. It has two variants: **PDGD-L** using a linear model and **PDGD-N** using a neural model.

Training and Tuning. IPS has two hyperparameters δ and γ in the range of 0–10. NRF has three hyperparameters: k_1 in the range of 0–2, b in the range of 0–1, and γ in the range of 0.5–2. We tune them on the validation set using grid search. PDGD and DRESSED require training. We train their models on the training set. For DRESSED we set epoch = 50 and batchsize = 1.

Initial summaries are generated using CD [26] throughout the experiment.

5.3   Metrics

Since we simulate a perfect user, it is meaningless to evaluate the quality of the final summary S_I which is exactly the ground-truth summary S_{gt}. Instead, we evaluate the iterative process, and we use two metrics for different elements of the process: NDCF for summaries, and NDCG for replacement triples.

NDCF. Following ESBM, we assess the quality of a computed summary S_i by comparing it with a ground-truth summary S_{gt} and calculating F1:

$$P(S_i) = \frac{|S_i \cap S_{gt}|}{|S_i|}, \quad R(S_i) = \frac{|S_i \cap S_{gt}|}{|S_{gt}|}, \quad F1(S_i) = \frac{2 \cdot P(S_i) \cdot R(S_i)}{P(S_i) + R(S_i)}. \quad (9)$$

Note that in the experiments we have P = R = F1 because $|S_i| = |S_{gt}| = 5$. We evaluate a sequence of summaries $S_1, S_2, \ldots, S_I$ computed during the iterative process. Considering that users will be better satisfied if high-quality summaries are computed earlier, we calculate the normalized discounted cumulative F1 (NDCF) over the first i iterations ($1 \le i \le I$):

$$\text{NDCF@}i = \frac{\sum_{j=1}^{i} F1(S_j) \cdot \beta^{j-1}}{\sum_{j=1}^{i} \beta^{j-1}}, \quad (10)$$

where $\beta \in [0, 1]$ is a discount factor representing the decay of importance. We set $\beta = 0.6$ to reduce the influence of summaries after 10 iterations below 1% (i.e., $0.6^{10-1} \approx 0.01$). The result of NDCF is in the range of 0–1. We are particularity interested in NDCF@I, which evaluates the entire iterative process.

NDCG. We can also assess the quality of a sequence of replacement triples $r_0, r_1, \ldots, r_{I-1}$ selected during the iterative process. We treat the sequence as a (partial) ranking of the triples in `Desc(e)`. Considering that users will be better satisfied if relevant triples are selected earlier, we calculate the normalized discounted cumulative gain (NDCG) of the ranking at position i ($1 \le i \le I$):

$$\text{NDCG@}i = \frac{\text{DCG@}i}{\text{IDCG@}i}, \quad \text{DCG@}i = \sum_{j=1}^{i} \frac{\text{rel}(r_{j-1})}{\log(j+1)}, \quad \text{IDCG@}i = \sum_{j=1}^{i} \frac{1}{\log(j+1)},$$

$$(11)$$

where `rel` is defined by Eq. (7). NDCG has been widely used in information retrieval. The result is in the range of 0–1. We are particularity interested in NDCG@I, which evaluates the entire iterative process.

Table 2. Overall results of offline evaluation (mean ± standard deviation). For each method, significant improvements and losses over other methods are indicated by ▲ ($p < 0.01$) or △ ($p < 0.05$), and by ▼ ($p < 0.01$) or ▽ ($p < 0.05$), respectively. Insignificant differences are indicated by ○.

	ESBM-D		ESBM-L		FED	
	NDCF@I	NDCG@I	NDCF@I	NDCG@I	NDCF@I	NDCG@I
FACES-E	.435±.022 –▲▲▼▼▼	.620±.017 –▲▲▼▼▼	.373±.028 –▲▲▼▼▼	.585±.027 –▲▲▼▼▼	.263±.067 –▲▲▼▼▼	.573±.063 –▲▲▼▼▼
IPS	.405±.026 ▼–○▼▼▼	.553±.023 ▼–○▼▼▼	.278±.030 ▼–▼▼▼▼	.410±.042 ▼–▼▼▼▼	.212±.027 ▼–○▼▼▼	.497±.009 ▼–▼▼▼▼
NRF	.407±.021 ▼○–▼▼▼	.554±.016 ▼○–▼▼▼	.325±.029 ▼▲–▼▼▼	.503±.034 ▼▲–▼▼▼	.218±.033 ▼○–▼▼▼	.510±.019 ▼▲–▼▼▼
PDGD-L	.445±.037 ▲▲▲–○▽	.632±.029 ▲▲▲–○▽	.446±.027 ▲▲▲–○▼	.699±.030 ▲▲▲–○▼	.300±.031 ▲▲▲–○▼	.628±.025 ▲▲▲–○▽
PDGD-N	.447±.037 ▲▲▲○–○	.636±.030 ▲▲▲○–▽	.446±.025 ▲▲▲○–▼	.698±.034 ▲▲▲○–▼	.303±.033 ▲▲▲○–▼	.630±.030 ▲▲▲○–▼
DRESSED	.455±.032 ▲▲▲△○–	.645±.028 ▲▲▲△▲–	.481±.030 ▲▲▲▲▲–	.760±.029 ▲▲▲▲▲–	.316±.038 ▲▲▲▲▲–	.644±.042 ▲▲▲▲▲–

5.4   Results

Table 2 presents the overall results of the offline evaluation. We compare DRESSED with the five baselines and we perform two-tailed t-test to analyze whether their differences are statistical significant ($p < 0.01$ and $p < 0.05$).

DRESSED significantly ($p < 0.01$) outperforms FACES-E, IPS, and NRF in terms of both NDCF@I and NDCG@I on all the three datasets. FACES-E is better than IPS. These results are consistent with the results of our online user study reported in Sect. 4. PDGD-L and PDGD-N are stronger baselines. These latest online learning to rank models achieve better results, but still, DRESSED significantly ($p < 0.01$) outperforms them in terms of both NDCF@I and NDCG@I on ESBM-L and FED. However, the difference between DRESSED and PDGD-N in NDCF@I is not significant ($p < 0.05$) on ESBM-D.

In Fig. 3 and Fig. 4, we plot NDCF@i and NDCG@i for $1 \leq i \leq 10$, respectively. The results reflect user experience over varying numbers of iterations. DRESSED is consistently above all the baselines in terms of both NDCF@i and NDCG@i on all the three datasets. It establishes superiority when i is very small, i.e., DRESSED better exploits early feedback to quickly improve computed summaries. In particular, NDCG@1 in Fig. 4 indicates the proportion of iterative processes where the first replacement triple is relevant. We observe a very high value NDCG@1 $= 0.782$ achieved by DRESSED on ESBM-L.

5.5   Discussion

We try to partially justify the performance of the participating systems.

FACES-E is a state-of-the-art entity summarizer but cannot exploit user feedback. Compared with FACES-E, the better performance of DRESSED demonstrates the usefulness of user feedback and the effectiveness of our exploitation.

IPS generates a summary having a similar word distribution to the original data. This feature is useful in document summarization but less useful when it is adapted to entity summarization. For example, entity descriptions in Linked-MDB often contain many triples about the `performance` property, which are thus favored by IPS but are rarely included in ground-truth summaries.

NRF relies on word distributions and exact word matching. Such simple text processing techniques are not very effective when processing the textual form of a triple, which can be very short and shows sparsity. By contrast, DRESSED concatenates word embeddings to represent a triple with both textual and structural features to more comprehensively exploit the semantics of the triple.

The two variants of PDGD represent the state of the art in relevance feedback research. Compared with PDGD, one possible reason for the better performance of DRESSED is that we directly and comprehensively model the interdependence of the current summary, user feedback, as well as the user feedback in history, whereas PDGD does not explicitly model all such interdependence.

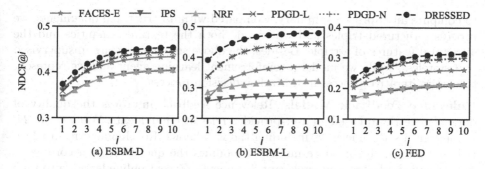

Fig. 3. Results of offline evaluation over varying numbers of iterations (NDCF@i).

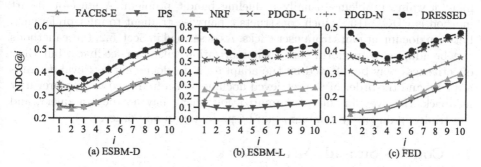

Fig. 4. Results of offline evaluation over varying numbers of iterations (NDCG@i).

6   Related Work

We discuss three related research topics.

Entity Summarization. Entity summarization has been studied for years. RELIN [4] computes informativeness. DIVERSUM [21] improves the diversity of an entity summary by choosing triples with different properties. CD [26] jointly optimizes informativeness and diversity. More than that, FACES [7] and its extension FACES-E [8] consider the frequency of property value, while LinkSUM [22] computes PageRank. ES-LDA [16,17] relies on a Latent Dirichlet Allocation (LDA) model. However, none of these methods could exploit user feedback to compute improved summaries. From a technical perspective, these methods are unsupervised, whereas our model is based on reinforcement learning. Some application-specific entity summarizers [10,23,28] are supervised based on a set of carefully designed features. Our approach avoids such manual feature engineering and learns deep representations of triples and their interdependence.

Document Summarization with User Feedback. Some document summarizers exploit user feedback to compute improved summaries. They allow users to select interesting topics [12], keywords [18], or concepts (e.g., named entities) [2]. IPS [27] is the most similar method to our approach. It supports clicking an interesting sentence in a document summary, and leverages this feedback to compute an improved summary. Compared with unstructured documents, we process structured triples and we encode both the textual semantics and the structural features of a triple. Besides, the above summarizers are unsupervised and stateless, while we model a reinforcement learning agent and we represent the entire iterative process as a Markov decision process.

Relevance Feedback Models. Relevance feedback improves the quality of document retrieval based on user-provided relevance judgments. Wang et al. [24] implement a set of methods including the well-known Rocchio algorithm which is based on the vector space model. It modifies the query vector according to user-specified relevant and irrelevant documents. Recent online learning to rank models formulate document retrieval with iterative user feedback as a reinforcement learning problem—usually a dueling bandit problem. A state-of-the-art method is PDGD [15], which constructs a pairwise gradient to infer preferences between document pairs from user clicks. As described in Sect. 5.2, these methods can be adapted to perform entity summarization with user feedback, but their effectiveness may be affected by the adaptation. In document retrieval, there is a query, and the order of the retrieved documents is often used to interpret user feedback. However, in entity summarization, there may not be any query, and the triples in an entity summary can be presented in any order.

7   Conclusion and Future Work

We presented the first attempt to improve entity summarization with user feedback. Our reinforcement learning based modeling of the task and, in particular, our deep neural policy network for representing triples and their interdependence, showed better performance than a wide variety of baselines. Our approach has the potential to replace static entity cards deployed in existing applications to facilitate task completion and improve user experience. Our encoder for triples and their interdependence may also find application in other knowledge graph based tasks like entity clustering.

We studied the cross-replace scenario but our implementation can be easily extended to support other scenarios, e.g., crossing off multiple triples in each iteration, crossing without replacement, or providing positive feedback. We will experiment with these extensions in future work. To further improve generalizability, e.g., to deal with paths and structures more complex than triples, one may extend the scope of entity summary with concepts like concise bounded description [19] or RDF sentence [29], to better process blank nodes in RDF.

Acknowledgments. This work was supported in part by the NSFC under Grant 61772264 and in part by the Qing Lan Program of Jiangsu Province.

References

1. Avinesh, P.V.S., Meyer, C.M.: Joint optimization of user-desired content in multi-document summaries by learning from user feedback. In: ACL 2017, Volume 1, pp. 1353–1363 (2017). https://doi.org/10.18653/v1/P17-1124

2. Avinesh, P.V.S., Meyer, C.M.: Joint optimization of user-desired content in multi-document summaries by learning from user feedback. In: ACL 2017, vol. 1: Long Papers, pp. 1353–1363 (2017). https://doi.org/10.18653/v1/P17-1124
3. Bojanowski, P., Grave, E., Joulin, A., Mikolov, T.: Enriching word vectors with subword information. TACL **5**, 135–146 (2017)
4. Cheng, G., Tran, T., Qu, Y.: RELIN: relatedness and informativeness-based centrality for entity summarization. In: Aroyo, L., Welty, C., Alani, H., Taylor, J., Bernstein, A., Kagal, L., Noy, N., Blomqvist, E. (eds.) ISWC 2011, Part I. LNCS, vol. 7031, pp. 114–129. Springer, Heidelberg (2011). https://doi.org/10.1007/978-3-642-25073-6_8
5. Cheng, G., Xu, D., Qu, Y.: C3D+P: a summarization method for interactive entity resolution. J. Web Sem. **35**, 203–213 (2015). https://doi.org/10.1016/j.websem.2015.05.004
6. Cheng, G., Xu, D., Qu, Y.: Summarizing entity descriptions for effective and efficient human-centered entity linking. In: WWW 2015, pp. 184–194 (2015). https://doi.org/10.1145/2736277.2741094
7. Gunaratna, K., Thirunarayan, K., Sheth, A.P.: FACES: diversity-aware entity summarization using incremental hierarchical conceptual clustering. In: AAAI 2015, pp. 116–122 (2015)
8. Gunaratna, K., Thirunarayan, K., Sheth, A., Cheng, G.: Gleaning types for literals in RDF triples with application to entity summarization. In: Sack, H., Blomqvist, E., d'Aquin, M., Ghidini, C., Ponzetto, S.P., Lange, C. (eds.) ESWC 2016. LNCS, vol. 9678, pp. 85–100. Springer, Cham (2016). https://doi.org/10.1007/978-3-319-34129-3_6
9. Gunaratna, K., Yazdavar, A.H., Thirunarayan, K., Sheth, A.P., Cheng, G.: Relatedness-based multi-entity summarization. In: IJCAI 2017, pp. 1060–1066 (2017). https://doi.org/10.24963/ijcai.2017/147
10. Hasibi, F., Balog, K., Bratsberg, S.E.: Dynamic factual summaries for entity cards. In: SIGIR 2017, pp. 773–782 (2017). https://doi.org/10.1145/3077136.3080810
11. Jagerman, R., Oosterhuis, H., de Rijke, M.: To model or to intervene: a comparison of counterfactual and online learning to rank from user interactions. In: SIGIR 2019, pp. 15–24 (2019). https://doi.org/10.1145/3331184.3331269
12. Leuski, A., Lin, C., Hovy, E.H.: iNeATS: interactive multi-document summarization. In: ACL 2003, pp. 125–128 (2003)
13. Liu, Q., Cheng, G., Gunaratna, K., Qu, Y.: Entity summarization: state of the art and future challenges. CoRR abs/1910.08252 (2019). http://arxiv.org/abs/1910.08252
14. Liu, Q., Cheng, G., Gunaratna, K., Qu, Y.: ESBM: an entity summarization benchmark. In: ESWC 2020 (2020)
15. Oosterhuis, H., de Rijke, M.: Differentiable unbiased online learning to rank. In: CIKM 2018, pp. 1293–1302 (2018). https://doi.org/10.1145/3269206.3271686
16. Pouriyeh, S.A., Allahyari, M., Kochut, K., Cheng, G., Arabnia, H.R.: Combining word embedding and knowledge-based topic modeling for entity summarization. In: ICSC 2018, pp. 252–255 (2018). https://doi.org/10.1109/ICSC.2018.00044
17. Pouriyeh, S.A., Allahyari, M., Kochut, K., Cheng, G., Arabnia, H.R.: ES-LDA: entity summarization using knowledge-based topic modeling. In: IJCNLP 2017, Volume 1, pp. 316–325 (2017)
18. Sakai, H., Masuyama, S.: A multiple-document summarization system with user interaction. In: COLING 2004 (2004)
19. Stickler, P.: CBD - concise bounded description (2005). http://www.w3.org/Submission/CBD/

20. Stoilos, G., Stamou, G., Kollias, S.: A string metric for ontology alignment. In: Gil, Y., Motta, E., Benjamins, V.R., Musen, M.A. (eds.) ISWC 2005. LNCS, vol. 3729, pp. 624–637. Springer, Heidelberg (2005). https://doi.org/10.1007/11574620_45

21. Sydow, M., Pikula, M., Schenkel, R.: The notion of diversity in graphical entity summarisation on semantic knowledge graphs. J. Intell. Inf. Syst. **41**(2), 109–149 (2013). https://doi.org/10.1007/s10844-013-0239-6

22. Thalhammer, A., Lasierra, N., Rettinger, A.: LinkSUM: using link analysis to summarize entity data. In: Bozzon, A., Cudre-Maroux, P., Pautasso, C. (eds.) ICWE 2016. LNCS, vol. 9671, pp. 244–261. Springer, Cham (2016). https://doi.org/10.1007/978-3-319-38791-8_14

23. Tonon, A., Catasta, M., Prokofyev, R., Demartini, G., Aberer, K., Cudré-Mauroux, P.: Contextualized ranking of entity types based on knowledge graphs. J. Web Sem. **37–38**, 170–183 (2016). https://doi.org/10.1016/j.websem.2015.12.005

24. Wang, X., Fang, H., Zhai, C.: A study of methods for negative relevance feedback. In: SIGIR 2008, pp. 219–226 (2008). https://doi.org/10.1145/1390334.1390374

25. Williams, R.J.: Simple statistical gradient-following algorithms for connectionist reinforcement learning. Mach. Learn. **8**, 229–256 (1992). https://doi.org/10.1007/BF00992696

26. Xu, D., Zheng, L., Qu, Y.: CD at ENSEC 2016: generating characteristic and diverse entity summaries. In: SumPre 2016 (2016)

27. Yan, R., Nie, J., Li, X.: Summarize what you are interested. In: An optimization framework for interactive personalized summarization. In: EMNLP 2011, pp. 1342–1351 (2011)

28. Zhang, L., Zhang, Y., Chen, Y.: Summarizing highly structured documents for effective search interaction. In: SIGIR 2012, pp. 145–154 (2012). https://doi.org/10.1145/2348283.2348306

29. Zhang, X., Cheng, G., Qu, Y.: Ontology summarization based on RDF sentence graph. In: WWW 2007, pp. 707–716 (2007). https://doi.org/10.1145/1242572.1242668

Incremental Multi-source Entity Resolution for Knowledge Graph Completion

Alieh Saeedi[✉], Eric Peukert, and Erhard Rahm

ScaDS.AI Dresden/Leipzig, University of Leipzig, Leipzig, Germany
saeedi@informatik.uni-leipzig.de

Abstract. We present and evaluate new methods for incremental entity resolution as needed for the completion of knowledge graphs integrating data from multiple sources. Compared to previous approaches we aim at reducing the dependency on the order in which new sources and entities are added. For this purpose, we consider sets of new entities for an optimized assignment of them to entity clusters. We also propose the use of a light-weight approach to repair entity clusters in order to correct wrong clusters. The new approaches are integrated within the FAMER framework for parallel and scalable entity clustering. A detailed evaluation of the new approaches for real-world workloads shows their high effectiveness. In particular, the repair approach outperforms other incremental approaches and achieves the same quality than with batch-like entity resolution showing that its results are independent from the order in which new entities are added.

1 Introduction

Knowledge graphs (KG) physically integrate numerous entities with their properties and relationships as well as associated metadata about entity types and relationship types in a graph-like structure [1]. The KG entities are typically integrated from numerous sources, such as other knowledge graphs or web pages. The initial KG may be created from a single source (e.g., a pre-existing knowledge graph such as DBpedia) or a static integration of multiple sources. KG completion (or extension) refers to the incremental addition of new entities and entire sources. The addition of new entities requires solving several challenging tasks, in particular an incremental entity resolution to match and cluster new entities with already known entities in the KG [2].

Most previous work on entity resolution (ER) deals with static ER to match entities from one or several static data sources. Such static approaches are not sufficient to add entities to an in-use KG where the majority of already integrated entities is largely unaffected by new entities and should not have to be re-integrated for every update. ER for entities of multiple sources typically groups or clusters matching entities and these clusters can then be used to fuse (merge) the properties of the matching entities to obtain an enriched entity description

© Springer Nature Switzerland AG 2020
A. Harth et al. (Eds.): ESWC 2020, LNCS 12123, pp. 393–408, 2020.
https://doi.org/10.1007/978-3-030-49461-2_23

for the KG. Incremental ER thus requires to update these entity clusters for new entities. A naive approach is to simply add a new entity either to the most similar existing cluster or to create a new cluster if there is no similar one [3,4]. However, this approach typically suffers from a strong dependency on the order in which new entities are added. In particular, wrong cluster decisions, e.g., due to data quality problems, will not be corrected and can lead to further errors when new entities are added. The overall ER quality can thus be much worse than for batch ER where all entities are simultaneously integrated.

We therefore propose and evaluate new approaches for incremental entity clustering that reduce the dependency on the order in which new entities and sources are added. The approaches have been developed for our framework FAMER that supports a parallel ER for entities from multiple sources [5]. For batch ER, FAMER first applies pairwise linking among entities and derives a so-called similarity graph. This graph is input for entity clustering that determines a set of clusters where each cluster groups the matching entities from several sources. These linking and clustering steps now need to become incremental while preserving a similarly high quality than for batch ER.

We make the following contributions:

- We propose several approaches for incremental linking and clustering. For an optimized cluster assignment, we consider the addition of sets of entities and so-called *max-both* assignments that add an entity to the most similar cluster only when there is no more similar new entity from the respective data source. Furthermore, we optionally can link new entities with themselves before updating entity clusters. We also support the fusion of cluster members to a single entity which simplifies and speed-ups incremental clustering as new entities need no longer be compared to several entities of a cluster.
- We propose a new method called *n-depth reclustering* for incremental ER that is able to repair existing clusters for improved quality and a reduced dependency on the insert order of new entities.
- We provide parallel implementations of all methods for improved runtimes and high scalability to large datasets.
- We evaluate the incremental approaches for datasets of three domains in terms of cluster quality and runtime efficiency. We also provide a comparison to a previous approach for incremental cluster repair [6] and with batch ER.

After a discussion of related work, we give an overview of the incremental methods within FAMER in Sect. 3. Section 4 presents the new methods in detail and Sect. 5 is the evaluation.

2   Related Work

ER and link discovery have been widely investigated and are the subject of several books and surveys [7–11]. Most previous approaches are static and focus on either finding duplicates in a single source or binary matching between entities of two sources. A few studies investigate multi-source ER and clustering [4,5,12,13].

Relatively little work has been done on incremental ER to deal with new entities which should be fast and not have to repeat the linkage of already linked entities. Most of these approaches [3,14,15] focus on a single data source only. In these approaches, new entities are either added to the most similar cluster (group) of entities or are considered as new entities. These approaches do neither aim at an optimized cluster assignment for sets of new entities nor do they repair previous match and cluster decisions.

Only little work coped with repairing previous cluster decisions for incremental ER and the previous approaches focus on a single source. Gruenheid et al. [6] maintain the clusters within a similarity graph and propose several approaches to update this graph based on different portions of the graph. Furthermore, a greedy method is introduced to use the updated graph to correct clusters by merging and splitting them or by moving entities among clusters. Nascimento et al. [16] extend the approach of [6] by defining six filters to limit the number of cluster updates. The filters improve runtime but also reduce the quality. The evaluations in both [6] and [16] are limited to small single-source datasets. In our evaluation we will also consider the greedy approach of [6].

To our knowledge, there is no previous method for multi-source incremental entity clustering except the initial approach introduced in [4]. This method assumes duplicate-free sources and provides an optimized addition for sets of new entities or entire new sources which was shown to achieve better cluster quality than the isolated addition of one new entity at a time. The most effective approach was a so-called *max-both* assignment where an entity e from a set S of new entities is only assigned to the cluster c with the highest similarity to e (above a minimal similarity threshold) if there is no other entity in S from the same source than e with a higher similarity.

Here, we substantially extend this simple approach by considering more options for incremental linkage, in particular the optional linkage among new entities and the use of cluster fusion. Moreover, we propose and evaluate a new repair method for incremental multi-source entity clustering. We also provide distributed implementations of the approaches for improved performance.

3   Overview of Incremental ER with FAMER

For batch ER of multiple sources, FAMER applies the two configurable phases of *linking* and *clustering* [5,12]. The linking phase determines a similarity graph containing links between pairs of similar entities. This phase starts with blocking [8] so that only entities of the same block need to be compared with each other. Pairwise matching is typically based on the combined similarity of several properties and a threshold for the minimal similarity. The second phase uses the similarity graph to determine entity clusters. It supports several clustering schemes to group similar entities that represent the same real-world object. The most effective clustering approaches such as CLIP [5] assume duplicate-free sources so that a cluster should at most contain one entity per source. While the proposed incremental approaches are largely independent of the specific clustering scheme we analyze them here in combination with the optimized approaches

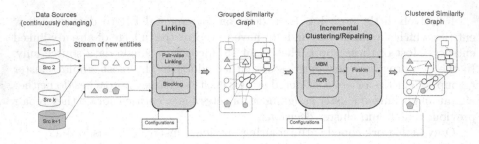

Fig. 1. FAMER workflow for incremental entity resolution

for duplicate-free data sources (assuming that dirty sources can first be dedupli-cated before their integration into a KG).

In this paper we propose significant extensions to FAMER for incremen-tal ER. The corresponding workflow is indicated in Fig. 1. The approach uses a so-called *clustered similarity graph*, i.e., a similarity graph reflecting already determined clusters. The input of the workflow is a stream of new entities from existing sources or from a new source plus the already determined clustered similarity graph from previous iterations. The *linking* part now focuses on the new entities and does not re-link among previous entities. We also support the linking among new entities to provide additional links in the similarity graph that may lead to better cluster results. The output of the linking is a *grouped similarity graph* composed of existing clusters and the group of new entities and the newly created links (the light-blue colored group in the middle of Fig. 1).

The *Incremental Clustering/Repairing* part supports two methods for inte-grating the group of new entities into clusters. In the base (non-repairing) app-roach called *Max-Both Merge* (MBM) the new entities are either added to a similar existing cluster or they form a new cluster. A more sophisticated app-roach is able to repair existing clusters to achieve a better cluster assignment for new entities by reclustering a portion of the existing clustered graph. The method is named *n-depth reclustering* (nDR) where n is a parameter to control the portion of the similarity graph that is considered for reclustering. The details of the incremental clustering approaches are explained in Sect. 4.

The output of incremental clustering is a fully clustered graph. The clus-ters can optionally be fused in the *Fusion* component so that all entities are represented by a single entity called cluster representative. Fusion can improve linking efficiency since new entities only have to be compared with the cluster representatives instead of all cluster members. On the other hand, we loose the possibility to recluster if we retain only a single fused entity per cluster. The fusion approach is outlined in Sect. 4.2 and the impact of fusion on quality and runtime is evaluated in Sect. 5.

FAMER and the new approaches for incremental entity linking and cluster-ing are implemented using the distributed execution framework Apache Flink. Hence, all match and clustering approaches can be executed in parallel on mul-tiple machines. We will evaluate our methods for different datasets and different numbers of worker machines.

4   Incremental Clustering Approaches

We first define the main concepts in Sect. 4.1. We then describe the general incremental ER process in Sect. 4.2 and the base approach MB in Sect. 4.3. Finally, the repairing method is described in Sect. 4.4.

4.1   Concepts

Similarity Graph: A similarity graph $\mathcal{G} = (\mathcal{E}, \mathcal{L})$ is a graph in which vertices of $\mathcal{E}$ represent entities and edges of $\mathcal{L}$ are links between similar entities. Edges have a property for the similarity value (real number in the interval $[0, 1]$) indicating the degree of similarity. Since we assume duplicate-free sources in this paper, there are no edges between entities of the same source.

Grouped Similarity Graph: A grouped similarity graph $\mathcal{GG}$ is a similarity graph where each entity can be associated to a group or cluster. Clustered entities have a cluster-id of the cluster they belong to. The grouped similarity graph allows us to maintain already determined clusters together with the underlying similarity graph as input for incremental changes such as adding new entities. A grouped similarity graph may also include new entities with their similarity links to other entities. Figure 2a shows a grouped similarity graph with four groups cg_0, cg_1, cg_2, cg_3 and group g_{new} with new entities. There are links between entities of the same group, so-called *intra-links*, as well as links between entities of different groups (*inter-links*) resulting in group neighborhoods.

Cluster: A cluster has a unique cluster-id and consists of a group of entities that are meant to represent to the same real-world object. With the assumption of duplicate-free sources, we require *source-consistent* clusters, i.e. there should be at most one entity per source in a cluster so that all cluster members are from different sources.

Clustered Similarity Graph: A clustered similarity graph $\mathcal{CG}$ is a similarity graph $\mathcal{G}$ such that all of its entities are clustered. The same cluster-id is assigned to all vertices of the same cluster.

Fused Similarity Graph: A fused similarity graph is a clustered similarity graph in that each cluster is only represented with a cluster representative. The cluster representative combines the property values of the original cluster members and also records the ids of the originating data sources as provenance information (see sample cluster representatives in Fig. 5a).

Max-Both Link: An entity from a source A may have several links to entities of a source B. From these links, the one with the highest similarity value is called maximum link. If a link is a maximum link from both sides, it is a max-both or strong link. In Fig. 2b, for entity a_1 the maximum link to source B is the one to entity b_1 (similarity 0.95). This link is also maximum for b_1 so that it is a max-both link. By contrast, the link between c_2 and b_1 is only the maximum link for one side (c_2) and the link between a_1 to b_0 for none of the sides.

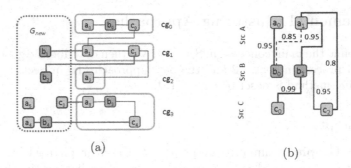

Fig. 2. a) Sample grouped similarity graph b) Max-Both concept

n-Depth Neighbor Graph: If a group in a grouped similarity graph is linked to the other groups via inter-links, the graphs directly linked to it are called 1-depth neighbor graphs. Recursively, the 1-depth neighbors of the n-depth neighbors are the (n + 1)-depth neighbors. For example in Fig. 2a, G_{new} is the 1-depth neighbor of cg_1 and cg_3 and also 2-depth neighbor of cg_0 and cg_2.

4.2   Incremental Entity Resolution

Incremental ER limits linking and clustering to the new entities rather than processing all entities as for batch ER. At the same time the resulting linkage and cluster quality should be similar to batch ER which means that the order in which entities are added should ideally have no impact on quality. The latter requirement is a main reason for re-clustering as otherwise wrong cluster decisions can impact further cluster decisions and thus lead to increasing quality problems.

As explained in Sect. 3, incremental ER entails the two main steps of *Linking* and *Clustering*. The input of linking is an existing clustered graph CG_{exist} and a set of new entities $\mathcal{E}_{new}$ from already known sources or from a new source. For illustration, we consider a running example with existing entities from four sources (shown in Fig. 3a) and new entities to be integrated (shown in Fig. 3b). As typical for real-world data, the entity properties are partly erroneous. Figure 4a shows the clustered similarity graph indicating that the previous entities form four clusters named cg_0 to cg_3. Note, that the colors indicate the originating source and that every cluster contains at most one entity per source.

For the linking of new entities we optionally support a linking among new entities. While this introduces additional computations, the additionally found links may lead to better clusters. Note that this *new-input-linking* is not applicable if all new entities are from the same source due to the assumption of duplicate-free sources. To limit the number of comparisons we apply blocking and only compare new entities with other entities of the same block. For the running example we assume that the two initial letters of the surname are used as blocking key (specified in the configuration) as shown in Fig. 3c. Without new-input-linking, we only compare new entities (marked in blue) with previous entities of the same block. With new-input-linking, we additionally link new

entities among each other, e.g., for blocking key *su*. All links between new entities with a similarity above a threshold (specified in the configuration) are added
to the similarity graph. Figure 4b and c illustrate the resulting grouped similarity graphs without and with new-input-linking, respectively. The only difference
occurs for the new entity 10 which is not linked with any previous entity but a
link with the new entity 12 is generated by new-input-linking so that entity 10
may be added to the same cluster.

The clustering part (second step of incremental ER) uses the determined
grouped similarity graph $\mathcal{GG}$ and the clustering configuration as input. The clustering configuration specifies either one of the base methods or the repair method
with their parameters (to be explained in Sects. 4.3 and 4.4). The output is an
updated clustered graph $\mathcal{CG}_{updated}$ that includes the new entities within updated
clusters.

The sketched process is similar when we choose to fuse all entities of a cluster
to build cluster representatives and when we use a fused similarity graph instead
of a clustered similarity graph. The reduced number of entities in this graph
reduces the number of comparisons and can thus lead to a more efficient linking.
Figure 5a shows the fused similarity graph of the running example to which the
new entities have to be compared. The cluster representatives (fused entities)
may contain per property multiple values from the original entities. When linking
a new entity we can choose to only link to cluster representatives that do not yet
include an entity from the same source. For example, in Fig. 5b, the link between
entity 9 and cluster cg_0 does not need to be created (indicated as dashed line)
since this cluster already contains an entity of the same source.

(a)				
id	name	surname	src	key
1	George	Walker	A	
2	george	Waker	B	wa
3	George	Wabel	A	
4	Frankie	Pollock	C	
5	Franklin	Pollock	B	po
6	Franklin	Pollim	A	
7	Berja	Summeahville	D	su

(b)			
id	name	surname	src
8	Franklin	Pollock	A
9	George	Wabel	B
10	Bertha	Summercille	C
11	Berta	Summeahville	A
12	Bertha	Summeahville	B

(c)			
key	wa	po	su
id	1 2 3 9	4 5 6 8	7 10 11 12

Fig. 3. Running example: existing entities, new entities and blocking

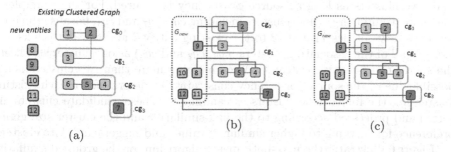

(a)   (b)   (c)

Fig. 4. a) Linking input b) w/o *new-input-linking* c) with *new-input-linking*

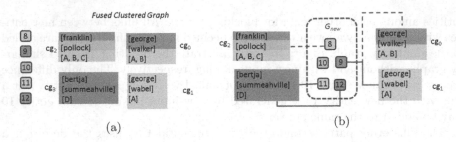

Fig. 5. a) Linking input b) linking output with fused clustered graph

4.3   Max-Both Merge

The max-both merge approach integrates new entities into already existing clusters or creates new clusters for them. The decision is based on the max-both (strong) links between new entities and already clustered entities. In case of new-input-linking, we first apply a pre-clustering among the linked new entities to create source-consistent clusters which may then be merged with the existing clusters. The case without new-input-linking can be viewed as a special case where each new entity forms a singleton cluster.

If $\mathcal{GG}$ is a grouped similarity graph consisting of $\mathcal{G}_{new}$, $\mathcal{CG}_{exist}$ and $\mathcal{L}_{exist\_new}$, the max-both approach merges a new cluster $n \in \mathcal{G}_{new}$ with an existing cluster $c \in \mathcal{CG}_{exist}$ if there is a max-both link $l(e_i, e_j) \in \mathcal{L}_{exist\_new}$ between a new entity $e_i \in n$ and an entity $e_j \in c$ and the two clusters n and c have only entities from different sources. Hence, max-both merge assigns a new cluster to the maximally similar existing cluster and merges them only if this does not violate source consistency. For the example in Fig. 6, we would assign entity 9 neither to cluster cg_0 nor to cg_1 if the link between entity 9 and entity 1 of cg_0 has a higher similarity than the link with entity 3 of cg_1.

The further processing of the selected max-both links has to consider that max-both links ensure the maximal entity similarity only w.r.t. a fixed pair of sources. Hence, it is possible that clusters can have several max-both links referring to entities of different sources. As a result, it may be possible to merge more than two clusters as long as source consistency is ensured. For the example in Fig. 6, we would merge three clusters including cg_6, cg_7 and cg_3, because the links from the new entities 11 and 12 to the existing entity 7 are max-both links and merging all of the associating clusters (cg_6, cg_7 and cg_3) as one cluster still keeps the source consistency constraint. When merging more than two clusters is not possible due to the source consistency constraint, we determine for each existing cluster cg_i, the linked new clusters as candidates. These candidate clusters are sorted and processed according to the link similarity and the cluster size giving preference for merging to higher similarity values and bigger candidate clusters.

Figure 6 illustrates the max-both merge algorithm for the grouped similarity graph of Fig. 4c. The left part of the Fig. 6 shows the result after pre-clustering the new entities resulting in clusters cg_4 to cg_7. Then the links are selected that are max-both and that connect mergeable clusters as shown in the middle part of

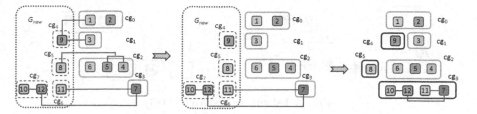

Fig. 6. Max-Both merge

Fig. 6 (the links from the new clusters cg_4 and cg_5 to clusters cg_0 and cg_2 would lead to source inconsistency and are thus removed). The right part of Fig. 6 indicates the final merge result with six instead of eight clusters. The existing cluster cg_3 is linked to two new clusters cg_0 and cg_7. Assuming that both links have the same similarity value, the sort order would first consider the bigger cluster cg_7 and merge it. Then cluster cg_6 is considered and also merged with cg_3 since source consistency is preserved.

For fused clusters, we use the provenance information in the cluster representatives to avoid linking new entities to clusters containing already an entity from the same source (Fig. 5b). This leads to an incremental clustering result corresponding to the one for the max-both approach.

4.4 n-Depth Reclustering

The approaches described so far cannot add a new entity to an existing cluster if there is already another entity of the respective source. This can lead to wrong cluster decisions, e.g., if the previously added entity is less similar to the other cluster members than the new entity. Our n-depth reclustering scheme addresses this problem to obtain better clusters and to become largely independent from the order in which new entities are added. At the same time, we want to limit the amount of reclustering in order to maintain good efficiency.

The approach reclusters the new entities in $\mathcal{G}_{new}$ with their neighbors in the existing clustered graph $\mathcal{CG}_{exist}$. The parameter n controls the depth up to which

---

Algorithm 1: n-Depth Reclustering

Input: grouped similarity graph $\mathcal{GG}$ ($\mathcal{G}_{new}$, $\mathcal{CG}_{exist}$, $\mathcal{L}_{exist\_new}$), configuration $config$

Output: updated Clustered Graph $\mathcal{CG}_{updated}$

1 $\mathcal{CG}_{neighbors} \leftarrow$ getNeighbors($\mathcal{GG}$, n)
2 $\mathcal{G}_{reclustering} \leftarrow \mathcal{CG}_{neighbors} \cup \mathcal{G}_{new} \cup \mathcal{L}_{exist\_new}$
3 $\mathcal{CG}_{new} \leftarrow$ batchClustering($\mathcal{G}_{reclustering}$, $conf.getClustering()$)
4 $\mathcal{CG}_{updated} \leftarrow \mathcal{GG}$
5 updateGraph($\mathcal{GG}$, $\mathcal{CG}_{new}$)
6 **return** $\mathcal{CG}_{updated}$

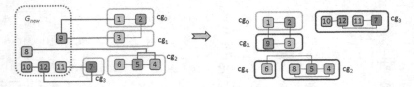

Fig. 7. 1-depth reclustering (1DR)

the neighboring clusters and their entities are reconsidered thereby allowing us to control the scope of processing and associated overhead. For $n = 1$, the algorithm only re-evaluates entities of the existing clusters directly connected to the new entities. For $n = 2$, the neighbors of 1-depth neighbors are also selected. The selected portion of the grouped similarity graph $\mathcal{GG}$, $\mathcal{G}_{new}$ and the neighbors, are reclustered using a static clustering scheme.

Algorithm 1 outlines this process. In line 1, the neighbors up to depth n are determined. The union of the found neighbor clusters (including their intra- and inter-links) with the subgraph of new entities $\mathcal{G}_{new}$ forms the portion ($\mathcal{G}_{reclustering}$) of the grouped similarity graph to be re-clustered (line 2). In line 3, the static clustering scheme is applied leading to an updated set of clusters. Any clustering algorithm can be used for the batchClustering. In our experiments in Sect. 5 we used the CLIP algorithm that was shown in [5] to achieve better quality than other ER clustering approaches.

Figure 7 illustrates the algorithm for $n = 1$. The portion of the input to be reclustered consists of the new graph $\mathcal{G}_{new}$ and its 1-depth neighbor clusters (cg_0 to cg_3). The output (right part of the Fig. 7) shows that the previous cluster cg_2 is changed so that the new entity 8 is included instead of the previous member 6 from the same source.

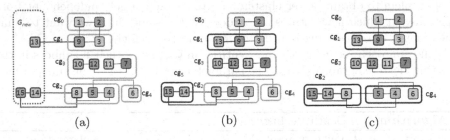

Fig. 8. a) 2nd increment input b) 1DR output c) 2DR output

Figure 8a shows the output of Fig. 7 as existing clustered graph and the next increment of new entities (13, 14 and 15). By performing 1-depth reclustering (1DR), a small portion of the graph including clusters cg_1 and cg_2 plus the new entities are reclustered. As illustrated in Fig. 8b only cluster cg_1 is modified and the entities 14 and 15 create a new cluster. For the same input choosing $n = 2$

would end to reclustering a bigger portion of the existing clustered graph compared with 1-depth reclustering. As illustrated in Fig. 8c, the 2-depth neighbour cluster cg_4 and the 1-depth neighbor clusters, cg_1 and cg_2 are modified by the reclustering.

The introduced reclustering of existing clusters depends on the intra-cluster links. Therefore, the repairing method is not applicable for fused clusters.

5   Evaluation

We now evaluate the effectiveness and efficiency of the proposed incremental clustering/repairing algorithms in comparison to the batch ER approach of FAMER and the Greedy incremental cluster repair of [6]. We first describe the used datasets from three domains. We then analyze comparatively the match quality of the proposed algorithms. Finally, we evaluate runtime performance.

We use datasets from three domains with different numbers of duplicate-free sources. The datasets are publicly available and have been used in prior ER studies[1]. Table 1 shows the main characteristics of the datasets in particular the number of clusters and match pairs of the perfect ER result. The smallest dataset G contains geographical real-world entities from four different data sources DBpedia (dp), Geonames (geo), Freebase (fb) and NYTimes (ny) and has already been used in the OAEI competition. For our evaluation, we focus on a subset of settlement entities as we had to manually determine the perfect clusters and thus the perfect match pairs. For the other larger evaluation datasets M and P we applied advanced data generation and corruption tools to be able to evaluate the ER quality and scalability for larger datasets and a controlled degree of corruption. M is based on real records about songs from the MusicBrainz database. We applied the DAPO data generator [17] to create five sources and duplicates for 50% of the original records in two to five sources as described for the initial evaluation of the FAMER framework [5,12]. P is based on real person records from the North-Carolina voter registry and synthetically generated duplicates using the tool GeCo [18]. We consider the configuration with 10 sources of 1 million entities each; i.e. we process up to 10 million person records.

We evaluate our proposed methods with two scenarios of incremental ER. In the first scenario, called *sources-wise*, a complete new source is added to the existing clustered graph in each increment. In the second scenario, called *entity-wise*, specific portions of new entities from already existing sources are added to the clustered graph. For this case, we consider the four configurations listed in Table 2. Each configuration specifies the percentage of entities from each source that is added to the knowledge base in each increment. For example, in configuration $conf1$, the initial KG only contains 20% of the entities from each source. In each of the following four increments 20% of the entities from each source are added.

For linking, we apply different configurations for each dataset (listed in Table 3). All configurations use standard blocking with different blocking keys.

---

[1] https://dbs.uni-leipzig.de/research/projects/object_matching/
benchmark_datasets_for_entity_resolution.

Table 1. Evaluation datasets

	General information		#Entity	#Src	Perfect result	
	Domain	Entity properties	#Entity	#Src	#Clusters	#Links
G	Geography	label, longitude, latitude	3,054	4	820	4,391
M	Music	artist, title, album, year, length	19,375	5	10,000	16,250
P	Persons	name, surname, suburb, postcode	10,000,000	10	6,625,848	14,995,973

The match rules rely on different attribute similarities using either string similarity functions (Jaro Winkler, Trigram) or geographical distance.

5.1   Evaluation Results

Initially we evaluate the quality and robustness of our proposed methods for source-wise incremental ER. As described in Sect. 4, we do not need to perform new-input-linking and pre-clustering in this scenario since sources are duplicate free.

To analyze the impact of the order in which we add sources, we start with the results for the real-world dataset G where the four sources differ strongly in size and quality. We compare our proposed incremental methods against the batch clustering approach of FAMER as well as the re-implemented Greedy algorithm from [6]. In Fig. 9 we show the obtained cluster quality results in terms of precision, recall and F-Measure for different similarity threshold of the linking phase which influences the number and the quality of generated links that are input to clustering. Lower thresholds produce more links (good recall) at a higher chance of wrong links (lower precision) while higher thresholds lead to the opposite behavior.

Table 2. Increment configurations

Conf	1	2	3	4
Base	20%	33%	50%	80%
inc 1	20%	33%	10%	10%
inc 2	20%	33%	10%	10%
inc 3	20%	–	10%	–
inc 4	20%	–	10%	–
inc 5	–	–	10%	–

Table 3. Linking configurations

	Blocking key	Similarity function
G	prefixLength1 (label)	Jaro Winkler (label) geographical distance
M	prefixLength1 (artist+title+album)	Trigram (artist+title+album)
P	prefixLength4 (surname) + prefixLength4 (name)	avg (Trigram (name) + Trigram (surname) + Trigram (postcode) + Trigram (suburb))

Twelve different orders of adding sources are possible. We examined all of them and report results for the best order "ny, fb, geo, dp" (conf1) and the worst order "dp, geo, ny, fb" (conf2) in Fig. 9. With a good insert order, the quality of all approaches including MB (max-both merge) are close together and as good as batch ER. However, for the worst order MB achieves substantially lower recall and F-measure values indicating its strong dependency on the insert order. By contrast, our proposed re-clustering approach nDR (n = 1) strongly reduces the dependency on the insert order and achieves the same quality as batch ER. The weakest results are observed for the Greedy approach [6]. Greedy initially tries to merge new entities to a randomly chosen neighboring cluster without considering the actual similarity value of the link. Then if merging is not possible, it tries to maximize the objective function of the clustering algorithm by iteratively splitting existing clusters and moving entities in between clusters until no the objective function is not improved further. However, the random assignment is problematic when a new entity has multiple neighboring clusters. We observed that even after many iterations of merge, split and move, some entities do not end up in the optimal cluster. Moreover, Greedy suffers from very long execution times due to its iterative nature and some experiments for larger datasets could not even finish. Therefore, the quality (particularly precision) results as well as the run-times are significantly lower than with our proposed approaches.

In Fig. 10 we compare the cluster quality of our proposed methods against the non-incremental batch clustering approach of FAMER for datasets M and P and different similarity thresholds for linking. In all experiments, our incremental methods are able to compete with batch clustering. For dataset M (first row in Fig. 10) all methods achieve high values for precision but lower recall values. The recall of the max-both approaches is consistently lower than nDR (n = 1) which is like for dataset G as effective as the batch approach. For the largest dataset P, the results are slightly different. Surprisingly, here all incremental methods could achieve better precision than batch clustering. This can be explained by the maximum possible cluster size of 10 while the average cluster size is only about 1.5 for this dataset. In batch clustering 10 entities from 10 different sources can be linked and considered as one cluster. Incremental methods do only touch the direct neighboring entities of the linked new entities. Hence, it is less likely for them to create clusters of non-matching entities.

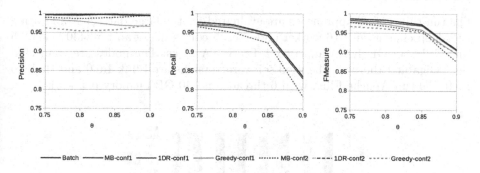

Fig. 9. Source-wise cluster quality for dataset G

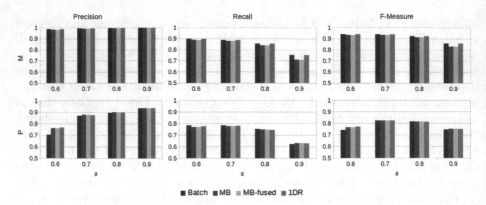

Fig. 10. Source-wise incremental ER for datasets M (1st row) and P (2nd row)

In Fig. 11 we report the F-Measure results for entity-wise incremental ER with the different increment configurations from Table 2. The results are reported for dataset M and we evaluate all methods with and without new-input-linking (we use subscript IL to indicate new-input-linking). MB_{IL} achieves higher F-Measure than MB due to better recall. The positive effect of new-input-linking is also visible in the results for 1DR so that $1DR_{IL}$ mostly achieves higher F-Measure than 1DR. The difference of methods with new-input-linking compared with their counterparts without new-input-linking in $conf3$ and $conf4$ is lower because a big portion of the dataset is already contained in the initial knowledge base and the data increments only contain 10% of the dataset. Therefore, when the volume of data in a new increment is much smaller than the volume of the existing knowledge graph, we may save the overhead of new-input-linking and pre-clustering. The approach $1DR_{IL}$ with new-input-linking consistently achieves the best results in all scenarios and newer achieves lower F-Measure than batch ER for our configurations.

5.2   Efficiency Evaluation

The run-times of all approaches are evaluated for the large dataset P and using a Hadoop cluster with 16 worker nodes, each consisting of an E5-2430 6(12) 2.5 Ghz CPU, 48 GB RAM and two 4 TB SATA disks. The nodes are connected via 1 Gigabit Ethernet. The used software versions are Flink 1.6.0 and Hadoop 2.6.0. We run Apache Flink with 6 threads and 40 GB memory per worker.

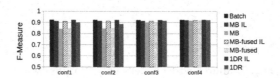

Fig. 11. F-Measure results for entity-wise incremental ER (dataset M)

Table 4 shows the accumulated runtimes when executing the methods on clusters with 4, 8 and 16 workers for the large dataset P with a linking threshold of 0.7. As expected, all incremental approaches are faster than Batch. Moreover, the MB approaches are faster than our 1DR method. The reason is, that MB methods just process newly computed links while 1DR relies on intra-links of already existing clusters and the newly computed links. All methods achieve their best runtime with 16 workers. Batch shows to have a better speedup, but starts at a much slower run-time. It is important to note that with less resources (less number of workers), the Batch runtime is significantly higher than the others. As expected, MB-fused performs slightly faster than MB.

In a further experiment we evaluated the runtimes of adding sources incrementally for dataset P. Figure 12 shows results of all 10 increments (adding 1 source per increment) for 16 workers. In every increment the incremental approaches are faster than the Batch method and MB-fused is faster than MB and both of them are faster than 1DR. In later increments the differences become higher. For example in the 10th increment the runtime of Batch is 5 times higher than 1DR. The reason is, that Batch clustering needs to process all vertices and links in each increment, whereas MB and 1DR only need to process a small fraction of links.

Table 4. Accumulated runtimes in seconds for source-wise ER

#W	P t_{min}0.7			
	Batch	MB	MB-fused	1DR
4	117 852	5 648	2220	21 179
8	33 791	2 178	1 562	4 283
16	8 542	1 778	1 184	2 513

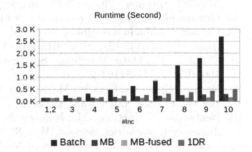

Fig. 12. Incremental runtimes

6   Conclusion and Outlook

Real-world data integration tasks such as the completion of knowledge graphs require efficient and effective incremental methods for entity resolution rather than batch-like approaches on static datasets. We proposed several new incremental methods for multi-source ER including a new method that can repair previous linking and cluster decisions. Our evaluation with datasets from different domains shows that the incremental approaches are much faster and similarly effective than batch ER. In particular, the introduced repair and re-clustering approach nDR achieves the same quality than batch ER while being still much faster. Its high effectiveness also shows that the quality does not depend on the order in which new entities are added in contrast to the non-repairing approaches such as max-both merge and previous repair schemes.

In future work, we plan to address further issues regarding knowledge graph completion such as the joint consideration of entities (and relationships) of different types, e.g., publications, authors and affiliations.

Acknowledgements. This work is partially funded by the German Federal Ministry of Education and Research under grant BMBF 01IS16026B in project ScaDS.AI Dresden/Leipzig.

References

1. Rahm, E.: The case for holistic data integration. In: Pokorný, J., Ivanović, M., Thalheim, B., Šaloun, P. (eds.) ADBIS 2016. LNCS, vol. 9809, pp. 11–27. Springer, Cham (2016). https://doi.org/10.1007/978-3-319-44039-2_2
2. Obraczka, D., Saeedi, A., Rahm, E.: Knowledge graph completion with FAMER. In: Proceedings of the DI2KG (2019)
3. Welch, M., Sane, A., Drome, C.: Fast and accurate incremental entity resolution relative to an entity knowledge base. In: CIKM (2012)
4. Nentwig, M., Rahm, E.: Incremental clustering on linked data. In: ICDMW. IEEE (2018)
5. Saeedi, A., Peukert, E., Rahm, E.: Using link features for entity clustering in knowledge graphs. In: Gangemi, A., et al. (eds.) ESWC 2018. LNCS, vol. 10843, pp. 576–592. Springer, Cham (2018). https://doi.org/10.1007/978-3-319-93417-4_37
6. Gruenheid, A., et al.: Incremental record linkage. PVLDB **7**(9), 697–708 (2014)
7. Getoor, L., Machanavajjhala, A.: Entity resolution: theory, practice & open challenges. PVLDB **5**(12), 2018–2019 (2012)
8. Christen, P.: Data Matching. Springer, Heidelberg (2012). https://doi.org/10.1007/978-3-642-31164-2
9. Volz, J., Bizer, C., Gaedke, M., Kobilarov, G.: Silk-a link discovery framework for the web of data. Ldow **538**, 53 (2009)
10. Nentwig, M., Hartung, M., Ngonga, N.A., Rahm, E.: A survey of current link discovery frameworks. Semant. Web **8**(3), 419–436 (2017)
11. Papadakis, G., et al.: The return of JedAI: end-to-end entity resolution for structured and semi-structured data. PVLDB **11**(12), 1950–1953 (2018)
12. Saeedi, A., Peukert, E., Rahm, E.: Comparative evaluation of distributed clustering schemes for multi-source entity resolution. In: Kirikova, M., Nørvåg, K., Papadopoulos, G.A. (eds.) ADBIS 2017. LNCS, vol. 10509, pp. 278–293. Springer, Cham (2017). https://doi.org/10.1007/978-3-319-66917-5_19
13. Bellare, K., et al.: WOO: a scalable and multi-tenant platform for continuous knowledge base synthesis. PVLDB **6**(11), 1114–1125 (2013)
14. Benjelloun, O., et al.: Swoosh: a generic approach to entity resolution. VLDB J. **18**(1), 255–276 (2009). https://doi.org/10.1007/s00778-008-0098-x
15. Costa, G., Manco, G., Ortale, R.: An incremental clustering scheme for data deduplication. Data Min. Knowl. Discov. **20**(1), 152 (2010). https://doi.org/10.1007/s10618-009-0155-0
16. do Nascimento, D., et al.: Heuristic-based approaches for speeding up incremental record linkage. J. Syst. Softw. **137**, 335–354 (2018)
17. Hildebrandt, K., Panse, F., Wilcke, N., Ritter, N.: Large-scale data pollution with Apache Spark. IEEE Trans. Big Data (2017)
18. Christen, P., Vatsalan, D.: Flexible and extensible generation and corruption of personal data. In: ACM CIKM. ACM (2013)

Building Linked Spatio-Temporal Data
from Vectorized Historical Maps

Basel Shbita[1]([⊠]), Craig A. Knoblock[1], Weiwei Duan[2], Yao-Yi Chiang[2],
Johannes H. Uhl[3], and Stefan Leyk[3]

[1] Information Sciences Institute and Department of Computer Science,
University of Southern California, Los Angeles, USA
{shbita,knoblock}@isi.edu
[2] Spatial Sciences Institute and Department of Computer Science,
University of Southern California, Los Angeles, USA
{weiweidu,yaoyic}@usc.edu
[3] Department of Geography, University of Colorado Boulder, Boulder, USA
{johannes.uhl,stefan.leyk}@colorado.edu

Abstract. Historical maps provide a rich source of information for
researchers in the social and natural sciences. These maps contain
detailed documentation of a wide variety of natural and human-made
features and their changes over time, such as the changes in the transportation networks and the decline of wetlands. It can be labor-intensive
for a scientist to analyze changes across space and time in such maps,
even after they have been digitized and converted to a vector format.
In this paper, we present an unsupervised approach that converts vector
data of geographic features extracted from multiple historical maps into
linked spatio-temporal data. The resulting graphs can be easily queried
and visualized to understand the changes in specific regions over time. We
evaluate our technique on railroad network data extracted from USGS
historical topographic maps for several regions over multiple map sheets
and demonstrate how the automatically constructed linked geospatial data enables effective querying of the changes over different time
periods.

Keywords: Linked spatio-temporal data · Historical maps ·
Knowledge graphs · Semantic web

1 Introduction

Historical map archives contain valuable geographic information on both natural and human-made features across time and space. The spatio-temporal data
extracted from these documents are important since they can convey where and

© Springer Nature Switzerland AG 2020
A. Harth et al. (Eds.): ESWC 2020, LNCS 12123, pp. 409–426, 2020.
https://doi.org/10.1007/978-3-030-49461-2_24

when changes took place. This type of data enables long-term analysis, such as detecting the changes in railroad networks between several map editions of the same region and can support decision-making related to the development of transportation infrastructure. Many applications assessing geographic changes over time typically require searching, discovering, and manually identifying relevant data. This is a difficult and laborious task that requires domain knowledge and familiarity with various data formats, and the task is often susceptible to human error.

Linked geospatial data has been receiving increased attention in recent years as researchers and practitioners have begun to explore the wealth of geospatial information on the Web. Recent technological advances facilitate the efficient extraction of vectorized information from scanned historical maps and other digital data to facilitate the integration of the extracted information with other datasets in Geographic Information Systems (GIS) [3–5,11].

Previous work on creating linked data from geospatial information has focused on the problem of transforming the vector data into RDF graphs [2,6,12]. However, this line of work does not address the issue of geospatial entity linkage, e.g., building linked geospatial data with a semantic relationship between vector data elements across maps of the same region. To better support analytical tasks and understand how map features change over time, we need more than just the extracted vector data from individual maps. In addition to the vector data extracted from historical maps, we need the relationship between the vector data elements (segments) composing the desired features across maps, and the detailed metadata and semantic properties that describe that data. To enable change analysis over time and across multiple spatial scales, we present an unsupervised approach to match, integrate, and relate vector data of map features using linked data principles and provide corresponding semantics for the representation of the data.

The task we address here is that given geospatial vector data extracted from numerous map editions covering the same region, we want to construct a knowledge graph depicting all the feature segments that represent the original data, their relations and their semantics across different points in time. Using the constructed knowledge graph, we enable tackling more specific downstream analysis tasks. These may include the visualization of feature changes over time and the exploration of supplementary information related to the region using additional knowledge bases we link to our graph.

As an example, consider the maps shown in Fig. 1a where changes in the Louisville, New Albany and Chicago railroad system have occurred between 1886 and 1904. Figure 1b shows the railroad segment changes between the different map editions. Segments that have been added are marked in red and segments that have been removed are marked in blue. Assuming we have the data available as vector data (which can be generated from scanned maps using [5]), our task in such a setting would be to construct a knowledge graph describing the different segment elements in these maps with a conventional semantic representation for the railroad line segments in each map edition. This would include objects

(a) Louisville, New Albany and Chicago railroad system maps in 1886 (left) and 1904 (right)

(b) Visual representation of the change in the railroad system; additions are in red, removals are in blue

Fig. 1. An example of a railroad system change over time (Color figure online)

from a list of common geographic features (points, lines, or polygons), their geocoordinates, and their matching temporal coverage to allow easy analysis and visualization.

Our approach is not only helpful in making the data widely available to researchers but also enables users to answer complex queries in an unsupervised manner, such as investigating the interrelationships between human and environmental systems. Our approach also benefits from the open and connective nature of linked data. Compared to existing tools such as PostGIS[1] that can only handle queries related to geospatial relationships within local databases, linked data can utilize many widely available knowledge sources, such as GeoNames and OpenStreetMap[2], in the semantic web and enable rich semantic queries.

Once we convert the map data into linked data, we can execute SPARQL queries to depict the changes in map segments over time and thus accelerate and improve spatio-temporal analysis tasks. Using a semantic representation that includes geospatial features, we are able to support researchers to query and visualize changes in maps over time and allow the development of data analytics applications that could have great implications for environmental, economic or societal purposes.

The rest of the paper is organized as follows. We present our proposed pipeline in Sect. 2. In Sect. 3 we evaluate our approach by automatically building a linked data representation for a series of railroad networks from historical maps covering two different regions from different time periods. Related work is discussed in Sect. 4. We conclude, discuss, and present future work in Sect. 5.

---

[1] https://postgis.net/.
[2] https://www.openstreetmap.org/.

2   Building and Querying Linked Spatio-Temporal Data

2.1   Taxonomy

Figure 2 shows the taxonomy of terms used in this paper. We refer to the elements composing the vector data extracted from historical maps as segments. These segments may be decomposed to small building blocks (we refer to these as segments or segment elements), which are encoded as WKT (well-known text representation of geometry) multi-line strings. These strings are composed from a collection of tuples of latitude and longitude coordinates.

2.2   Overall Approach

The unsupervised pipeline we propose for constructing linked data from vector data of extracted map feature segments consists of several major steps as illustrated in Fig. 3. These steps can be summarized as follows:

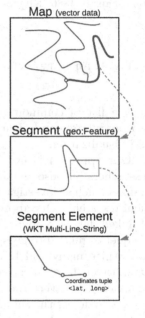

1. Automatically partition the feature segments from the original shapefiles (vector data) into collections of segments using a spatially-enabled database service (i.e., PostGIS) to form groups of segments (see Sect. 2.3).
2. Utilize a reverse-geocoding service (i.e., OpenStreetMap) to map the partitioned feature segment geometric literals to existing instances in the semantic web (i.e., LinkedGeoData [1]) (see Sect. 2.4)
3. Construct the knowledge graph by generating RDF triples following a pre-defined semantic model using the data we generated from previous steps (see Sects. 2.5 and 2.6)

Fig. 2. Taxonomy of terms used in the paper

Once the RDF data is deployed, users can easily interact with the feature segment data and perform queries (Sect. 2.7), which allow end-users to visualize the data and supports the development of spatio-temporal applications.

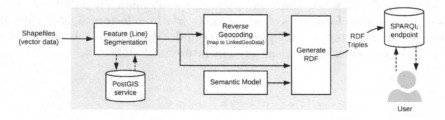

Fig. 3. Pipeline for constructing linked data from vector data

2.3 Automatic Feature Segmentation

The first task in our pipeline is the creation of segment partitions (elements) that can represent the various geographic features (e.g., railroad network) across different maps (same region, different map editions) in a granular and efficient fashion. This task can be classified as a common entity matching/linking and entity "partitioning" task. Given two segment elements from two map editions of the same region, we want to identify which parts of those elements coincide and thus represent the same parts of the feature. This allows us to generate segment groups of elements that are more granular and can be used to represent the common and the distinct parts of features.

Consider a simplified example consisting of segments (geometry of line type) from two map editions (Fig. 4a), where segment A is from an older map edition and segment B is from the latest map edition with a part of the feature that has been changed. In order to detect those parts that exist in both segments, we split each of these segments into several sub-segments based on the intersection of the segments, as shown in Figs. 4b and 4c. When a third source (another map edition also containing the feature), C, is added, a similar segmentation process is executed as shown in Figs. 4d and 4e.

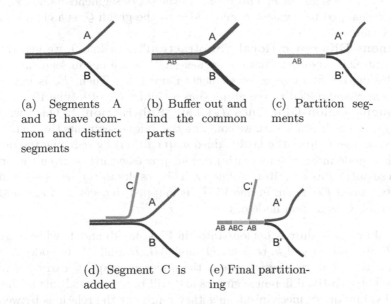

(a) Segments A and B have common and distinct segments

(b) Buffer out and find the common parts

(c) Partition segments

(d) Segment C is added

(e) Final partitioning

Fig. 4. Segments partitioning process: spatial buffers are used to identify the same segments considering potential positional offsets of the data

As we mentioned earlier, we use a spatially-enabled database service to simplify handling data manipulations over feature segments. PostGIS is a powerful PostgreSQL extension for spatial data storage and query. It offers various functions to manipulate and transform geographic objects in databases. To handle the task mentioned earlier efficiently and enable an incremental addition of maps over time, we implemented Algorithm 1. The algorithm performs the segmentation tasks by employing several PostGIS application programming interface (API) calls over the geometries of our segments that we loaded in the database.

In detail, the procedure works as follows. The **for** loop in line 1 iterates over each collection of vector data (segment geometries) in each map edition. For each iteration, lines 2–3 extract the set of feature segments from a given shapefile and map them to a node i (representing the segment) which is then added to the directed acyclic graph (data structure) $\mathcal{G}$. The graph $\mathcal{G}$ will eventually hold our final set of segments and record their relations in a data structure within the graph. Line 4 retrieves the leaf nodes from graph $\mathcal{G}$ to list $\mathcal{L}$. In the first iteration list $\mathcal{L}$ is empty. In the next iterations it will include the nodes which represent the segments that are similar to and distinct from segments from other map editions in the same degree (distance in the graph from the root) as their parent node. Then, for each "leaf" node we execute the following steps:

1. **Segment Intersection.** Line 6 extracts the set of feature segments from the leaf segment k. Line 7 performs an intersection of segment i with segment k by creating a buffer for the vector data and intersecting this buffer with the vector data in segment k. This results in the set of segments named F_α which is then mapped to segment α and added to the graph $\mathcal{G}$ as a child node of i and k (line 8).
2. **Segment Difference (local "Subtraction").** In line 9, we generate the segment elements of the data in segment k that are not in segment i, which results in the set of segment elements named F_γ. Then, F_γ is mapped to segment γ and added to the graph $\mathcal{G}$ as a child node of k (line 10).
3. **Segment Union-Difference (global "Subtraction").** Once we finish going over the list of leaves, we compute the unique segments that exist in the added segment (from the lastly added map edition) by reducing the union of the leaf node intersections (with previous processed maps) from the original map segment i as described in line 12. This results in the set of segment elements named F_δ. Then, in line 13, F_δ is mapped to segment δ and added to the graph $\mathcal{G}$ as a child node of i.

The above procedure is demonstrated in Figs. 4a, 4b and 4c where segments A and B are nodes i and k, respectively and AB, B' and A' are nodes α, γ and δ, respectively. The relations between the nodes in graph $\mathcal{G}$ carry a semantic meaning between the different segments and will play a critical role in the RDF generation and query mechanism since they represent the relations between the segment elements across different time extents of the same region. The hierarchical relationship is built with respect to these attributes and allows us to retrieve the segments that will represent the changes in feature segments when running a query.

Data: a set $\mathcal{M}$ of segments for different map editions of the same region (shapefiles)

Result: a directed acyclic graph $\mathcal{G}$ of feature segment objects (nodes) and their relations

1 **foreach** $i \in \mathcal{M}$ **do**
2      $\mathcal{F}_i$ = set of geometry features (segment elements) in i;
3      $\mathcal{G}.\text{add}(i \mapsto F_i)$;
4      $\mathcal{L}$ = list of current leaf nodes in $\mathcal{G}$;
5   **foreach** $k \in \mathcal{L}$ **do**
6          $\mathcal{F}_k$ = set of geometry features (segment elements) in k;
7          $\mathcal{F}_\alpha = \mathcal{F}_i \bigcap \mathcal{F}_k$;
8          $\mathcal{G}.\text{add}(\alpha \mapsto F_\alpha)$ and set i, k as parents of α;
9          $\mathcal{F}_\gamma = \mathcal{F}_k \setminus \mathcal{F}_\alpha$;
10         $\mathcal{G}.\text{add}(\gamma \mapsto F_\gamma)$ and set k as parent of γ;
11   **end**
12     $\mathcal{F}_\delta = \mathcal{F}_i \setminus (\bigcup_{j \in \mathcal{L}} F_j)$;
13     $\mathcal{G}.\text{add}(\delta \mapsto F_\delta)$ and set i as parent of δ;
14 **end**

Algorithm 1: The feature segments partitioning algorithm

2.4 Reverse Geocoding and Linking to Linked Open Vocabularies

In the last two decades there has been a major effort in publishing data following semantic web and linked data principles. There are now tens of billions of facts spanning hundreds of linked datasets on the web covering a wide range of topics. To better describe the semantics of data and reuse well-documented vocabularies in the linked data ecosystem, we propose a simple mechanism to allow linking the extracted segments from the processed historical maps to additional knowledge bases on the web. This is again a task of entity matching; this time it is with an entity in an external knowledge base.

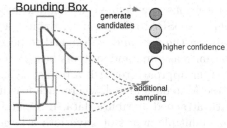

Our proposed method is based on reverse geocoding. Reverse geocoding is the process of mapping the latitude and longitude measures of a point or a bounding box to a readable address or place name. Examples of these services include the GeoNames reverse geocoding web service[3] and OpenStreetMap's API.[4] These services permit for a given location the identification of nearby street addresses, places, areal subdivisions, etc.

Fig. 5. Method for acquiring external knowledge base instances

The "geo-linking" process is depicted in Algorithm 2 and illustrated in Fig. 5. We start with individual features extracted from the original maps that are of

---

[3] http://www.geonames.org/export/reverse-geocoding.html.
[4] https://wiki.openstreetmap.org/wiki/API.

known type (T in Algorithm 2). In the case of the data we present later in the evaluation section, we are starting with the extracted segments of **railroads**, so we know the feature type we are searching for. Each input segment s here is an individual node in graph $\mathcal{G}$ from Sect. 2.3. We first generate a global bounding box for segment s and execute a reverse-geocoding API call to locate instances of type T on the external knowledge base, as described in lines 1–2. Some of these instances do not share any geometry parts with our inspected segment. Thus, we randomly sample a small number ($N = 30$) of coordinate pairs (`Points`), from those composing the segment s, as seen in lines 3–5, to gain more confidence in the detected instances. Finally, we reduce the list by filtering out the candidates that have a single appearance (high confidence that it is not part of the segment but is found in the bounding box). These resulting instances are used in later stages to enrich the knowledge graph we are constructing with additional semantics.

> **Data**: segment s, number of samples N, feature type T
> **Result**: list $\mathcal{L}$ of instances on LinkedGeoData composing our input segment s
> 1 B_s = bounding box wrapping s;
> 2 $\mathcal{L}$ = reverse-geocoding(B_s, T); // returns LinkedGeoData instances of T in B_s
>   **for** 1...N **do**
> 3 | e = randomly sample a `Point` in segment s;
> 4 | E = reverse-geocoding(e, T);
> 5 | $\mathcal{L}$.add(E);
> 6 **end**
> 7 filter out instances with a single appearance in $\mathcal{L}$;
> 8 **return** $\mathcal{L}$;

Algorithm 2: The "geo-linking" algorithm

2.5   Semantic Model

In order to provide a representation with useful semantic meaning and universal conventions, we defined a semantic model that builds on GeoSPARQL.[5] The OGC GeoSPARQL standard defines a vocabulary for representing geospatial data on the web and is designed to accommodate systems based on qualitative spatial reasoning and systems based on quantitative spatial computations.

Our approach towards a robust semantic model was motivated by the Open-StreetMap data model, where each feature is described as one or more geometries with attached attribute data. In OpenStreetMap, `relations` are used to organize multiple `nodes` or `ways` into a larger whole. For example, an instance of a bus route running through three different `ways` would be defined as a `relation`.

In GeoSPARQL, the class type `geo:Feature` represents the top-level feature type. It is a superclass of all feature types. In our model, each instance of this class represents a single segment (element) extracted from the original vector data. It is possible to compose different collections of segments representing the specified feature in some time extent using this instance and a property of type `geo:sfWithin` or `geo:sfContains` to denote a decomposition to smaller

---

[5] https://www.opengeospatial.org/standards/geosparql.

elements. The use of such properties enables application-specific queries with a backward-chaining spatial "reasoner" to transform the query into a geometry-based query that can be evaluated with computational geometry. Additionally, we use the property `geo:sfOverlaps` with subjects that are instances from the LinkedGeoData knowledge base in order to employ the web as a medium for data and spatial information integration following linked data principles. Furthermore, each instance has properties of type `dcterms:date`, to denote the time extent of the segment, and `dcterms:created`, to denote the time in which this segment was generated to record provenance data.

Complex geometries are not human-readable as they consist of hundreds or thousands of coordinate pairs. Therefore, we use dereferenceable URIs to represent the geometric objects instead. Using a named node in this capacity means that each geometric object has its own URI as opposed to the common blank-node approach often used with linked geometric objects. Thus, each segment instance holds a property of type `geo:hasGeometry` with a subject that is an instance of the

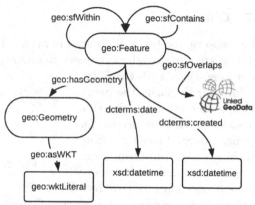

Fig. 6. Semantic model for linked maps

class `geo:Geometry`. This property refers to the spatial representation of a given feature. The class `geo:Geometry` represents the top-level geometry type and is a superclass of all geometry types.

In order to describe the geometries in a compact and human-readable way we use the WKT format for further pre-processing. The `geo:asWKT` property is defined to link a geometry with its WKT serialization and enable downstream applications to use SPARQL graph patterns. The semantic model we described above is shown in Fig. 6.

2.6   Incremental Linked Data

Following the data extraction and acquisition tasks described in the previous section, we can now produce a structured standard ontologized output in a form of a knowledge graph that can be easily interpreted by humans and machines, as linked data.

This hierarchical structure of our directed acyclic graph $\mathcal{G}$ and its metadata management allows us to avoid an update across all the existing published geographic vector data as linked data and instead handle the computations incrementally once a new map edition of the feature is introduced.

The approach we present is complete and follows the principles of Linked Open Data by:

- Generating URIs as names for things, without the need to modify any of the previously published URIs once further vector data from the same region is available and processed
- Maintaining existing relations (predicates) between instances (additional relations may be added, but they do not break older ones)
- Generating data as a machine-readable structured data
- Using standard namespaces and semantics (e.g., GeoSPARQL)
- Linking to additional resources in the web of Linked Open Data.

2.7   Querying

The semantic model we presented in Sect. 2.5 and its structure provide a robust solution enabling a coherent query mechanism to allow a user-friendly and efficient interaction with the data.

In order to clarify the query construction idea, we describe the elements that are needed for a general query "skeleton" from which we can establish more complicated queries to achieve

```
1  SELECT ?f ?wkt
2  WHERE {
3     ?f a geo:Feature ;
4        geo:hasGeometry [ geo:asWKT ?wkt ] .
5     FILTER NOT EXISTS { ?f geo:sfContains _:_ } }
```

Fig. 7. Our SPARQL query "skeleton"

different outcomes as required. Figure 7 shows a query which retrieves all the leaf node segments (i.e., the "skeleton" query). As shown in the figure, we first denote that we are interested in a geo:Feature that has a geometry in WKT format which gets stored in the variable ?wkt as shown in lines 3–4 (the variable we visualize in Fig. 14). Line 5 restricts the queried segments (geo:Features) to leaf nodes only (in graph G). This is done by discarding all the nodes that hold a predicate of type geo:sfContains, which means that we retrieve only the nodes that are the "building blocks".

This is important due to the incremental nature (and the way graph G "grows"): as we mentioned previously, every time we add an additional map edition of the feature, we decompose the existing leaf segments (smallest building blocks) to a new layer of leaf segments (newer and smaller building blocks, if subject to decomposition) and its metadata migrates to the lowest level of segment leaves. This property makes our solution robust and suggests an efficient way of querying, avoiding the need to "climb up" the graph for more complicated ("composed") segments.

If, for example, we are interested to see the full version of the segment from a specific time, we can add the clause {?f dcterms:date <...> .} inside the WHERE block (lines 2–6). If we are interested to see the changes from a different time, we can add an additional clause {MINUS { ?f dcterms:date <...> . }} as well. The syntax and structure of the query allows an easy adaptation for additional tasks such as finding the distinct segment parts from a specific time or finding the segment parts that are shared over three, four or even more points in time or map editions. The nature of our knowledge graph provides an intuitive approach towards writing simple and complex queries.

3   Evaluation

We tested two datasets of vector railroad data (the inspected feature) that were extracted from the USGS historical topographic map archives,[6],[7] each of which covers a different region and is available for different time periods.

In this section, we present the results, measures and outcomes of our pipeline when executed on railroad data from a collection of historical maps of a region in Bray, California from the years 1950, 1954, 1958, 1962, 1984, 1988, and 2001 (shown in Fig. 8) and from a region in Louisville, Colorado from the years 1942, 1950, 1957 and 1965. Our primary goal is to show that our proposal provides a complete, robust, tractable, and efficient solution for the production of linked data from vectorized historical maps.

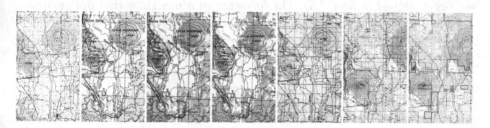

Fig. 8. Historical maps in Bray, California from 1950, 1954, 1958, 1962, 1984, 1988 and 2001 (left to right, respectively)

3.1   Evaluation on the Feature Segmentation Process

In order to evaluate the performance of this task, we look into the runtime and the number of generated nodes (in graph $\mathcal{G}$) for each region. The number of vector lines in the segment geometry (column '# vecs'), resulting runtimes (column 'Runtime', measured in seconds) and total number of nodes following each sub-step of an addition of another map edition (column '# nodes') are depicted in Tables 1 and 2 for each region.

As seen in Tables 1 and 2, the railroad segments extracted from these maps vary in terms of "quality". That is, they have a different number of vector lines that describe the railroads and each one has a different areal coverage. This is caused by the vector extraction process (see [5]) and is not within

Table 1. Segmentation Statistics for Bray

Year	# vecs	Runtime (s)	# nodes
1954	2382	<1	1
1962	2322	36	5
1988	11134	1047	11
1984	11868	581	24
1950	11076	1332	43
2001	497	145	57
1958	1860	222	85

---

[6] https://viewer.nationalmap.gov.

[7] http://historicalmaps.arcgis.com/usgs/.

the scope of this paper. We also acknowledge that the quality and scale of the original images used for the extraction affects
these parameters but we do not focus on such
issues. We treat these values and attributes
as a ground truth for our process.

Table 2. Segmentation Statistics for Louisville

Year	# vecs	Runtime (s)	# nodes
1965	838	<1	1
1950	418	8	5
1942	513	5	8
1957	353	4	10

First, we notice that the growth of the
number of nodes in graph $\mathcal{G}$ is reasonable
due to the way the railroad network changes
in practice. Further, the runtime of each sub-step is also reasonable and tractable.
As expected, the first two map editions (for both areas) generate results within
less than a minute, requiring at most three computations: one geometry intersection between two elements and two additional subtractions: a local and a global
one (as explained in Sect. 2.3). The following runtimes show that our computation cost is not exponential in practice. By inspecting Tables 1 and 2 we observe
that the segmentation runtime somewhat depends on two factors: the number
of vectors in the geometries and the number of nodes that exist in the graph.
The more geometry elements we have and the more geometries exist, the more
operations we need to run.

These results are not surprising because "leaves" in the graph will only be
partitioned in case it is "required", that is, they will be partitioned to smaller
unique parts to represent the different segments they need to compose. With the
addition of map editions, we do not necessarily add unique parts since changes
do not occur between all map editions. This shows that the data processing is not
necessarily becoming more complex in terms of space and time, thus, providing
a solution that is feasible and systematically tractable.

3.2 Evaluation on Linking to LinkedGeoData

In the process of linking our data to LinkedGeoData, we are interested in the
evaluation of the running time and correctness (precision and recall) of this task.

The running time is linearly dependent on the number of nodes in graph $\mathcal{G}$,
the number of samples using the OpenStreetMaps API, and the availability of
the API. The API response time averages 2 s for each sample. The execution
time for the set of maps from the region in Bray took approximately an hour (85
nodes) and only a few minutes for Louisville (10 nodes). This provides a feasible
solution to a process that runs only once for a collection of map editions.

Due to the unsupervised characteristic of the linking task, we had to manually
inspect and label the sets of instances found in each bounding box that we
query for each segment. The measure we present here is in terms of coverage.
It is the number of instances we detected out of the number of instances that
are available on the external knowledge base and which make up the inspected
railroad segment. Nonetheless, in terms of detecting which railroad it is (label),
we are able to achieve 100% accuracy (by taking a majority vote on the labels
of instances we queried).

As an example, let us observe the instances in the LinkedGeoData knowledge base that are linked to a segment that holds railroad lines in the map edition from 1950 in the data from Bray, as shown in Fig. 9. All of the Linked-GeoData instances linked to this segment show an rdf:type of type lgdo:-AbandonedRailway, as seen in red in Fig. 10. This shows our ability to enrich and link our graph to the web of linked data.

We have set up a baseline for comparison with our "geo-linking" method. The baseline approach returns the set of all instances found in the bound-

```
<http://linkedmaps.isi.edu/69> a geo:Feature ;
    dcterms:created "2019-12-10T15:23:23"^^xsd:dateTime ;
    dcterms:date "1950-01-01T00:00:00"^^xsd:dateTime ;
    geo:hasGeometry <http://linkedmaps.isi.edu/69_sc_m_2091b7b4c0> ;
    geo:sfOverlaps <http://linkedgeodata.org/triplify/way177559134>,
        <http://linkedgeodata.org/triplify/way177559138> ;
    geo:sfWithin <http://linkedmaps.isi.edu/41> .
```

Fig. 9. A segment representation in RDF

ing box. This is the list of candidates we generate in the first step of our method, without the additional sampling and filtering steps we have described in Sect. 2.4.

The precision, recall and F1 scores of each method over each dataset are shown in Table 3. The first row (BRA-baseline) provides the baseline's results applied on the Bray dataset. The second row (BRA) shows the results of our method when applied on the Bray dataset. The third (LOU-baseline) and fourth rows (LOU) show the results of the baseline method and our method, respectively, applied on the Louisville dataset. Due to the different geometries, areal coverage and avail-

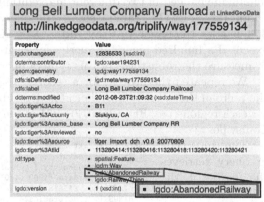

Fig. 10. Screenshot of an instance at LinkedGeo-Data knowledge base (Color figure online)

able data in the external knowledge base for each region, our measure shows different scores for each dataset. However, our method achieves much higher F1 scores than the baseline (0.774 and 0.909 compared to 0.323 and 0.625 respectively) and achieves an acceptable score for this task.

Table 3. "Geo-linking" Results

	Precision	Recall	F1
BRA-baseline	0.193	1.000	0.323
BRA	0.800	0.750	**0.774**
LOU-baseline	0.455	1.000	0.625
LOU	0.833	1.000	**0.909**

3.3 Evaluation on Querying the Data

We execute several query examples over the knowledge graph we constructed in order to measure our model in terms of query time, validity, and effectiveness. We had a total of 914 triples for the Bray region dataset and 96 triples for Louisville.

The generated RDF triples would be appropriate to use with any Triplestore. We hosted our triples in Apache Jena.[8] Jena is relatively lightweight, easy to use, and provides a programmatic environment. Each SPARQL query response was visualized using the Google Maps API.

```
SELECT ?f ?wkt WHERE {
  ?f a geo:Feature ;
    geo:hasGeometry [ geo:asWKT ?wkt ] ;
    dcterms:date "1962-01-01T00:00:00"^^xsd:dateTime ;
    dcterms:date "2001-01-01T00:00:00"^^xsd:dateTime .
  FILTER NOT EXISTS { ?f geo:sfContains _:_ } }
```

Fig. 11. SPARQL query generating similar railroad segments in both 1962 and 2001

In the first type of query we want to identify the parts of the railroad that remain unchanged in two different map editions (different time periods) for each region (i.e., Fig. 11). Table 4 shows the query-time results in the row labelled SIM-BRA for the region in Bray and by SIM-LOU for the region in Louisville. We executed a hundred identical queries for each area across different time extents to measure the robustness of this type of query.

We repeated the process for a second type of query to identify the parts of the railroad that were removed or abandoned between two different map editions for each region (i.e., Fig. 12). DIFF-BRA is the result for Bray and DIFF-LOU for Louisville.

The third type of query retrieves the parts of the railroad that are unique to a specific edition of the map (i.e., Fig. 13). UNIQ-BRA is the result for Bray and UNIQ-LOU for Louisville.

```
SELECT ?f ?wkt WHERE {
  ?f a geo:Feature ;
    geo:hasGeometry [ geo:asWKT ?wkt ] ;
    dcterms:date "1962-01-01T00:00:00"^^xsd:dateTime .
  FILTER NOT EXISTS { ?f geo:sfContains _:_ }
  MINUS { ?f dcterms:date "2001-01-01T00:00:00"^^xsd:dateTime . } }
```

Fig. 12. SPARQL query generating railroad segments present in 1962 but not in 2001

The execution times (average, minimum and maximum) are shown in Table 4. We notice that the query times are all in the range of 8–28 (ms) and do not seem to change significantly with respect to the number of map editions we process or the complexity of the query we compose. This is based on the fact that the data from Bray was constructed from 7 map editions compared to the data from Louisville, which was constructed from 4 map editions.

---

[8] https://jena.apache.org/.

In order to evaluate the validity of our graph we observe the visualized results of the query in Fig. 11, which are shown in Fig. 14a. This figure shows in red the unchanged seg-

```
SELECT ?f ?wkt WHERE {
  ?f a geo:Feature ;
    geo:hasGeometry [ geo:asWKT ?wkt ] ;
    dcterms:date "1958-01-01T00:00:00"^^xsd:dateTime .
  FILTER NOT EXISTS { ?f geo:sfContains _:_ }
  ?f dcterms:date ?date . }
GROUP BY ?f ?wkt
HAVING (COUNT(DISTINCT ?date) = 1)
```

Fig. 13. SPARQL query generating unique railroad parts that are present only in 1958

ments between the years 1962 and 2001 for Bray. We notice that the geometries we retrieve do match what we observe in the original shapefiles (the line marked in black over the two maps represents the current railway, which has not changed since 2001). The results of the query in Fig. 12 are shown in Fig. 14b. This figure shows in blue the parts of the railroad that were abandoned between 1962 to 2001.

The query results above establish high confidence in our model, showing that we can easily and effectively answer complex queries in a robust manner. Overall, we demonstrated that our approach and the proposed pipeline can be effectively used to automatically construct linked data from geospatial information.

Table 4. Query Time Statistics (in milliseconds)

	Avg	Min	Max
SIM-BRA	12	10	18
SIM-LOU	11	9	20
DIFF-BRA	10	8	20
DIFF-LOU	10	9	14
UNIQ-BRA	14	8	28
UNIQ-LOU	15	9	17

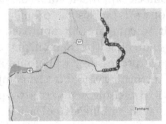

(a) The parts of the railroad that are similar in 1962 and 2001, marked in red

(b) The parts of the railroad that are present in 1962 but are not present in 2001, marked in blue

Fig. 14. Examples of railroad system changes over time (Color figure online)

4   Related Work

Much work has been done on mapping vector data into RDF graphs. Kyzirakos et al. [6] developed a semi-automated tool for transforming geospatial data from their original formats into RDF using R2RML mapping. Usery et al. [12] presented a method for converting point and vector data to RDF for supporting query and analysis of geographic data. Our work differs by building linked geospatial data with a meaningful semantic relations between vector segments across map editions of the same region and thus for different points in time whereas prior approaches focus on the publication of data from raw files or relational databases.

Existing work on geographical data conflation [7,9] focuses on reconciling different sources for improving data accuracy and in combining incompatible geospatial data. This line of work does not consider the semantics and nature of linked data as we address it. Their work can be used within our framework to strengthen our geometric entity-matching tasks.

Bernard et al. [2] present a semantic matching algorithm for automatically detecting, describing and publishing descriptions of changes occurring in region partitions, and their geometries, in the linked open data web. Their work focuses on Territorial Statistical Nomenclatures (TSNs) which are used for the collection of regional statistics. Their semantic matching algorithm is bounded to an ontology where geometric changes are described either as deformed, expanded or contracted with no regard to composition or decomposition of geometries as we do. Our approach goes further since it provides a richer semantic capability, decomposition of geometries and data interlinking.

Prudhomme et al. [8] present an automatic approach for geospatial data integration in the web. Although this line of work tackles the problem of entity resolution for geospatial data, it is difficult to compare our approach to theirs because they tackle the task of ontology-matching (by maximizing semantic information from files using natural language processing) while ours addresses a complementary problem to that theirs. Our primary goal is the completeness and tractability of building the linked geodata, using semantics to provide a model that is linked to other online sources such as LinkedGeoData.

5   Discussion and Future Work

With the increasing availability of digitized geospatial data from historical map archives, better techniques are required to enable end-users and non-experts to easily understand and analyze geographic information across time and space. Existing techniques rely on human interaction and expert domain knowledge. In this paper, we addressed this issue and presented an unsupervised, effective approach to integrate, relate and interlink geospatial data from digitized resources and publish it as semantic-rich, structured linked data that follows the Linked Open Data principles.

The evaluation we presented in Sect. 3 shows that our approach is feasible and effective in terms of processing time, completeness and robustness. The segmentation process runs only once for newly added resource, and does not require re-generation of "old" data since our approach is incremental. In case a new map edition emerges for the same region, we only need to process the newly added segments. Thus, data that has been previously published will continue to exist with a proper URI and will be preserved over time.

In a scenario that includes contemporary maps that change very quickly, we expect our method to require longer computation time, but would still be tractable with respect to the changes happening in the map geometries. As we mentioned in Sect. 2.3, the breakdown of segments depends on the complexity of the actual changes in the original topographic map. Further, the quality and level of detail of the original vector data play a significant role in the final RDF model as we mentioned in Sect. 3.1. In our ongoing work on this topic, we are looking into techniques to normalize and denoise the original vector data for the purpose of higher quality output.

Our approach has several limitations, one of them is in a form of a hyper-parameter that governs the buffer size we use in the process of the partitioning of segments to smaller parts. We currently set this parameter manually but we believe such parameter can be learned from the data or estimated using some heuristics. Another limitation in the system is the usage of a single external knowledge base. We will address this issue by expanding the ability to utilize additional knowledge bases to enrich our linked data with more semantics from Linked Open Vocabularies [13].

Although we only evaluated railroad data, it can be easily extended for highways, wetlands, forests and additional natural or man-made features with minor adjustments of their geometries and the filtering term that is used in the geocoding API (e.g., railroads). Since the topological relations of the geometries are expressed (via GeoSPARQL) and computed (via PostGIS) according to the DE-9IM model [10], a 2D model, it allows us to apply it over polygon geometries in addition to line geometries. For continuous 2D surfaces, such as wetlands and forests, that are expressed in polygon geometries, we can handle their boundaries similarly. We already started exploring this line of work.

In future work, we also plan to investigate the possibility of using multiple machines for faster processing. This is possible since there are computations in the segment-partitioning algorithm that are independent of each other and can be executed in parallel in the same iteration over a single map edition (lines 7 and 9 for different ks in Algorithm 1). This will enable a faster processing time and strengthen the effectiveness of our solution.

Resources. The source code, original datasets and the resulting RDF, can be found here: https://github.com/usc-isi-i2/linked-maps.

Acknowledgements. This material is based upon work supported by the National Science Foundation under Grant Nos. IIS 1564164 (to the University of Southern California) and IIS 1563933 (to the University of Colorado at Boulder).

References

1. Auer, S., Lehmann, J., Hellmann, S.: LinkedGeoData: adding a spatial dimension to the web of data. In: Bernstein, A., et al. (eds.) ISWC 2009. LNCS, vol. 5823, pp. 731–746. Springer, Heidelberg (2009). https://doi.org/10.1007/978-3-642-04930-9_46
2. Bernard, C., Plumejeaud-Perreau, C., Villanova-Oliver, M., Gensel, J., Dao, H.: An ontology-based algorithm for managing the evolution of multi-level territorial partitions. In: Proceedings of the 26th ACM SIGSPATIAL International Conference on Advances in Geographic Information Systems, pp. 456–459. ACM (2018)
3. Chiang, Y.-Y., Duan, W., Leyk, S., Uhl, J.H., Knoblock, C.A.: Using Historical Maps in Scientific Studies: Applications, Challenges, and Best Practices. SG. Springer, Cham (2020). https://doi.org/10.1007/978-3-319-66908-3
4. Chiang, Y.Y., Leyk, S., Knoblock, C.A.: A survey of digital map processing techniques. ACM Comput. Surv. (CSUR) 47(1), 1–44 (2014)
5. Duan, W., Chiang, Y., Knoblock, C.A., Leyk, S., Uhl, J.: Automatic generation of precisely delineated geographic features from georeferenced historical maps using deep learning. In: Proceedings of the AutoCarto (2018)
6. Kyzirakos, K., Vlachopoulos, I., Savva, D., Manegold, S., Koubarakis, M.: GeoTriples: a tool for publishing geospatial data as RDF graphs using R2RML mappings. In: Terra Cognita, 6th International Workshop on the Foundations, Technologies and Applications of the Geospatial Web, in Conjuction with ISWC, pp. 33–44 (2014)
7. Li, L., Goodchild, M.F.: An optimisation model for linear feature matching in geographical data conflation. Int. J. Image Data Fusion 2(4), 309–328 (2011)
8. Prudhomme, C., Homburg, T., Ponciano, J.J., Boochs, F., Cruz, C., Roxin, A.M.: Interpretation and automatic integration of geospatial data into the semantic web. Computing 102, 1–27 (2019)
9. Ruiz, J.J., Ariza, F.J., Urena, M.A., Blázquez, E.B.: Digital map conflation: a review of the process and a proposal for classification. Int. J. Geogr. Inf. Sci. 25(9), 1439–1466 (2011)
10. Strobl, C.: Dimensionally extended nine-intersection model (DE-9IM). In: Shekhar, S., Xiong, H. (eds.) Encyclopedia of GIS, pp. 240–245. Springer, Boston (2008). https://doi.org/10.1007/978-0-387-35973-1_298
11. Uhl, J.H., Leyk, S., Chiang, Y.Y., Duan, W., Knoblock, C.A.: Automated extraction of human settlement patterns from historical topographic map series using weakly supervised convolutional neural networks. IEEE Access (2019)
12. Usery, E.L., Varanka, D.: Design and development of linked data from the national map. Semant. Web 3(4), 371–384 (2012)
13. Vandenbussche, P.Y., Atemezing, G.A., Poveda-Villalón, M., Vatant, B.: Linked open vocabularies (LOV): a gateway to reusable semantic vocabularies on the web. Semant. Web 8(3), 437–452 (2017)

Integration, Services and APIs

QAnswer KG: Designing a Portable Question Answering System over RDF Data

Dennis Diefenbach[1]([✉])[iD], José Giménez-García[2], Andreas Both[3,4],
Kamal Singh[2], and Pierre Maret[2]

[1] The QA Company SAS, Saint-Etienne, France
`dennis.diefenbach@qanswer.eu`
[2] CNRS UMR 5516 Laboratoire Hubert Curien, Université de Lyon, Lyon, France
`{jose.gimenez.garcia,kamal.singh,pierre.maret}@univ-st-etienne.fr`
[3] DATEV eG, Nuremberg, Germany
`andreas.both@datev.de`
[4] Anhalt University of Applied Science, Köthen, Germany
`andreas.both@hs-anhalt.de`

Abstract. While RDF was designed to make data easily readable by machines, it does not make data easily usable by end-users. Question Answering (QA) over Knowledge Graphs (KGs) is seen as the technology which is able to bridge this gap. It aims to build systems which are capable of extracting the answer to a user's natural language question from an RDF dataset.

In recent years, many approaches were proposed which tackle the problem of QA over KGs. Despite such efforts, it is hard and cumbersome to create a Question Answering system on top of a new RDF dataset. The main open challenge remains portability, i.e., the possibility to apply a QA algorithm easily on new and previously untested RDF datasets.

In this publication, we address the problem of portability by presenting an architecture for a portable QA system. We present a novel approach called QAnswer KG, which allows the construction of on-demand QA systems over new RDF datasets. Hence, our approach addresses non-expert users in QA domain.

In this paper, we provide the details of QA system generation process. We show that it is possible to build a QA system over any RDF dataset while requiring minimal investments in terms of training. We run experiments using 3 different datasets.

To the best of our knowledge, we are the first to design a process for non-expert users. We enable such users to efficiently create an on-demand, scalable, multilingual, QA system on top of any RDF dataset.

Keywords: Question Answering · RDF · Knowledge Graphs · Portability · QAnswer · On-demand

© Springer Nature Switzerland AG 2020
A. Harth et al. (Eds.): ESWC 2020, LNCS 12123, pp. 429–445, 2020.
https://doi.org/10.1007/978-3-030-49461-2_25

1   Introduction

In the last decade, a large number of datasets were published using the RDF standard. RDF allows storing data using a flexible and extensible schema, thus making it possible to store very heterogeneous data. An RDF dataset is generally referred to as a Knowledge Graph (KG). Nowadays, there are KGs about general knowledge, publications, music, geography, life sciences, and many more[1]. The data published, using the RDF standard, and accessible on the World Wide Web is part of the Semantic Web or Web 3.0.

One of the main goals of the Semantic Web is that data can be easily processed by machines. In contrast, the Web 2.0 concepts mostly address end-users. Semantic Web makes data easily accessible by machines. However, it becomes relatively difficult to interpret for end users, although the contained information is extremely valuable for them.

End-users can access RDF data in different ways. Formats and methods like Turtle, N-triples, JSON-LD, etc., make it possible to access RDF data through serialization. Other possibilities include user interfaces for faceted search on RDF data (like LodLive[2]). Moreover, there exists SPARQL[3], a standardized query language for RDF that allows to retrieve complex information from any RDF dataset. All these possibilities require considerable technical knowledge. Thus, they are restricted only to expert users.

In contrast, Question Answering (QA) over Knowledge Graphs (KGs) aims at accessing RDF data using natural language questions. This is generally accomplished by converting a user's question (expressed in natural language) to a corresponding SPARQL query, whose result set is the answer to the question. This process should be performed in an automatic way. This allows also the non-expert users to access RDF data. While a lot of research was done in the last decade addressing this problem, in general, all proposed solutions queried one or a very few specific RDF datasets. The main problem that was not addressed was portability, i.e., the ability to easily apply and port the developed algorithm to new datasets. This observation is the motivation of our research question: *Is it possible to develop a QA approach which can be easily applied to new datasets with little to no manual work?*

We build on top of a recently proposed approach, namely QAnswer [5] to construct a portable QA system that is multilingual, robust, scalable and supports multiple KGs. The QAnswer approach has already been successfully applied to a number of different, well-known datasets including Wikidata, DBpedia, DBLP, Freebase, MusicBrainz, SciGraph and LinkedGeoData [9].

We design and present an architecture for training and running a QA system. This actually results in an out-of-the-box QA system for a user-defined RDF dataset. We call it *QAnswer KG*. Using our approach, we enable any (non-expert)

---

[1] A comprehensive overview of open RDF datasets is available at http://lod-cloud. net.

[2] http://en.lodlive.it.

[3] see https://www.w3.org/TR/rdf-sparql-query/.

dataset owners to efficiently create a QA system on top of their dataset, so that it can be accessed and consumed by end users.

This paper is organized as follows. First, we examine related works in Sect. 2. Then we summarize the approach of QAnswer in Sect. 3. In Sect. 4, we present our perspective on the relation between RDF data and the questions that can be answered on top of it. This section also describes the process of constructing a portable QA system based on the QAnswer approach and the process of training it is using new questions. Additionally, the limitations of the current approach are discussed. We conclude with Sect. 5.

2   Related Work

Question Answering (QA) over Knowledge Graphs (KGs) is an extensive research area with many challenges. For a global overview, we refer to [8]. The main challenge that is addressed in this work is *portability*, i.e., the ability to easily adapt a QA system to a new RDF dataset. The lack of portability of existing approaches is mainly caused by two problems:

Problem 1). Many approaches rely on machine learning algorithms having a large number of learning parameters and requiring a lot of data. Among them, especially deep learning approaches became very popular in recent years like Bordes et al. [3] and Zhang et al. [18]. The main drawback of these approaches is the training data itself. Creating a new training dataset for a new KG is very expensive. For example, Berant et al. [2], report that they spent several thousand US dollars for the creation of the WebQuestions dataset using an online crowd-sourcing marketplace (Amazon Mechanical Turk). This dataset contains 5810 questions. The systems evaluated over the SimpleQuestions[4] dataset (one of the most commonly used benchmarks for studying single-relation factoid questions) use 75910 question-answer pairs for training. The dependency on such large training datasets makes these approaches non-portable unless it is possible to spend very significant effort.

Problem 2). Existing question answering systems depend on KG-specific external tools like entity linkers. Moreover, these works often use manually implemented rules adapted to the addressed KG. This is the case of Xser [17], gAnswer [19] or QuerioDali [14]. These factors limit portability.

For these reasons, *portability problem is not solved* (i.e., existing approaches working on one RDF dataset cannot be easily ported to a new dataset). Hence, up to now the goal of making any RDF dataset accessible via natural language has still not been achieved.

The observation that it is hard and cumbersome to build a QA system from scratch, leads to the idea of creating frameworks that allow the integration of existing techniques and services in a modular way. At least four frameworks tried to achieve this goal: QALL-ME [12], openQA [15], the Open Knowledge Base and Question-Answering (OKBQA) challenge[5] and Qanary [4,10,16]. While Qanary

---

[4] c.f., https://research.fb.com/downloads/babi/.
[5] http://www.okbqa.org/.

achieved to integrate a consistent number of tools, most of them only work for specific KGs and the portability problem is carried over from the integrated tools.

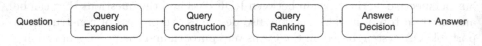

Fig. 1. QAnswer workflow

3   QAnswer Approach

In this section, we describe the workflow used by the QAnswer system to retrieve the answers for a given question formulated in natural language. For more details please refer to [5]. Figure 1 illustrates the QAnswer workflow, consisting of four steps: (1) Query Expansion, (2) Query Construction, (3) Query Ranking, and (4) Answer Decision, described in the following subsections. For the rest of this section, we use a running example "What planets belong to the solar system", queried over Wikidata[6] to describe our approach.

(1) Query Expansion: In this step, all possible n-grams from the textual question (with n taking values ranging from 1 to the number of words in the question) are mapped, if possible, to resources in the given KG. Hence, we intend to identify all possible interpretations of n-grams in a given question. Considering our example, the 1-gram sequences "solar" and "system" are mapped to the resources Q29441547 (ID of "family name") and Q58778 ("set of interacting or interdependent components"), among others; but the 2-gram "solar system" is mapped to Q544 ("planetary system of the Sun"). The 1-gram "belong" is mapped to Q4884518 (a band with that name), while the 2-gram "belong to" is mapped to the property P361 ("part of"). Consequently, there are many possible mappings from the question to resources, but only a small subset of them is the correct one. In the following steps, all the possible combinations of mappings to resources are created, and then one of them is chosen in order to get the correct answer.

(2) Query Construction: In the second step, all possible SPARQL queries are generated from combinations of the resources identified in the previous step. To that end, we extract triple patterns from the KG by using the distance in the graph between the resources in it. Then each query is created by combining triple patterns that share a variable. In Fig. 2, some example queries (i.e., candidates for a correct interpretation) for our running example are shown.[7]

---

[6] http://www.wikidata.org.

[7] We use the following RDF prefixes:
```
PREFIX wdt: <http://www.wikidata.org/prop/direct/>
PREFIX wd: <http://www.wikidata.org/entity/>.
```

#	SPARQL query	Interpretation

1.	SELECT DISTINCT ?s1 WHERE {
	  ?s1 wdt:P398 wd:Q544 .
	}
		this query gives the astronomical bodies of the solar system

2.	SELECT DISTINCT ?o1 where {
	  wd:Q37532538 wdt:P282 ?o1 .
	}
		this outputs the writing system of the family name "belong"

3.	?s1 wdt:31 wd:Q634 . ?s1 ?p1 wd:Q544 . }	the searched query gives back the planets that have any relation with the Solar System
4.	VALUES ?s0 { wde:Q544 } }	the query just gives back the resource of the Solar System which would correspond to the question "Solar System?"

Fig. 2. Examples of queries, generated by QAnswer, with their corresponding interpretation of the question: "What planets belong to the solar system?".

(3) Query Ranking: In this step, the queries created in the previous step are ranked by a pre-trained machine learning component using a set of features. The goal is to rank the correct query in the top position. Among others, the following features are used for this purpose:

- Number of words in the question string that are associated with resources in the SPARQL query.
- Similarity of the resource's label to the associated n-gram.

(4) Answer Decision: Finally, the query ranked in the top position from the previous step is analyzed. The goal is to decide if it is an appropriate answer to the question, i.e., to determine if it expresses the user's intention. For example, if the first ranked query would be Query 4 in Fig. 2 (i.e., the query which just returns the information about "what the solar system is"), then the confidence should be low and no answer should be given. On the contrary, if the first ranked query is Query 1 in Fig. 2, the confidence model should output that this is the right interpretation and provide the corresponding answer set.

This concludes the general description of the approach. For more details please see [9].

Advantages: The QAnswer approach departs from the traditional ways used in Question Answering domain (e.g., using linguistic features for Entity Recognition and Entity Disambiguation). However, it provides a number of advantages:

- **Robustness:** users are not limited to questions formulated using correct natural language. Our system supports keyword-based questions (e.g., "planets solar

system"), or malformed questions (e.g., "planets that solar system belong").
The algorithm is robust enough to deal with all these scenarios [5][8].

- **Multilingualism:** our approach can be applied to other languages without changes. In a previous work, it was shown that the algorithm works for English, German, French, Italian, Spanish, Portuguese, Arabic, and Chinese [9].
- **Multi-Knowledge-base:** our approach allows querying multiple knowledge bases at the same time [5].
- **Precision and Recall:** our approach has been tested on multiple benchmarks and can compete with most of the existing approaches [5].

```
PREFIX vsw:    <http://vocabulary.semantic-web.at/cocktails>
PREFIX vswo:   <http://vocabulary.semantic-web.at/cocktail-ontology>
PREFIX sch:    <http://schema.org/>
PREFIX rdf:    <http://www.w3.org/1999/02/22-rdf-syntax-ns#>
PREFIX rdfs:   <http://www.w3.org/2000/01/rdf-schema#>


vsw:2d85fb1b     rdf:type        vswo:Cocktail ;
                 rdfs:label      "Margarita"@en,"Upside Down Margarita"@en ;
                 sch:description "The margarita is a Mexican ..."@en ;
                 vswo:consistsOf vsw:1439e6c3, vsw:7dede323, vsw:88f5de3d .
vswo:Cocktail    rdfs:label      "Cocktail"@en .
vsw:1439e6c3     rdfs:label      "Cointreau"@en .
vsw:7dede323     rdfs:label      "Tequila"@en .
vsw:88f5de3d     rdfs:label      "Lime juice"@en .
vswo:consistsOf  rdfs:label      "ingredients"@en, "consists of"@en,
                                 "contains"@en, "made up"@en .
```

Question	Answer
Give me all cocktails.	Margarita
What is Margarita?	The margarita is a Mexican cocktail ...
Margarita cocktail?	The margarita is a Mexican cocktail ...
What are the ingredients of Margarita?	Cointreau, Tequila, Lime juice
What is Margarita made of?	Cointreau, Tequila, Lime juice
The ingredients of Margarita are what?	Cointreau, Tequila, Lime juice
ingredients Margarita?	Cointreau, Tequila, Lime juice
Give me cocktails containing tequila.	Margarita
Which cocktails have as ingredient Cointreau?	Margarita
cocktails containing tequila and cointreau	Margarita

Fig. 3. Upper part: A snippet of the Cocktail KG with information about a cocktail that, in English, is called "Margarita" or "Upside Down Margarita". It contains the facts that we are speaking about a cocktail, some names are described, a description and the ingredients are provided. **Lower Part:** Questions that can be answered using the snippet above. Note that many more questions can be answered, including the different variations of the questions above.

---

[8] Note that spelling mistakes are treated in a separated process.

In conclusion, QAnswer is designed to work with any RDF dataset and has several crucial features distinguishing it from QA systems designed for single datasets.

4   QAnswer KG: A RDF to QA Approach

In this section, we describe the relation between an RDF dataset and the questions that can be answered by using QAnswer KG. In Sect. 4.2, we will describe the limitations of the proposed approach and will discuss how these limitations position our work with respect to the state-of-the-art.

In the following, another running example is used that is the small KG *cocktails*[9] providing information about cocktails. A snippet can be found in Fig. 3 (above). The KG contains some cocktails including a short description, an image, and the ingredients. The triples contained in the snippet in Fig. 3 (above) can be used to answer the questions of Fig. 3 (below) as well as their variations. Note that there is a clear correspondence between the information encoded into the RDF dataset and the questions that can be answered using this information.

4.1   QAnswer KG

We are now going to describe the QAnswer KG process which encapsulates QAnswer for generating a QA system on top of an RDF dataset. The global architecture is depicted in Fig. 4.

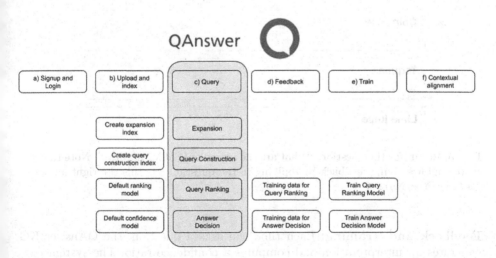

Fig. 4. Overview of QAnswer KG. The gray box shows the original QAnswer pipeline of Fig. 1.

---

[9] The full KB is available at https://qanswer.univ-st-etienne.fr/cocktails.nt. It is published under a CC BY-NC license.

Initiation: The system reserves space for the new QA system and creates directories to allow the upload of new datasets (Fig. 4a).

Indexing: After the dataset is uploaded (see Fig. 4b), it is parsed and indexed. In particular, the indexes for query expansion step (1) and query construction step (2) are created. Both the query ranking step (3) and the answer decision step (4) are models built using machine learning. We already provide some default models for these steps. Moreover, we construct a SPARQL endpoint that is used to execute the generated SPARQL queries.

Query: Now, by means of its default algorithms provided initially, QAnswer KG can already answer user's natural language queries on the dataset. This step corresponds to the original QA pipeline of QAnswer (Fig. 4c). For the "cocktails" dataset, QAnswer KG can, for example, answer to "What is a Margarita?" or "What are the ingredients of Margarita?" (see Fig. 5).

The achieved initial and ad-hoc results may not be satisfying. The next section introduces the training of a machine learning model to adapt it to the particular dataset uploaded. Without this learning step, the initial default model can always be used.

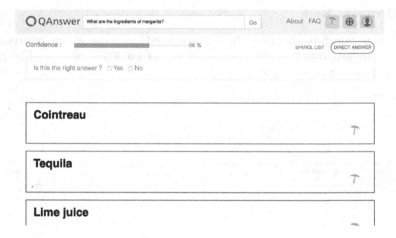

Fig. 5. Result for the question "What are the ingredients of Margarita?". Note that the system allows giving feedback by replying to the question: "Is this the right answer?" (options: Yes/No).

Feedback and Training: Each time one asks a question, the QAnswer KG generates an interpretation and computes a confidence ratio. The system considers the answer to be correct if the confidence is higher or equal than 50% and wrong if it is lower than 50%. By using the feedback functionality, i.e., by getting the user's feedback to the question: "Is this the right answer?" (see Fig. 5), QAnswer KG learns to choose the right interpretation and correctly compute the confidence.

For example, the default model, which is provided initially, responds "Cocktail" to the query "Give me all cocktails?". However, all generated interpretations can be shown to the user. By capturing the click on the right interpretation, QAnswer KG learns to deliver the right answer (in this case: a long list of cocktails), but with low confidence. Using the feedback functionality, the system stores the given example for training (Figure 4d). After processing a set of questions, and by capturing the feedback, the system creates a training set. Such a training set for the cocktail dataset can be downloaded at https://qanswer.univ-st-etienne. fr/questions_cocktail.nt. For the questions on which feedback was given, QAnswer KG also provides an overview of how it performs on these questions (see Fig. 6, "Training Evaluation"). At this stage, QAnswer KG is able to create an improved model that adapts to the specific training dataset (Fig. 4e). This is done by retraining the underlying machine learning models. Note that this training process demands very light investment. This is because the system is only asking users to, optionally, provide feedback in the form of yes and no.

Details

	ID	Question	Validated	Ranking	Confidence
SELECT TRUE	SELECT FALSE	UNSELECT ALL	REMOVE	TRAIN	

Hello

	ID	Question	Validated	Ranking	Confidence
☐	681575	how to prepare margerita	False	0	0.25
☐	681587	what are the ingredients of margerita	False	1	0.64
☐	681607	which cocktails contains salt	False	1	0
☐	681627	margerita	False	1	1
☐	681636	give me all cocktails	False	0	1

Fig. 6. Evaluation screen for the questions where feedback was provided. Red questions indicate that they will not be answered correctly according to the current model while questions marked green will be answered correctly. By clicking on the button "train", the model will be retrained and will learn from the given feedback.

Contextual Information Display: In the default setup, the system output is always provided by displaying the resulting `rdfs:label`. However, depending on the RDF datasets, there is potentially lot of contextual information that can be shown like descriptions, images, maps, and videos. QAnswer KG allows the display of these contextual pieces of information when the properties in the KG are specified (Fig. 4f). Examples of properties in the case of the cocktail KG are:

- http://www.w3.org/2004/02/skos/core#definition gives a short description of the entity,
- http://vocabulary.semantic-web.at/cocktail-ontology/image indicates an image of the resource and
- http://www.w3.org/2004/02/skos/core#exactMatch indicates a DBpedia out-link.

There are two options to make QAnswer KG aware of such semantics: (1) One aligns the KG with the default properties of Wikidata described in the next paragraph[10], and (2) One can specify the properties with the mapping interface, as shown in Fig. 7. Figure 8 shows the displayed information with contextual information.

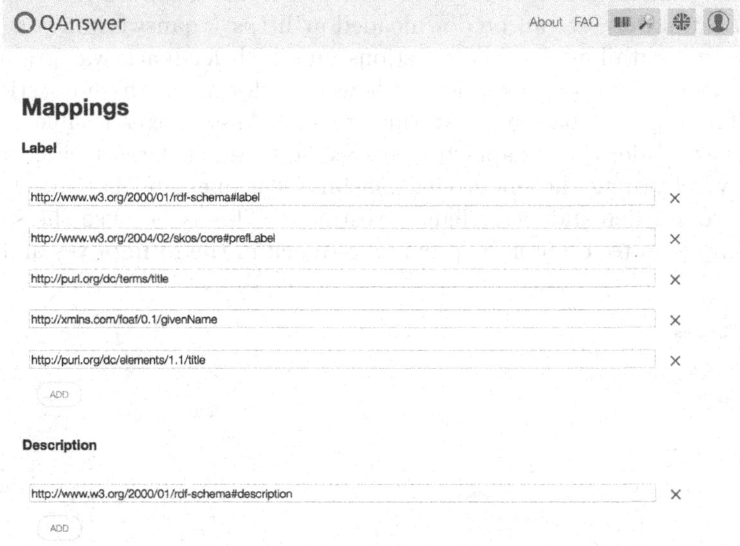

Fig. 7. This interface allows specifying properties that should be taken into consideration when displaying contextual information. For example, by adding a property "P" to the description section, QAnswer KG will use the information attached to "P" to render a description.

As for the option (1), by default, we align the KG with the following Wikidata properties:

- http://schema.org/description, to provide a description
- http://www.wikidata.org/prop/direct/P18, to provide an image. The object is expected to be a link to an online available image file.
- http://www.wikidata.org/prop/direct/P625, to visualize a geographic location. The object is expected to be a literal with datatype http://www.opengis.net/ont/geosparql\#wktLiteral like `Point(12.482777777778 41.893055555556)^^`http://www.opengis.net/ont/geosparql#wktLiteral.
- External links can be expressed using the following properties:
  - http://www.wikidata.org/prop/direct/P856 to show a link to the homepage

---

[10] The cocktail KG where the above URIs are substituted can be downloaded at https://qanswer.univ-st-etienne.fr/cocktails_align.nt.

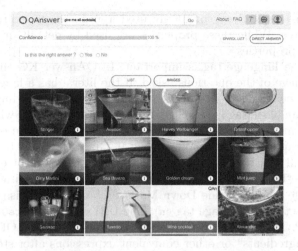

Fig. 8. Result set with contextual information.

```
vsw:2d85fb1b      rdfs:label   "Margarita" .
vswo:consistsOf   rdfs:label   "consists of"@en, "contains"@en,
                               "made up"@en, "ingredients"@en .
```

Fig. 9. Example graph (a subset of the triples provided in the cocktail KG).

- http://www.wikidata.org/prop/direct/P1651 to show a YouTube link
- http://www.wikidata.org/prop/direct/P2037 to show a GitHub link
- http://www.wikidata.org/prop/direct/P2002 to show a Twitter link
- http://www.wikidata.org/prop/direct/P2013 to show a Facebook link
- http://www.wikidata.org/prop/direct/P2003 to show an Instagram link
- http://www.wikidata.org/prop/direct/P496 to show an ORCID link
- http://www.wikidata.org/prop/direct/P356 to show a DOI link

4.2 Limitations

In this section, we describe the current limitations of QAnswer KG and discuss how these limitations can be positioned with respect to the state of the art QA research.

Limitation 1: A URI will only be used to generate SPARQL queries if the question contains (up to stemming) the literal attached via one of the following properties:

- http://www.w3.org/2000/01/rdf-schema#label
- http://purl.org/dc/elements/1.1/title
- https://schema.org/name
- http://www.w3.org/2004/02/skos/core#prefLabel
- http://www.w3.org/2004/02/skos/core#altLabel

The intention is inspired by commonly used approaches to express the corresponding resource. While these properties are used by default, it is possible to specify custom properties.

Moreover, the language tag is important. In QAnswer KG the user has to select the language of the questions asked. If the literal has a language tag, the label will only be searched in questions where the corresponding language is selected. If no language tag is attached, the corresponding label will be searched in all questions independently of the selected language. For example, we assume that an RDF graph is given as shown in Fig. 9. Given the listed triples, the URI `vsw:2d85fb1b` will only be used in a SPARQL query if the question either contains "Margarita" or "Upside Down Margarita". Moreover, "Margarita" will be used for any language while "Upside Down Margarita" only if English is selected as a language (due to the language tag `en`). The URI `vswo:consistsOf` will be used to construct SPARQL queries if the question contains "consistsOf", "contains", "made up", "ingredients" or other equivalent expressions after stemming. This is for example the case for the expression "contained" which, after stemming, is same as "contains".

In particular, note that with a graph similar to as follows, it will not be possible to answer any question since no labels are attached:

```
vsw:Margarita vswo:consistsOf vsw:Cointreau .
```

Additionally, note that, for humans, even if the name of the URI is meaningful, according to RDF standard the above graph is equivalent to:

```
vsw:2d85fb1b  vswo:1234  vsw:1439e6c3 .
```

Hence, even for human users, it does not express the previous information.

Limitation 2: We assume that the RDF dataset does not use any form of reification. Recall that, RDF is perfectly suited to represent binary statements like "Margarita contains Cointreau" which can be represented as the triple (Margarita, contains, Cointreau). Reified statements are used when there is the need to speak about a binary statement like in: "Margarita contains 50 ml of Cointreau". In this case, a triple is not enough to represent this piece of information. The Semantic Web Community proposed a series of models to represent this type of information. For a full overview of the presented models, we refer to [13]. One of the models is *n-ary relations* (the reification model used by Wikidata), where the knowledge would be represented as:

```
vsw:Margarita  vswo:consistsOf_IN  _:b1 .
_:b1 vswo:consistsOf_OUT vsw:Cointreau .
_:b1 vswo:quantity "50 ml" .
```

Another model is RDF reification which was proposed during the standardization of RDF. The knowledge would be represented as:

```
vsw:Statement
    rdf:type        rdf:Statement ;
    rdf:subject     vsw:Margarita ;
    rdf:predicate   vswo:consistsOf ;
```

```
rdf:object      vsw:Cointreau ;
vswo:quantity   "50 ml" .
```

QAnswer KG was not designed to cope with such representations and it is not clear how it behaves when they are indexed in QAnswer KG. We consider this as a future challenge.

Querying KGs, which contain reified statements, is a poorly addressed research topic. Let's consider the three main QA benchmarks and the systems evaluated on them, namely SimpleQuestions, QALD, and WebQuestions. SimpleQuestions is based on a non-reified version of Freebase so this problem is not addressed in the benchmark. QALD is based on DBpedia which does not contain reified statements. Consequently, all systems evaluated over QALD also do not tackle this problem. Finally, WebQuestions considers full Freebase and therefore its reified structure. However, by reviewing the QA systems evaluated over WebQuestions, it can be seen that more than 60% of the systems ignore the reified structure by deleting the contextual information (like it is done in Bordes et al. [3]). The remaining approaches were only evaluated over Freebase and none among them was evaluated over KGs.

Limitation 3: The complexity of the SPARQL query that can be generated is limited. The queries can be of type ASK, COUNT, and SELECT and may contain up to 3 triple patterns.

Again let's compare this with respect to the state-of-the-art with three main QA benchmarks. All questions over SimpleQuestions are SELECT queries with one triple pattern. WebQuestions does not contain the answer queries, but only the labels of the answers. However, [1] achieved high accuracy by only matching to a non-reified or a reified statement which corresponds to SPARQL queries with a maximum of 3 triple patterns. Finally, the QALD benchmark contains some queries with aggregates or SPARQL operators like ORDER BY and FILTER. Anyways, our analysis shows that 66 % of the questions in QALD-9 can be answered using the syntax supported by QAnswer KG. Moreover, most of proposed approaches over QALD do not generate these kind of queries.

We above, we described the three main limitations of QAnswer KG and explained how our work can be positioned in the state-of-the-art after considering such limitations.

4.3   Experiment

To prove the portability of our approach, we let users test our system on three datasets.

- A **cocktails** dataset: the dataset used as a running example in the previous sections, i.e., a dataset containing cocktails with their ingredients and preparation.

– An **HR** dataset: the dataset contains information about employees of a company. The information includes their skills, the spoken languages, the languages they can program and their images.
– A **EU** dataset: i.e., a dataset containing information on the European Union
about their member states, their capitals and ministries. This dataset is
multilingual.

The users who set up the systems were knowledge engineers, i.e., persons who
are familiar with knowledge representation, but not with question answering.
The users checked the datasets beforehand to know which information they
encode, i.e., which questions can be answered using it. The users generated
some benchmarks for the datasets using the feedback functionality described in
Sect. 4.1. The statistics of the three datasets and the statistics of the benchmarks
are reported in Fig. 10.

In many cases, the users do not need to know the answer, but can make
an educated guess about the correctness. This can be done by verifying the
generated SPARQL query. For example, assume the user asks "What is the
capital of Slovenia?", but he/she does not know the capital. The user can check
the SPARQL query if it is "Slovenia capital ?o" then he/she can click on yes
to provide feedback to express that the SPARQL query correctly reflects the
question. It is assumed that the data and knowledge encoded in the KG are
correct.

The efforts in re-training the system can be quantified with the number of
questions asked by the users. These are reported in Fig. 10. The number of
questions for the EU dataset is higher than the others. But only 1/6th of the
questions were formulated. The remaining 5/6th were automatically translated
to 5 different languages to ensure that the system also works in other languages.

We report the F-Measure of the 3 benchmarks by using the default model
and the trained model in Fig. 10. We can see that, before training, the default
model generalizes quite well, while after training we get very good performances.
This shows that it is possible to reuse the described QA system across different
domains.

Dataset	#Triples	#Properties	#Questions	F-Measure default	F-Measure train
Cocktails	10.253	90	27	0.37	0.92
HR	4394	48	259	0.52	0.97
EU	4.835.856	992	844	0.70	0.90

Fig. 10. Statistics of the three considered datasets and their benchmark. Note that the
benchmark over the EU dataset is multilingual.

4.4   Service and Demo

An online tutorial describing the process is available at https://qanswer.univ-st-etienne.fr/docs/doc0. The QAnswer KG approach was implemented as a service and is available for public use. A demo is available at https://www.qanswer.eu/qa. It facilitates access to several datasets using the QAnswer KG technology. Many well-known and widely used datasets, such as DBpedia, Wikidata, DBLP, OpenStreetMap, MusicBrainz, and ORCID are provided. Thus, users can ask questions using natural language to retrieve information from these datasets. The demo supports the following languages: English, German, French, Italian, Spanish, Portuguese, Dutch, Chinese, Arabic, and Japanese. The quality of the created question answering system is inherited from the QAnswer approach (cf., [5] for details on the benchmark results).

5   Conclusion and Future Work

We have presented QAnswer KG, a novel approach that is able to generate on-demand QA systems for any RDF dataset. It addresses one of the major open challenges in the domain of QA over KGs, namely, portability.

The QAnswer KG approach is designed on top of the QAnswer technology that is in turn encapsulated inside the QAnswer KG. QAnswer provides major features, e.g., it is robust with respect to new questions from the user, allows multilingual question, and can be used to query multiple KGs at the same time. The QAnswer technology was extensively tested on a wide variety of benchmarks showing that it can compete with most of the state-of-the-art solutions.

Our approach enabled non-expert users to create QA systems on top of new RDF datasets. There is little to no knowledge about QA required to establish a system by a user as shown in the demo. Therefore, QAnswer KG achieves portability for RDF-driven QA system. We believe that QAnswer KG represents an important contribution for the Semantic Web Community since it will enable data owners to expose their datasets directly to end-users, and therefore make the Semantic Web more useful and popular.

In the future, we plan to extend the functionality of the QAnswer KG service by integrating additional services: (A) SPARQLtoUser (cf., [6]), a service capable of transforming a SPARQL query into a user understandable representation, (B) SummaServer [11], a service that selects between all triples associated to an RDF entity, the most important ones, (C) a service to allow users to disambiguate between different entities, as described in [7]. Note that these services are already used when querying some KGs like Wikidata, DBpedia and DBLP, but they are not sufficiently generalized to work over any KG.

Note: There is a patent pending for the presented approach. It was filed on January 18th, 2018 at the EPO (number EP18305035.0).

Acknowledgment. We want to thank Semantic Web Company to let us use the cocktails dataset.

References

1. Bast, H., Haussmann, E.: More accurate question answering on freebase. In: Proceedings of the 24th ACM International on Conference on Information and Knowledge Management. ACM (2015)
2. Berant, J., Chou, A., Frostig, R., Liang, P.: Semantic parsing on freebase from question-answer pairs. In: EMNLP (2013)
3. Bordes, A., Usunier, N., Chopra, S., Weston, J.: Large-scale simple question answering with memory networks. arXiv preprint arXiv:1506.02075 (2015)
4. Both, A., Diefenbach, D., Singh, K., Shekarpour, S., Cherix, D., Lange, C.: Qanary – a methodology for vocabulary-driven open question answering systems. In: Sack, H., Blomqvist, E., d'Aquin, M., Ghidini, C., Ponzetto, S.P., Lange, C. (eds.) ESWC 2016. LNCS, vol. 9678, pp. 625–641. Springer, Cham (2016). https://doi.org/10.1007/978-3-319-34129-3_38
5. Diefenbach, D., Both, A., Singh, K.D., Maret, P.: Towards a question answering system over the semantic web. Semant. Web J. (2019)
6. Diefenbach, D., Dridi, Y., Singh, K.D., Maret, P.: SPARQLtoUser: did the question answering system understand me? In: Joint Proceedings of BLINK2017: 2nd International Workshop on Benchmarking Linked Data and NLIWoD3: Natural Language Interfaces for the Web of Data co-located with 16th ISWC (2017). http://ceur-ws.org/Vol-1932/paper-01.pdf
7. Diefenbach, D., Hormozi, N., Amjad, S., Both, A.: Introducing feedback in qanary: how users can interact with QA systems. In: Blomqvist, E., Hose, K., Paulheim, H., Ławrynowicz, A., Ciravegna, F., Hartig, O. (eds.) ESWC 2017. LNCS, vol. 10577, pp. 81–86. Springer, Cham (2017). https://doi.org/10.1007/978-3-319-70407-4_16
8. Diefenbach, D., Lopez, V., Singh, K., Pierre, M.: Core techniques of question answering systems over knowledge bases: a survey. Knowl. Inf. Syst. **55**, 529–569 (2017)
9. Diefenbach, D., Migliatti, P.H., Qawasmeh, O., Lully, V., Singh, K., Maret, P.: QAnswer: a question answering prototype bridging the gap between a considerable part of the LOD cloud and end-users. In: The World Wide Web Conference, pp. 3507–3510. ACM (2019)
10. Diefenbach, D., Singh, K., Both, A., Cherix, D., Lange, C., Auer, S.: The qanary ecosystem: getting new insights by composing question answering pipelines. In: Cabot, J., De Virgilio, R., Torlone, R. (eds.) ICWE 2017. LNCS, vol. 10360, pp. 171–189. Springer, Cham (2017). https://doi.org/10.1007/978-3-319-60131-1_10
11. Diefenbach, D., Thalhammer, A.: PageRank and generic entity summarization for RDF knowledge bases. In: Gangemi, A., et al. (eds.) ESWC 2018. LNCS, vol. 10843, pp. 145–160. Springer, Cham (2018). https://doi.org/10.1007/978-3-319-93417-4_10
12. Ferrández, Ó., Spurk, C., Kouylekov, M., al.: The QALL-ME framework: a specifiable-domain multilingual Question Answering architecture. J. Web Semant. (2011)
13. Giménez-García, J.M., Zimmermann, A., Maret, P.: NdFluents: an ontology for annotated statements with inference preservation. In: Blomqvist, E., Maynard, D., Gangemi, A., Hoekstra, R., Hitzler, P., Hartig, O. (eds.) ESWC 2017. LNCS, vol. 10249, pp. 638–654. Springer, Cham (2017). https://doi.org/10.1007/978-3-319-58068-5_39

14. Lopez, V., Tommasi, P., Kotoulas, S., Wu, J.: QuerioDALI: question answering over dynamic and linked knowledge graphs. In: Groth, P., et al. (eds.) ISWC 2016. LNCS, vol. 9982, pp. 363–382. Springer, Cham (2016). https://doi.org/10.1007/978-3-319-46547-0_32

15. Marx, E., Usbeck, R., Ngonga Ngomo, A., Höffner, K., Lehmann, J., Auer, S.: Towards an open question answering architecture. In: Semantics (2014)

16. Singh, K., Both, A., Diefenbach, D., Shekarpour, S.: Towards a message-driven vocabulary for promoting the interoperability of question answering systems. In: ICSC 2016 (2016)

17. Xu, K., Feng, Y., Zhao, D.: Xser@ QALD-4: answering natural language questions via phrasal semantic parsing (2014)

18. Zhang, Y., et al.: Question answering over knowledge base with neural attention combining global knowledge information. arXiv preprint arXiv:1606.00979 (2016)

19. Zou, L., Huang, R., Wang, H., Yu, J.X., He, W., Zhao, D.: Natural language question answering over RDF: a graph data driven approach. In: Proceedings of the 2014 ACM SIGMOD International Conference on Management of Data. ACM (2014)

Equivalent Rewritings on Path Views
with Binding Patterns

Julien Romero[1(✉)], Nicoleta Preda[2], Antoine Amarilli[1], and Fabian Suchanek[1]

[1] LTCI, Télécom Paris, Institut Polytechnique de Paris, Palaiseau, France
{julien.romero,antoine.amarilli,fabian.suchanek}@telecom-paris.fr
[2] Université de Versailles, Versailles, France
nicoleta.preda@uvsq.fr

Abstract. A view with a binding pattern is a parameterized query on a database. Such views are used, e.g., to model Web services. To answer a query on such views, the views have to be orchestrated together in execution plans. We show how queries can be rewritten into equivalent execution plans, which are guaranteed to deliver the same results as the query on all databases. We provide a correct and complete algorithm to find these plans for path views and atomic queries. Finally, we show that our method can be used to answer queries on real-world Web services.

1   Introduction

In this paper, we study views with binding patterns [25]. Intuitively, these can be seen as functions that, given input values, return output values from a database. For example, a function on a music database could take as input a musician, and return the songs by the musician stored in the database.

Several databases on the Web can be accessed only through such functions. They are usually presented as a form or as a Web service. For a REST Web service, a client calls a function by accessing a parameterized URL, and it responds by sending back the results in an XML or JSON file. The advantage of such

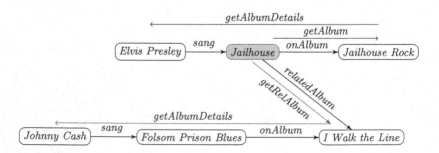

Fig. 1. An equivalent execution plan (blue) and a maximal contained rewriting (green) executed on a database (black). (Color figure online)

© Springer Nature Switzerland AG 2020
A. Harth et al. (Eds.): ESWC 2020, LNCS 12123, pp. 446–462, 2020.
https://doi.org/10.1007/978-3-030-49461-2_26

an interface is that it offers a simple way of accessing the data without downloading it. Furthermore, the functions allow the data provider to choose which data to expose, and under which conditions. For example, the data provider can allow only queries about a given entity, or limit the number of calls per minute. According to programmableWeb.com, there are over 20,000 Web services of this form – including LibraryThing, Amazon, TMDb, Musicbrainz, and Lastfm.

If we want to answer a user query on a database with such functions, we have to *compose* them. For example, consider a database about music – as shown in Fig. 1 in black. Assume that the user wants to find the musician of the song *Jailhouse*. One way to answer this query is to call a function *getAlbum*, which returns the album of the song. Then we can call *getAlbumDetails*, which takes as input the album, and returns all songs on the album and their musicians. If we consider among these results only those with the song *Jailhouse*, we obtain the musician *Elvis Presley* (Fig. 1, top, in blue). We will later see that, under certain conditions, this plan is guaranteed to return exactly all answers to the query on all databases: it is an *equivalent rewriting* of the query. This plan is in contrast to other possible plans, such as calling *getRelatedAlbum* and *getAlbumDetails* (Fig. 1, bottom, in green). This plan does not return the exact set of query results. It is a *maximally contained rewriting*, another form of rewriting, which we will discuss in the related work.

Equivalent rewritings are of primordial interest to the user because they allow obtaining exactly the answers to the query – no matter what the database contains. Equivalent rewritings are also of interest to the data provider: For example, in the interest of usability, the provider may want to make sure that equivalent plans can answer all queries of importance. However, finding equivalent rewritings is inherently non-trivial. As observed in [2,4], the problem is undecidable in general. Indeed, plans can recursively call the same function. Thus, there is, a priori, no bound on the length of an execution plan. Hence, if there is no plan, an algorithm may try forever to find one – which indeed happens in practice.

In this paper, we focus on path functions (i.e., functions that form a sequence of relations) and atomic queries. For this scenario, we can give a correct and complete algorithm that decides in PTIME whether a query has an equivalent rewriting or not. If it has one, we can give a grammar that enumerates all of them. Finally, we show that our method can be used to answer queries on real-world Web services. After reviewing related work in Sect. 2 and preliminaries in Sect. 3, we present our problem statement in Sect. 4 and our algorithm in Sect. 5, concluding with experiments in Sect. 6. This paper is complemented by an extended version [27] that contains the proofs for our theorems.

2   Related Work

Formally, we aim at computing *equivalent rewritings* over views with binding patterns [25] in the presence of inclusion dependencies. Our approach relates to the following other works.

Equivalent Rewritings. Checking if a query is *determined* by views [16], or finding possible equivalent rewritings of a query over views, is a task that has been intensively studied for query optimization [4,15], under various classes of constraints. In our work, we are specifically interested in computing equivalent rewritings over views with binding patterns, i.e., restrictions on how the views can be accessed. This question has also been studied, in particular with the approach by Benedikt et al. [2] based on logical interpolation, for very general classes of constraints. In our setting, we focus on path views and unary inclusion dependencies on binary relations. This restricted (but practically relevant) language of functions and constraints has not been investigated in [2]. We show that, in this context, the problem is solvable in PTIME. What is more, we provide a self-contained, effective algorithm for computing plans, for which we provide an implementation. We compare experimentally against the PDQ implementation by Benedikt et al. [3] in Sect. 6.

Maximally Contained Rewritings. Another line of work has studied how to rewrite queries against data sources in a way that is not equivalent but maximizes the number of query answers [17]. Unlike equivalent rewritings, there is no guarantee that all answers are returned. For views with binding patterns, a first solution was proposed in [13,14]. The problem has also been studied for different query languages or under various constraints [7,8,12,20]. We remark that by definition, the approach requires the generation of relevant but not-so-smart call compositions. These call compositions make sure that no answers are lost. Earlier work by some of the present authors proposed to prioritize promising function calls [21] or to complete the set of functions with new functions [22]. In our case, however, we are concerned with identifying only those function compositions that are guaranteed to deliver answers.

Orthogonal Works. Several works study how to optimize given execution plans [29,32]. Our work, in contrast, aims at *finding* such execution plans. Other works are concerned with mapping several functions onto the same schema [10,18,31]. Our approach takes a Local As View perspective, in which all functions are already formulated in the same schema.

Federated Databases. Some works [24,28] have studied *federated databases*, where each source can be queried with any query from a predefined language. By contrast, our sources only publish a set of preset parameterized queries, and the abstraction for a Web service is a view with a binding pattern, hence, a predefined query with input parameters. Therefore, our setting is different from theirs, as we cannot send arbitrary queries to the data sources: we can only call these predefined functions.

Web Services. There are different types of Web services, and many of them are not (or cannot be) modeled as views with binding patterns. AJAX Web services use JavaScript to allow a Web page to contact the server. Other Web services are used to execute complex business processes [11] according to protocols or choreographies, often described in BPEL [30]. The Web Services Description Language (WSDL) describes SOAP Web services. The Web Services Modeling Ontology (WSMO) [33], in the Web Ontology Language for Services (OWL-S)

[19], or in Description Logics (DL) [26] can describe more complex services. These descriptions allow for Artificial Intelligence reasoning about Web services in terms of their behavior by explicitly declaring their preconditions and effects. Some works derive or enrich such descriptions automatically [6,9,23] in order to facilitate Web service discovery.

In our work, we only study Web services that are querying interfaces to databases. These can be modeled as views with binding patterns and are typically implemented in the Representational State Transfer (REST) architecture, which does not provide a formal or semantic description of the functions.

3 Preliminaries

Global Schema. We assume a set $\mathcal{C}$ of constants and a set $\mathcal{R}$ of relation names. We assume that all relations are binary, i.e., any n-ary relations have been encoded as binary relations by introducing additional constants[1]. A *fact* $r(a, b)$ is formed using a relation name $r \in \mathcal{R}$ and two constants $a, b \in \mathcal{C}$. A *database instance* I, or simply *instance*, is a set of facts. For $r \in \mathcal{R}$, we will use r^- as a relation name to mean the inverse of r, i.e., $r^-(b, a)$ stands for $r(a, b)$. More precisely, we see the inverse relations r^- for $r \in \mathcal{R}$ as being relation names in $\mathcal{R}$, and we assume that, for any instance I, the facts of I involving the relation name r^- are always precisely the facts $r^-(b, a)$ such that $r(a, b)$ is in I.

Inclusion Dependencies. A *unary inclusion dependency* for two relations r, s, which we write $r \rightsquigarrow s$, is the following constraint:

$$\forall x, y : r(x, y) \Rightarrow \exists z : s(x, z)$$

Note that one of the two relations or both may be inverses. In the following, we will assume a fixed set $\mathcal{UID}$ of unary inclusion dependencies, and we will only consider instances that satisfy these inclusion dependencies. We assume that $\mathcal{UID}$ is closed under implication, i.e., if $r \rightsquigarrow s$ and $s \rightsquigarrow t$ are two inclusion dependencies in $\mathcal{UID}$, then so is $r \rightsquigarrow t$.

Queries. An *atom* $r(\alpha, \beta)$ is formed with a relation name $r \in \mathcal{R}$ and α and β being either constants or variables. A *query* takes the form

$$q(\alpha_1, ..., \alpha_m) \leftarrow B_1, ..., B_n$$

where $\alpha_1, ... \alpha_m$ are variables, each of which must appear in at least one of the body atoms $B_1, ... B_n$. We assume that queries are *connected*, i.e., each body atom must be transitively linked to every other body atom by shared variables. An *embedding* for a query q on a database instance I is a substitution σ for the variables of the body atoms so that $\forall B \in \{B_1, ..., B_n\} : \sigma(B) \in I$. A *result* of a query is an embedding projected to the variables of the head atom. We write $q(\alpha_1, ..., \alpha_m)(I)$ for the results of the query on I. An *atomic query* is a query that takes the form $q(x) \leftarrow r(a, x)$, where a is a constant and x is a variable.

---

[1] https://www.w3.org/TR/swbp-n-aryRelations/.

Functions. We model functions as views with binding patterns [25], namely:

$$f(\underline{x}, y_1, ..., y_m) \leftarrow B_1, ..., B_n$$

Here, f is the function name, x is the *input variable* (which we underline), $y_1, ..., y_m$ are the *output variables*, and any other variables of the body atoms are *existential variables*. In this paper, we are concerned with *path functions*, where the body atoms are ordered in a sequence $r_1(\underline{x}, x_1), r_2(x_1, x_2), ..., r_n(x_{n-1}, x_n)$, the first variable of the first atom is the input of the plan, the second variable of each atom is the first variable of its successor, and the output variables are ordered in the same way as the atoms.

Example 3.1. *Consider again our example in Fig. 1. There are 3 relations names in the database: onAlbum, sang, and relAlbum. The relation relAlbum links a song to a related album. The functions are:*

$$getAlbum(\underline{s}, a) \leftarrow onAlbum(\underline{s}, a)$$
$$getAlbumDetails(\underline{a}, s, m) \leftarrow onAlbum^-(\underline{a}, s), sang^-(s, m)$$
$$getRelAlbum(\underline{s}, a) \leftarrow relAlbum(\underline{s}, a)$$

The first function takes as input a song s, and returns as output the album a of the song. The second function takes as input an album a and returns the songs s with their musicians m. The last function returns the related albums of a song.

Execution Plans. Our goal in this work is to study when we can evaluate an atomic query on an instance using a set of path functions, which we will do using *plans*. Formally, a *plan* is a finite sequence $\pi_a(x) = c_1, \ldots, c_n$ of *function calls*, where a is a constant, x is the output variable. Each function call c_i is of the form $f(\underline{\alpha}, \beta_1, \ldots, \beta_n)$, where f is a function name, where the input α is either a constant or a variable occurring in some call in $c_1, \ldots, c_{i-1}$, and where the outputs $\beta_1, \ldots, \beta_n$ are either variables or constants. A *filter* in a plan is the use of a constant in one of the outputs β_i of a function call; if the plan has none, then we call it *unfiltered*. The *semantics* of the plan is the query:

$$q(x) \leftarrow \phi(c_1), \ldots, \phi(c_n)$$

where each $\phi(c_i)$ is the body of the query defining the function f of the call c_i in which we have substituted the constants and variables used in c_i, where we have used fresh existential variables across the different $\phi(c_i)$, and where x is the output variable of the plan.

To *evaluate* a plan on an instance means running the query above. Given an execution plan π_a and a database I, we call $\pi_a(I)$ the answers of the plan on I. In practice, evaluating the plan means calling the functions in the order given by the plan. If a call fails, it can potentially remove one or all answers of the plan. More precisely, for a given instance I, the results $b \in \pi_a(I)$ are precisely the elements b to which we can bind the output variable when matching the semantics of the plan on I. For example, let us consider a function $f(\underline{x}, y) = r(x, y)$ and a plan $\pi_a(x) = f(\underline{a}, x), f(\underline{b}, y)$. This plan returns the answer a' on the instance $I = \{r(a, a'), r(b, b')\}$, and returns no answer on $I' = \{r(a, a')\}$.

Example 3.2. *The following is an execution plan for Example 3.1:*

$$\pi_{Jailhouse}(m) = getAlbum(\underline{Jailhouse}, a), getAlbumDetails(\underline{a}, Jailhouse, m)$$

The first element is a function call to getAlbum with the constant Jailhouse as input, and the variable a as output. The variable a then serves as input in the second function call to getAlbumDetails. The plan is shown in Fig. 1 on page 1 with an example instance. This plan defines the query:

$$onAlbum(Jailhouse, a), onAlbum^-(a, Jailhouse), sang^-(Jailhouse, m)$$

For our example instance, we have the embedding:

$$\sigma = \{a = JailhouseRock, m = ElvisPresley\}.$$

Atomic Query Rewriting. Our goal is to determine when a given atomic query $q(x)$ can be evaluated as a plan $\pi_a(x)$. Formally, we say that $\pi_a(x)$ is a *rewriting* (or an *equivalent plan*) of the query $q(x)$ if, for any database instance I satisfying the inclusion dependencies $\mathcal{UID}$, the result of the plan π_a is equal to the result of the query q on I.

4   Problem Statement and Main Results

The goal of this paper is to determine when a query admits a rewriting under the inclusion dependencies. If so, we compute a rewriting. In this section, we present our main high-level results for this task. We then describe in the next section (Sect. 5) the algorithm that we use to achieve these results, and show in Sect. 6 our experimental results on an implementation of this algorithm.

Remember that we study *atomic* queries, e.g., $q(x) \leftarrow r(a, x)$, that we study plans on a set $\mathcal{F}$ of path functions, and that we assume that the data satisfy integrity constraints given as a set $\mathcal{UID}$ of *unary inclusion dependencies*. In this section, we first introduce the notion of *non-redundant plans*, which are a specific class of plans that we study throughout the paper; and we then state our results about finding rewritings that are non-redundant plans.

4.1   Non-redundant Plans

Our goal in this section is to restrict to a well-behaved subset of plans that are *non-redundant*. Intuitively, a *redundant plan* is a plan that contains function calls that are not useful to get the output of the plan. For example, if we add the function call $getAlbum(m, a')$ to the plan in Example 3.2, then this is a redundant call that does not change the result of $\pi_{Jailhouse}$. We also call *redundant* the calls that are used to remove some of the answers, e.g., for the function $f(\underline{x}, y) = r(x, y)$ and the plan $\pi_a(x) = f(a, x), f(b, y)$ presented before, the second call is redundant because it does not contribute to the output (but can filter out some results). Formally:

Definition 4.1 (Redundant plan). *An execution plan* $\pi_a(x)$ *is* redundant *if it has no call using the constant a as input, or if it contains a call where none of the outputs is an output of the plan or an input to another call. If the plan does not satisfy these conditions, it is* non-redundant.

Non-redundant plans can easily be reformulated to have a more convenient shape: the first call uses the input value as its input, and each subsequent call uses as its input a variable that was an output of the previous call. Formally:

Property 4.2. *The function calls of any non-redundant plan* $\pi_a(x)$ *can be organized in a sequence* $c_0, c_1, \ldots, c_k$ *such that the input of* c_0 *is the constant a, every other call* c_i *takes as input an output variable of the previous call* c_{i-1}, *and the output of the plan is in the call* c_k.

Non-redundant plans seem less potent than redundant plans, because they cannot, e.g., filter the outputs of a call based on whether some other call is successful. However, as it turns out, we can restrict our study to non-redundant plans without loss of generality, which we do in the remainder of the paper.

Property 4.3. *For any redundant plan* $\pi_a(x)$ *that is a rewriting to an atomic query* $q(x) \leftarrow r(a, x)$, *a subset of its calls forms a non-redundant plan, which is also equivalent to* $q(x)$.

4.2   Result Statements

Our main theoretical contribution is the following theorem:

Theorem 4.4. *There is an algorithm which, given an atomic query* $q(x) \leftarrow r(a, x)$, *a set* $\mathcal{F}$ *of path function definitions, and a set* $\mathcal{UID}$ *of UIDs, decides in polynomial time if there exists an equivalent rewriting of* q. *If so, the algorithm enumerates all the non-redundant plans that are equivalent rewritings of* q.

In other words, we can efficiently decide if equivalent rewritings exist, and when they do, the algorithm can compute them. Note that, in this case, the generation of an equivalent rewriting is *not* guaranteed to be in polynomial time, as the equivalent plans are not guaranteed to be of polynomial size. Also, observe that this result gives a *characterization* of the equivalent non-redundant plans, in the sense that *all* such plans are of the form that our algorithm produces. Of course, as the set of equivalent non-redundant plans is generally infinite, our algorithm cannot actually write down all such plans, but it provides any such plan after a finite time. The underlying characterization of equivalent non-redundant plans is performed via a context-free grammar describing possible paths of a specific form, which we will introduce in the next section.

Our methods can also solve a different problem: given the query, path view definitions, unary inclusion dependencies, and given a candidate non-redundant plan, decide if the plan is correct, i.e., if it is an equivalent rewriting of the query. The previous result does not provide a solution as it produces all non-redundant equivalent plans in some arbitrary order. However, we can show using similar methods that this task can also be decided in polynomial time:

Proposition 4.5. *Given a set of unary inclusion dependencies, a set of path functions, an atomic query $q(x) \leftarrow r(a,x)$ and a non-redundant execution plan π_a, one can determine in PTIME if π_a is an equivalent rewriting of q.*

That proposition concludes the statement of our main theoretical contributions. We describe in the next section the algorithm used to show our main theorem (Theorem 4.4) and used for our experiments in Sect. 6. The extended version of this paper [27] contains the proofs for our theorems.

5   Algorithm

We now present the algorithm used to show Theorem 4.4. The presentation explains at a high level how the algorithm can be implemented, as we did for the experiments in Sect. 6. However, some formal details of the algorithm are deferred to the extended version of this paper [27], as well as the formal proof.

Our algorithm is based on a characterization of the non-redundant equivalent rewritings as the intersection between a context-free grammar and a regular expression (the result of which is itself a context-free language). The context-free grammar encodes the UID constraints and generates a language of words that intuitively describe forward-backward paths that are guaranteed to exist under the UIDs. As for the regular expression, it encodes the path functions and expresses the legal execution plans. Then, the intersection gets all non-redundant execution plans that satisfy the UIDs. We first detail the construction of the grammar, and then of the regular expression.

5.1   Defining the Context-Free Grammar of Forward-Backward Paths

Our context-free grammar intuitively describes a language of forward-backward paths, which intuitively describe the sequences of relations that an equivalent plan can take to walk away from the input value on an instance, and then walk back to that value, as in our example on Fig. 1, to finally use the relation that consists of the query answer: in our example, the plan is *getAlbum(Jailhouse, a)*, *getAlbumDetails(a, Jailhouse, m)*. The grammar then describes all such back-and-forth paths from the input value that are guaranteed to exist thanks to the unary inclusion dependencies that we assumed in $\mathcal{UID}$. Intuitively, it describes such paths in the *chase* by $\mathcal{UID}$ of an answer fact. We now define this grammar, noting that the definition is independent of the functions in $\mathcal{F}$:

Definition 5.1 (Grammar of forward-backward paths). *Given a set of relations $\mathcal{R}$, given an atomic query $q(a,x) \leftarrow r(a,x)$ with $r \in \mathcal{R}$, and given a set of unary inclusion dependencies $\mathcal{UID}$, the grammar of forward-backward paths is a context-free grammar $\mathcal{G}_q$, whose language is written $\mathcal{L}_q$, with the non-terminal symbols $S \cup \{L_{r_i}, B_{r_i} \mid r_i \in \mathcal{R}\}$, the terminals $\{r_i \mid r_i \in \mathcal{R}\}$, the start symbol S, and the following productions:*

$$S \to B_r r \tag{5.1}$$

$$S \to B_r r B_{r^-} r^- \tag{5.2}$$

$$\forall r_i, r_j \in \mathcal{R} \; s.t. \; r_i \rightsquigarrow r_j \; in \; \mathcal{UID} : B_{r_i} \to B_{r_i} L_{r_j} \tag{5.3}$$

$$\forall r_i \in \mathcal{R} : B_{r_i} \to \epsilon \tag{5.4}$$

$$\forall r_i \in \mathcal{R} : L_{r_i} \to r_i B_{r_i^-} r_i^- \tag{5.5}$$

The words of this grammar describe the sequence of relations of paths starting at the input value and ending by the query relation r, which are guaranteed to exist thanks to the unary inclusion dependencies $\mathcal{UID}$. In this grammar, the B_{r_i}s represent the paths that "loop" to the position where they started, at which we have an outgoing r_i-fact. These loops are either empty (Rule 5.4), are concatenations of loops which may involve facts implied by $\mathcal{UID}$ (Rule 5.3), or may involve the outgoing r_i fact and come back in the reverse direction using r_i^- after a loop at a position with an outgoing r_i^--fact (Rule 5.5).

5.2 Defining the Regular Expression of Possible Plans

While the grammar of forward-backward paths describes possible paths that are guaranteed to exist thanks to $\mathcal{UID}$, it does not reflect the set $\mathcal{F}$ of available functions. This is why we intersect it with a regular expression that we will construct from $\mathcal{F}$, to describe the possible sequences of calls that we can perform following the description of non-redundant plans given in Property 4.2.

The intuitive definition of the regular expression is simple: we can take any sequence of relations, which is the semantics of a function in $\mathcal{F}$, and concatenate such sequences to form the sequence of relations corresponding to what the plan retrieves. However, there are several complications. First, for every call, the output variable that we use may not be the last one in the path, so performing the call intuitively corresponds to a prefix of its semantics: we work around this by adding some backward relations to focus on the right prefix when the output variable is not the last one. Second, the last call must end with the relation r used in the query, and the variable that precedes the output variable of the whole plan must not be existential (otherwise, we will not be able to filter on the correct results). Third, some plans consisting of one single call must be handled separately. Last, the definition includes other technicalities that relate to our choice of so-called *minimal filtering plans* in the correctness proofs that we give in the extended version [27]. Here is the formal definition:

Definition 5.2 (Regular expression of possible plans). *Given a set of functions $\mathcal{F}$ and an atomic query $q(x) \leftarrow r(a, x)$, for each function $f :$ $r_1(x_0, x_1), ... r_n(x_{n-1}, x_n)$ of $\mathcal{F}$ and input or output variable x_i, define:*

$$w_{f,i} = \begin{cases} r_1 \ldots r_i & \text{if } i = n \\ r_1 \ldots r_n r_n^- \ldots r_{i+1}^- & \text{if } 0 \leq i < n \end{cases}$$

For $f \in \mathcal{F}$ and $0 \leq i < n$, we say that a $w_{f,i}$ is final when:

- *the last letter of $w_{f,i}$ is r^-, or it is r and we have $i > 0$;*
- *writing the body of f as above, the variable x_{i+1} is an output variable;*
- *for $i < n-1$, if x_{i+2} is an output variable, we require that f does not contain the atoms: $r(x_i, x_{i+1}).r^-(x_{i+1}, x_{i+2})$.*

The regular expression of possible plans is then $P_r = W_0|(W^*W')$, where:

- *W is the disjunction over all the $w_{f,i}$ above with $0 < i \leq n$.*
- *W' is the disjunction over the final $w_{f,i}$ above with $0 < i < n$.*
- *W_0 is the disjunction over the final $w_{f,i}$ above with $i = 0$.*

5.3   Defining the Algorithm

We can now present our algorithm to decide the existence of equivalent rewritings and enumerate all non-redundant equivalent execution plans when they exist, which is what we use to show Theorem 4.4:

Input: a set of path functions $\mathcal{F}$, a set of relations $\mathcal{R}$, a set of $\mathcal{UID}$ of UIDs, and an atomic query $q(x) \leftarrow r(a, x)$.
Output: a (possibly infinite) list of rewritings.

1. Construct the grammar $\mathcal{G}_q$ of forward-backward paths (Definition 5.1).
2. Construct the regular expression P_r of possible plans (Definition 5.2).
3. Intersect P_r and $\mathcal{G}_q$ to create a grammar $\mathcal{G}$
4. Determine if the language of $\mathcal{G}$ is empty:
       If <u>no</u>, then no equivalent rewritings exist and stop;
       If <u>yes</u>, then continue
5. For each word w in the language of $\mathcal{G}$:
   - For each execution plan $\pi_a(x)$ that can be built from w (intuitively decomposing w using P_r, see extended version [27] for details):
     - For each subset S of output variables of $\pi_a(x)$:
       * If adding a filter to a on the outputs in S gives an equivalent plan, then output the plan (see extended version [27] for how to decide this)

Our algorithm thus decides the existence of an equivalent rewriting by computing the intersection of a context-free language and a regular language and checking if its language is empty. As this problem can be solved in PTIME, the complexity of our entire algorithm is polynomial in the size of its input. The correctness proof of our algorithm (which establishes Theorem 4.4), and the variant required to show Proposition 4.5, are given in the extended version of this paper [27].

6   Experiments

We have given an algorithm that, given an atomic query and a set of path functions, generates all equivalent plans for the query (Sect. 5). We now compare our approach experimentally to two other methods, Susie [22], and PDQ [3], on both synthetic datasets and real functions from Web services.

6.1 Setup

We found only two systems that can be used to rewrite a query into an equivalent execution plan: Susie [22] and PDQ (Proof-Driven Querying) [3]. We benchmark them against our implementation. All algorithms must answer the same task: given an atomic query and a set of path functions, produce an equivalent rewriting, or claim that there is no such rewriting.

We first describe the Susie approach. Susie takes as input a query and a set of Web service functions and extracts the answers to the query both from the functions and from Web documents. Its rewriting approach is rather simple, and we have reimplemented it in Python. However, the Susie approach is not complete for our task: she may fail to return an equivalent rewriting even when one exists. What is more, as Susie is not looking for equivalent plans and makes different assumptions from ours, the plan that she returns may not be equivalent rewritings (in which case there may be a different plan which is an equivalent rewriting, or no equivalent rewriting at all).

Second, we describe PDQ. The PDQ system is an approach to generating query plans over semantically interconnected data sources with diverse access interfaces. We use the official Java release of the system. PDQ runs the chase algorithm [1] to create a canonical database, and, at the same time, tries to find a plan in that canonical database. If a plan exists, PDQ will eventually find it; and whenever PDQ claims that there is no equivalent plan, then indeed no equivalent plan exists. However, in some cases, the chase algorithm used by PDQ may not terminate. In this case, it is impossible to know whether the query has a rewriting or not. We use PDQ by first running the chase with a timeout, and re-running the chase multiple times in case of timeouts while increasing the search depth in the chase, up to a maximal depth. The exponential nature of PDQ's algorithm means that already very small depths (around 20) can make the method run for hours on a single query.

Our method is implemented in Python and follows the algorithm presented in the previous section. For the manipulation of formal languages, we used pyform-lang[2]. Our implementation is available online[3]. All experiments were run on a laptop with Linux, 1 CPU with 4 cores at 2.5 GHz, and 16 GB RAM.

6.2 Synthetic Functions

In our first experiments, we consider a set of artificial relations $\mathcal{R} = \{r_1, ..., r_n\}$, and randomly generate path functions up to length 4. Then we tried to find a equivalent plan for each query of the form $r(c, x)$ for $r \in \mathcal{R}$. The set $\mathcal{UID}$ consists of all pairs of relations $r \rightsquigarrow s$ for which there is a function in whose body r^- and s appear in two successive atoms. We made this choice because functions without these UIDs are useless in most cases.

For each experiment that we perform, we generate 200 random instances of the problem, run each system on these instances, and average the results of

---

[2] https://pyformlang.readthedocs.io.
[3] https://github.com/Aunsiels/query_rewriting.

each method. Because of the large number of runs, we had to put a time limit of 2 minutes per chase for PDQ and a maximum depth of 16 (so the maximum total time with PDQ for each query is 32 min). In practice, PDQ does not strictly abide by the time limit, and its running time can be twice longer. We report, for each experiment, the following numbers:

- Ours: The proportion of instances for which our approach found an equivalent plan. As our approach is proved to be correct, this is the true proportion of instances for which an equivalent plan exists.
- Susie: The proportion of instances for which Susie returned a plan which is actually an equivalent rewriting (we check this with our approach).
- PDQ: The proportion of instances for which PDQ returned an equivalent plan (without timing out): these plans are always equivalent rewritings.
- Susie Requires Assumption: The proportion of instances for which Susie returned a plan, but the returned plan is not an equivalent rewriting (i.e., it is only correct under the additional assumptions made by Susie).
- PDQ Timeout: The proportion of instances for which PDQ timed out (so we cannot conclude whether a plan exists or not).

In all cases, the two competing approaches (Susie and PDQ) cannot be better than our approach, as we always find an equivalent rewriting when one exists, whereas Susie may fail to find one (or return a non-equivalent one), and PDQ may timeout. The two other statistics (Susie Requires Assumption, and PDQ Timeout) denote cases where our competitors fail, which cannot be compared to the performance of our method.

In our first experiment, we limited the number of functions to 15, with 20% of existential variables, and varied the number n of relations. Both Susie and our algorithm run in less than 1 min in each setting for each query, whereas PDQ may timeout. Figure 2a shows which percentage of the queries can be answered. As expected, when the number of relations increases, the rate of answered queries decreases as it becomes harder to combine functions. Our approach can always answer strictly more queries than Susie and PDQ.

In our next experiment, we fixed the number of relations to 7, the probability of existential variables to 20%, and varied the number of functions. Figure 2b shows the results. As we increase the number of functions, we increase the number of possible function combinations. Therefore, the percentage of answered queries increases both for our approach and for our competitors. However, our approach answers about twice as many queries as Susie and PDQ.

In our last experiment, we fixed the number of relations to 7, the number of functions to 15, and we varied the probability of having an existential variable. Figure 2c shows the results. As we increase the probability of existential variables, the number of possible plans decreases because fewer outputs are available to call other functions. However, the impact is not as marked as before, because we have to impose at least one output variable per function, which, for small functions, results in few existential variables. As Susie and PDQ use these short functions in general, changing the probability did not impact them too much. Still, our approach can answer about twice as many queries as Susie and PDQ.

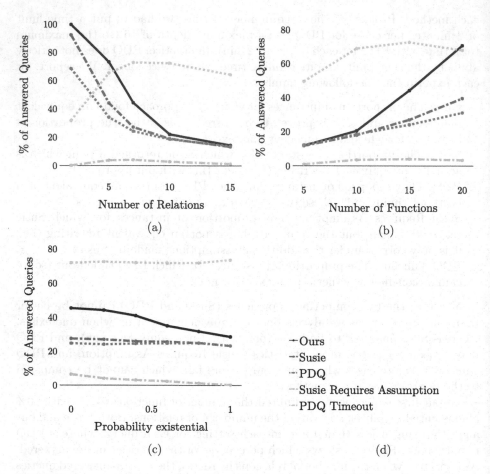

Fig. 2. Percentage of answered queries with varying number of (a) relations, (b) functions, and (c) existential variables; (d) key to the plots.

6.3   Real-World Web Services

We consider the functions of Abe Books (http://search2.abebooks.com), ISB-NDB (http://isbndb.com/), LibraryThing (http://www.librarything.com/), and MusicBrainz (http://musicbrainz.org/), all used in [22], and Movie DB (https://www.themoviedb.org) to replace the (now defunct) Internet Video Archive used in [22]. We add to these functions some other functions built by the Susie approach. We group these Web services into three categories: Books, Movies, and Music, on which we run experiments separately. For each category, we manually map all services into the same schema and generate the UIDs as in Sect. 6.2. Our dataset is available online (see URL above).

The left part of Table 1 shows the number of functions and the number of relations for each Web service. Table 2 gives examples of functions. Some of

Table 1. Web services and results

Web service	Functions	Relations	Susie	PDQ (timeout)	Ours
Movies	2	8	13%	**25% (0%)**	**25%**
Books	13	28	57%	64% (7%)	**68%**
Music	24	64	22%	22% (25%)	**33%**

Table 2. Examples of real functions

GetCollaboratorsByID(<u>artistId</u>, collab, collabId) ←
    hasId⁻(artistId,artist), isMemberOf(artist,collab), hasId(collab,collabId)
GetBookAuthorAndPrizeByTitle(<u>title</u>, author, prize) ←
    isTitled⁻(title, book), wrote⁻(book,author), hasWonPrize(author,prize)
GetMovieDirectorByTitle(<u>title</u>, director) ←
    isTitled⁻(title,movie), directed⁻(movie,director)

---

them are recursive. For example, the first function in the table allows querying for the collaborators of an artist, which are again artists. This allows for the type of infinite plans that we discussed in the introduction, and that makes query rewriting difficult.

For each Web service, we considered all queries of the form $r(c,x)$ and $r^-(c,x)$, where r is a relation used in a function definition. We ran the Susie algorithm, PDQ, and our algorithm for each of these queries. The runtime is always less than 1 min for each query for our approach and Susie but can timeout for PDQ. The time limit is set to 30 min for each chase, and the maximum depth is set to 16. Table 1 shows the results, similarly to Sect. 6.2. As in this case, all plans returned by Susie happened to be equivalent plans, we do not include the "Susie Requires Assumption" statistic (it is 0%). Our approach can always answer more queries than Susie and PDQ, and we see that with more complicated problems (like Music), PDQ tends to timeout more often.

In terms of the results that we obtain, some queries can be answered by rather short execution plans. Table 3 shows a few examples. However, our results show that many queries do not have an equivalent plan. In the Music domain, for example, it is not possible to answer $produced(c,x)$ (i.e., to know which albums

Table 3. Example plans

Query	Execution plan
released	GetArtistInfoByName, GetReleasesByArtistID, GetArtistInfoByName, GetTracksByArtistID, GetTrackInfoByName, GetReleaseInfoByName
published	GetPublisherAuthors, GetBooksByAuthorName
actedIn	GetMoviesByActorName, GetMovieInfoByName

a producer produced), $hasChild^-$ (c,x) (to know the parents of a person), and $rated^-(c, x)$ (i.e., to know which tracks have a given rating). This illustrates that the services maintain control over the data, and do not allow arbitrary requests.

7   Conclusion

In this paper, we have addressed the problem of finding equivalent execution plans for Web service functions. We have characterized these plans for atomic queries and path functions, and we have given a correct and complete method to find them. Our experiments have demonstrated that our approach can be applied to real-world Web services and that its completeness entails that we always find plans for more queries than our competitors. All experimental data, as well as all code, is available at the URL given in Sect. 6. We hope that our work can help Web service providers to design their functions, and users to query the services more efficiently. For future work, we aim to broaden our results to non-path functions. We also intend to investigate connections between our theoretical results and the methods by Benedikt et al. [2], in particular possible links between our techniques and those used to answer regular path queries under logical constraints [5].

Acknowledgements. Partially supported by the grants ANR-16-CE23-0007-01 ("DICOS") and ANR-18-CE23-0003-02 ("CQFD").

References

1. Abiteboul, S., Hull, R., Vianu, V.: Foundations of Databases. Addison-Wesley, Boston (1995)
2. Benedikt, M., Leblay, J., ten Cate, B., Tsamoura, E.: Generating plans from proofs: the interpolation-based approach to query reformulation. Synth. Lect. Data Manag. **8**(1), 1–205 (2016)
3. Benedikt, M., Leblay, J., Tsamoura, E.: PDQ: proof-driven query answering over web-based data. Proc. VLDB Endow. **7**(13), 1553–1556 (2014)
4. Benedikt, M., Leblay, J., Tsamoura, E.: Querying with access patterns and integrity constraints. Proc. VLDB Endow. **8**(6), 690–701 (2015)
5. Bienvenu, M., Ortiz, M., Simkus, M.: Regular path queries in lightweight description logics: complexity and algorithms. JAIR **53**, 315–374 (2015)
6. Bozzon, A., Brambilla, M., Ceri, S.: Answering search queries with crowdsearcher. In: WWW (2012)
7. Calì, A., Calvanese, D., Martinenghi, D.: Dynamic query optimization under access limitations and dependencies. J. UCS **15**(1), 33–62 (2009)
8. Calì, A., Martinenghi, D.: Querying data under access limitations. In: ICDE (2008)
9. Ceri, S., Bozzon, A., Brambilla, M.: The anatomy of a multi-domain search infrastructure. In: Auer, S., Díaz, O., Papadopoulos, G.A. (eds.) ICWE 2011. LNCS, vol. 6757, pp. 1–12. Springer, Heidelberg (2011). https://doi.org/10.1007/978-3-642-22233-7_1
10. Choi, N., Song, I.-Y., Han, H.: A survey on ontology mapping. ACM SIGMOD Rec. **35**(3), 34–41 (2006)

11. Deutch, D., Milo, T.: Business processes: a database perspective. Synth. Lect. Data Manag. **4**(5), 1–103 (2012)
12. Deutsch, A., Ludäscher, B., Nash, A.: Rewriting queries using views with access patterns under integrity constraints. Theor. Comput. Sci. **371**(3), 200–226 (2007)
13. Duschka, O.M., Genesereth, M.R.: Answering recursive queries using views. In: PODS (1997)
14. Duschka, O.M., Genesereth, M.R., Levy, A.Y.: Recursive query plans for data integration. J. Logic Program. **43**(1), 49–73 (2000)
15. Florescu, D., Levy, A.Y., Manolescu, I., Suciu, D.: Query optimization in the presence of limited access patterns. In: SIGMOD (1999)
16. Gogacz, T., Marcinkowski, J.: Red spider meets a rainworm: conjunctive query finite determinacy is undecidable. In: SIGMOD (2016)
17. Halevy, A.Y.: Answering queries using views: a survey. VLDB J. **10**(4), 270–294 (2001). https://doi.org/10.1007/s007780100054
18. Koutraki, M., Vodislav, D., Preda, N.: Deriving intensional descriptions for web services. In: CIKM (2015)
19. Martin, D., et al.: Bringing semantics to web services: the OWL-S approach. In: Cardoso, J., Sheth, A. (eds.) SWSWPC 2004. LNCS, vol. 3387, pp. 26–42. Springer, Heidelberg (2005). https://doi.org/10.1007/978-3-540-30581-1_4
20. Nash, A., Ludäscher, B.: Processing unions of conjunctive queries with negation under limited access patterns. In: Bertino, E., et al. (eds.) EDBT 2004. LNCS, vol. 2992, pp. 422–440. Springer, Heidelberg (2004). https://doi.org/10.1007/978-3-540-24741-8_25
21. Preda, N., Kasneci, G., Suchanek, F.M., Neumann, T., Yuan, W., Weikum, G.: Active knowledge: dynamically enriching RDF knowledge bases by web services. In: SIGMOD (2010)
22. Preda, N., Suchanek, F.M., Yuan, W., Weikum, G.: SUSIE: search using services and information extraction. In: ICDE (2013)
23. Pu, K.Q., Hristidis, V., Koudas, N.: Syntactic rule based approach to Web service composition. In: ICDE (2006)
24. Quilitz, B., Leser, U.: Querying distributed RDF data sources with SPARQL. In: Bechhofer, S., Hauswirth, M., Hoffmann, J., Koubarakis, M. (eds.) ESWC 2008. LNCS, vol. 5021, pp. 524–538. Springer, Heidelberg (2008). https://doi.org/10.1007/978-3-540-68234-9_39
25. Rajaraman, A., Sagiv, Y., Ullman, J.D.: Answering queries using templates with binding patterns. In: PODS (1995)
26. Rao, J., Küngas, P., Matskin, M.: Logic-based web services composition: from service description to process model. In: ICWS (2004)
27. Romero, J., Preda, N., Amarilli, A., Suchanek, F.: Equivalent rewritings on path views with binding patterns (2020). Extended version with proofs. https://arxiv.org/abs/2003.07316
28. Schwarte, A., Haase, P., Hose, K., Schenkel, R., Schmidt, M.: FedX: optimization techniques for federated query processing on linked data. In: Aroyo, L., et al. (eds.) ISWC 2011. LNCS, vol. 7031, pp. 601–616. Springer, Heidelberg (2011). https://doi.org/10.1007/978-3-642-25073-6_38
29. Srivastava, U., Munagala, K., Widom, J., Motwani, R.: Query optimization over web services. In: VLDB (2006)
30. OASIS Standard: Web services business process execution language, April 2007. https://docs.oasis-open.org/wsbpel/2.0/wsbpel-v2.0.pdf

31. Taheriyan, M., Knoblock, C.A., Szekely, P., Ambite, J.L.: Rapidly integrating services into the linked data cloud. In: Cudré-Mauroux, P., et al. (eds.) ISWC 2012. LNCS, vol. 7649, pp. 559–574. Springer, Heidelberg (2012). https://doi.org/10.1007/978-3-642-35176-1_35

32. Thakkar, S., Ambite, J.L., Knoblock, C.A.: Composing, optimizing, and executing plans for bioinformatics web services. VLDB J. **14**(3), 330–353 (2005). https://doi.org/10.1007/s00778-005-0158-4

33. WSML Working Group: WSML language reference (2008). http://www.wsmo.org/wsml/

Resources

Resources

A Knowledge Graph for Industry 4.0

Sebastian R. Bader[1,3(✉)] ⓘ, Irlan Grangel-Gonzalez[2], Priyanka Nanjappa[3],
Maria-Esther Vidal[4], and Maria Maleshkova[3] ⓘ

[1] Fraunhofer IAIS, Schloss Birlinghoven, 53757 Sankt Augustin, Germany
sebastian.bader@iais.fraunhofer.de
[2] Corporate Research Robert Bosch GmbH, Robert-Bosch-Campus 1,
71272 Renningen, Germany
Irlan.GrangelGonzalez@de.bosch.com
[3] University of Bonn, Endenicher Allee 19a, 53115 Bonn, Germany
priyanka.nanjappa@uni-bonn.de, maleshkova@cs.uni-bonn.de
[4] TIB Leibniz Information Centre for Science and Technology, Welfengarten 1 B,
30167 Hannover, Germany
maria.vidal@tib.eu

Abstract. One of the most crucial tasks for today's knowledge workers is to get and retain a thorough overview on the latest state of the art. Especially in dynamic and evolving domains, the amount of relevant sources is constantly increasing, updating and overruling previous methods and approaches. For instance, the digital transformation of manufacturing systems, called Industry 4.0, currently faces an overwhelming amount of standardization efforts and reference initiatives, resulting in a sophisticated information environment. We propose a structured dataset in the form of a semantically annotated knowledge graph for Industry 4.0 related standards, norms and reference frameworks. The graph provides a Linked Data-conform collection of annotated, classified reference guidelines supporting newcomers and experts alike in understanding how to implement Industry 4.0 systems. We illustrate the suitability of the graph for various use cases, its already existing applications, present the maintenance process and evaluate its quality.

Keywords: Industry 4.0 · Knowledge graph · Standards · Knowledge representation

1 Introduction

Industrial processes are driven by norms and standards. While other domains and communities rely on common agreements and best practices, the specific reliability and safety requirements of industrial manufacturing demand strict and formal specifications. International institutions such as ISO, IEC, or ETSI together with national organizations such as NIST, DIN, or ANSI face this demand and form a network of highly recognised authorities, ensuring the quality of published standards and norms.

The rising popularity of digitizing processes, components, and complete production lines has consequently led to an increasing number of standards targeting

© Springer Nature Switzerland AG 2020
A. Harth et al. (Eds.): ESWC 2020, LNCS 12123, pp. 465–480, 2020.
https://doi.org/10.1007/978-3-030-49461-2_27

Table 1. Resource overview

Resource type	RDF-based Knowledge graph
Location	https://github.com/i40-Tools/I40KG
Namespace	https://w3id.org/i40/sto#
Topic	Standards, norms and frameworks for Industry 4.0
License	Creative Common License 3

the various related aspects. The so-called Industry 4.0 (I40) has drawn significant attention not only inside the manufacturing companies but also in academia and government. The result is an already overwhelming but further growing amount of relevant norms, standards, and specifications. The necessary effort for both domain experts and newcomers is also increased by the lack of suitable guidance and limited meta data. The interested reader can only evaluate the significance of a specific publication after examining the complete text – a substantial challenge regarding the amount of available specifications. Therefore, we identify a rising need for a structuring approach to better organize the relevant entities and to explicitly outline their interlinks and attributes.

We propose a publicly available knowledge graph containing the latest state of I40 specifications with respect to standards, reference frameworks as well as key requirements (cf. Table 1). The inter-linked nature of the content and its various relations to outside topics led to the design of an RDF-based knowledge graph for I40 standards and reference frameworks. Utilizing the information content of the proposed knowledge graph, the following types of relevant information can be retrieved:

1. Where can additional information about a certain topic be found?
2. Which specification is most appropriate for establishing a secure data exchange between Industry 4.0 devices?
3. What are the requirements related to a specific Industry 4.0 challenge and where can appropriate guidance to solving them be found?

A key feature of this work is the provisioning of relations to external data sources. Openly available information, for instance from DBpedia, enhances the understanding and points the user to further data sources in the Linked Open Data Cloud. The thereby accessible content makes the knowledge graph relevant for several potential consumer groups: *System architects* are interested in finding and learning about suitable design patterns, *I40 experts* working in standardization groups need to be aware of and observe related initiatives, *component developers* require best practices for interfaces and models, *system integrators* need to understand common data models and interaction patterns, *machine manufacturers* need to ensure the sustainability of their digital interfaces, and *I40 newcomers* want to reduce their onboarding time.

We contribute to the outlined challenges with the following: (1) present the Industry 4.0 Knowledge Graph (I40KG), (2) present its maintenance and curation processes, and (3) discuss its applicability as the basis for other resources and applications. The I40KG helps to overcome hindrances related to realizing the Industry 4.0 vision, which prerequisites not only comprehensive knowledge about distinct standards but needs to consider the semantics and relations between standards, standardization framework as well as their requirements.

The remainder of this paper is structured as follows: Sect. 2 gives an overview on the evolution of the resource and comparable approaches in the literature. The following section explains the I40KG principles, and how it is provisioned (Sect. 4). Section 5 presents intended use cases and evaluates the I40KG. We conclude the paper and outline future work in Sect. 6.

2 Application Domains and Impact of the Resource

This section explains the background of the proposed Industry 4.0 knowledge graph, portrays its development and compares it to similar approaches from the community.

2.1 State of the Art

The targeted challenge – to support newcomers, domain experts and any other stakeholder to establish and curate a proper overview on the published standards, frameworks, and concerns is one of the key obstacles hindering the wider adoption and successful fulfilment of the potential of I40 ideas. The hereby presented work extends previous efforts on creating an overall ontology for Industry 4.0 standards. Grangel-González et al. [7] introduced a first ontology for Industry 4.0 components, in particular for the Asset Administration Shell model. Extending this work, the basic structure and scheme of the graph has been developed, together with a first approach to structure the Industry 4.0-related standards and norms in terms of a unified landscape [6]. These publications introduced the initial definitions of the standard and standardization framework concepts. Further progress has been presented by Bader et al. [2], enhancing the graph with Industry 4.0 reference frameworks and new application patterns of Web-based visualization services and interactive views.

The I40KG is the first structured approach applying machine-readable data interlinking the textual, normative and informative resources containing the knowledge of I40 standardization. In comparison to the earlier evolution steps, the hereby presented I40KG has been significantly extended in terms of contained entities, from less than 80 as presented by Grangel-González et al. to more than 300 described instances. Furthermore, a vast number of Industry 4.0 affecting requirements has been introduced and implemented in order to allow use case-driven filtering and context-dependent discovery of relevant entities.

The I40KG constitutes a machine-readable resource of interrelated standards, reference frameworks, and concerns. It thereby comprises an extendable representation of the whole topic. In contrast to the more common format of literature reviews, the I40KG is a semantically enriched and openly accessible resource, which represents the state of the domain at its publication date and beyond. To the best of our knowledge, no comparable knowledge graph or similar resource is currently available.

The principles of Linked Data, especially of openly accessible data through established Web technologies, are at the core of the Semantic Web Community. The proposed knowledge graph utilizes these practices and connects previously independent information sources with the Linked Open Data Cloud, in particular DBpedia. Thereby, the Semantic Web Community can use the knowledge graph to structure and extend the various related works in the context of I40. However, the targeted users of the I40KG are not limited to the Semantic Web community. As the major trend of digitization affects any domain, but in particular currently the manufacturing industry, multiple further communities can benefit from the proposed work as the insights gained in I40 radiate for instance into Smart Cities, new mobility solutions, Smart Homes and many more.

As the I40KG follows the principles for provisioning Linked Data, it also may serve as a way to spread semantic technologies to other communities. The recommendations and guidelines as for instance formulated by Noy et al. have been followed to ensure the quality of the graph [12]. The target groups are usually not too familiar with the Semantic Web in general and RDF-based knowledge graphs in particular, therefore the adaption of the I40KG can further support the dissemination of the mature practices of the Semantic Web and Linked Open Data.

2.2   Related Work

Overview works comparable to the one proposed in this paper usually appear in one of two forms. On the one hand, experts with an academic background collect relevant publications and comprise them in literature reviews. On the other hand, industry experts and consortia publish their views on the domain through reference frameworks and white papers. Both approaches require extensive efforts for the interested reader to discover, filter, and understand the provided content. Furthermore, the provided knowledge is only valid for a limited time around the publication date. Updates in terms of extensions and adjustments to recent developments are not common practice. Especially in the research community, updating survey papers – to reflect developments since the original publication – usually does not happen.

Still, a significant number of reviews on Industry 4.0 and the very much related IoT emerges each year. For instance, Xu et al. present a comprehensive overview on the major drivers and also standardization activities [16], mentioning the key developments and concerns. Martinez et al. outline the relations of Industry 4.0 with cyber-physical systems and (Industrial) IoT [14]. However, as typical for academic reviews, references to technical standards are omitted. This habit does not the reflect the actual relevance of standards and norms for the engineering and implementation processes.

Searching for technical information in the internet is mainly executed through the established search engines. Even though more and more search queries can be answered directly returning related information, for instance by displaying Wikipedia abstracts, in general only collections of web sites are provided. The user then has to manually discover and examine the sources. Especially for technical information needs, this approach is highly inefficient as it is time-consuming

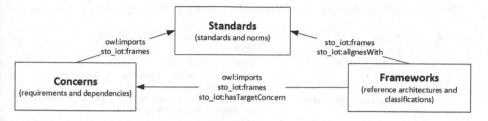

Fig. 1. The three partitions of the I40KG. The I40KG is designed in interconnected parts representing the I40 domain: Standards, Concerns, and Frameworks.

and requires considerable prior knowledge. Lafia, Turner and Kuhn [10] show how semantic annotations and mappings on open data improves the discovery process. Nevertheless, the search for targeted, domain-specific information as regarded in this work, presents a significant burden.

Several works address the challenge of structuring the landscapes of industrial standards. For instance, Lu *et al.* [11] describe a landscape of Smart Manufacturing Systems. Similarly, Andreev *et al.* [1] provide several visual comparisons of radio connectivity standards and technologies. However, none of these surveys are published in an accessible data set as the contributions and insights are only represented written text and cannot be processed by further tools and applications.

3 Design and Technical Quality

The I40KG design follows best practices of publishing resources as Linked Data. As stated in Table 2, the resource conforms to the FAIR principles and is created, curated and accessible in an transparent and open manner. The required characteristics are listed in brackets using the notation of Wilkinson *et al.* [15]. The graph also reuses common RDF vocabularies wherever possible. Upper level ontologies, such as DUL or DCTERMS, support the understanding of classes and properties. Relations to DBpedia resources help to identify the intended entity but also provide valuable directions for further lookups.

3.1 Ontology Description

In this section, we present the relevant parts that form the I40KG. The I40KG is designed in a modular way in order to ensure the maintainability of the sources and increase the readability for the users. As recommended by Parent and Spaccapietra [13], each partition focuses on one of the mentioned sub-domains – *Standards*, *Concerns*, and *Reference Frameworks* (cf. Fig. 1), published in respective Turtle files. The partitions themselves depend on each other utilizing *owl:imports* statements.

The original standards ontology has been extended but still serves as the foundation for the other modules. It is focused on the description of a *standard*

Table 2. *I40KG* **details.** Relevant aspects of the *I40KG* and related resources.

General	Name	Industry 4.0 Knowledge Graph (I40KG)
	DL Expressivity	SHOIF(D)
	Licence (R1.1)	Creative Commons 3
	Size	44 classes, 35 object properties, 22 data properties, 1335 individuals
	Standards and Norms (R1.2)	338 standards and standard parts, 49 ISO standards, 67 IEC standards, 11 DIN standards
	Frameworks	18 reference frameworks divided into 138 classification sections
	Concerns	160 interrelated Industry 4.0 concerns in 6 categories
	External Links (F3, I3)	286 to DBpedia resources, 271 to Wikipedia pages
	Reasoning	4.257 derived triples
	Total size	16.447 unique triples without derived ones
Reuse	Reused Ontologies (I2, R1)	DCTERMS, DCELEMS, PROV, DUL, FOAF, OM, etc
	Reused ODPs	Componency ODP
Documentation	Element description (F2, R1)	By means of rdfs:label, rdfs:comment, skos:prefLabel and rdfs:isDefinedBy
	Ontology Documentation	http://i40.semantic-interoperability.org/sto/
Conventions	Naming pattern	CamelCase notation for the schema and Ada for instances
	Linked Data (R1.3)	5 Star Linked Data
Multilinguality	English labels for all terms	rdfs:label and rdfs:comment with the @en notation
Availability	PersistentURI (F1)	https://w3id.org/i40/sto
	Serialisations (I1)	Turtle, RDF/XML
	GitHub (A1)	https://github.com/i40-Tools/I40KG/
	LOV (F4)	http://lov.okfn.org/dataset/lov/vocabs/sto
	OntoPortal (A2)	http://iofportal.ncor.buffalo.edu/ontologies/STO
	Licence	Creative Commons 3.0
	VoCol Instance (A2)	http://vocol.iais.fraunhofer.de/sto/

as a logical concept, defines attributes and relations, and contains all standard instances (cf. Fig. 2). Concerns, as defined in ISO 42010 [9], can be understood as domain requirements, motives or issues, which a stakeholder can have about an IT system in general and – in the context of this paper – an Industry 4.0 setting. To increase readability, we further use the terms 'concern' and 'requirement' synonymously, even though the definitions in ISO 42010 slightly differ.

While ISO 42010 defines the terminology of a concern itself, it lacks an approach to supply a set of usable instances. The I40KG therefore contains a taxonomy for I40-related concerns, which is intended as a first outline undergoing further refinements. Starting with six top-level concerns (*Data Sovereignty, Internet of Things, Trustworthiness, Data Analytics, Interoperability, Business Context*), cycle-free dependencies of sub-concerns are formed. Further details about the concerns themselves have been presented also by Bader *et al.* [2].

3.2 I40KG Example Instances

Figure 3 shows a set of I40KG instances. The *IEC 62714* about AutomationML has various links (*sto:uses, sto:isComponentOf, sto:relatedTo*) to other standards. In addition, annotations (green, values yellow) explain the entity itself,

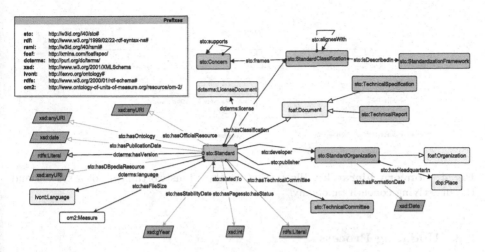

Fig. 2. Core classes and properties of the Standards Module. I40KG-specific classes (light blue), imported properties (blue) and classes (white) from FOAF, DCTERMS, and RAMI4.0 ontologies. (Color figure online)

containing among others the official location of the source document. For IEC standards, this is usually the IEC webstore site of the respective standard. More relations to external resources are also supplied, mainly to Wikipedia/DBpedia.

As depicted in Fig. 3, IEC 62714 is classified as relevant for the *RAMI Control Device*, a *Standard Classification* scheme related to the *RAMI4.0 Standardization Framework*. A user can traverse these links and discover another *Standard Classification* instance of RAMI4.0 frames *Trustworthiness*, the *Concern* also presented in Fig. 4. In this way, further information can be accessed and the user is able to further explore the I40KG.

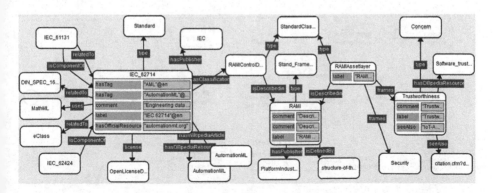

Fig. 3. Contained entities: Standards (IEC 62714) link to standard classifications (RAMI Asset Layer) with frameworks (RAMI) and requirements (Trustworthiness).

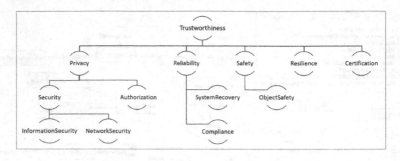

Fig. 4. Concern hierarchy. Illustration for the "Trustworthiness" of a system and the underlying concern taxonomy.

3.3 Updating Process

The knowledge graph is maintained following three different insertion processes. As depicted in Fig. 5, one process for the selection, examination and annotation for standards (top) and reference frameworks (bottom) have been established. Details about the selection criteria have already been explained [3,6] and are therefore omitted here. Both approaches are transparently executed using the GitHub repository and its commit history.

In addition to the manual extensions, an automated update process has been introduced (cf. Fig. 5). As the frequency of new standards and updates of already published ones is too high, a bot searches for such events, maps the metadata to RDF, filters relevant standards and norms, and proposes the resulting entities for insertion into the I40KG. Currently, only IEC standards are monitored but a further generalization is intended. The automated proposals require a manual approval, usually together with additional annotations to external resources, for instance to DBpedia resources.

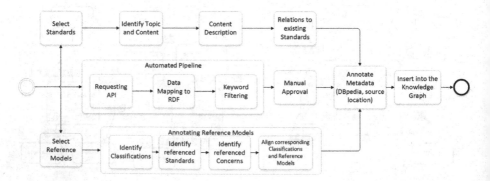

Fig. 5. Insertion process: Three different sub-processes to create the I40KG content.

4   Availability of I40KG

The I40KG is documented following the established best practices for ontologies and Linked Data resources. We supply a human readable documentation page for all classes, properties and instances[1]. Furthermore, several serializations, e.g., RDF-XML, Turtle, N-Triples, etc. are provided, where the Turtle-files act as the single source of truth. Redirects and content negotiation is in place to supply each client with the most appropriate serialisation.

The I40KG and its entities are defined in the STO namespace, using W3IDs for long-term accessibility. STO was the original acronym for "standards ontology" and is retained for sustainability reasons. The knowledge graph is available under the **Creative Commons 3.0 license** and can be reused by anyone and for any purpose. Extensions to the original graph in terms of A- and T-Box are possible but require approval of the graph creators in order to ensure the consistency and quality of the content. Change requests can be placed at its official location, a publicly available **GitHub repository** (cf. Table 1).

The maintenance and further development of the knowledge graph is organized in the mentioned GitHub repository, in particular through GitHub issues. The issue system is also the main communication channel in order to propose changes, document errors and outline extensions. The complete sources are accessible and all changes and updates are executed in a publicly visible and transparent manner. Following best practices of the Semantic Web, each entity is annotated with well-known annotation properties, i.e., `rdfs:label`, `rdfs:comment` and is linked to DBpedia resources, wherever a suitable entry exists.

5   Reusability of the Graph Content

The described knowledge graph is used in several projects. In the context of the International Data Spaces (IDS)[2], it is used in its data model but also as a reference resource for the I40 domain in general and the most up-to-date reference frameworks and architectures. We use knowledge graph embeddings on top of the I40KG to automatically exploiting the meaning of the relationships between standards[3]. We then employed unsupervised Machine Learning methods, e.g., Clustering, to unveil existing relations of standards in the I40KG. A visualisation tool has been developed in order to support and outline the use of the provided information content[4]. The various preconfigured views allow the interactive selection and comparison of I40KG's entities. The website provides a hierarchical overview of the contained standards, a timeline, network views visualizing the various inter-relations and a comparison tools utilizing Venn diagrams and co-occurrence matrices. Figure 6 and Fig. 7 show the capabilities of

---

[1]   http://i40.semantic-interoperability.org/sto/.
[2]   https://www.internationaldataspaces.org/.
[3]   https://github.com/i40-Tools/I40KG-Embeddings/.
[4]   https://i40-tools.github.io/StandardOntologyVisualization/.

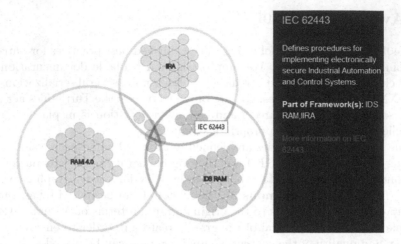

Fig. 6. Venn diagrams for reference frameworks and standards. The Venn diagrams localise the standards (e.g. IEC 62443) in regard to the reference frameworks, for instance to recognize the overlaps but also uniquely covered areas.

this tool. Furthermore, a public SPARQL endpoint[5] provides the latest version of I40KG, also hosted at a VoCol instance[6] [8] for additional documentation purposes.

All generally available RDF tools can work with the I40KG and its source files. Its core classes are, wherever suitable, linked to upper level ontologies. In particular, the linking to commonly-known DBpedia resources allows its direct integration with other knowledge graphs and especially the Linked Open Data Cloud. However, the I40KG does not intend to fully cover the domain, nor represent or judge the internal quality of the referred standards, norms and frameworks. It is – and always has to be – in the responsibility of the user to finally decide on the suitability of a certain standard or norm regarding the specific context or use case. The I40KG can support the user to effectively gain an overview and discover unknown resources. While we constantly extend and update the graph, a perfect coverage is neither possible nor intended. Nevertheless, a sufficient completeness of the domain is necessary and has been examined by Bader et al. [2]. The presented selection criteria show how academic and industry impact have been examined to optimally discover and filter the I40KG entities.

Nevertheless, a comprehensive overview with as much content as possible is desirable. The supplied content must comply to best practices and meet the expectations of potential users in order to provide value. We therefore evaluated the knowledge graph by two approaches. Section 5.1 explains potential use cases, shows which tasks can be solved and how the I40KG is capable of supporting the target groups. Section 5.2 describes the executed tests and quality metrics.

---

[5] https://dydra.com/mtasnim/stoviz/.
[6] https://vocol.iais.fraunhofer.de/sto/.

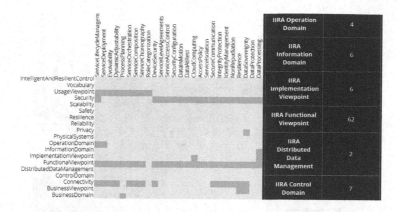

Fig. 7. Co-occurrence matrix between concerns and classification categories. The co-occurrence matrix enables insights which concerns are targeted by which classification categories of the presented frameworks.

5.1 User Stories

The outlined information content is without comparison regarding its relations to the Linked Open Data Cloud resources and the amount of described technical standards and architectural propositions. The knowledge graph can be used in various ways. We further give adoption examples by describing several user stories. Alice, Bob and Charlie represent typical users, each with a different background and information need in the context of Industry 4.0.

Alice, who is just starting with Industry 4.0 applications, needs to quickly gain an overview of the most influential reference frameworks. She has to communicate with consultants, suppliers and developers using the correct terminology and concepts in order to effectively manage the project resources. Alice looks through the hierarchy view of the mentioned web service, learning which frameworks contain which categories and standards. She gains a quick overview of which standards are the most prevalent in almost all the frameworks. She follows the relations between the classifications and traverses the links to standards and other publications but also to new reference frameworks. This process gives her a general understanding of the structure of the domain, the relevant technical standards and the their relations. Alice also executes unsupervised Machine Learning algorithms on top of the I40KG. The output of those algorithms provide knowledge about non existing relations of standards that can be used to improve the classification that the frameworks provides w.r.t standards. This also enables the enrichment of the current landscape of Industry 4.0 standards. Thus, enhancing the understanding Alice of this complex domain.

Another user of the I40KG is Bob, an industry expert working in a standardization council. He is aware of all the details of the group's works and ideas, and knows which arguments led to the proposed solution of this council. For further iterations of their guidelines, Bob would like to know about the focus and state

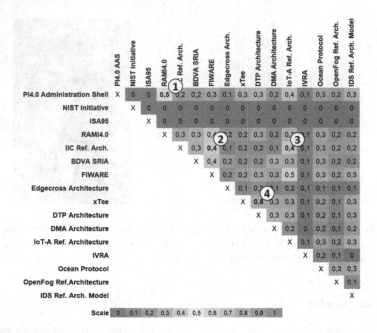

Fig. 8. Overlap of reference frameworks. Symmetric matrix displaying similar frameworks based on the amount of targeted Industry 4.0 concerns.

of complementary but also competing approaches. Furthermore, Bob searches for good ideas for his own standardization work.

Bob uses the I40KG to create the analysis shown in Fig. 8. A quick look at the results tells him (cf. Fig. 8 (1)), that for instance the concepts defined in the Plattform Industrie 4.0 Asset Administration Shell model are closely related to the Reference Architecture Model Industry 4.0 (RAMI4.0). This quite obvious discovery is due to the fact that both models are published by the same organization, which Bob quickly recognizes by following the relations between the two entities in the knowledge graph. In addition, Bob also identifies a significant overlap between the Reference Architecture of the Industrial Internet Consortium (IIC) and the FIWARE platform specification[7] and IoT-A Reference Architecture [4] (cf. Fig. 8 (2) and (3)). He is already familiar with the work of the IIC, therefore he decides to also examine the publications from FIWARE and IoT-A, as they might provide further suitable insights.

Charlie, a senior system architect, is aware of the concerns and requirements that his customer will face in his next project. With the aim to ensure the data security and protection of his customer's data, he searches for best practices for implementing upcoming technologies. The co-occurrence matrix of the already mentioned web service depicts which reference frameworks and which respective classifications frame Charlie's concerns.

---

[7] https://www.fiware.org/.

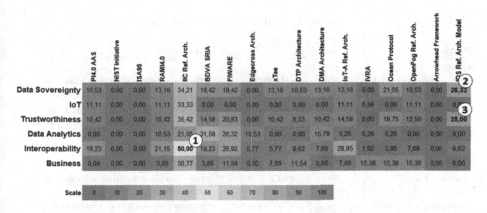

Fig. 9. Focus comparison. Calculated total coverage of Industry 4.0 requirements by reference frameworks. Higher scores do not indicate higher quality but broader coverage of a topic.

Furthermore, he uses the concern hierarchy to aggregate the information of the I40KG (cf. Fig. 9). With this query, Charlie is able to see that the IIC Reference Architecture surpasses the others in terms of its interoperability references (cf. Fig. 9 (1)). However, as data protection is his major target, the IDS Reference Architecture Model seems like a valuable information source (cf. Fig. 9 (2) and (3)).

5.2   Technical Evaluation

The syntactic quality has been checked by commonly used tools such as the Ontology Pitfall Checker[8] and RDF-TripleChecker[9]. These tools indicate that the I40KG is consistent and correct in terms of common RDF and ontology pitfalls. Wherever the mentioned tools indicated potential for improvement, the respective sections have undergone an intense manual evaluation. The reports are also hosted in the GitHub repository.

The reports, for instance, mention two issues. Several properties miss domain and/or range attributes and sometimes the disjointness of classes is not sufficiently declared. However, it has been explicitly decided to not set the range and domain to all properties, as their implications for reasoning on the I40KG can easily result in inconsistencies. Complete disjointness statements, on the other hand, are rather uncommon, adding only limited added value to the graph itself but requiring extensive maintenance.

Furthermore, we evaluated the quality of the I40KG by using metrics as proposed by Färber et al. [5]. Table 3 contains all metrics grouped by the categories from Färber et al. in order to provide as much information as possible. Nevertheless, the expressiveness of several of the suggest criteria is certainly

---

[8] http://oops.linkeddata.es/.
[9] http://graphite.ecs.soton.ac.uk/checker/.

Table 3. *I40KG* evaluation results.

Metric	Result	Explanation
Accuracy		
Synt. validity of RDF doc	$m_{synRDF}(\text{I40KG}) = 1$	RDF documents are syntactically valid
Synt. validity of literals	$m_{synLit}(\text{I40KG}) = 1$	Literals conform to their datatype
Semant. validity of triples	$m_{sem}(\text{I40KG}) = 1$	No gold standard available. References to original information sources applied
Trustworthiness		
KG level	$m_{graph}(\text{I40KG}) \geq 0.5$	Manual data curation but also automated process in place
Statement level	$m_{fact}(\text{I40KG}) = 0.5$	Provenance information provided on resource level
Unknown/empty values	$m_{NoVal}(\text{I40KG}) = 0$	Unknown values are not indicated
Consistency		
Schema restr. at insertion	$m_{checkRestr}(\text{I40KG}) = 1$	Schema restrictions are (partly) checked
Class constraints	$m_{conClass}(\text{I40KG}) = 1$	Empty set of class constraints
Relation constraints	$m_{conRelat}(\text{I40KG}) = 1$	Domain and range are consistent
Relevancy		
Ranking of statements	$m_{Ranking}(\text{I40KG}) = 0$	Ranking of statements is not feasible
Completeness	–	No gold standard available
Timeliness		
Frequency of the KG	$m_{Freq}(\text{I40KG}) = 0.5$	Discrete periodic updates, also through the automated pipeline
Validity period of stmts	$m_{Validity}(\text{I40KG}) = 0$	Provisioning of validity statements is not intended
Modification date of stmts	$m_{Change}(\text{I40KG}) = 0$	Modification dates are only supplied on knowledge graph level
Ease of understanding		
Description of resources	$m_{Descr}(\text{I40KG}) = 1$	All resources have a label and comment
Labels in multiple lang	$m_{Lang}(\text{I40KG}) = 0$	Only some resources have multi-language annotations
RDF serialization	$m_{uSer}(\text{I40KG}) = 1$	Serializations in Turtle and RDF/XML
Self-describing URIs	$m_{uURI}(\text{I40KG}) = 1$	Self-describing URIs are always used
Interoperability		
Blank nodes & RDF reification	$m_{Reif}(\text{I40KG}) = 1$	No blank nodes or RDF reification
Serialization formats	$m_{iSerial}(\text{I40KG}) = 1$	RDF/XML and Turtle are supplied when dereferencing URIs
Using external vocabulary	$m_{extVoc}(\text{I40KG}) = 0.65$	Ratio of external properties
Used proprietary vocab	$m_{propVoc}(\text{I40KG}) = 0.63$	34 classes and 23 proprietary properties without relations to external definitions out of 66 overall classes and 88 properties
Accessibility	$m_{access}(\text{I40KG}) = 1$	see Table 2
License	$m_{macLicense}(\text{I40KG}) = 1$	Machine-readable licensing available
Interlinking		
Interlinking via owl:sameAs	$m_{Inst}(\text{I40KG}) = 0$	owl:sameAs not appropriate for external linking. *sto:hasDBpediaResource* used wherever possible (for instance)
Validity of external URIs	$m_{URIs}(\text{I40KG}) = 1$	External URIs are resolvable

limited. One reason is that the I40KG covers a new domain for structured or open data, therefore no gold standard exists (cf. *Completeness*). In addition, it has been explicitly decided to avoid certain statements and relations. For instance, the validity time of standards is not determined by the publishers, making any inserted information wrong by default (cf. *Validity period*). Regarding the suggestions for interlinking resources, *owl:sameAs* would result in wrong inferences, leading to the introduction of, for instance, *sto:hasDBpediaResource* and *sto:hasWikipediaResource*.

In summary, we are confident that the I40KG meets the expectations and standards of the community, even though some metrics could not be met. We argue that the outlined characteristics support the potential user to better estimate the strengths and limits of the I40KG. Best practices and recommendations have been implemented wherever feasible. Deviations have been analyzed and consciously addressed in order to retain the best possible quality of the overall resource and to support the adoption by the community.

6 Conclusion and Future Work

In this paper, we present the Industry 4.0 Knowledge Graph depicting the latest status of standards, reference frameworks and concerns. The resource describes, connects, and outlines the most relevant information sources. We have explained the characteristics of I40KG, presented its content and outlined its various applications. The I40KG has been created following best practices, conforms by design to the Linked Data principles and is enhanced with a set of supporting tools, documentation and hosting services. It is transparently maintained and open to the community.

We identify the cumbersome search and structuring of the information resources for each involved participant as one of the most crucial obstacles for efficiently realizing Industry 4.0 use cases. The presented approach addresses precisely this challenge. The benefits of the Semantic Web technology stack can support the industrial community and furthermore reach new application areas. We have outlined how the I40KG can solve some of these issues and create added value for various target groups.

The knowledge graph will be further maintained and extended. After having reached a certain maturity level, the next steps focus on the application of I40KG in higher-level applications. The formalized knowledge of the graph can, for instance, be used to improve the performance of ML-based recommender systems. The main target was and will remain the support of the modern knowledge worker in the manufacturing industry. The faced obstacles and efforts are still too high and prevent the easy and wide implementation of Industry 4.0.

Acknowledgement. This work has been supported by the German Federal Ministry of Education and Research through the research project "Industrial Data Space Plus" (grant no. 01IS17031) and the EU H2020 project "BOOST4.0" (grant no. 780732).

References

1. Andreev, S., Galinina, O., Pyattaev, A., Gerasimenko, M., Tirronen, T., Torsner, J., et al.: Understanding the IoT connectivity landscape: a contemporary M2M radio technology roadmap. IEEE Commun. Mag. **53**(9), 32–40 (2015)
2. Bader, S.R., Grangel-González, I., Tasnim, M., Lohmann, S.: Structuring the industry 4.0 landscape. In: International Conference on Emerging Technologies and Factory Automation (ETFA), pp. 224–231. IEEE (2019)
3. Bader, S.R., Maleshkova, M., Lohmann, S.: Structuring reference architectures for the industrial internet of things. Future Internet **11**(7), 151 (2019)
4. Bassi, A., et al.: Enabling Things to Talk: Designing IoT Solutions with the IoT Architectural Reference Model. Springer, Heidelberg (2013). https://doi.org/10.1007/978-3-642-40403-0
5. Färber, M., Bartscherer, F., Menne, C., Rettinger, A.: Linked data quality of DBpedia, Freebase, OpenCyc, Wikidata, and YAGO. Seman. Web **9**(1), 77–129 (2018)
6. Grangel-González, I., et al.: The industry 4.0 standards landscape from a semantic integration perspective. In: ETFA 2017, pp. 1–8. IEEE (2017)
7. Grangel-González, I., Halilaj, L., Auer, S., Lohmann, S., Lange, C., Collarana, D.: An RDF-based approach for implementing industry 4.0 components with administration shells. In: ETFA 2016, pp. 1–8. IEEE (2016)
8. Halilaj, L., et al.: VoCol: an integrated environment to support version-controlled vocabulary development. In: Blomqvist, E., Ciancarini, P., Poggi, F., Vitali, F. (eds.) EKAW 2016. LNCS (LNAI), vol. 10024, pp. 303–319. Springer, Cham (2016). https://doi.org/10.1007/978-3-319-49004-5_20
9. Hilliard, R., et al.: ISO/IEC/IEEE 42010: Systems and Software Engineering - Architecture Description, December 2011
10. Lafia, S., Turner, A., Kuhn, W.: Improving discovery of open civic data. In: 10th International Conference on Geographic Information Science, GIScience. LIPIcs, vol. 114, pp. 9:1–9:15. Schloss Dagstuhl (2018)
11. Lu, Y., Morris, K.C., Frechette, S.: Current standards landscape for smart manufacturing systems. NIST, no. 8107, p. 39 (2016)
12. Noy, N.F., McGuinness, D.L., et al.: Ontology Development 101: A Guide to Creating Your First Ontology (2001)
13. Parent, C., Spaccapietra, S.: An overview of modularity. In: Stuckenschmidt, H., Parent, C., Spaccapietra, S. (eds.) Modular Ontologies. LNCS, vol. 5445, pp. 5–23. Springer, Heidelberg (2009). https://doi.org/10.1007/978-3-642-01907-4_2
14. Saucedo-Martínez, J.A., Pérez-Lara, M., Marmolejo-Saucedo, J.A., Salais-Fierro, T.E.: Industry 4.0 framework for management and operations: a review. J. Ambient Intell. Humaniz. Comput. **9**(3), 789–801 (2018)
15. Wilkinson, M.D., et al.: The FAIR guiding principles for scientific data management and stewardship. Sci. Data **3** (2016)
16. Xu, L.D., Xu, E.L., Li, L.: Industry 4.0: state of the art and future trends. Int. J. Prod. Res. **56**(8), 2941–2962 (2018)

MetaLink: A Travel Guide to the LOD Cloud

Wouter Beek[1], Joe Raad[2(✉)], Erman Acar[2], and Frank van Harmelen[2]

[1] Triply Ltd., Amsterdam, The Netherlands
wouter@triply.cc
[2] Knowledge Representation and Reasoning Group, Vrije Universiteit Amsterdam,
Amsterdam, The Netherlands
{j.raad,erman.acar,frank.van.harmelen}@vu.nl
https://triply.cc, https://krr.cs.vu.nl

Abstract. Graph-based traversal is an important navigation paradigm
for the Semantic Web, where datasets are interlinked to provide context. While following links may result in the discovery of complementary data sources and enriched query results, it is widely recognized
that traversing the LOD Cloud indiscriminately results in low quality
answers. Over the years, approaches have been published that help to
determine whether links are trustworthy or not, based on certain criteria. While such approaches are often useful for specific datasets and/or
in specific applications, they are not yet widely used in practice or at
the scale of the entire LOD Cloud. This paper introduces a new resource
called *MetaLink*. MetaLink is a dataset that contains metadata for a very
large set of `owl:sameAs` links that are crawled from the LOD Cloud. MetaLink encodes a previously published error metric for each of these links.
MetaLink is published in combination with LOD-a-lot, a dataset that is
based on a large crawl of a subset of the LOD Cloud. By combining
MetaLink and LOD-a-lot, applications are able to make informed decisions about whether or not to follow specific links on the LOD Cloud.
This paper describes our approach for creating the MetaLink dataset. It
describes the vocabulary that it uses and provides an overview of multiple
real-world use cases in which the MetaLink dataset can solve non-trivial
research and application challenges that were not addressed before.

Keywords: Semantic Web · Linked Open Data · Identity
management · Graph navigation

1 Introduction

The ability to follow links between datasets is perhaps the most important theo-
retic benefit of Linked Open Data. The following of links in order to learn more
about a data item is laid down in the fourth Linked Open Data rule [2] and it
is the fifth star of Linked Open Data [10]. Unfortunately, in practice it is widely
recognized that traversing the LOD Cloud indiscriminately may result in following incorrect links. Since the validity of an entire dataset can be jeopardized
by following such incorrect links, LOD clients are often hesitant to follow links

© Springer Nature Switzerland AG 2020
A. Harth et al. (Eds.): ESWC 2020, LNCS 12123, pp. 481–496, 2020.
https://doi.org/10.1007/978-3-030-49461-2_28

at all. The fear of following bad links undermines the basic purpose of Linked Data: the reuse of other people's datasets and the interpretation of a data item in the context of other people's assertions about that same item.

Over the past decade various approaches have been published that help determine whether links are trustworthy or not based on certain criteria. While such approaches are often useful for specific datasets and/or in specific applications, they are not yet widely used by clients in practice. The reason for this is that existing identity resolution approaches are relatively complex to implement, computationally expensive to use, make assumptions that are valid for some but not all datasets, and rely on properties like text labels and/or ontological axioms that are present in some but not all datasets. As such, existing identity resolution approaches are inherently at odds with graph-based navigation clients, which are generally light-weight, run on commodity hardware (e.g., within a web browser), and are expected to be so generic as to be able to navigate the entire LOD Cloud, or at least a significant subset of it.

This paper introduces *MetaLink*, a new resource that helps light-weight clients navigate the links of LOD Cloud-sized graphs. MetaLink is a dataset that contains metadata for a very large set of `owl:sameAs` links that are crawled from the LOD Cloud. It encodes a previously published error metric for each of these identity links and also publishes the grouping of links in terms of the originally asserted equivalence sets as well as in terms of so-called communities that are the result of an existing clustering algorithm. As such, MetaLink provides detailed metadata about the trustworthiness of specific identity links, as well as an overview of high-trust links for specific nodes in the LOD Cloud.

MetaLink is a meta-dataset that contains *metadata* about `owl:sameAs` assertions that have been published publicly. As such, MetaLink only becomes truly useful when combined with *data* that contains nodes that are described in MetaLink. For example, we will use LOD-a-lot, a dataset that is based on a crawl of a very large subset of the LOD Cloud. By combining MetaLink and LOD-a-lot (or any other Linked Dataset that uses terms that appear in the LOD Cloud), applications are able to make informed decisions about whether or not to follow specific links on the LOD Cloud. This results in multiple real-world use cases in which the MetaLink dataset can be used to solve non-trivial research and application challenges that were not addressed before.

This paper makes the following contributions:

1. A specification of the requirements for a meta-dataset of identity links.
2. An approach for generating MetaLink, a meta-dataset of identity links that follows these requirements.
3. An implementation of the approach that is able to generate instances of MetaLink in a repeatable, low-cost, and scalable way.
4. Illustrations of use cases that are enabled by the availability of MetaLink.

The rest of this paper is structured as follows: Sect. 2 gives the motivation for creating MetaLink, discusses related work, and provides a list of design requirements. In Sect. 3, the approach for generating, storing and querying MetaLink is described. The implementation of MetaLink is described in Sect. 4. Some of the uses that are enabled by the availability of MetaLink are presented in Sect. 5. Section 6 concludes the paper.

2 Motivation

Graph-based traversal is an important navigation paradigm for the Semantic Web[1]. The basic idea behind Linked Data is that datasets are not only semantically described on an individual basis, but also they are interlinked with one another. Indeed, the use of links in order to interconnect datasets is specified by the fourth and last Linked Data rule [2]: *"Include links to other URIs, so that [data clients] can discover more things"*. As such, the creation of links is more than a courtesy sign of Linked Data etiquette. Links are necessary in order to express the full meaning of a dataset. Full meaning is achieved by positioning formally described nodes in the context of the wider fabric of meaning that is asserted by the ever expanding Web of Data. This essential semantic step of contextualizing a dataset by connecting it to the global fabric of meaning, is also known as the fifth star of Linked Open Data [2]: *"Link your data to other data to provide context"*.

The formal correlate of the practice of linking is specified in the Web Ontology Language (OWL) by the `owl:sameAs` predicate [12]. This predicate denotes the identity relation (i.e., the smallest equivalence relation). Had the Semantic Web been an isolated Knowledge Representation system, there would have been no need for an identity-denoting predicate in the first place. Indeed, in such a closed system each distinct concept could have been expressed by a distinct name, and that would have lifted the need for any kind of linking (such knowledge representation systems are said to adhere to the Unique Name Assumption (UNA)). But the Semantic Web is not an isolated system, it is a world-wide collaborative effort that already includes hundreds of thousands of datasets that are specifically intended to be interpreted and used in the context of each other.

While Linked Open Data *theory* focuses on the necessity to traverse links in order to interpret the meaning of data within a wider context, in *practice* it is widely recognized that traversing the LOD Cloud indiscriminately may result in following incorrect links and – by combining Linked Data that maybe should not have been combined – that may result in low-quality answers.

---

[1] In this paper we use the following RDF prefix declarations for brevity:

- `dbc`: http://dbpedia.org/resource/Category:
- `dbr`: http://dbpedia.org/resource/
- `fb`: http://rdf.freebase.com/ns/
- `owl`: http://www.w3.org/2002/07/owl#
- `rdfs`: http://www.w3.org/2000/01/rdf-schema#
- `skos`: http://www.w3.org/2004/02/skos/core#
- `meta`: https://krr.triply.cc/krr/sameas-meta/def/.

Let us take a concrete example. Suppose that we are traversing the LOD-a-lot dataset, starting out with the DBpedia IRI dbr:President_Barack_Obama. By following an owl:sameAs link we reach the Freebase IRI fb:m.05b6w1g, and from there we follow another owl:sameAs link to reach another DBpedia IRI: dbr:Barack_Obama_cabinet. We have only followed two identity links and we are already in big semantic trouble! We are now conflating a person who is an important member of a group with the entirety of that group[2].

While the notion of providing context by following links should be the main benefit of using Linked Data, the validity of an entire dataset can be jeopardized by following only one incorrect link. As a result of this extremely high cost of following one single potentially erroneous link, Linked Data clients are hesitant in following links at all. This is unfortunate, because a plethora of valid owl:sameAs links can be followed into a vast number of possibly relevant datasets, encapsulating potentially useful information.

2.1 Related Work

Over time, an increasing number of studies in Semantic Web have shown that the identity predicate is used incorrectly for various reasons (e.g. heuristic entity resolution techniques, lack of suitable alternatives for owl:sameAs, context-independent classical semantics). This misuse has resulted in the presence of a number of incorrect owl:sameAs statements in the LOD Cloud, with some studies estimating this number to be around 2.8% [11] or 4% [17], whilst others suggesting that possibly one out of five owl:sameAs in the Web is erroneous [9].

Some vocabularies have proposed alternatives to owl:sameAs with different or no semantics. For example, umbel:isLike statements denote similarity instead of identity and are symmetric but not transitive; skos:exactMatch statements are symmetric and transitive, but indicate "a high degree of confidence that the concepts can be used interchangeably across a wide range of information retrieval applications," which is semantically very different from the notion of identity. As a result, the semantics of the closure that is calculated over this variety of statements is unclear.

Various approaches have been proposed for detecting erroneous identity statements, based on the similarity of textual descriptions associated to a pair of linked names [5], UNA violations [14,20], logical inconsistencies [11,16], network metrics [8], and crowd-sourcing [1]. However, existing approaches either do not scale in order to be applied to the LOD Cloud as a whole, or they make assumptions about the data that may be valid in some datasets but not in others (we refer the reader to [19] for more details). For example, in the LOD Cloud not all names have textual descriptions, many datasets do not include vocabulary mappings, or they lack ontological axioms and assertions that are strong enough to yield inconsistencies. While all of the here mentioned approaches for erroneous identity links detection are useful in some cases, this paper presents a solution that can be applied to all datasets of the entire LOD Cloud.

---

[2] Notice that such conflations are generally allowed in natural language semantics, where policies enacted by the Obama administration are commonly denoted by phrases like "Obama's policies".

2.2   Requirements

While a large number of identity resolutions approaches exist, such approaches are relatively complex to implement, computationally expensive to use, make assumptions that are valid for some but not all datasets, and rely on properties like text labels and/or ontological axioms that are present in some but not in all datasets. As such, existing identity resolution approaches are inherently at odds with graph-based navigation clients, which are generally light-weight, run on commodity hardware (e.g., within a web browser), and are expected to be so generic as to be able to navigate the entire LOD Cloud, or at least a significant subset of it. Since light-weight LOD clients can already be assumed to implement basic Linked Data querying mechanisms like SPARQL or Linked Data Fragments (LDF) [21], it makes sense to publish a solution to the identity resolution problems in the form of a Linked Open Dataset. Such an identity meta-dataset must meet the following requirements in order to be truly usable for a wide variety of LOD clients:

1. **Scalable.** The approach for generating the identity meta-dataset must be applicable on a very large scale. This requirement is needed in order to be able to apply the here presented approach on an increasingly larger scale, ultimately at the scale of the entire LOD Cloud.
2. **Reliable.** The metric that indicates the trustworthiness or error degree of identity links must be good enough to be relied upon in many client applications. This requirement is a trade-off with respect to Requirement 1: since the meta-dataset must be applicable on the scale of the LOD Cloud, it cannot extensively rely on dataset-specific features.
3. **Ordered.** It is often interesting to know the order in which an identity between two terms has been asserted. For example, even though formal semantics states that identity assertions are entirely symmetric, in practice most linkset publishers put their own terms in the subject position and the terms they link to in the object position.
4. **Modular.** An identity meta-dataset must be able to integrate with existing datasets. It must not put an unnecessary burden on the client that wishes to use it, but must tap into the dataset that the client is already using.
5. **Standards-compliant.** An identity meta-dataset must be encoded using open standards[3]. This allows light-weight clients that already implement LOD standards to interpret and process the identity meta-dataset with relatively small implementation changes.
6. **Broadly applicable.** It must be possible to use the identity meta-dataset in order to achieve a broad range of research goals and applications that cannot be achieved (or very difficult to achieve) by existing means.
7. **Low-cost.** Since it is very difficult to sustain resources within an academic setting, the cost of generating, hosting, and using the identity meta-dataset must be very low. Specifically, it must be much lower than the traditional approach of loading all the dataset into a (memory-intensive) triple store and/or processing all data in memory.

---

[3] https://www.w3.org/standards/.

3   MetaLink Data Model

This section details the data model of MetaLink, an identity meta-dataset that implements the requirements specified in Sect. 2.2. Figure 1 gives an overview of the MetaLink vocabulary, and Fig. 2 shows an example of two identity assertions together with their corresponding MetaLink metadata.

3.1   Implicit and Explicit Identity Assertions

MetaLink distinguishes between two types of identity statements: those that are explicitly asserted (Definition 1), and those that can be derived from such explicit assertions through entailment (Definition 2).

Definition 1 (Explicit Identity Relation). *The explicit identity relation for an RDF graph G is represented by the tuple $\langle V, E, w \rangle$. E is the set of directed edges $\{(x, y) \mid \langle x, owl\!:\!sameAs, y \rangle \in G\}$. V is the set of vertices $\{x \mid (x, y) \in E \vee (y, x) \in E\}$. $w : E \to \{1, 2\}$ is the weight function:*

$$w((x, y)) := \begin{cases} 1 & \text{if } (y, x) \notin E \\ 2 & \text{if } (y, x) \in E \end{cases}$$

The order in which assertions have been made (Requirement 3) is preserved by reifying explicit identity assertions using the properties rdf:subject and rdf:object. While there is some overhead in also asserting the predicate term (rdf:predicate) for each identity assertion, doing so keeps the application of the RDF vocabulary recognizable (Requirement 5), while at the same time opening up the possibility for storing links that do not use the owl:sameAs property in the future.

Definition 2 (Implicit Identity Relation). *The implicit identity relation for an RDF graph G is represented by the tuple $\langle V', E' \rangle$. E' is the closure of E under equivalence (reflexivity, symmetry, transitivity). V' is the set of vertices $\{x \mid (x, y) \in E' \vee (y, x) \in E'\}$.*

While it is essential to store explicit identity assertions, this is not the case for implicit identity assertions. Firstly, assertions that only belong to the implicit identity relation follow from the explicit identity relation in systematic ways, i.e., according to OWL entailment rules. An identity meta-dataset can rely on the same systematicity in order to derive metadata about implicit assertions from the recorded metadata about explicit assertions. Secondly, the implicit identity relation is impractically large to store. In general, an identity set of size N can be expressed by $N - 1$ explicit identity assertions, but the corresponding closure contains N^2 implicit identity assertions. Since identity sets can contain tens of thousands of terms, the difference between the implicit and the explicit identity relation for one identity set can already amount to billions of assertions.

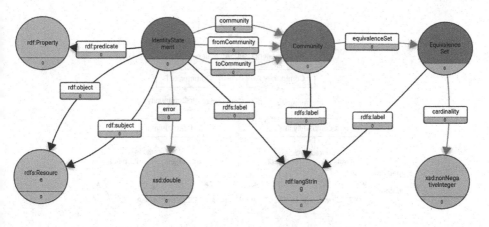

Fig. 1. Vocabulary of the MetaLink dataset. Classes are displayed by circles and properties are displayed by arcs. The MetaLink-specific classes and properties are displayed in red, the blue classes and properties are reused from existing vocabularies. The vocabulary can be accessed at https://krr.triply.cc/krr/metalink/graphs. (Color figure online)

3.2 Singleton and Non-singleton Equivalence Sets

The implicit identity relation assigns exactly one equivalence set to every term (Definition 3). The set of all equivalence sets forms a partition of the domain of discourse V'. Because MetaLink only records explicit identity links, it also only records non-singleton equivalence sets.

Definition 3 (Equivalence set). *For a specific term* x, *the corresponding equivalence set is* $[x]_\sim := \{y \mid (x, y) \in E'\}$.

3.3 Communities

In order to implement the scalability and reliability requirements (Requirements 1 and 2), MetaLink uses the community detection approach for identity links that is introduced in Raad et al. [18]. This approach uses the Louvain algorithm in order to cluster every connected component of the explicit identity relation into one or more communities. Communities partition equivalence sets, which partition the domain of discourse. Once the communities have been detected, an error metric is calculated (Sect. 3.4). This results in the only identity metric that has been calculated at the required scale and that has acceptable accuracy. In addition, this metric is calculated by an efficient, low-cost algorithm (Requirement 7). MetaLink distinguishes between explicit identity assertions that form intra-community links and ones that form inter-community links (Definition 4). MetaLink uses the :community property to relate identity assertions to the communities to which their subject and object terms belong. The subproperties :fromCommunity and :toCommunity are used to relate inter-community links to their respective communities. MetaLink uses the :equivalenceSet property

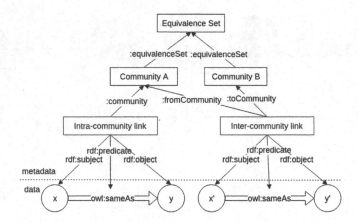

Fig. 2. An example of two `owl:sameAs` assertions (below the dotted line) in combination with the corresponding MetaLink annotations (above the dotted line).

in order to relate communities to their corresponding equivalence sets (see the top half of Fig. 2).

Definition 4 (Intra- and Inter-Community Links). *An intra-community link is an edge* $(x, y) \in E$ *such that* x *and* y *belong to the same community. An inter-community link is an edge* $(x, y) \in E$ *such that* x *and* y *belong to different communities.*

3.4 Error Metric

After detecting the community structure in each equivalence set, an error degree for each identity link is computed. This error degree, described in details in [18], is computed based on two elements: (a) the density of the community for intra-community links or the density of both communities for inter-community links, and (b) whether the link is reciprocally asserted ((x, y) and (y, x)). Overall, reciprocally asserted links have a lower error degree than non-reciprocally asserted identity links. Furthermore, links that belong to more densely connected communities are more likely to be correct. This results in an error degree for each identity link ranging from 0.0 (most likely correct) till 1.0 (most likely incorrect). The experiments in [18] show that indeed the higher an error degree of an identity link is, the more likely it is erroneous. Specifically, the manual evaluation conducted by the authors in [18] show that links with error degree >0.99 are in most cases erroneous (~1M identity links), whilst identity links with error degree <0.4 are in most cases correct (~400M identity links). MetaLink uses the `:error` property to store the error degree.

3.5 Separation Between Metadata and Data

In line with the modularity requirement (Requirement 4), MetaLink makes a clean separation between data and metadata. The data (displayed below the dotted line in Fig. 2) is intended to be delivered by the data consumer, either up-front or during the process of online link traversal.

The relationship between data and metadata is established with the RDF reification properties (`rdf:subject`, `rdf:predicate`, and `rdf:object`). The reification properties clearly communicate to data consumers that they are traversing the boundary between data and metadata. Notice that it would have been possible to establish links between terms in the data (x, x', y, and y' in Fig. 2), but doing so would have made the distinction between metadata and data less noticeable to a modest data consumer.

The link assertion on the left-hand side ($\langle x, \texttt{owl:sameAs}, y \rangle$) is an example of an intra-community link, so the generic `:community` property is used to relate (the subject and object terms in) the identity link to Community A. The link assertion on the right-hand side ($\langle x', \texttt{owl:sameAs}, y' \rangle$) is an example of an inter-community link, so the more specific `:fromCommunity` and `:toCommunity` properties are used to relate (the subject and object terms in) the identity link to Communities A and B. Both communities have the same equivalence set (property `:equivalenceSet`).

4   Implementation

MetaLink is created based on the TSV file[4] published as a part of [18]. This TSV file contains rows for over 330M non-reflexive `owl:sameAs` assertions that are drawn from the LOD-a-lot dataset [6]. The TSV file has the following columns:

- The subject or object term, whichever comes lexicographically first.
- The subject or object term, whichever comes lexicographically last.
- The calculated error degree: a value between 0.0 (probably correct) and 1.0 (probably incorrect).
- The weight of the link: 2 if the symmetric link also appears in LOD-a-lot, and 1 if this is not the case.
- A unique identifier for the equivalence set to which the link belongs.
- The cardinality of the equivalence set.
- Either a unique identifier for a community (for inter-community links), or a pair of from/to (in that order) unique community identifiers (for intra-community links).

The TSV file is used as the input for the MetaLink creation script. Because the order of the terms within links is relevant in MetaLink (Requirement 3), we use the original LOD-a-lot file in order to determine the order for each row in the TSV file. The script is written in SWI-Prolog that has extensive support for RDF, and is publicly available[5]. The script generates an N-Triples file that contains 4,352,602,452 unique triples and describes 556,152,454 non-reflexive `owl:sameAs` links.

---

[4]   https://krr.triply.cc/krr/sameas/assets/5c16733d68c97e02a691c19a.
[5]   https://github.com/wouterbeek/sameas_script.

Table 1. Overview of the size of the composition of the MetaLink dataset in terms of its classes and properties.

Class	# instances
meta:IdentityStatement	556,152,454
meta:Community	55,697,160
meta:EquivalenceSet	48,999,148

Property	# triples
meta:cardinality	48,999,148
meta:community	410,706,139
meta:equivalenceSet	55,697,160
meta:error	556,152,454
meta:fromCommunity	145,446,315
meta:toCommunity	145,446,315

4.1 HDT: Low-Cost Usage

In order to implement the low-cost requirement (Requirement 7) we cannot publish the MetaLink dataset in a traditional triple store. Even though there are triple stores that are able to store 4.3 B triples, such services are relatively costly to set up. Also, MetaLink is only truly useful when combined with a dataset in which the identity metadata can be used. Since we want people to use the MetaLink meta-dataset in the context of the LOD-a-lot dataset, it would be preferable to expose MetaLink together with the 28.3 B LOD-a-lot triples. For this reason we create a Header Dictionary Triples (HDT) [7] file. HDT provides a popular low-cost alternative to memory-intensive Linked Data publication approaches. By working almost exclusively from disk, HDT allows the MetaLink meta-dataset and the LOD-a-lot dataset to be queried from commodity hardware such as a regular consumer laptop. Table 1 shows statistics about the MetaLink classes and properties that are obtained from the HDT file. The MetaLink HDT file and its index (36 GB each) are published at persistent URI with a citable DOI:

- MetaLink HDT file (https://doi.org/10.5281/zenodo.3227976)

Since it has been made available online in April 2019 as part of the Zenodo Linked Data and Semantic Web communities, this dataset has attracted[6] more than 161 views (131 unique), 42 downloads (15 unique), and a number of tweets by members of the Semantic Web community.

4.2 TriplyDB: Low-Cost Hosting

MetaLink and LOD-a-lot are published in a TriplyDB[7] instance over at https:// krr.triply.cc:

- MetaLink (https://krr.triply.cc/krr/metalink)
- LOD-a-lot (https://krr.triply.cc/krr/lod-a-lot)
- MetaLink with LOD-a-lot (https://krr.triply.cc/krr/lod-a-lot-plus)

---

[6] Statistics collected by Zenodo and visible on the dataset's web page.

[7] https://triply.cc.

TriplyDB is an HDT-based Linked Data hosting platform. Human users can navigate the MetaLink and LOD-a-lot datasets with an HTML-based browser. Machine users can use a Linked Data Fragments (LDF) API (Requirement 5).

5 Use Cases

This section briefly describes five concrete use cases for which MetaLink is an enabler. While we do not have the space here to expand on these use cases in great detail, they do show the impact and utility of MetaLink for academic research and LOD client applications (Requirement 6).

5.1 Follow-Your-Nose

In Sect. 2, we saw that performing a Follow-Your-Nose approach quickly resulted in following incorrect links such as the following:

fb :m.05b6w1g owl:sameAs dbr:President_Barack_Obama .

A light-weight Linked Data client typically does not have a module that can estimate the trustworthiness of links. However, such a client is probably able to query the MetaLink dataset with the following query:

```
select ?err {
  [ rdf:subject fb:m.05b6w1g;
    rdf:object dbr:President_Barack_Obama;
    :error ?err ]. }
```

For example, this query can be performed with the Comunica SPARQL engine (http://comunica.linkeddatafragments.org/) by using the MetaLink Triple Pattern Fragments API as a backend (https://api.krr.triply.cc/datasets/ krr/metalink/fragments). The result for ?err is 1.0, in other words: most likely an incorrect link. Based on this information, a client may choose to not follow this link.

5.2 Question Answering

The Follow-Your-Nose use case can be extended to cover queries of arbitrary complexity. We will illustrate this based on two SPARQL queries from the literature. The first question is "Who are the band members of ABBA?", which appears in Buistra et al. [3] as the following SPARQL query:

```
select distinct ?member ?label {
  ?member
    skos:subject dbc:ABBA_members;
    rdfs:label ?label.
  filter(lang(?label) = 'en')}
```

In order to follow identity links into the LOD Cloud, we change this into the following query:

Table 2. Results of the ABBA band member query using different error degrees in MetaLink.

Result	≤1.0	≤0.8	≤0.6	≤0.4	≤0.2	≤0.0
Björn Ulvaeus (band member)	28	8	8	3	2	2
Agnetha Fältskog (band member)	26	4	4	2	1	1
Anni-Frid Lyngstad (band member)	9	3	3	2	1	1
Benny Andersson (band member)	6	2	2	1	1	1
Ola Brukert (drummer)	3	2	2	1	1	1
Agnetha Ulvaeus (Agnetha F. married name)	2	0	0	0	0	0
Stig Andersson (band manager)	9	4	4	1	1	1
Gert van der Graaf (stalker of Agnetha Fältskog)	2	0	0	0	0	0
Benny Anderssons Orkester (new band)	5	3	3	0	0	0
Stig Andersson (sportsman)	2	2	2	0	0	0

```
select distinct ?member ?label {
  ?member
    owl:sameAs*/skos:subject/owl:sameAs* dbc:ABBA_members;
    rdfs:label/owl:sameAs* ?label.
  filter(lang(?label) = 'en')}
```

Table 2 shows the number of results for different error degrees in MetaLink. The column under ≤1.0 shows the results when all available links are followed, i.e., without distinguishing between high and low error degrees. These results include the four correct answers (display in the first four rows), offering many alternative names/IRIs from DBpedia, Wikidata, OpenCyc, New York Times, and other datasets. The table also shows that there are many results that may be considered incorrect, like the drummer of ABBA, the manager, and stalker of one of the ABBA band members. The subsequent columns lower the error degree, resulting in more trustworthy links. The use of MetaLink for this query is inconclusive: the number of incorrect results decreases, but the number of alternative names for the correct results decreases too.

Our second question is "Through which countries does the Yenisei river flow?" which appears in Lopez et al. [13] as the following SPARQL query:

```
select distinct ?uri ?string {
  dbr:Yenisei_River dbp:country ?uri.
  optional {
    ?uri rdfs:label ?string.
    filter(lang(?string) = 'en')}}
```

When this query is performed with error degree ≤0.3, the two correct answers are returned: Russia and Mongolia. When the error degree is above 0.3, more than 30 K results are returned, including hundreds of unrelated geographic places, the concept of creative writing, and the mythical creature Gorgon. For this query it is clear that the LOD Cloud contains incorrect links that destroy the value of following links, and that MetaLink can be used to circumvent this risk.

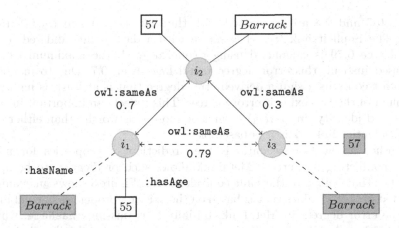

Fig. 3. An example of fuzzy reasoning over the error degrees in MetaLink. Solid edges denote explicit assertions; dashed lines denote implicit assertions. The derived error degree is calculated with t-conorm f_p. The predicted properties are displayed in red boxes. (Color figure online)

5.3 Fuzzy Reasoning

In Sect. 2.1, we saw that there have been ample attempts at replacing the role of `owl:sameAs` with less strict alternatives that denote various shades of relatedness. Unfortunately, such alternative linking properties fail to oil the wheels of Semantic Web when they seek to replace potentially faulty identity links with links that have no semantics whatsoever. Since MetaLink assigns a specific error degree between 0.0 and 1.0 to each `owl:sameAs` link, it can be used in order to assign a fuzzy alternative to the classical binary OWL semantics.

For example, by borrowing the notion of *t-conorm* from Fuzzy Logic [15] we can assign fuzzy error degrees to the implicit (i.e., missing) identity statements. A t-conorm is a function $f : [0, 1] \times [0, 1] \to [0, 1]$ that is commutative, monotonic, associative, and that treats 0.0 as the identity element. As such, t-conorm is often used as the fuzzy correspondence of the binary logic operator $\vee$.

We now give two examples of t-conorms in the context of the MetaLink metadataset. Firstly, the standard maximum t-conorm is defined as $f_{\max}(a, b) :=$ $\max(\{a, b\})$. Intuitively, $f_{\max}$ adopts a pessimistic perspective on errors; considering all explicit identity links with known error degree, it assigns the maximum error degree to the corresponding implicit identity link. This perspective is useful if we are entirely skeptical about the truth values of the implicit or missing identity links. The downside of that perspective is that, it results in a less diverse set of truth values, since larger values are copied throughout the graph. Secondly, the probabilistic sum t-conorm, defined as $f_p(a, b) := a + b - a \cdot b$, results in the assignment of more diverse fuzzy truth values to implicit identity links.

Figure 3 shows an example of three instances that belong to the same equivalence set. Solid lines denote explicit `owl:sameAs` statements. MetaLink error degrees 0.7 and 0.3 are associated with the links (i_1, i_2) and (i_2, i_3), respectively. The implicit link (i_1, i_3) is shown with a dashed line and red text: its error degree 0.79 is calculated using t-conorm f_p. If the maximum t-conorm were used instead, this error degree would have been 0.7. Due to monotonicity, both t-conorms assign a derived error degree that is at least as high as the maximum of the two explicit error degrees. This reflects an important intuition: the derived identity link (i_1, i_3) cannot be more trustworthy than either of the explicit identity links that it is based on.

Another application scenario is the prediction of properties for missing and/or conflicting properties. MetaLink allows such predication to be applied to entities that belong to the same equivalence set. Figure 3 shows an example of predicted property values that is based on the existing properties in combination with the error degrees in MetaLink. Initially i_1 is missing :hasName, which is completed based on the information in i_2. Moreover, i_3 is initially missing both :hasName and :hasAge. For the latter, there is a conflict with respect to the age value (i_1 has value 55 but i_2 has value 57), and priority is given to the value that is associated with the equivalent entity that has the lower error degree.

5.4   Erroneous Identity Link Detection

The error degrees attributed to each owl:sameAs link in MetaLink is computed based on the recent approach by Raad et al. [18]. In this work, the authors showed that when the threshold is fixed at 0.99 (i.e. links higher than this threshold are considered erroneous), the approach enables detection of a large number of erroneous owl:sameAs (93% recall). However, the evaluation also shows that a number of correct identity links were attributed to such a high error degree (precision between 40% and 73%). As a consequence, correct links with such high error degree would be also discarded from applications aiming at using a higher quality subset of the LOD cloud, hence leading to the unwanted loss of additional information. Therefore, one possible and direct use case would be to apply more computationally expensive approaches to this smaller subset of owl:sameAs links for minimizing this information loss. Most importantly, since MetaLink is published in combination with LOD-a-lot, these approaches can rely on additional information besides the owl:sameAs network topology, in which these error degrees were computed from.

5.5   Erroneous Identity Link Benchmarking

In recent years, a number of approaches aiming at detecting erroneous identity links were introduced. Such approaches tend to make certain trade-offs, either by leveraging scalability over the accuracy of the approach [11,14,20], or the other way around [4,5,16]. These two categories of approaches are traditionally applied to different datasets, with the former generally applied to large real-world datasets (e.g., DBpedia), whilst the latter usually applied to smaller, mostly synthetic datasets (e.g., subset of links from the Ontology Alignment Evaluation Initiative OAEI). In addition, results generated from such approaches (e.g., the erroneous/correct links detected/validated by the approach, their error/confidence score, the dataset, the manually evaluated gold standard by the authors) become hardly accessible after publication due to several technical and social factors. As a consequence, the current situation shows that these results are hardly reproducible and comparable in practice. MetaLink can be deployed as a platform for solving this problem. Firstly, it allows both categories of approaches to be tested on the same dataset, where less scalable approaches can be tested on a subset of these links. Secondly, the vocabulary of MetaLink can be extended in a way that allows different approaches to publish their error degree and manually evaluated links. This will allow approaches to be directly compared and deployed long past the publication of their results.

6   Conclusion and Future Work

This paper has presented MetaLink, an identity meta-dataset that stores the error degree of a large number of `owl:sameAs` statements that occur in the LOD Cloud. The availability of such an error degree is valuable, especially for light-weight Linked Data clients that currently do not have alternative means for determining the validity of identity links. The MetaLink approach is complementary to existing identity resolution approaches that may be more accurate, but that are not (yet) published for the scale of the LOD Cloud. We have presented several use cases for which MetaLink is an enabler, including question/answering systems, error link detection/benchmarking, and research into alternative identity semantics. The version of MetaLink presented in this paper is based on the data collected from the LOD Laundromat 2015 crawl. Since the construction of this dataset is completely automated, an updated version will be published as soon as a new crawl of the LOD Cloud is made available.

References

1. Acosta, M., Zaveri, A., Simperl, E., Kontokostas, D., Auer, S., Lehmann, J.: Crowdsourcing linked data quality assessment. In: Alani, H., et al. (eds.) ISWC 2013. LNCS, vol. 8219, pp. 260–276. Springer, Heidelberg (2013). https://doi.org/10.1007/978-3-642-41338-4_17
2. Berners-Lee, T.: Linked data-design issues (2011). http://www.w3.org/DesignIssues/LinkedData.html
3. Buikstra, A., Neth, H., Schooler, L., Teije, A.T., Harmelen, F.V.: Ranking query results from linked open data using a simple cognitive heuristic. In: IJCAI 2011 (2011)
4. CudreMauroux, P., Haghani, P., Jost, M., Aberer, K., De Meer, H.: idmesh: graph-based disambiguation of linked data. In: International Conference WWW, pp. 591–600. ACM (2009)
5. Cuzzola, J., Bagheri, E., Jovanovic, J.: Filtering inaccurate entity co-references on the linked open data. In: Chen, Q., Hameurlain, A., Toumani, F., Wagner, R., Decker, H. (eds.) DEXA 2015. LNCS, vol. 9261, pp. 128–143. Springer, Cham (2015). https://doi.org/10.1007/978-3-319-22849-5_10

6. Fernández, J.D., Beek, W., Martínez-Prieto, M.A., Arias, M.: LOD-a-lot. In: d'Amato, C., et al. (eds.) ISWC 2017. LNCS, vol. 10588, pp. 75–83. Springer, Cham (2017). https://doi.org/10.1007/978-3-319-68204-4_7
7. Fernández, J.D., Martínez-Prieto, M.A., Gutiérrez, C., Polleres, A., Arias, M.: Binary RDF representation for publication and exchange (HDT). Web Seman.: Sci. Serv. Agents World Wide Web 19, 22–41 (2013)
8. Guéret, C., Groth, P., Stadler, C., Lehmann, J.: Assessing linked data mappings using network measures. In: Simperl, E., Cimiano, P., Polleres, A., Corcho, O., Presutti, V. (eds.) ESWC 2012. LNCS, vol. 7295, pp. 87–102. Springer, Heidelberg (2012). https://doi.org/10.1007/978-3-642-30284-8_13
9. Halpin, H., Hayes, P.J., McCusker, J.P., McGuinness, D.L., Thompson, H.S.: When owl:sameAs isn't the same: an analysis of identity in linked data. In: Patel-Schneider, P.F., et al. (eds.) ISWC 2010. LNCS, vol. 6496, pp. 305–320. Springer, Heidelberg (2010). https://doi.org/10.1007/978-3-642-17746-0_20
10. Hausenblas, M.: 5 ⋆ open data (2012). http://5stardata.info/
11. Hogan, A., Zimmermann, A., Umbrich, J., Polleres, A., Decker, S.: Scalable and distributed methods for entity matching, consolidation and disambiguation over linked data corpora. Web Seman.: Sci. Serv. Agents World Wide Web 10, 76–110 (2012)
12. Horrocks, I., Patel-Schneider, P.F., Harmelen, F.V.: From SHIQ and RDF to OWL: the making of a web ontology language. Web Seman.: Sci. Serv. Agents World Wide Web 1(1), 7–26 (2003)
13. Lopez, V., Unger, C., Cimiano, P., Motta, E.: Evaluating question answering over linked data. Web Seman.: Sci. Serv. Agents World Wide Web 21, 3–13 (2013)
14. de Melo, G.: Not quite the same: identity constraints for the web of linked data. In: AAAI. AAAI Press (2013)
15. Novák, V., Perfilieva, I., Mockor, J.: Mathematical Principles of Fuzzy Logic, vol. 517. Springer, Boston (2012). https://doi.org/10.1007/978-1-4615-5217-8
16. Papaleo, L., Pernelle, N., Saïs, F., Dumont, C.: Logical detection of invalid SameAs statements in RDF Data. In: Janowicz, K., Schlobach, S., Lambrix, P., Hyvönen, E. (eds.) EKAW 2014. LNCS (LNAI), vol. 8876, pp. 373–384. Springer, Cham (2014). https://doi.org/10.1007/978-3-319-13704-9_29
17. Raad, J.: Identity management in knowledge graphs. Ph.D. thesis, University of Paris-Saclay (2018)
18. Raad, J., Beek, W., van Harmelen, F., Pernelle, N., Saïs, F.: Detecting erroneous identity links on the web using network metrics. In: Vrandečić, D., et al. (eds.) ISWC 2018. LNCS, vol. 11136, pp. 391–407. Springer, Cham (2018). https://doi.org/10.1007/978-3-030-00671-6_23
19. Raad, J., Pernelle, N., Saïs, F., Beek, W., van Harmelen, F.: The sameas problem: a survey on identity management in the web of data. arXiv preprint arXiv:1907.10528 (2019)
20. Valdestilhas, A., Soru, T., Ngomo, A.C.N.: CEDAL: time-efficient detection of erroneous links in large-scale link repositories. In: International Conference on Web Intelligence, pp. 106–113. ACM (2017)
21. Verborgh, R., et al.: Triple pattern fragments: a low-cost knowledge graph interface for the web. Web Seman.: Sci. Serv. Agents World Wide Web 37, 184–206 (2016)

Astrea: Automatic Generation of SHACL Shapes from Ontologies

Andrea Cimmino[✉][iD], Alba Fernández-Izquierdo[iD], and Raúl García-Castro[iD]

Ontology Engineering Group, Universidad Politécnica de Madrid, Madrid, Spain
{cimmino,albafernandez,rgarcia}@fi.upm.es

Abstract. Knowledge Graphs (KGs) that publish RDF data modelled using ontologies in a wide range of domains have populated the Web. The SHACL language is a W3C recommendation that has been endowed to encode a set of either value or model data restrictions that aim at validating KG data, ensuring data quality. Developing shapes is a complex and time consuming task that is not feasible to achieve manually. This article presents two resources that aim at generating automatically SHACL shapes for a set of ontologies: (1) Astrea-KG, a KG that publishes a set of mappings that encode the equivalent conceptual restrictions among ontology constraint patterns and SHACL constraint patterns, and (2) Astrea, a tool that automatically generates SHACL shapes from a set of ontologies by executing the mappings from the Astrea-KG. These two resources are openly available at Zenodo, GitHub, and a web application. In contrast to other proposals, these resources cover a large number of SHACL restrictions producing both value and model data restrictions, whereas other proposals consider only a limited number of restrictions or focus only on value or model restrictions.

Keywords: SHACL shapes · RDF validation · Ontology

Resource type: Dataset & Software
Astrea-KG: http://astrea.helio.linkeddata.es/
Astrea-KG DOI: https://doi.org/10.5281/zenodo.3571009
Astrea application: http://astrea.linkeddata.es/

1 Introduction

Knowledge Graphs (KGs) are becoming pervasive on the Web [5]. Since 2014 there is a growing number of KGs from different domains that publish a quite large amount of data using RDF and modelled with ontologies [19]. As a result, in the last decade a considerable effort has been put in developing ontologies for specific domains [21]. Due to the growth of these public available KGs, the W3C has promoted a recommendation called SHACL (Shapes Constraint Language) to validate the RDF graphs [2]. In the last years KGs validation by means of SHACL shapes has gained momentum and has become a relevant research topic [14].

© Springer Nature Switzerland AG 2020
A. Harth et al. (Eds.): ESWC 2020, LNCS 12123, pp. 497–513, 2020.
https://doi.org/10.1007/978-3-030-49461-2_29

A shape defines a set of restrictions that data from a KG must fulfil. There are two kinds of restrictions [15], those that refer to the data model, e.g., cardinality, and those that apply to the data values, e.g., string patterns. Due to this reason developing shapes has become the cornerstone solution to validate KG data. Nevertheless, developing data shapes is a complex task due to the potential size of the data and all the available restrictions that require a deep domain knowledge (like the one encoded in ontologies); in addition, developing shapes manually is a dull-task and error-prone.

Different proposals to assist shapes generation have been proposed. Some focus on learning shapes from a set of data [1,7,16,22]; these proposals cover a small amount of the restrictions, and most of the learnt restrictions refer to value restrictions. Nevertheless, since KGs are modelled by ontologies, when these proposals learn model restrictions from data they do not take such ontologies into account, leading to a potential discordance with the model. A lower number of proposals aim at aligning the restrictions encoded by OWL constructs with those of SHACL [12,17]. Unfortunately, these proposals cover a small number of constructs, and do not generate any shapes.

In this paper two resources to generate automatically SHACL shapes [13] from a set of ontologies are introduced. The resources are: A) the Astrea-KG[1] that contains 158 mappings, each of which relates an ontology constraint pattern with an equivalent SHACL constraint pattern; and B) the Astrea[2] tool that automatically generates SHACL shapes for a set of input ontologies by using the mappings provided by the Astrea-KG. The mappings in the Astrea-KG are endowed from a theoretical point of view, presented as ontology and SHACL construct patterns; in addition, the Astrea-KG also contains an implementation as SPARQL CONSTRUCT queries for such mappings. These queries issued over a set of ontologies produce their SHACL shapes, which is the task performed by Astrea.

The shapes generated with the resources presented in this paper contain data and model restrictions, covering 60% of the SHACL available restrictions. Astrea has been evaluated by performing two experiments. The former consists in generating the SHACL shapes of 5 well-known ontologies, such as SAREF or SSN, and two ontologies developed in the context of two European projects. The latter consists in analysing the expressivity and richness of the generated shapes. For the sake of readability, Table 1 shows the prefixes and their associated namespaces that are used through the paper.

The rest of this article is structured as follows. Section 2 reports an analysis of some proposals from the literature; Sect. 3 introduces and details the mappings published in the Astrea-KG; Sect. 4 reports the implementation of Astrea that produces shapes using the Astrea-KG; Sect. 5 explains the experiments carried out in this article; finally, Sect. 6 recaps our findings and conclusions.

---

[1] https://astrea.helio.linkeddata.es.
[2] https://astrea.linkeddata.es.

Table 1. Summary of the prefixes used through the paper

Prefix	Namespace
sh	http://www.w3.org/ns/shacl/
owl	http://www.w3.org/2002/07/owl/
rdfs	http://www.w3.org/2000/01/rdf-schema/
xsd	http://www.w3.org/2001/XMLSchema/

2   Related Work

The increasing uptake of SHACL shapes as a mechanism for validating RDF data has lead to the proposal of several approaches to assist practitioners in their generation. Approaches can be classified into two types: A) Automatic generation of shapes from data, which aim at learning shapes from a training data set; and B) Analysis of the equivalence between ontology and SHACL restrictions. Table 2 summarises these approaches indicating the source of the shapes and whether they support their automatic generation.

Table 2. Comparison of approaches that deal with shapes generation

Proposal	Extracted from data	Extracted from ontologies	Automatically generated
Mihindukulasooriya et al.	✓	✗	✓
Fernández-Alvarez et al.	✓	✗	✓
Spahiu et al.	✓	✗	✓
Boneva et al.	✓	✗	✓
Pandit et al.	✗	✓	✗
Knublauch	✗	✓	✗
Astrea	✗	✓	✓

✓Supported
✗Not supported

Regarding the approaches oriented to the generation of shapes through data, Mihindukulasooriya et al. [16] aim at using machine learning techniques to produce RDF Shapes. The authors propose a data-driven approach for inducing integrity constraints for RDF data using data profiling, which are then combined into RDF Shapes. Although the proposed approach is defined in a generic way, it is validated using only cardinality and range constraints.

Another work related to the generation of shapes from data is the one presented by Fernández-Alvarez et al. [7], which infers Shape expressions associated to the classes in an RDF graph. This approach consists in the following steps: (1) find all the instances of the target classes; (2) for each class, find all the triples whose subject is one of its instances and use them all to build a profile of the class; and (3) turn each profile into a shape written in ShEx language[3].

The work of Spahiu et al. [22] was also designed to generate shapes from RDF data. It uses semantic profiles, i.e., a summary that provides an abstract but complete description of the dataset content and statistics, of a given RDF graph and translates them into SHACL shapes.

Finally, Boneva et al. [1] presented Shape Designer, a graphical tool for building SHACL or ShEx constraints for an existing RDF graph. Shape Designer provides a set of queries and shape patterns that can be selected by the user to generate a shape constraint. Such shape constraint can then be added to the SHACL or ShEx schema under construction.

Concerning the analysis of the equivalence between ontology and SHACL restrictions, the position paper presented by Pandit et al. [17] encourages the reuse of Ontology Design Patterns (ODPs) [8] beyond the data modelling phase to generate SHACL shapes. The authors discuss the similarity that could be obtained between the axioms used to model ODPs and the constraints within SHACL shapes. However, this work does not identify such equivalences between ontologies and SHACL.

To conclude, Knublauch [12] proposes a comparison between OWL and SHACL. This work associates each OWL constraint with its similar SHACL constraint, claiming that a syntactic translation between OWL and SHACL is feasible. Although the author of this work identified similarities between OWL and SHACL, he relates an OWL construct with at most two SHACL constructs. Therefore, it is not taken into account the use of patterns, which hinders the translation.

The resources presented in this paper aim at assisting the automatic generation of SHACL shapes from ontologies, taking into account OWL 2, RDFS, and XSD restrictions. As it is illustrated in Table 2, although there are approaches that deal with shapes extracted from ontologies, only Astrea supports their automatic generation. However, this work is grounded on these previous works that discuss the similarity between OWL and SHACL constraints.

3   Astrea-KG Mappings

The cornerstone element to automatically generate shapes from a set of ontologies are the mappings within the Astrea-KG. These mappings relate one or more ontology construct patterns with the equivalent SHACL construct patterns that validate such ontology construct pattern. However, OWL and SHACL are not considered equivalent in their interpretation. There are differences in how OWL interprets restrictions (for inferencing), and how SHACL interprets constraints (for validation) [12].

The ontology construct patterns include constructs from the well-known OWL 2, RDFS, and XSD specifications. In addition, the mappings have been

---

implemented as SPARQL CONSTRUCT queries in which the WHERE clause contains the ontology construct patterns and the CONSTRUCT clause contains the SHACL construct patterns.

Notice that from a conceptual point of view the mappings are bi-directional, since they relate construct patterns. Nevertheless, their implementation is not bi-directional: the current SPARQL queries identify ontology construct patterns and translate them into the equivalent SHACL construct pattern.

Previous works already stated the similarity between OWL and SHACL constructs. However, during the development of the mappings we noticed that the relation between single constructs was not enough to generate the shapes. The reason is that an ontology construct may be specified within different contexts and the equivalent SHACL construct may change depending on such context. As a result, the mappings relate patterns of constructs rather than just constructs.

For instance, the RDFS construct *rdfs:range* can be considered equivalent to the SHACL construct *sh:class*. But in order for such equivalence to be correct the *rdfs:range* has to be defined in the context of an *owl:ObjectProperty*. Listing 1.1 shows the SHACL construct pattern of the *sh:class* that is related to the ontology construct *rdfs:range*. Notice that this SHACL construct makes only sense in the context of a *sh:PropertyShape*.

```
?shapeUrl a sh:PropertyShape;
    sh:class ?rangeURI .
```

Listing 1.1. SHACL construct pattern for *sh:class*

Listing 1.2 reports the ontology construct pattern for *rdfs:range* that is equivalent to the one of Listing 1.1. However, the statement *rdfs:range* could be expressed alternatively: instead of having an URL in its range it may have a blank node that has different properties (*owl:unionOf, owl:someValuesFrom,* or *owl:allValuesFrom* among others). For these cases other ontology construct patterns must be specified, like the one reported in Listing 1.3. Both ontology construct patterns are different yet they are equivalent to the same SHACL construct pattern.

```
?subject a owl:ObjectProperty;
    rdfs:range ?rangeURL .
```

Listing 1.2. Ontology construct pattern for *rdfs:range*

```
?subject a owl:ObjectProperty;
    rdfs:range [
        owl:unionOf ?rangeURL
    ] .
```

Listing 1.3. Alternative ontology construct pattern for *rdfs:range*

As it can be noticed the constructs are not enough to automatically generate shapes, patterns of constructs are required in the mappings to generate them. Also, it is worth mentioning that different ontology construct patterns may generate the same SHACL construct pattern, or vice versa.

3.1   Methodology for Mappings Generation

The mappings were designed and written following a thorough process, which consist in the following steps:

1. **To manually list OWL 2, RDFS, XSD constructs.** Based on the OWL 2 specification [11], a list of OWL 2 constructs were gathered from the OWL 2 Web Ontology Language Primer [11]. It was decided to consider every OWL 2 construct except for the versioning constructs and the instance ones. Thus, this list includes 55 constructs out of the 88 total constructs defined in the OWL 2 specification. The same process was performed for the RDFS [3] and XSD [18] specifications obtaining 8 and 37 constructs, respectively.
2. **To manually list SHACL constructs.** Based on the SHACL specification [13], the list of SHACL restrictions was collected from the Shapes Constraint Language specification. It was decided to consider every SHACL restriction except for those related to Validation Report restrictions, since they do not add additional content to the shape. Thus, the list includes 58 constructs out of the 301 defined in the SHACL specification document.
3. **To review existing relations among ontologies and SHACL.** Some previous works have attempted to relate OWL 2 constructs with the SHACL constructs [12,17]. Some authors hypothesised that construct patterns would be required to automatically generate shapes [17]. These proposals were taken as starting point to develop the Astrea-KG mappings.
4. **To generate mappings between ontology construct patterns and their equivalent SHACL construct patterns.** For each ontology construct pattern, the equivalent pattern in SHACL has been proposed. It should be mentioned that an ontology construct pattern can be equivalent to multiple SHACL construct patterns, and vice versa.
5. **To include data restrictions.** The only restrictions over data that ontologies encode is the *xsd:pattern* one. Nevertheless, the XSD schema specifies different datatypes that have specific restrictions over values [18], such as their maximum, minimum, or lexical pattern. We incorporated to the mappings the restrictions specified by the XSD datatype anytime in an ontology a XSD datatype was specified. For instance, when a *xsd:nonNegativeInteger* is defined as datatype for a literal it means that it follows the pattern "$[-\backslash+]?[0-9]+$", an has a minimum inclusive of 0.
6. **To implement executable-mappings.** Finally, all the identified equivalences between the ontology construct patterns (OWL, RDFS, and XSD) and the SHACL construct patterns were implemented as SPARQL queries.

3.2   Mappings Ontology

The Astrea-KG contains and publishes the information of the 157 defined mappings. A vocabulary to model these mappings has been defined[4]. Figure 1 shows an overview of such vocabulary, which models the relation between the mappings

---

[4] https://w3id.org/def/astrea.

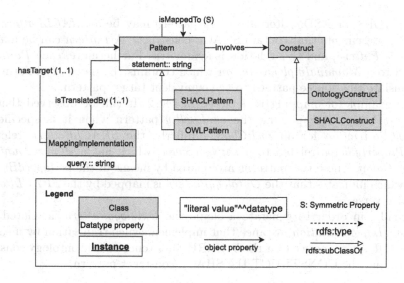

Fig. 1. Overview of the vocabulary.

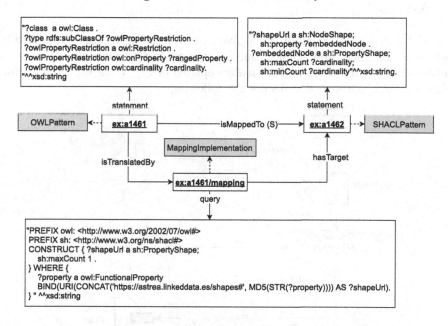

Fig. 2. Example of SPARQL query using the vocabulary proposed in this work

between ontology and SHACL construct patterns, and the mapping implementations as SPARQL queries.

As depicted in Fig. 1, two *Patterns* can be mapped by each other, which indicates that they are equivalent. Any of these patterns could be an *OntologyPattern*, if the pattern includes statements that contain any construct from

OWL, RDFS, or XSD. Alternatively, a pattern may be a *SHACLPattern* if it includes statements that contain SHACL constructs. A *Pattern* can be mapped by other *Pattern*, and this relation is symmetric. Furthermore, each *Pattern* is related to a *MappingImplementation* which contains the necessary information to translate this source pattern to the equivalent target pattern.

An example of mapping is depicted in Fig. 2. It can be observed that the *OntologyPattern* is capturing the *cardinality* pattern when it is specified as an *owl:Restriction* for an *owl:Class*. Similarly, the *SHACLPattern* refers to a *sh:PropertyShape* related to a *sh:NodeShape*, which has a *sh:minCount* and *sh:maxCount*. These two patterns are related by means of the *isMappedBy* relation, which indicates that the *OntologyPattern* is mapped by the *SHACLPattern* and vice versa.

Finally, in order to generate a shape the *OntologyPattern* is related to a *MappingImplementation* instance that implements such translation by means of a SPARQL query; notice that the WHERE clause encodes the ontology construct pattern and the CONSTRUCT the SHACL construct pattern.

4   Astrea

The tool Astrea aims at reading the Astrea-KG, fetching the mappings within, and executing their implementation, i.e., the SPARQL queries, over a set of ontologies. The architecture of Astrea is depicted in Fig. 3; the depicted components and their performed tasks are the following:

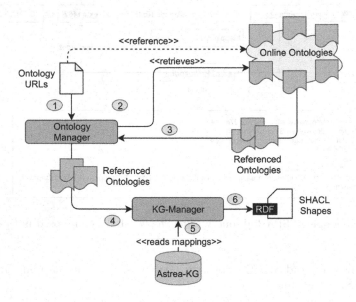

Fig. 3. Astrea architecture.

OntologyManager: this component is fed with a set of ontology URLs provided as input (step 1 in Fig. 3). These ontologies are downloaded and, then, for each ontollogy the *OntologyManager* checks if the statement *owl:import* is present. When such statement is present, the ontology URL specified is downloaded by the *OntologyManager* (steps 2 and 3 in Fig. 3). Finally, all the ontologies retrieved are sent to the *KG-Manager* (step 4 in Fig. 3).

Astrea-KG: the Astrea-KG is the KG previously described and available online. The Astrea tool reads the latest version of this KG, entailing that anytime a mapping is included, or modified, Astrea is aware of such update.

KG-Manager: Then, all the mapping implementations are retrieved from the Astrea-KG (step 5 in Fig. 3). Since the implementations of the mappings are CONSTRUCT queries, they produce as result an RDF graph that contains the SHACL shapes associated to the ontology construct mapping encoded in the CONSTRUCT query. The *KG-Manager* issues all these queries over the ontologies provided by the *OntologyManager*, during step 4. As a result, the output of each query is stored in the same RDF graph. Finally the RDF graph containing all the generated SHACL shapes is returned (step 6 in Fig. 3).

4.1   Expressivity of the SHACL Shapes Generated by Astrea

Table 3 summarises the SHACL restrictions that are supported by Astrea using the Astrea-KG mappings. The symbol "✓" indicates that Astrea supports the restriction, while "≈" indicates that Astrea supports it partially, and "×" that it is out of scope of Astrea.

From Table 3 it can be observed that Astrea covers 60% of the SHACL restrictions and 40% are not supported. Notice that the *sh:pattern* restriction is only partially covered. In addition, the unsupported restrictions can be classified as follows: data value restrictions, practitioner-required restrictions, and unfeasible restrictions. Next, we provide an insight for the partially covered restrictions and for the three unsupported types of restrictions.

Partially Covered: ontologies infrequently contain patterns for data values, although they could be specified by means of the *xsd:pattern* statement. Nevertheless, it is common to assign a *XSD* datatype to data values; these datatypes have restrictions defined by the W3C [18]. The mappings are endowed to cover the patterns specified by the *xsd:pattern* statement. Additionally, when a data value has a *XSD* datatype with no pattern defined, the mappings automatically inject the restrictions defined by the W3C. As a result, Astrea covers *sh:pattern* restrictions under these two circumstances.

In addition, the *sh:qualifiedValueShape* restriction specifies the condition that a specified number of value nodes needs to conform to. Thus, the range of this construct could be any shape that refers to a constraint, e.g., the class of the node, the possible list of values of the node or the pattern that the node should follow. Astrea only covers the *sh:qualifiedValueShape* restriction when it defines the specific class of the node.

Table 3. List of SHACL restrictions supported by Astrea

SHACL restriction	Coverage	SHACL restriction	Coverage
sh:Shape	✓	sh:maxInclusive	✓
sh:NodeShape	✓	sh:maxLength	✓
sh:PropertyShape	✓	sh:minCount	✓
sh:nodeKind	✓	sh:minExclusive	✓
sh:targetClass	✓	sh:minInclusive	✓
sh:targetNode	×[b]	sh:minLength	✓
sh:targetObjectsOf	×[a]	sh:node	×[b]
sh:targetSubjectsOf	×[a]	sh:not	✓
sh:value	×[b]	sh:or	✓
sh:path	✓	sh:pattern	≈
sh:inversePath	✓	sh:flags	×[b]
sh:alternativePath	×[a]	sh:property	✓
sh:zeroOrMorePath	×[a]	sh:qualifiedMaxCount	✓
sh:oneOrMorePath	×[a]	sh:qualifiedValueShape	≈
sh:zeroOrOnePath	×[a]	sh:qualifiedValueShapesDisjoint	×[b]
sh:and	✓	sh:qualifiedMinCount	✓
sh:class	✓	sh:uniqueLang	×[c]
sh:closed	×[b]	sh:xone	×[c]
sh:datatype	✓	sh:defaultValue	×[b]
sh:ignoredProperties	×[a]	sh:description	✓
sh:maxCount	✓	sh:group	×[b]
sh:disjoint	✓	sh:name	✓
sh:equals	✓	sh:order	×[a]
sh:hasValue	✓	sh:BlankNode	×[a]
sh:in	✓	sh:BlankNodeOrIRI	✓
sh:languageIn	×[c]	sh:BlankNodeOrLiteral	×[a]
sh:lessThan	×[a]	sh:IRI	✓
sh:lessThanOrEquals	×[a]	sh:IRIOrLiteral	✓
sh:maxExclusive	✓	sh:Literal	✓

✓ Covered
≈ Partially covered
× Not covered
[a] Not covered due to data value restrictions
[b] Not covered due to practitioner-required restrictions
[c] Not covered due to unfeasible restrictions

Data Value Restrictions: the majority of the restrictions from Table 3 are not supported because they refer to data instances; which are 20.7% of the unsupported restrictions. Due to the fact that Astrea only takes ontologies into account, and they are not expected to have data instances, supporting these restrictions is not feasible. These restrictions are: *sh:targetObjectsOf*, *sh:targetSubjectsOf*, *sh:alternativePath*, *sh:zeroOrMorePath*, *sh:oneOrMorePath*, *sh:zeroOrOnePath*, *sh:ignoredProperties*, *sh:lessThan*, *sh:BlankNode*, *sh:order*, *sh:lessThanOrEquals*, and *sh:BlankNodeOrLiteral*.

Practitioner-Required Restrictions: a smaller amount of restrictions, i.e., 13.8%, require a practitioner to establish them. These restrictions depend on a domain problem and the granularity of the desired validation using shapes. These restrictions are: *sh:targetNode*, *sh:value sh:flags*, *sh:defaultValue*, *sh:group*, *sh:qualifiedValueShape*, *sh:qualifiedValueShapeDisjoint*, and *sh:close*.

Unfeasible Restrictions: 5.5% of the restrictions were not supported because their equivalent ontology construct patterns were not found. These restrictions are: *sh:languageIn*, *sh:uniqueLang*, and *sh:xone*.

4.2 Availability, Sustainability, Extensibility and Maintenance of the Resources

The Astrea tool is available as an online web application (see Footnote 2). This web application also provides a REST API and its documentation[5]. Furthermore, the code of the tool is also available in GitHub[6] under the Apache 2.0 licence[7]. The maintenance of the tool will be facilitated through the continuous update of the mappings, and the fact that the architecture is automatically aware of these changes.

The current version of the Astrea-KG is available as a Zenodo resource. It has a canonical citation using a DOI (https://doi.org/10.5281/zenodo.3571009) and is published under the Creative Commons Attribution 4.0 International[8] (CC BY 4.0) license. In addition, the KG is publicly available for third-party contributions or reusability (see Footnote 1). A further analysis will be performed in order to include, if possible, new mappings.

5   Experiments

In order to validate the two resources of this paper, i.e., Astrea-KG and Astrea, we performed two experiments. Both experiments rely on a set of well-known ontologies, most of which are standards, namely: *W3C Time* [4], *ETSI SAREF* [6], *ETSI SAREF* extension for environment[9] (S4ENVI), *ETSI SAREF* extension for buildings [20] (S4BLDG)[10], and *W3C SSN* [10] and *DBpedia*

---

[5] https://astrea.linkeddata.es/swagger-ui.html.
[6] https://github.com/oeg-upm/Astrea.
[7] https://www.apache.org/licenses/LICENSE-2.0.
[8] https://creativecommons.org/licenses/by/4.0.
[9] https://saref.etsi.org/saref4envi.
[10] https://saref.etsi.org/saref4bldg.

2016-10[11]. In addition, experiments relied on two ontologies developed in the context of the European Projects VICINITY and DELTA, namely: the VICINITY ontology[12] and the DELTA ontology[13]. All the shapes generated during both experiments using Astrea were manually validated in term of syntax correctness using the SHACL playground[14].

Bear in mind that whether an ontology uses the term *owl:imports* the referenced ontology will be loaded and its shapes generated; for example, SAREF imports W3C Time or SSN imports SOSA [9], or VICINITY imports other well-known ontologies. Consider that the restrictions in the shapes depend directly on how the ontologies are expressed, using third-party ontologies provides a fair input for Astrea since they have not been biased to produce especially expressive and rich shapes.

In addition to these experiments the Astrea implementation has been tested by means of 108 JUnit tests, available on its GitHub repository (see Footnote 6). For each test the expected SHACL shape was defined, and an ontology fragment was provided as input to Astrea. As a result, the expected output was compared to the actual result of Astrea.

5.1   SHACL Shapes of Public Available Ontologies

The first experiment consists in generating the SHACL shapes of all the ontologies previously mentioned, measuring the number of classes and properties (data and object properties) within and the number of *sh:NodeShape* and *sh:PropertyShape* generated. In addition, the total number of SHACL restrictions and the average time that took generating 10 times each of the shapes is reported. Table 4 recaps the results of this experiment.

Table 4. SHACL shapes generated with Astrea from a set of ontologies

Ontology	Classes	Properties	Node shapes	Property shapes	Total restrictions	Generation time (s)
DELTA	74	100	74	166	1,269	0.77
DBpedia	760	2,865	760	3,247	26,940	4.73
SAREF	112	97	112	238	2,076	2.05
S4BLDG	71	263	71	570	3,533	0.48
S4ENVI	30	37	30	86	699	0.35
SSN	22	38	22	87	628	1.23
Time	20	61	20	113	807	0.92
VICINITY	94	155	94	210	1,728	1.49

---

[11] http://downloads.dbpedia.org/2016-10/dbpedia_2016-10.owl.
[12] http://iot.linkeddata.es.
[13] http://delta.iot.linkeddata.es.
[14] https://shacl.org/playground/.

The generation times for the ontologies are quite low. Figure 4 depicts how the generation times are related to the number of total SHACL restrictions generated in the shapes. No correlation can be analysed since Astrea requests to remote servers the code of the ontologies when generating shapes on the fly. As a result, some servers can answer faster with large ontologies and others slower with smaller ones. This action introduces noise that prevents studying the scalability or the correlation between SHACL restrictions and generation time.

Conclusions: the ratio of classes is held in the generated shapes. The ratio of properties is lower than the property shapes, the reason is the existence of restrictions for properties that apply only when they are used by a specific class producing more property shapes. Unfortunately, analysing the scalability is unfeasible in this scenario as previously explained. Nevertheless, generating shapes is not a critical task and the generation times for large ontologies such as DBpedia are rather low; less than 5 s for producing 26,940 SHACL restrictions.

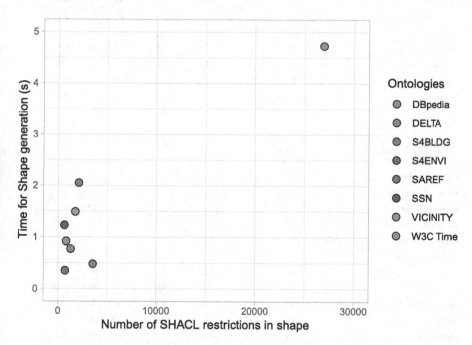

Fig. 4. Shape generation time and number of SHACL restrictions for given ontologies

5.2   SHACL Restrictions Produced by Astrea

In this experiment the expressiveness and richness of the generated shapes for the ontologies considered are analysed; the expressiveness and richness refer to the variety of SHACL constructs that a generated shape may contain. For this purpose, Table 5 reports all the restrictions that can be defined in SHACL and, for each, which were produced for the given ontologies. Notice that the last row reports the total number of SHACL restrictions that a shape has.

Conclusions: the results reported in Table 5 show how expressive and rich the SHACL shapes produced by Astrea are. The shape of the Time ontology contains 65% of all the supported constructs, SAREF 77%, SAREF for environment and for building contain both 68%, SSN 56%, DBpedia 38%, and VICINITY and DELTA contain both 65%. It is worth mentioning that some of the SHACL

Table 5. Expressivity of the generated SHACL shapes

SHACL restriction	DBpedia	DELTA	SAREF	S4BLDG	S4ENVI	SSN	Time	VICINITY
sh:NodeShape	760	74	112	71	30	22	20	94
sh:PropertyShape	3,247	166	238	570	86	87	113	210
sh:nodeKind	4,037	240	350	641	116	109	133	304
sh:targetClass	760	74	112	71	30	22	20	94
sh:path	–	67	141	307	49	49	52	60
sh:inversePath	–	–	1	–	1	1	–	2
sh:and	–	–	–	–	–	–	–	–
sh:class	828	42	84	218	37	41	33	89
sh:datatype	1,760	33	37	172	24	1	32	28
sh:disjoint	25	1	5	2	11	23	1	6
sh:equals	634	1	–	–	–	–	–	3
sh:hasValue	–	–	15	–	3	–	5	–
sh:in	–	–	–	–	–	–	–	–
sh:maxCount	30	–	42	1	9	15	38	16
sh:maxExclusive	–	–	–	–	–	–	–	–
sh:maxInclusive	2	–	–	–	–	–	–	–
sh:maxLength	–	–	–	–	–	–	–	–
sh:minCount	–	–	19	–	–	–	19	–
sh:minExclusive	–	–	–	–	–	–	–	–
sh:minInclusive	285	–	4	1	–	–	4	–
sh:minLength	–	–	–	–	–	–	–	–
sh:not	–	30	49	42	15	17	9	29
sh:name	11,780	154	209	333	66	57	81	221
sh:BlankNodeOrIRI	–	62	63	179	24	36	33	121
sh:IRI	–	74	112	71	30	22	20	94
sh:Literal	–	38	34	84	13	2	28	29
sh:IRIOrLiteral	–	67	141	307	49	49	52	60
sh:pattern	1,560	22	28	82	9	1	24	24
sh:property	–	29	49	42	15	17	9	28
sh:qualifiedMaxCount	–	1	2	2	5	–	–	4
sh:qualifiedMinCount	–	1	10	2	5	–	–	–
sh:description	1,232	92	208	333	67	57	80	208
sh:or	–	–	1	–	–	–	1	–
sh:qualifiedValue-Shape	–	1	10	2	5	–	–	4
Total restrictions	26,940	1,269	2,076	3,533	699	628	807	1,728

constructs where not generated although they are supported, the reason is that their associated ontologies lacked of the ontology construct patterns required to generate such SHACL constructs.

6   Discussion and Conclusions

Nowadays, data has been published as Knowledge Graphs in a wide number of environments and domains. The data of these KGs is expressed in RDF and modelled by means of ontologies. SHACL shapes have been endowed with the goal of providing a validation mechanism to guarantee data quality for these Knowledge Graphs. Producing SHACL shapes manually is an unfeasible task, due to the data size, to the need for expert knowledge, and to the need to use as much different restrictions as possible. Astrea generates SHACL shapes taking as input ontologies, which encode the expert knowledge of a domain, and produces either data model and data value restrictions.

In this article two main contributions were presented: A) The Astrea-KG, that contains a set of mappings that allow the generation of SHACL shapes from one or more ontologies; and B) Astrea, which is a tool that using the Astrea-KG produces the shapes. We carried out two experiments, the former aims at evaluating the generation time, whereas the second evaluates the expressiveness of the SHACL shapes produced.

The mappings presented in this article are bi-directional; however, the implementation provided in Astrea-KG works only from ontology construct patterns to SHACL construct patterns. A further analysis will be performed in the future to design the mapping implementations that produce ontologies from SHACL shapes. Implementing the round-trip translation will enable an interesting research path that may settle the basis to establish potential new quality measurements for shapes; checking how aligned their restrictions are regarding a given ontology.

Finally, during the experiments carried out we realised that there is not an automatic way to compare shapes, which could report which one has richer expressiveness or which is more restrictive. Similarly, we noticed that there is no way to combine two or more shapes, which is a rather interesting issue; this experience led to endow the definition of operators that combine shapes. For instance, defining an operator *restrictive* whose input are two shapes, and which output will be a new shape with the hardest restrictions from both inputs.

Astrea is meant to offer different extension points: including new patterns, applying other shape-learning techniques that are not ontology-based to enhance output shapes, or derived research lines that use automatic-shape generation.

Acknowledgements. The paper was written in the context of the European project DELTA (https://www.delta-h2020.eu/) and, thus, was partially funded by the European Union's Horizon 2020 research and innovation programme under grant agreement No 773960. Additionally, this article was also partially funded by a Predoctoral grant from the I+D+i program of the Universidad Politécnica de Madrid.

References

1. Boneva, I., Dusart, J., Fernández-Álvarez, D., Labra-Gayo, J.E.: Shape Designer for ShEx and SHACL Constraints (2019)
2. Boneva, I., Labra-Gayo, J.E., Hym, S., Prud'hommeau, E.G., Solbrig, H.R., Staworko, S.: Validating RDF with shape expressions. CoRR, abs/1404.1270 (2014)
3. Brickley, D., Guha, R.V., McBride, B.: RDF Schema 1.1. Technical report (2014)
4. Cox, S., Little, C.: Time ontology in OWL. Technical report (2017)
5. Debattista, J., Lange, C., Auer, S., Cortis, D.: Evaluating the quality of the LOD cloud: an empirical investigation. Seman. Web **9**(6), 859–901 (2018)
6. ETSI, TS: 264 411–v1. 1.1: SmartM2M; smart appliances; reference ontology and oneM2M mapping. Technical report, ETSI (2015)
7. Fernández-Álvarez, D., García-González, H., Frey, J., Hellmann, S., Labra-Gayo, J.E.: Inference of latent shape expressions associated to DBpedia ontology. In: Proceedings of the ISWC 2018 Posters & Demonstrations, Industry and Blue Sky Ideas Tracks co-located with 17th International Semantic Web Conference (ISWC 2018), Monterey, USA, 8th–12th October 2018 (2018)
8. Gangemi, A., Presutti, V.: Ontology design patterns. In: Staab, S., Studer, R. (eds.) Handbook on Ontologies. IHIS, pp. 221–243. Springer, Heidelberg (2009). https://doi.org/10.1007/978-3-540-92673-3_10
9. Haller, A., Janowicz, K., Cox, S., Le Phuoc, D., Taylor, K., Lefrançois, M.: Semantic sensor network ontology. W3C recommendation, W3C (2017)
10. Haller, A., et al.: The modular SSN ontology: a joint W3C and OGC standard specifying the semantics of sensors, observations, sampling, and actuation. Seman. Web **10**(1), 9–32 (2019)
11. Hitzler, P., Krötzsch, M., Parsia, B., Patel-Schneider, P.F., Rudolph, S., et al.: OWL 2 web ontology language primer. W3C recommendation (2009)
12. Knublauch, H.: SHACL and OWL Compared (2017). https://spinrdf.org/shacl-and-owl.html
13. Knublauch, H., Kontokostas, D.: Shapes Constraint Language (SHACL). W3C recommendation (2017)
14. Labra-Gayo, J.E., García-González, H., Fernández-Alvarez, D., Prud'hommeaux, E.: Challenges in RDF validation. In: Alor-Hernández, G., Sánchez-Cervantes, J.L., Rodríguez-González, A., Valencia-García, R. (eds.) Current Trends in Semantic Web Technologies: Theory and Practice. SCI, vol. 815, pp. 121–151. Springer, Cham (2019). https://doi.org/10.1007/978-3-030-06149-4_6
15. Labra-Gayo, J.E., Prud'Hommeaux, E., Boneva, I., Kontokostas, D.: Validating RDF data. Synth. Lect. Seman. Web: Theory Technol. **7**(1), 1–328 (2017)
16. Mihindukulasooriya, N., Rashid, M.R.A., Rizzo, G., García-Castro, R., Corcho, O., Torchiano, M.: RDF shape induction using knowledge base profiling. In: Proceedings of the 33rd Annual ACM Symposium on Applied Computing, pp. 1952–1959. ACM (2018)
17. Pandit, H.J., O'Sullivan, D., Lewis, D.: Using ontology design patterns to define SHACL shapes. In: Proceedings of the 9th Workshop on Ontology Design and Patterns (WOP 2018) co-located with 17th International Semantic Web Conference (ISWC 2018), Monterey, USA, 9th October 2018, pp. 67–71 (2018)
18. Peterson, D., Gao, S., Malhotra, A., Sperberg-McQueen, C.M., Thompson, H.S., Biron, P.: W3C XML schema definition language (XSD) 1.1 part 2: datatypes. World Wide Web Consortium, Working Draft, June 2008 (2012)

19. Schmachtenberg, M., Bizer, C., Paulheim, H.: State of the LOD Cloud 2014. University of Mannheim, Data and Web Science Group, 30 August 2014
20. SmartM2M: SAREF extension investigation Technical Report (TR 103 411). Technical report, ETSI (2017)
21. Spahiu, B., Maurino, A., Meusel, R.: Topic profiling benchmarks in the linked open data cloud: issues and lessons learned. Seman. Web (Preprint) **10**, 1–20 (2019)
22. Spahiu, B., Maurino, A., Palmonari, M.: Towards improving the quality of knowledge graphs with data-driven ontology patterns and SHACL. In: Proceedings of the 9th Workshop on Ontology Design and Patterns (WOP 2018) co-located with 17th International Semantic Web Conference (ISWC 2018), pp. 103–117 (2018)

SemTab 2019: Resources to Benchmark Tabular Data to Knowledge Graph Matching Systems

Ernesto Jiménez-Ruiz[1,2]([✉]), Oktie Hassanzadeh[3], Vasilis Efthymiou[5],
Jiaoyan Chen[4], and Kavitha Srinivas[3]

[1] City, University of London, London, UK
ernesto.jimenez-ruiz@city.ac.uk
[2] SIRIUS, University of Oslo, Oslo, Norway
ernestoj@uio.no
[3] IBM Research, Yorktown Heights, NY, USA
hassanzadeh@us.ibm.com, kavitha.srinivas@ibm.com
[4] University of Oxford, Oxford, UK
jiaoyan.chen@cs.ox.ac.uk
[5] IBM Research, San Jose, CA, USA
vasilis.efthymiou@ibm.com

Abstract. Tabular data to Knowledge Graph matching is the process of assigning semantic tags from knowledge graphs (e.g., Wikidata or DBpedia) to the elements of a table. This task is a challenging problem for various reasons, including the lack of metadata (e.g., table and column names), the noisiness, heterogeneity, incompleteness and ambiguity in the data. The results of this task provide significant insights about potentially highly valuable tabular data, as recent works have shown, enabling a new family of data analytics and data science applications. Despite significant amount of work on various flavors of this problem, there is a lack of a common framework to conduct a systematic evaluation of state-of-the-art systems. The creation of the *Semantic Web Challenge on Tabular Data to Knowledge Graph Matching* (SemTab) aims at filling this gap. In this paper, we report about the datasets, infrastructure and lessons learned from the first edition of the SemTab challenge.

Keywords: Tabular data · Knowledge graphs · Matching

1 Introduction

Tabular data in the form of CSV files is the common input format in a data analytics pipeline. However, a lack of understanding of the semantic structure and meaning of the content may hinder the data analytics process. Thus, gaining this semantic understanding will be very valuable for data integration, data cleaning, data mining, machine learning and knowledge discovery tasks. For example, understanding what the data is can help assess what sorts of transformation are appropriate on the data. Tables on the Web may also be the source of highly valuable data. The addition of semantic information to Web tables may

© Springer Nature Switzerland AG 2020
A. Harth et al. (Eds.): ESWC 2020, LNCS 12123, pp. 514–530, 2020.
https://doi.org/10.1007/978-3-030-49461-2_30

enhance a wide range of applications, such as web search, question answering, and knowledge base construction.

Tabular data to Knowledge Graph (KG) matching is the process of assigning semantic tags from KGs (e.g., Wikidata or DBpedia) to the elements of the table. This task however is often difficult in practice due to metadata (e.g., table and column names) being missing, noisy, incomplete or ambiguous. There exist several systems that address the tabular data to KG matching problem (e.g., [5, 8, 26]) and use state-of-the-art datasets with ground truths (e.g., [8, 19, 20]) or custom datasets. However, there does not exist a common framework to conduct a systematic evaluation of these systems, which leads to experimental results that are not easy to compare as they use different notions for true/false positives and performance measures. Furthermore, available datasets are either small in size (e.g., [19, 20]) or low in quality and messy (e.g., [8]). The creation of the *Semantic Web Challenge on Tabular Data to Knowledge Graph Matching* (SemTab) [12] aims at filling this gap.

The main contributions of this paper are summarized as follows:

(i) We introduce an automated method for generating benchmark datasets for tabular data to KG matching.

(ii) We release 4 generated benchmark datasets (see Zenodo repository [13]), and the code for evaluating the systems results (see GitHub repository [3]).

(iii) We report and analyze the results of the systems that participated in the first edition of the SemTab challenge, using our 4 benchmark datasets.

The rest of the paper is organized as follows. Section 2 introduces the matching problems and its challenges. In Sect. 3, we discuss related initiatives. The automatic dataset generator is described in Sect. 4. Section 5 presents the SemTab evaluation. Finally, Sect. 6 provides the lessons learned and experiences from the SemTab challenge and points to future lines.

2   Background

In this section, we provide some basic definitions about KGs and tabular data. We also introduce the selected matching tasks and their associated challenges.

Knowledge Graph (KG). We consider RDF-based KGs which are represented as a set of RDF triples $\langle s, p, o \rangle$, where s represents a subject (a class or an instance), p represents a predicate (a property) and o represents an object (a class, an instance or a data value, e.g., text, date and number). RDF entities (i.e., classes, properties and instances) are represented by Uniform Resource Identifiers (URIs). A KG consists of a terminological component (TBox) and an assertion component (ABox). The TBox is often composed of RDF Schema constructs like class subsumption (e.g., dbo:Scientist rdfs:subClassOf dbo:Person) and property domains (e.g., dbo:doctoralAdvisor rdfs:domain dbo:Scientist). The ABox contains relationships among entities and semantic type definitions (e.g., dbr:Albert_Einstein rdf:type dbo:Scientist). An OWL 2 ontology associated to the KG may provide more expressive constructors without a direct

Table 1. Excerpts of *(a)* a Web table about countries and capitals, *(b)* a real CSV file about broadband data, and *(c)* a custom table with start-ups from Oxford and their foundation year.

(a) Web table		(b) CSV file		(c) Custom table	
China	Beijing	Virgin	60	London	OST	2017
Indonesia	Jakarta	BT	60	East	DeepReason.ai	2018
Congo	Kinshasa	BT	40	Scotland	Oxstem	2011
Brazil		Virgen	40	Wales	Oxbotica	2014
Congo	Brazzaville	Orange	30	West Midlands	DeepMind	2010

translation into triples, which will contribute to the inference of new triples via logical reasoning. A KG can typically be accessed via a SPARQL endpoint[1] and via fuzzy matching based on an index of the lexical information associated to the KG entities. The latter is often referred to as KG lookup (*e.g.*, Spotlight for DBpedia [21] and OpenTapioca for Wikidata [7]).

Tabular Data. Tabular data can be seen as a set of columns $C = \{c_1, \ldots, c_m\}$, a set of rows $R = \{r_1, \ldots, r_n\}$, or a matrix of cells $T = \{t_{1,1}, \ldots, t_{n,m}\}$, where a column $c_k = \{t_{1,k}, \ldots, t_{n,k}\}$ and a row $r_k = \{t_{k,1}, \ldots, t_{k,m}\}$ are tuples of cells. We assume that all columns and rows have the same size, with possibly cells with empty values. In arbitrary tabular data, unlike in relational tables, column names and row identifiers (*i.e.*, primary keys) may be missing. In Web tables and relational tables, rows typically characterize an entity, while in arbitrary tabular data (*e.g.*, typical CSV files in data science) there may not be a leading entity in each row (see for example Table 1b).

Matching Tasks. We have selected the following tasks for the semantic annotation of tabular data: *(i)* Column-Type Annotation (CTA), *(ii)* Cell-Entity Annotation (CEA), and *(iii)* Columns-Property Annotation (CPA). These matching tasks can be seen as subtasks that can serve the larger purpose of matching an entire table to a class, or matching a row of a table to an entity. The CTA task expects the prediction of the semantic types (*i.e.*, KG classes) for every given table column c_k in a table T, *i.e.*, $CTA(T, c_k, KG) = \{st_1, \ldots, st_a\}$.[2] The CEA task requires the prediction of the entity or entities (*i.e.*, instances) that a cell $t_{i,j} \in T$ represents, *i.e.*, $CEA(T, t_{i,j}, KG) = \{e_1, \ldots, e_b\}$. Finally, the CPA task expects as output a set of KG properties that represent the relationship between the elements of the input columns c_k and c_l, *i.e.*, $CPA(T, c_k, c_l, KG) = \{p_1, \ldots, p_c\}$. Note that CTA (resp. CEA) task focuses on categorical columns (resp. cells) that can be represented with a KG class (resp. KG entity). Some numerical values may also represent entities if they play a *foreign key* role, but this would involve a different data wrangling task not considered in this work.

---

[1] For example, DBpedia Endpoint: http://dbpedia.org/sparql.
[2] Note that one could annotate with more than one KG and merge the results.

Challenges. The above matching tasks are challenging for various reasons including but not limited to: *(i)* Lack of metadata or uninformative table and column names, a typical scenario in Web tables and real-world tabular data. *(ii)* Noisiness in the data (*e.g.*, "Virgen" in Table 1b). *(iii)* Knowledge gap, cells without a correspondence to the KG (*e.g.*, Oxford start-ups in Table 1c). *(iv)* Ambiguous cells pointing to more than one possible entity (*e.g.*, "Congo" in Table 1a or "Virgin" and "Orange" in Table 1b). *(v)* Missing data (*i.e.*, cells without a value) increasing the effect of the knowledge gap (*e.g.*, capital of "Brazil" in Table 1a). *(vi)* Short labels or acronyms, which typically bring more ambiguity to KG matching (*e.g.*, "BT" in Table 1b).

3 Related Work

Several benchmarks have been proposed for semantic table annotation.

T2Dv2 [19] includes common tables drawn from the Web.[3] It contains 779 tables, with around 400 entity columns covering contents about place, work, organization, person, species, etc., around 26,000 DBpedia entity matches, and around 420 DBpedia property matches.

Limaye et al. [20] proposed a benchmark containing tables from Wikipedia pages.[4] It has 428 entity columns, each of which has 23 cells in average, and around 5,600 DBpedia entity matches.

Efthymiou et al. [8] created a benchmark containing 485,000 Wikipedia page tables. It has around 485,000 tables, with around 4,500,000 DBpedia entity matches. 620 of its entity columns are annotated with DBpedia classes by [4].

IMDB and Musicbrainz are other popular benchmarks. IMDB contains over 7,000 tables from IMDB movie web pages, and Musicbrainz contains some 1,400 tables from MusicBrainz web pages [29]. The entity mention cells are annotated with Freebase topics.

Viznet [15] contains 31 million datasets mined from open data repositories and visualization data repositories. Although Viznet was initially derived for use in visualizations, it has been used in the context of column-to-type matching (CTA task) of tables in a system called SHERLOCK [16]. SHERLOCK provides a total of 11,700 crowdsourced annotations from 390 human participants. However the annotations are not publicly available yet.

NumDB [18] is a dataset of 389 tables generated from DBpedia where the primary emphasis is on creating tables for identifying numerical columns. It allows the varying of the size of the table, as well as injection of different degrees of noise in the data, particularly in the textual data that can be used to match 'key' columns to test the robustness of any numerical matching approach.

Although these benchmarks are widely used in recent studies, they still suffer from a few shortcomings: *(i)* some benchmarks like Limaye and T2Dv2 are quite

---

[3] http://webdatacommons.org/webtables/goldstandardV2.htm.

[4] There have been different versions of this dataset. The one by [8] is described here.

SPARQL Endpoint → Profiling → Raw Table Generation → Refinement → Table Collection + Ground Truth Mappings

Fig. 1. Steps for automatic dataset generation.

small, with only limited contents; *(ii)* those large benchmarks like Efthymiou are often in short of high quality ground truths, especially when all the three tasks need to be evaluated at the same time; *(iii)* large benchmarks often have a large number of rows but simple relations and contents (classes); *(iv)* most benchmarks have ground truth annotations from only one KG.[5] Meanwhile, using a fixed benchmark limits the evaluation of some special cases, such as the big knowledge gap when a large part of cells have no entity correspondences, while a system for generating benchmarks with an ad-hoc configuration enables researchers to evaluate the performance in face of these special cases. Our efforts target this lacuna in benchmarks.

Benchmarks have been also developed for the related task of ontology matching, which is a well studied problem [10,11]. Our benchmarking effort was inspired by the yearly Ontology Alignment Evaluation Initiative (OAEI).[6] The main difference between our benchmarks and the OAEI benchmarks is the level of heterogeneity involved in the two data sources to be matched. Instead of two semantically rich ontologies, as those in the OAEI benchmarks, we consider one rich ontology corresponding to the KG, and one typically shallow table in terms of semantics. This heterogeneity creates an additional challenge, which ontology matching tools were not originally designed to cope with, but we believe that those tools can also benefit from our benchmarks. Therefore, we also provide our benchmark data in RDF format and experiment with publicly available ontology matching tools (e.g., LogMap [17]), to better evaluate their potential strengths and weaknesses from a different perspective than OAEI (cf. Sect. 4.4).

4   Benchmark Data Generation

To overcome the limitations of the existing benchmark datasets, and to create new benchmark datasets for each round of the challenge without extensive human annotation, we designed an automated data generator that creates tabular data given a SPARQL endpoint. The idea is to create tabular data similar to tables found on the Web, but ensure a reasonable diversity in terms of size and coverage of classes and properties from various domains. In what follows, we describe each of the steps in the data generation pipeline summarized in Fig. 1.

---

[5] To ease participation SemTab 2019 only used DBpedia as the target KG; however, as described in Sect. 4, the data generator can be fed with other KGs.

[6] http://oaei.ontologymatching.org.

4.1 Profiling

Although we used the English DBpedia as our source for this edition of the challenge, given that most state-of-the-art systems and the most widely used benchmarks use DBpedia mappings, our goal was to design a generic method of creating benchmark data that can go beyond DBpedia annotations. This way, DBpedia can be replaced with e.g. Wikidata, or a domain-specific KG. We can also switch to other languages or create a multilingual collection. Given this goal, the first step in data generation is a profiling step in which the list of classes, properties, and some basic statistics are extracted. The output of the profiling step is: *1)* a list of classes along with the number of instances per class; *2)* a list of properties for each class along with: *(i)* the number of instances that have a value for the property; *(ii)* the datatype for datatype properties and the range class for object properties. This information will be used in the next step to construct SPARQL queries.

Although our current profiling is simple, performing the necessary SPARQL queries over existing RDF stores could still be slow, and so a raw processing of RDF dumps may be required. Another option is to use a profiling tool such as Loupe [22]. For table generation with numeric columns, refer to [18].

4.2 Raw Table Generation

In this step, we go through the list of classes from the output of the profiling, and generate a set of SPARQL queries for each class. This way, each table will have one class as the main topic with each row containing values from the properties of an instance of the class (or its subclasses, if any). In order to pick a set of properties for each class to turn into a set of columns in the output table, we use a simple randomized method. We use the gathered statistics only to avoid properties with very few instance values that could in turn result in SPARQL queries with empty or very small result set. For each class, we randomly select a number of properties within a predefined range. For the tables generated for the challenge, we select a minimum of 3 and a maximum of 7 columns for each table. We then create a query to retrieve the (primary) label of the instance along with labels of object properties and values of data type properties. When multiple values are present, we only select a single value for the corresponding cell. We also ensure in the query that the type of the object property matches the expected range in the ontology (if any) since, particularly in DBpedia, there might be objects of various types as property values of the same property.

Finally, we need to ensure a diversity of classes in the output and a balanced collection in terms of table size so that we avoid very small tables, and larger classes (e.g. Person in DBpedia) do not end up dominating the collection. For small query result sets (less than 5 rows for this edition), we drop the query and try selecting a new random subset and repeat the process until all properties are included or no new tables can be generated. To deal with larger classes, we break larger query results into randomly sized subsets, and ensure that we do not have more than a fixed number (5 for this edition) of tables for the same query, and no more than a fixed number (2,000 for this edition) of rows across the collection for a given class.

The final outcome is a collection of SPARQL queries, each resulting in tabular data with *(i)* columns that can be annotated with the expected type (class for the case of object properties), *(ii)* cell values that can be annotated with instance URIs, and *(iii)* pairs of columns that can be annotated with a property.

4.3   Refinement

The outcome of the previous step is a collection of tables with all their contents completely based on values in the source (English DBpedia for this edition) which is somewhat unrealistic as real tables often have noise as well as columns/rows/values that cannot be matched with our knowledge source. For this edition, we implemented only a few simple refinement strategies to make the tables more realistic and so the matching task more difficult. We plan to significantly improve this refinement step to create more realistic collections and also collections geared towards particular features, e.g., the ability to handle certain kinds noise or the so-called "NIL detection".

The first simple refinement step includes adjusting some label values in a rule-based approach. For this edition, we do this only for Person entities, by abbreviating first names. It is possible to do this string value manipulation based on introducing errors (e.g. typos, using the method used in the UIS data generator [14]) or using sources of synonym terms and alternative labels.

To further make the matching tasks more challenging, we have used another refinement process which is applied over a number of automatically generated collections (which differ due to the random creation of SPARQL queries described above). The goal of this refinement is to retain only a subset of benchmark tables from the generated collections, after discarding fairly easy matching cases. This process can be further divided into three sub-processes: *(i)* identifying tables in which the matching tasks is more challenging, *(ii)* identifying rows in a challenging table that are still fairly easy to match (CEA task), and *(iii)* adapting the benchmark tables and the ground truths accordingly.

For sub-process *(i)*, we use the so-called refined lookup approach [8] to identify more challenging tables. In summary, this two-step approach first looks up the contents of each table cell in a KB index, and for each top-ranked result, it stores its rdf:type. In the second step, it performs the same lookup operation, but this time, it restricts the results to only those belonging to the 5 most frequent types per column, as retrieved from the first step. Despite its simplicity, this approach provided decent effectiveness results compared to more sophisticated methods. We set an empirical threshold for F1-score (0.4), and we report all the tables for which the simple lookup method returns an F1-score lower than the threshold. The tables in the final benchmark dataset will only consist of tables that are reported in this step, i.e., easier tables are ignored.

For sub-process *(ii)*, we scan in depth the error logs of the previous sub-process, in which we report how many wrong results were reported per row and per column in a table. We remove the rows for which the simple baseline method provided only correct results (0 errors), as long as the pruned table has more than 3 rows. Finally, for sub-process (*iii*), we adapt the ground truth files to reflect the refinement step. We first remove all the information about tables that were entirely discarded, and for the remaining tables, we adapt the row numbering to reflect the changes made in sub-process (*ii*).

4.4 RDF Data

In order to allow ontology matching tools to use our benchmark datasets, we also provide our datasets in RDF format, as described by a simple OWL ontology that we generate automatically from the tables [9]. Note that this process is currently only applicable when column headers are available in a table.

In summary, we assume that each table corresponds to an OWL Class, with each row being an instance of this class. The table columns correspond to either data type or object properties, which have as domain the class corresponding to the table. We detect a special label column (using heuristics, as in [8,26]), which we use as the rdfs:label property. Based on the values of each column we define the range of each data property (e.g., xsd:integer, xsd:date, xsd:string) and object property. In the case of object properties, the range class is defined as a new class, named after the header of the corresponding column. This way, the values for the columns that describe object properties are treated as instances of the OWL class, which is the range of this column.

In the example of Table 1a, assume that we have an additional row at the beginning, with the values: "Country", "Capital". In that example, we would create an OWL ontology with the classes *Country* and *Capital*, and the object property *hasCapital*. The OWL class describing the table would be *Country*, and this class would also be the domain of all the properties (in this case only *hasCapital*). The range of *hasCapital* would be the class *Capital*. Finally, each row in the table corresponds to an instance of a Country, with the rdfs:label of each instance defined from the value of the *Country* column (which is determined as the label column). For example, the RDF triples generated for the first row would be: `:China rdf:type :Country`, `:China rdfs:label "China"`, `:China :hasCapital :Beijing`, and `:Beijing rdf:type :Capital`.

5 Benchmarking Systems

The 2019 edition of the SemTab challenge was collocated with the *18th International Semantic Web Conference* as a Semantic Web Challenge and with the *14th Ontology Matching workshop* as a special OAEI evaluation track.

5.1 Evaluation Methodology

The SemTab challenge started in mid April and closed in mid October 2019. It was organised into four evaluation rounds where we aimed at testing different datasets with increasing difficulty.

Table 2. Statistics of the datasets in each SemTab round.

	Round 1	Round 2	Round 3	Round 4
Tables #	64	11,924	2,161	817
Avg. rows # (± Std Dev)	142 ± 139	25 ± 52	71 ± 58	63 ± 52
Avg. columns # (± Std Dev)	5 ± 2	5 ± 3	5 ± 1	4 ± 1
Avg. cells # (± Std Dev)	696 ± 715	124 ± 281	313 ± 262	268 ± 223
Target cells # (CEA)	8,418	463,796	406,827	107,352
Target columns # (CTA)	120	14,780	5,752	1,732
Target column pairs # (CPA)	116	6,762	7,575	2,747

Evaluation Framework. We relied on Alcrowd[7] as the platform to manage the SemTab challenge tasks: CTA, CEA and CPA. Alcrowd provides a number of useful functionalities such as challenge presentation, participant registration, automatic evaluation, ranking, submission limitation, and so on. For the (automatic) evaluation, an Alcrowd Python code template was provided, according to which the SemTab evaluation interface and metrics were implemented and deployed [3].

Datasets and Rounds. Table 2 provides a summary of the statistics of the datasets. For example, Round 3 dataset was composed of 2,161 tables; there were 406,827 target cells in CEA, 5,752 target columns in CTA, and 7,575 target column pairs in CPA. Round 1 was based on the T2Dv2 dataset [19] and served as *sandbox* for the participating systems. As T2Dv2 provides only class annotations at table level, for CTA, we extended the annotation of types for the other (entity) columns. We also manually revised the original and the new column types. Round 2 dataset was composed of *(i)* 10,000 relatively clean tables from the Wikipedia tables presented in [8] (i.e., not including tables with multiple column/row span, and large textual cell contents as in [8], and *(ii)* an automatically generated dataset of 1,924 tables as described in Sect. 4. Rounds 3 and 4 were composed of an automatically generated dataset with enhanced characteristics and a focus on non-trivial annotations. The ground truth for all four rounds was based on DBpedia. In this edition of the challenge, the ground truth was blind during the competition; but the target cells, columns and column pairs were provided to the participants.

Format of Solutions. Participants executed the matching tasks as defined in Sect. 2 for each of the given target table elements. The solutions for the CEA task were expected in a file with lines having these fields: "Table ID", "Column ID", "Row ID" and "DBpedia entity (only one)" (*e.g.*, "table1", "0", "121", "dbr:Norway"). Similarly, CPA solutions had the following fields per line: "Table ID", "Head Column ID", "Tail Column ID" and "DBpedia property (only one)" (*e.g.*, "table1", "0", "1", "dbo:releaseDate"). For CTA, more than

---

[7] https://www.aicrowd.com/.

Table 3. Schedule of submissions in each round.

	Round 1	Round 2	Round 3	Round 4
Opening	April 15	July 17	Sept. 23	Oct. 15
Closing	June 30	Sept. 22	Oct. 14	Oct. 20

one type annotations, separated by a space, were accepted: 'Table ID", "Column ID" and "DBpedia classes (1 or more)" (*e.g.*, "table1", "0", "1", "dbo:Country dbo:Place"). Note that those annotations outside the targets were ignored. Multiple annotations to one target cell or column pair, and multiple lines associated to the same target element returned an error.

Submission and Schedule. Participants had to submit their solutions for the three matching tasks via the Alcrowd platform. The performance scores were automatically computed and systems were publicly ranked in the Alcrowd webpages.[8] In Rounds 1 and 2, the number of submissions was unlimited so that participants could fine-tune their systems. The number of submissions per day was limited in Rounds 3 and 4 to avoid the effect of over-tuning. Table 3 shows the opening and closing dates for each round. The objective of Round 4 and the limited time also aimed at identifying potential over-tuning in the participating systems.

Evaluation Metrics for CEA and CPA. For CEA and CPA, we compute Precision P, Recall R and $F1$ Score (primary score) as follows:

$$P = \frac{|\text{Correct Annotations}|}{|\text{System Annotations}|} \quad R = \frac{|\text{Correct Annotations}|}{|\text{Target Annotations}|} \quad F1 = \frac{2 \times P \times R}{P + R} \quad (1)$$

where target annotations refer to the target cells for CEA and the target column pairs for CPA. Note that it is possible that one target cell or column pair has multiple ground truths, as modern KGs often have duplicate components. One example is the wiki page redirected entities in DBpedia. An annotation is regarded as true if it is equal to one of the ground truths. The comparison for equality is case insensitive. Recall that at most one annotation was submitted for each target cell or column pair.

Evaluation Metrics for CTA. For CTA we used a different set of metrics to take into account the taxonomy (hierarchy) of classes in the KG, namely *Average Hierarchical Score (AH)* and *Average Perfect Score (AP)*:

$$AH = \frac{|P| + 0.5 \times |O| - |W|}{|T|} \quad AP = \frac{|P|}{|P| + |O| + |W|} \quad (2)$$

T denotes all the columns for annotation. We refer as *perfect* annotations (P) the most fine-grained classes in the (ontology) hierarchy that also appear in

---

[8] E.g., CEA leaderboard: https://www.aicrowd.com/challenges/iswc-2019-cell-entity-annotation-cea-challenge/leaderboards.

Table 4. Participation in the SemTab challenge.

	Round 1	Round 2	Round 3	Round 4
Overall	17	11	9	8
CEA task	11	10	8	8
CTA task	13	9	8	7
CPA task	5	7	7	7

the ground truth, while annotations involving the super-classes (excluding very generic top classes like *owl:Thing*) of perfect classes are referred to as *okay* annotations (O). Other annotations not in the ground truths are considered as *wrong* (W). *AH* gives a full score to the *perfect* annotation, a half score to the *okay* annotations, and a negative score to *wrong* class annotation. *AH* is used as the primary score as it considers both correct and wrong annotations, while *AP* is used as secondary score as it only considers the rate of perfect annotations.

5.2   Challenge Participation

Table 4 shows the participation per round. We had a total of 17 systems participating in Round 1. Round 2 had a reduction of participating systems (from 17 to 11), which helped us identify the core systems and groups actively working in tabular data to KG matching. Round 3 and Round 4 preserved the 7 core participants across rounds and all three tasks. It is worth mentioning that LogMap [17], a pure ontology alignment system, participated in Round 2. LogMap was given as input *(i)* the tabular data in RDF format as described in Sect. 4.4, and *(ii)* a relevant portion of the DBpedia KG. The obtained results were reasonable, but far from the specialised system in the challenge. This is expected as systems like LogMap rely on the semantics of the input ontologies or KGs, which is missing in the input tabular data.

Next, we provide a brief description of the core participants, who also submitted a system paper to the challenge.

MTab [24]. MTab is a system that can jointly deal with the three tasks CTA, CEA and CPA. It is based on the joint probability distribution of multiple table to KG matching, following the probabilistic graph model by [20]. However, the team improves the matching by using multiple services including DBpedia Lookup, DBpedia endpoint, Wikipedia and Wikidata, as well as a cross-lingual matching strategy.

IDLab [27]. The IDLab team developed an iterative matching procedure named CSV2KG with the following steps: *(i)* gets crude entity matching with cells; *(ii)* determines the column types and column relations with these entities; *(iii)* corrects the cell to entity matching with the column types and column relations; *(iv)* corrects the remaining cells with the head cells; and *(v)* calculates the column type again with all the corrected cell to entity matching.

ADOG [25]. This systems utilizes a NoSQL database named ArangoDB[9] to load DBpedia and index its components. ADOG then matches tabular data with the entities of DBpedia using Levenshtein distance, a string similarity metric.

Tabularisi [28]. The team developed a system with two steps: candidate generation and selection. The former uses the Wikidata API and a search index based on DBpedia labels to obtain a list of entities for each cell, while the later scores the candidates with lexical features which are based on lexical similarity metrics, and semantic features which capture the cell coherence of each column.

DAGOBAH [2]. This participant system proposes an embedding approach which assumes that entities in the same column should be closed in the embedding space. It gets candidate entities by KG lookup, and uses pre-trained Wikidata embeddings for entity clustering and cluster type scoring. The challenge of this method lies in the setting of hyper parameters such as the cluster number.

Team_sti [6]. This team developed a tool named MantisTable that can automatically annotate, manage and make the semantics of tables accessible to humans and machines. The tool has some built in functions for the three matching tasks, including a SPARQL query for entity matching, a relation annotator based on maximum frequency and a class annotator based on voting by entities. Note that this system also provides a web interface for manual annotation.

LOD4ALL [23]. This system implements a pipeline for the three tasks with five steps: *(i)* extracts ranked candidate entities of cells with direct search by ASK SPARQL queries and keywords; *(ii)* gets the type of each entity; *(iii)* determines the type of each column with a weighted combination of ratio score and a normalized class score; *(iv)* determines the entity of each cell with the type constraint; and *(v)* extracts the relation of entities in each row and select the inter-column relation by frequency.

5.3   Challenge Evaluation

In this section, we report the results of the challenge Rounds 2–4 for the systems participating in at least two rounds, which include the above core participants and a system called *saggu* that only participated in CEA. Complete evaluation results are available from the challenge website [12].

The results for all three matching tasks are presented in Fig. 2. MTab and IDLab were the clear dominants in all three tasks. Tabularisi was in a clear overall 3rd position in CTA and CPA. The overall 3rd position in CEA was shared among Tabularisi and ADOG. Special mention requires Team_sti which had an outstanding performance in Round 4 of CEA.

In terms of average scores, Round 2 was the most challenging one, although it is not comparable to Rounds 3 and 4 as it includes a different source dataset. Rounds 3 and 4 completely rely on the dataset generator. Round 4 aimed at being more challenging than Round 3 by only including non-trivial cases. This was partially achieved for CEA, with the exception of MTab and Team_sti.

---

[9] https://www.arangodb.com.

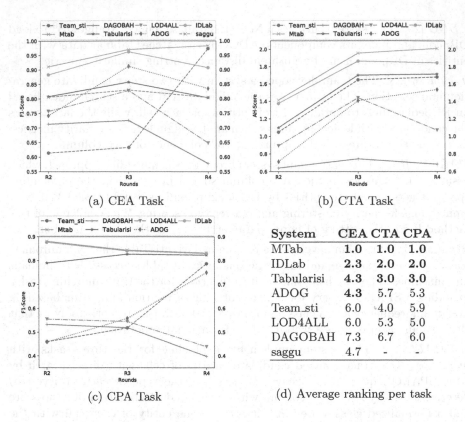

(a) CEA Task

(b) CTA Task

(c) CPA Task

(d) Average ranking per task

System	CEA	CTA	CPA
MTab	1.0	1.0	1.0
IDLab	2.3	2.0	2.0
Tabularisi	4.3	3.0	3.0
ADOG	4.3	5.7	5.3
Team_sti	6.0	4.0	5.9
LOD4ALL	6.0	5.3	5.0
DAGOBAH	7.3	6.7	6.0
saggu	4.7	-	-

Fig. 2. Results of systems competing in challenge Rounds 2, 3 and 4.

The relative performance of systems across rounds is similar in CEA and CTA with the exception of Team_sti in CEA, where there is an important improvement in Round 4, and LOD4ALL that decreased performance in Round 4 of CTA.

According to the results, complementing DBpedia with additional resources like Wikidata (e.g., MTab and Tabularisi) brings an important value. In general, the use of elaborated lexical techniques seems to be the key for a good performance. Other approaches based on more sophisticated methods like semantic embeddings (e.g., DAGOBAH) do not seem to bring the expected value to the final performance, but they may suffer a lighter impact with respect to changes in the datasets and the KG. Another factor that may impact their performance is the long time spent for learning or fine tuning the embeddings of a large KG like Wikidata and DBpedia.

Sponsorship and Awards. SIRIUS[10] and IBM Research[11] sponsored the prizes for the challenge. This sponsorship was important not only for the challenge awards, but also because it shows a strong interest from industry. Figure 2d shows the

---

[10] SIRIUS: Norwegian Centre for Research-driven Innovation: https://sirius-labs.no.
[11] https://www.research.ibm.com/.

average ranking of the participating systems in each task. MTab, IDLab and Tabularisi obtained the *1st*, *2nd* and *3rd* prize, respectively, across the three matching task. ADOG shared the *3rd* prize in CEA with Tabularisi. Finally, Team_sti obtained the *Outstanding Improvement* prize in CEA.

6 Lessons Learned and Future Work

In this paper, we have presented the datasets and the results of the first edition of the SemTab challenge. The experience has been successful and has served to start creating a community interested in the semantic enrichment of tabular data. Both from the organization side and the participation side, we aim at preparing a new edition of the SemTab challenge in 2020. Next, we summarize the issues we encountered during the different evaluation rounds, the lessons learned, and some ideas for the future editions of the challenge.

Importance of the Challenge. We received very positive feedback from the participants with respect to the necessity of a challenge like SemTab to conduct a systematic evaluation of their systems. Our challenge was also well-received from industry via the sponsorship of IBM Research and SIRIUS.

Minor Issues. We faced a few minor issues during the evaluation rounds, which will help us improve the future editions of the challenge. Next, we summarise some of them: *(i)* explicit reference to the version of the KG used; *(ii)* incompatible encodings when merging different datasets; *(iii)* low quality of the DBpedia wikiredirects; *(iv)* Wikipedia disambiguation pages as annotations; *(v)* property hierarchy was not considered; *(vi)* the average Hierarchical Score (AH) was not easy to interpret for participants as, in the way it is currently defined, it does not have a clear upper bound. Nevertheless, we believe these issues affected all participants in a similar way and they did not have an important impact in the relative comparison among systems.

Evaluation Platform. On the one hand, the Alcrowd platform makes the management of submissions, evaluation and ranking very easy. On the other hand, it has no interface for automatic deployment of the evaluation codes and data, which makes it inconvenient to deal with online errors or changes, as challenge organisers depend on the Alcrowd team. It was also hard to communicate with participants not using the Alcrowd discussion forum. For next editions, we may consider alternative solutions.

Number of Submissions. The limitation of number of submission per day was not welcomed by all participants. However, we find that unlimited submissions may lead to over-tuning the matching model that will have limited generalization performance. In future editions, we will try to better split the datasets for fine-tuning from the ones for testing.

Instance Matching. We produced an RDF version of the dataset in Round 2, but we did not attract the expected attention in the OAEI community and the participation of (ontology) instance matching or link discovery systems was limited to LogMap. In future editions of the challenge, we aim at facilitating the participation of OAEI systems.

Real-World Datasets. Several participants highlighted the necessity of more realistic datasets, however manually annotated datasets are limited in quantity and size. A possible solution is to create a consensual ground truth by combining the output of several systems. This solution has already been used in several evaluation tracks of the OAEI campaign [1].

Reproducibility. As SemTab 2019 was the first edition of the challenge, our priority was to facilitate participation and allow participants to directly submit their solutions for each matching task. This plays a negative role in terms of reproducibility of the results. In future editions, we are considering to require from participants *(i)* the submission of a running system as in the OAEI campaign, or *(ii)* the publication of their system as a (Web) service.

Matching Targets. In SemTab 2019 we advocated to provide this information to the users to make the matching and the evaluation easier. In future editions we may hide this information to the participants. Participants will have less guidance which will especially be reflected in the CPA task. Evaluation will also be more challenging as incompleteness of the ground truth should not penalize potentially correct predictions.

Improved Data Generator. As outlined in Sect. 4, there are a number of ways to improve our data generator to create more realistic datasets. In particular, much work needs to be done in creating tables that are more challenging to match, and contain more variety of representations and contents that cannot be matched to the source KG. Also, our data generator has a number of parameters which can be adjusted to create different benchmarks each suitable for a different use case. We intend to work on these extensions, create more diverse and realistic collections, and make our data generator publicly available which will allow us to seek contributions from the community.

Acknowledgements. We would like to thank the challenge participants, the ISWC & OM organisers, the Alcrowd team, and our sponsors (SIRIUS and IBM Research) that played a key role in the success of SemTab. This work was also supported by the AIDA project (Alan Turing Institute), the SIRIUS Centre for Scalable Data Access (Research Council of Norway), Samsung Research UK, Siemens AG, and the EPSRC projects AnaLOG, OASIS and UK FIRES.

References

1. Algergawy, A., et al.: Results of the ontology alignment evaluation initiative 2018. In: 13th International Workshop on Ontology Matching, pp. 76–116 (2018)
2. Chabot, Y., Labbe, T., Liu, J., Troncy, R.: DAGOBAH: an end-to-end context-free tabular data semantic annotation system. In: SemTab, ISWC Challenge (2019)
3. Chen, J., Efthymiou, V., Hassanzadeh, O., Jiménez-Ruiz, E., Srinivas, K.: AIcrowd Evaluation Codes (Python code). https://github.com/sem-tab-challenge/aicrowd-evaluator. Accessed 6 Mar 2020

4. Chen, J., Jimenez-Ruiz, E., Horrocks, I., Sutton, C.: Learning semantic annotations for tabular data. In: IJCAI (2019)
5. Chen, J., Jiménez-Ruiz, E., Horrocks, I., Sutton, C.A.: ColNet: embedding the semantics of web tables for column type prediction. In: AAAI, pp. 29–36 (2019)
6. Cremaschi, M., Avogadro, R., Chieregato, D.: MantisTable: an automatic approach for the semantic table interpretation. In: SemTab, ISWC Challenge (2019)
7. Delpeuch, A.: OpenTapioca: lightweight entity linking for Wikidata. arXiv preprint arXiv:1904.09131 (2019)
8. Efthymiou, V., Hassanzadeh, O., Rodriguez-Muro, M., Christophides, V.: Matching web tables with knowledge base entities: from entity lookups to entity embeddings. In: d'Amato, C., et al. (eds.) ISWC 2017. LNCS, vol. 10587, pp. 260–277. Springer, Cham (2017). https://doi.org/10.1007/978-3-319-68288-4_16
9. Efthymiou, V., Hassanzadeh, O., Sadoghi, M., Rodriguez-Muro, M.: Annotating web tables through ontology matching. In: OM, pp. 229–230 (2016)
10. Euzenat, J., Rosoiu, M., dos Santos, C.T.: Ontology matching benchmarks: generation, stability, and discriminability. J. Web Semant. 21, 30–48 (2013)
11. Euzenat, J., Shvaiko, P.: Ontology Matching, 2nd edn. Springer, Heidelberg (2013). https://doi.org/10.1007/978-3-642-38721-0
12. Hassanzadeh, O., Efthymiou, V., Chen, J., Jiménez-Ruiz, E., Srinivas, K.: Semantic Web Challenge on Tabular Data to Knowledge Graph Matching (SemTab 2019) (2019). http://www.cs.ox.ac.uk/isg/challenges/sem-tab/2019. Accessed 6 Mar 2020
13. Hassanzadeh, O., Efthymiou, V., Chen, J., Jiménez-Ruiz, E., Srinivas, K.: SemTab2019: Semantic Web Challenge on Tabular Data to Knowledge Graph Matching - 2019 Data Sets (2019). https://doi.org/10.5281/zenodo.3518539. Accessed 6 Mar 2020
14. Hernández, M.A., Stolfo, S.J.: The merge/purge problem for large databases. In: ACM SIGMOD Conference on Management of Data, pp. 127–138 (1995)
15. Hu, K., et al.: VizNet: towards a large-scale visualization learning and benchmarking repository. In: CHI. ACM (2019)
16. Hulsebos, M., et al.: Sherlock: a deep learning approach to semantic data type detection. In: Knowledge Discovery and Data Mining (KDD) (2019)
17. Jiménez-Ruiz, E., Cuenca Grau, B.: LogMap: logic-based and scalable ontology matching. In: Aroyo, L., et al. (eds.) ISWC 2011. LNCS, vol. 7031, pp. 273–288. Springer, Heidelberg (2011). https://doi.org/10.1007/978-3-642-25073-6_18
18. Kacprzak, E., et al.: Making sense of numerical data - semantic labelling of web tables. In: Faron Zucker, C., Ghidini, C., Napoli, A., Toussaint, Y. (eds.) EKAW 2018. LNCS (LNAI), vol. 11313, pp. 163–178. Springer, Cham (2018). https://doi.org/10.1007/978-3-030-03667-6_11
19. Lehmberg, O., Ritze, D., Meusel, R., Bizer, C.: A large public corpus of web tables containing time and context metadata. In: WWW (2016)
20. Limaye, G., Sarawagi, S., Chakrabarti, S.: Annotating and searching web tables using entities, types and relationships. VLDB Endow. 3(1–2), 1338–1347 (2010)
21. Mendes, P.N., Jakob, M., García-Silva, A., Bizer, C.: DBpedia spotlight: shedding light on the web of documents. In: I-Semantic, pp. 1–8. ACM (2011)
22. Mihindukulasooriya, N., Poveda-Villalón, M., García-Castro, R., Gómez-Pérez, A.: Loupe - an online tool for inspecting datasets in the linked data cloud. In: ISWC Posters & Demos (2015)
23. Morikawa, H.: Semantic table interpretation using LOD4ALL. In: SemTab, ISWC Challenge (2019)

24. Nguyen, P., Kertkeidkachorn, N., Ichise, R., Takeda, H.: MTab: matching tabular data to knowledge graph using probability models. In: SemTab, ISWC Challenge (2019)
25. Oliveira, D., d'Aquin, M.: ADOG - anotating data with ontologies and graphs. In: SemTab, ISWC Challenge (2019)
26. Ritze, D., Lehmberg, O., Bizer, C.: Matching HTML Tables to DBpedia. In: WIMS, pp. 10:1–10:6 (2015)
27. Steenwinckel, B., Vandewiele, G., De Turck, F., Ongenae, F.: CSV2KG: transforming tabular data into semantic knowledge. In: SemTab, ISWC Challenge (2019)
28. Thawani, A., et al.: Entity linking to knowledge graphs to infer column types and properties. In: SemTab, ISWC Challenge (2019)
29. Zhang, Z.: Effective and efficient semantic table interpretation using tableminer+. Semant. Web 8(6), 921–957 (2017)

VQuAnDa: Verbalization QUestion ANswering DAtaset

Endri Kacupaj[1](✉)(iD), Hamid Zafar[1](✉)(iD), Jens Lehmann[1,2](✉)(iD),
and Maria Maleshkova[1](✉)(iD)

[1] University of Bonn, Bonn, Germany
{kacupaj,hzafarta,jens.lehmann,maleshkova}@cs.uni-bonn.de
[2] Fraunhofer IAIS, Dresden, Germany
jens.lehmann@iais.fraunhofer.de

Abstract. Question Answering (QA) systems over Knowledge Graphs (KGs) aim to provide a concise answer to a given natural language question. Despite the significant evolution of QA methods over the past years, there are still some core lines of work, which are lagging behind. This is especially true for methods and datasets that support the verbalization of answers in natural language. Specifically, to the best of our knowledge, none of the existing Question Answering datasets provide any verbalization data for the question-query pairs. Hence, we aim to fill this gap by providing the first QA dataset VQuAnDa that includes the verbalization of each answer. We base VQuAnDa on a commonly used large-scale QA dataset – LC-QuAD, in order to support compatibility and continuity of previous work. We complement the dataset with baseline scores for measuring future training and evaluation work, by using a set of standard sequence to sequence models and sharing the results of the experiments. This resource empowers researchers to train and evaluate a variety of models to generate answer verbalizations.

Keywords: Verbalization · Question Answering · Knowledge Graph · Dataset

Resource Type: Dataset
Website: http://vquanda.sda.tech/
License: Attribution 4.0 International (CC BY 4.0)
Permanent URL: https://figshare.com/projects/VQuAnDa/72488.

1 Introduction

Knowledge Graphs (KGs) have been gaining in popularity and adoption during the past years and have become an established solution for storing large-scale data, in both domain-specific (i.e., Knowlife [17]) and open-domain areas (i.e, Freebase [7], DBpedia [21] and Wikidata [34]). Despite the success of KGs, there are still some adoption hurdles that need to be overcome. In particular, users

© Springer Nature Switzerland AG 2020
A. Harth et al. (Eds.): ESWC 2020, LNCS 12123, pp. 531–547, 2020.
https://doi.org/10.1007/978-3-030-49461-2_31

need the expertise to use the formal query language supported by the KG in order to access the data within the KG. Question Answering (QA) systems aim to address this issue by providing a natural language-based interface to query the underlying KG. Thus, QA systems make KG data more accessible by empowering the users to retrieve the desired information via natural language questions rather than using a formal query language.

The early Knowledge Graph based Question Answering (KGQA) systems were mostly template or rule-based systems with limited learnable modules [14,32], mainly due to the fact that the existing QA datasets were small-scaled [9]. Consequently, researchers in the QA community are working on expanding QA datasets from two perspectives: (i) size: to support machine learning approaches that need more training data [8] and (ii) complexity: to move on from simple factoid questions to complex questions (e.g. multi-hop, ordinal, aggregation, etc.) [6]. Note that while there are some QA datasets that are automatically generated [28], most QA datasets are manually created either by (i) using in-house workers [31] or crowd-sourcing [12] (ii) or extract questions from online question answering platforms such as search engines, online forum, etc. [6]. The goal is to create datasets that are representative in terms of the types of questions that users are likely to ask.

These large-scale and complex QA datasets enable researchers to develop end-to-end learning approaches [25] and support questions with various features of varying complexity [1]. As a result, the main focus of many competitive QA methods is to enhance the performance of QA systems in terms of the accuracy of answer(s) retrieval. However, the average accuracy of the current state of the art QA approaches on manually created QA datasets is about 0.49, hence, there is plenty of room for improvement (See Fig. 1).

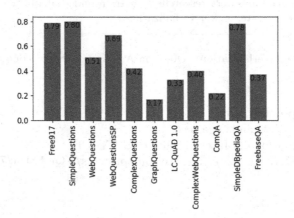

Fig. 1. The accuracy of the state of the art QA over KGs systems

Consequently, given this accuracy, the answers provided by a QA system need to be validated to assure that the questions are understood correctly and that the right data is retrieved. For instance, assuming that the answer to the exemplary question *"What is the longest river in Africa?"* is not known by the user. If the QA system only provides a name with no further explanation, the user might need to refer to an external data source to verify the answer. In an attempt to enable the users to verify the answer provided by a QA system, researchers employ various techniques such as (i) revealing the generated formal query [18], (ii) graphical visualizations of the formal query [36] and (iii) verbalizing the formal query [11,15,24]. We take a different approach to addressing the problem of validating the answers given by the QA system. We aim to verbalize the answer in a way that it conveys not only the information requested by the user but also includes additional characteristics that are indicative of how the answer was determined. For instance, the answer verbalization for the example question should be *"The longest river in Africa is Nile"* and given this verbalization, the user can better verify that the system is retrieving a *river* that is the *longest* river, which is located in *Africa*.

In this context we make the following contributions:

- We provide a framework for automatically generating the verbalization of answer(s), given the input question and the corresponding SPARQL query, which reduces the needed initial manual effort. The questions generated by the framework are subsequently manually verified to guarantee the accuracy of the verbalized answers.
- We present VQuAnDa – Verbalization QUestion ANswering DAtaset – the first QA dataset, which provides the verbalization of the answer in natural language.
- Evaluation baselines, based on a set of standard sequence to sequence models, which can serve to determine the accuracy of machine learning approaches used to verbalize the answers of QA systems.

The further advantages of having a dataset with accurate verbalization of the answer are multi-fold. Users do not need to understand RDF/the formalization of the results, which decreases the adoption barriers of using KGs and QA systems. In addition, by providing indications of how the answer was derived as part of the verbalization, we enhance the explainability of the system. Furthermore, VQuAnDa serves as the basis for training and developing new ML models, which was up to date difficult due to the lack of data. Finally, our dataset lays the foundation for new lines of work towards extending VQuAnDa by the community.

The remainder of the paper is structured as follows. The next section presents the impact of our dataset within the QA community and its differences in comparison to the existing QA datasets. We introduce the details of our dataset and the generation workflow in Sect. 3. Section 4 discusses availability of the dataset, followed by the reusability study in Sect. 5, and Sect. 6 concludes our contributions.

2   Impact

Question Answering (QA) datasets over Knowledge Graphs (KG) commonly contain natural language questions, corresponding formal queries and/or the answer(s) from the underlying KG. Table 1 summarizes the features of all existing QA datasets over KGs. All QA datasets (except for [28]) are created using human annotators to ensure the quality of the results. In some datasets (such as FreebaseQA [20] and Free917 [9]), the questions are collected from search engines or other online question answering platforms and were subsequently adapted to an open-domain knowledge graph by human annotators. Others formulate the questions from a list of keywords (for instance LC-QuAD 1.0 [31]), or compose the question given a template-based automatically generated pseudo-question (for instance LC-QuAD 2.0 [12]).

Table 1. Summary of QA datasets over knowledge graphs

Dataset	KG	Size	Year	Formal rep.	Creation
Free917 [9]	Freebase	917	2013	SPARQL	Manual
WebQuestions [6]	Freebase	5810	2013	None	Manual
SimpleQuestions [8]	Freebase	100K	2015	SPARQL	Manual
WebQuestionsSP [35]	Freebase	5810	2016	SPARQL	Manual
ComplexQuestions [5]	Freebase	2100	2016	None	Manual
GraphQuestions [29]	Freebase	5166	2016	SPARQL	Manual
30M Factoid Questions [28]	Freebase	30M	2016	SPARQL	Automatic
QALD (1–9)[a]	DBpedia	500	2011–2018	SPARQL	Manual
LC-QuAD 1.0 [31]	DBpedia	5000	2017	SPARQL	Manual
ComplexWebQuestions [30]	Freebase	33K	2018	SPARQL	Manual
ComQA [2]	Wikipedia	11K	2018	None	Manual
SimpleDBpediaQA [3]	DBpedia	43K	2018	Inferential Chain	Manual
CSQA [27]	Wikidata	200K	2018	Entities/Relations	Manual
LC-QuAD 2.0 [12]	Wikidata	30K	2019	SPARQL	Manual
FreebaseQA [20]	Freebase	28K	2019	Inferential Chain	Manual

[a]http://qald.aksw.org/

The general trend in QA datasets is to work on the following aspects: (i) to increase the size of the dataset, (ii) to expand the question types to cover various features such as boolean queries, aggregations, ordinals in queries, etc. (iii) to increase the complexity of question by using compound features such as comparison or unions. Most recently, in an attempt to provide human-like conversations on a single topic, researchers expanded QA datasets to cover multiple utterances turns by introducing CSQA [27] – a sequential QA dataset in which instead of isolated questions, the benchmark contains a sequence of related questions along with their answers. However, the dataset contains only plain answers with no further verbalization to mimic human conversation.

On the one hand, recent advances in task-oriented dialogue systems resulted in releasing multi-turn dialogue datasets that are grounded through knowledge bases [16]. The intention is to provide training data for models allowing them to have a coherent conversion. However, users cannot validate whether the provided answer at each step is correct. Moreover, the underlying knowledge graphs are significantly smaller than open-domain knowledge graphs such as DBpedia in terms of the number of entities and relations.

Considering the existing QA datasets and task-oriented dialogue datasets, we observe that the verbalization of answers with the intention to enable the users to validate the provided answer is neglected in the existing datasets. Consequently, the existing works cover either (i) the verbalization of the answer as in the dialog dataset, however, without empowering the users to validate the answer, (ii) or they enable the user to validate the answer, however, without a human like conversation [11].

We fill this gap in the question answering community by providing VQuAnDa, thus facilitating the research on semantic-enabled verbalization of answers in order to engage the users in human-like conversations while enabling them to verify the answers as well. We provide the verbalization of the answers by compiling all the necessary elements from the formal query and the answers into a coherent statement. Given this characterization of the answer, the user is enabled to verify whether the system has understood the intention of the question correctly. Furthermore, the dataset can be beneficial in dialog systems to not only hold the conversation but also to augment it with relevant elements that explain how the system comprehends the intention of the question.

We provide details on the dataset and the generation workflow in the next section.

3   VQuAnDa: Verbalization QUestion ANswering DAtaset

We introduce a new dataset with verbalized KBQA results called VQuAnDa. The dataset intends to completely hide any semantic technologies and provide a fluent experience between the users and the Knowledge Base. A key advantage of the verbalization is to support the answers given for a question/query. By receiving a complete natural language sentence as an answer, the user can understand how the QA system interpreted the question and what is the corresponding result. Table 2 shows some verbalization examples from our dataset. In the first example, the question *"What is the common school of Chris Marve and Neria Douglass?"* is translated to the corresponding SPARQL query, which retrieves the result dbr:Vanderbilt_University from the KB. In this case, the full verbalization of the result is *"[Vanderbilt University] is the alma mater of both Chris Marve and Neria Douglass."*. As it can be seen, this form of answer provides us the query result as well as details about the intention of the query.

Our dataset is based on the Largescale Complex Question Answering Dataset (LC-QuAD), which is a complex question answering dataset over DBpedia containing 5,000 pairs of questions and their SPARQL queries. The dataset was

Table 2. Examples from VQuAnDa

Question	What is the common school of Chris Marve and Neria Douglass?

Query	SELECT DISTINCT ?uri
	WHERE {
	dbr:Chris_Marve dbo:school ?uri .
	dbr:Neria_Douglass dbo:almaMater ?uri .
	}

Query result	dbr:Vanderbilt_University
Verbalization	[Vanderbilt University] is the alma mater of both Chris Marve and Neria Douglass
Question	List all the faiths that British Columbian politicians follow?

Query	SELECT DISTINCT ?uri
	WHERE {
	?x dbp:residence dbr:British_Columbia .
	?x dbp:religion ?uri .
	?x a dbo:Politician .
	}

Query result	dbr:{Anglican, Anglicanism, Catholic Church, United Church of Canada, Fellowship of Evangelical Baptist Churches in Canada, Mennonite Brethren Church, story.html, Sikh, Roman Catholic}
Verbalization	The religions of the British Columbia politicians are [Anglican, Anglicanism, Catholic Church, United Church of Canada, Fellowship of Evangelical Baptist Churches in Canada, Mennonite Brethren Church, story.html, Sikh, Roman Catholic]

generated using 38 unique templates together with 5,042 entities and 615 predicates. To create our dataset, we extended the LC-QuAD by providing verbalizations for all results. Furthermore, we improved the quality of the dataset by fixing grammar mistakes in the questions and, in some cases where the wording was unclear, completely rewriting them.

Given that Freebase is no longer publicly maintained, we decided to focus on the QA datasets that are based on other KGs such as DBpedia or Wikidata. Therefore, QALD, LC-QuAD 1.0, LC-QuAD 2.0 and CSQA are the only viable options. However, the size of the QALD dataset is significantly smaller in comparison to the other datasets (See Table 1). Moreover, in contrast to LC-QuAD 2.0 and CSQA that have not been yet used by any QA system, LC-QuAD 1.0 was the benchmarking dataset in more than 10 recent QA systems. Thus, we choose to built our dataset over LC-QuAD because of the large variety of questions and the manageable size that it has, which allows us to estimate the effectiveness of the produced results.

3.1   Generation Workflow

We followed a semi-automated approach to generate the dataset. The overall architecture of the approach is depicted in Fig. 2.

Extract Results and Set Limit. Initially, we retrieved the answers to all questions by using the DBpedia endpoint. Since some questions had multiple results, we had to set a limit on how many answers will be shown as part of the verbalization. In the dataset, there are questions with one result and others with thousands. Creating a verbalization with a long list of all results is not intuitive, often not readable, and it is not contributing to the main focus of our work. Therefore we set a limit of a maximum of 15 results that are shown as part of the verbalization sentence. This limit was chosen by considering the different types of questions within the dataset and their complexity. In *Sect. 3.2 Statistics* we provide further details about the characteristics of the results. To handle the cases with more than 15 results we decided to replace them with an answer token ([*answer*]). For instance, for the question *"Which comic characters are painted by Bill Finger?"* the corresponding query retrieves 23 comic characters, therefore, the verbalization will include the answer token and it will be *"Bill Finger painted the following comic characters, [answer]."*. In this way, we can guarantee the sentence fluency for the particular example and we can still consider it for the verbalization task.

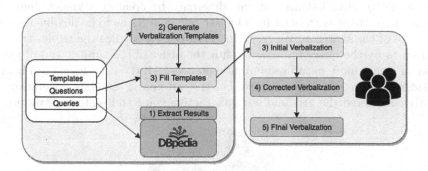

Fig. 2. Overview of dataset generation

Generate Verbalization Templates. Next, we generated the templates for the verbalized answers. In this step, we used the question templates from the LC-QuAD dataset. We decided to paraphrase them using a rule-based approach (see *Section Verbalization Rules*) and generate an initial draft version of the verbalizations.

Create Initial Verbalization. In the following, we filled the templates with entities, predicates, and query results. To be able to distinguish the query results from the remaining parts of the verbalization sentence we decided to annotate them using box brackets. This provides us the flexibility whether we want to include, cover or exclude the results while working with the dataset.

Correct and Final Verbalizations. While all initial draft versions of the verbalized answers were automatically generated, the last 2 steps had to be done manually in order to ensure the correctness of the verbalizations. First, we corrected and, if necessary, rephrased all answers to sound more natural and fluent. Finally, to ensure the grammatical correctness of the dataset, we peer-reviewed all the generated results.

Verbalization Rules

During the generation workflow, we followed 4 rules on how to produce proper, fluent and correct verbalizations. These rules are:

- Use active voice;
- Use paraphrasing and synonyms;
- Construct the verbalization by using information from both the question and the query;
- Allow for rearranging the triple's order in verbalization.

The first and most important rule is the use of active voice as much as possible. In this way, we produce clean results that are close to human spoken language. The second rule is to paraphrase the sentences and use synonyms for generating different alternatives. The third rule is to base the verbalization on both questions and queries. We have many examples where the question is not directly related to a query from the aspect of structure and words it uses. During the process, we tried to balance out this difference by creating verbalizations that are closer to one or both of them. The last rule enables us to be flexible with the structure of the sentence. We tried not to directly verbalize the triple structure referred to by the query but also to shift the order of the subject and object in order to create more natural sounding sentences. All the rules have been heavily considered during the manual steps. For the automatic template generation, we mostly considered the first and last rule (active voice and sentence structure).

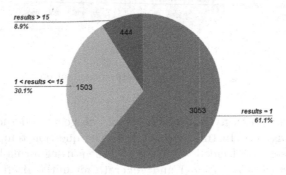

Fig. 3. Number of results returned per query

3.2   Statistics

In this section we provide more details on the data contained in VQuAnDa, specifically focusing on the distribution of the query results. The dataset consists of 3053 (61.1%) questions that retrieve only one result from the knowledge base. These examples include also boolean and count questions. There are 1503 (30.1%) examples that have more than one answer but less or equal to 15, which is the maximum number that we display as part verbalization. Finally, only 444 (8.9%) examples have more than 15 answers and are replaced with an answer token. Figure 3 depicts the result distribution.

Regarding the modified questions in the dataset –340 (6.8%) examples in the LC-QuAD were revised to better represent the intention of the query. Some of the modifications are grammatical mistakes, while for others we had to completely restructure or even rewrite the questions. Figure 4 shows the number of modified questions, per question type and modification type.

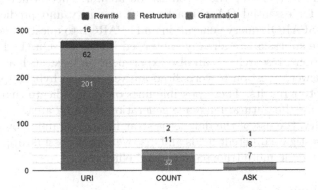

Fig. 4. Modified questions in the dataset

4   Availability and Sustainability

The dataset is available at AskNowQA[1] GitHub repository under the Attribution 4.0 International (CC BY 4.0) license. As a permanent URL, we also provide our dataset through figshare at https://figshare.com/projects/VQuAnDa/72488. The repository includes the training and test JSON files, where each of them contains the ids, questions, verbalized answers, and the queries.

The sustainability of the resource is guaranteed by the Question and Answering team of the Smart Data Analytics (SDA) research group at the University of Bonn and at Fraunhofer IAIS. A core team of 3 members is committed to taking care of the dataset, with a time horizon of at least 3 years. The dataset is crucial for currently ongoing PhD research and project work, and will, therefore, be maintained and kept up to date.

---

[1] https://github.com/AskNowQA/VQUANDA.

We are planning to have six-months release cycles, regularly updating the dataset based on improvement suggestions and corrections. However, we also plan to further extend VQuAnDa with more verbalization examples. We also aim to make the dataset a community effort, where researchers working in the domain of verbalization can update the data and also include their own evaluation baseline models. VQuAnDa should become an open community effort. Therefore, ESWC is the perfect venue for presenting and sharing this resource.

5   Reusability

The dataset can be used in multiple areas of research. The most suitable one is the knowledge base question answering area, since the initial purpose of the dataset was to support a more reliable QA experience. VQuAnDa allows researchers to train end-to-end models from generating the query, extracting the results and formulating the verbalization answer. Furthermore, the dataset can be used for essential QA subtasks such as entity and predicate recognition/linking, SPARQL query generation and SPARQL to question language generation. These subtasks are already supported by the LC-QuAD dataset. With the verbalizations, researchers can also experiment on tasks such as SPARQL to verbalized answer, question to verbalized answer or even hybrid approaches for generating better results. These possible lines of work indicate that the dataset is also useful for the natural language generation research area.

In summary, the use of the dataset is straightforward and allows researchers to further investigate different fields and discover other possible approaches were KBQA can be done more transparently and efficiently.

5.1   Experiments

To ensure the quality of the dataset but also to support its reuse we decided to perform experiments and provide some baseline models. These baseline models can be used as a reference point by anyone working with the dataset.

The experiments are done for the natural language generation task. We would like to test how easy it is for common neural machine translation or sequence to sequence models to generate the verbalized answers using as input only the question or the SPARQL query. To keep the task simple and because the answers appear only in the output verbalization part, we prefer to hide them with an answer token ($<ans>$). In this way, it will be enough for the model to predict only the position of the answer in the verbalization sentence.

We perform the experiments in two ways – i) the question or SPARQL query will be the input to our models and the expected output will be the correct verbalization; ii) we cover the entities in both input (question or query) and verbalization, so we allow the model to focus on other parts such as the sentence structure and the word relations. For the second experiment approach, we use the EARL framework [13] for recognizing the entities in both the question and answer sentences, and we cover them with an entity token ($<ent>$). For the queries, we can directly cover the entities, since we already know their positions.

As we might expect, not all entities will be recognized correctly, but this can happen with any entity recognition framework and especially with datasets with complex sentences that contain one or multiple entities.

In the following subsections, we provide more details about the baseline models, the evaluation metrics, training details, and the results.

Baseline Models

For the baseline models, we decided to employ some standard sequence to sequence models. We first experiment with two RNN models that use different attention mechanisms [4,22]. For both RNN models we use bidirectional gated recurrent units (Bi-GRU) [10]. Next, we experiment with a convolutional sequence to sequence model, which is based on the original approach [19] where they employ a convolutional neural network (CNN) architecture for machine translation tasks. Finally, we use a transformer neural architecture, which is based on the original paper [33] where they create a simple attention-based sequence to sequence model.

Evaluation Metrics

BLEU: The first evaluation metric we use is the Bilingual Evaluation Understudy (BLEU) score introduced by [26]. The idea of the BLEU score is to count the n-gram overlaps in the reference; it takes the maximum count of each n-gram and it clips the count of the n-grams in the candidate translation to the maximum count in the reference. Essentially, BLEU is a modified version of precision to compare a candidate with a reference. However, candidates with a shorter length than the reference tend to give a higher score, while candidates that are longer are already penalized by the modified n-gram precision. To face this issue a brevity penalty (BP) was introduced, which is 1 if the candidate length c is larger or equal to the reference length r. Otherwise, the brevity penalty is set to $\exp(1 - r/c)$. Finally, a set of positive weights $\{w_1, ..., w_N\}$ is determined to compute the geometric mean of the modified n-gram precisions. The BLEU score is calculated by:

$$BLEU = BP \cdot \exp(\sum_{n=1}^{N} w_n \, log \, p_n), \qquad (1)$$

where N is the number of different n-grams. In our experiments, we employ $N = 4$ and uniform weights $w_n = 1/N$.

Perplexity: To estimate how well our models predict the verbalization we are using the perplexity metric. For measuring the similarity of a target probability distribution p and an estimated probability distribution q, we are using cross entropy $H(p, q)$ which is defined by

$$H(p, q) = - \sum_{x} p(x) \, log \, q(x), \qquad (2)$$

where x indicates the possible values in the distribution. The perplexity is defined as the exponentiation of cross entropy:

$$Perplexity(p, q) = 2^{H(p,q)}. \tag{3}$$

In our case, the target distribution p is the encoding vector of the verbalization vocabulary and q is the prediction output of the decoder. We calculate perplexity after every epoch using the averaged cross entropy loss of the batches. Researchers have shown [23] that perplexity strongly correlates with the performance of machine translation models.

Training

To keep the comparison fair across the models we employ the same training parameters for all. We split the data into 80-10-10 where 80% is used for training, 10% for validation and the last 10% for testing. The batch size is set to 100 and we train for 50 epochs. During the training, we save the model state with the lowest loss on the validation data.

We tried to keep the models almost of the same size regarding their trainable parameters. More precisely, for the first RNN model we use an embedding dimension of 256, the hidden dimension is 512 and we use 2 layers. We also apply dropout with probability 0.5 on both encoder and decoder. For the second RNN model, we keep everything the same except the embedding dimension where we decided to double it to 512. For the convolutional model, we set the embedding dimension to 512, we keep all the channels in the same dimension of 512 and we use a kernel size of 3. We use 3 layers for the encoder and decoder. Similar to RNNs, the dropout here is set to 0.5. Finally, for the transformer model, the embedding dimension is 512, we use 8 heads and 2 layers. The dropout here is set to 0.1. For the first two RNN models we use a teacher forcing value of 1.0 so we can compare the results with the other models.

We do not use any pretrained embedding model. For building the vocabularies we use a simple one-hot encoding approach. For all the models we use Adam optimizer, and cross entropy as a loss function. All our experiments are publicly available here https://github.com/endrikacupaj/VQUANDA-Baseline-Models.

Results

Beginning with the perplexity results, in Table 3 we can see that the convolutional model outperforms all other models and is considered the best. The transformer model comes second and is pretty close to the convolutional. The RNN models perform considerably worse comparing the other two.

Since perplexity is the exponentiation of cross entropy, the lower the value the better the results, which means that the best possible value is 1. The convolutional model using the question as input achieves 4.1 with entities and 3.4 with covered entities on validation and test data. When we use the SPARQL query as input the perplexity gets a lower value, which means the model performs slightly better. In particular, for the convolutional model, we obtain 3.3 with

Table 3. Perplexity experiment results

Models	Input	With entities		Covered entities	
		Validation	Test	Validation	Test
RNN-1 [4]	Question	8.257	8.865	5.709	5.809
	Query	6.823	7.029	5.212	5.335
RNN-2 [22]	Question	8.494	8.802	5.799	5.891
	Query	6.727	6.999	5.259	5.394
Convolutional [19]	Question	**4.137**	**4.194**	**3.409**	**3.451**
	Query	**3.175**	**3.311**	**3.158**	**3.201**
Transformer [33]	Question	5.232	5.464	3.716	3.727
	Query	3.978	4.062	3.229	3.292

Table 4. BLEU score experiment results

Models	Input	With entities		Covered entities	
		Validation	Test	Validation	Test
RNN-1 [4]	Question	14.00	12.86	25.09	24.88
	Query	18.40	17.76	30.74	29.25
RNN-2 [22]	Question	15.53	15.43	27.63	26.95
	Query	22.29	21.33	**34.34**	30.78
Convolutional [19]	Question	**21.49**	**21.30**	28.21	**27.73**
	Query	**26.02**	**25.95**	32.61	**32.39**
Transformer [33]	Question	19.00	18.38	25.67	26.58
	Query	24.16	22.98	31.65	29.14

entities and 3.2 with covered entities on test data. The improved performance using the query as input is expected since the model receives the same pattern of queries every time.

In any case, there is still a lot of space for improvement until we can say that the task is solved. The BLEU score further supports this fact. By looking at Table 4 with the BLEU score results we can see that again the convolutional model performs best with a value of up to 32 with covered entities. Without covering entities the best we get on test data is almost 26, which is not really an adequate result. The best possible value for the BLEU metric is 100. A score of more than 60 is considered a perfect translation that often outperforms humans. For our dataset, there is still a lot of research required until we produce models that can reach these numbers.

5.2   Use by the Community

Currently, we are actively developing and sharing the dataset within the scope of two projects – SOLIDE and CLEOPATRA. The work is very well received, however, our ultimate goal is to make VQuAnDa an open community effort.

SOLIDE[2]. In major disastrous situations such as flooding, emergency services are confronted with a variety of information from different sources. The goal of the SOLIDE project is to analyze and process the information from multiple sources in order to maintain a knowledge graph that captures an overall picture of the situation. Furthermore, using a voice-based interface, users can ask various questions about the ongoing mission, for instance, *"How many units are still available?"*. Given the dangerous circumstances, it is vital to assert the user that the provided answer is complete and sound. Hence, the system needs to verbalize its internal representation of the question (e.g. SPARQL) with the answer as *"There are 2 units with the status available"*. Thus, VQuAnDa is essential for being able to learn a verbalization model as part of the solution framework of the SOLIDE project.

CLEOPATRA ITN[3]. As European countries become more and more integrated, an increasing number of events, such as the Paris shootings and Brexit, strongly affect the European community and the European digital economy across language and country borders. As a result, there is a lot of event-centric multilingual information available from different communities in the news, on the Web and in social media. The Cleopatra ITN project aims to enable effective and efficient analytics of event-centric multilingual information spread across heterogeneous sources and deliver results meaningful to the users. In particular in the context of question answering, Cleopatra advances the current state of the art by enabling user interaction with event-centric multilingual information. Considering this challenge, the VQuAnDa dataset serves as a basis for learning a question answering model, while the verbalizations are employed to enhance the interactivity of the system.

In addition to using the dataset in order to conduct research and enable the work within projects, we also use it for teaching purposes. VQuAnDa and pre-trained models are given to the students so that they can try out machine learning approaches by themselves and evaluate the produced results by looking at the quality of the generated verbalizations. While the dataset already has a solid level of reuse, we see great potential for further adoption by the Semantic Web community, especially in the areas of applied and fundamental QA research.

6   Conclusion and Future Work

We introduce VQuAnDa – the first QA dataset including the verbalizations of answers in natural language. We complement the dataset by a framework for

---

[2] http://solide-projekt.de.
[3] http://cleopatra-project.eu/.

automatically generating the verbalizations, given the input question and the corresponding SPARQL query. Finally, we also share a set of evaluation baselines, based on a set of standard sequence to sequence models, which can serve to determine the accuracy of machine learning approaches used to verbalize the answers of QA systems. Without a doubt, the dataset presents a very valuable contribution to the community, providing the foundation for multiple lines of research in the QA domain.

As part of future work, we plan to develop an end-to-end model that will use the question to obtain the correct answer and at the same time to generate the correct verbalization. Moreover, we would like to focus on the verbalization part by researching possible models that can improve the results. The baseline models we used for the dataset receive as input the question or the query. We assume that a hybrid approach can make the model benefit from both input types and possibly produce better results. Finally, we will also work on continuously extending and improving VQuAnDa.

Acknowledgments. This work was supported by the European Union H2020 founded project CLEOPATRA (ITN, GA. 812997).

References

1. Abdelkawi, A., Zafar, H., Maleshkova, M., Lehmann, J.: Complex query augmentation for question answering over knowledge graphs. In: Panetto, H., Debruyne, C., Hepp, M., Lewis, D., Ardagna, C.A., Meersman, R. (eds.) OTM 2019. LNCS, vol. 11877, pp. 571–587. Springer, Cham (2019). https://doi.org/10.1007/978-3-030-33246-4_36
2. Abujabal, A., Roy, R.S., Yahya, M., Weikum, G.: ComQa: a community-sourced dataset for complex factoid question answering with paraphrase clusters. arXiv preprint arXiv:1809.09528 (2018)
3. Azmy, M., Shi, P., Lin, J., Ilyas, I.: Farewell freebase: migrating the simple questions dataset to DBpedia. In: Proceedings of the 27th International Conference on Computational Linguistics, pp. 2093–2103 (2018)
4. Bahdanau, D., Cho, K., Bengio, Y.: Neural machine translation by jointly learning to align and translate. arXiv e-prints arXiv:1409.0473, September 2014
5. Bao, J., Duan, N., Yan, Z., Zhou, M., Zhao, T.: Constraint-based question answering with knowledge graph. In: Proceedings of COLING 2016, the 26th International Conference on Computational Linguistics: Technical Papers, pp. 2503–2514 (2016)
6. Berant, J., Chou, A., Frostig, R., Liang, P.: Semantic parsing on freebase from question-answer pairs. In: Proceedings of the 2013 Conference on Empirical Methods in Natural Language Processing, pp. 1533–1544 (2013)
7. Bollacker, K., Evans, C., Paritosh, P., Sturge, T., Taylor, J.: Freebase: a collaboratively created graph database for structuring human knowledge. In: Proceedings of the 2008 ACM SIGMOD International Conference on Management of Data (2008)
8. Bordes, A., Usunier, N., Chopra, S., Weston, J.: Large-scale simple question answering with memory networks. arXiv preprint arXiv:1506.02075 (2015)
9. Cai, Q., Yates, A.: Large-scale semantic parsing via schema matching and Lexicon extension. In: Proceedings of the 51st Annual Meeting of the Association for Computational Linguistics (2013)

10. Cho, K., et al.: Learning phrase representations using RNN encoder-decoder for statistical machine translation. arXiv e-prints arXiv:1406.1078, June 2014
11. Diefenbach, D., Dridi, Y., Singh, K., Maret, P.: SPARQLtoUser: did the question answering system understand me? (2017)
12. Dubey, M., Banerjee, D., Abdelkawi, A., Lehmann, J.: LC-QuAD 2.0: a large dataset for complex question answering over Wikidata and DBpedia. In: Ghidini, C., et al. (eds.) ISWC 2019. LNCS, vol. 11779, pp. 69–78. Springer, Cham (2019). https://doi.org/10.1007/978-3-030-30796-7_5
13. Dubey, M., Banerjee, D., Chaudhuri, D., Lehmann, J.: EARL: joint entity and relation linking for question answering over knowledge graphs. In: Vrandečić, D., et al. (eds.) ISWC 2018. LNCS, vol. 11136, pp. 108–126. Springer, Cham (2018). https://doi.org/10.1007/978-3-030-00671-6_7
14. Dubey, M., Dasgupta, S., Sharma, A., Höffner, K., Lehmann, J.: AskNow: a framework for natural language query formalization in SPARQL. In: Sack, H., Blomqvist, E., d'Aquin, M., Ghidini, C., Ponzetto, S.P., Lange, C. (eds.) ESWC 2016. LNCS, vol. 9678, pp. 300–316. Springer, Cham (2016). https://doi.org/10.1007/978-3-319-34129-3_19
15. Ell, B., Harth, A., Simperl, E.: SPARQL query verbalization for explaining semantic search engine queries. In: Presutti, V., d'Amato, C., Gandon, F., d'Aquin, M., Staab, S., Tordai, A. (eds.) ESWC 2014. LNCS, vol. 8465, pp. 426–441. Springer, Cham (2014). https://doi.org/10.1007/978-3-319-07443-6_29
16. Eric, M., Manning, C.D.: Key-value retrieval networks for task-oriented dialogue. arXiv preprint arXiv:1705.05414 (2017)
17. Ernst, P., Meng, C., Siu, A., Weikum, G.: KnowLife: a knowledge graph for health and life sciences. In: 2014 IEEE 30th International Conference on Data Engineering (2014)
18. Ferré, S.: SPARKLIS: an expressive query builder for SPARQL endpoints with guidance in natural language. Semant. Web 8(3), 405–418 (2017)
19. Gehring, J., Auli, M., Grangier, D., Yarats, D., Dauphin, Y.N.: Convolutional sequence to sequence learning. arXiv e-prints arXiv:1705.03122, May 2017
20. Jiang, K., Wu, D., Jiang, H.: FreebaseQA: a new factoid QA data set matching Trivia-style question-answer pairs with freebase. In: Proceedings of the 2019 Conference of the North American Chapter of the Association for Computational Linguistics (2019)
21. Lehmann, J., et al.: DBpedia - a large-scale, multilingual knowledge base extracted from Wikipedia. Semant. Web J. 6, 167–195 (2015)
22. Luong, M.T., Pham, H., Manning, C.D.: Effective approaches to attention-based neural machine translation. arXiv e-prints arXiv:1508.04025, August 2015
23. Luong, T., Kayser, M., Manning, C.D.: Deep neural language models for machine translation. In: Proceedings of the 19th Conference on Computational Natural Language Learning, Beijing, China. Association for Computational Linguistics (2015)
24. Ngonga Ngomo, A.C., Bühmann, L., Unger, C., Lehmann, J., Gerber, D.: SPARQL2NL: verbalizing SPARQL queries. In: Proceedings of the 22nd International Conference on World Wide Web, pp. 329–332. ACM (2013)
25. Chakraborty, N., Lukovnikov, D., Maheshwari, G., Trivedi, P., Lehmann, J., Fischer, A.: Introduction to neural network based approaches for question answering over knowledge graphs (2019)
26. Papineni, K., Roukos, S., Ward, T., Zhu, W.J.: BLEU: a method for automatic evaluation of machine translation. In: Proceedings of the 40th Annual Meeting of the Association for Computational Linguistics (2002)

27. Saha, A., Pahuja, V., Khapra, M.M., Sankaranarayanan, K., Chandar, S.: Complex sequential question answering: towards learning to converse over linked question answer pairs with a knowledge graph. In: Thirty-Second AAAI Conference (2018)
28. Serban, I.V., et al.: Generating factoid questions with recurrent neural networks: the 30m factoid question-answer corpus. arXiv preprint arXiv:1603.06807 (2016)
29. Su, Y., et al.: On generating characteristic-rich question sets for QA evaluation. In: Proceedings of the 2016 Conference on Empirical Methods in Natural Language Processing (2016)
30. Talmor, A., Berant, J.: The web as a knowledge-base for answering complex questions. arXiv preprint arXiv:1803.06643 (2018)
31. Trivedi, P., Maheshwari, G., Dubey, M., Lehmann, J.: LC-QuAD: a corpus for complex question answering over knowledge graphs. In: d'Amato, C., et al. (eds.) ISWC 2017. LNCS, vol. 10588, pp. 210–218. Springer, Cham (2017). https://doi. org/10.1007/978-3-319-68204-4_22
32. Unger, C., Bühmann, L., Lehmann, J., Ngonga Ngomo, A.C., Gerber, D., Cimiano, P.: Template-based question answering over RDF data. In: Proceedings of the 21st International Conference on World Wide Web, pp. 639–648. ACM (2012)
33. Vaswani, A., et al.: Attention is all you need. arXiv e-prints arXiv:1706.03762
34. Vrandečić, D., Krötzsch, M.: Wikidata: a free collaborative knowledge base (2014)
35. Yih, W.t., Richardson, M., Meek, C., Chang, M.W., Suh, J.: The value of semantic parse labeling for knowledge base question answering. In: Proceedings of the 54th Annual Meeting of the Association for Computational Linguistics (2016)
36. Zheng, W., Cheng, H., Zou, L., Yu, J.X., Zhao, K.: Natural language question/answering: let users talk with the knowledge graph. In: Proceedings of the 2017 ACM on Conference on Information and Knowledge Management (2017)

ESBM: An Entity Summarization BenchMark

Qingxia Liu[1], Gong Cheng[1(✉)], Kalpa Gunaratna[2], and Yuzhong Qu[1]

[1] National Key Laboratory for Novel Software Technology, Nanjing University, Nanjing, China
qxliu2013@smail.nju.edu.cn, {gcheng,yzqu}@nju.edu.cn
[2] Samsung Research America, Mountain View, CA, USA
k.gunaratna@samsung.com

Abstract. Entity summarization is the problem of computing an optimal compact summary for an entity by selecting a size-constrained subset of triples from RDF data. Entity summarization supports a multiplicity of applications and has led to fruitful research. However, there is a lack of evaluation efforts that cover the broad spectrum of existing systems. One reason is a lack of benchmarks for evaluation. Some benchmarks are no longer available, while others are small and have limitations. In this paper, we create an Entity Summarization BenchMark (ESBM) which overcomes the limitations of existing benchmarks and meets standard desiderata for a benchmark. Using this largest available benchmark for evaluating general-purpose entity summarizers, we perform the most extensive experiment to date where 9 existing systems are compared. Considering that all of these systems are unsupervised, we also implement and evaluate a supervised learning based system for reference.

Keywords: Entity summarization · Triple ranking · Benchmarking

1 Introduction

RDF data describes entities with triples representing property values. In an RDF dataset, the description of an entity comprises all the RDF triples where the entity appears as the subject or the object. An example entity description is shown in Fig. 1. Entity descriptions can be large. An entity may be described in dozens or hundreds of triples, exceeding the capacity of a typical user interface. A user served with all of those triples may suffer information overload and find it difficult to quickly identify the small set of triples that are truly needed. To solve the problem, an established research topic is *entity summarization* [15], which aims to compute an optimal compact summary for the entity by selecting a size-constrained subset of triples. An example entity summary under the size constraint of 5 triples is shown in the bottom right corner of Fig. 1.

© Springer Nature Switzerland AG 2020
A. Harth et al. (Eds.): ESWC 2020, LNCS 12123, pp. 548–564, 2020.
https://doi.org/10.1007/978-3-030-49461-2_32

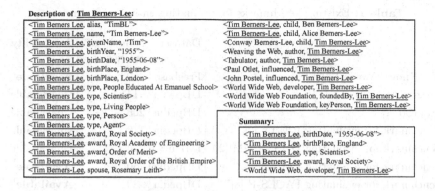

Fig. 1. Description of entity `Tim Berners-Lee` and a summary thereof.

Entity summarization supports a multiplicity of applications [6,21]. Entity summaries constitute entity cards displayed in search engines [9], provide background knowledge for enriching documents [26], and facilitate research activities with humans in the loop [3,4]. This far-reaching application has led to fruitful research as reviewed in our recent survey paper [15]. Many entity summarizers have been developed, most of which generate summaries for general purposes.

Research Challenges. However, two challenges face the research community. First, there is a *lack of benchmarks* for evaluating entity summarizers. As shown in Table 1, some benchmarks are no longer available. Others are available [7,8,22] but they are small and have limitations. Specifically, [22] has a task-specific nature, and [7,8] exclude classes and/or literals. These benchmarks could not support a comprehensive evaluation of general-purpose entity summarizers. Second, there is a *lack of evaluation efforts* that cover the broad spectrum of existing systems to compare their performance and assist practitioners in choosing solutions appropriate to their applications.

Contributions. We address the challenges with two contributions. First, we create an **E**ntity **S**ummarization **B**enchMark (ESBM) which overcomes the limitations of existing benchmarks and meets the desiderata for a successful benchmark [18]. ESBM has been published on GitHub with extended documentation and a permanent identifier on `w3id.org`[1] under the ODC-By license. As the largest available benchmark for evaluating general-purpose entity summarizers, ESBM contains 175 heterogeneous entities sampled from two datasets, for which 30 human experts create 2,100 general-purpose ground-truth summaries under two size constraints. Second, using ESBM, we evaluate 9 existing general-purpose entity summarizers. It represents the most extensive evaluation effort to date. Considering that existing systems are unsupervised, we also implement and evaluate a supervised learning based entity summarizer for reference.

In this paper, for the first time we comprehensively describe the creation and use of ESBM. We report ESBM v1.2—the latest version, while early

---

[1] https://w3id.org/esbm.

Table 1. Existing benchmarks for evaluating entity summarization.

	Dataset	Number of entities	Availability
WhoKnows?Movies! [22]	Freebase	60	**Available**[a]
Langer et al. [13]	DBpedia	14	Unavailable
FRanCo [1]	DBpedia	265	Unavailable
Benchmark for evaluating RELIN [2]	DBpedia	149	Unavailable
Benchmark for evaluating DIVERSUM [20]	IMDb	20	Unavailable
Benchmark for evaluating FACES [7]	DBpedia	50	**Available**[b]
Benchmark for evaluating FACES-E [8]	DBpedia	80	**Available**[b]

[a] http://yovisto.com/labs/iswc2012
[b] http://wiki.knoesis.org/index.php/FACES

versions have successfully supported the entity summarization shared task at the EYRE 2018 workshop[2] and the EYRE 2019 workshop.[3] We will also educate on the use of ESBM at an ESWC 2020 tutorial on entity summarization[4].

The remainder of the paper is organized as follows. Section 2 reviews related work and limitations of existing benchmarks. Section 3 describes the creation of ESBM, which is analyzed in Sect. 4. Section 5 presents our evaluation. In Sect. 6 we discuss limitations of our study and perspectives for future work.

2   Related Work

We review methods and evaluation efforts for entity summarization.

Methods for Entity Summarization. In a recent survey [15] we have categorized the broad spectrum of research on entity summarization. Below we briefly review *general-purpose* entity summarizers which mainly rely on generic technical features that can apply to a wide range of domains and applications. We will not address methods that are domain-specific (e.g., for movies [25] or timelines [5]), task-specific (e.g., for facilitating entity resolution [3] or entity linking [4]), or context-aware (e.g., contextualized by a document [26] or a query [9]).

RELIN [2] uses a weighted PageRank model to rank triples according to their statistical informativeness and relatedness. DIVERSUM [20] ranks triples by property frequency and generates a summary with a strong constraint that avoids selecting triples having the same property. SUMMARUM [24] and LinkSUM [23] mainly rank triples by the PageRank scores of property values that are entities. LinkSUM also considers backlinks from values. FACES [7], and its extension FACES-E [8] which adds support for literals, cluster triples by their bag-of-words based similarity and choose top-ranked triples from as many different clusters as

---

[2] https://sites.google.com/view/eyre18/sharedtasks.
[3] https://sites.google.com/view/eyre19/sharedtasks.
[4] https://sites.google.com/view/entity-summarization-tutorials/eswc2020.

possible. Triples are ranked by statistical informativeness and property value frequency. CD [28] models entity summarization as a quadratic knapsack problem that maximizes the statistical informativeness of the selected triples and in the meantime minimizes the string, numerical, and logical similarity between them. In ES-LDA [17], ES-LDA$_{ext}$ [16], and MPSUM [27], a Latent Dirichlet Allocation (LDA) model is learned where properties are treated as topics, and each property is a distribution over all the property values. Triples are ranked by the probabilities of properties and values. MPSUM further avoids selecting triples having the same property. BAFREC [12] categorizes triples into meta-level and data-level. It ranks meta-level triples by their depths in an ontology and ranks data-level triples by property and value frequency. Triples having textually similar properties are penalized to improve diversity. KAFCA [11] ranks triples by the depths of properties and values in a hierarchy constructed by performing the Formal Concept Analysis (FCA). It tends to select triples containing infrequent properties but frequent values, where frequency is computed at the word level.

Limitations of Existing Benchmarks. For evaluating entity summarization, compared with task completion based *extrinsic evaluation*, ground truth based *intrinsic evaluation* is more popular because it is easy to perform and the results are reproducible. Its idea is to create a benchmark consisting of human-made ground-truth summaries, and then compute how much a machine-generated summary is close to a ground-truth summary.

Table 1 lists known benchmarks, including dedicated benchmarks [1,13,22] and those created for evaluating a particular entity summarizer [2,7,8,20]. It is not surprising that these benchmarks are not very large since it is expensive to manually create high-quality summaries for a large set of entities. Unfortunately, some of these benchmarks are not publicly available at this moment. Three are available [7,8,22] but they are relatively small and have limitations. Specifically, WhoKnows?Movies! [22] is not a set of ground-truth summaries but annotates each triple with the ratio of movie questions that were correctly answered based on that triple, as an indicator of its importance. This kind of task-specific ground truth may not be suitable for evaluating general-purpose entity summarizers. The other two available benchmarks were created for evaluating FACES/-E [7,8]. Classes and/or literals are not included because they could not be processed by FACES/-E and hence were filtered out. Such benchmarks could not comprehensively evaluate most of the existing entity summarizers [2,11,12,20,27,28] that can handle classes and literals. These limitations of available benchmarks motivated us to create a new ground truth consisting of *general-purpose summaries* for a *larger set of entities* involving *more comprehensive triples* where property values can be entities, classes, or literals.

3   Creating ESBM

To overcome the above-mentioned limitations of existing benchmarks, we created a new benchmark called ESBM. To date, it is the largest available benchmark for evaluating general-purpose entity summarizers. In this section, we will first specify our design goals. Then we describe the selection of entity descriptions and the creation of ground-truth summaries. We partition the data to support cross-validation for parameter fitting. Finally we summarize how our design goals are achieved and how ESBM meets standard desiderata for a benchmark.

3.1 Design Goals

The creation of ESBM has two main design goals. First, a successful benchmark should meet seven desiderata [18]: accessibility, affordability, clarity, relevance, solvability, portability, and scalability, which we will detail in Sect. 3.5. Our design of ESBM aims to satisfy these basic requirements. Second, in Sect. 2 we discussed the limitations of available benchmarks, including task specificness, small size, and triple incomprehensiveness. Besides, all the existing benchmarks use a single dataset and hence may weaken the generalizability of evaluation results. We aim to overcome these limitations when creating ESBM. In Sect. 3.5 we will summarize how our design goals are achieved.

3.2 Entity Descriptions

To choose entity descriptions to summarize, we sample entities from selected datasets and filter their triples. The process is detailed below.

Datasets. We sample entities from two datasets of different kinds: an encyclopedic dataset and a domain-specific dataset. For the encyclopedic dataset we choose DBpedia [14], which has been used in other benchmarks [1,2,7,8,13]. We use the English version of DBpedia 2015-10[5]—the latest version when we started to create ESBM. For the domain-specific dataset we choose LinkedMDB [10], which is a popular movie database. The movie domain is also the focus of some existing benchmarks [20,22] possibly because this domain is familiar to the lay audience so that it would be easy to find qualified human experts to create ground-truth summaries. We use the latest available version of LinkedMDB.[6]

Entities. For DBpedia we sample entities from five large classes: Agent, Event, Location, Species, and Work. They collectively contain 3,501,366 entities (60%) in the dataset. For LinkedMDB we sample from Film and Person, which contain 159,957 entities (24%) in the dataset. Entities from different classes are described by very different properties as we will see in Sect. 4.3, and hence help to assess the generalizability of an entity summarizer. According to the human efforts we could afford, from each class we randomly sample 25 entities. The total number of selected entities is 175. Each selected entity should be described in at least 20 triples so that summarization would not be a trivial task. This requirement follows common practice in the literature [1,2,7,20] where a minimum constraint in the range of 10–20 was posed.

---

[5] http://wiki.dbpedia.org/dbpedia-dataset-version-2015-10.

[6] http://www.cs.toronto.edu/~oktie/linkedmdb/linkedmdb-latest-dump.zip.

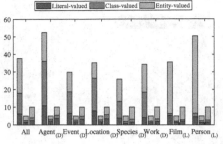
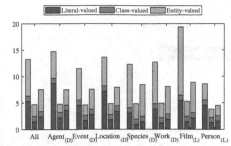

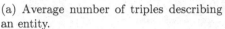

(a) Average number of triples describing an entity.   (b) Average number of distinct properties describing an entity.

Fig. 2. Composition of entity descriptions (the left bar in each group), top-5 ground-truth summaries (the middle bar), and top-10 ground-truth summaries (the right bar), grouped by class in DBpedia (D) and LinkedMDB (L).

Triples. For DBpedia, entity descriptions comprise triples in the following dump files: *instance types, instance types transitive, YAGO types, mappingbased literals, mappingbased objects, labels, images, homepages, persondata, geo coordinates mappingbased,* and *article categories.* We do not import dump files that provide metadata about Wikipedia articles such as *page links* and *page length.* We do not import *short abstracts* and *long abstracts* as they provide handcrafted textual entity summaries; it would be inappropriate to include them in a benchmark for evaluating entity summarization. For LinkedMDB we import all the triples in the dump file except **sameAs** links which do not express facts about entities but are of more technical nature. Finally, as shown in Fig. 2a (the left bar in each group), the mean number of triples in an entity description is in the range of 25.88–52.44 depending on the class, and the overall mean value is 37.62.

3.3   Ground-Truth Summaries

We invite 30 researchers and students to create ground-truth summaries for entity descriptions. All the participants are familiar with RDF.

Task Assignment. Each participant is assigned 35 entities consisting of 5 entities randomly selected from each of the 7 classes in ESBM. The assignment is controlled to ensure that each entity in ESBM is processed by 6 participants. A participant creates two summaries for each entity description by selecting different numbers of triples: a *top-5 summary* containing 5 triples, and a *top-10 summary* containing 10 triples. Therefore, we will be able to evaluate entity summarizers under different size constraints. The choice of these two numbers follows previous work [2,7,8]. Participants work independently and they may create different summaries for an entity. It is not feasible to ask participants to reach an agreement. It is also not reasonable to merge different summaries into a single version. So we keep different summaries and will use all of them in the evaluation. The total number of ground-truth summaries is $175 \cdot 6 \cdot 2 = 2,100$.

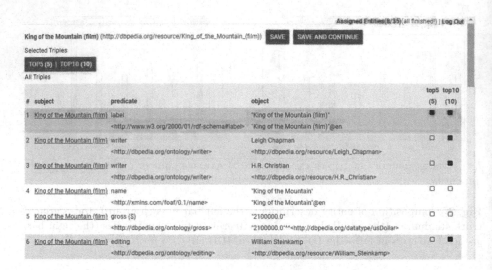

Fig. 3. User interface for creating ground-truth entity summaries.

Procedure. Participants are instructed to create *general-purpose summaries* that are not specifically created for any particular task. They read and select triples using a Web-based user interface shown in Fig. 3. All the triples in an entity description are listed in random order but those having a common property are placed together for convenient reading and comparison. For IRIs, their human-readable labels (`rdfs:label`) are shown if available. To help participants understand a property value that is an unfamiliar entity, a click on it will open a pop-up showing a short textual description extracted from the first paragraph of its Wikipedia/IMDb page. Any triple can be selected into the top-5 summary, the top-10 summary, or both. The top-5 summary is not required to be a subset of the top-10 summary.

3.4 Training, Validation, and Test Sets

Some entity summarizers need to tune hyperparameters or fit models. To make their evaluation results comparable with each other, we specify a split of our data into training, validation, and test sets. We provide a partition of the 175 entities in ESBM into 5 equally sized subsets $P_0, \ldots, P_4$ to support 5-fold cross-validation. Entities of each class are partitioned evenly among the subsets. For $0 \leq i \leq 4$, the i-th fold uses $P_i, P_{i+1 \bmod 5}, P_{i+2 \bmod 5}$ as the training set (e.g., for model fitting), uses $P_{i+3 \bmod 5}$ for validation (e.g., tuning hyperparameters), and retains $P_{i+4 \bmod 5}$ as the test set. Evaluation results are averaged over the 5 folds.

3.5 Conclusion

ESBM overcomes the limitations of available benchmarks discussed in Sect. 2. It contains 175 entities which is 2–3 times as large as available benchmarks [7,8,22].

In ESBM, property values are not filtered as in [7,8] but can be any entity, class, or literal. Different from the task-specific nature of [22], ESBM provides general-purpose ground-truth summaries for evaluating general-purpose entity summarizers.

Besides, ESBM meets the seven desiderata proposed in [18] as follows.

- **Accessibility.** ESBM is publicly available and has a permanent identifier on w3id.org.
- **Affordability.** ESBM is with an open-source program and example code for evaluation. The cost of using ESBM is minimized.
- **Clarity.** ESBM is documented clearly and concisely.
- **Relevance.** ESBM samples entities from two real datasets that have been widely used. The summarization tasks are natural and representative.
- **Solvability.** An entity description in ESBM has at least 20 triples and a mean number of 37.62 triples, from which 5 or 10 triples are to be selected. The summarization tasks are not trivial and not too difficult.
- **Portability.** ESBM can be used to evaluate any general-purpose entity summarizer that can process RDF data.
- **Scalability.** ESBM samples 175 entities from 7 classes. It is reasonably large and diverse to evaluate mature entity summarizers but is not too large to evaluate research prototypes.

However, ESBM has its own limitations, which we will discuss in Sect. 6.

4 Analyzing ESBM

In this section, we will first characterize ESBM by providing some basic statistics and analyzing the triple composition and heterogeneity of entity descriptions. Then we compute inter-rater agreement to show how much consensus exists in the ground-truth summaries given by different participants.

4.1 Basic Statistics

The 175 entity descriptions in ESBM collectively contain 6,584 triples, of which 37.44% are selected into at least one top-5 summary and 58.15% appear in at least one top-10 summary, showing a wide selection by the participants. However, many of them are selected only by a single participant; 20.46% and 40.23% are selected by different participants into top-5 and top-10 summaries, respectively. We will further analyze inter-rater agreement in Sect. 4.4.

We calculate the overlap between the top-5 and the top-10 summaries created by the same participant for the same entity. The mean overlap is in the range of 4.80–4.99 triples depending on the class, and the overall mean value is 4.91, showing that the top-5 summary is usually a subset of the top-10 summary.

4.2   Triple Composition

In Fig. 2 we present the composition of entity descriptions (the left bar in each group) and their ground-truth summaries (the middle bar for top-5 and the right bar for top-10) in ESBM, in terms of the average number of triples describing an entity (Fig. 2a) and in terms of the average number of distinct properties describing an entity (Fig. 2b). Properties are divided into literal-valued, class-valued, and entity-valued. Triples are divided accordingly.

In Fig. 2a, both class-valued and entity-valued triples occupy a considerable proportion of the entity descriptions in DBpedia. Entity-valued triples predominate in LinkedMDB. Literal-valued triples account for a small proportion in both datasets. However, they constitute 30% in top-5 ground-truth summaries and 25% in top-10 summaries. Entity summarizers that cannot process literals [7,17,23,24] have to ignore these notable proportions, thereby significantly influencing their performance.

DBpedia

	Work	Species	Location	Event
Agent	0.088	0.065	0.066	0.081
Event	0.089	0.090	0.102	
Location	0.090	0.077		
Species	0.087			

LinkedMDB

	Film
Person	0.085

Fig. 4. Jaccard similarity between property sets describing different classes.

Table 2. Popular properties in ground-truth summaries.

In top-5 summaries							In top-10 summaries						
Agent	Event	Location	Species	Work	Film	Person	Agent	Event	Location	Species	Work	Film	Person
type	type	type	type	type	director	type	type	type	type	family	type	director	type
birthDate	date	country	family		type	actor	subject	subject	country	type	subject	actor	actor
							birthDate	date	subject	order	genre	type	label
							label			class		writer	page
										genus		producer	
										subject		date	
										kingdom		language	

In Fig. 2b, in terms of distinct properties, entity-valued and literal-valued triples have comparable numbers in entity descriptions since many entity-valued properties are multi-valued. Specifically, an entity is described by 13.24 distinct properties, including 5.31 literal-valued (40%) and 6.93 entity-valued (52%). Multi-valued properties appear in every entity description and they constitute 35% of the triples. However, in top-5 ground-truth summaries, the average number of distinct properties is 4.70 and is very close to 5, indicating that the participants are not inclined to select multiple values of a property. Entity summarizers that prefer diverse properties [7,8,12,20,27,28] may exhibit good performance.

4.3   Entity Heterogeneity

Entities from different classes are described by different sets of properties. For each class we identify the set of properties describing at least one entity from the class. The Jaccard similarity between properties sets for each pair of classes is very low, as shown in Fig. 4. Such heterogeneous entity descriptions help to assess the generalizability of an entity summarizer.

Table 2 shows popular properties that appear in at least 50% of the ground-truth summaries for each class. Some universal properties like `rdf:type` and `dct:subject` are popular for most classes. We also see class-specific properties, e.g., `dbo:birthDate` for `Agent`, `dbo:family` for `Species`. However, the results suggest that it would be unrealistic to generate good summaries by manually selecting properties for each class. For example, among 13.24 distinct properties describing an entity, only 1–2 are popular in top-5 ground-truth summaries. The importance of properties is generally contextualized by concrete entities.

4.4   Inter-rater Agreement

Recall that each entity in ESBM has six top-5 ground-truth summaries and six top-10 summaries created by different participants. We calculate the average overlap between these summaries in terms of the number of common triples they contain. As shown in Table 3, the results are generally comparable with those reported for other benchmarks in the literature. There is a moderate degree of agreement between the participants.

Table 3. Inter-rater agreement.

	ESBM	[2]	[7]	[8]
Overlap between top-5 summaries	1.99 (39.8%)	2.91 (58.2%)	1.92 (38.4%)	2.12 (42.4%)
Overlap between top-10 summaries	5.42 (54.2%)	7.86 (78.6%)	4.64 (46.4%)	5.44 (54.4%)
Ground-truth summaries per entity	6	4.43	≥7	≥4

5   Evaluating with ESBM

We used ESBM to perform the most extensive evaluation of general-purpose entity summarizers to date. In this section, we will first describe evaluation criteria. Then we introduce the entity summarizers that we evaluate. Finally we present evaluation results.

5.1   Evaluation Criteria

Let S_m be a machine-generated entity summary. Let S_h be a human-made ground-truth summary. To compare S_m with S_h and assess the quality of S_m based on how much S_m is close to S_h, it is natural to compute precision (P), recall (R), and F1. The results are in the range of 0–1:

$$P = \frac{|S_m \cap S_h|}{|S_m|}, \quad R = \frac{|S_m \cap S_h|}{|S_h|}, \quad F1 = \frac{2 \cdot P \cdot R}{P + R}. \tag{1}$$

In the experiments we configure entity summarizers to output at most k triples and we set $k = |S_h|$, i.e., $k = 5$ and $k = 10$ are our two settings corresponding to the sizes of ground-truth summaries. We will trivially have P=R=F1 if $|S_m| = |S_h|$. However, some entity summarizers may output less than k triples. For example, DIVERSUM [20] disallows an entity summary to contain triples having the same property. It is possible that an entity description contains less than k distinct properties and hence DIVERSUM has to output less than k triples. In this case, $P \neq R$ and one should rely on F1.

In the evaluation, for each entity in ESBM, we compare a machine-generated summary with each of the 6 ground-truth summaries by calculating F1, and take their aggregation value. Finally we report the mean F1 over all the entities. For aggregation function, we report the results of average, to show an overall match with all the different ground truths; on the website we also give the results of maximum, to show the best match with each individual ground truth.

5.2   Participating Entity Summarizers

We not only evaluate existing entity summarizers but also compare them with two special entity summarizers we create: an oracle entity summarizer which is used to show the best possible performance on ESBM, and a new supervised learning based entity summarizer.

Existing Entity Summarizers. We evaluate 9 out of the 12 general-purpose entity summarizers reviewed in Sect. 2. We re-implement RELIN [2], DIVER-SUM [20], LinkSUM [23], FACES [7], FACES-E [8], and CD [28], while MPSUM [27], BAFREC [12], and KAFCA [11] are open source. We exclude SUMMARUM [24], ES-LDA [17], and ES-LDA$_{ext}$ [16] because LinkSUM represents an extension of SUMMARUM, and MPSUM represents an extension of ES-LDA and ES-LDA$_{ext}$.

We follow the original implementation and suggested configuration of existing entity summarizers as far as possible. However, for RELIN, we replace its Google-based relatedness measure with a string metric [19] because Google's search API is no longer free. We also use this metric to replace the unavailable UMBC's SimService used in FACES-E. For DIVERSUM, we ignore its witness count measure since it does not apply to ESBM. For LinkSUM, we obtain backlinks between entities in LinkedMDB via their corresponding entities in DBpedia.

RELIN, CD, and LinkSUM compute a weighted combination of two scoring components. We tune these hyperparameters in the range of 0–1 in 0.01 increments. Since these summarizers are unsupervised, we use both the training set and the validation set described in Sect. 3.4 for tuning hyperparameters.

Oracle Entity Summarizer. We implement an entity summarizer denoted by ORACLE to approximate the best possible performance on ESBM and form a reference point used for comparisons. ORACLE simply outputs k triples that are selected by the most participants into ground-truth summaries.

Supervised Learning Based Entity Summarizer. Existing general-purpose entity summarizers are unsupervised. We implement a supervised learning based entity summarizer with features that are used by existing entity summarizers. A triple with property p and value v describing entity e is represented by the following features:

- gf_T: the number of triples in the dataset where p appears [12,23],
- lf: the number of triples in the description of e where p appears [20,23],
- vf_T: the number of triples in the dataset where v appears [7,8,12], and
- si: the self-information of the triple [2,7,8,28].

We also add three binary features:

- isC: whether v is a class,
- isE: whether v is an entity, and
- isL: whether v is a literal.

Based on the training and validation sets described in Sect. 3.4, we implement and tune 6 pointwise learning to rank models provided by Weka: SMOreg, LinearRegression, MultilayerPerceptron, AdditiveRegression, REPTree, and RandomForest. Each model outputs k top-ranked triples as a summary.

5.3 Evaluation Results

We first report the overall evaluation results to show which entity summarizer generally performs better. Then we break down the results into different entity types (i.e., classes) for detailed comparison. Finally we present and analyze the performance of our supervised learning based entity summarizer.

Overall Results of Existing Entity Summarizers. Table 4 presents the results of all the participating entity summarizers on two datasets under two size constraints. We compare nine existing summarizers using one-way ANOVA post-hoc LSD and we show whether the difference between each pair of them is statistical significant at the 0.05 level. Among existing summarizers, BAFREC achieves the highest F1 under $k = 5$. It significantly outperforms six existing summarizers on DBpedia and outperforms all the eight ones on LinkedMDB. It is also among the best under $k = 10$. MPSUM follows BAFREC under $k = 5$ but performs slightly better under $k = 10$. Other top-tier results belong to KAFCA on DBpedia and FACES-E on LinkedMDB.

Table 4. Average F1 over all the entities in a dataset. For the nine existing entity summarizers, significant improvements and losses over each other are indicated by ▲ and ▼ ($p < 0.05$), respectively. Insignificant differences are indicated by ○.

	DBpedia		LinkedMDB	
	$k = 5$	$k = 10$	$k = 5$	$k = 10$
RELIN	0.242 -○○▼▼▼▼▼▼	0.455 -▼○○▼○▼▼▼	0.203 -○○▼○▲▼○▼	0.258 -▼○▼▼○▼▼▼
DIVERSUM	0.249 ○-○○▼▼▼▼▼	0.507 ▲-▲○○○○○○	0.207 ○-○▼○▲▼○▼	0.358 ▲-▲○○▲▼○▼
FACES	0.270 ○○-○○○▼▼▼	0.428 ○▼-▼▼▼▼▼▼	0.169 ○○-▼▼○▼▼▼	0.263 ○▼-▼▼○▼▼▼
FACES-E	0.280 ▲○○-○○▼▼▼	0.488 ○○▲-○○○○○	0.313 ▲▲▲-▲▲▼▲○	0.393 ▲○▲-▲▲○○○
CD	0.283 ▲▲○○-○▼○○	0.513 ▲○▲○-○○○○	0.217 ○○▲▼-▲▼○▼	0.331 ▲○▲▼-▲▼▼▼
LinkSUM	0.287 ▲▲○○○-▼○○	0.486 ○○▲○○-○○○	0.140 ▼▼○▼▼-▼▼▼	0.279 ○▼○▼▼-▼▼▼
BAFREC	0.335 ▲▲▲▲▲▲-○○	0.503 ▲○▲○○○-○○	0.360 ▲▲▲▲▲▲-▲▲	0.402 ▲▲▲○▲▲-○○
KAFCA	0.314 ▲▲▲▲○○○-○	0.509 ▲○▲○○○○-○	0.244 ○○▲▼○▲▼-○	0.397 ▲○▲○▲▲○-○
MPSUM	0.314 ▲▲▲▲○○○○-	0.512 ▲○▲○○○○○-	0.272 ▲▲▲○▲▲▼○-	0.423 ▲▲▲○▲▲○○-
ORACLE	0.595	0.713	0.619	0.678
SMOreg	0.279	0.543	0.403	0.472
LinearRegression	0.319	0.556	0.401	0.471
MultilayerPerceptron	0.340	0.560	0.390	0.477
AdditiveRegression	0.345	0.558	0.415	0.510
REPTree	0.392	0.570	0.455	0.538
RandomForest	0.399	0.576	0.449	0.506

The F1 scores of ORACLE are in the range of 0.595–0.713. It is impossible for ORACLE or any other summarizer to reach $F1 = 1$, because for each entity in ESBM there are six ground-truth summaries which are often different and hence cannot simultaneously match a machine-generated summary. However, the gap between the results of ORACLE and the best results of existing summarizers is still as large as 0.20–0.26, suggesting that there is much room for improvement.

Results on Different Entity Types. We break down the results of existing entity summarizers into 7 entity types (i.e., classes). When $k = 5$ in Fig. 5, there is no single winner on every class, but BAFREC and MPSUM are among top three on 6 classes, showing relatively good generalizability over different entity types. Some entity summarizers have limited generalizability and they perform not well on certain classes. For example, RELIN and CD mainly rely on the self-information of a triple, while for Location entities their latitudes and longitudes are often unique in DBpedia but such triples with large self-information rarely appear in ground-truth summaries. Besides, most summarizers generate low-quality summaries for Agent, Film, and Person entities. This is not surprising since these entities are described in more triples and/or by more properties according to Fig. 2. Their summarization is inherently more difficult. When $k = 10$ in Fig. 6, MPSUM is still among top three on 6 classes. KAFCA also shows relatively good generalizability—among top three on 5 classes.

Results of Supervised Learning. As shown in Table 4, among the six supervised learning based methods, RandomForest and REPTree achieve the highest

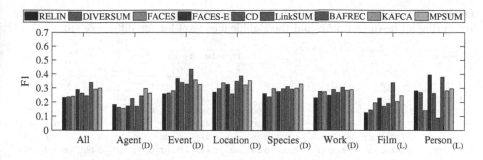

Fig. 5. Average F1 over all the entities in each class under $k = 5$.

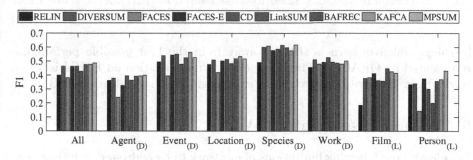

Fig. 6. Average F1 over all the entities in each class under $k = 10$.

F1 on DBpedia and LinkedMDB, respectively. Four methods (MultilayerPerceptron, AdditiveRegression, REPTree, and RandomForest) outperform all the existing entity summarizers on both datasets under both size constraints, and two methods (SMOreg and LinearRegression) only fail to outperform in one setting. The results demonstrate the powerfulness of supervised learning for entity summarization. Further, recall that these methods only use standard models and rely on features that are used by existing entity summarizers. It would be reasonable to predict that better results can be achieved with specialized models and more advanced features. However, creating a large number of ground-truth summaries for training is expensive, and the generalizability of supervised methods for entity summarization still needs further exploration.

Moreover, we are interested in how much the seven features contribute to the good performance of supervised learning. Table 5 shows the results of RandomForest after removing each individual feature. Considering statistical significance at the 0.05 level, two features gf_T and lf show effectiveness on both datasets under both size constraints, and two features vf_T and si are only effective on LinkedMDB. The usefulness of the three binary features isC, isE, and isL is not statistically significant.

Conclusion. Among existing entity summarizers, BAFREC generally shows the best performance on ESBM while MPSUM seems more robust. However, none of them are comparable with our straightforward implementation of supervised

Table 5. F1 of RandomForest after removing each individual feature, its difference from using all features ($\Delta\%$), and the significance level for the difference (p).

DBpedia								LinkedMDB							
$k=5$				$k=10$				$k=5$				$k=10$			
	F1	$\Delta\%$	p		F1	$\Delta\%$	p		F1	$\Delta\%$	p		F1	$\Delta\%$	p
All	0.399	—	—	All	0.576	—	—	All	0.449	—	—	All	0.506	—	—
-gf$_T$	0.346	−5.360	0.000	-lf	0.546	−0.030	0.000	-gf$_T$	0.383	−0.066	0.000	-lf	0.473	−0.033	0.008
-lf	0.366	−3.307	0.000	-gf$_T$	0.551	−0.025	0.000	-lf	0.413	−0.036	0.025	-vf$_T$	0.477	−0.029	0.010
-isC	0.392	−0.720	0.261	-vf$_T$	0.569	−0.007	0.198	-vf$_T$	0.414	−0.035	0.022	-gf$_T$	0.479	−0.027	0.007
-isE	0.397	−0.267	0.720	-isE	0.570	−0.006	0.262	-si	0.442	−0.007	0.574	-si	0.486	−0.020	0.009
-si	0.400	+0.027	0.973	-isC	0.571	−0.005	0.303	-isE	0.455	+0.005	0.651	-isL	0.491	−0.015	0.079
-isL	0.401	+0.160	0.816	-si	0.572	−0.004	0.402	-isL	0.456	+0.007	0.504	-isE	0.492	−0.014	0.148
-vf$_T$	0.407	+0.720	0.346	-isL	0.578	+0.002	0.683	-isC	0.463	+0.013	0.281	-isC	0.514	+0.008	0.396

learning, which in turn is still far away from the best possible performance represented by ORACLE. Therefore, entity summarization on ESBM is a non-trivial task. We invite researchers to experiment with new ideas on ESBM.

6   Discussion and Future Work

We identify the following limitations of our work to be addressed in future work.

Evaluation Criteria. We compute F1 score in the evaluation, which is based on common triples but ignores semantic overlap between triples. A triple t in a machine-generated summary S may partially cover the information provided by some triple t' in the ground-truth summary. It may be reasonable to not completely penalize S for missing t' but give some reward for the presence of t. However, it is difficult to quantify the extent of penalization for all possible cases, particularly when multiple triples semantically overlap with each other. In future work, we will explore more proper evaluation criteria.

Representativeness of Ground Truth. The ground-truth summaries in ESBM are not supposed to represent the view of the entire user population. They are intrinsically biased towards their creators. Besides, these ground-truth summaries are created for general purposes. Accordingly, we use them to evaluate general-purpose entity summarizers. However, for a specific task, these summaries may not show optimality, and the participating systems may not represent the state of the art. Still, we believe it is valuable to evaluate general-purpose systems not only because of their wide range of applications but also because their original technical features have been reused by task-specific systems. In future work, we will extend ESBM to a larger scale, and will consider benchmarking task-specific entity summarization.

Form of Ground Truth. ESBM provides ground-truth summaries, whereas some other benchmarks offer ground-truth scores of triples [1,13,22]. Scoring-based ground truth may more comprehensively evaluate an entity summarizer than our set-based ground truth because it not only considers the triples in a machine-generated summary but also assesses the rest of the triples. However, on the other hand, a set of top-scored triples may not equal an optimal summary because they may cover limited aspects of an entity and show redundancy. Therefore, both methods have their advantages and disadvantages. In future work, we will conduct scoring-based evaluation to compare with the current results.

Acknowledgments. This work was supported in part by the NSFC under Grant 61772264 and in part by the Qing Lan Program of Jiangsu Province.

References

1. Bobic, T., Waitelonis, J., Sack, H.: FRanCo - a ground truth corpus for fact ranking evaluation. In: SumPre 2015 & HSWI 2015 (2015)
2. Cheng, G., Tran, T., Qu, Y.: RELIN: relatedness and informativeness-based centrality for entity summarization. In: Aroyo, L., et al. (eds.) ISWC 2011, Part I. LNCS, vol. 7031, pp. 114–129. Springer, Heidelberg (2011). https://doi.org/10.1007/978-3-642-25073-6_8
3. Cheng, G., Xu, D., Qu, Y.: C3D+P: a summarization method for interactive entity resolution. J. Web Semant. **35**, 203–213 (2015). https://doi.org/10.1016/j.websem.2015.05.004
4. Cheng, G., Xu, D., Qu, Y.: Summarizing entity descriptions for effective and efficient human-centered entity linking. In: WWW 2015, pp. 184–194 (2015). https://doi.org/10.1145/2736277.2741094
5. Gottschalk, S., Demidova, E.: EventKG - the hub of event knowledge on the web - and biographical timeline generation. Semant. Web **10**(6), 1039–1070 (2019). https://doi.org/10.3233/SW-190355
6. Gunaratna, K.: Semantics-based summarization of entities in knowledge graphs. Ph.D. thesis, Wright State University (2017)
7. Gunaratna, K., Thirunarayan, K., Sheth, A.P.: FACES: diversity-aware entity summarization using incremental hierarchical conceptual clustering. In: AAAI 2015, pp. 116–122 (2015)
8. Gunaratna, K., Thirunarayan, K., Sheth, A., Cheng, G.: Gleaning types for literals in RDF triples with application to entity summarization. In: Sack, H., Blomqvist, E., d'Aquin, M., Ghidini, C., Ponzetto, S.P., Lange, C. (eds.) ESWC 2016. LNCS, vol. 9678, pp. 85–100. Springer, Cham (2016). https://doi.org/10.1007/978-3-319-34129-3_6
9. Hasibi, F., Balog, K., Bratsberg, S.E.: Dynamic factual summaries for entity cards. SIGIR **2017**, 773–782 (2017). https://doi.org/10.1145/3077136.3080810
10. Hassanzadeh, O., Consens, M.P.: Linked movie data base. In: LDOW 2009 (2009)
11. Kim, E.K., Choi, K.S.: Entity summarization based on formal concept analysis. In: EYRE 2018 (2018)
12. Kroll, H., Nagel, D., Balke, W.T.: BAFREC: balancing frequency and rarity for entity characterization in linked open data. In: EYRE 2018 (2018)
13. Langer, P., et al.: Assigning global relevance scores to DBpedia facts. In: ICDE Workshops 2014, pp. 248–253 (2014). https://doi.org/10.1109/ICDEW.2014.6818334
14. Lehmann, J., et al.: DBpedia - a large-scale, multilingual knowledge base extracted from Wikipedia. Semant. Web **6**(2), 167–195 (2015). https://doi.org/10.3233/SW-140134

15. Liu, Q., Cheng, G., Gunaratna, K., Qu, Y.: Entity summarization: state of the art and future challenges. CoRR abs/1910.08252 (2019), http://arxiv.org/abs/1910.08252

16. Pouriyeh, S.A., Allahyari, M., Kochut, K., Cheng, G., Arabnia, H.R.: Combining word embedding and knowledge-based topic modeling for entity summarization. In: ICSC 2018, pp. 252–255 (2018). https://doi.org/10.1109/ICSC.2018.00044

17. Pouriyeh, S.A., Allahyari, M., Kochut, K., Cheng, G., Arabnia, H.R.: ES-LDA: entity summarization using knowledge-based topic modeling. In: IJCNLP 2017, vol. 1, pp. 316–325 (2017)

18. Sim, S.E., Easterbrook, S.M., Holt, R.C.: Using benchmarking to advance research: a challenge to software engineering. In: ICSE 2003, pp. 74–83 (2003). https://doi.org/10.1109/ICSE.2003.1201189

19. Stoilos, G., Stamou, G.B., Kollias, S.D.: A string metric for ontology alignment. In: ISWC 2005, pp. 624–637 (2005). https://doi.org/10.1007/11574620_45

20. Sydow, M., Pikula, M., Schenkel, R.: The notion of diversity in graphical entity summarisation on semantic knowledge graphs. J. Intell. Inf. Syst. **41**(2), 109–149 (2013). https://doi.org/10.1007/s10844-013-0239-6

21. Thalhammer, A.: Linked data entity summarization. Ph.D. thesis, Karlsruher Institut für Technologie (2017)

22. Thalhammer, A., Knuth, M., Sack, H.: Evaluating entity summarization using a game-based ground truth. In: Cudré-Mauroux, P., et al. (eds.) ISWC 2012, Part II. LNCS, vol. 7650, pp. 350–361. Springer, Heidelberg (2012). https://doi.org/10.1007/978-3-642-35173-0_24

23. Thalhammer, A., Lasierra, N., Rettinger, A.: LinkSUM: using link analysis to summarize entity data. In: Bozzon, A., Cudre-Maroux, P., Pautasso, C. (eds.) ICWE 2016. LNCS, vol. 9671, pp. 244–261. Springer, Cham (2016). https://doi.org/10.1007/978-3-319-38791-8_14

24. Thalhammer, A., Rettinger, A.: Browsing DBpedia entities with summaries. In: Presutti, V., Blomqvist, E., Troncy, R., Sack, H., Papadakis, I., Tordai, A. (eds.) ESWC 2014. LNCS, vol. 8798, pp. 511–515. Springer, Cham (2014). https://doi.org/10.1007/978-3-319-11955-7_76

25. Thalhammer, A., Toma, I., Roa-Valverde, A.J., Fensel, D.: Leveraging usage data for linked data movie entity summarization. In: USEWOD 2012 (2012)

26. Tonon, A., et al.: Contextualized ranking of entity types based on knowledge graphs. J. Web Semant. **37–38**, 170–183 (2016). https://doi.org/10.1016/j.websem.2015.12.005

27. Wei, D., Gao, S., Liu, Y., Liu, Z., Huang, L.: MPSUM: entity summarization with predicate-based matching. In: EYRE 2018 (2018)

28. Xu, D., Zheng, L., Qu, Y.: CD at ENSEC 2016: generating characteristic and diverse entity summaries. In: SumPre 2016 (2016)

GEval: A Modular and Extensible Evaluation Framework for Graph Embedding Techniques

Maria Angela Pellegrino[1]([✉]), Abdulrahman Altabba[2], Martina Garofalo[1], Petar Ristoski[3], and Michael Cochez[4][ID]

[1] Department of Computer Science, University of Salerno, Fisciano, Italy
mapellegrino@unisa.it, margar1994@gmail.com
[2] Information Systems and Databases, RWTH Aachen University, Aachen, Germany
abdulrahman.altabba@rwth-aachen.de
[3] IBM Research Almaden, San Jose, CA, USA
petar.ristoski@ibm.com
[4] VU Amsterdam, Amsterdam, The Netherlands
m.cochez@vu.nl

Abstract. While RDF data are graph shaped by nature, most traditional Machine Learning (ML) algorithms expect data in a vector form. To transform graph elements to vectors, several graph embedding approaches have been proposed. Comparing these approaches is interesting for 1) developers of new embedding techniques to verify in which cases their proposal outperforms the state of art and 2) consumers of these techniques in choosing the best approach according to the task(s) the vectors will be used for. The comparison could be delayed (and made difficult) by the choice of tasks, the design of the evaluation, the selection of models, parameters, and needed datasets. We propose *GEval*, an evaluation framework to simplify the evaluation and the comparison of graph embedding techniques. The covered tasks range from ML tasks (Classification, Regression, Clustering), semantic tasks (entity relatedness, document similarity) to semantic analogies. However, GEval is designed to be (easily) extensible. In this article, we will describe the design and development of the proposed framework by detailing its overall structure, the already implemented tasks, and how to extend it. In conclusion, to demonstrate its operating approach, we consider the parameter tuning of the KGloVe algorithm as a use case.

Keywords: Evaluation framework · Knowledge graph embedding · Machine Learning · Semantic tasks

Resource type Software Framework
GitHub link https://github.com/mariaangelapellegrino/Evaluation-Framework
Permanent URL https://doi.org/10.5281/zenodo.3715267

© Springer Nature Switzerland AG 2020
A. Harth et al. (Eds.): ESWC 2020, LNCS 12123, pp. 565–582, 2020.
https://doi.org/10.1007/978-3-030-49461-2_33

1   Introduction

A graph embedding technique takes an RDF graph as its input and creates a low-dimensional feature vector representation of nodes and edges of the graph. Formally, a graph embedding technique aims to learn a function $f : G(V, E) \rightarrow \mathbb{R}^d$ which is a mapping from the graph $G(V, E)$, where V is the set of vertices and E is the set of edges, to a set of numerical embeddings for the vertices and edges, where d is the dimension of the embedding. The purpose of such a graph embedding technique is to represent each node and edge in a graph (or a subset of them) as a low-dimensional vector; often while preserving semantic properties (e.g., keeping similar entities close together) and/or topological features. If only nodes are embedded, it is called node embedding.

A desirable property for the obtained vectors is that they would be task-independent, meaning that they can be reused for other applications as they were created for. Therefore, it is useful to have an idea of how the vectors perform on different tasks to broaden the insight into the information the embedding algorithm is able to preserve. It is also important to know whether the vectors show very good performance on a given task while their performance degrades significantly on others. It is important to bear in mind that the *extrinsic* evaluation is not the only (and probably it is not the best) way to elect the best embedding approach. However, this kind of evaluation is extremely useful to choose the best set of vectors according to the tasks they will be used for. Besides the evaluation and comparison, a systematic evaluation is also useful in parameter tuning. In fact, many embedding algorithms have various parameters, which are difficult to set. Therefore, in this scenario, it is interesting to compare different versions of the same algorithm and check how the parameters affect extrinsic evaluations.

By considering extrinsic evaluation and comparison, one of the first aspects to take into account is the choice of the tasks. Systematic comparative evaluations of different approaches are scarce; approaches are rather evaluated on a handful of often project-specific data sets. Usually, they do not show how the algorithm performs on large and less regular graphs, such as DBpedia[1] or Wikidata[2].

To simplify the evaluation phase while providing a wider comparison, we present the design and open-source implementation of GEval (Graph Embeddings Evaluation), a software *evaluation framework* for knowledge graph (KG) embedding techniques. The provided tasks range from machine learning (ML) (classification, regression, and clustering) and semantic tasks (entity relatedness and document similarity) to semantic analogies. Furthermore, the framework is designed to be extended with additional tasks. It is useful both for embedding algorithm developers and users. On one side, when a new embedding algorithm is defined, there is the need to evaluate it upon tasks it was created for. On the other side, users can be interested in performing particular tests and choosing the embedding algorithm that performs best for their application. Our goal is

---

[1] https://dbpedia.org/.
[2] https://www.wikidata.org.

to address both situations providing a ready-to-use framework that can be customized and easily extended. This work is a continuation on our earlier work [13].

This paper is structured as follows: in Sect. 2, we present related work; in Sect. 3, we describe our evaluation framework, detailing the implemented tasks in Sect. 4; in Sect. 5, we present a practical use case, i.e., how to exploit the proposed framework in parameter tuning; then, we conclude with considerations and some final observation.

2 Related Work

The easiest way to categorize software evaluation frameworks is related to the provided tasks. Moreover, frameworks can be distinguished according to the expected input. In the case of embedding algorithms, an evaluation framework can take as input the model and train it before starting the evaluation. In the alternative, it could expect pre-computed vectors. The input format can influence the type of covered tasks. For example, for a fair comparison in link prediction, it is important to know the input graph used to train the model. Only by bounding the training set, it is possible to fairly test unknown edges and verify the ability of the embedding algorithm to forecast only positive edges. In this section, we will focus on frameworks to evaluate graph embedding approaches by pointing out the covered tasks. In Table 1, we will list frameworks by reporting the publication year, the covered tasks, and if they expect the model or the pre-trained vectors.

Table 1. For each evaluation framework, we report 1) the publication year, 2) the available tasks, and 3) the input format. *Task label: Clas* for Classification, *Clu* for Clustering, *DocSim* for Document Similarity, *EntRel* for Entity Relatedness, *LP* for Link Prediction, *Net Comp* for Network Compression, *Reg* for Regression, *SemAn* for Semantic Analogies, *Vis* for Visualization.

	Year	Tasks	Embedding technique
Bonner et al. [3]	2017	Topological structure	Model
GEM [7]	2018	Clas, Clu, LP, Net Comp, Vis	Model
Rulinda et al. [16]	2018	Clu, LP, Vis	Model
OpenNE	2019	Clas, Vis	Model
EvalNE [11]	2019	LP	Model
AYNEC [2]	2019	LP	-
Bogumil et al. [9]	2019	Clu	Model
GEval	2019	Clas, Clu, DocSim, EntRel, Reg, SemAn	Vectors

Goyal and Ferrara [7] released an open-source Python library, GEM (Graph Embedding Methods), which provides a unified interface to train many state-of-the-art embedding techniques on the Zachary's Karate graph and test them on network compression, visualization, clustering, link prediction, and node classification. GEM modular implementation should help users to introduce new datasets. This library is bounded to the embedding methods provided by the authors, while the introduction of new embedding approaches requires compliance with an interface defined within the library. It focuses more on the implementation of embedding approaches than on the effective evaluation workflow.

Bonner et al. [3] provide a framework to assess the effectiveness of graph embeddings approaches in capturing detailed topological structure, mainly at the vertex level. For instance, they hypothesize that a good graph embedding should be able to preserve the vertex centrality. The evaluation is based on empirical and synthetic datasets. Also this task needs to be aware of the graph used during the training phase of the model to verify the presence of topological structure in the vectors. The authors do not state if further tasks can be added.

Rulinda et al. [16] implement a collection of graph embedding techniques and, once trained, they evaluate the resulting vectors on clustering, link prediction, and visualization. The framework focuses only on uniform graphs.

Even if OpenNE[3] is an open-source package to train and test graph embedding techniques on node classification and network visualization, it is more focused on the generation phase than on the evaluation aspect.

EvalNE [11] focuses on the Link Prediction task. It starts from an incomplete training graph along with a (more) complete version of the graph to test and verify the prediction power. EvalNE interprets the link prediction task as a binary classification task and it can be extended by adding other binary classifiers.

Also AYNEC [2] focuses on the link prediction task. It provides some incomplete graphs as a training set. The user, on his/her behalf, can train a graph embedding algorithm on these datasets and run the link prediction task on the testing datasets. AYNEC takes as input the forecast edges and evaluate them by considering the complete graph. It provides all the useful phases to evaluate the link prediction task, but the link prediction step is charged to the user.

Bogumil et al. [9] focus on the clustering task and they define a divergence score that can be used to distinguish good and bad embeddings. They test a pool of embeddings of synthetic and real datasets. From their work it appears that they plan to extend the framework to hypergraphs. They do not state how or whether the framework can be used and extended for other tasks.

We propose GEval, an evaluation framework that combines both ML and semantic tasks. The advantage of considering also semantic tasks in the evaluation is due to the recent trend to extend neural embedding techniques, traditionally introduced only for natural language word sequences, also to KGs. Besides the wider diffusion of this kind of embedding techniques, to the best of our knowledge, they are not incorporated in a KG evaluation framework. Our tool is designed to be modular and extensible. It takes as input already pre-trained vectors without constraint on the way these vectors are produced.

---

[3] https://github.com/thunlp/OpenNE.

3   GEval: Evaluation Framework for Graph Embeddings

GEval is a software framework to perform evaluation and comparison of graph embedding techniques. It takes as input a file containing pre-computed vectors. More in detail, the input file must provide pairs of an embedded node (represented by its IRI) and the related vector. For each task, ground truth is modeled as a gold standard, which will be further referred to as *gold standard datasets*. They contain the tested entities and its ground truth. In Fig. 1, there is a diagrammatic representation of the involved parts in the framework and their interactions. The starting point is the *Evaluation Manager* which is the orchestrator of the whole evaluation and it is in charge of 1) verifying the correctness of the parameters set by the user, 2) instantiating the correct data manager according to the data format provided by the user, 3) determining which task(s) the user asked for, and 4) managing the storage of the results.

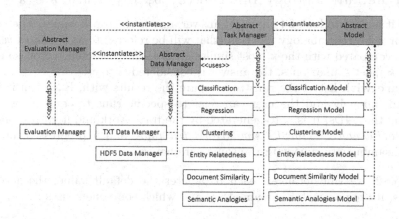

Fig. 1. The diagram represents the components of the framework. The blue boxes represent abstract classes, while the white boxes represent concrete classes. If A <<extends>> B, A is the concrete class which extends and makes the abstract behaviour of A concrete. If A <<instantiates>> B, A creates an instance of B. If A <<uses>> B, A is dependent on B.

Running Details. GEval can be run from the command line and by APIs. As stressed before, most of the actions performed by the evaluator strictly depend on the user settings and preferences. Users can customize the evaluation settings by: i) specifying them on the command line (useful when only a few settings must be specified and the user desires to use the default value for most of the parameters); ii) organizing them in an XML file (especially useful when there is the need to define most of the parameters); iii) passing them to a function that starts the evaluation. In the **example** folder of the project on GitHub, there are examples for the different ways to provide the parameters. The parameters are:

vectors_file path of the file where the embedded vectors are stored;

vector_file_format data format of the input file;

vectors_size length of the embedded vectors;

tasks list of the tasks to execute;

parallel task execution mode;

debugging_mode True to run the tasks by reporting all the information collected during the run, False otherwise;

similarity_metric metric used to compute the distance among vectors. When an embedding technique is created, there is often also a specific distance metric which makes sense to measure similarity in the created space. This measure is a proxy for the similarity between the entities in the graph;

analogy_function function to compute the analogy among vectors. By specifying None, the default function is used. To customize it, the programmatically provided function handler must take 3 parameters and return a number.

def default_analogy_function(a, b, c){return b − a + c}

top_k it is used to look for the *right* answer among the top_k values. The vector returned by the analogy function (that will be referred to as *predicted vector*) gets compared with the k most similar ones. If the predicted vector is among the k most similar ones, the answer is considered correct;

compare_with list of the runs to compare the results with. Each run is identified uniquely and the user can refer to specific runs to compare with by using these IDs. It is auto-generated by the framework and it corresponds to *vectorFilename_vectorSize_similarityMetric_topK* and a progressive number to disambiguate runs with the same parameters.

In Table 2, we will detail for each parameter the default value, the accepted options, if the parameter is mandatory, and which component uses it.

Data Management. The input file can be provided either as a plain text (also called TXT) file or as a HDF5. In particular, the TXT file must be a white-space separated value file with a line for each embedded entity. Each row must contain the IRI of the embedded entity and its vector representation. Since most of the tasks implemented in the evaluation framework need to intersect (inner join) the data set(s) used as gold standard and the input file, we also work with an indexed file format to speed up the merging phase. Indeed, the direct access to the entities of interest gives us the chance to save time during the merging step and also to save space since we do not read the complete vectors file into the memory. Among the available formats, we decided to work with HDF5[4]. The HDF5 vectors file must provide one group called *vectors*. In this group there must be a dataset for each entity with the base32 encoding of the entity name as the dataset name and the embedded vector as its value. Depending on the file format, the data manager decides to read the whole content or not. For instance, the TXT file will be completely read. HDF5, instead, provides an immediate access to vectors

---

[4] https://www.hdfgroup.org/solutions/hdf5/.

Table 2. The table reports details for each parameter: the parameter name, the default value, the accepted options, if it is mandatory, and which component/task uses it. The * means that the parameter is used by all the tasks.

Parameter	Default	Options	Mandatory	Used_ by
vectors_file			✓	*
vector_file_format	TXT	TXT, HDF5		data_manager
vectors_size	200	numeric value		data_manager
tasks	_all	Class, Reg, Clu, EntRel, DocSim, SemAn		evaluation_manager
parallel	False	boolean		evaluation_manager
debugging_mode	False	boolean		*
similarity_metric	cosine	Sklearn affinity metrics[a]		Clu, DocSim
analogy_function	None	handler to function		semantic_analogy
top_k	2	numeric value		SemAn
compare_with	_all	list of run IDs		evaluation_manager

[a] https://scikit-learn.org/stable/modules/classes.html#module-sklearn.metrics.pairwise

of interest. Each data manager has to i) read the gold standard datasets, ii) read the input file and iii) determine how to merge each gold standard dataset and the input file. The behaviour of the data manager is modelled by the **abstract data manager**, implemented by a concrete data manager based on the input file format and it refined by task data managers.

Task Management. Once data have been accessed, the task(s) can be run. Each task is modelled as a pair of task manager and model. The task manager is in charge of 1) merging the input file and each gold standard file (if more than one is provided) (by exploiting the data manager), 2) instantiating and training a model for each configuration to test, and 3) collecting and storing results computed by the model. Therefore, the framework is in charge of retrieving entities of interest, i.e., entities listed in gold standard datasets, and the related vectors. Only the intersection of entities provided by the input file and the ones required by gold standard datasets will be considered into the evaluation. Each task can decide if the missing entities (i.e., the entities required into the gold standard file, but absent into the input file) will affect the final result of the task or not. According to the user preferences, tasks can be run in sequential or in parallel. The parallelization is trivially handled: by asking for the parallel execution, a new process is created for each task and it is immediately run. Once results are returned, they are collected and stored by the Evaluation Manager.

Out-of-the-Box Tasks and Extension Points. The provided tasks range from ML tasks (Classification, Regression, Clustering), semantic tasks (entity relatedness and document similarity) to semantic analogies. Each task is kept separate, by satisfying the modularity requirement. By the usage of abstraction, it is easy to add new tasks and/or data manager. The `abstract data manager` defines the interface of a data manager, while `abstract task manager` and `abstract model` define the interface of a new task. Extending the framework with new data formats and/or new tasks is as simple as creating a class implementing these interfaces. To further enrich an already implemented task, it is easy to retrieve the exact point to modify since each task is limited to its task manager and model. Moreover, to extend the evaluation also to edges, it is enough to create gold standard dataset containing edges and related ground truth.

Results Storage. For each task and for each file used as gold standard, GEval will create i) an output file that contains a reference to the file used as gold standard and all the information related to evaluation metric(s) provided by each task, ii) a file containing all the *missing* entities, iii) a log file reporting extra information, occurred problems, and execution time, and iv) information related to the comparison with previous runs. In particular, about the comparison, it reports the values effectively considered in the comparison and the ranking of the current run upon the other ones. The results of each run are stored in the directory `results/result_<starting time of the execution>` generated by the evaluation manager in the local path.

4   Out of the Box Available Tasks

The available tasks are Classification, Regression and Clustering that belong to the ML field, and Entity Relatedness, Document Similarity and Semantic Analogies, more related to the semantic field. Each task is implemented as a concrete task manager that implements functionalities modelled by the `Abstract Task Manager`. Each task follows the same workflow:

1. the task manager asks data manager to merge each gold standard dataset and the input file and keeps track of both the retrieved vectors and the *missing* entities, i.e., entities required by the gold standard dataset, but absent in the input file;
2. a model for each configuration is instantiated and trained;
3. the missing entities are managed: it is up to the task to decide if they should affect the final result or they can be simply ignored;
4. the scores are calculated and stored.

We will separately analyse each task, by detailing the gold standard datasets, the configuration of the model(s), and the computed evaluation metrics.

4.1 Classification

Table 3 contains details related to the gold standard datasets used for the Classification task, the trained models and its parameter(s) (if any), and the evaluated metric. The gold standard datasets have been designed for use in quantitative performance testing and systematic comparisons of approaches. They can be freely downloaded from the author's website.[5] The missing entities are simply ignored. The results are calculated using stratified 10-fold cross-validation.

Table 3. Details of the Classification task.

	Dataset	Semantic of classes	Classes	Size	Source
INPUT	Cities	Living style	3	212	Mercer
	AAUP	Salary of professors	3	960	JSE
	Forbes	Agency income	3	1,585	Forbes
	Albums	Album popularity	2	1,600	Metacritic
	Movies	Movie popularity	2	2,000	Metacritic
MODEL	**Model**			**Conf**	
	Naive Bayes (NB)			-	
	C4.5 decision tree			-	
	k-NN			k=3	
	SVM			$C \in \{10^{-3}, 10^{-2}, 0.1, 1, 10, 10^2, 10^3\}$	
OUTPUT	**Metric**		**Range**	**Optimum**	
	Accuracy		[0,1]	Highest	

4.2 Regression

Table 4 contains details related to the gold standard datasets used for the Regression task, the trained models and its parameter(s) (if any), and the evaluated metric. The gold standard datasets used for the Regression tasks are the same used for the Classification task. The missing entities are simply ignored. The results are calculated using stratified 10-fold cross-validation.

4.3 Clustering

Table 5 contains details related to the gold standard datasets used for the Clustering task, the trained models and its parameter(s) (if any), and the evaluated metrics.

---

[5] http://data.dws.informatik.uni-mannheim.de/rmlod/LOD_ML_Datasets/data/datasets/.

Table 4. Details of the Regression task.

	Dataset	Semantic of values	Size	Source
INPUT	Cities	Living style	212	Mercer
	AAUP	Salary of professors	960	JSE
	Forbes	Agency income	1,585	Forbes
	Albums	Album popularity	1,600	Metacritic
	Movies	Movie popularity	2,000	Metacritic
	Model		**Conf**	
MODEL	Linear Regression		-	
	M5Rules		-	
	k-NN		k=3	
OUTPUT	**Metric**		**Range**	**Optimum**
	Root Mean Squared Error (RMSE)		[0,1]	Lowest

The gold standard datasets encompass different domains:

- the *Cities, Metacritic Movies, Metacritic Albums, AAUP* and *Forbes datasets* are the datasets already used for the Classification and Regression task, here used as a single dataset. Since these datasets contain resources belonging to distinct class (City, Music Album, Movie, University, and Company), the goal of the clustering approach on this dataset is verifying the ability to distinguish elements belonging to completely different classes. Therefore, the entities from each set are considered member of the same cluster;
- *Cities* and *Countries* are retrieved by SPARQL queries over DBpedia, asking for all dbo:City[6] and dbo:PopulatedPlace, respectively.
- the small version of the dataset *Cities* and *Countries* is defined as before, but balancing the clusters by retrieving only 2,000 Cities. The balancing operation has been performed since the majority of clustering approaches (k-means is an example in this direction) attempt to balance the size of the clusters while minimising the interaction between dissimilar nodes [17]. Therefore, unbalanced clusters could strongly affect the final results.
- *Football* and *Basketball teams* are retrieved by SPARQL queries run against the DBpedia SPARQL endpoint, asking for all dbo:SportsTeam whose identifier contains respectively football_team or basketball_team.

All the models but k-Means allow to customize the distance function. Therefore, we exploit the similarity_metric given in input by the user. Only k-Means is bounded (due to its implementation) to the euclidean distance.

For each missing entities a *singleton cluster* is created, i.e., a cluster which contains only the current entity. Further, soft clustering approaches, such as DBscan, do not cluster all entities. We call these entities *miss-clustered entities*

---

[6] dbo is the prefix of http://dbpedia.org/ontology/.

Table 5. Details of the Clustering task.

	Dataset	Interpretation of clusters	Clusters	Size
	Teams	{Football T., Basketball T.}	2	4,206
INPUT	Cities and Countries	{Cities, Countries}	2	4,344
	Cities, Albums, Movies,	{Cities, Albums, Movies,	5	6,357
	AAUP, Forbes	Universities, Societies}		
	Cities and Countries	{Cities, Countries}	2	11,182

	Model	Conf
	Agglomerative Clu.	*similarity_metric*
MODEL	Ward Hierarchical Clu.	*similarity_metric*
	DBscan	*similarity_metric*
	k-Means	-

	Metric	Range	Optimum
	adjusted rand score	[-1,1]	Highest
	adjusted mutual info score	[0,1]	Highest
OUTPUT	Fowlkes Mallow index	[0,1]	Highest
	v_measure score	[0,1]	Highest
	homogeneity score	[0,1]	Highest
	completeness score	[0,1]	Highest

and manage them exactly as the missing entities, i.e., we create a singleton cluster for each of them. The evaluation metrics are applied to the combination of the clusters returned by the clustering algorithm and all the *singleton clusters*.

4.4 Entity Relatedness

In the entity relatedness task we assume that two entities are related if they often appear in the same context [15]. The goal of this task is to check if embedded vectors are able to preserve the semantic relatedness which can be detected from the original entities. The relatedness between vectors is brought back to the computation of the similarity metric among them.

Table 6 contains details related to the gold standard dataset used for the Entity Relatedness task, the model, and the evaluated metrics. The original version of the gold standard dataset KORE [8] consists of 420 pairs of words: for each of 21 main words, there are 20 words whose relatedness has been manually assessed. The dataset has been adapted by manually resolving each word as DBpedia entities. The main entities belong to four distinct categories: Actors, Companies, TV series, and Video-games. Missing entities are managed as follows:

- if a main entity is missing, it is simply ignored;
- if one or more related entities attached to the same main entity are missing, first, the task compute the similarity among the available entities as reported in the model described in the Table 6; then, all the missing related entities are randomly put in the tail of the sorted list, and, finally, the evaluation metric

Table 6. Details of the Entity Relatedness task.

	Dataset	Structure	Size
INPUT	KORE [8]	*main entity* with a	420
		sorted list of 20 related entities	

	Model		Conf
MODEL	sim_scores = [ ]		*similarity_metric*
	for each main entity as *me*:		
	for each related entity as *re*:		
	sim_scores.add(similarity(*me*, *re*))		
	sort(sim_scores) //from more to less similar		

	Metric	Range	Interpretation
	Kendall's tau	[-1,1]	Extreme values:
OUTPUT	correlation coefficient		correlation
			Values close to 0:
			no correlation

is calculated on the ranking obtained by the similarity score among all the available pairs concatenated with the missing entities.

4.5   Document Similarity

Table 7 contains details related to the gold standard datasets used for the Document Similarity task and the evaluated metric. The original dataset used as gold standard is the LP50 data set [10], a collection of 50 news articles from the Australian Broadcasting Corporation. It were pairwise annotated manually by 8 to 12 different university students who evaluated the similarity among documents assigning to each pair a point in the range [1, 5] where 5 means maximum similarity. To create the gold standard dataset, we worked as follows. For each pair of documents, the average of the manually assessed rates is computed. Then, we the extract the entities from the documents using the annotator xLisa[7].

Model. The algorithm takes two documents d_1 and d_2 as its input and calculates their similarity as follows:

- For each document, the related set of entities is retrieved. The output of this step are the sets E_1 and E_2, respectively.
- For each pair of entities (i.e., for the cross product of the sets), the similarity score is computed.
- Only the maximum value is preserved for determining the document similarity evaluation. Therefore, for each entity in E_1 the maximum similarity to an entity in E_2 is kept and vice versa.

---

[7] http://km.aifb.kit.edu/sites/xlisa/.

Table 7. Details of the Document Similarity task.

INPUT	Dataset	Structure	Size
	LP50 [10]	doc1 doc2 avg	50 docs

MODEL	Model		Conf
	it is described into *the Doc. Sim. section*		*similarity_metric*

	Metric	Range	Interpretation
	Pearson correlation (P_cor)	[-1,1]	Extreme: correlation Close to 0: no correlation
OUTPUT	Spearman correlation (S_cor)	[-1,1]	Extreme: correlation Close to 0: no correlation
	Harmonic mean of P_cor and S_cor	[-1,1]	Extreme: correlation Close to 0: no correlation

- The similarity score between the two documents is calculated by averaging the sum of all these maximum similarities.

The annotators also provided weights. Hence, the previous procedure is repeated by considering the weights to normalise the distances. The Document Similarity task simply ignores any missing entities and computes the similarity only on entities that both occur in the gold standard dataset and in the input file.

4.6 Semantic Analogies

The Semantic Analogies task is based on quadruplets of words ($word_1, word_2, word_3, word_4$) and it checks whether it is possible to predict the last word based on the first three ones, given that the same analogy exists between $word_1$ and $word_2$ as between $word_3$ and $word_4$. A practical example [12] is the quadruplet (king, queen, man, woman). Then, one can compute X = vector("queen")-vector("woman") + vector("man") and check if X is near to the embedding of "king". In Word2Vec both syntactic and semantic analogies are considered. However, in our evaluation framework we consider only semantic analogies as KGs do generally not provide conjugated verbs, female and male nouns, singular and plural words, which are required information to perform the syntactic analogy evaluation. The original datasets used as gold standard can be freely be downloaded[8]. To create the gold standard datasets for the Semantic Analogies task, all the words have been manually substituted with DBpedia entities (Table 8).

Model. The task takes the quadruplets (v_1, v_2, v_3, v_4) and works on the first three vectors to predict the fourth one. Among all the vectors, the nearest to the predicted one is retrieved, where the *nearest* is computed by the dot product.

---

[8] https://sites.google.com/site/semeval2012task2/download.

Table 8. Details of the Semantic Analogies task.

	Dataset	Structure	Size	Source
	Capitals and countries	ca1 co1 ca2 co2	505	Word2Vec [12]
INPUT	Currency (and Countries)	cu1 co1 cu2 co2	866	Word2Vec [12]
	Cities and State	ci1 st1 ci2 st2	2,467	Word2Vec [12]
	(All) capitals and countries	ca1 co1 ca2 co2	4,523	Word2Vec [12]
MODEL	Model			Conf
	it is described into the Sem. An. section			analogy_function
OUTPUT	Metric		Range	Optimum
	accuracy		[0,1]	Highest

The analogy function to compute the predicted vector can be customised. The vector returned by the function (the *predicted vector*) gets compared with the *top_k* most similar ones. If the actual fourth vector is among the *top_k* most similar ones, the answer is considered correct. *top_k* can be customised by the user.

5 Evaluation and Use Case

Execution Time Evaluation. We have already tested the execution time of each task both in sequential and in parallel [13]. We are interested in estimating how the vector size affects the computational time for the Classification and Regression tasks. The experiments are performed on a system with an Intel(R) Core(TM) i7-8700T CPU at 2.40 GHz and 16 GB RAM. We evaluated vectors produced by RDF2Vec [6] and by KGloVe [5]. Here, we report only results related to KGloVe since in both cases we observed the same trend. We extrapolated only vectors required by the Classification and Regression tasks, because of memory limitations. Then, we crop the filtered vectors by considering $[10, 20, 50, 100, 150, 180, 200]$ as size. We perform the Classification and the Regression tasks on all the obtained vectors. In Fig. 2, you can observe the actual execution times of the ML tasks and you can note that the execution time of Classification and Regression tasks is linearly correlated with the vector size.

Use Case. In this use case, we focus on parameter tuning and we will use results produced by ML tasks to detect the best combination of hyper-parameters. In this evaluation, we consider a modified version of KGloVe [4] where the difference with the original algorithm lies in the parallel implementation (GPU based) of the underlying GloVe [1]. Our goal is to optimize KGloVe parameters to find out the values that produce vectors which gain the best results in ML tasks. In Fig. 3, the entire pipeline is visible. Starting from DBpedia 2016, the *graph walks* produces a co-occurrence matrix for the nodes of the graph [4]. The parameters that affect the co-occurrence matrix are α, ϵ, and the *weighting function* which is applied once on the graph (forward weighting function) and once

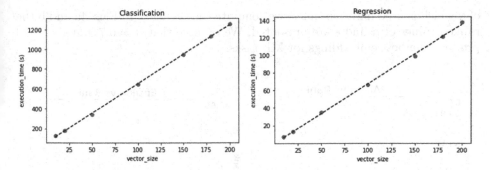

Fig. 2. It represents how vector size affects the execution time of the Classification and Regression tasks: they are linearly correlated.

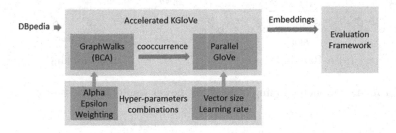

Fig. 3. Pipeline of hyper-parameter tuning

on the graph with reversed edges (backward weighting function). The *Parallel GloVe* [1] implementation takes the co-occurrences matrix as input and trains the vectors in parallel by minimising the loss function defined by GloVe [14]. The produced embeddings are affected by GloVe parameters, i.e., the vector size and the learning rate. To reduce the employed resources in finding the optimum parameters combination, we opt for a random search. We performed the evaluation by considering a set of 105 uniformly random generated combinations: we tested $\alpha \in \{0.4, 0.45, 0.5, 0.55, 0.6, 0.65, 0.7, 0.75, 0.8, 0.85, 0.9, 0.95\}$; *learning rate*= 0.01; *vector size*= 50; $\epsilon \in \{10^{-6}, 10^{-5}, 10^{-4}, 10^{-3}\}$; *weighting functions* (forward, backward) |weighers| × |weighers| = 12 options × 12 options. Once produced vectors, we evaluate them on the Classification and Regression tasks implemented by GEval. GEval runs 10 times both the Classification and the Regression task and returns the average result. By considering the combination of models and their configurations (see Table 3), the classification task produces 10 accuracy scores, while the regression task produces 2 RMSE scores (k-NN and LR). For each run, we take the average of the results produced by the 5 datasets used as a gold standard.

Then, we rank the runs (and therefore the parameter combination) according to the 12 different scores. The average rank is taken for evaluating the corresponding parameter combination. To find out the performance according to a given parameter y, we plot the performance for each run of y (if there is a value of y which is used multiple times, we compute the average). In Figs. 4a and b the ranked values of α and ϵ are presented. We observe that $\alpha = 0.7$ and $\epsilon = 10^{-5}$ produce the best embeddings for ML tasks.

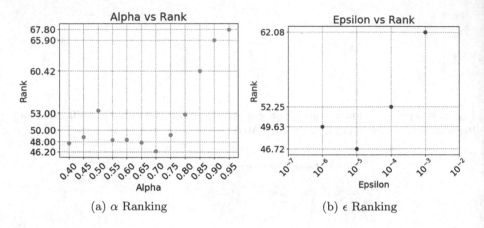

(a) α Ranking   (b) ϵ Ranking

Fig. 4. Parameter tuning of KGloVe. Lower results are the best ones.

6   Conclusion

GEval aims to simplify the evaluation phase of KG embedding techniques providing tasks ranging from ML to semantic ones. To the best of our knowledge, our proposal is one of the most comprehensive frameworks to evaluate KG embedding techniques for heterogeneous graphs. GEval can be used in evaluation and comparison over multiple tasks. Moreover, it can be also used in parameters tuning, as shown in the presented use case. The modularity of GEval is achieved by keeping each task separated, but still abstracting away the commonalities.

Our software framework can be used to perform benchmarks, but it is not designed as a benchmark itself. We provide the framework as a command-line tool and by APIs[9]. We do not provide server-side execution, since the computation of tasks and the memory requirements can be onerous and can not be determined apriori. In our opinion, it is more beneficial to provide the software and give the opportunity of choosing the hardware requirements adapt to the size of the managed vectors. GEval is not bounded to evaluate only node embeddings. By incorporating also edges into the gold standard datasets, it is possible to consider graph embeddings which embed both nodes and edges. Our default gold standard datasets contain DBpedia entities. However, this is not a framework requirement; it is possible to evaluate different sets of entities (and embeddings of other KGs) by adding gold standard datasets.

---

[9] https://pypi.org/project/evaluation-framework/.

The framework has been published with an open-source licence in order to be used by the whole community. GEval is already of interest for experimentation with graph embedding techniques by the authors' institutes (Fraunhofer FIT, the RWTH Aachen University, the University of Salerno, and IBM research). Moreover, other institutes show an interest in collaborating to this project. The Télécom ParisTech is interested in extending the already available tasks to incorporate gold standard datasets related to (French) museums. We are now working to create the gold standard of interest. Moreover, we are working with the University of Madrid to incorporate the Link Prediction task in GEval. We are certain that also others will benefit from this valuable resource.

References

1. Altabba, A.: Accelerating KGloVe graph embedding (2019). Unpublished thesis
2. Ayala, D., Borrego, A., Hernández, I., Rivero, C.R., Ruiz, D.: AYNEC: all you need for evaluating completion techniques in knowledge graphs. In: Hitzler, P., et al. (eds.) ESWC 2019. LNCS, vol. 11503, pp. 397–411. Springer, Cham (2019). https://doi.org/10.1007/978-3-030-21348-0_26
3. Bonner, S., Brennan, J., Kureshi, I., Theodoropoulos, G., McGough, A.S., Obara, B.: Evaluating the quality of graph embeddings via topological feature reconstruction. In: 2017 IEEE International Conference on Big Data, pp. 2691–2700 (2017)
4. Cochez, M., Ristoski, P., Ponzetto, S.P., Paulheim, H.: Global RDF vector space embeddings. In: d'Amato, C., et al. (eds.) ISWC 2017. LNCS, vol. 10587, pp. 190–207. Springer, Cham (2017). https://doi.org/10.1007/978-3-319-68288-4_12
5. Cochez, M., Ristoski, P., Ponzetto, S.P., Paulheim, H.: KGloVe DBpedia uniform embeddings (2017). https://doi.org/10.5281/zenodo.1320148
6. Cochez, M., Ristoski, P., Ponzetto, S.P., Paulheim, H.: RDf2Vec DBpedia uniform embeddings (2017). https://doi.org/10.5281/zenodo.1318146
7. Goyal, P., Ferrara, E.: Graph embedding techniques, applications, and performance: a survey. Knowl. Based Syst. **151**, 78–94 (2018)
8. Hoffart, J., Seufert, S., Nguyen, D.B., Theobald, M., Weikum, G.: KORE: keyphrase overlap relatedness for entity disambiguation. In: Proceedings of the 21st ACM CIKM, pp. 545–554 (2012)
9. Kaminski, B., Pralat, P., Théberge, F.: An unsupervised framework for comparing graph embeddings. CoRR abs/1906.04562 (2019)
10. Lee, M.D., Welsh, M.: An empirical evaluation of models of text document similarity. In: XXVII Annual Conference of the Cognitive Science Society (2005)
11. Mara, A., Lijffijt, J., Bie, T.D.: EvalNE: a framework for evaluating network embeddings on link prediction. In: Reproducibility in Machine Learning, ICLR (2019)
12. Mikolov, T., Sutskever, I., Chen, K., Corrado, G.S., Dean, J.: Distributed representations of words and phrases and their compositionality. In: 27th Annual Conference on Neural Information Processing Systems, pp. 3111–3119 (2013)
13. Pellegrino, M.A., Cochez, M., Garofalo, M., Ristoski, P.: A configurable evaluation framework for node embedding techniques. In: Hitzler, P., et al. (eds.) ESWC 2019. LNCS, vol. 11762, pp. 156–160. Springer, Cham (2019). https://doi.org/10.1007/978-3-030-32327-1_31
14. Pennington, J., Socher, R., Manning, C.D.: GloVe: global vectors for word representation. In: Proceedings of the Conference on Empirical Methods in Natural Language Processing, pp. 1532–1543 (2014)

15. Ristoski, P., Rosati, J., Noia, T.D., Leone, R.D., Paulheim, H.: RDF2Vec: RDF graph embeddings and their applications. Semant. Web **10**(4), 721–752 (2019)
16. Rulinda, J., de Dieu Tugirimana, J., Nzaramba, A., Aila, F.O., Langat, G.K.: An integrated platform to evaluate graph embedding. Int. J. Sci. Eng. Res. **9**, 665–676 (2018)
17. White, S., Smyth, P.: A spectral clustering approach to finding communities in graph. In: Proceedings of the SIAM International Conference on Data Mining (2005)

YAGO 4: A Reason-able Knowledge Base

Thomas Pellissier Tanon[1]($\boxtimes$), Gerhard Weikum[2], and Fabian Suchanek[1]

[1] Télécom Paris, Institut Polytechnique de Paris, Palaiseau, France
thomas@pellissier-tanon.fr, suchanek@telecom-paris.fr
[2] Max Planck Institute for Informatics, Saarbrücken, Germany

Abstract. YAGO is one of the large knowledge bases in the Linked Open Data cloud. In this resource paper, we present its latest version, YAGO 4, which reconciles the rigorous typing and constraints of schema.org with the rich instance data of Wikidata. The resulting resource contains 2 billion type-consistent triples for 64 Million entities, and has a consistent ontology that allows semantic reasoning with OWL 2 description logics.

1 Introduction

A knowledge base (KB) is a machine-readable collection of knowledge about the real world. A KB contains entities (such as organizations, movies, people, and locations) and relations between them (such as *birthPlace*, *director*, etc.). KBs have wide applications in search engines, question answering, fact checking, chatbots, and many other NLP and AI tasks. Numerous projects have constructed KBs automatically or by help of a community. Notable KBs include YAGO [17], DBpedia [1], BabelNet [14], NELL [2], KnowItAll [3], and Wikidata [18]. On the industry side, giants such as Amazon, Google, Microsoft, Alibaba, Tencent and others are running KB technology as a background asset, often referred to as knowledge graphs.

YAGO [10,13,16,17] was one of the first academic projects to build a knowledge base automatically. The main idea of YAGO was to harvest information about entities from the infoboxes and categories of Wikipedia, and to combine this data with an ontological backbone derived from classes in WordNet [4]. Since Wikipedia is an excellent repository of entities, and WordNet is a widely used lexical resource, the combination proved useful. YAGO sent each fact through a pipeline of filtering, constraint checking, and de-duplication steps. This procedure scrutinized noisy input and boosted the quality of the final KB, to a manually verified accuracy of 95%. This precision was possible thanks to the tight control that the YAGO creators had over the extraction process, the filtering process, the ontological type system, the choice of the relations, and the semantic constraints. However, despite new versions YAGO2 and YAGO3 with substantial jumps in scope and size, the focus on Wikipedia infoboxes meant that YAGO has not arrived at the same scale as Freebase or Wikidata.

Meanwhile, Wikidata [18] has evolved into the world's foremost publicly available KB. It is a community effort where anybody can contribute facts – either

© Springer Nature Switzerland AG 2020
A. Harth et al. (Eds.): ESWC 2020, LNCS 12123, pp. 583–596, 2020.
https://doi.org/10.1007/978-3-030-49461-2_34

by manually adding or curating statements in the online interface, or by bulk-loading data. Wikidata has motivated more than 40,000 people who contribute at least once a month. The result is a public KB with 70M named entities, very good long-tail coverage, and impressive detail.[1]

At the same time, Wikidata understands itself as a collection of information, not as a collection of universally agreed-upon knowledge. It may intentionally contain contradictory statements, each with different sources or validity areas. Therefore, Wikidata does not enforce semantic constraints, such as "each person has exactly one father". Furthermore, the large user community has led to a proliferation of relations and classes: Wikidata contains 6.7k relations, of which only 2.6K have more than 1000 facts, and it comprises around 2.4M classes[2], of which 80% have less than 10 instances. Many instances (e.g., all cities) are placed in the taxonomy under more than 60 classes, with three-fold multiple inheritance. This complexity is the trade-off that Wikidata has found to accommodate its large user community. For downstream applications, the convoluted and often confusing type system of Wikidata make browsing and question answering tedious. Moreover, there is little hope to run strict classical reasoners (e.g., for OWL 2) in a meaningful way, as the KB contains many small inconsistencies so that every possible statement is deducible regardless of whether it is intuitively correct or false. Some of these issues have been pointed out in the comprehensive study of KB quality by [19].

Example. To illustrate the shortcomings by the verbose and sometimes confusing type hierarchy of Wikidata, consider the entities *Notre Dame de Paris* (http://www.wikidata.org/entity/Q2981) and *Potala Palace* (http://www.wikidata.org/entity/Q71229) both landmarks of two world religions.

Notre Dame is an instance of types *catholic cathedral* and *minor basilicas*, with a rich set of superclasses. The Potala Palace in Lhasa is an instance of *palace* and *tourist attraction*. Interestingly, the latter does not have Notre Dame de Paris as an instance, neither directly nor indirectly. So a query for tourist attractions would find the Potala Palace but not Notre Dame.

Moreover, the class *tourist attraction* is a subclass of *geographic object* which is an instance of the class *geometric concept* which in turn has superclass *mathematical concept*. As a consequence, a query for mathematical concepts returns entities like tensor, polynomial, differential equation... and the *Potala Palace* as answers.

Contribution. In this resource paper, we describe the new YAGO version, YAGO 4, which aims to combine the best of the two worlds: It collects the facts about instances from Wikidata, but it forces them into a rigorous type hierarchy with semantic constraints. The complex taxonomy of Wikidata is replaced by

---

[1] All the numbers given in the paper about Wikidata are valid as of Feb. 24, 2020.

[2] Wikidata does not have a strong concept of a "class"; we use this term to denote entities that have superclasses (i.e., appear as left-hand argument of "subclass of" triples).

the simpler and clean taxonomy of schema.org [8]. The classes are equipped with SHACL constraints [12] that specify disjointness, applicable relations, and cardinalities. This way, YAGO 4 transfers the rationale of the original YAGO from the combination of Wikipedia and WordNet to the combination of Wikidata and schema.org. The result is a new knowledge base, which is not just large, but also logically consistent, so that OWL-based reasoning is feasible. Hence we call YAGO 4 a "reason-able" knowledge base. The new resource is available at http://yago-knowledge.org under a permissive license (Creative Commons Attribution-ShareAlike). YAGO 4 also comes with a browser and a SPARQL endpoint. Figure 1 shows an excerpt of the new YAGO in the online browser.

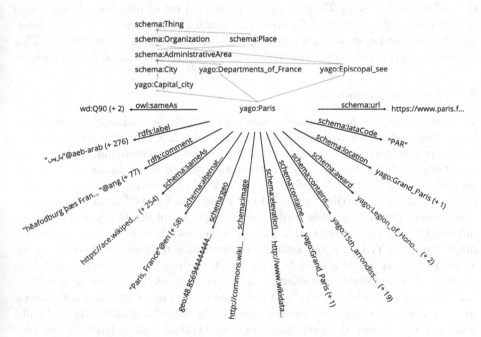

Fig. 1. The YAGO 4 Browser. Hovering reveals the full name of abbreviated items; all red and blue items are clickable. (Color figure online)

2   Related Work

The Linked Open data cloud contains several dozen general-purpose KBs[3]. YAGO 4 is not intended to replace these KBs, but rather as an addition to this ecosystem with unique characteristics that complement the other players. For example, DBpedia also has a new version that ingests facts from Wikidata [11], with a well-designed pipeline that allows harvesting different knowledge sources [5]. This new DBpedia and YAGO 4 have made different design

---

[3] https://www.lod-cloud.net/.

choices, resulting in different strengths and limitations. Our key priority has been to strengthen the logical rigor of the KB, so as to support OWL and other reasoners. This is why YAGO 4 builds on schema.org and adds its own constraint system which is much more elaborate than what DBpedia enforces.

3   Design

The construction of the YAGO 4 knowledge base is driven by several design decisions, which we explain and motivate next. The overarching point is to center YAGO 4 around a well-founded notion of classes. For example, a *Person* is defined as a subclass of *Thing*, and has an explicit set of possible relations such as *birthDate, affiliation*, etc.[4] Conversely, other relations such as *capitalOf, headquarter* or *population* are not applicable to instances of the class *Person*. This overarching principle of semantic consistency unfolds into several design choices.

3.1   Concise Taxonomy

Wikidata contains a very detailed taxonomy to which the community contributes by adding *instanceOf* and *subclassOf* statements. However, the resulting class hierarchy is so deep and convoluted that it is not easy to grasp and that browsing it is rather tedious. For example, Paris is an instance of 60 classes, 20 of which are called "unit", "entity", "subject", or "object". Moreover, the class hierarchy is not stable: any contributor can add or remove *subclassOf* links between any two classes. Potentially, this could lead to millions of entities being classified differently, just by a single edit. On the other hand, schema.org, the second major input to YAGO 4, has established itself as a reference taxonomy on the Web, beyond its initial aim at helping search engines to index web pages. It is stable, well maintained, and changes are made only by agreement in the W3C Schema.org Community Group[5]. At the same time, schema.org does not provide fine-grained classes such as "electric cars" or "villages" – which only Wikidata has. Schema.org also does not have any biochemical classes (such as proteins etc.).

We address the latter problem by using *Bioschemas* [7][6]. This project extends schema.org in the field of the life sciences – a field that is not covered in schema.org, and that is very prominent in Wikidata. We manually merged 6 Bioschemas classes into schema.org, referring to the merged taxonomy as the "schema.org taxonomy" for simplicity.

To obtain the stability of schema.org while preserving the fine-grained classes of Wikidata, we found the following solution: The top-level taxonomy of YAGO 4 is taken from schema.org (incl. Bioschemas), and leaf-level classes are taken from Wikidata. For this purpose, we manually mapped 235 classes of schema.org to Wikidata classes. Classes of schema.org that could not be mapped,

---

[4] For readability, we omit namespace prefixes in this paper.

[5] https://www.w3.org/community/schemaorg/.

[6] https://bioschemas.org.

mostly shopping-related or social-media classes such as *schema:LikeAction*, were removed. With these inputs, the YAGO 4 taxonomy is then constructed as follows:

- For each instance in Wikidata, we consider each possible path in the Wikidata taxonomy to the root node. If the first class on the path has a Wikipedia article, we include it in YAGO 4. The rationale is that only classes with an English Wikipedia article are of sufficient interest for a wider audience and use cases.
- We then continue the path to the root in the Wikidata taxonomy, discarding all classes on the way, until we hit a class that has been mapped to schema.org. We continue our path to the root in the schema.org taxonomy, adding all classes on the way to YAGO 4.
- If we do not hit a class that has been mapped to schema.org, we discard the entire path. If an instance has no path with a class that qualifies for these criteria, we discard the instance.

We discard all Wikidata classes that have less than 10 direct instances. This threshold serves to ignore classes that have little value in use cases or are rather exotic. We further remove subclasses of a small list of meta-level Wikidata classes such as Wikipedia categories, disambiguation pages, etc. Finally, we drop sub-classes of pair of classes for which we enforce disjointness constraints. These design choices allow us to model villages and cars, while significantly reducing the size of the taxonomy. From the 2.4M original Wikidata classes, we kept only 10k classes, shrinking the taxonomy by 99.6%. We also discard 11M instances (14%) – two thirds of which (7.5M) are Wikipedia-specific meta-entities (disambiguation page, category, wikitext template, etc.). Our strategy capitalizes on the stable backbone of schema.org, while being able to augment YAGO 4 with new data coming from Wikidata.

3.2 Legible Entities and Relations

YAGO 4 is stored in the RDF format. Unlike Wikidata, we chose to give human-readable URIs to all entities, in order to make the KB more accessible for inter-active use. If an entity has a Wikipedia page (which we know because Wikidata links it to Wikipedia), we take the Wikipedia title as the entity name. Otherwise, we concatenate the English label of the entity with its Wikidata identifier (e.g., *Bischmisheim_Q866094*). Studies like [15] suggest that the Wikidata labels are fairly stable, leading to fairly stable YAGO URIs. If the entity has no English label, we stay with the Wikidata identifier. We make the necessary changes to arrive at a valid local IRI name, and add the namespace of YAGO, http://yago-knowledge.org/resource/. This gives the vast majority of entities human-readable names, without introducing duplicates or ambiguity.

Wikidata has a very rich set of relations, but many of these have only very few facts. Indeed 61% of them have less than 1000 facts and 85% of them less than 10k. For YAGO 4, we chose to follow the successful model of previous YAGO versions, which have been parsimonious on the relations per class. We chose the relations from schema.org, which are each attached to a class. While these relations are conservative in coverage, they have emerged as a useful reference. We mapped 116 of these relations manually to the relations of Wikidata. We simply add this information to our schema, by using two new relations, *yago:fromClass* and *yago:fromProperty*, as shown here:

> *schema:Person yago:fromClass wd:Q215627*
> *yago:birthPlaceProperty yago:fromProperty wdt:P569*

The pipeline for KB construction takes care to implement these mappings (Sect. 4.1). This process discards around 7k relations from Wikidata. As a byproduct, it gives human-readable names to all relations. Example relations are *schema:birthPlace, schema:founder*, and *schema:containedInPlace*. We use RDF and RDFS relations whenever possible, including *rdfs:label* and *rdfs:comment* instead of *schema:name* and *schema:description*. For example, the fact "wd:Q42 wdt:P31 wd:Q5" from Wikidata becomes

> *yago:Douglas_Adams rdf:type schema:Person*

3.3   Well-Typed Values

YAGO 4 has not just well-typed entities, but also well-typed literals. For this purpose, we translate the data values of Wikidata to RDF terms. References to Wikidata entities are converted to references to the YAGO entities as explained in Sect. 3.2. External URIs are converted into *xsd:anyURI* literals after normalizing them.[7] We chose to keep external URIs as literals and not as entities, because we do not make any statements about URIs. Time values are converted to *xsd:dateTime, xsd:date, xsd:gYearMonth* or *xsd:gYear*, depending on the time precision. We discard the other time values whose precision could not be mapped to an XML schema type. Globe coordinates are mapped to *schema:GeoCoordinates* resources. Quantities are mapped to *schema:QuantitativeValue* resources (keeping the unit and precision). If there is no unit and an empty precision range, we map to *xsd:integer* where possible. If the unit is a duration unit (minutes, seconds...) and the precision range is empty, we map to *xsd:duration*. In this way, the vast majority of values are migrated to standard RDF typed literals.

3.4   Semantic Constraints

YAGO 4 has hand-crafted semantic constraints that not just keep the data clean, but also allow logical reasoning on the data. We model constraints in the W3C standards SHACL [12] and OWL. YAGO 4 currently has the following constraints:

---

[7] We follow the normalization suggested by RFC 2986 Section 6.2.

Disjointness. We specify 6 major top-level classes: *schema:BioChemical-Entity*, *schema:Event*, *schema:Organization*, *schema:Person*, *schema:Place*, and *schema:CreativeWork*. With the exception of *schema:Organization/schema: Place*, these are pairwise disjoint; so that these classes cannot have any instances in common. We use OWL to express, for example:

> *schema:Person owl:disjointWith schema:CreativeWork*

Note that organizations are not disjoint from places, because many organizations are also located somewhere.

Domain and Range. Each relation comes with a domain and range constraint, meaning that a relation such as *birthPlace* can apply only to a person and a place. RDFS can specify the domain and range of relations by help of the predicates *rdfs:domain* and *rdfs:range*, but our constraints are different: If a KB contained the fact *birthPlace (London, Paris)*, then the statement *rdfs:domain (birthPlace,Person)* would simply deduce that London must be a person. In contrast, our constraints would flag the KB as inconsistent. We use SHACL to express these constraints, as in this example:

> *schema:Person sh:property yago:birthPlaceProperty*
> *yago:birthPlaceProperty sh:path schema:birthPlace*
> *yago:birthPlaceProperty sh:node schema:Place*

The same property can be used to describe entities of different classes. For example *telephone* can be used to describe both persons and organizations. In this case, the same property is going to be in the shapes of several classes. The domain of the property then is the union of all these classes.

In the same spirit, we also support disjunction in property ranges. For example, the range of *author* is *Person* union *Organization*. Following the same argument, the range of the *birthDate* property is the union of datatypes *xsd:dateTime*, *xsd:date*, *xsd:gYearMonth* and *xsd:gYear* to allow different calendar value precisions. Our range constraints also include the validation of *xsd:string* literals via regular expressions, as in this example:

> *schema:Person sh:property yago:telephoneProperty*
> *yago:telephoneProperty sh:path schema:telephone*
> *yago:telephoneProperty sh:pattern "+\d{1,3} ..."*

Functional Constraints. A functional constraint says that a relation can have at most one object for a subject. Several of our relations are functional, e.g., *birthPlace* or *gender*. Again, we use SHACL:

> *yago:Person sh:property yago:birthPlaceProperty*
> *yago:birthPlaceProperty sh:maxCount "1"^^xsd:integer*

Cardinality Constraints. Going beyond functional constraints, we can also specify the maximal number of objects in general. For example, people can have only two parents in YAGO 4. We use again the SHACL *sh:maxCount* property.

YAGO 4 assumes that no other properties are allowed for each class, thereby interpreting the SHACL constraints under a "closed world assumption". The constraints are automatically enforced during the construction of the KB (see Sect. 4.1), and so the data of YAGO 4 satisfies all constraints. Overall, the enforcement of constraints leads to the removal of 132M facts from Wikidata (i.e. 28% of all the facts). Since the constraints are enforced at KB-construction time, we can then add the deductive *rdfs:domain* and *rdfs:range* facts to YAGO 4 without risking that these deduce anything that violates the constraints.

The generated ontology uses the OWL 2 axioms *DisjointClasses*, *ObjectPropertyDomain*, *DataPropertyDomain*, *ObjectPropertyRange*, *DataPropertyRange*, *ObjectUnionOf*, *FunctionalDataProperty*, *FunctionalObjectProperty*, and falls into the OWL DL flavor. Statistics about the mapping and constraints are shown in Table 1.

Table 1. Schema and mapping statistics

Item	Number
Schema.org classes	235
Bioschemas.org classes	6
Object properties	100
Datatype properties	41
Node shapes	49
Property shapes	217
Domain constraints	217
Object range constraints	132
Datatype range constraints	57
Regex constraints	21
Disjoint constraints	18

3.5 Annotations for Temporal Scope

Following previous YAGO versions, YAGO 4 also attaches temporal information to its facts. We harvest these from the Wikidata qualifier system, which annotates facts with their validity time, provenance, and other meta information. We express the temporal scopes of facts by the relations *schema:startDate* and *schema:endDate*. Instead of relying on a custom format for these annotations, we made use of the RDF* model proposal [9], which has received good traction in recent years. For example, we state that Douglas Adams lived in Santa Barbara until 2001 as follows:

<< *Douglas_Adams schema:homeLocation Santa_Barbara* >> *schema:endDate 2001*
We cannot use the usual Property Graph (PG) semantics of RDF*, because this
would assert that Douglas Adams still lives in Santa Barbara. Rather, we use
the "separate-assertions mode" (SA mode), which asserts only that he lived in
Santa Barbara until 2001 – without saying where he currently lives.

4 Knowledge Base

4.1 Construction

We have designed a system that builds YAGO 4 automatically from (1) a Wikidata dump and (2) the SHACL shapes definitions of Sect. 3. We keep only the
"truthy" Wikidata statements, i.e. for each subject and predicate we keep only
the statements with the "best" rank (a.k.a. "preferred" if a statement with such
a rank exists, "normal" if not).

The KB building system constructs the class hierarchy, the entities, and the
facts as outlined in Sect. 3. Its main purpose is then to enforce the constraints
(Sect. 3.4). If a resource is an instance of disjoint classes, we drop the two *rdf:type*
relations leading to this conflict. We drop all instances that are not instances
of any class. We enforce domain, range and regular-expression constraints by
pruning all candidate facts that would violate a constraint. Finally, we check the
cardinality constraints, removing all objects if there are too many for a given
subject.

Our system is implemented in the Rust programming language[8], using
the `Iterator` infrastructure to ingest and output data streams. We use the
already existing stream operators, which resemble those of relational algebra
(map/project, filter, flat map, collect/materialize into a hash structure). We also
implemented new operators particularly for YAGO 4 (stream-hash join, stream-
hash anti join, group-by, and transitive closure). For example, the *owl:sameAs*
links between YAGO 4 and Freebase can be extracted from Wikidata by the
following algebraic operator plan:

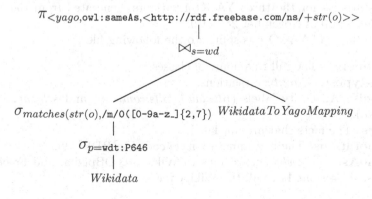

$$\pi_{<yago,\text{owl:sameAs},<\text{http://rdf.freebase.com/ns/}+str(o)>>}$$

$$\bowtie_{s=wd}$$

$$\sigma_{matches(str(o),\text{/m/0(}[\text{0-9a-z\_}]\{2,7\})}\quad WikidataToYagoMapping$$

$$\sigma_{p=\text{wdt:P646}}$$

Wikidata

---

[8] https://www.rust-lang.org/.

Here, π is the projection operator, σ the selection, $\bowtie$ the inner join, $Wikidata$ the table of all Wikidata triples (s, p, o), and $WikidataToYagoMapping$ the mapping between Wikidata and YAGO instances $(wd, yago)$. To avoid reading the full Wikidata N-Triples dump each time, we first load the Wikidata dump into the RocksDB key-value store to index its content[9]. This index allows for efficiently selecting triples based on a predicate or a (predicate, subject) tuple, and getting back a stream of triples from the database.

The advantage of having operator plans in Rust is that we can benefit from declarative programs where performance optimizations are carried out by the compiler, generating highly efficient native code. After having loaded the data into RocksDB, our execution plan generates the Wikipedia-flavored YAGO 4 (see below) in two hours on a commodity server.

We ran our system on a dump of 78M Wikidata items. 8M of these are entities about Wikimedia Websites-related entities, such as categories. From the 474M Wikidata facts whose property has been mapped to schema.org, we filtered out 89M of them because of the domain constraints and 42M more because of the range and regex constraints. The cardinality constraints lead to the removal of an extra 0.6M facts.

4.2 Data

YAGO 4 is made available in three "flavors":

- **Full:** This flavor uses all data from Wikidata, resulting in a very large KB.
- **Wikipedia:** This smaller flavor of YAGO 4 contains only the instances that have a Wikipedia article (in any language).
- **English Wikipedia:** This is an additional restriction of the Wikipedia flavor, containing only instances that have an English Wikipedia article.

All three flavors of YAGO 4 are built in the same way, and have the same schema, with 116 properties and the same taxonomy of 140 top-level classes from schema.org and bioschemas.org, and the same subset of Wikidata classes. Table 2 shows statistics for the three YAGO 4 variants, generated from the Wikidata N-Triples dump of November 25, 2019.

Each flavor of YAGO 4 is split into the following files:

- **Taxonomy:** The full taxonomy of classes.
- **Full-types:** All *rdf:type* relations.
- **Labels:** All entity labels (*rdfs:label, rdfs:comment* and *schema: alternate-Name*).
- **Facts:** The facts that are not labels.
- **Annotations:** The fact annotations encoded in RDF* [9].
- **SameAs:** The *owl:sameAs* links to Wikidata, DBpedia, and Freebase and the *schema:sameAs* to all the Wikipedias.

---

[9] https://rocksdb.org/.

- **Schema:** The schema.org classes and properties, in OWL 2 DL.
- **Shapes:** The SHACL constraints used to generate YAGO 4.

Each file is a compressed N-Triples file, so that standard tools can directly ingest the data.

Table 2. Size statistics for YAGO 4 in the flavors Full, Wikipedia (W), and English Wikipedia (E), Wikidata and DBpedia (per DBpedia SPARQL server on 2020-03-04).

	Yago Full	Yago W	Yago E	Wikidata	DBpedia
Classes	10124	10124	10124	2.4M	484k
Classes from Wikidata	9883	9883	9883	2.4M	222
Individuals	67M	15M	5M	78M	5M
Labels (*rdfs:label*)	303M	137M	66M	371M	22M
Descriptions (*rdfs:comment*)	1399M	139M	50M	2146M	12M
Aliases (*schema:alternateName*)	68M	21M	14M	71M	0
rdf:type (without transitive closure)	70M	16M	5M	77M	114M
Facts	343M	48M	20M	974M	131M
Avg. # of facts per entity	5.1	3.2	4	12.5	26
sameAs to Wikidata	67M	15M	5M	N.A	816k
sameAs to DBpedia	5M	5M	5M	0	N.A.
sameAs to Freebase	1M	1M	1M	1M	157k
sameAs to Wikipedia	43M	43M	26M	66M	13M
Fact annotations	2.5M	2.2M	1.7M	220M	0
Dump size	60 GB	7 GB	3 GB	127 GB	99 GB

4.3 Access

Web Page. The YAGO 4 knowledge base is available at http://yago-knowledge. org. The Web page offers an introduction to YAGO, documentation ("Getting started"), and a list of publications and contributors. The Web page also has a schema diagram that lists all top-level classes with their associated relations and constraints.

License. The entire YAGO 4 knowledge base, as well as all previous versions and the logo, can be downloaded from the Web page. YAGO 4 is available under a Creative Commons Attribution-ShareAlike License. The reason for this choice is that, while Wikidata is in the public domain, schema.org is under a Creative Commons Attribution-ShareAlike License.[10]

Source Code. We have released the source code for constructing YAGO 4 on GitHub at https://github.com/yago-naga/yago4 under the GNU GPL v3+ license.

SPARQL Endpoint. YAGO 4 comes with a responsive SPARQL endpoint, which can be used as an API or interactively. The URL is http://yago-knowledge.org/sparql/query. The YAGO URIs are also all dereferencable, thus complying with the Semantic Web best practice.

Browser. YAGO 4 comes with a graphical KB browser, with an example shown in Fig. 1. For each entity, the browser visualizes the outgoing relationships in a star-shape around the entity. Above the entity, the browser shows the hierarchy of all classes of which the entity is a (transitive) instance, including those with multiple inheritance. If an entity has more than one object for a given relation, a relation-specific screen shows all objects of that relation for the entity. For size reasons, the browser shows only the Wikipedia flavor of YAGO.

Applications. YAGO has already been used in quite a number of projects [16], including question answering, entity recognition, and semantic text analysis. We believe that the new version of YAGO opens up the door to an entire array of new applications, because it is possible to perform logical reasoning on YAGO 4. Not only is the KB equipped with semantic constraints, but it is also provably consistent. We have checked the "English Wikipedia" flavor of YAGO 4 with the OWL 2 DL reasoner HermiT [6], proving its logical consistency.[11] This makes it possible to perform advanced kinds of logical inference on YAGO 4.

5   Conclusion

This paper presents YAGO 4, the newest version of the YAGO knowledge base. The unique characteristics of YAGO 4 is to combine the wealth of facts from Wikidata with the clean and human-readable taxonomy from schema.org, together with semantic constraints that enforce logical consistency. This way, the resulting KB can be processed with OWL and other reasoners, and is also more user-friendly for browsing and question answering. We hope that the YAGO 4 resource fills a gap in the landscape of public KBs, and will be useful in downstream applications.

We plan to release updates of YAGO 4 to reflect the changes in Wikidata. A change of the schema vocabulary would require human intervention, and could

---

[10] http://schema.org/docs/terms.html.
[11] HermiT was unable to load the "Full" flavor due to a memory overflow, but it contains the same taxonomy and the same constraints as the "English Wikipedia" flavor.

be done a few times a year. Future work includes extending the set of semantic constraints to capture inverse functions, symmetric and transitive properties, and more. We also consider tapping into additional data sources, beyond Wikidata, to further enrich the factual knowledge of YAGO 4.

Acknowledgements. This work was partially supported by the grant ANR-16-CE23-0007-01 ("DICOS").

References

1. Auer, S., Bizer, C., Kobilarov, G., Lehmann, J., Cyganiak, R., Ives, Z.: DBpedia: a nucleus for a web of open data. In: Aberer, K., et al. (eds.) ASWC/ISWC -2007. LNCS, vol. 4825, pp. 722–735. Springer, Heidelberg (2007). https://doi.org/10. 1007/978-3-540-76298-0_52
2. Carlson, A., Betteridge, J., Kisiel, B., Settles, B., Jr. Hruschka, E.R., Mitchell, T.M.: Toward an architecture for never-ending language learning. In: AAAI (2010). http://www.aaai.org/ocs/index.php/AAAI/AAAI10/paper/view/1879
3. Etzioni, O., et al.: Web-scale information extraction in knowitall. In: WWW, pp. 100–110 (2004). https://doi.org/10.1145/988672.988687
4. Fellbaum, C. (ed.): WordNet: An Electronic Lexical Database. MIT Press, Cambridge (1998). https://mitpress.mit.edu/books/wordnet
5. Frey, J., Hofer, M., Obraczka, D., Lehmann, J., Hellmann, S.: DBpedia FlexiFusion the best of Wikipedia > Wikidata > your data. In: Ghidini, C., et al. (eds.) ISWC 2019. LNCS, vol. 11779, pp. 96–112. Springer, Cham (2019). https://doi.org/10. 1007/978-3-030-30796-7_7
6. Glimm, B., Horrocks, I., Motik, B., Stoilos, G., Wang, Z.: HermiT: An OWL 2 Reasoner. J. Autom. Reasoning **53**(3), 245–269 (2014). https://doi.org/10.1007/ s10817-014-9305-1
7. Gray, A.J.G., Goble, C.A., Jimenez, R.: Bioschemas: from potato salad to protein annotation. In: ISWC (2017). http://ceur-ws.org/Vol-1963/paper579.pdf
8. Guha, R.V., Brickley, D., Macbeth, S.: Schema.org: evolution of structured data on the web. Commun. ACM **59**(2), 44–51 (2016). https://doi.org/10.1145/2844544
9. Hartig, O.: Foundations of RDF* and SPARQL* (an alternative approach to statement-level metadata in RDF). In: Alberto Mendelzon Workshop on Foundations of Data Management and the Web (2017). http://ceur-ws.org/Vol-1912/ paper12.pdf
10. Hoffart, J., Suchanek, F.M., Berberich, K., Lewis-Kelham, E., de Melo, G., Weikum, G.: YAGO2: exploring and querying world knowledge in time, space, context, and many languages. In: WWW, pp. 229–232 (2011). https://doi.org/10. 1145/1963192.1963296
11. Ismayilov, A., Kontokostas, D., Auer, S., Lehmann, J., Hellmann, S.: Wikidata through the eyes of dbpedia. Semant. Web **9**(4), 493–503 (2018). https://doi.org/ 10.3233/SW-170277
12. Knublauch, H., Kontokostas, D.: Shapes constraint language (SHACL). W3C Candidate Recommendation, **11**(8) (2017). https://www.w3.org/TR/shacl/
13. Mahdisoltani, F., Biega, J., Suchanek, F.M.: YAGO3: a knowledge base from multilingual Wikipedias. In: CIDR (2015). http://cidrdb.org/cidr2015/Papers/CIDR15_ Paper1.pdf

14. Navigli, R., Ponzetto, S.P.: Babelnet: Building a very large multilingual semantic network. In: ACL, pp. 216–225 (2010). https://www.aclweb.org/anthology/P10-1023/

15. Pellissier Tanon, T., Kaffee, L.: Property label stability in wikidata: evolution and convergence of schemas in collaborative knowledge bases. In: WikiWorkshop, WWW, pp. 1801–1803 (2018). https://doi.org/10.1145/3184558.3191643

16. Rebele, T., Suchanek, F.M., Hoffart, J., Biega, J., Kuzey, E., Weikum, G.: YAGO: a multilingual knowledge base from Wikipedia, Wordnet, and Geonames. In: ISWC, pp. 177–185 (2016). https://doi.org/10.1007/978-3-319-46547-0_19

17. Suchanek, F.M., Kasneci, G., Weikum, G.: YAGO: a core of semantic knowledge. In: WWW, pp. 697–706 (2007). https://doi.org/10.1145/1242572.1242667

18. Vrandecic, D., Krötzsch, M.: Wikidata: a free collaborative knowledgebase. Commun. ACM 57(10), 78–85 (2014). https://doi.org/10.1145/2629489

19. Zaveri, A., Rula, A., Maurino, A., Pietrobon, R., Lehmann, J., Auer, S.: Quality assessment for linked data: a survey. Semant. Web 7(1), 63–93 (2016). https://doi.org/10.3233/SW-150175

In-Use

On Modeling the Physical World as a Collection of Things: The W3C Thing Description Ontology

Victor Charpenay[1]([✉])[iD] and Sebastian Käbisch[2][iD]

[1] FAU Erlangen-Nürnberg, Nuremberg, Germany
victor.charpenay@fau.de
[2] Siemens AG, Munich, Germany
sebastian.kaebisch@siemens.com

Abstract. This document presents the Thing Description ontology, an axiomatization of the W3C Thing Description model. It also introduces an alignment with the Semantic Sensor Network ontology and evaluates how this alignment contributes to semantic interoperability in the Web of Things.

Keywords: Web of Things · Thing Description · SSN · RDF

1 Introduction

The Web of Things (WoT) is an architectural principle that aims at bringing sensor and actuator data on the Web in order to increase interoperability between connected devices and develop arbitrarily complex mash-ups on that basis [4,19]. The World Wide Web Consortium (W3C) embraced that vision and recently started a standardization activity around WoT with two main outcomes: a set of architectural guidelines [12] and a model to describe 'things' and their interface, the Thing Description (TD) model [8].

As both specifications are about to be officially released, the present paper provides an analysis of the role played by RDF and other Semantic Web technologies in WoT. In particular, RDF shall improve the interoperability across sensors and actuators at the semantic level, such that autonomous Web agents can build their own representation of the physical world from data exposed by various WoT devices.

In practice, semantic interoperability in the TD model translates into an annotation mechanism such that TD documents—instances of the TD model serialized in JSON—link to RDF terms defined in domain-specific vocabularies. To permit it, the TD model was designed on top of a Web ontology, which is being introduced in this paper: the TD ontology. The paper also introduces a formal alignment between the TD ontology and the Semantic Sensor Network

© Springer Nature Switzerland AG 2020
A. Harth et al. (Eds.): ESWC 2020, LNCS 12123, pp. 599–615, 2020.
https://doi.org/10.1007/978-3-030-49461-2_35

(SSN) ontology [6]. It is indeed expected that most relevant vocabularies will be defined as specializations of SSN, as suggested by recent trends in ontology engineering for WoT [1,2].

Both the TD ontology and its alignment with SSN were designed as per the requirement that the TD annotation mechanism should remain as easy to use as possible, especially for developers with no particular knowledge of Semantic Web technologies. In practice, developers are only asked to provide semantic "tags" at several places of a TD document. As a consequence, the axiomatization we present in this paper favors simplicity over completeness. We provide an evaluation on its effectiveness at the end of the paper, by looking at a collection of TD documents that serves as a test set in the W3C standardization process.

The paper is structured as follows: Sect. 2 contextualizes the TD ontology by providing a short review of the state-of-the-art in WoT ontology engineering, Sect. 3 presents the vocabulary it defines and Sect. 4 introduces an alignment of the TD ontology with SSN. Finally, in Sect. 5, the W3C TD test set is being analyzed in more detail.

2   Ontologies for the Web of Things: State-of-the-Art

Over the last decade, research on WoT systems has moved from pre-defined sensor mash-ups to autonomous agents capable of selecting what sensor measurements to read and what actuator commands to activate to fulfill a global goal [3,11,13,18]. This agent-oriented vision for WoT requires a detailed ontological view on the physical world, such that agents can take informed decisions on what interaction to initiate.

In parallel, a significant effort has been put to providing Web ontologies for WoT [5]. The SSN ontology, recently standardized, is now the pivot to any ontology engineering work in the domain. By analyzing the network formed by alignments between more than 80 WoT ontologies, SSN stands out as the most central point in the network [1,2]. Among others, it aligns with the ontology for units of measure (OM) [17] and the ontology for Quantity Kinds, Units and Datatypes[1] (QUDT), which both provide an extensive list of physical properties in OWL. SSN also aligns with domain-specific ontologies, like the Building Topology Ontology (BOT) [16]. In particular, a range of ontologies derived from the Smart Appliance Reference (SAREF) ontology is currently under construction[2]. All these ontologies are designed with compatibility with SSN in mind [14].

While SSN and the ontologies that align to it model the physical world, the TD ontology shall provide metadata to guide autonomous Web agents in the network of interconnected devices that quantify it. In particular, it formalizes the concept of 'affordance', introduced in the next section.

---

[1] http://qudt.org/.

[2] https://saref.etsi.org/.

3   The Thing Description Model

The TD model is a schema to which TD documents must comply when exposing the capabilities of a 'thing' on the Web [8]. We briefly presents its main components on an example. The following TD document, serialized in JSON, describes a lamp:

```
1   {
2     "@context": "https://www.w3.org/...",
3     "id": "http://lamp.local/#it",
4     "title": "Some lamp",
5     "properties": {
6       "state": {
7         "type": "boolean",
8         "forms": [
9           { "href": "http://lamp.local/st" }
10        ]
11      }
12    },
13    "actions": {
14      "on": {
15        "output": { "type": "boolean" },
16        "forms": [
17          { "href": "http://lamp.local/on" }
18        ]
19      },
20      "off": {
21        "output": { "type": "boolean" },
22        "forms": [{
23          "href": "http://lamp.local/off" }
24        ]
25      }
26    },
27    "events": {}
28  }
```

The mandatory @context key makes this document a JSON-LD 1.1 document, such that it complies to the Linked Data principles and can be turned into RDF in a standard way [9]. In order for the 'thing' (here, the physical lamp) to become a Web resource, it can be assigned an IRI with the key id, an alias for the JSON-LD keyword @id.

The three keys properties, actions and events are the main elements of a TD document. Here, the lamp exposes its on/off state as a property (state), which can be changed by calling two actions (on and off). The on/off state could also have been exposed as an event. Every possible interaction with the lamp starts by submitting a Web form to the 'thing', as specified under the forms key. Here, agents must only know the target URI of each form (href) to start interacting with the lamp.

This approach centered around Web forms is inspired by the Representational State Transfer (REST) principles, fundamental to the Web. The values under property, actions and events are 'interaction affordances', which can be seen informally as "invitations" to interact with the 'thing'. The concept of affordance has a well-defined meaning in the context of REST: it relates to hypermedia controls, that is, links and forms embedded in a message [15].

3.1   Requirements

Requirements for the TD model have been collected in the WoT architecture recommendation document [12]. The main requirements can be found in Sect. 6.4 of that document as a series of assertions, which can be turned into formal axioms with little effort. All model elements listed in these assertions (i.e. the TD terminology) were turned into an RDF class. Assertions that include the keyword

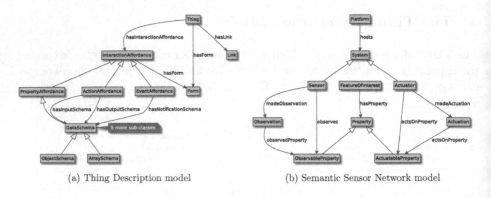

(a) Thing Description model   (b) Semantic Sensor Network model

Fig. 1. Overview of the TD and SSN ontologies

'may' have been axiomatized using the lightweight schema.org semantics[3]. Assertions including the keyword 'must' have been turned into RDF shapes, using the SHACL language [10]. The later part is however not presented in this paper. One can indeed argue that it contributes little to semantic interoperability.

It is however important to introduce the RDF classes and properties of the TD model (loosely referred to as the TD ontology), in order to then provide an alignment with SSN, the key element of semantic interoperability. It is indeed in SSN terms that the internal state of a 'thing' is to be specified. Contrary to other RESTful systems, the internal state of WoT systems is not purely informational but is instead derived from observing physical world objects. Before developing this aspect in Sect. 4, we first introduce the details of the TD ontology axiomatization.

3.2 Axiomatization

An overview of the classes and properties of the TD ontology is provided on Fig. 1a. The Figure shows sub-class relations and property relations whenever instances of two classes may be related in a TD document. The terms 'property affordance', 'action affordance' and 'event affordance' are respectively the abbreviation of 'affordance to retrieve/update a property', 'affordance to invoke an action' and 'affordance to subscribe to an event'.

As shown on the figure, the TD ontology refers to classes that may be used in another context. In particular, it relies on JSON Schema, a language under standardization[4], and on hypermedia controls (links and forms), which may be used in other RESTful systems, outside the scope of WoT. To encourage reusability, these two aspects were put in their own modules, separate from the TD core module[5]. We present them next.

---

[3] https://meta.schema.org/.

[4] https://tools.ietf.org/html/draft-handrews-json-schema.

[5] A fourth module for security configurations is included in the W3C standard but not covered in this paper.

Core Module. The core module defines two main classes: the class `td:Thing`[6] is the entry point of the ontology and its instances are anything that provides affordances to interact with it (`td:InteractionAffordance`). The concept of interaction is further refined into three sub-classes: it can be a basic state transfer, i.e. a retrieval or an update of the exposed state of the 'thing', it can be an invocation with input parameters and expected result or it can be an asynchronous notification after subscribing to a particular event. Any of these three interaction patterns translate into a certain kind of affordance, which must include the appropriate metadata for an agent to be able to properly submit the associated form. The three affordance classes are `td:PropertyAffordance`, `td:ActionAffordance` and `td:EventAffordance`.

As per architectural requirements, an action may manipulate the exposed state of a 'thing' but it may as well leave it unchanged. Similarly, event notifications may include parts of the exposed state or not. Conversely, properties (which represent the exposed state of the 'thing') may be retrieved asynchronously if they are 'observable'. As a result, these concepts are *not* mutually exclusive. A state can be retrieved either as properties or via events, while it can be updated by manipulating properties or via action invocation. This versatility shall account for the diversity of communication paradigms that coexist on WoT.

All interaction affordances are composed of two kinds of objects: data schema, which are to be understood as specifications of abstract data structures, and hypermedia controls (forms). They are each described next.

Data Schema Module. The data schema module is a port of JSON Schema to RDF. JSON Schema was favored over e.g. schema.org's property/value specification mechanism[7], mostly designed for HTML forms. As its name suggests, JSON Schema is a language whose type system relies on the basic JSON types (object, array, number, string, boolean and null), to which it adds the integer type. In RDF, each type becomes a class: `jsonschema:ObjectSchema`, `jsonschema:ArraySchema`, etc. The language also includes constraints specific to each type, like minimum and maximum values for numbers or a maximum length for strings. Contrary to schema.org's property/value specifications, JSON Schema is a recursive language, via the `jsonschema:properties` and `jsonschema:items` relations, for JSON values of the object and array type.

The goal of this ontological module is less to provide axioms for logical inference than to offer a simple transformation from JSON to RDF (using a JSON-LD standard processor). It is therefore merely a set of RDF terms. An alternative design would have been to embed JSON Schema definitions as literal, leveraging the newly introduced `rdf:JSON` datatype[8].

---

[6] All prefixes in the paper can be found on https://prefix.cc/.

[7] https://schema.org/PropertyValueSpecification.

[8] https://w3c.github.io/json-ld-syntax/#the-rdf-json-datatype.

Yet, the chosen approach has mainly two benefits over literal schemas. First, sub-schemas can be semantically tagged in an individual fashion, which will be later illustrated in Sect. 4. Second, the RDF entities resulting from JSON-LD transformation could then carry both schema information and denote actual properties of physical world objects. An example is given later in Sect. 5.3.

Hypermedia Controls Module. Classical Web applications make use of two kinds of hypermedia controls: links and forms. Both links and forms include a target IRI and a "type". This type is alternatively called a *relation* type for links and an *operation* type for forms. The TD ontology defines operation types specific to WoT: `td:readProperty`, `td:writeProperty`, `td:invokeActtion`, `td:subscribeEvent` and a few others. The hypermedia controls module, however, only includes generic classes and properties that are needed to express links and forms in RDF. A link can also be thought of as a reification of an RDF triple, e.g. to add provenance or temporal metadata.

The JSON-LD context that maps terms from this module to JSON keys was designed in such a way that links have the same format as specified in JSON Hyper-Schema[9].

4   Alignment with the Semantic Sensor Network

4.1   Requirements

The TD model serves primarily communication purposes. The axiomatization presented in the previous section therefore concentrates on the concept of 'interaction affordance'. Contrary to what one may think at first sight, it provides only few axioms on the concept of 'thing'. Yet, as previously mentioned, the peculiarity of WoT systems is that they do not have a purely informational state but rather maintain a virtual representation of the state of physical world objects (the actual 'things').

According to the state-of-the-art, the state of physical world objects will likely be modeled using ontologies aligned with SSN. It therefore calls for an alignment of the TD ontology itself to SSN, in order to derive an SSN "view" on instances of `td:Thing`.

To this end, we provide four competency questions from the point of view of Web agents that process TD documents (Table 1). Our assumption is that agents are autonomous and rely solely on the RDF statements included in a TD document to select affordances. An example of an affordance selection task is provided later in Sect. 5.3.

---

[9] https://tools.ietf.org/html/draft-handrews-json-schema-hyperschema.

Table 1. Competency questions for autonomous Web agents

Competency questions	
Q1	How to identify affordances exposed by a 'thing' that have the same effects on the physical world?
Q2	How to identify 'things' that fulfill the same function?
Q3	How to map complex property affordances to simpler representations of physical world objects and their properties?
Q4	How to differentiate between active 'things' (like sensors) and passive 'things' (like feature of interest under observation)?

4.2   Axiomatization

An overview of SSN is given on Fig. 1b. The ontology is mostly centered around the concepts of 'observations' and 'actuations' performed by sensors and actuators. However, in the context of WoT, the most relevant classes are sosa:FeatureOfInterest and ssn:Property. These two classes roughly denote physical world objects and their properties (or characteristics). This basic object model is meant to be specialized for concrete domains of application, as is the case in the ontologies mentioned in Sect. 2.

The alignment between TD and SSN consists mostly in existential restrictions on the classes td:Thing and td:InteractionAffordance. These axioms, like the TD axioms themselves, were not designed for automatic inference but rather as 'may' statements on the SSN entities to include in TD documents. The two main alignment axioms are given below[10] (OWL Manchester syntax [7]):

```
1    Class: td:Thing
2        SubClassOf: ssn:System or sosa:Platform or sosa:FeatureOfInterest
3    Class: td:InteractionAffordance
4        SubClassOf: ssn:forProperty some ssn:Property
```

We review each in the following and then move on to a review of how competency questions can be addressed with SSN.

As provided in our alignment, a 'thing' can be any of the following: a sensor (for illuminance, temperature, air quality, etc.); an actuator (like a binary switch); a composite system; a platform that hosts a system (like a electronic board with pluggable sensors); a feature of interest (like a room). The list is not exhaustive. Yet, it covers all 'things' described in the W3C implementation report we review in Sect. 5.

SSN does not define systems, platforms and features of interest as mutually exclusive. In fact, having systems being themselves features of interest is a common pattern. It is the case e.g. of consumer electronics products like light bulbs or air conditioning units: they are connected devices and thus instances of ssn:System but they are neither sensors, nor actuators and they are more

---

[10] Other axioms can be found in the TD ontology documentation, served under its namespace URI: https://www.w3.org/2019/wot/td.

than simply a combination of both (because the coupling of sensing and actuation follows some internal logic). They can however be modeled as features of interest with their own properties (on/off status, wind speed, etc.).

The second alignment axiom we reported implies a restriction on what parts of a 'thing' should be exposed via affordances. Indeed, the axiom states that every affordance relates to the property of some physical world object, that is, to part of the physical world. In contrast, some properties like a software version number, a product ID or a writable label only belong to some informational space, without any tangible extent. Despite the fact that neither SSN axioms nor the alignment axioms are restrictive on what instances of ssn:Property should be, exposing informational properties as plain RDF statements should be favored over exposing affordances to these properties.

We now illustrate with examples how the competency questions of Table 1 can be addressed. In each case, the existential restrictions that exist between TD and SSN classes were "instantiated" with blank nodes that have ssn:forProperty-relations with TD entities. Portions of TD documents can be found on Fig. 2.

The first competency question (Q1) refers to the fact that the exposed state of a 'thing' may be retrieved via readable properties or events and updated via writable properties or actions, often exposed within the same TD document. The example on Fig. 2a makes the relation explicit between the state property affordance and the on and off action affordances, by pointing at the same actuatable property (an on/off status).

In this example, Web agents must also be able to differentiate between the on and off actions, as they may have the same signature. For that purpose, a set of basic command types can be found in SAREF ('turn on', 'turn off', 'toggle', 'set level', 'setp up', 'step down', etc.). This aspect is however not directly solvable by an alignment with SSN.

Regarding Q2, it is also possible to use properties of physical world objects as connectors between 'things'. For instance, two sensors may provide measurements for the same observable property, as on Fig. 2b. In this example, two light sensors observe the same illuminance property, e.g. because they are in the same room. This modeling is an approximation, as the two sensors cannot strictly provide measurements for the same illuminated surface but it suffices in most home automation applications.

Regarding Q3, the need to individually characterize parts of a data schema arises from the observation that certain developers expose data of different nature under the same URI. For instance, sensor boards designed to provide environmental data (temperature, humidity, compass direction, etc.) may expose only one complex property in which a value for all physical quantities is provided in a single JSON message.

It is the case in the example of Fig. 2c which offers only one measurement property affordance. The temperature and humidity values in the provided schema however point to SSN properties of different types (type statements are not shown for the sake of brevity).

```
 1   {
 2     "properties": {
 3       "state": {
 4         "ssn:forProperty": "_:status"
 5       }
 6     },
 7     "actions": {
 8       "on": {
 9         "ssn:forProperty": "_:status"
10       },
11       "off": {
12         "ssn:forProperty": "_:status"
13       }
14     }
15   }
```

(a) Q1

```
 1   [
 2     {
 3       "properties": {
 4         "light1": {
 5           "ssn:forProperty": "_:light"
 6         }
 7       }
 8     }, {
 9       "properties": {
10         "light2": {
11           "ssn:forProperty": "_:light"
12         }
13       }
14     }
15   ]
```

(b) Q2

```
 1   {
 2     "properties": {
 3       "measurement": {
 4         "type": "object",
 5         "properties": {
 6           "temperature": {
 7             "ssn:forProperty": "_:temp"
 8           },
 9           "humidity": {
10             "ssn:forProperty": "_:humid"
11           }
12         }
13       }
14     }
15   }
```

(c) Q3

```
 1   [
 2     {
 3       "title": "Some sensor",
 4       "properties": {
 5         "measure": {
 6           "ssn:forProperty": "_:light"
 7         }
 8       },
 9       "sosa:observes": "_:light"
10     }, {
11       },
12       "title": "Some room",
13       "properties": {
14         "measure": {
15           "ssn:forProperty": "_:light"
16         }
17       "ssn:hasProperty": "_:light"
18     }
19   ]
```

(d) Q4

Fig. 2. Examples of annotation for each competency question

The last competency question (Q4) is relevant to Web agents insofar as selecting interactions may require knowledge about the underlying sensing or actuation mechanism. In the last example (Fig. 2d), the upper definition describes the sensor that produces measurements itself while in the lower one, the room in which the sensor is located is exposed instead, hiding the sensing device from the agent. Yet, the two definitions include the same affordance.

Exposing (inanimate) physical world objects instead of sensors is relevant in certain cases, though. It is for instance simpler when the object is observed by numerous devices, whose measurements are combined into a single state. In the implementation report presented in the next section, a TD document describes a water tank that embeds three sensor: a water level sensor at its top, another at its bottom and a radar that provides the absolute level.

5   Evaluation

Every W3C standard must be associated with a technical implementation report, which proves interoperability between distinct implementations of the standard. Over the course of the standardization of WoT at W3C, the working group gathered implementation experience by putting existing devices on the Web and thus collected a number of TD documents that were then included in the implementation report for the TD model. In the following, we analyze these TD documents with respect to semantic interoperability and evaluate the role of our axiomatization on that aspect.

In this section, we first give an overview of the set of TD documents that are available. We then report on the semantic tagging approach chosen by implementers and evaluate whether the competency questions of Table 1 are properly addressed by this approach. To this end, we chose a specific task among those tested by the W3C working group, which consists in automatically selecting specific affordances from all affordances included in the set of TD documents.

5.1   The W3C Thing Description Implementation Report

The implementation report for the W3C TD specification[11] relies on a set of 95 TD documents that each implement specific aspects of the TD model. All examples mentioned in this paper come from this test set.

Among the 95 documents, we identified 65 that relate to actual devices (or simulations). The other documents are synthetic and designed for pure testing. Table 2 provides a list of all devices under test. Most of them are small devices (lamp, illuminance sensor, switch, sensor board, electric meter) but the test set includes various other devices, like air conditioning units, blinds, cars and an industrial plant model. Some of the TD documents were generated from other specifications, standardized by other consortia like the Open Connectivity Foundation[12] and ECHONET[13]. One of the two cars exposes data via its on-board diagnostics interface, specified by the International Organization for Standardization.

Some of the TD documents are copies of each other, in which only id and href values differ. If we discard duplicates, there remains 44 unique sets of interaction affordances. They were designed by 8 distinct organizations (all members of the W3C working group). We could observe notable differences in the data schema definitions, despite referring to similar properties. In particular, the test set includes four different schema definitions for a brightness property: either a number in the intervals $[0, 100]$, $[0, 254]$ or $[-64, 64]$ or an enumeration of the 100 integers in the interval $[0, 100]$[14]. This observation motivates the need for some further input by WoT developers to guarantee interoperability.

---

[11] https://w3c.github.io/wot-thing-description/testing/report.html.
[12] https://openconnectivity.org/.
[13] https://echonet.jp/.
[14] This uncommon representation is due to an automatic translation from ECHONET schemas to TD documents.

Table 2. List of 'things' under test

Type	Unique	All	Type	Unique	All
Light switch	2	13	Blinds	2	2
Lamp	7	9	Camera	2	2
Illuminance sensor	5	5	Car	1	2
Generic switch	5	5	Pump	1	2
Motion sensor	4	4	Electric meter	1	1
Generic sensor board	4	4	Robot cleaner	1	1
Bulletin board	2	4	Industry automation model	1	1
Temperature sensor	1	3	Water tank	1	1
Buzzer	2	2	Boiler	1	1
Air conditioning unit	2	2	Medical device	1	1
Total				44	65

Interoperability among these devices was tested in different scenarios by the working group members: home appliances are turned off when the owner leaves the house; industrial equipment is put in safety mode when an accident is detected; the electric consumption of devices in a large building is adapted to real-time electric supply. Other ad-hoc interoperability tests have been performed, e.g. between generic switches and various actuators (like a car's honk). For practical reasons, all interoperability tests were performed among specific instances of 'things', involving manual annotation, as opposed to relying on semantic annotations of TD documents. The next two sections address the question of pure semantic interoperability, without human intervention.

Note that all figures in the remainder of the evaluation are based on the 44 TD documents with unique sets of interaction affordances, rather than on all 65 documents.

5.2 Semantic Tagging

Every TD document is a JSON-LD document. Objects that map to RDF entities can therefore be added arbitrary statements in the JSON-LD syntax, as in the examples of Sect. 4. However, this principle seems to be hardly understood by developers with no particular knowledge of Semantic Web technologies. Consequently, the decision has been made among the group that semantic annotations be limited to the tagging of certain model elements with type statements, using the JSON-LD @type keyword. Such @type tags should be put on instances of three classes: td:Thing, td:InteractionAffordance and jsonschema:DataSchema. One implementation of the WoT standards documents them as "the names of schemas for types of capabilities a device supports,"[15].

---

[15] https://iot.mozilla.org/wot/#type-member.

Table 3. Summary of @type tagging in the W3C test set (t: thing, p: property, a:action, e: event, sc: data schema, x: resource not found, ∅: no tag)

	t	p	a	e	sc	x	∅
td:Thing	10	1				12	33
td:PropertyAffordance		29	2	11	6	264
td:ActionAffordance			5			7	41
td:EventAffordance				1		1	4
jsonschema:DataSchema		2			14	22	258

Although developers are generally aware of the necessity of semantic tagging to increase interoperability in WoT, the concept of "schema" has remained ambiguous. To ease the tagging effort developers must provide, an initiative to provide a unified vocabulary adapted to TD documents has been launched in parallel to the W3C standardization activity. This initiative, referred to as iot.schema.org, aims at reproducing the success of schema.org in the WoT domain[16]. The upper-level classes of iot.schema.org are aligned with those of the TD model and are meant to later align both with schema.org and with ontologies like SSN and SAREF. It includes a total of 194 classes at the time of writing, some of them having no equivalent class in other WoT ontologies yet (e.g. for individual red/green/blue components of a color).

Some of the TD documents of the W3C implementation report include @type tags from iot.schema.org. An overview of how tagging was performed is given in Table 3. What the table first shows is that the majority of TD entities were still not tagged (84% of property affordances and 86% of data schemas). It also shows how many tags can be considered as erroneous because the corresponding URI does not exist in iot.schema.org (resource not found): they represent 39% of the tags.

Some of the erroneous tags are undoubtedly spelling mistakes (like iot:PropertyChangeEvent instead of iot:PropertyChangedEvent), which appropriate tooling can mitigate. However, some of these tags seem to result from conceptual discrepancies with the original iot.schema.org vocabulary. For example, the tag iot:RunModeChanged does not exist in iot.schema.org although iot:RunMode does. Moreover, the former is used as annotation for a data schema, although its name suggests it should apply to event affordances.

This assumption is supported by the fact that the confusion between properties and events can also be observed for a tag that does exist in the vocabulary: iot:MotionDetected. This class is defined as a sub-class of iot:Event but despite this axiom, two independent contributors to the implementation report used it to tag an instance of iot:Property, which is semantically inconsistent. We identified two more cases of semantic inconsistency: a sub-class

---

[16] http://iotschema.org/ (incubated domain name for http://iot.schema.org).

of iot:Property used to tag a 'thing' entity and two other sub-classes of iot:Property to annotate data schemas.

One of the original design choices of iot.schema.org was to introduce a certain level of redundancy to ensure developers would find the appropriate tag for a given level of abstraction. As a result, the vocabulary includes e.g. the classes iot:IlluminanceSensing, iot:Illuminance and iot:IlluminanceData, to respectively tag a 'thing', a property affordance and a data schema. What our review suggests, however, is that developers tend not to make the distinction.

To mitigate the risk of confusion, an alternative design would consist in keeping property classes only: iot:Motion and iot:Illuminance, for example. Our alignment of the TD ontology with SSN becomes then relevant to retain conceptual consistency. These two classes can indeed be both defined as subclasses of sosa:ObservableProperty.

It is worth mentioning two further observations on that topic. First, most entities in TD documents are either data schemas or property affordances (which are also instances of data schemas, as constrained by the TD model's RDF shapes). The modeling effort of iot.schema.org should therefore give priority to properties. Second, although Table 3 shows that 'things' are entities with the highest tagging ratio, all 'things' with tags also include tags at the affordance or the data schema level. It suggests again that properties are the most important entities in a TD document. Existing WoT ontologies already include a number of classes for the physical properties of physical world objects (OM and QUDT, in the first place). Our alignment with SSN details how affordances and properties should relate.

In the next section, we review how SSN statements can be derived from @type tags in order to perform an affordance selection task. Tags originate from existing WoT ontologies, as per the above conclusion.

5.3 Affordance Selection Task

The following three-step process was part of a larger home automation scenario in the W3C implementation report: 1. start if motion is detected in some room, 2. turn on the lamp in this room, 3. after some time, end if illuminance is above a certain threshold, 4. otherwise, retry.

This relatively simple mash-up requires affordances of three different kinds to be properly selected. Selection can be reduced to a single query that matches the pattern depicted on Fig. 3, which is formulated using SSN and BOT terms, mostly. This choice is motivated by our review of the state-of-the-art. The goal of the evaluation for this task is to compare a manual affordance selection with an automatic procedure which only takes @type tags as input.

We manually annotated the relevant TD documents with SSN statements, assuming all 'things' were located in the same room. The task involves 16 'things', about one third of the whole test set, and 21 affordances in total: 3 for motion, 14 for updating the on/off state of the lamp and 4 for illuminance. We used five classes for the annotation: saref:Motion, saref:LightingDevice, saref:OnOffState, saref:OnCommand and saref:Light. We assume developers provide

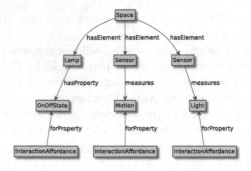

Fig. 3. Query pattern for the affordance selection task

the appropriate @type tagging for these classes. Given that baseline, we can compare our manual annotation with an inference-based procedure which derives SSN statements from a combination of TD statements and type statements. We further assume that the classes listed above are aligned with SSN.

The first inference rule that is needed for that purpose is given by the following axiom (OWL Manchester syntax):

```
1   Class: :SelfAffordance
2     SubClassOf: (ssn:PropertyAffordance or jsonschema:DataSchema) and
3               ssn:Property
4   Class: :SelfAffordance
5     SubClassOf: ssn:forProperty Self
```

This rule states that whenever a property affordance or a data schema is annotated with a sub-class of `ssn:Property`, it then has an `ssn:forProperty`-relation with itself. In other words, it is as if the SSN property carries its own schema information.

We now look at the competency questions of Table 1 one by one to bridge the gap between @type tags and our baseline. Looking at Q1, the challenge is here to find the correspondance between property affordancs on the (writable) on/off state of a lamp and actions affordance to turn the same lamp on. This occurs in 4 TD documents. This equivalence between property and action can be turned into an inference rule that is triggered whenever the tags `saref:OnOffState` and `saref:OnCommand` co-occur in a TD document[17].

Interestingly, 2 TD documents expose two distinct property affordances for the same on/off state. The rule above would also merge them if we add the constraint that lamps can only have one on/off state. However, another TD document exposes a total of 4 affordances tagged with `saref:OnCommand`. Yet, not all these affordances are for the same property. The 'thing' is indeed composed of three LED strips which can be individually controlled. Only one affordance turns all LEDs on. Inference remains sound e.g. if the 'thing' is tagged as a

---

[17] Because most inference rules mentioned in this section are tedious to write in OWL, we do not represent them in the paper; they can be found online, along with the set of annotated TD at https://www.vcharpenay.link/talks/td-sem-interop.html.

platform instead of a feature of interest (such that the rule is not triggered). It is however a fragile assumption.

As for Q2, the relation between 'things' that is required for our lighting task is a relation stating that devices are in the same building space (to prevent that the process runs into infinite loops). Because this aspect is not addressed in the W3C implementation report, we assume that all devices are in the same room for the sake of this evaluation, without further annotation.

Regarding Q3, @type tagging is satisfactory. It does not require further inference. However, @type is necessary: 7 TD documents embed the values required for the task in complex schemas.

Finally, regarding Q4, we can observe that most TD documents follow the same pattern: if the 'thing' is a feature of interest, it provides affordances for its own properties; if it is a sensor or an actuator, its affordances refer to the properties it measures or acts on. Again, these rules can be expressed as OWL axioms such that SSN relations be inferred from td:hasInteractionAffordance-relations.

In a similar fashion to the inference rule fulfilling Q1, the inferred statements would not hold in the general case. For instance, when a 'thing' is a complex system as are a car or an industrial automation system, if it is tagged as an instance of sosa:FeatureOfInterest as well, it would be inferred that it exposes affordances to its own properties. However, it would be more likely that the exposed properties are those of its subsystems. It remains sound in our lighting task, though.

To summarize our comparison between a manual annotation and automatically inferred statements from @type annotations, we can state that all 21 affordances could be correctly selected as expected. However, as noted while looking at Q1, 3 more affordances would be wrongly selected as well depending on the value of a single @type tag. On a different aspect, to arrive at the expected result, it is worth noting that only a tractable OWL fragment was needed (OWL RL), which provides certain guarantees in terms of scalability.

6   Conclusion

This paper, along with introducing the TD ontology, underlines that the alignment with SSN is essential for autonomous agents to be developed in future WoT systems. Most of the standardization conducted by the W3C was put on interoperability at the protocol level. The TD standard that results from this work includes certain assumptions on how interoperability at the semantic level can also be guaranteed. In particular, it is assumed that relying on the JSON-LD syntax and allowing for @type tagging will allow agents to implement arbitrarily complex form selection procedures to drive applications.

This paper provides an initial evaluation of this claim, based on the TD documents included in the W3C implementation report associated with the standard. Under certain conditions, a lighting process involving motion sensors, lamps and illuminance sensors could be executed on the sole basis of @type tags, provided that OWL axioms specify how SSN statements can be inferred from these annotations (Sect. 5.3).

Even in this simple task, certain limitations could be shown: substituting one tag with another may threaten the soundness of inference. Mitigating that risk will require appropriate tooling to show WoT developers the potential effects of their tagging when 'things' are combined. In particular, members of the W3C working group on WoT expressed several times the lack of tools that can detect semantic inconsistencies introduced by @type tags. A few inconsistencies could indeed be shown in the implementation report, as mentioned in Sect. 5.2. However, we could identify an alternative conceptualization, centered around SSN's features of interests and their properties, that could help limit these inconsistencies.

As the W3C is already preparing for the future version of the TD standard, the Semantic Web community may embrace this question of tooling to improve the quality of input annotations.

Acknowledgments. The authors would like to thank all participants of the W3C WoT Working Group, particularly María Poveda-Villalón and Maxime Lefrançois, for their contribution to the TD ontology. This work was partially funded by the German Federal Ministry of Education and Research through the MOSAIK project (grant no. 01IS18070-A).

References

1. Charpenay, V.: Semantics for the web of things: modeling the physical world as a collection of things and reasoning with their descriptions (2019)
2. Charpenay, V., Käbisch, S., Kosch, H.: Introducing thing descriptions and interactions: an ontology for the web of things. In: Joint Proceedings of SR and SWIT 2016, vol. 1783, pp. 55–66 (2016)
3. Ciortea, A., Mayer, S., Michahelles, F.: Repurposing manufacturing lines on the fly with multi-agent systems for the web of things. In: Proceedings of the 17th International Conference on Autonomous Agents and MultiAgent Systems, AAMAS 2018, Stockholm, Sweden, 10–15 July 2018, pp. 813–822 (2018)
4. Guinard, D., Trifa, V.: Towards the web of things: web mashups for embedded devices. In: Workshop on Mashups, Enterprise Mashups and Lightweight Composition on the Web (MEM 2009), Proceedings of WWW (International World Wide Web Conferences), Madrid, Spain, vol. 15
5. Gyrard, A., Bonnet, C., Boudaoud, K., Serrano, M.: LOV4IoT: a second life for ontology-based domain knowledge to build semantic web of things applications. In: 2016 IEEE 4th International Conference on Future Internet of Things and Cloud (FiCloud), pp. 254–261. IEEE (2014)
6. Haller, A., Janowicz, K., Cox, S., Le Phuoc, D., Taylor, K., Lefrançois, M.: Semantic sensor network ontology. https://www.w3.org/TR/vocab-ssn/
7. Horridge, M., Patel-Schneider, P.F.: OWL 2 web ontology language manchester syntax
8. Kaebisch, S., Kamiya, T., McCool, M., Charpenay, V., Kovatsch, M.: Web of things (WoT) thing description. https://www.w3.org/TR/wot-thing-description/

9. Kellogg, G., Champin, P.A., Longley, D.: JSON-LD 1.1. https://www.w3.org/TR/json-ld11/
10. Knublauch, H., Kontokostas, D.: Shapes constraint language (SHACL). https://www.w3.org/TR/shacl/
11. Kovatsch, M., Hassan, Y.N., Mayer, S.: Practical semantics for the internet of things: physical states, device mashups, and open questions. In: 2015 5th International Conference on the Internet of Things (IOT), pp. 54–61. IEEE (2015)
12. Kovatsch, M., Matsukura, R., Lagally, M., Kawaguchi, T., Toumura, K., Kajimoto, K.: Web of things (WoT) architecture. https://www.w3.org/TR/wot-architecture/
13. Käfer, T., Harth, A.: Rule-based programming of user agents for Linked Data. In: LDOW 2018 (2018)
14. Lefrançois, M.: Planned ETSI SAREF extensions based on the W3C&OGC SOSA/SSN-compatible SEAS ontology patterns. In: Workshop on Semantic Interoperability and Standardization in the IoT, SIS-IoT, Proceedings of Workshop on Semantic Interoperability and Standardization in the IoT, SIS-IoT. 11p
15. Pautasso, C., Wilde, E., Alarcon, R. (eds.): REST: Advanced Research Topics and Practical Applications. Springer, New York (2014). https://doi.org/10.1007/978-1-4614-9299-3
16. Rasmussen, M.H., Lefrançois, M., Pauwels, P., Hviid, C.A., Karlshøj, J.: Managing interrelated project information in AEC knowledge graphs. Autom. Constr. **108**, 102956 (2019). Please check and confirm the edit made in Ref. [16]
17. Rijgersberg, H., van Assem, M., Top, J.: Ontology of units of measure and related concepts. Semant. Web **4**(1), 3–13 (2013)
18. Verborgh, R., et al.: Functional composition of sensor web APIs. In: SSN, pp. 65–80 (2012)
19. Wilde, E.: Putting things to REST (2007)

Applying Knowledge Graphs as Integrated Semantic Information Model for the Computerized Engineering of Building Automation Systems

Henrik Dibowski$^{(\boxtimes)}$ ⓘ and Francesco Massa Gray ⓘ

Corporate Research, Robert Bosch GmbH, 71272 Renningen, Germany
`henrik.dibowski@de.bosch.com`

Abstract. During the life cycle of a smart building, an extensive amount of heterogeneous information is required to plan, construct, operate and maintain the building and its technical systems. Traditionally, there is an information gap between the different phases and stakeholders, leading to information being exchanged, processed and stored in a variety of mostly human-readable documents. This paper shows how a knowledge graph can be established as integrated information model that can provide the required information for all phases in a machine-interpretable way. The knowledge graph describes and connects all relevant information, which allows combining and applying it in a holistic way. This makes the knowledge graph a key enabler for a variety of advanced, computerized engineering tasks, ranging from the planning and design phases over the commissioning and the operation of a building. The computerized engineering of building automation systems (BAS) with an advanced software tool chain is presented as such a use case in more detail. The knowledge graph is based on standard semantic web technologies and builds on existing ontologies, such as the Brick and QUDT ontologies, with various novel extensions presented in this paper. Special attention is given to the rich semantic definition of the entities, such as the equipment and the typically thousands of datapoints in a BAS, which can be achieved as a combination of contextual modeling and semantic tagging.

Keywords: Building automation system · Knowledge graph · Information model · Semantic definition · Semantic tagging · Building controls · Analytics

1 Introduction

Several trends in the building domain, such as the increasing ubiquitousness and interconnectivity of IoT devices [1], an energy or cost efficient operation guaranteed through the well-orchestrated control of heterogeneous technical equipment and systems [2] and the adaptation of the indoor climate to individual needs [3], have led to the concept of "smart buildings". A central part of a smart building is the building automation system (BAS), which can be understood as the combination of software and hardware required

© Springer Nature Switzerland AG 2020
A. Harth et al. (Eds.): ESWC 2020, LNCS 12123, pp. 616–631, 2020.
https://doi.org/10.1007/978-3-030-49461-2_36

to operate and monitor the building [4]. BAS can consist of hundreds or thousands of sensors, actuators and control functions, and a complex communication system connecting all these devices into an interoperable, functioning system.

During the life cycle of a smart building, an extensive amount of different kinds of heterogeneous information is required. Traditionally, there is an information gap between the different phases (e.g. planning, installation, operation) and stakeholders, leading to information being exchanged, processed and stored in a variety of mostly human-readable documents of different types. This leads to a large amount of time and effort required to organize and integrate the data, and it makes it very hard or impossible for computers to make use of the information.

In practice, the planning and design of building automation systems is hence a complex, predominantly manual process. BAS planners must typically extract and interpret requirements and information about the building and its technical systems from heterogeneous sources, translate this information into a general or functional plan of the system and finally design and program the complex, highly-connected BAS, including the necessary software and hardware components and the communication between them. This has several disadvantages: The manual data collection is cumbersome and error-prone, certain tasks are repetitive and time consuming, and the manual BAS setup can result in configuration and parameterization issues. Moreover, the current lack of qualified technicians in the building automation field is forecasted to increase in the next years [5].

Empowered by the strength of semantic technologies for describing information and knowledge in a holistic, consistent and machine-interpretable way, this paper presents a semantic model developed for an automated BAS engineering solution. The fundamental concept behind the solution, which is called "BIM2BA", is to gather digital information through all planning and engineering phases and use it in order to automatically configure and parameterize the BAS, which is up to now a highly manual process that requires skilled engineers. The information can stem from various sources, including a Building Information Model (BIM), a requirement definition tool, digital product catalogues or digital parts lists. By storing all the BAS planning data using semantic technologies, information silos are avoided and errors and inconsistencies can be automatically detected by employing reasoning on the resulting knowledge graph.

This paper specifically focuses on the semantic model and knowledge graph of the BIM2BA solution. For this purpose we built upon existing ontologies, such as Brick [6], and extended them where necessary. Moreover, we explain why we consider semantic tagging to be an enabler for automating complex engineering tasks in the building domain.

2   The BIM2BA Solution and Workflow

The overall objective of the BIM2BA solution is to plan and generate working BAS control networks automatically with only minimal manual effort. The development of the BIM2BA solution was triggered by the current digitalization trend in the building industry. An embodiment of this trend can be found in Building Information Modeling (BIM) [7], a digital planning process for buildings that has been gaining strength in the past decades. At the core of the BIM process lies the Building Information Model[1], which is typically understood as a machine-readable, digital representation of the building and its subsystems. By ingesting data stemming from a BIM, BIM2BA extracts, interprets and stores the relevant architectural and engineering data automatically.

An overview of BIM2BA's workflow and software architecture is shown in Fig. 1. BIM2BA consists of a RESTful backend with four microservices, which represent and implement the four phases of the BIM2BA workflow. The knowledge graph is the core element of the BIM2BA backend and stores all relevant information. A browser-based frontend acts as the interface for the user, typically planners and system integrators. On the technical infrastructure level, the backend is powered by a Jena Fuseki triple store, the Jena ontology API and the TopBraid SHACL API.

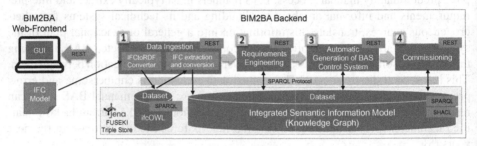

Fig. 1. Workflow and software architecture of the BIM2BA solution

In the following, we explain the four phases of BIM2BA for the automatic generation of a BAS.

1) Data Ingestion

The BIM2BA workflow starts with the ingestion of a BIM file in the IFC format [8]. The IFC file must contain the building geometry and the HVAC system topology, including information regarding the characteristics of the HVAC components.

The IFC file is automatically converted to ifcOWL [9] by using the IFCtoRDF converter software [10], with the resulting triples stored in a separate dataset in the triple store. Since ifcOWL is an automatic one-to-one translation of the complicated IFC EXPRESS schema into RDF, the resulting structures stay complicated and are not straightforward to navigate and search. To overcome these issues and drastically reduce the model complexity (IFC models describe the entire geometry), our solution performs a further model transformation from ifcOWL to our semantic model via a set of transformation rules encoded as SPARQL update queries. This results in a much leaner semantic model, which is optimized for following causalities and for performing semantic search and reasoning.

---

[1] Also abbreviated as "BIM".

Additionally, information from other sources can be ingested and stored in the knowledge graph via dedicated ingestion pipelines (not shown in Fig. 1), along with information manually entered with dedicated tools.

2) Requirements Engineering

In addition to the technical data contained in the BIM, the BA planner must define the functional and non-functional requirements for the BAS to be built. For this purpose, he or she can use the requirements engineering web-frontend, which allows the context-sensitive definition of requirements, given all known information about the building and HVAC system. The requirements are stored in the knowledge graph and checked for consistency and completeness with SHACL. An example of the requirements engineering web-frontend can be seen in Fig. 2.

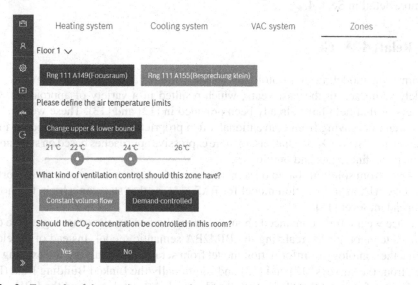

Fig. 2. Example of the requirements engineering web-frontend in the BIM2BA solution

In the simplified example presented there, the requirements comprise the following: the type of control used in each control zone; the parameters of the controllers, such as the upper and lower temperature bounds or the maximum CO_2 concentration; the desired operation schedule of the HVAC system.

3) Automatic Generation of BAS Control System

Based on the information about the building, HVAC system and requirements available in the knowledge graph, the control system of the BAS is automatically generated by the BIM2BA solution and a description of it is added to the knowledge graph. At first, the necessary control functions for each control zone are determined. The control functions are then configured for the specific HVAC system. This includes setting up all required connections for the communication between the control functions and the sensors and actuators. Additionally, the controller's parameters and the actuation ranges for the different actuators have to be defined. This includes the inclusion of parameters defined by the user during the requirements engineering, e.g. the desired temperature bounds, and the post-processing and transformation of specific user requirements into control parameters. The latter requires transformations and calculations, which can be done directly on the knowledge graph via SHACL rules (see Sect. 5).

4) Commissioning
In a final commissioning step, the generated BAS control system can be deployed to the HVAC system. Tridium Niagara [11] is the currently supported target system.

In summary, the BIM2BA solution allows the user to create a BAS software without requiring advanced knowledge about the inner workings of the control functions nor the target system. A central part of BIM2BA is its rich semantic model, which is described in more detail in Sect. 4.

3 Related Work

Information modeling and ontologies in the building automation domain have been widely addressed in the past years, which resulted in a variety of approaches. Good surveys of that field have already been provided in [12] and [13]. These works show a clear trend in moving from conventional, often proprietary information models, mostly based on text files or XML dialects, to more expressive approaches based on standardized semantic technologies and ontologies.

Apart from solutions based on semantic technologies, there is some recent work that uses OPC/UA as information model for BAS [14], or that stays on a high, technology-independent level [15].

Since we are fully convinced about the strength of semantic technologies, we chose them as technology for realizing the BIM2BA semantic model. Instead of developing yet another ontology or information model from scratch, we analyzed the existing solutions from the surveys [12] and [13] and additionally the Linked Building Data (LBD) ontologies[2] for suitability. Brick [6], the Haystack 4.0 ontology[3] and the LBD ontologies appeared content-wise to be the best candidates with respect to completeness and conciseness. Further evaluation criteria we applied were accuracy, clarity, adaptability and the user community behind. We finally selected the Brick ontologies as the most suitable approach. Brick allows for modeling a building from a structural point of view (topological building), and of its BAS components and datapoints, which is a good fit to what we need to model. Furthermore, there is a broad community of both industrial and academic contributors and supporters behind Brick.

The Haystack 4.0 ontology on the contrary was not as convincing, since, due to its claim of ensuring full backward compatibility to older Haystack versions, inherent issues from Haystack from a sound and good modeling perspective kept on existing in it. Such negative aspects are the strongly typed relations, poorly defined tags and the low expressivity. Nevertheless, the Haystack-typical tagging mechanism, which found

---

[2] https://w3c-lbd-cg.github.io/lbd/UseCasesAndRequirements/.
[3] https://project-haystack.dev/doc/docHaystack/Rdf.

its way into Brick as well, inspired us for our semantic modeling approach as a simple but powerful way of defining semantics and enabling semantic search (see Sect. 4.6). Despite the good intentions behind the emerging LBD ontology and initiative, it was not ready for being used at the time, but meanwhile it is worth reconsidering it.

We made several extensions to Brick for customizing it to the needs of the BIM2BA solution (see Sect. 4). The main differentiation of the BIM2BA semantic model, described in this paper, and other existing solutions is the intended coverage of the whole building life cycle in a holistic knowledge graph, including requirements, and the way how a rich semantic definition of BAS entities is achieved by a combination of contextual modeling and semantic tagging. This will be explained in the next section.

4   Integrated Semantic Information Model

The semantic model of the BIM2BA solution acts as an integrated information model that can cover all life cycle phases of a building, making the information combinable and applicable in a holistic way. As the information backbone, it is positioned at the core of the BIM2BA software architecture, as can be seen in Fig. 1. It can contain all the required information, including the building geometry, interior architectural layout, technical details of the HVAC system, the controllers and their functional description, the datapoints, parameters and the BAS requirements etc.

As was mentioned in the last chapter, we chose the Brick ontologies as foundation for the semantic model. We made several extensions to Brick to customize it to the needs of the BIM2BA solution. For this purpose, we used the professional ontology IDE TopBraid Composer. The customizations extend the coverage of Brick from the operation phase of buildings towards the planning and engineering phase, by adding capabilities for modeling and storing requirements for the BAS to be built, and for expressing the functionality of the control network.

The following sections describe the semantic model of BIM2BA in detail, from its structure over extensions made to Brick up to different use cases that were addressed. The ontology examples will show excerpts from a semantic model of a building at the Bosch site in Renningen, Germany, which served as one of the demonstrator buildings for the BIM2BA solution.

4.1   Ontology Layer Architecture

Semantic technologies provide powerful, flexible means of reusing and extending existing vocabularies. Ontologies can be (re-)used by simply importing them into a model, and they can be extended by subclassing, by defining (sub-)properties and by enriching them with further axioms and constraints. As mentioned in the previous section, the Brick ontologies were one starting point for the BIM2BA semantic model.

Apart from Brick, two more groups of ontologies were (re-)used: the QUDT (Quantities, Units, Dimensions and Types) ontologies[4] and the Open PHACTS Units

---

[4] http://www.qudt.org/release2/qudt-catalog.html.

ontology[5,6] (OPS). QUDT defines an extensive list of units, quantities, dimensions and types of more than a thousand in number, and is a de-facto standard for expressing units and currencies. Still, not all units are defined in QUDT, which is why OPS is also employed. OPS uses the QUDT ontology vocabulary and defines additional units, for example parts per million (ppm), which was needed by BIM2BA to define CO_2 concentrations.

The integration and extension of these ontologies resulted in a layered ontology model, which is shown in Fig. 3. Arrows from one ontology block (the source) to another (the target) represent an import relationship between both (groups of) ontologies, i.e. all triples defined in the target model are imported into the source model. Those arrows labeled with "*uses*" import and leave the models as they are, whereas arrows labeled with "*extends*" import, extend and hence enrich the models. Figure 3 shows also the namespace prefixes used in all following examples for the respective ontologies.

The Brick Extensions ontology presented in this paper combines all aforementioned ontologies and customizes the Brick ontologies in order to address aspects that were not adequately supported, but needed (see Sect. 4.5).

The bottom layer comprises the building instance ontologies, each of which models and represents a specific building of the real world, and each of which uses a part of the ontology vocabulary defined in the upper ontology layers. Some insights on these vocabularies and several example knowledge graphs will be explained in the following.

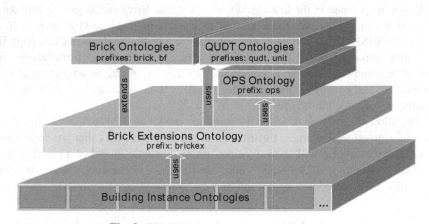

Fig. 3. BIM2BA ontology layer architecture

4.2   Use Case: Modeling of the Hierarchical Building Structure

Brick defines the necessary concepts and object properties to define a structural building model. This is shown in Fig. 4 for the Bosch site in Renningen[7]. There, the concepts brick:Building, brick:Floor, brick:Room and brick:HVAC_Zone

---

[5] http://www.openphacts.org/specs/2013/WD-units-20130913/.

[6] https://github.com/openphacts/jqudt/blob/master/src/main/resources/onto/ops.ttl.

[7] This and all following figures were created with TopBraid Composer.

are used to model the building Rng111 with its first floor and two rooms in it. The `bf:hasPart` object property defines the hierarchical containment structure, i.e. building contains floor, floor contains rooms etc. Properties of the rooms, such as area and volume, are modeled as specific static types of properties, which is one of the extensions made to Brick (see Sect. 4.5). They are attached to the rooms via the Brick object property `bf:hasPoint`.

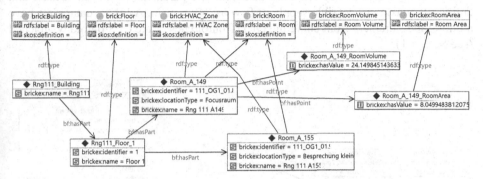

Fig. 4. Structural building model example with some static properties (See footnote 7)

4.3 Use Case: Modeling of the HVAC System and Energy Flows

Brick furthermore enables the modeling of HVAC plants and equipment and their up- and downstream relationships. Figure 5 shows that for a section of the BAS in building Rng111: An air handling unit supplies two downstream VAV[8] boxes, which supply the rooms they are located in. The supply relationships are modeled with the Brick object property `bf:feeds`, which represents the supply of material and energy (here: heated or cooled air) from an upstream to a downstream plant or building element.

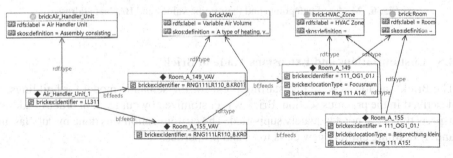

Fig. 5. Model of the material and energy flow from plants to zones

4.4 Use Case: Modeling of Datapoints

Datapoints, such as inputs and outputs of sensors, controllers or actuators in the building, can be represented as instances of the various specializing subclasses of

---

[8] Variable Air Volume, a type of ventilating and air-conditioning system.

brick:Point. They are associated with an HVAC plant, equipment or build-ing element via bf:hasPoint object property. Figure 6 shows an example of three modeled datapoints that are associated with a room. Two of them are sensor datapoints of type brick:Return_Air_Temperature_Sensor and brick:Return_Air_ CO2_Sensor. They have a BACnet address and identi-fier assigned via two new datatype properties brickex:bacnetAddress and brickex:identifier. The third datapoint is a parameter of the room itself and defines its maximum possible supply airflow as 240.5 m³/h. All three datapoints have a unit of measurement from either the QUDT ontologies or the OPS ontology attached (see Sect. 4.1).

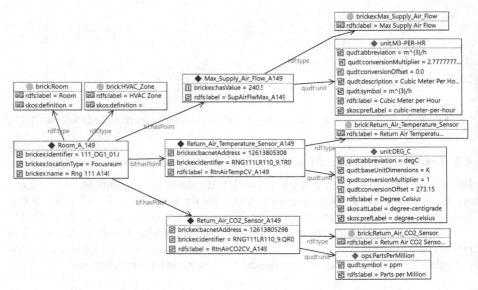

Fig. 6. Model of datapoints and their units, values and BACnet addresses

4.5 Customizations and Extensions Made to Brick

The Brick ontologies were one starting point for the semantic model for buildings, as described in the previous section. Brick was customized by our team in order to address aspects that were not adequately supported. The customization was done by subclassing and by defining entirely new class trees and properties.

Static Properties

An important concept that was missing in Brick is the concept of static properties. Unlike time series based datapoints, such as sensor values, commands or alarms (which are widely addressed by Brick), static properties do not change over time. Therefore we added a new subclass brickex:StaticValue to the brick:Point class, as can be seen in Fig. 7. By defining new subclasses of brickex:StaticValue, such as brickex:RoomArea, brickex:RoomVolume, new types of static properties can now be defined and used, and they are semantically distinguishable from conventional datapoints. The usage of these added classes was shown already in Fig. 4.

Datatype Properties

Brick itself does not define any datatype properties. We had to import and define a couple of datatype properties for modeling required attributes, such as names, identifier, BACnet addresses etc.

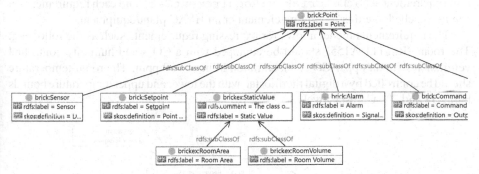

Fig. 7. New concept brickex:StaticValue and subclasses for modeling static properties

Control Functions

Brick is also missing concepts for control functions, i.e. classes for expressing the functionality of field and automation devices. We added such concepts by introducing a new class `brickex:ControlFunction` and a tree of subclasses underneath it, as displayed in Fig. 8. This class hierarchy is not exhaustive, but extensible as needed.

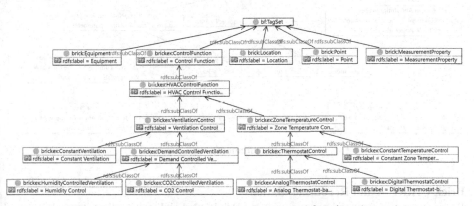

Fig. 8. New class hierarchy for modeling control functions (extract)

New Datapoint Subclasses and Tags

Additional extensions comprise new and more specific datapoint subclasses (`brick: Point`) for some missing types of datapoints, and new tags (e.g. `Area`, `Constant`, `StaticValue`) needed for tagging some of the new classes.

Requirements Model

Furthermore, a comprehensive requirements model, shown in Fig. 9, was developed. It comprises classes and properties for modeling requirements of a BAS that is to be planned and built. A requirement (class `brickex:Requirement`) can define a control function as required feature to be implemented (object property `brickex:requiredFeature`). Optionally, it can define one or more parameter values relevant for the control function to be realized. Related requirements can be bundled into requirement sets (class `brickex:RequirementSet`), and each requirement set can be attached to either a building element or an HVAC plant/equipment.

The requirements model allows for expressing requirements such as the following: The room "Rng111 A155" should be equipped with a CO_2- and humidity-controlled ventilation with an upper CO_2 concentration limit of 800 ppm. The room temperature should be controlled by a digital thermostat, with the lower and upper temperature bounds being 18 and 23 °C, respectively.

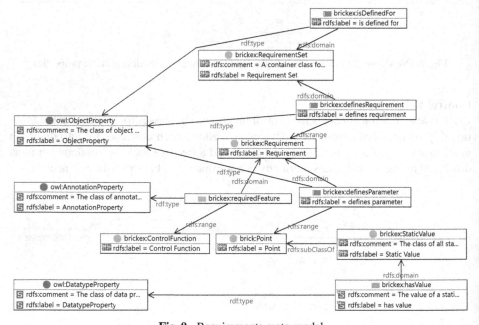

Fig. 9. Requirements meta-model

Brick Criticism and Recommendations

We recommend further improvements to Brick, especially regarding its usability and human interpretability. What is completely missing in Brick are human readable labels (`rdfs:label`) and descriptions (`rdfs:comment`) of the defined classes and object properties, which compromises clarity. Furthermore, there are several occurrences of duplicate class definitions that should be resolved.

Brick at its current state abstracts from the specific hardware of devices and sensors, as well as from their specific software functionality, as it mainly focuses on the modeling of the HVAC equipment and their datapoints. If that was required, such a device layer and relevant properties would need to be added to Brick.

4.6 Machine-Interpretable Semantic Definition

Semantics is the philosophical and linguistic study of meaning in language, be it natural language or computational languages, such as programming languages and formal logics. It is concerned with the meaning of words or symbols and what they stand for in reality. In this section, we want to focus on the semantics of human readable words that are stored and used in a computer system as names or labels for real-world entities.

Consider the following example: The strings "RtnAirCO2CV_A149", "SupAir-FlwMax_A149" and "RtnAirTempCV_A149" are examples of datapoint names (rdfs:labels in Fig. 6). Such natural-language based texts carry some implicit semantics, which is interpretable by a person reading it, albeit this much depends on the person's background and contextual knowledge he or she has. The meaning of such labels is however not (directly) interpretable for machines, as it requires natural language processing and knowledge about the domain and context.

Ontologies and knowledge graphs are an adequate means to model knowledge and context in a machine-interpretable way, and they can define the semantics of symbols. One way of capturing semantics is by applying rich logical formalisms that describe entities and their semantics formally, such as with description logics. However, this can become extremely complex, and may still not be able to capture the complete semantics. A more manageable, yet powerful alternative way of defining semantics is contextual modeling by means of a rich, interconnected knowledge graph. All relevant entities are to be modeled therein with all relationships and property values that are relevant for understanding their meaning, in the extent that is required for the particular use cases.

Yet, some semantic aspects of certain entities cannot be fully captured by modeling the context alone. The meaning of the various types of datapoints, for example, be it the current value of a return air temperature or a chilled water supply temperature setpoint etc., cannot be adequately expressed by modeling the surroundings of the datapoints, such as the equipment they belong to. In addition to the contextual modeling, the solution for capturing the particular semantics of such entities is semantic tagging.

Semantic tagging is a concept that first appeared in the BAS domain in Project Haystack, and it is also supported by Brick. Semantic tags are the underlying, elementary building blocks that ideally cannot be further split down into smaller semantic units. In Brick, semantic tags are defined as direct subclasses of bf:Tag class, and there are 313 of them predefined, from A like Acceleration to Z like Zone. Based on the requirements of the BIM2BA use case, we added several new tags to Brick.

Figure 10 shows the semantic tagging approach of Brick on the three datapoints from Fig. 6. While Fig. 6 shows the surrounding knowledge graph, i.e. contextual knowledge, of the datapoints, Fig. 10 shows their semantic tags. The tags are attached via bf:usesTag annotation properties to the classes of the datapoints. By that, instantiating a class means that all the tags of the class are applicable to their instances. The combination of all tags of an entity then describes the semantics of the entity. The semantics of the datapoint "RtnAirTempCV_A149" (instance Room_A_149_Return_Air_Temperature_Sensor), for example, is Return

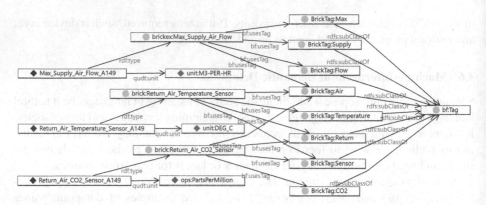

Fig. 10. Semantic definition of datapoints with semantic tags and units

AND Air AND Temperature AND Sensor. Based on the tags, the datapoint is a sensor datapoint that measures a return air temperature. Semantic tagging is applied in the same way to semantically describe HVAC plants and equipment, or any other type of entities.

Semantic tagging is superior to the conventional definition of (large) class hierarchies, whenever the classes are defined by combining atomic concepts to more complex ones. The datatypes of BAS are such an example, where several tags from multiple dimensions are combined to express the overall semantics of datapoints (see examples from Fig. 10). Expressing the entirety of possible datapoint types in a class hierarchy would result in a highly complex, and very likely never complete taxonomy, along with thousands of rdfs:subclassOf relations and multiple inheritance. Semantic tagging however does not require to predefine all possible classes, i.e. combinations of tags (despite Brick does so, which is in our opinion the wrong approach). Instead, a set of tags should be in place that allows for selecting and combining the required ones.

We herewith propose, as an additional improvement of Brick and in general, to organize the tags into orthogonal tag categories (i.e. dimensions), such as measurement (tags "temperature", "pressure", "mass flow" etc.), material (tags "air", "water" etc.), control (tags "current value", "setpoint", "command" etc.), plant (tags "VAV", "air handler unit" etc.) and so on. Consistency rules can then be imposed on the tags, such as the rule that an entity can be tagged with maximum one tag per category, or rules that constrain the combination of specific tags from different dimensions etc.

Besides the tags and the contextual model, the unit of measurement adds another dimension to the semantic definition of a datapoint. Physical units such as degree centigrade (°C) and cubic meter per hour (m³/h), or pseudo-units such as part per million (ppm) comprise certain semantics on their own, namely that it is a temperature, a volume flow or a concentration of some substance.

5 Semantic Model as Key-Enabler for Automating Engineering Tasks and Advanced Features

A rich semantic model of a BAS, forming an interconnected knowledge graph, can provide many advantages. The knowledge graph is a key enabler for the computerized automation of a variety of engineering tasks that previously could only be realized by qualified engineers. In the following, different use cases are explained.

Contextual modeling and semantic tagging enables semantic search, i.e. the search for entities based on their semantic definition, instead of a primitive string matching. It is straightforward to write SPARQL queries that search for all entities related to air temperature by defining a SPARQL graph pattern that searches for all entities that have both the tag `Air` and `Temperature` attached. This simple but powerful mechanism allows for searching for all temperature-related setpoints, for all hot-water-related plants and equipment, for all datapoints that are not alarms and many more scenarios.

Semantic search can simplify and automate the task of finding the equipment and datapoints of interest in a building. Currently it is a complicated task to find the required datapoints amongst couple of thousands in a building by using a string search on their names. The hits are often wrong (false positives) or many datapoints are not matched by the search (incomplete results), so that an engineer has to try different terms to improve the search results, but finally still has to go through a list of datapoint names, interpret their meaning and make the right selection. Semantic search dramatically improves that situation by returning exact matches and complete search results, at the push of a button. It enables software and algorithms to take over this task of finding and selecting the right equipment and datapoints, and by that releases the engineers from this repetitive and laborious task. That is a key enabler for several advanced features, such as building management dashboards that are composed and visualized automatically, or building analytics (e.g. fault detection, predictive maintenance) that are self-enabled, i.e. get configured and commissioned completely automatically [16]. Even virtual sensors that compute unavailable measurements virtually from other available data, can be created automatically from such a knowledge graph [17].

In the BIM2BA use case, the knowledge graph is the key enabler for automating the planning and engineering of BAS. The knowledge graph provides all required information and makes it accessible and retrievable within one repository, with one query language (SPARQL). Information is no longer kept in separated silos, without a semantic definition, but it is totally integrated, connected and has a rich semantics. That enables computers to query and process the information, make sense out of it and automate important engineering tasks. By storing the BAS requirements in the same knowledge graph, with the same concepts, requirements can be mapped directly to matching equipment, devices etc., which were described with the same ontologies. All that relieves engineers to process the requirement documents, study product catalogs and specifications and match requirements to suitable control structures and equipment.

Queries and reasoning allow for performing operations and computations directly in the knowledge graph. For a constant volume flow control to be realized for a zone, for example, knowing the desired hourly air change rate[9] (requirement entered by the user)

---

[9] The amount of time the air in a zone is completely replaced.

and the volume of the control zone (information from BIM), a SPARQL Insert query or SHACL rule can calculate and materialize the equivalent volume flow in m^3/h. It can then be used as setpoint parameter for the controller, and it also defines the required minimum volume flow of a ventilation damper to be chosen. Such computations can automatically run in the background and expand the knowledge graph by additional information, which otherwise had to be calculated and provided by engineers.

Reasoning is another key benefit of knowledge graphs. A reasoner can process axioms and rules on the knowledge graph and derive new information that enriches it. That has been applied and patented for a rule-based fault propagation and root cause analysis for BAS [18]. It is based on a set of rules (e.g. SHACL rules) that formalize the causalities of how faults can physically (via material flow) or logically (via control network) propagate in the building and affect other equipment, zones and datapoints.

6 Conclusion

In this paper we presented the semantic model developed for the BIM2BA solution, a software for the automated engineering of building automation systems (BAS). Creating a BAS is typically a highly manual task requiring the extraction and combination of information from heterogeneous sources from different phases in the building's lifecycle. By harmonizing, combining and integrating BAS information into a rich, interconnected knowledge graph, all information is made available in one repository and usable in a holistic way. This overcomes information silos and enables semantic search and reasoning over the complete set of triples.

As a basis for the semantic model we used the Brick ontologies and extended them by different aspects, such as capabilities for modeling BAS requirements and the functionality of the control network. The customizations extend the coverage of Brick from the operation phase of BAS towards the planning and engineering phase. Furthermore, we found certain issues with Brick, which we clarified and recommend to improve.

The resulting knowledge graph is a key-enabler for the automated engineering of BAS, which was realized with the BIM2BA solution, as well as for a variety of other advanced functionalities, such as automatically enabled fault detection and analytics. The basis for such advanced use cases is the rich semantic definition of entities, achieved with a combination of contextual modelling in the knowledge graph and semantic tagging. This enables the precise retrieval of datapoints and other BAS entities of interest with semantic search. Furthermore, it supports rule-based inferences on the knowledge graph (SHACL rules), such as the creation and calculations of BAS parameters, the propagation of faults, or plausibility and consistency checks.

In summary, the developed semantic model provides a universally applicable, formal vocabulary for the building automation domain. It has proven to be suitable for automating the engineering of BAS, as well as for realizing automatically enabled and advanced analytics, which can lead to a strong reduction in cost and time and to an increased energy efficiency of the buildings.

References

1. Gupta, A., Tsai, T., Rueb, D., Yamaji, M., Middleton, P.: Forecast: Internet of Things— Endpoints and Associated Services, Worldwide. Gartner Research (2017)
2. Henze, G.P., Kalz, D.E., Liu, S., Felsmann, C.: Experimental analysis of model-based predictive optimal control for active and passive building thermal storage inventor. HVAC&R Res. 11(2), 189–213 (2005)
3. Feldmeier, M., Paradiso, J.A.: Personalized HVAC control system. In: IEEE Internet of Things (IOT), Tokyo, Japan (2010)
4. ISO 16484-2: Building Automation and Control Systems (BACS) – Part 2: Hardware. International Organization for Standardization (2004)
5. Seefeldt, F., Rau, D., Hoch, M.: Fachkräftebedarf für die Energiewende in Gebäuden. Prognos, Study comissioned by VdZ: Forum für Energieeffizienz in der Gebäudetechnik e.V. (2018)
6. Balaji, B., et al.: Brick: towards a unified metadata schema for buildings. In: Proceedings of the 3rd ACM International Conference on Systems for Energy-Efficient Built Environments, Stanford, California (2016)
7. buildingSMART International. https://www.buildingsmart.org/. Accessed 28 Oct 2019
8. Industry Foundation Classes – An Introduction (buildingSMART). https://technical.buildings mart.org/standards/ifc/. Accessed 12 March 2020
9. Beetz, J., van Leeuwen, J., de Vries, B.: IfcOWL: A Case of Transforming EXPRESS Schemas into Ontologies. Artif. Intell. Eng. Des. Anal. Manuf. 23(1), 89–101 (2009)
10. Pauwels, P.: IFCtoRDF. GitHub. https://github.com/pipauwel/IFCtoRDF. Accessed 27 Nov 2019
11. Tridium Inc. https://www.tridium.com/en/products-services. Accessed 10 Dec 2019
12. Butzin, B., Golatowski, F., Timmermann, D.: A survey on information modeling and ontologies in building automation. In: 43rd Annual Conference of the IEEE Industrial Electronics Society (IECON 2017), Beijing, China (2017)
13. Dibowski, H., Ploennigs, P., Wollschlaeger, M.: Semantic device and system modeling for automation systems and sensor networks. IEEE Trans. Ind. Informat. 14(4), 1298–1311 (2018)
14. Fernbach, A., Kastner, W.: Semi-automated engineering in building automation systems and management integration. In: 26th IEEE International Symposium on Industrial Electronics (ISIE), Edinburgh, UK (2017)
15. Lehmann, M., Andreas, J., Mai, T. L., Kabitzsch, K.: Towards a comprehensive life cycle approach of building automation systems. In: 26th IEEE International Symposium on Industrial Electronics (ISIE), Edinburgh, UK (2017)
16. Dibowski, H., Vass, J., Holub, O., Rojicek, J.: Automatic setup of fault detection algorithms in building and home automation. In: 21st IEEE International Conference on Emerging Technologies and Factory Automation (ETFA 2016), Berlin, Germany (2016)
17. Dibowski, H., Holub, O., Rojicek, J.: Ontology-based automatic setup of virtual sensors in building automation systems. In: International Congress on Ultra Modern Telecommunications & Control Systems (ICUMT 2016), Lisbon, Portugal (2016)
18. Dibowski, H., Holub, O., Rojicek, J.: Knowledge-based fault propagation in building automation systems. In: Second International Conference on System Informatics, Modeling and Simulation (SIMS 2016), Riga, Latvia (2016)

Supporting Complex Decision Making by Semantic Technologies

Stefan Fenz[✉]

SBA Research and TU Wien, Floragasse 7, 1040 Vienna, Austria
stefan.fenz@tuwien.ac.at

Abstract. Complex decisions require stakeholders to identify potential decision options and collaboratively select the optimal option. Identifying potential decision options and communicating them to stakeholders is a challenging task as it requires the translation of the decision option's technical dimension to a stakeholder-compliant language which describes the impact of the decision (e.g., financial, political). Existing knowledge-driven decision support methods generate decision options by automatically processing available data and knowledge. Ontology-based methods emerged as a sub-field in the medical domain and provide concrete instructions for given medical problems. However, the research field lacks an evaluated practical approach to support the full cycle from data and knowledge assessment to the actual decision making. This work advances the field by: (i) a problem-driven ontology engineering method which (a) supports creating the necessary ontology model for the given problem domain and (b) harmonizes relevant data and knowledge sources for automatically identifying decision options by reasoners, and (ii) an approach which translates technical decision options into a language that is understood by relevant stakeholders. Expert evaluations and real-world deployments in three different domains demonstrate the added value of this method.

Keywords: Semantic technologies · Ontology engineering · Decision support

1 Introduction and Problem Statement

Making complex decisions is fundamental to business activities. In the context of this work, decisions are defined as complex if (i) they are unique, i.e., non-repeatable, (ii) they involve uncertainty, (iii) they require multiple decision makers to make the decision, (iv) the necessary domain knowledge is not present amongst all required decision makers, and (v) decision makers may not understand the full impact of their decision (cf. [7]). For example, the top management of a company has to decide about different IT security strategies, risk mitigation measures, or building refurbishment projects. In these scenarios, management may knowledgeable about maximum investment costs, business/political

© Springer Nature Switzerland AG 2020
A. Harth et al. (Eds.): ESWC 2020, LNCS 12123, pp. 632–647, 2020.
https://doi.org/10.1007/978-3-030-49461-2_37

impact, and acceptable risks, but they may not know how an optimization in one dimension affects the remaining decision dimensions. For instance, reducing the investment costs may result in lower energy efficiency in building refurbishment projects and spending less money on IT security may result in a higher IT security risk level. The challenge in complex decision making is to quantify these observations in such a way that a decision maker – who is not fully knowledgeable about the underlying technical issue – can still identify the options which maximize the cost/benefit ratio of the decision.

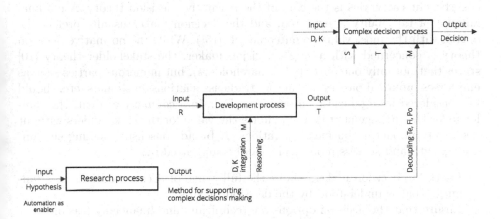

Fig. 1. Interaction of research, development and decision process

In general, a complex decision process (cf. Fig. 1) requires data (D) and knowledge (K) as well as stakeholders (i.e., decision makers) (S) using tools (T) and methods (M) to process the input (D, K), with the final goal of reaching a decision. The necessary tools are the output of a development process which uses methods and requirements (R) to generate the decision support tool, i.e., the output. The research process of this work is driven by the hypothesis that only an increased degree of automation of the necessary data/knowledge integration and the subsequent automated reasoning can efficiently support the complex decision making process. Automation requires that (i) the knowledge necessary to identify decision options has to be available in a machine-readable way (e.g., in the form of ontologies), and (ii) automated reasoning engines have to automatically derive decision options based on this machine-readable knowledge body. The main challenges in achieving this goal is on the one hand to efficiently create the machine-readable knowledge body, and on the other hand to communicate the decision options identified by reasoning engines in a stakeholder-comprehensible way.

As a result, this work contributes the following methods to support complex decision making via semantic technologies: (i) data/knowledge integration and a reasoning method for efficiently querying the knowledge body to identify decision options, and (ii) a method which separates the relevant dimensions (e.g., technical, financial, and political) in the decision process to provide the stakeholders with comprehensible decision options.

2   Theoretical Background

The theoretical background of this work stems from the normative decision theory and the stakeholder theory. The comparison of options in terms of their cost/benefit categories is the core of the normative decision theory. A minimal amount of rationality is expected, and the decision maker usually prefers the option with the most valuable outcome (cf. [15]). While the normative decision theory is concerned with a single decision maker, the stakeholder theory [10] states that not only one party (e.g., shareholders), but numerous parties such as employees, political parties, financiers, trade associations, customers, etc. should be considered in organizational decisions. E.g., in a company context, the challenge for the management is to maximize the value for the stakeholders without negatively impacting business operations. A broad consensus, making sustainable growth and success more likely, can be supported by:

- Informing decision makers about the full range of decision options in a language that is understood by the decision makers
- Ensure that the decision options are technically and financially feasible
- Provide comprehensible information relevant for the decision option (cost, benefits)
- Support collaborative decision making

To efficiently meet these requirements in complex decision making scenarios (involving a large number of decision alternatives), a decision support system with the following characteristics is required:

- Knowledge relevant to the decision making is available in a machine-readable way to ensure processing in a timely manner
- Potential decision options on the basis of the knowledge body are identified by automated means
- Decision options are presented in a comprehensible way to the decision makers

In the following section we review the state of the art and derive the field's research gap.

3   State of the Art and Research Gap

According to [13] existing decision support systems (DSS) can be classified as follows: *Model-driven DSS* access and manipulate finance, optimization or simulation models (examples: production planning management decision system [6] and production scheduling application [5]). *Data-driven DSS* access and manipulate time series of internal and external data (example: analytical airline information management system [8]). *Communication-driven DSS* [3] support decision-relevant communication by using information and network technology as the main architectural component (examples: groupware, video conferencing and Wikis). *Document-driven DSS* support decision making through document retrieval and analysis (examples: full-text document search engines and document organization systems). *Knowledge-driven DSS* store the knowledge about a specific domain in a machine-readable form and are capable of automatically using this knowledge to support the decision maker in identifying solutions for a given problem. The roots of knowledge-driven DSS date back to 1965 (cf. [4]) and it has been steadily improved since.

Ontology-based DSS are a sub-field of knowledge-driven systems and use an ontology together with a reasoning engine to support the decision making. Ontologies are a formal way to define the structure of knowledge for a certain domain. Classes are used to represent and define concepts of the domain, and properties are used to establish relations between the classes. OWL[1] is currently the dominant language to encode ontologies.

Personal recommendation system (e.g., [9]) and clinical decision support systems (e.g., [1,11]) are examples for ontology-based decision support systems. These systems use ontologies to encode the underlying knowledge body (e.g., symptoms and diseases) and reasoners to infer new knowledge (e.g., potential diseases based on observed symptoms).

The role of the ontology in these systems is critical because its capabilities (formally describing domain concepts, their relation/dependencies to each other, description logic statements which can be used to evaluate a certain state with a reasoner, etc.) are required to efficiently support the complex decision-making process by automatically finding technically feasible solutions for the decision problem. Ontologies enable us to define the domain once and reuse it in similar context with minimal additional costs. As OWL is used to encode the ontology, a wide range of editors and reasoners can be used and a vendor lock-in is prevented. Not using ontologies would require us to develop all these functionalities/tools from scratch and the reusability of the artifacts would suffer. The main strength of the reasoner is that it supports description logics. Intersection/union/negation of concepts, universal/existential restrictions, etc. are provided out of the box by OWL and compatible reasoners. These concepts can be combined to powerful description logic statements which go beyond basic matching of criteria. Examples are building renovation measures which have alternative requirement sets and each requirement set contains mandatory and optional components.

E.g., a heating system of a building can be renovated by replacing it by a heat pump or a gas condensing boiler. A heat pump ready building has at least, one floor heating system or wall heating system, and at least, one surface collector or deep drilling, and, a power grid connection which is greater than X kilowatts. A gas condensing boiler ready building needs at least, one chimney and at least, one access to the gas network with a capacity that is greater than the heating and warm water demand of the building. Such requirements can be

---

[1] W3C web ontology language. See https://www.w3.org/OWL/ for further details.

formally described by description logics and reasoners can be used to evaluate the statements in a specific context (such as a concrete building modelled inside the ontology).

Based on the requirements derived from the theoretical background of our work, we identified the following research gap to increase the practical value of ontology-based decision support systems:

- A problem-driven ontology engineering method which provides a design pattern for how to structure the ontology in order to maximize its value and expressiveness in a given decision support scenario.
- Stakeholder communication to present the output of the ontology-based DSS in a comprehensible form to enable the stakeholders to collaboratively identify the most suitable decision.

In the following sections we outline our research contribution to these challenges and show how we have evaluated our research results in practice.

4   Integration and Reasoning

The main challenge of ontology-based decision support systems is to model the ontology in a way that it supports problem-solving reasoning. Existing ontology engineering methods support (i) the creation of general ontologies (e.g., [12,14, 17]), (ii) specific user groups such as non-experts (e.g., [2]), (iii) specific scenarios such as ontology re-use (e.g., [16]), and (iv) specific organizational settings such as collaboration (e.g., [18]). While all of these approaches work in their intended fields, they do not give explicit guidance on how to build an ontology which is capable to assist in complex decision support scenarios.

We developed a problem-driven ontology engineering method which (i) uses the decision problem and available data/knowledge as design foundation, (ii) harmonizes knowledge sources with regard to the decision problem, and (iii) evaluates the maintainability of and contribution to problem solving in order to rate the quality of the produced ontology. The following paragraphs outline each step of the developed method:

4.1   State Decision Problem

The problem which should be addressed by the decision support system and the underlying ontology have to be clearly stated, since the ontology competency questions in Step 4 are derived from the stated problem. Examples: What energy efficiency measures have the best cost/benefit ratio in terms of costs and CO_2 emissions with regard to a specific building? What IT security measures have to be implemented in a given organization to reduce risks to an acceptable level and to not exceed allocated budgets?

4.2   Review Relevant Knowledge Sources

To address the stated decision problem, it is necessary to review relevant knowledge sources such as guidelines, handbooks, laws, and process knowledge. The review process should strictly focus on understanding and extracting the knowledge which is necessary to solve the problem. This step is completed when the method of how to identify potential solutions to a given problem is fully understood. Examples: (i) identifying appropriate insulation products for a building refurbishment requires an understanding of the building heating demand calculation and all associated calculation parameters, (ii) identifying useful information security products requires an understanding which vulnerabilities are mitigated by these products.

4.3   Model-Relevant Problem Parameters on an Abstract Layer

The knowledge source review in the previous step is used as input for the modeling process. The goal is to model only the most relevant problem parameters which are necessary to solve the stated problem on an abstract layer. Holistically model the domain or to include knowledge which goes beyond the purpose of solving the problem is a clear non-goal in this step. Figure 2 shows an example from the building energy efficiency domain. The building (refurbishment project) is characterized as a class which is connected to (i) existing building components (windows, roof, etc.) with specified thermal conductivity levels, (ii) access to energy networks, (iii) existing housing technology such as photovoltaics (PV), heat distribution systems, etc., and (iv) refurbishment candidate classes which allow an ontology reasoner to classify the building according to its specific refurbishment needs (see Step 4 for further details). Example: a building equipped with a very inefficient heating system would be classified as a heating system modernization candidate.

In general, the final model has to include:

- Ontology classes, properties, and individuals which can be used to describe the status quo in sufficient detail. If it is for example required to identify heating system replacement options, the model has to provide the necessary components to formally express the current heating system status and heating-relevant building parameters such as heat demand.
- Ontology classes, properties, and individuals to describe potential solutions to the problem. In the context of the heating system example, the model has to allow the integration of new heating systems including their technical and financial characteristics such as cost or efficiency parameters.
- Ontology classes which can be used to map potential solutions to the status quo. See Step 4 for further details.

4.4   Create Description Logic Statements to Validate the Model

The goal of this step is to create description logic statements which can be used to validate the model with competency questions that are suited to solve the

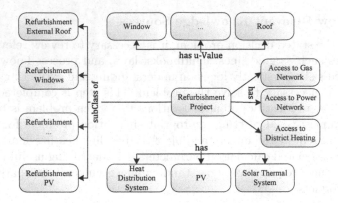

Fig. 2. Step 3 - output example

problem stated in Step 1. Figure 3 shows an example of statements to analyse whether the heating system of a building can be replaced with a modern gas-driven one, therefore checking if the building has (i) a chimney to get the exhaust out of the building, (ii) access to the gas network, and (iii) a heat distribution system which would work with a gas-driven system (floor/wall heating system or radiators). We used the Protege ontology editor to create the description logic statements and a reasoner to validate the model created in Step 3. The validation is successful if the reasoner classifies the building into the correct refurbishment candidate categories.

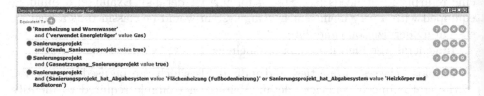

Fig. 3. Step 4 - output example (Translation: Raumheizung - space heating, Warmwasser - hot water, verwendet Energietraeger - uses energy carrier, Gas - natural gas, Sanierungsprojekt - renovation project, Kamin - chimney, Gasnetzzugang - natural gas network access, hat Abgabesystem - has delivery system, Flaechenheizung - panel heating, Fussbodenheizung - underfloor heating, Heizkoerper - radiators)

In general, the following pattern is applied to create the description logic statements based on the ontology classes, properties and individuals defined in Step 3:

- Define the technical requirements which have to be met in order to map a status quo element to a potential solution. Example: classifying a building as a candidate for a modern gas-driven heating system requires that the building is already equipped with a chimney, has access to the gas network, and has a compatible heat distribution system.
- Express these requirements by description logic statements as anonymous classes which are defined as equivalent to the mapping class. See Fig. 3 for an example.
- Test the statements by running the reasoner and checking if the classification was done as intended. Extend and modify the statements until the reasoner produces correct results.

4.5 Harmonize and Integrate Relevant Knowledge Sources Based on the Model

Based on the abstract model created in the previous steps, concrete and relevant knowledge necessary for solving the problem is harmonized and integrated. Examples: integration of concrete building refurbishment products including feature and price data, compatibility information such as heating technology and heating distribution systems, and legal requirements regarding minimal thermal conductivity values of insulation products.

4.6 Validate the Model

In Step 6 the ontology contains all necessary components (domain knowledge, domain model, environment data, solution data, and description logic statements) to assist, in combination with a reasoner, with solving the stated decision problem. The validation of the ontology reasoner output is done by modeling concrete environment data (e.g., data of a concrete building we have to refurbish) in the ontology. After running the reasoner, the output (see Fig. 4 for an example) is validated by experts with regard to its correctness and usability in further decision support operations.

5 Decoupling

The output of the reasoner defines potential solutions for the stated problem. For instance, as shown in Fig. 4, the energy efficiency of the building can be improved by putting insulation on the outer walls, switching to a modern gas heating system or putting photovoltaics on the roof. All measures suggested by the reasoner comply with the building and the requirements which have been modeled in the ontology (e.g., legal or technical requirements).

Every suggested measure can be part of the final solution which has to be identified by the decision makers based on their preferences. The following process ensures that the correct solution data is presented in a comprehensible way:

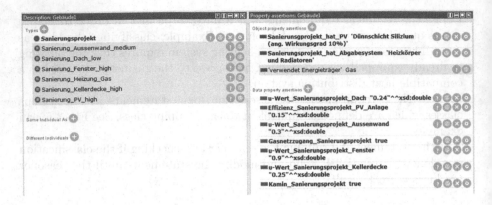

Fig. 4. Step 6 - output example

1. Extract cost and benefit data for each measure from the ontology
2. Identify feasible solution sets by creating all combinations of the identified measures (e.g., solution set X would be to put photovoltaics on the roof and insulate the outer walls, solution set Y would be solution set X plus replacing the heating system)
3. Visualize each solution set with data which is relevant to the decision maker (costs, break even, etc.)
4. Enable the decision maker to sort and filter the solution sets

Figure 5 shows the user interface of a building refurbishment decision support system which was built based on the developed methods. The user specifies the maximum investment costs, relevant goals such as minimum CO_2 emission reduction and renewable energy share. By clicking on the optimization button the system conducts the aforementioned steps and presents a list of solution sets which can be filtered and sorted. By selecting a specific solution set the user learns about its specific measures. The main benefit of this method is that all presented solution sets are completely compatible to the given technical and financial requirements (only feasible measures are suggested by the reasoner based on the knowledge and data modeled in the ontology).

By decoupling the technical from the financial/political dimension we enable stakeholders to focus on the decision parameters they understand. The developed semantic decision support methods ensure that potential solutions are identified in an automated way and fully compatible with the actual problem environment (e.g., the concrete building stock).

The implemented data visualization enables stakeholders to explore the solution space in an interactive way and to find the most suited solution by collaboratively evaluating the consequences in relevant cost/benefit categories. As such, the developed method supports the stakeholder theory (see Sect. 2).

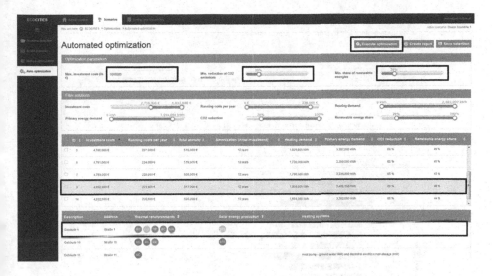

Fig. 5. User interface

6   Evaluation

The developed methods have been evaluated in four European small- and medium-sized companies (three different productive application fields) and two governmental institutions.

6.1   Single Building Refurbishment

Semergy.net is a decision support system for single building refurbishment which addresses both home owners and professionals. The user models the building and sets maximum investment costs; based on that the system calculates numerous ways of how to improve the building energy efficiency at certain investment resp. running energy costs and payback periods (see Fig. 6).

Within an extensive validation phase, experts checked the system output regarding technical and financial feasibility and confirmed that the system provides refurbishment suggestions which are compliant with their respective expectations. 38 of these expert tests were conducted. Currently 590 users are registered on semergy.net and use it for their personal and professional energy efficiency calculations. Semergy.net reduces the time for identifying the most suitable energy efficiency strategy for a given building by up to 81% compared to traditional energy performance certificate (EPC) tools. This substantial time reduction is based on the high automation level w.r.t. the identification of appropriate energy efficiency measures. Table 1 shows the evaluation results.

Please note that traditional EPC tools do not provide an automated extensive search for refurbishment options. The user has to manually adjust the building parameters (e.g., outer wall insulation) to see how they affect the output in terms

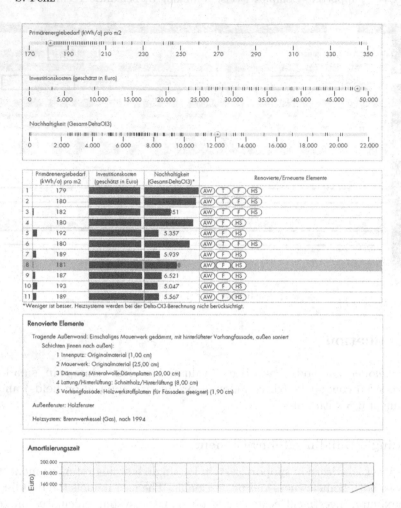

Fig. 6. Semergy.net - decision support user interface

Table 1. Semergy.net evaluation results - times on average across 38 test runs

	Semergy.net	EPC tools
Entering building data	9 min	10 min
Identifying solutions	2 min	75 min (limited to 15 solutions)
Decision making	6 min	9 min
Total	17 min	94 min

of energy efficiency. Costs of the energy efficiency measures are also not provided
by these tools and the compatibility of measure combinations has to be judged
manually by the user. Because of this high manual effort at traditional tools, we
required experts to identify only 15 refurbishment strategy options and measured

Table 2. Semergy.net - candidates per construction type on the example of a two story single family home with heated basement

Construction type	Candidates
Outer walls	268
Inner walls (load bearing)	77
Inner walls (non-load bearing)	77
Earth-facing walls	30
Earth-facing floor	216
Subceiling	6
Basement ceiling	250
Roof	467
Door	2
Window	5
Roof top window	5
Heating system	6
Total combinations	2.16×10^{18}

the corresponding execution time. The evaluation has shown that the semantic knowledge base of semergy.net enabled the reasoner to identify all potential measure combinations and to prepare the data (investment costs and energy efficiency) for a comprehensible visualization of the decision options. Compared to traditional methods, the developed method provides not only significant time savings but also a broader range of decision options and a comprehensible of the decision dimensions (Table 2).

6.2 Multiple Building and Energy Network Refurbishment

Ecocities.at (see the UI in Fig. 5) is a decision support system for identifying energy efficiency measures in large building groups. Compared to semergy.net, the system operates in the context of multiple buildings (e.g., 30), potential synergies/dependencies among these buildings, and energy networks within a building group. The solution set of ecocities.at (concrete energy efficiency measures on each building of the building group and global impact data such as costs and CO_2 emission reduction) was validated together with experts and pilot customers. The validation phase showed that a lot of feasible energy efficiency strategies were overlooked in non-automated considerations of the problem. The calculated solution space was much bigger and allowed the users to collaboratively identify the most suitable solution. Ecocities.at is the first product of its kind on the market. In comparison to traditional methods – which combine manual and tool work – ecocities.at reduces the time required for identifying

Table 3. Ecocities.at evaluation results - times on average across 7 test runs

	Ecocities.at	EPC tools and Excel
Entering building data	370 min	330 min
Identifying solutions	47 min	1350 min (limited to 150 solutions)
Decision making	15 min	15 min
Total (10 buildings)	432 min	1695 min

Table 4. Ecocities.at - candidates per construction type

Construction type	Candidates
Outer walls	4
Earth-facing walls	4
Uppermost ceiling/roof	4
Window	4
Heating system	71
PV and solar thermal	10
Total combinations	181.760

appropriate energy efficiency strategies by 74%. Table 3 shows the evaluation results which are average times based on 7 test runs including 10 to 32 buildings (Table 4).

Please note that because of the large number of possibilities a full identification of refurbishment options across the entire building group is not feasible by manual means. Therefore, we measured the time necessary to manually calculate the effect of a single refurbishment measure and extrapolated it to all potential measures. The manual calculation task includes the decision which refurbishment measure to implement (e.g., putting 20 cm wall insulation on building X and replacing the heating systems at building Y) and checking how this affects the energy efficiency of the entire building group. Conducting this single task by traditional EPC tools and Microsoft Excel requires on average 9 min. However, for each building ecocities.at considers 218.700 refurbishment strategies based on the following refurbishment options: (i) three different qualities for earth-facing floor, outer wall and uppermost ceiling insulation, (ii) three different window qualities, (iii) three different photovoltaic systems, (iv) six different solar thermal systems, (v) ten different heating systems, and (vi) 15 different hot water production systems. By manual means this would results in a time effort of around 1 year for one building only. In reality an expert would not calculate all possible combinations, but would choose feasible combinations based on her/his experience (around 15 combinations per building). Compared to traditional methods, the developed method identifies a much larger space of refurbishment options and significantly reduces the time which is necessary to conduct the entire planning process.

6.3 IT Security Risk Management

AURUM is the first ontology-driven IT security risk management product. It supports organizations in identifying the optimal information security measures in terms of costs, effectiveness, and compliance to standards. It is designed to (i) minimize the necessary interaction between user and system, and (ii) provide decision makers with an intuitive solution that can be used without in-depth information security knowledge. The integration and reasoning components of AURUM make sure that only technically and financially feasible security measures are suggested to the decision maker. The selection of the final security measure strategy is based on its investment, running costs, and organization-wide risk level after implementation (see Fig. 7). 18 test runs were conducted with experts and end-users, one productive installation is currently deployed at an governmental institution in Europe. The evaluation results have shown that AURUM provides no time savings but a deeper and broader range of comprehensible security measure strategies compared to traditional risk and compliance management tools.

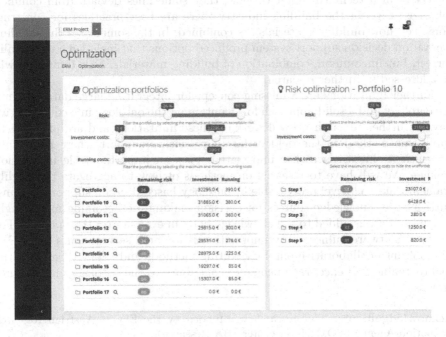

Fig. 7. AURUM

7 Discussion and Further Research

The purpose of this research is the development of methods to enable sustainable decisions by stakeholder inclusion. Especially in complex decision scenarios, stakeholders need decision options to be presented in a language they understand.

In order to process detailed domain knowledge and create comprehensible decision options in an automated way, we have developed an ontology engineering method that supports researchers and practitioners to efficiently build the required ontologies independently of the application field. The decoupling approach translates detailed technical knowledge into financial/political dimensions and therefore enables decision makers to identify adequate options. The added value of the research results was assessed in an extensive evaluation phase, including several real-world deployments. The evaluation showed that the method supports the full cycle from data/knowledge assessment to the actual decision making, independent of the application field. Compared to traditional methods, the developed method provides (i) a broader range of technically feasible decision options, (ii) substantial time savings at identifying the decision options, and (iii) the possibility to visualize the decision options in a comprehensible way to relevant stakeholders. While users valued the time savings and comprehensible presentation of decision options, some users criticized the broad range of decision options. While all the options were compliant to the underlying rule sets and correct from a technical point of view, they sometimes deviate from common solutions. E.g., in the building industry there are best practices for constructions, i.e., how building materials are combined. In the some cases the building renovation decision support system produced options that included a technically correct, but uncommon, combination of building materials. This limitation will be addressed in further research.

Further limitations are a missing concept for integrating large data sets into the ontology and a solid approach for maintaining the ontology in a collaborative way. In further research we will work on these limitations and are planning to apply this method in the field of farming decision support where large data sets such as historic weather information play an important role in decision making. We will have to research on methods of how to aggregate this highly granular data to a level processable by ontology-based decision support systems. Furthermore, knowledge sources for decision making are becoming increasingly dynamic – data is added to the knowledge body in ever shorter time periods. For instance, software vulnerability information is updated several times a day. We will look into collaborative ontology editing methods and adapt them with the goal to enable and encourage people to contribute to the ontology maintenance process.

Acknowledgements. This research was funded by the FFG – Austrian Research Promotion Agency (COMET K1 center SBA Research).

References

1. Bouamrane, M.M., Rector, A., Hurrell, M.: Using owl ontologies for adaptive patient information modelling and preoperative clinical decision support. Knowl. Inf. Syst. **29**(2), 405–418 (2011)
2. De Nicola, A., Missikoff, M.: A lightweight methodology for rapid ontology engineering. Commun. ACM **59**(3), 79–86 (2016)

3. Engelbart, D.C.: Augmenting human intellect: a conceptual framework (1962). Packer, R., Jordan, K.: Multimedia: from wagner to virtual reality, WW Norton & Company, New York, pp. 64–90 (2001)

4. Feigenbaum, E.A., Buchanan, B.G.: Dendral and meta-dendral: roots of knowledge systems and expert system applications. Artif. Intell. 59(1–2), 233–240 (1993)

5. Ferguson, R.L., Jones, C.H.: A computer aided decision system. Manage. Sci. 15(10), B-550 (1969)

6. Gorry, G.A., Scott Morton, M.S.: A framework for management information systems. Sloan Manage. Rev. 13, 510–571 (1971)

7. Keane, M., Thorp, S.: Chapter 11 - complex decision making: The roles of cognitive limitations, cognitive decline, and aging. In: Piggott, J., Woodland, A. (eds.) Handbook of the Economics of Population Aging, vol. 1, pp. 661–709. Elseiver, North-Holland (2016). https://doi.org/10.1016/bs.hespa.2016.09.001

8. Klaas, R.L.: A DSS for airline management. ACM SIGMIS Database 8(3), 3–8 (1977)

9. Liang, T.P., Yang, Y.F., Chen, D.N., Ku, Y.C.: A semantic-expansion approach to personalized knowledge recommendation. Decis. Support Syst. 45(3), 401–412 (2008)

10. Mitroff, I.I.: Stakeholders of the Organizational Mind. Jossey-Bass Inc Pub, San Francisco (1983)

11. Musen, M.A., Middleton, B., Greenes, R.A.: Clinical decision-support systems. In: Shortliffe, E.H., Cimino, J.J. (eds.) Biomedical Informatics, pp. 643–674. Springer, London (2014). https://doi.org/10.1007/978-1-4471-4474-8_22

12. Noy, N.F., McGuinness, D.L., et al.: Ontology development 101: A guide to creating your first ontology (2001)

13. Power, D.J.: Decision support systems: a historical overview. Handb. Decis. Support Syst. 1, 121–140 (2008). https://doi.org/10.1007/978-3-540-48713-5_7

14. Spyns, P., Tang, Y., Meersman, R.: An ontology engineering methodology for dogma. Appl. Ontol. 3(1–2), 13–39 (2008)

15. Steele, K., Stefánsson, H.O.: Decision theory. In: Zalta, E.N. (ed.) The Stanford Encyclopedia of Philosophy, winter 2016 edn edn. Metaphysics Research Lab, Stanford University, Stanford (2016)

16. Suarez-Figueroa, M.C., Gomez-Perez, A., Fernandez-Lopez, M.: The neon methodology framework: a scenario-based methodology for ontology development. Appl. Ontol. 10(2), 107–145 (2015)

17. Sure, Y., Staab, S., Studer, R.: Ontology engineering methodology. In: Staab, S., Studer, R. (eds.) Handbook on Ontologies. IHIS, pp. 135–152. Springer, Heidelberg (2009). https://doi.org/10.1007/978-3-540-92673-3_6

18. Tempich, C., Simperl, E., Luczak, M., Studer, R., Pinto, H.S.: Argumentation-based ontology engineering. IEEE Intell. Syst. 22(6), 10 (2007)

Piveau: A Large-Scale Open Data Management Platform Based on Semantic Web Technologies

Fabian Kirstein[1,2(✉)], Kyriakos Stefanidis[1], Benjamin Dittwald[1],
Simon Dutkowski[1], Sebastian Urbanek[1,2], and Manfred Hauswirth[1,2,3]

[1] Fraunhofer FOKUS, Berlin, Germany
{fabian.kirstein,kyriakos.stefanidis,benjamin.dittwald,simon.dutkowski,
sebastian.urbanek,manfred.hauswirth}@fokus.fraunhofer.de
[2] Weizenbaum Institute for the Networked Society, Berlin, Germany
[3] TU Berlin, Open Distributed Systems, Berlin, Germany

Abstract. The publication and (re)utilization of Open Data is still facing multiple barriers on technical, organizational and legal levels. This includes limitations in interfaces, search capabilities, provision of quality information and the lack of definite standards and implementation guidelines. Many Semantic Web specifications and technologies are specifically designed to address the publication of data on the web. In addition, many official publication bodies encourage and foster the development of Open Data standards based on Semantic Web principles. However, no existing solution for managing Open Data takes full advantage of these possibilities and benefits. In this paper, we present our solution "Piveau", a fully-fledged Open Data management solution, based on Semantic Web technologies. It harnesses a variety of standards, like RDF, DCAT, DQV, and SKOS, to overcome the barriers in Open Data publication. The solution puts a strong focus on assuring data quality and scalability. We give a detailed description of the underlying, highly scalable, service-oriented architecture, how we integrated the aforementioned standards, and used a triplestore as our primary database. We have evaluated our work in a comprehensive feature comparison to established solutions and through a practical application in a production environment, the European Data Portal. Our solution is available as Open Source.

Keywords: Open Data · DCAT · Scalability

Electronic supplementary material The online version of this chapter (https://doi.org/10.1007/978-3-030-49461-2_38) contains supplementary material, which is available to authorized users.

© The Author(s) 2020
A. Harth et al. (Eds.): ESWC 2020, LNCS 12123, pp. 648–664, 2020.
https://doi.org/10.1007/978-3-030-49461-2_38

1   Introduction

Open Data constitutes a prospering and continuously evolving concept. At the very core, this includes the publication and re-utilization of datasets. Typical actors and publishers are public administrations, research institutes, and non-profit organizations. Common users are data journalists, businesses, and governments. The established method of distributing Open Data is via a web platform that is responsible for gathering, storing, and publishing the data. Several software solutions and specifications exist for implementing such platforms. Especially the Resource Description Framework (RDF) data model and its associated vocabularies represent a foundation for fostering interoperability and harmonization of different data sources. The Data Catalog Vocabulary (DCAT) is applied as a comprehensive model and standard for describing datasets and data services on Open Data platforms [1]. However, RDF is only a subset of the Semantic Web stack and Open Data publishing does not benefit from the stack's full potential, which offers more features beyond data modeling. Therefore, we developed a novel and scalable platform for managing Open Data, where the Semantic Web stack is a first-class citizen. Our work focuses on two central aspects: (1) The utilization of a variety of Semantic Web standards and technologies for covering the entire life-cycle of the Open Data publishing process. This covers particularly data models for metadata, quality verification, reporting, harmonization, and machine-readable interfaces. (2) The application of state-of-the-art software engineering approaches for development and deployment to ensure production-grade applicability and scalability. Hence, we integrated a tailored microservice-based architecture and a suitable orchestration pattern to fit the requirements in an Open Data platform.

It is important to note, that currently our work emphasizes the management of metadata, as intended by the DCAT specification. Hence, throughout the paper the notion of data is used in terms of metadata.

In Sect. 2 we describe the overall problem and in Sect. 3 we discuss related and existing solutions. Our software architecture and orchestration approach is described in Sect. 4. Section 5 gives a detailed overview of the data workflow and the applied Semantic Web standards. We evaluate our work in Sect. 6 with a feature analysis and an extensive use case. To conclude, we summarize our work and give an outlook for future developments.

2   Problem Statement

A wide adoption of Open Data by data providers and data users is still facing many barriers. Beno et al. [7] conducted a comprehensive study of these barriers, considering legal, organizational, technical, strategic, and usability aspects. Major technical issues for users are the limitations in the Application Programming Interfaces (APIs), difficulties in searching and browsing, missing information about data quality, and language barriers. Generally, low data quality is also a fundamental issue, especially because (meta)data is not machine-readable or, in many cases, incomplete. In addition, low responsiveness and bad performance of the portals have a negative impact on the adoption of Open Data. For publishers, securing the integrity and authenticity, enabling resource-efficient provision, and clear licensing are highly important issues. The lack of a definite standard and technical solutions is listed as a core barrier.

The hypothesis of our work is, that **a more sophisticated application of Semantic Web technologies can lower many barriers in Open Data publishing and reuse.** These technologies intrinsically offer many aspects, which are required to improve the current support of Open Data. Essentially, the Semantic Web is about defining a common standard for integrating and harnessing data from heterogeneous sources [2]. Thus, it constitutes an excellent match for the decentralized and heterogeneous nature of Open Data.

Widespread solutions for implementing Open Data platforms are based on canonical software stacks for web applications with relational and/or document databases. The most popular example is the Open Source solution Comprehensive Knowledge Archive Network (CKAN) [10], which is based on a flat JSON data schema, stored in a PostgreSQL database. This impedes a full adoption of Semantic Web principles. The expressiveness of such a data model is limited and not suited for a straightforward integration of RDF.

3   Related Work

Making Open Data and Linked Data publicly available and accessible is an ongoing process that involves innovation and standardization efforts in various topics such as semantic interoperability, data and metadata quality, standardization as well as toolchain and platform development.

One of the most widely adopted standards for the description of datasets is DCAT and its extension DCAT Application profile for data portals in Europe (DCAT-AP) [12]. The latter adds metadata fields and mandatory property ranges, making it suitable for use with Open Data management platforms. Its adoption by various European countries led to the development of country-specific extensions such as the official exchange standard for open governmental data in Germany [17] and Belgium's extension [24]. Regarding Open Data management platforms, the most widely known Open Source solution is CKAN [10]. It is considered the de-facto standard for the public sector and is also used by private organizations. It does not provide native Linked Data capabilities but only a mapping between existing data structures and RDF. Another widely adopted platform is uData [23]. It is a catalog application for collecting data and metadata focused on being more contributive and inclusive than other Open Data platforms by providing additional functionality for data reuse and community contributions. Other Open Source alternatives include the repository solution DSpace which dynamically translates [13] relational metadata into native RDF metadata and offers it via a SPARQL endpoint. WikiData also follows a similar approach [36]; it uses a custom structure for identifiable items, converts them to native RDF and provides an API endpoint. Another, proprietary, solution is

OpenDataSoft [26], which has limited support for Linked Data via its interoperability mode. There are also solutions that offer native Linked Data support following the W3C recommendation for Linked Data Platforms (LDPs). Apache Marmotta [38] has native implementation of RDF with a pluggable triplestore for Linked Data publication. Virtuoso [27] is a highly scalable LDP implementation that supports a wide array of data access standards and output formats. Fedora [21] is a native Linked Data repository suited for digital libraries. Recent research efforts [30] focuses on the notion of dynamic Linked Data where context aware services and applications are able to detect changes in data by means of publish-subscribe mechanisms using SPARQL.

A core feature of most big commercial platforms is the Extract, Transform, Load (ETL) functionality. It refers to the three basic data processing stages of reading data (extract) from heterogeneous sources, converting it (transform) to a suitable format, and storing it (load) into a database. Platforms that offer ETL as a core functionality include IBM InfoSphere [16] with its DataStage module, Oracle Autonomus Data Warehouse [28] with its Data Integrator module and SAS Institute's data warehouse [31]. Moreover, various Open Source solutions such as Scriptella [35] and Talend Open Studio [32] are based on ETL. The above data warehouses offer highly scalable ETL functionality but do not support Linked Data and DCAT. On the other hand, the previously mentioned Linked Data platforms do not offer any real ETL capabilities. Bridging this gap was the main objective that led to the development of the Piveau pipeline as a core part of our architecture. Similar data pipelines can be found as stand-alone services and applications such as AWS Data Pipeline [5], Data Pipes from OKFN [25], North Concepts Data Pipeline [22], and Apache Airflow [33].

4   A Flexible Architecture for Semantic Web Applications

Semantic Web technologies are mainly supported by specifications, standards, libraries, full frameworks, and software. The underlying concept of our architecture is the encapsulation of Semantic Web functionalities to make them reusable and interoperable, which is considered a classical software engineering principle. Our Open Data platform introduces a state-of-the-art, tailored architecture to orchestrate these encapsulations and make them easy to apply in production environments. It is based on a microservice architecture and a custom pipeline system, facilitating a flexible and scalable feature composition of Open Data platforms. This enables the application of Piveau for various use cases and audiences. Furthermore, it enables the re-use of features in other environments and applications.

4.1   The Piveau Pipeline

The basic requirements of our architecture were the use of microservices, high scalability, lightweight in application and management, and suitable for large-scale data processing. Existing workflow engines and ETL systems are either not designed for Linked Data and/or limited solely to extensive data integration tasks (see Sect. 3). To lower complexity and maintenance needs, we aimed for an unifying architecture and data processing concept, which targets specifically our needs. Therefore, we designed and implemented the Piveau pipeline (PPL). The PPL builds upon three principal design choices: (1) All services and features expose RESTful interfaces and comply with the microservice style. (2) The services can be connected and orchestrated in a generic fashion to implement specific data processing chains. (3) There is no central instance, which is responsible for orchestrating the services.

A PPL orchestration is described by a *descriptor*, which is a plain JSON document, including a list of segments, where each segment describes a step (a service) in the data processing chain. Every segment includes at least meta-information, targeting the respective service and defining the consecutive service(s).[1] The entire descriptor is passed from service to service as state information. Each service identifies its segment by a service identifier, executes its defined task and passes the descriptor to the next service(s). Hence, the descriptor is a compilation and self-contained description of a data processing chain. Each microservice must expose an endpoint to receive the descriptor and must be able to parse and execute its content. The processed data itself can be embedded directly into the descriptor or passed via a pointer to a separate data store, e.g. a database, file system or other storage. This depends on the requirements and size of data and can be mixed within the process.

The PPL has been proven to be a fitting middle ground between ETL approaches and workflow engines. On an architectural level, it allows to harvest data from diverse data providers and orchestrate a multitude of services. Its production-level implementation in the European Data Portal (EDP) supports millions of open datasets with tens of thousands updates per day (see Sect. 6.2).

4.2   Architecture, Stack and Deployment

The development of Piveau follows the reactive manifesto, which requires a system to be responsive, resilient, elastic, and message driven [9]. The platform is divided into three logical main components, each one responsible for a phase within the life-cycle of the datasets: Consus, Hub and Metrics. Figure 1 illustrates the overall architecture and structure.

---

[1] The PPL descriptor schema can be found at: https://gitlab.com/piveau/pipeline/ piveau-pipe-model/-/blob/master/src/main/resources/piveau-pipe.schema.json.

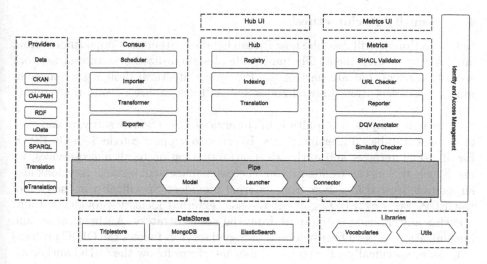

Fig. 1. Piveau high-level architecture

Consus is responsible for the data acquisition from various sources and data providers. This includes scheduling, transformation and harmonization. Hub is the central component to store and register the data. Its persistence layer consists of a Virtuoso triplestore[2] as the principal database, Elasticsearch[3] as the indexing server and a MongoDB[4] for storing binary files. Metrics is responsible for creating and maintaining comprehensive quality information and feeding them back to the Hub. Two web applications based on Vue.js[5] are available for browsing the data. The services are written with the reactive JVM framework Vert.x[6] and orchestrated with the PPL within and across the logical components. Several libraries for common tasks, RDF handling and the PPL orchestration are re-used in all services.

In order to enable native cloud deployment, we use the Docker[7] container technology. Each service is packaged as a container, supporting easy and scalable deployment. In addition, Piveau was tested with Kubernetes-based[8] container management solutions like Rancher[9] and OpenShift[10]. Hence, our architecture supports a production-grade development scheme and is ready for DevOps practices.

---

[2] https://virtuoso.openlinksw.com/.
[3] https://www.elastic.co/products/elasticsearch.
[4] https://www.mongodb.com/.
[5] https://vuejs.org/.
[6] https://vertx.io/.
[7] https://www.docker.com/.
[8] https://kubernetes.io/.
[9] https://rancher.com/.
[10] https://www.openshift.com/.

4.3   Security Architecture

In this section we will describe how Piveau handles authentication, authorization, and identity management. The multitude of standardized system and network security aspects that are part of the Piveau architectural design, such as communication encryption, firewall zones and API design, are beyond the scope of this paper.

Piveau is comprised of multiple microservices, Open Source software and a set of distinct web-based user interfaces. In order to support Single Sign-On (SSO) for all user interfaces and authentication/authorization to all microservices, we use Keycloak[11] as central identity and access management service. Keycloak also supports federated identities from external providers. Specifically, in the case of the EDP, we use "EU Login" as the sole external identity provider without allowing any internal users apart from the administrators. Authentication and authorization on both front-end and back-end services follows the OIDC protocol [34]. More specifically, all web-based user interfaces follow the OIDC authorization code flow. This means that when a user tries to login to any of Piveau's user interfaces, they are redirected to the central Keycloak authentication form (or the main identity provider's authentication form) and, upon successful login, they are redirected back to the requested web page. This provides a uniform user experience and minimizes the risk of insecure implementation of custom login forms.

All back-end services also follow OIDC by requiring valid access tokens for each API call. Those tokens follow the JSON Web Token (JWT) standard. In contrast to static internal API keys, this design pattern supports arbitrary back-end services to be open to the public without any change to their authentication mechanisms. Moreover, since the JWT tokens are self-contained, i.e. they contain all the required information for user authentication and resource authorization, the back-end services can perform the required checks without the need of communication with a database or Keycloak. Not requiring round-trips greatly enhances the performance of the whole platform.

The fine-grained authorization follows the User-Managed Access (UMA) specification [18], where resource servers (back-end services) and a UMA-enabled authorization server (Keycloak) can provide uniform management features to user-owned resources such as catalogs and datasets.

5   Semantic Data Workflow

In the following, a typical data flow in our Open Data platform is described to illustrate our solution in detail. This covers the process of acquiring the data from the original providers, evaluating the quality of that data, and presenting and managing the data (see Fig. 2). We focus on the used Semantic Web technologies and specifications. The presented order reflects roughly the order of execution. But since many processes run asynchronously, the order can vary depending on their execution time.

---

[11] https://www.keycloak.org/.

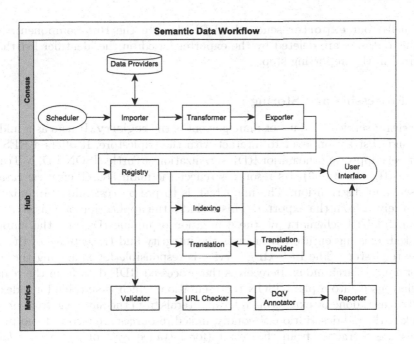

Fig. 2. Semantic data workflow

5.1 Data Acquisition

The main entry point for any data workflow and orchestration is the **scheduler**.
Each data workflow, defined as a PPL descriptor (see Sect. 4.1), is assigned a list
of triggers. A trigger may define a periodical execution (hourly, daily, weekly,
bi-weekly, yearly, etc.), number of execution times, a list of specific date and
times to execute, or an immediate execution. Each trigger is able to pass its own
process configuration in order to individualize the workflow depending on the
execution time. Upon execution, the scheduler passes the descriptor to the first
service in line, typically an **importer**.

An importer retrieves the metadata from the source portal(s). We have implemented a range of importers to support a variety of interfaces and data formats,
e.g. CKAN-API, OAI-PMH, uData, RDF, and SPARQL. The importer is responsible for extracting records of metadata from either an API or a dump file and for
sending it to the next processing step. This covers the generation of a complete
list of identifiers of all datasets, which will be required for a final synchroniza-
tion, including the deletion of datasets, which are not present in the source portal
anymore.

The principal data format of Piveau is RDF, therefore non-RDF or not supported RDF dialects sources require a transformation. A **transformer** generates RDF from such source data, by applying light-weight transformation scripts
written in JavaScript. The final output is always DCAT-compliant RDF. The
scripts can be managed externally (e.g. in Git) to ensure maintainability.

Finally, our **exporter** sends the RDF data to the Hub component. Non-existing datasets are deleted by the exporter based on the identifier list that is acquired in the importing step.

5.2 Processing and Storing

The central service for dataset management is the **registry**. It acts as a middleware and abstraction layer to interact with the triplestore. It offers a RESTful interface, supporting the major RDF serializations (Turtle, JSON-LD, N-Triples, RDF/XML, Notation3). Its resources reflect the main DCAT entities: catalog, dataset, and distribution. The main task is to pre-process and harmonize the data received from the exporter. This includes the application of consistent and meaningful URI schemata [6], the generation of unique IDs, and the mapping to linked, existing entities. It ensures the integrity and traceability of the data in the triplestore. The **indexing** service is responsible for managing the high-performance search index. It receives the processed RDF data from the registry and flattens it into a plain JSON representation, which is suitable for indexing. Firstly, this is done by extracting relevant literals from the data, e.g. from properties like title and description. Secondly, linked resources are resolved and proper literals are extracted from the result (for instance by looking for *rdfs:label*). The service supports the use of existing and well-maintained vocabularies and ontologies for that purpose. Piveau ships with a selection of vocabularies, e.g. for human languages, licenses, and geolocations. The result of the search service constitutes one of the main access points to the data, because it is much more human-readable than native RDF.

The **translation** service manages the machine translation of literals into multiple languages. It represents a middleware to third-party translations services, bundling strings from multiple datasets to an integrated request. After completion the service stores the translation by applying the native multi-language features of RDF. As soon as a dataset is retrieved, the existing original languages are identified and added to the text information using a language tag inside the dataset. This labeling is based on ISO 639-1 language codes. In addition, metadata about the translation status are stored in the dataset, indicating when a translation was started and when it was completed. Translated text information are labeled with an extended language tag to differentiate them from the original text. It follows the schema *en-t-de-t0-abc* [11], where the target language is named first, followed by a *t* and the original language.

Finally, the data is accessible via multiple means. The triplestore exposes a SPARQL endpoint, which offers raw und direct access to the data. A RESTful API allows the access to the RDF serializations, provided by the registry and to the indexed serializations, provided by the search service. A web **user interface** offers access to end users and interacts directly with the RESTful API.

5.3 Quality Evaluation

In parallel with the main data processing steps, the data is processed by dedicated services to assess its quality. Semantic Web technologies offer mature tools and standards to conduct this task.

The **validator** provides a formal validation of each dataset. We apply the W3C Shapes Constraint Language (SHACL) [20], where a pre-defined set of rules is tested against a dataset. Currently the DCAT-AP SHACL rules [15] are included. The validation results include detailed information about issues and violations. This result covers the exact paths and reasons for the identified deficits. The applied rules can also be extended or replaced. In addition, the **URL checker** performs accessibility tests on each linked distribution (the actual data) and assesses its availability via HTTP status codes.

The **DQV annotator** [4] provides a qualitative assessment for each dataset. It is based on a custom metrics scheme, which is inspired by the FAIR principles [39]. The findability dimension refers to completeness of the metadata, e.g. whether keywords, geo data or time information are provided. Accessibility refers to the results from the URL checker. Interoperability is assessed by evaluating the format and type of data, which is referenced in a dataset (distribution). For instance, if the data is in a machine-readable and/or non-proprietary format. Reusability is mostly confirmed by checking the availability of licensing information. Beyond this FAIR evaluation, the similarity of a dataset to other datasets is calculated based on locality-sensitive hashing (LSH) algorithm.

The results of the validation and annotator services are summarized in a quality report and attached as RDF to the concerned dataset in the triplestore. This report uses a custom quality vocabulary, which applies the W3C Data Quality Vocabulary (DQV) and reflects our metric scheme. In addition, an aggregated report is attached to the respective catalog.

The **reporter** offers a variety of human-readable versions of the quality reports. It collects all data from the triplestore and renders visually appealing reports of the information. It supports PDF, XLS or ODS. In addition, a comprehensive web front-end is available, and is integrated into the front-end of the Hub component.

6 Evaluation

We have evaluated our work according to three quantitative and qualitative aspects. In Sect. 6.1 we compare Piveau with two well-known Open Data solutions. In Sect. 6.2 we describe a real-world application based on Piveau. Finally, in Sect. 6.3 we present an analysis of the impact of Semantic Web technologies on the perceived barriers of Open Data.

6.1 Feature Comparison with Open Data Solutions

No definite metric exists to specifically assess the technical performance of Open Data technologies and infrastructures. However, a lot of work and research was conducted in the field of requirements and evaluation modeling for Open Data. An extensive review covering a broad variety of dimensions (economical, organizational, ergonomic, etc.) is presented by Charalabidis et al. [3] This includes an overview of "Functional Requirements of an Open Data Infrastructure", which acts as the main basis for our feature matrix [3]. It is supplemented by indicators from the outcome of "Adapting IS [Information Systems] Success Model on Open Data Evaluation" [3]. Furthermore, we translated the W3C recommendation for best practices for publishing data on the web into additional indicators [37]. Finally, the matrix is complemented by custom indicators to reflect our experiences in designing and developing Open Data infrastructures. In the selection process we only focused on indicators, which were applicable to measurable technical aspects that reflect the overall objective of managing metadata. More personal indicators, like "The web pages look attractive", were not considered. Still, this approach led to a large number of indicators (>50), which we semantically combined to generate a compact and meaningful feature matrix.[12]

We compared Piveau with the popular Open Data solutions CKAN and uData (see Sect. 3). The selection criteria were: (1) Must be freely available as Open Source software; (2) Must not be a cloud- or hosting-only solution; (3) Has a high rate of adoption and (4) Primarily targets public sector data. Table 1 shows the final feature matrix and the result of the evaluation. Each measure was rated with the following scale: 0 - not supported, 1 - partially supported, 2 - fully supported. An explanation is given for each rating, where required.

The overall result indicates that our solution can match with existing and established solutions and even reaches the highest score. Piveau offers strong features regarding searching and finding datasets and data provision. The comprehensive metadata is a great foundation for analyses and visualizations. Our features for quality assurance are unrivaled and we support the most scalable architecture. Yet, uData offers unique features for interaction and CKAN is very mature and industry-proven.

6.2   The European Data Portal

The EDP[13] is a central portal, publishing all metadata of Open Data provided by public authorities of the European Union (EU). It gathers the data from national Open Data portals and geographic information systems. It was initially launched in November 2015 by the European Commission (EC). Its design and development was driven by the DCAT-AP specification.

The EDP was one of the first implementations of the DCAT-AP specification. In order to comply with established Open Data publishing concepts, the first version was based on an extended CKAN with an additional layer for transforming and replicating all metadata into RDF. This setup required additional mechanisms to transform data and, thus, proved to be too complex and limited for the growing amounts of Open Data in Europe [19]. We successfully

---

[12] The exact provenance and creation process of the feature matrix is available as supplementary material: https://zenodo.org/record/3571171.

[13] https://www.europeandataportal.eu.

Table 1. Feature comparison

	Piveau		CKAN		uData	
Searching and Finding Data						
Support for data federation	2	Native support through SPARQL	1	Indirect through harvesting	1	Indirect through harvesting
Integration of controlled vocabularies	2	Support for structured controlled vocabulary	1	Support for simple controlled vocabulary	1	Support for simple controlled vocabulary
Filtering, sorting, structuring, browsing and ordering search results by diverse dimensions	2	Application of search engine	2	Application of search engine	2	Application of search engine
Offer a strong and interoperable API	2	DCAT compliant REST	2	DCAT compliant REST	2	DCAT compliant REST
Support multiple languages	2	On interface and dataset level	1	Only on interface level	2	On interface and dataset level
Linked Data interface	2	SPARQL endpoint	0		0	
Geo-search	2	Available	2	Available	2	Available
Data Provision and Processing						
Data upload	1	Binary data upload	2	Binary and structured data upload	1	Binary data upload
Data enrichment and cleansing	0		0		0	
Support for linking and referring other data	2	Any number of links possible	1	Restrictive schema	1	Restrictive schema
Analysis and Visualization						
Provide comprehensive metadata	2	Complete and extensible schema	1	Restricted schema	1	Restricted schema
Offer tools for analyses	0		1	Preview of tabular data	0	
Visualizing data on maps	1	Visualization of geo metadata	1	Visualization of geo metadata	1	Visualization of geo metadata
Detailed reuse information	0		0		1	Indicates purpose and user
Quality Assurance						
Information about data quality	2	Comprehensive quality evaluation	0		1	Simple quality evaluation
Provide quality dimensions to compare datasets and its evolution	2	Comprehensive quality evaluation	0		0	
Interaction						
Support interaction and communication between various stakeholders	0		0		2	Discussion platform
Enrich data	0		0		1	Additional community resources
Support revisions and version history	0		1	Metadata revision	0	
Track reuse	0		0		2	Linked reuse in dataset

(continued)

Table 1. *(continued)*

	Piveau		CKAN		uData	
Performance and Architecture						
Maturity	1	*Application in a few portals*	2	*Application in many portals*	1	*Application in a few portals*
Personalization and custom themes	1	*Replaceable themes*	2	*Use of theme API*	1	*Replaceable themes*
Scalable architecture	2	*Microservice architecture*	1	*Monolithic architecture*	1	*Monolithic architecture*
Score	28		21		24	

improved this first version with our solution Piveau. This successfully enrolled our solution in a large-scale production environment. Our translation middleware integrates the eTranslation Service of the EU Commission [29], enabling the provision of metadata in 25 European languages. As of December 2019 the EDP offers approximately one million DCAT datasets, in total consisting of more than 170 million RDF triples, fetched from more than 80 data providers. Open Data is considered to be a key building block of Europe's data economy [14], indicating the practical relevance of our work.

6.3   Impact of Semantic Web Technologies

The initially required development effort was higher and partly more challenging than with more traditional approaches. Some artifacts of the Semantic Web have not yet reached the required production readiness or caught up with latest progresses in software development. This increased integration effort and required some interim solutions for providing a production system. For instance, integrating synchronous third-party libraries into our asynchronous programming model. Particularly challenging was the adoption of a triplestore as primary database. The access is implemented on a very low level via SPARQL, since a mature object-relational mapping (ORM) tool does not exist. Most of the integrity and relationship management of the data is handled on application level and needed to be implemented there, since the triplestore, unlike relational databases, cannot handle constraints directly. In addition, the SPARQL endpoint should be openly available. This currently prevents the management of closed or draft data and will require a more elaborated approach. To the best of our knowledge no (free) production triplestore is available, supporting that kind of access control on the SPARQL endpoint. Furthermore, in the Open Data domain there is no suitable and mature method to present RDF in a user interface. Hence, the transformation and processing of RDF is still required before final presentation. Usually, this presentation is domain-depended and builds on custom implementations. We solved this by applying our search service for both, strong search capabilities and immediate presentation of the data in a user front-end.

However, the overall benefits outweigh the initial barriers and efforts. With our native application of the Semantic Web data model and its definite standards via a triplestore as principal data layer, we are much more able to harness the full potential of many Open Data specifications. This particularly concerns the required implementation of DCAT-AP. The direct reuse and linking to existing vocabularies or other resources enable a more expressive and explicit description of the data, e.g. for license, policy, and provenance information. In addition, this approach increases the machine-readability. The good supply of tools for working with RDF simplifies the integration into third-party applications and creates new possibilities for browsing, processing, and understanding the data. Especially, the availability of tools for reasoning can support the creation of new insights and derived data. The native capabilities of RDF to handle multiple languages support the cross-national aspect of Open Data. The application of SHACL in connection with DQV allowed us to generate and provide comprehensive quality information in a very effective fashion. In general, the strong liaison of the Semantic Web technologies facilitates a seamless integration of the data processing pipe.

7   Conclusions and Outlook

In this paper we have presented our scalable Open Data management platform Piveau. It provides functions for Open Data publication, quality assurance, and reuse, typically conducted by public administrations, research institutes and journalists. We applied a wide range of Semantic Web technologies and principles in our solution to overcome barriers and to address functional requirements of this domain. Although the Open Data community has always leveraged specifications of the Semantic Web, our work takes a previously untaken step by designing our platform around Semantic Web technologies from scratch. This allows for a much more efficient and immediate application of existing Open Data specifications. Hence, Piveau closes a gap between formal specifications and their utilization in production. We combined this with a new scalable architecture and an efficient development lice-cycle approach. Our orchestration approach enables a sustainable and flexible creation of Open Data platforms. Furthermore, it fosters the reuse of individual aspects of Piveau beyond the scope of Open Data. We have shown that our work can compete with existing Open Data solutions and exceed their features in several aspects. We have improved the generation and provision of quality information, enhanced the expressiveness of the metadata model and the support for multilingualism. As the core technology of the European Data Portal, Piveau promotes the Semantic Web as a highly relevant concept for Europe's data economy and has proven to be ready for production and reached a high degree of maturity. Finally, our work is a relevant contribution to the 5-star deployment scheme of Open Data, which supports the concept of Linked Open Data [8]. The source code of Piveau can be found on GitLab.[14]

In the next steps, Piveau will be extended with additional features. This includes support for user interaction, data enrichment, and data analysis. The support for further Semantic Web features is also planned, e.g. compliance with the LDP specifications and the extension beyond metadata to manage actual data as RDF. Open research questions are the implementation of revision and access control on triplestore level, which cannot be satisfied yet on production-grade. In general, we aim to increase the overall readiness, broaden the target group beyond the Open Data community, and strengthen the meaning of Semantic Web technologies as core elements of data ecosystems.

Acknowledgments. This work has been partially supported by the Federal Ministry of Education and Research of Germany (BMBF) under grant no. 16DII111 ("Deutsches Internet-Institut") and by the EU Horizon 2020 project "Reflow" under grant agreement no. 820937. The implementation and provision of the European Data Portal is funded by the European Commission under contracts DG CONNECT SMART 2014/1072 and SMART 2017/1123.

References

1. Data Catalog Vocabulary (DCAT). https://www.w3.org/TR/vocab-dcat/
2. W3C Semantic Web Activity Homepage. https://www.w3.org/2001/sw/
3. Charalabidis, Y., Zuiderwijk, A., Alexopoulos, C., Janssen, M., Lampoltshammer, T., Ferro, E.: The World of Open Data Concepts, Methods, Tools and Experiences. PAIT, vol. 28. Springer, Cham (2018). https://doi.org/10.1007/978-3-319-90850-2
4. Albertoni, R., Isaac, A.: Data on the web best practices: Data quality vocabulary. https://www.w3.org/TR/vocab-dqv/. Accessed 3 Dec 2019
5. Amazon Web Services Inc.: Aws data pipeline. https://aws.amazon.com/datapipeline/. Accessed 3 Dec 2019
6. Archer, P., Goedertier, S., Loutas, N.: D7.1.3 - Study on persistent URIs, with identification of best practices and recommendations on the topic for the MSs and the EC, December 2012. https://joinup.ec.europa.eu/sites/default/files/document/2013-02/D7.1.3%20-%20Study%20on%20persistent%20URIs.pdf
7. Beno, M., Figl, K., Umbrich, J., Polleres, A.: Perception of key barriers in using and publishing open data. JeDEM - eJournal of eDemocracy and Open Government **9**(2), 134–165 (2017). https://doi.org/10.29379/jedem.v9i2.465
8. Berners-Lee, T.: Linked Data. https://www.w3.org/DesignIssues/LinkedData.html. Accessed 11 Mar 2019
9. Bonér, J., Farley, D., Kuhn, R., Thompson, M.: The ractive manifesto. https://www.reactivemanifesto.org/. Accessed 5 Dec 2019
10. CKAN Association: CKAN. https://ckan.org/
11. Davis, M., Phillips, A., Umaoka, Y., Falk, C.: Bcp 47 extension t - transformed content. https://tools.ietf.org/html/rfc6497. Accessed 3 Dec 2019
12. Dragan, A.: DCAT Application Profile for data portals in Europe, November 2018. https://joinup.ec.europa.eu/sites/default/files/distribution/access_url/2018-11/014bde52-eb3c-4060-8c3c-fcd0dfc07a8a/DCAT_AP_1.2.pdf

---

[14] https://gitlab.com/piveau.

13. DuraSpace Wiki: Linked (Open) Data. https://wiki.duraspace.org/display/DSDOC6x/Linked+%28Open%29+Data. Accessed 11 Mar 2019

14. European Commision: Open data — Digital Single Market. https://ec.europa.eu/digital-single-market/en/open-data. Accessed 11 Mar 2019

15. European Commission: DCAT-AP 1.2.1. https://joinup.ec.europa.eu/solution/dcat-application-profile-data-portals-europe/distribution/dcat-ap-121-shacl. Accessed 3 Dec 2019

16. IBM: Ibm infosphere datastage. https://www.ibm.com/products/infosphere-datastage. Accessed 3 Dec 2019

17.]init[AG und SID Sachsen: DCAT-AP.de Spezifikation. https://www.dcat-ap.de/def/dcatde/1.0.1/spec/specification.pdf. Accessed 11 Mar 2019

18. Kantara Initiative: Federated authorization for user-managed access (uma) 2.0. https://docs.kantarainitiative.org/uma/wg/oauth-uma-federated-authz-2.0-09.html. Accessed 3 Dec 2019

19. Kirstein, F., Dittwald, B., Dutkowski, S., Glikman, Y., Schimmler, S., Hauswirth, M.: Linked data in the European data portal: A comprehensive platform for applying dcat-ap. In: International Conference on Electronic Government, pp. 192–204 (2019). https://academic.microsoft.com/paper/2967218146

20. Knublauch, H., Kontokostas, D.: Shapes constraint language (shacl). https://www.w3.org/TR/shacl/. Accessed 3 Dec 2019

21. LYRASIS: Fedora - the flexible, modular, open source repository platform. https://duraspace.org/fedora/. Accessed 22 Nov 2019

22. North Concepts Inc.: Data pipeline. https://northconcepts.com/. Accessed 3 Dec 2019

23. Open Data Team: Customizable and skinnable social platform dedicated to (open) data. https://github.com/opendatateam/udata. Accessed 11 Mar 2019

24. Open Knowledge BE: Dcat-be. linking data portals across Belgium. http://dcat.be/. Accessed 22 Nov 2019

25. Open Knowledge Foundation Labs: Data pipes. https://datapipes.okfnlabs.org/. Accessed 3 Dec 2019

26. OpenDataSoft: Open Data Solution. https://www.opendatasoft.com/solutions/open-data/. Accessed 11 Mar 2019

27. OpenLink Software: About OpenLink Virtuoso. https://virtuoso.openlinksw.com/. Accessed 11 Mar 2019

28. Oracle: Oracle autonomous data warehouse. https://www.oracle.com/de/database/data-warehouse.html. Accessed 3 Dec 2019

29. Publications Office of the EU: Authority tables. https://publications.europa.eu/en/web/eu-vocabularies/authority-tables. Accessed 11 Mar 2019

30. Roffia, L., Azzoni, P., Aguzzi, C., Viola, F., Antoniazzi, F., Cinotti, T.: Dynamic linked data: a sparql event processing architecture. Future Internet 10, 36 (2018). https://doi.org/10.3390/fi10040036

31. SAS Institue: Sas. https://www.sas.com/. Accessed 3 Dec 2019

32. Talend: Talend open studio. https://www.talend.com/products/talend-open-studio/. Accessed 3 Dec 2019

33. The Apache Software Foundation: Apache airflow. https://airflow.apache.org/. Accessed 3 Dec 2019

34. The OpenID Foundation: Openid connect core 1.0 incorporating errata set 1. https://openid.net/specs/openid-connect-core-1_0.html. Accessed 3 Dec 2019

35. The Scriptella Project Team: Scriptella etl project. https://scriptella.org/. Accessed 3 Dec 2019

36. Vrandečić, D., Krötzsch, M.: Wikidata: a free collaborative knowledgebase. Commun. ACM **57**(10), 78–85 (2014). https://doi.org/10.1145/2629489
37. W3C: Data on the web best practices. https://www.w3.org/TR/dwbp/. Accessed 02 Dec 2019
38. W3C Wiki: LDP Implementations. https://www.w3.org/wiki/LDP_Implementations. Accessed 11 Mar 2019
39. Wilkinson, M., Dumontier, M., Aalbersberg, I., et al.: The fair guiding principles for scientific data management and stewardship. Sci. Data **3**, 160018 (2016). https://doi.org/10.1038/sdata.2016.18

Open Access This chapter is licensed under the terms of the Creative Commons Attribution 4.0 International License (http://creativecommons.org/licenses/by/4.0/), which permits use, sharing, adaptation, distribution and reproduction in any medium or format, as long as you give appropriate credit to the original author(s) and the source, provide a link to the Creative Commons license and indicate if changes were made.

The images or other third party material in this chapter are included in the chapter's Creative Commons license, unless indicated otherwise in a credit line to the material. If material is not included in the chapter's Creative Commons license and your intended use is not permitted by statutory regulation or exceeds the permitted use, you will need to obtain permission directly from the copyright holder.

StreamPipes Connect: Semantics-Based Edge Adapters for the IIoT

Philipp Zehnder[✉], Patrick Wiener, Tim Straub, and Dominik Riemer

FZI Research Center for Information Technology,
Haid-und-Neu-Str. 10-14, 76131 Karlsruhe, Germany
{zehnder,wiener,straub,riemer}@fzi.de

Abstract. Accessing continuous time series data from various machines and sensors is a crucial task to enable data-driven decision making in the Industrial Internet of Things (IIoT). However, connecting data from industrial machines to real-time analytics software is still technically complex and time-consuming due to the heterogeneity of protocols, formats and sensor types. To mitigate these challenges, we present *StreamPipes Connect*, targeted at domain experts to ingest, harmonize, and share time series data as part of our industry-proven open source IIoT analytics toolbox StreamPipes. Our main contributions are (i) a semantic adapter model including automated transformation rules for pre-processing, and (ii) a distributed architecture design to instantiate adapters at edge nodes where the data originates. The evaluation of a conducted user study shows that domain experts are capable of connecting new sources in less than a minute by using our system. The presented solution is publicly available as part of the open source software Apache StreamPipes.

Keywords: Industrial Internet of Things · Edge processing · Self-service analytics

1 Introduction

In order to exploit the full potential of data-driven decision making in the Industrial Internet of Things (IIoT), a massive amount of high quality data is needed. This data must be integrated, harmonized, and properly described, which requires technical as well a domain knowledge. Since these abilities are often spread over several people, we try to enable domain experts with little technical understanding to access data sources themselves. To achieve this, some challenges have to be overcome, such as the early pre-processing (e.g. reducing) of the potentially high frequency IIoT data close to the sensor at the edge, or to cope with high technological complexity of heterogeneous data sources. The goal of this paper is to simplify the process of connecting new sources, harmonize data, as well as to utilize semantic meta-information about its meaning, by providing a system with a graphical user interface (GUI).

© Springer Nature Switzerland AG 2020
A. Harth et al. (Eds.): ESWC 2020, LNCS 12123, pp. 665–680, 2020.
https://doi.org/10.1007/978-3-030-49461-2_39

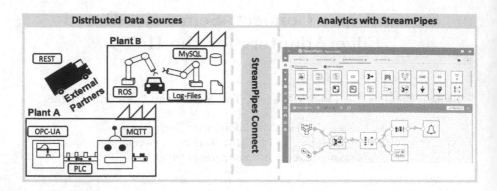

Fig. 1. Motivating scenario of a manufacturing company

Our solution, StreamPipes Connect, is made publicly available as part of the open-source, self-service data analytics platform *Apache StreamPipes (incubating)*[1]. StreamPipes [14] provides a complete toolbox to easily analyze and exploit a variety of IoT-related data without programming skills. Therefore, it leverages different technologies especially from the fields of big data, distributed computing and semantic web (e.g. RDF, JSON-LD). StreamPipes is widely adopted in the industry and is an incubating project at the Apache Software Foundation.

Figure 1 shows a motivating scenario of a production process in a company with several plants. It further illustrates the potentially geo-distributed heterogeneous data sources that are available in such a company. However, the challenge is how to enable domain experts to connect and harmonize these distributed heterogeneous industrial streaming data sources. First we show how our approach differs from existing related work in Sect. 2. To cope with the distributed setting we leverage a master worker paradigm with a distributed architecture (Sect. 3). Adapters are deployed on edge devices located within a close proximity to sources, to early filter and transform events. We use a semantics based model to describe adapters and to employ transformation rules on events (Sect. 4). The model covers standard formats and protocols as well as the possibility to connect proprietary data sources. In Sect. 5, the implementation of our approach and the GUI is explained in detail. We present results of a conducted user study to evaluate the usability of our system, in addition to the performance tests carried out in Sect. 6. Lastly Sect. 7 concludes our work and presents an outline of planned future work.

---

[1] https://streampipes.apache.org/.

2 Related Work

Data flow tools with a GUI are commonly used to process and harmonize data from various sources. Applications like Talend[2], or StreamSets[3] can be used for Extract, Transform, Load (ETL) tasks, wich is a well elaborated field where the goal is to gather data from many heterogeneous sources and store it in a database. Using such tools still requires a lot of technical knowledge, especially because they are not leveraging semantic technologies to describe the meaning of data. Another tool in this field is Node-RED[4], which describes itself as a low-code solution for event-driven applications. Node-RED is designed to run on a single host. However, our approach targets distributed IIoT data sources like machines or sensors. Therefore, data can be processed directly on edge devices, potentially reducing network traffic. There are also approaches leveraging semantic technologies for the task of data integration and harmonization. WInte.r [9] supports standard data formats, like CSV, XML, or RDF, further it supports several strategies to merge different data sets with a schema detection and unit harmonization. In contrast to our approach, it focuses on data sets instead of IIoT data sources. The goal of Spitfire [12] is to provide a Semantic Web of Things. It focuses on REST-like sensor interfaces, not on the challenge of integrating sensors using industrial protocols and high-frequency streaming data, that require local preprocessing. The Big IoT API [6] enables interoperability between IoT platforms. Thus the paper has a different focus, we focus on domain experts to connect data, especially from IIoT data sources.

Distributed architectures like presented in [8] are required to cope with the distributed nature of IIoT data sources. In the paper, a lightweight solution to ease the adoption of distributed analytics applications is presented. All raw events are stored in a distributed storage and are later used for analytics. The authors try to adopt a very lightweight approach and do not describe the semantics of events or transform them. In our approach, data is transformed and harmonized directly in the adapter at the edge. This eases the analytics tasks downstream usually performed by a (distributed) stream processing engine, such as Kafka Streams. Such engines provide solutions to connect to data sources with Kafka Connect[5]. It is possible to create connectors that publish data directly to Kafka. They provide a toolbox of already integrated technologies, such as several databases or message brokers. Still, a lot of configuration and programming work is required to use them.

Other industry solutions to cope with the problem of accessing machine data are to build custom adapters, e.g. with Apache PLC4X[6]. This requires a lot of development effort and often is targeted at a specific use case. We leverage such tools to enable an easy to configure and re-usable approach. Another way to

---

[2] https://www.talend.com/.
[3] https://streamsets.com/.
[4] https://nodered.org/.
[5] https://www.confluent.io/connectors/.
[6] https://plc4x.apache.org/.

access machine data is to use a unified description, like the Asset Administration Shell (AAS) [2]. It is introduced by the Platform Industry 4.0 and provides a unified wrapper around assets describing its representation and technical functionality. There are also some realizations of the concept, as described in [16]. In our approach we try to automatically create an adapter by extracting sample data and meta-data from the data source. Thus, this allows us to work with data sources that do not have a specific description like the AAS.

3   Architecture

The main design decisions for our architecture are based on the goal of creating a system for both small, centralized as well as large, distributed environments. Therefore, we decided to implement a master/worker paradigm, where the master is responsible for the management and controlling of the system and the workers actually access and process data. To achieve this, we need a lightweight approach to run and distribute services. Container technologies offer a well suited solution and are particularly suitable for edge and fog processing scenarios [7]. Figure 2 provides an overview of our architecture showing the data sources and the compute units located close to the sources, running the services of the system. The StreamPipes backend communicates with the master, which manages all the worker containers, as well as the adapter instances running in the workers. For the communication between the individual components we use JSON-LD. The master persists the information about the workers and running adatpers in a triple store.

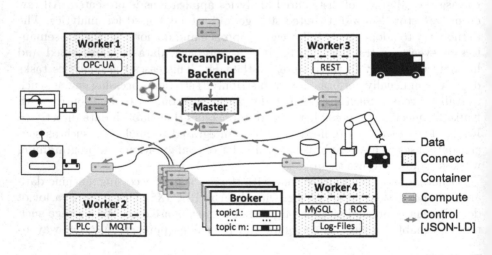

Fig. 2. Architectural overview of our system

Once a new worker is started, it is registered at the master, providing information which adapter types (e.g. PLC, MQTT) are supported. When an adapter instance is instantiated to connect a new machine, the data is directly forwarded to a distributed message broker, as shown in Fig. 2. New worker instances can be added during runtime to extend the system and the master schedules new adapters accordingly. The master coordinates and manages the system. For the transmission of the harmonized data we rely on already existing broker technologies, e.g. Apache Kafka.

4 Adapters

The adapter model is the core of our approach and provides a way to describe time series data sources. Based on this model, adapters are instantiated, to connect and harmonize data according to pre-processing rules applied to each incoming event. Such adapter descriptions are provided in RDF serialized as JSON-LD.

4.1 Adapter Model

Figure 3 shows our semantic adapter model. The *Adapter* concept is at the core of the model. Each adapter has a *StreamGrounding* describing the protocol and format used to publish the harmonized data. Additionally to sending unified data to a message broker, adapters are capable of applying *Transformation Rules*.

DataSets and *DataStreams* are both supported by the model. For a better overview of the Figure, we present a compact version of the model with the notation {*Stream, Set*}, meaning there is one class for streams and one for sets. From a modeling and conceptual point of view, there is no difference in our approach between the two types. We treat data sets as bounded data streams, which is why we generally refer to data streams from here onwards.

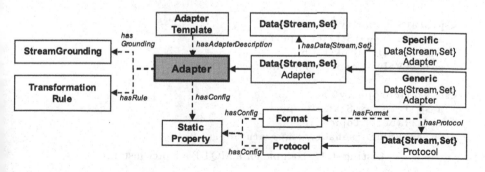

Fig. 3. Core of our adapter model

Further, there are two types of Data Stream Adapters, *GenericDataStreamAdapters* and *SpecificDataStreamAdapters*. A GenericDataStreamAdapter consists of a combination of a *DataStreamProtocol* (e.g. MQTT), responsible for connecting to data sources and formats (e.g. JSON) that are required to convert the connected data into the internal representation of events. Since not all data sources comply with those standards (e.g. PLC's, ROS, OPC-UA), we added the concept of a *SpecificDataStreamAdapter*. This can also be used to provide custom solutions and implementations of proprietary data sources. User configurations for an adapter can be provided via *StaticProperties*. They are available for *Formats*, *Protocols*, and *Adapters*. There are several types of static properties, that allow to automatically validate user inputs (e.g. strings, URLs, numeric values). Configurations of adapters (e.g., protocol information or required API keys) can be stored in *Adapter Templates*, encapsulating the required information. Listing 1.1 shows an instance of a *GenericDataStreamAdapter*, with MQTT as the protocol and JSON as a format.

```
1   @prefix sp: <https://streampipes.apache.org/vocabulary/v1/> .
2
3
4   <sp:adapter1>
5     a sp:GenericDataStreamAdapter ;
6     rdfs:label "Temperature Sensor" ;
7     sp:hasProtocol <sp:protocol/stream/mqtt> ;
8     sp:hasFormat <sp:format/json> ;
9     sp:hasDataStream <sp:dataStream1> ;
10    sp:hasRule <sp:transformationrule1> .
11
12  <sp:protocol/stream/mqtt>
13    a sp:DataStreamProtocol ;
14    rdfs:label "MQTT" ;
15    sp:config <sp:staticproperty1>, <sp:staticproperty2> .
16
17  <sp:format/json>
18    a sp:Format ;
19    rdfs:label "JSON" .
20
21  <sp:staticproperty1>
22    a sp:FreeTextStaticProperty ;
23    rdfs:label "Broker URL" ;
24    sp:hasValue "tcp://mqtt-host.com:1883" .
25
26  <sp:staticproperty2>
27    a sp:FreeTextStaticProperty ;
28    rdfs:label "Topic" ;
29    sp:hasValue "sensor/temperature" .
```

Listing 1.1. Example for a MQTT adapter instance

4.2   Transformation Rule Model

Oftentimes, it is not sufficient to only connect data, it must also be transformed, reduced, or anonymized. Therefore we introduce transformation rules, visualized in Fig. 4, to either change the value of properties, schema, or the stream itself.

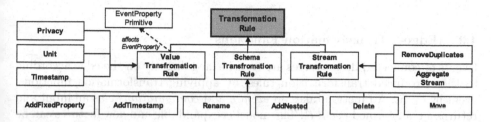

Fig. 4. Model of the transformation rules with all Value-, Schema-, and StreamTransformationRules

Our approach uses transformation rules to describe the actual transformation of events. Based on these rules, pre-processing pipelines are automatically configured in the background, which run within an adapter instance. The following table presents an overview of an extensible set of transformation rules, which are already integrated.

Scope	Rule	Example
Schema	Add Fix Property	{} → { "id": "sensor5"}
	Add Nested	{} → { "a": {}}
	Move	{ "a": { "b": 1}} → { "a": {}, "b": 1}
	Add Timestamp	{} → { "timestamp": 1575476535373}
	Rename	{ "old": 1} → { "new": 1}
	Delete	{ "a": 1} → {}
Value	Privacy (SHA-256)	{ "name": "Pia"} → { "name": "ca9..."}
	Unit ($°C → °F$)	{ "temp": 41} → { "temp": 5}
	Timestamp	{ "time": "2019/12/03 16:29"} →{ "time": 1575476535373}
Stream	Remove Duplicates	{ "a": 1},...,{ "a": 1} → { "a": 1}
	Aggregate	{ "a": 2},...,{ "a": 1} → { "a": 1.5}

Listing 1.2 shows an example instance of the *UnitTransformationRule*. It is part of the adapter model in Listing 1.1 and describes how to transform the temperature value form the unit degree celsius into degree Fahrenheit. All instances of the rules look similar. The configuration parameters of the individual rules differ, for example instead of the fromUnit and toUnit, the rename rule contains the old and the new runtime name.

```
1  <sp:transformationrule1>
2    a sp:UnitTransformRule ;
3    sp:runtimeKey "temperature" ;
4    sp:fromUnit "http://qudt.org/vocab/unit#DegreeFahrenheit" ;
5    sp:toUnit "http://qudt.org/vocab/unit#DegreeCelsius" .
```

Listing 1.2. Unit transformation rule instance example

4.3   (Edge-) Transformation Functions

Events of connected data sources are transformed directly on the edge according to the introduced transformation rules, by applying transformation functions, event by event. A function takes an *event e* and *configurations c* as an input and returns a transformed *event e'*. The model is expandable and new features can be added by a developer. An instance of an adapter contains a set of functions which are concatenated to a pre-processing pipeline. Equation (1) shows how an event is transformed by multiple functions. Each function represents a transformation rule from our model. To ensure that the transformations are performed correctly the rules must be applied in a fixed order. First the schema, then the value, and last the stream transformations.

$$F(e) = f_n(f_{...}(f_1(e, c), ...), c) = e' \tag{1}$$

The unit transformation function for example takes the property name, the original unit and the new unit as a configuration input. Within the function the value of the property is transformed according to the factors in the qudt ontology[7]. Figure 5 shows a complete pre-processing pipeline of our running example. On the left the raw input *event e* is handed to the first function f_1 that changes the schema. The result of each function is handed to the next function in addition to the configurations. In the end, the final *event e'* is sent to the defined *StreamGrounding* of the adapter.

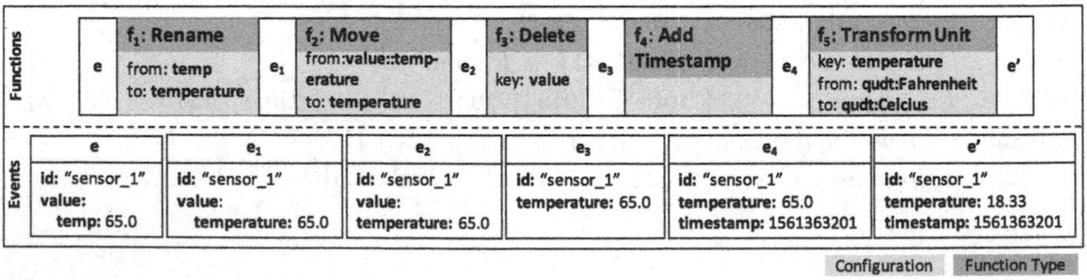

| Functions | e | f_1: Rename
from: temp
to: temperature | e_1 | f_2: Move
from:value::temp-erature
to: temperature | e_2 | f_3: Delete
key: value | e_3 | f_4: Add
Timestamp | e_4 | f_5: Transform Unit
key: temperature
from: qudt:Fahrenheit
to: qudt:Celcius | e' |

Events	e	e_1	e_2	e_3	e_4	e'
	id: "sensor_1" value: temp: 65.0	id: "sensor_1" value: temperature: 65.0	id: "sensor_1" value: temperature: 65.0	id: "sensor_1" temperature: 65.0	id: "sensor_1" temperature: 65.0 timestamp: 1561363201	id: "sensor_1" temperature: 18.33 timestamp: 1561363201

Configuration   Function Type

Fig. 5. Example of a pre-processing pipeline

---

[7] https://www.qudt.org/.

5   Implementation

We integrated our implementation into the open source software Apache StreamPipes (incubating), which is publicly available on GitHub[8].

5.1   Adapter Marketplace

Figure 6 shows the adapter marketplace containing an overview of all protocols, specific adapters, and adapter templates. Currently, we integrated 25 different adapters and we continually integrate new ones. For streaming protocols, PLCs (e.g. Siemens S7), OPC-UA[9], ROS [13], MQTT [3], FTP, REST (iterative polling), MySQL (subscribing to changes), InfluxDB, Kafka, Pulsar are integrated. Further we support several data set protocols like files (can be uploaded), HDFS, FTP, REST, MySQL, InfluxDB. Additionally to those generic adapters, we have integrated several open APIs, like openSenseMap[10] resulting in specific adapters. This number is also constantly growing, since adapters can be stored and shared as adapter templates. Templates are serialized into JSON-LD, that can be exported and imported into other systems. They are also listed in the data marketplace.

5.2   Adapter Modeling Process

Once a user selects the adapter that should be connected, a guided configuration process is started. This process is the same for data sets and data streams and just differs slightly between generic and specific adapters. We illustrate the

Fig. 6. Overview of the data marketplace

---

[8] https://github.com/apache/incubator-streampipes.
[9] https://opcfoundation.org/.
[10] https://opensemap.org/.

modeling process of a generic adapter with the example of a temperature sensor introduced in Fig. 5. The sensor values are provided over MQTT and are serialized in JSON:

1. **Select adapter/protocol:** First a user must select the specific adapter or protocol form the marketplace, shown in Fig. 6.
2. **Configure adapter/protocol:** In the next step a configuration menu is presented to the user. In ❶ of Fig. 7 an example for the MQTT protocol is shown. The broker URL, optional credentials for authentication and the topic must be provided.
3. **Configure format (optional):** For generic adapters additionally the format must be configured. In our example a user must select JSON.
4. **Refine event schema:** So far the technical configurations to connect data sources were described, now the content of the events must be specified. Figure 7 in ❷ shows the event schema. Users can add, or delete properties, as well as change the schema via a drag-and-drop user interface. Further shown in ❸ additional information can be added to individual properties, like a description, the domain property, or the unit. Based on the user interaction the transformation rules are derived in the background.
5. **Start adapter:** In the last step a name for the adapter must be provided. Additionally a description or an icon can be added. In this step it is also possible to define a maximum frequency for the resulting data stream, or to filter duplicate events. Again, rules are derived from the user interaction. Users just interact with the GUI and the system creates the rules, resulting in an intuitive way of interacting with the system without worrying about the explicit modeling of the rules.

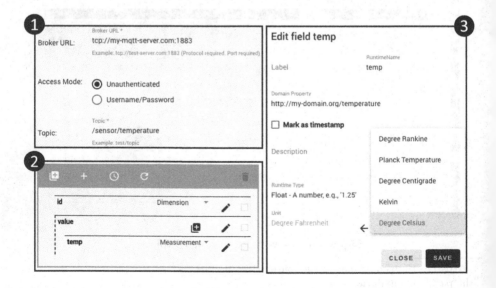

Fig. 7. Screenshots of adapter modeling process

5.3   Semantics Based User Guidance

We try to use the semantic model and meta-data as much as possible to help and guide the user through the system. All user inputs are validated in the GUI according to the information provided in the adapter model (e.g. ensure correct data types or URIs). Additionally, the system uses information of the data sources, when available, during the configuration steps 2./3., described in the previous section. Unfortunately, the usefulness of those interfaces highly depends on the selected adapter/protocol, since not all provide the same amount of high quality information. For example, some message brokers provide a list of available topics. Other technologies, like PLCs often have no interface like that and the users have to enter such information manually. But still, this user input is checked and when an error occurs during the connection to the source a notification with the problem is provided to the user.

Furthermore, the schema of the events is guessed by reading sample data from the source. Once the endpoint of the source is connected, we establish a connection to gather some sample data. Based on this data a guess of the schema is provided and suggested to the user in the GUI. The realization for the individual implementations of this schema guess is again very different. For CSV files for example it depends if they have a header line or not. For message brokers sending JSON a connection has to be established to gather several events to get the structure of the JSON objects. Other adapters like the one for OPC-UA can leverage the rich model stored in the OPC server to already extract as much meta-information as possible. All of this information is harmonized into our semantic adapter model, where we also integrate external vocabularies, and presented in the GUI to the user. Users are able to refine or change the model.

Also on the property level we try to leverage the semantics of our model to easily integrate different representations of timestamps, by providing a simple way to harmonize them to the internal representation of UNIX timestamps. Another example are unit transformations. Based on the qudt ontology only reasonable transformations are suggested to the user.

6   Evaluation

In our evaluation we show that domain experts with little technical knowledge are able to connect new sources. Additionally, we present performance results of adapters and where the system is already deployed in production.

6.1   User Study

Setup: For our user study, we recruited 19 students from a voluntary student pool of the Karlsruhe Institute of Technology (KIT) using hroot [4]. The user study took place at the Karlsruhe Decision & Design Lab (KD²Lab)[11] at the KIT. The overall task was to connect two data sources with measurements of environment sensors as a basis, to create a live air quality index, similar to the one in [1]. Since most of the participants did not have a technical background and never worked with sensor data before, we gave a 10 min introduction about the domain, the data sources, what it contains (e.g. particulate matter PM2.5/PM10, nitrogen dioxide NO_2, . . .), and how an air quality index might look like. After that, the participants went into an isolated cabin to solve the tasks on their own, without any further assistance by the instructors. As a first task, they had to connect data from the openSenseMap API [11], an online service for environmental data. The goal of the second task was to connect environmental data from official institutions, therefore data provided by the 'Baden-Wuerttemberg State Institute for the Environment, Survey and Nature Conservation' was used. This data is produced by officially standardized air measuring stations distributed all over the state. After finishing the two tasks, the participants were forwarded to an online questionnaire, where they had to answer several questions to assess how usable the system was in their experience. For the questions, we used three standardized questionnaires as well as additional questions. To ensure that the participants answer the questions carefully, we added control questions to the questionnaire. Three participants answered those control questions wrong, resulting in a total of 16 valid answers.

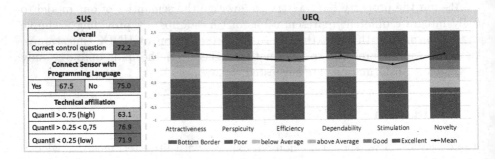

Fig. 8. Results of SUS & UEQ

Results: First, we present the results of the System Usability Scale (SUS) [5], which measures how usable a software system is by comparing results to the average scores of 500 websites[12]. A score above 71.4 is considered as good result. We use the same colors to indicate how well the score is compared to the other

[11] http://www.kd2lab.kit.edu/.
[12] https://www.trymyui.com/sus-system-usability-scale.

systems. On the left of Fig. 8, the overall result of 72.2 can be seen. Since we have a high variance of technical expertise within our participants we grouped the results according to the technical experience. First we grouped them into two groups, whether they stated to be able to connect sensors with any programming language of their choice or not. Participants not able to develop a connector for sensors with a programming language find the system more useful (good system, mean: 75.0) than participants who are able to connect a sensor with a programming language of their own choice (acceptable system, mean: 67.5). Second, we grouped them according to their technological affinity from high to low. For that, we adopted the items of the Technology Readiness Index (TRI) [10] in order to frame the questions on the expertise in using programming IDE's and data tools. We can use this as a control to measure how affine participants are in using technologies (e.g. IDE's). Participants with a high technology affinity (quantile > 0.75) find the system not as useful as less technology affine participants, but still acceptable (mean: 63.1). Participants with an average technology affinity find the system the most useful (good system: mean: 76,9). Participants with a low technology affinity (quantile < 0.25) find the system good as well, however a bit less useful as the average class (mean: 71,9). This is in line with the assumption, that such a tool is especially useful for non-technical users. The SUS gives the tool a rating of a good system. The participants used the system for the first time and only for a duration of 15 to 20 min. In this respect, this is already a very good score and it is likely to assume that the score would be higher when more experienced users would have participated.

For the second questionnaire, the User Experience Questionnaire (UEQ) was chosen [15]. It consists of six categories: Attractiveness, Perspicuity, Efficiency, Dependability, Stimulation, and Novelty. For each of these categories, a Likert scale is provided to indicate how good the system is compared to other systems evaluated with the UEQ. Figure 8 shows the results of the UEQ on the right. All the results of the individual categories are above average. The results of the categories Attractiveness, Perspicuity, Efficiency, and Dependability are considered as good. The result of the Novelty of the system is even rated as excellent. The figure also reveals that the results of all categories are equally good meaning we do not have to focus on a single aspect. It also suggests that there is still room for further improvement, but for a first user study the results are already very promising. Together with the results from the SUS, this means that the system is not only usable (i.e. fulfils its purpose) but also gives a good experience when using it (i.e. fun experience).

Additionally, we added own questions to the questionnaire to get some information which is especially relevant for our work. To see how technical the students were, we asked them whether they are able to connect new sensors in a programming language of their choice or not. Just 5 of the participants answered with yes, while 11 gave a negative answer. This indicates we had a good mix of technical experience of the participants, as our system focuses on less technical users with little to no programming experience. We asked the participants, if they think, once they are more familiar with the system, they are able to connect new data sources in under one minute. 14 answered with yes and 2 with no. This shows that our approach is simple to use and efficient, as even the less technical participants state they can connect new data sources in under one minute, which is usually a technical and time-consuming task. Regarding the question whether they think they are capable of connecting new real-time sensor data with our system, all of the participants answered with yes. This means all participants are capable of creating new adapters with the system. We also monitored the interaction of the users with the system to find out how long they approximately needed to complete the individual tasks. The result was that users took between 3 to 5 min for each task. Overall, the results of the user study show that StreamPipes Connect is already rated as a good system, which can be used by domain experts to quickly connect new data sources.

6.2   Performance Evaluation

Setup: For the evaluation we connected the events of the joint states of a robot arm via ROS. The frequency of the data stream is 500 Hz and the event size is 800 Bytes. This data was connected and processed with the ROS adapter without any delays. To discover the limits of our system we created an adapter with a configurable data generator. Therefore, we used the temperature event and transformed it with the same rules as in our example in Fig. 5. For the test setup we used a server running the StreamPipes backend and two different commonly used edge devices for the worker instance. We used a Raspberry Pi 4 and an Intel NUC. To test the maximum performance of an adapter within a worker we produced events as fast as the worker could process them. For each device we ran 6 different set-ups, all with a different lengths of the pipeline shown in Fig. 5.

Results: Figure 9 shows the results of the performance test. Each test ran 15 times and the mean of sent Events per second is plotted in the chart. For the NUC we produced 10.000.000 events per test and for the Raspberry Pi 5.000.000 events.

The results of the figure show that if no pre-processing pipeline is used the events are transmitted the fastest and the longer the pre-processing pipeline is, the less events are processed. The only exception is the delete function, which removes a property of the event and thus increases the performance. The NUC performs significantly better then the raspberry Pi, but for many real-world use cases a Pi is still sufficient, since it also processes 54.000 events per second (with no pre-processing function). The add timestamp and transform unit functions have an higher impact on the performance than the other tested functions.

6.3   Usage

Apache StreamPipes (incubating) was developed as an open source project over the last couple of years by the authors of this paper at the FZI Research Center for Information Technology. Since November 2019, we transitioned the tool to the Apache Software Foundation as a new incubating project.

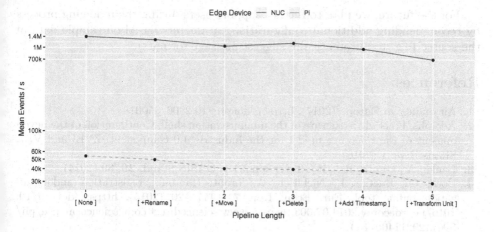

Fig. 9. Performance test results over 15 test runs

We successfully deployed StreamPipes in multiple projects in the manufacturing domain. One example is condition monitoring in a large industrial automation company. We connected several robots (Universal Robots) and PLCs to monitor a production process and calculate business-critical KPIs, improving the transparency on the current health status of a production line.

7 Conclusion and Future Work

In this paper, we presented StreamPipes Connect, a self-service system for ingestion and harmonization of IIoT time series data, developed as part of the open source IoT toolbox Apache StreamPipes (incubating).

We presented a distributed, event-based data ingestion architecture where services can be directly deployed on edge devices in form of worker nodes. Workers send real-time data from a variety of supported industrial communication protocols (e.g., PLCs, MQTT, OPC-UA) to a centralized message broker for further analysis.

Our approach makes use of an underlying semantics-based adapter model, which serves to describe data sources and to instantiate adapters. Generated adapters connect to the configured data sources and pre-process data directly at the edge by applying pipelines consisting of user-defined transformation rules. In addition, we further presented a graphical user interface which leverages semantic information to better guide domain experts in connecting new sources, thus reducing development effort.

To achieve the goal of providing a generic adapter model that covers the great heterogeneity of data sources and data types, the flexibility of semantic technologies was particularly helpful. Especially the reuse of vocabularies (e.g. QUDT) facilitates the implementation significantly. The user study has shown us that modeling must be easy and intuitive for the end user.

For the future, we plan to further support users during the modeling process by recommending additional configuration parameters based on sample data of the source (e.g. to automatically suggest message formats).

References

1. Air quality in Europe (2017). https://doi.org/10.2800/850018
2. Adolphs, P., et al.: Structure of the administration shell. Continuation of the development of the reference model for the Industrie 4.0 component. ZVEI and VDI, Status Report (2016)
3. Banks, A., Gupta, R.: MQTT version 3.1.1. OASIS Stand. **29**, 89 (2014)
4. Bock, O., Baetge, I., Nicklisch, A.: hroot: Hamburg registration andorganization online tool. Eur. Econ. Rev. **71**, 117–120 (2014). https://doi.org/10.1016/j.euroecorev.2014.07.003. http://www.sciencedirect.com/science/article/pii/S0014292114001159
5. Brooke, J., et al.: SUS-A quick and dirty usability scale. In: Brooke, J., Jordan, P.W., Thomas, B., Weerdmeester, B.A., McClelland, I.L. (eds.) Usability Evaluation Industry, pp. 184–194. CRC Press, London (1996)
6. Bröring, A., et al.: The big IoT API - semantically enabling iot interoperability. IEEE Pervasive Comput. **17**(4), 41–51 (2018). https://doi.org/10.1109/MPRV.2018.2873566
7. Ismail, B.I., et al.: Evaluation of docker as edge computing platform, pp. 130–135. IEEE (2015). https://doi.org/10.1109/ICOS.2015.7377291
8. Kirmse, A., Kraus, V., Hoffmann, M., Meisen, T.: An architecture for efficient integration and harmonization of heterogeneous, distributed data sources enabling big data analytics. In: Proceedings of the 20th International Conference on Enterprise Information Systems, Funchal, Madeira, Portugal, pp. 175–182. SCITEPRESS - Science and Technology Publications (2018). https://doi.org/10.5220/0006776701750182
9. Lehmberg, O., Brinkmann, A., Bizer, C.: WInte.r - a web data integration framework, p. 4 (2017)
10. Parasuraman, A.: Technology readiness index (TRI) a multiple-item scale to measure readiness to embrace new technologies. J. Serv. Res. **2**(4), 307–320 (2000)
11. Pfeil, M., Bartoschek, T., Wirwahn, J.A.: Opensensemap-a citizen science platform for publishing and exploring sensor data as open data. In: Free and Open Source Software for Geospatial (FOSS4G) Conference Proceedings. vol. 15, p. 39 (2015)
12. Pfisterer, D., et al.: Spitfire: toward a semantic web of things. IEEE Commun. Mag. **49**(11), 40–48 (2011). https://doi.org/10.1109/MCOM.2011.6069708
13. Quigley, M., et al.: ROS: an open-source robot operating system. In: ICRA workshop on open source software. vol. 3, p. 5. Kobe, Japan (2009)
14. Riemer, D., Kaulfersch, F., Hutmacher, R., Stojanovic, L.: Streampipes: solving the challenge with semantic stream processing pipelines. In: Proceedings of the 9th ACM International Conference on Distributed Event-Based Systems, pp. 330–331. ACM (2015)
15. Schrepp, M., Hinderks, A., Thomaschewski, J.: Applying the user experience questionnaire (UEQ) in different evaluation scenarios. In: Marcus, A. (ed.) DUXU 2014. LNCS, vol. 8517, pp. 383–392. Springer, Cham (2014). https://doi.org/10.1007/978-3-319-07668-3_37
16. Tantik, E., Anderl, R.: Integrated data model and structure for the asset administration shell in Industrie 4.0. Proc. CIRP **60**, 86–91 (2017)

Author Index

Printed in the United States
by Baker & Taylor Publisher Services

Printed in the United States
By Bookmasters